THE SOCIAL SCIENCES

Library and Information Science Text Series

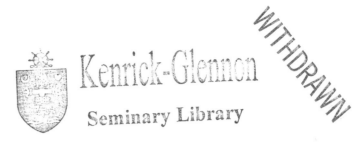
The Social Sciences

A Cross-Disciplinary Guide to Selected Sources

THIRD EDITION

General Editor

Nancy L. Herron

2002
LIBRARIES UNLIMITED
A Division of Greenwood Publishing Group, Inc.
Greenwood Village, Colorado

LIBRARIES UNLIMITED
A Division of Greenwood Publishing Group, Inc.
7730 East Belleview Avenue, Suite A200
Greenwood Village, CO 80111
1-800-225-5800
www.lu.com

Library of Congress Cataloging-in-Publication Data

The social sciences : a cross-disciplinary guide to selected sources / general editor Nancy
L. Herron -- 3rd ed.
      p. cm. -- (Library and information science text series)
   Includes bibliographical references and index.
   ISBN 1-56308-882-7 (pbk.) -- ISBN 1-56308-985-8 (cloth)
      1. Social sciences--References books--Bibliography. 2. Social sciences--Bibliography.
I. Herron, Nancy L., 1942- II. Series.

Z7161 .S648 2002
[H61]
016.3--dc21
                                                                                    2001050748

Contents

Part 1
General Literature of the Social Sciences

Part 2
Literature of the Established Disciplines of the Social Sciences

6—LAW AND JUSTICE 195

Kevin R. Harwell

Part 3
Those Disciplines with a Social Origin or That Have Acquired a Social Aspect

9—EDUCATION **289**

Justina O. Osa

Part 4
Those Disciplines with Recognized Social Implications

12—COMMUNICATION. **433**

Christine A. Whittington

12—COMMUNICATION (*continued*)

Acknowledgments

Gratitude and acknowledgments are extended to the excellent staffs of the libraries of The Pennsylvania State University, the University of Maine, and the University of Washington for their many contributions to the identification and location of quality resources outlined in this text. These institutions also provided research grant support and release time for authors to develop their disciplinary craft and produce their chapters.

Thanks are expressed to the many students in library science undergraduate and graduate reference service courses and their instructors, who provided suggestions and additions to the third edition.

Special acknowledgment is made to the authors of the second edition, Cynthia Faries, Sally G. W. Kalin, Kay Harvey, Karl H. Proehl, and Robert F. Rose, whose excellent scholarship provided the primary building blocks upon which the work of the third edition was constructed.

And finally, appreciation is expressed to Eugene W. Herron, M.D. for his careful and complete copy reading and numerous editorial suggestions made over the three editions of this book.

Introduction

Welcome to the third edition of *The Social Sciences: A Cross-Disciplinary Guide to Selected Sources!* Like the two editions that precede it, this volume is designed as a working text to serve two distinct groups of users. First, it is a carefully structured and up-to-date guide to the literature prepared by practicing librarians for fast and easy access to some of the best resources in the social science literature. Second, it is a teaching textbook for students wanting a clear, straightforward approach to learning about the most used and the most important reference sources in the social sciences, both print and electronic.

Also like its predecessors, this volume does not attempt to examine philosophical foundations of the social sciences, nor does it explore the nature of science and the differences between the social and natural sciences; neither does it consider various traditions of social science and the concepts and the assumptions that underlie them. These important elements the reader will discover as the resources outlined in this guide are located, explored, and used.

In searching for a modern and up-to-date definition of the social sciences, the broad definition that Peter Mayer expressed in November 1999[1] seems appropriate to this volume: "the rational systematic study of human society in all its forms with the aim of arriving at an enduring understanding, acknowledged as such by a broad consensus of researchers of social phenomena." From this definition it is not difficult to envision the enormous amount of information centered around "human society" today.

In *Creative Marginality: Innovation at the Intersections of Social Sciences*, Kattei Dogan and Robert Pahre state that "no one can possibly master the social sciences today."[2] Their observation a decade ago certainly has been highlighted and intensified by a decade of proliferation of electronic access points to resources in the social sciences. The potential for interaction across the social sciences, greatly enhanced by computer technologies, Boolean search strategies, and the ability of the searcher to regularly tailor searches for information using specific search terms and search engines, has increased geometrically in proportion to the number of Web sites. Frank Newman and Jamie Scurry have outlined how more than 1,100 colleges and universities in the United States, as well as hundreds in institutions in other countries, are now offering courses on the Internet.[3] Their enrollments are soaring. And a growing body of research is demonstrating that learning online can be both effective and satisfying for students. In the next few years we can expect even more spectacular growth in virtual education.

With all the online access tools presently existing for delivery of social science information, why, you may ask, have we decided to develop a new print edition of this book? The answer is simple. Many people have asked us for an updated text. As librarian-educators we want to provide the same "quick and easy" access for a new generation of social science information-seekers, many of whom will be seeking online access to the social science literature. We want to provide the same careful and rational look at the disciplinary structure of the social sciences literature as was provided in the first and the second editions of this text but with an expanded view to the virtual classroom and the virtual library. We hope to continue to do just that by the suggested chapter arrangement, a robust potential for creative interfaces and interactions across social science disciplines. We also believe that identifying quality resources is one of the most helpful and useful things we can do as information professionals, more critical now than ever in this age of overwhelming information "overload." And finally, having worked with students for a very long time, we understand the value, convenience, and portability of a printed text as a complement and an enhancement to online teaching and learning. Jason Epstein has underscored the value of the book format: "Books as physical objects will not pass away to be replaced by electronic signals read from glowing, hand-held screens. Nor will bookstores vanish. But they will coexist hereafter with a vast multilingual directory of digitized texts, assembled from a multitude of sources."[4]

The balance of chapter lengths in the book reflects changing societal trends. The sources listed in each one of the twelve chapters have been selected because of their value to the student/researcher. In this edition, all chapters have been revised, the essays expanded, and the annotated lists of resources changed to better reflect currency. Dated sources have been replaced by more up-to-date publications, and the amount of change across chapters, as in the second edition, is discipline-specific; the increased length of specific chapters is directly proportional to the amount of new knowledge produced in each subject area since the second edition was published in 1996. Electronic sources have multiplied geometrically, and most annotations have been rewritten to reflect changes in scope of new editions. This text is designed to serve the research needs of students/researchers in the year 2002 and beyond.

Of course, many popular Web sites for the "Social Sciences" field of inquiry exist and can be found by searching the World Wide Web (WWW) using simply the term "social sciences." Some interesting sites are the following:

Universal Codex for the Social Sciences (http/:socsciresearch.com)

Origin Myths in the Social Sciences (http://www.ualberta.ca/~cjscopy/articles/mclaughlin.html)

Social Science Data Center (http://www.lib.virginia.edu/socsci/)

Social Studies & Social Sciences (http://www.indiana.edu/~ssdc/eric_shess.htm)

Social Sciences Resources Homepage (http://www.nde.state.ne.us/SS/ss.html)

MSN Encarta-Social Sciences (http://encarta.msn.com/find/Concise.asp?ti=00FBB000)

Scout Report, The Scout Report for Social Sciences (http://scout.cs.wisc.edu/report/socsci /current/index.html)

Social Science Computer and Social Science Data Terms (http://odwin.ucsd.edu/glossary/)

NESSTAR—Network Social Science Tools and Resource (http://www.nesstar.org/)

Part 1 is a general section composed of reference sources applicable across all disciplines. **Part 2** contains the literature of disciplines firmly established by scholarly tradition among the social sciences (although some disciplines, such as history, are often still debated as to their appropriateness for inclusion in the literature of the social sciences as opposed to the humanities). **Part 3** contains the literature of disciplines defined as "emerging" from roots in the humanities or pure sciences into the social science disciplines; **Part 4** contains the literature of the disciplines related to the social sciences or those with recognized social implications for the other disciplines covered in parts 1 through 3.

Like the first and second editions, this text is a cooperative, collaborative enterprise undertaken by subject specialist librarians. As a result, it reflects throughout an academician's appreciation for the importance of a cross-disciplinary approach to reference service and the need on the part of professional information providers for a clear understanding of the multifaceted relationships that exist among the varied and diverse literatures that constitute the works of the social sciences. The content of this text also suggests that often innovation with important results in the social sciences occurs at the intersection of disciplines. This is both the cause and the effect of a continual fragmentation of the social sciences into narrow specialties and the recombination of these specialties across disciplinary lines into what Dogan and Pahre termed "hybrid" fields. Information professionals, like their business and academic counterparts, will continue to devise new strategies to provide better and faster service for researchers. This book, like the two that preceded it, attempts to support this idea; it looks at newly emerging disciplines alongside established ones with a cross-disciplinary perspective to provide a realistic, pragmatic approach to the exploration of the broad literature of the social sciences.

NOTES

1. *An Essay in the Philosophy of Social Science*, http://serendipity.cia.com.au/jsmill/pss2.htm (November 1999).

2. (Boulder, CO: Westview Press, 1990), preface.

3. "On-line Technology Pushes Pedagogy to the Forefront," *Chronicle of Higher Education* (July 13, 2001).

4. *Book Business: Publishing Past, Present and Future* (New York: W. W. Norton, 2000), preface.

Nancy L. Herron, General Editor
The Pennsylvania State University
University Park
April 2002

Contributing Authors

Christine Avery, BSS, MSS, MLS
Head of Reference and Assistant Access Services Librarian
Head, Commonwealth College Libraries
University Libraries
The Pennsylvania State University
Christine Avery has been a librarian at the Pennsylvania State University since 1990. She is the head of Commonwealth College Libraries, which consists of the libraries of the twelve Penn State campuses across the state. Prior to this appointment she served as a social sciences and business librarian at the University Park campus. She is co-author of *The Flexible Workplace: A Sourcebook of Information and Research* (2001) and *The Quality Management Sourcebook: An International Guide to Materials and Resources* (1997). Her research interests relate to assessment of library services.

Debora Cheney, BA, MLS
Head, Social Sciences Library
University Libraries
The Pennsylvania State University
Associate Librarian Debora Cheney is currently on sabbatical at Oxford University. Her work has focused on government and political science research and teaching. She teaches a course on the use of government and political information at the University Park campus, has co-authored articles on government information and library instruction and treaty research, and has prepared a citation guide to citing government information resources.

Kevin R. Harwell, BA, MLIS
Government Documents Librarian
University Libraries
The Pennsylvania State University
Kevin Harwell is the subject specialist for business law, economics, and intellectual property resources at the Schreyer Business Library. He joined the faculty of the Penn State University Libraries in 1990 after previously being librarian at Oklahoma State University. As an active member and past president of the Patent & Trademark Depository Library Association, he keeps busy; he is also a member of the Legal Division and the Business and Finance Division of the Special Libraries Association. Recent publications include "Resources for Searching Common Law Trademarks," *Reference and User Services Quarterly* (2000), and "Legal Issues Relating to Patent Searching in Publicly Accessible Libraries," *Journal of Government Information* (1998). He works to make legal information resources and processes understandable and approachable to nonspecialist users and to minimize obstacles in accessing patent and trademark information.

Kristi Jensen, BA, MLS
Head, Earth and Mineral Sciences Librarian
University Libraries
The Pennsylvania State University
In her current position in the Earth and Mineral Sciences Library, Kristi Jensen works with subject matter in the earth sciences and mineral, energy, and environmental economics. Before coming to Penn State, she participated in the University of Michigan Library Residency Program and completed projects related to GIS services in a distributed academic setting. Her primary research interest is access issues related to changes in technology, with an emphasis on modifying existing or creating new tools to increase user access to library resources. Her recent article in *Science and Technology Libraries* explores the impact of the online publishing of government documents on users' access.

Her other recent publications include "Preparing Problem Maps for Cataloging: Reflections on a New Earth Sciences Librarian," *GIS Newsletter* (February 2001), and "Creating Resources for GIS Support to Remote Users" for the Geoscience Information Society (June 2001).

Daniel C. Mack, BA, MA, MLS
Humanities Librarian
Arts and Humanities Library
University Libraries
The Pennsylvania State University
Humanities librarian Daniel Mack is the subject specialist for classics and ancient Mediterranean studies, Jewish studies, philosophy, and religious studies for the Pennsylvania State University, University Libraries. In these areas he is responsible for collection development, library instruction, reference work, and research assistance. He also coordinates reference collections and services for the Arts and Humanities Library.

Joyce L. Ogburn, BA, MA, MSLS
Associate Director of Libraries for Resources and Collection Management Services
University of Washington
Joyce Ogburn's background encompasses managing many areas of technical services and collection development activities in addition to serving as anthropology bibliographer at both The Pennsylvania State University and Yale University. She has chaired the Anthropology and Sociology Sections of the Association of College and Research Libraries and is founder/editor of ANSSWeb. In 1999 she was a member of a committee of the American Anthropological Association that redesigned their Web site. Her publications and presentations span a wide range of subjects, including anthropology reference and resources, library acquisitions and cataloging, and intellectual property.

Justina O. Osa, MSLS, M ED, EdD
Education and Behavioral Sciences Librarian
University Libraries
The Pennsylvania State University
Dr. Osa is a member of the Board of Examiners, National Council for the Accreditation of Teacher Education (NCATE); co-chair of the Collection Development Education Committee of the Reference and User Services Association; and a committee member of the American Library Association, International Relations Committee, Africa Subcommittee. Dr. Osa has recently contributed articles to the American Library Association, International Relations Committee online conference proceedings and the Jackson State University *Researcher: An Interdisciplinary Journal.* Current research interests focus on delivery of quality reference services to patrons.

Joanne M. Perry, BS, MA, MSLS
Maps Librarian and Head, Cartographic Services
University Libraries
The Pennsylvania State University
Before coming to Penn State, Joanne Perry served as map librarian at Oregon State University and map reference librarian at the University of Arizona. Her research interests lie in map storage methods, map bibliography, book reviews, and the history of American cartography, specifically the work of Richard Edes Harrison. She has been a member of many map and map librarianship organizations, including the Special Libraries Association, the Geography and Maps Division; the Western Association of Map Libraries; the Association of Canadian Map Libraries and Archives; North American Cartographic Society; and the International Map Trade Association. She is currently book review editor for *Cartographic Perspectives*, journal of NACIS, and for many years was editor and book review editor for the Special Libraries Association, Geography and Maps Division.

Gary W. White, MBA, MLS

Head, Schreyer Business Library
University Libraries
The Pennsylvania State University

Gary White is editor of the Web review column in the *Journal of Business & Finance Librarianship* and is co-author of *Using Microsoft PowerPoint: A How-To-Do-It Manual for Librarians* (Neal-Schuman, 1998). He has published numerous book chapters and articles, including publications in *College & Research Libraries, Journal of Academic Librarianship, Reference & User Services Quarterly, Reference Librarian, Collection Building*, and *The Journal of Marketing Management*. In addition, he has published proceedings and made presentations at many national conferences, including National Online, Internet Librarian, Computers in Libraries, Online World, and Integrated Online Library Systems.

White is an active member of the American Library Association, especially in the Business Reference and Services Section (BRASS) of the Reference and User Services Association of ALA. He served as chair of BRASS's 1999 conference program committee and is chair of the 2003 preconference program. He would like to thank Christopher D. Greiner for his editorial assistance.

Christine A. Whittington, BA, MSLS

Head, Reference Services and Assistant Access Librarian
Raymond H. Fogler Library
University of Maine

Reference Department Head Christine Whittington's responsibilities include reference service, collection development, and instruction in the use of information resources with specialization in the areas of anthropology, art and art history, communication and journalism, theater, and the dance. She is active in several important American Library Association committees, reviews regularly reference books for "Reference Books Bulletin" in *Booklist*, and has authored articles, contributed book chapters, and delivered presentations, including on the history of tattooing within the contexts of folklore and popular culture. She is a member of the Popular Culture Association, the American Culture Association, and the American Folklore Society.

Diane Zabel, M UP, MSLIS

Endowed Librarian for Business
Schreyer Business Library
University Libraries
The Pennsylvania State University

Diane Zabel, business librarian in the Schreyer Business Library at Penn State, is the first Endowed Librarian for Business in the University Libraries. She holds the rank of librarian. Diane is a member of the American Library Association, having chaired committees relating to continuing education, information literacy, and building library collections. She has authored numerous articles and co-authored several books, including *The Flexible Workplace: A Sourcebook for Information and Research* (2001) with Christine Avery for Quorum Books, *The Quality Management Sourcebook: An International Guide to Materials and Resources* for Routledge (1997) (with Avery), and *Bridging the Gap: Examining Polarity in America* (1995) for Libraries Unlimited with Nancy L. Herron. Since 1999, she has served as the editor of the "Alert Collector" column in *Reference & User Services Quarterly*.

General Editor

Nancy L. Herron, BS, MLS, PhD
Associate Dean for Academic Programs, Commonwealth College
Librarian, University Libraries
The Pennsylvania State University

Dr. Nancy L. Herron joined Penn State as a head librarian in 1984. She was named administrative fellow in 1990, serving in the Office of the Executive Vice President and Provost of the University. In 1991 she was appointed director of academic affairs at Penn State McKeesport, a position she held for eight years; in 1992 she was promoted to full professional rank. In 1999 Dr. Herron was appointed as associate dean for academic programs for the Commonwealth College. In spring she was awarded the Achieving Woman Award from the Penn State Commission for Women, an organization she chaired in 1997. She has received the Advisory Board Campus Leadership Award and the Advocacy Award from the Department of Continuing Education and has been a member of Beta Phi Mu since 1972. As an academic scholar, she has served as general editor for reference texts edited for Libraries Unlimited since 1986. She is a member of the American Association of Higher Education and the American Library Association.

Part 1

General Literature of the Social Sciences

General Social Sciences

Christine A. Whittington

ESSAY

Defining the Social Sciences in the 21st Century

     In the introduction to the chapter on general social sciences in the first edition of this guide, we endeavored to pin down a definition of the social sciences and to define the disciplines they encompass. We cited the 1930 definition by R. A. Seligman, editor-in-chief of *Encyclopedia of the Social Sciences* (A-52) as "those mental or cultural sciences, which deal with the activities of the individual as a member of a group."[1] Seligman divided the social sciences into three groups. The older, purely social sciences are political science, economics, history, and jurisprudence. Those "of more recent origin" are anthropology, penology, sociology, and social work. The semi-social sciences are social in origin or have acquired a social aspect: ethics, education, philosophy, and psychology. A third category consists of natural and cultural sciences with recognized social implications: biology, geography, linguistics, and art.[2] In the second edition of the *Social Science Encyclopedia*, Ralf Dahrendorf presented a more contemporary definition:

> The social sciences include economics, sociology (and anthropology) and political science. At their boundaries, the social sciences reach into the study of the individual (social psychology) and of nature (social biology, social geography). Methodologically, they straddle normative (law, social philosophy, political theory) and historical approaches (social history, economic history). In terms of university departments, the social sciences have split up into numerous areas of teaching and research, including not only the central disciplines, but also such subjects as industrial relations, international relations, business studies, and social (public) administration.[3]

3

Although reference book editors continue to include different disciplines and fields of study within their definitions of the social sciences, the importance of trying to reach a consensus about which disciplines are or are not included seems inconsequential next to the new theoretical approaches, applications and methodology, and the social dimensions and implications of a vast array of other disciplines, from genetics to spatial engineering. Adam Kuper and Jessica Kuper have noted that "[m]any fields have moved on from the preoccupations of the 1980s."[4] It no longer seems as crucial to establish whether business, philosophy, or demography are indeed social sciences as it is to examine new or freshly approached fields of study such as post-modernism, subcultures, sex and gender, environmental and resource economics, media studies, and cultural studies.

Scholarly Communication in the Social Sciences

The 1989 edition of this guide included mostly print resources. The 1996 edition included relatively few new print titles but listed electronic equivalents of print sources and resources available only in electronic format. This edition includes more resources available electronically only (such as the *World Biographical Index* and *FedStats*) and focuses on electronic, rather than print, versions because those are the versions that most researchers are using. Although all librarians should be aware of the existence of the print version of *Dissertation Abstracts* or the *Monthly Catalog of Government Publications*, for example, not many librarians or researchers choose to perform comprehensive searches in those indexes if an electronic version is available. At the time the 1996 edition of this guide was being written, use of the World Wide Web in the reference environment was still in its infancy. Librarians depended on electronic discussion lists such as LIBREF-L and GOVDOC-L to keep in touch with developments in the world of electronic information. Librarians watched in fascination while an image of a butterfly loaded on the Web browser Mosaic over a period of several minutes. At the turn of the millennium, electronic versions of reference sources not only replicate their print versions but also use interactivity and hyperlinking features to link to resources elsewhere on the Web. For example, *Statistical Universe*, the electronic equivalent of the *American Statistics Index*, not only provides the SuDocs numbers needed to retrieve publications in government documents collections but also links to full-text publications available on the Internet. The *Catalog of Government Publications* is more than the Web version of the *Monthly Catalog of Government Publications*, providing links to full-text publications and to agency Web sites. Librarians and social scientists still share information on e-mail and electronic discussion lists but also routinely check portals like *FedStats*, the *Scout Report*, and the *Librarians' Index to the Internet* to keep up with technology.

Electronic publishing has not completely superseded print publishing in the social sciences. The 1996 edition of this guide noted the continued use of print classics such as the *Dictionary of the History of Ideas*, the *Encyclopedia of the Social Sciences*, and the *International Encyclopedia of the Social Sciences*, and this guide retains those classic sources. Although it has not yet been published as of this writing, the new *International Encyclopedia of the Social and Behavioral Sciences* (*IESBS*) (Elsevier, 2001) has the potential to become the social sciences encyclopedia of the new millennium. Like many other massive reference works (the *Dictionary of Art*, for example), the *IESBS* is preceded by and accompanied by a Web page that includes plans for publication, abstracts of articles, several sample articles, and a list of topics. After the print version has been published, the Web site will continue to offer updates and special features.

Internet resources have given research not so much an electronic substitute for print resources as additional options. Librarians still serve as leaders, teaching their users how to determine whether their information needs will be best served by using print sources, electronic sources, or a combination of both. Because university professors and high school teachers have expressed dismay at student papers citing only Internet sources—and not always good ones—librarians have also begun to teach their users to evaluate critically material they find on the Internet. In the second edition of our book, we mentioned the freewheeling nature of and lack of quality control on the Internet and the various tools used to gain access to it. The tools mentioned—Gopher, Archie, Veronica, and Mosaic—have long since gone to the Internet vocabulary graveyard, replaced by Google, Northern Light, Yahoo, and Inference Find, as well as a number of specialized portals, such as University of Michigan's Document Center.

One thing that has not changed is the assumption among many library users that all information needed is free on the Internet and that all the librarian (or user) needs to do is "punch it into the computer and get it from the Web." Although a great deal of information is indeed free, database vendors, periodical publishers, and producers of market research and financial records are not about to make their expensive products available free to all Internet users. On the other hand, scholars are exploring refereed electronic publishing ventures and ownership of their own work to address the high price tag that information often carries. Initiatives such as SPARC (Scholarly Publishing and Academic Resources Coalition) hope to "return science to the scientists" by using technology to bring quality research to a broader audience at a lower cost. Social science initiatives include electronic publications such as the *Electronic Journal of Communication* (*EJC/REC*), e-published by the Communication Institute for Online Scholarship.

Much research in the social sciences is recorded in unpublished papers; in conferences whose proceedings are not always published; and in materials produced by national and international organizations, research centers, and corporations. As information has become increasingly available on the Internet, librarians and other information professionals have created sources that identify and control this information. Because many social science disciplines depend on recent information, prompt access to these materials is essential. Primary sources and review articles are usually more useful to the social scientist than books, which may not be as up-to-date or as specialized. Reference sources provide access to both types of materials, and if the source is online on a commercial database or the Internet, information is usually even more timely. A need for very recent materials often involves online database searching or identifying people or organizations that the researcher can contact to initiate networking activity.

The interdisciplinary nature of much social science research requires the use of sources involving several disciplines both within and outside the social sciences. For example, an economist working on valuation of natural resources will study human needs for recreation and scenic areas. The social sciences librarian must be aware of reference sources covering tangential disciplines so users will not miss relevant materials that may not be included in reference sources specific to their disciplines.

Research in the social sciences is complicated by terminology that varies according to discipline, reference source, chronological period, geographic location, and individual author. Terminology in the natural sciences is much better defined and more consistent. Controlled subject headings exist for many sources, but others, such as the *Social Sciences Citation Index* (A-23), *Dissertation Abstracts International* (A-39), *NTIS Database* (A-48), and the online periodical index CARL *UnCover* (A-17), have little controlled vocabulary, and access is dependent upon the titles and abstracts authors have written for their papers. Even when controlled vocabulary is present, as in online public access catalogs or general periodical indexes, many users do not use it, preferring to search by keywords. The "softness" of social science terminology, although not as problematic as in the humanities, can be a challenge for reference librarians.

Once information has been located, its delivery is the next issue to be addressed. The Internet has revolutionized document delivery. Most periodical articles can be faxed or delivered to a researcher's computer desktop, if the researcher is willing to pay the price of document delivery through databases such as *UnCover*. Material retrieved on the Internet can be e-mailed, downloaded, or printed. Some "chat" reference services offer technology that enables a librarian to "push" a Web page to the person at the other end of the "chat." In the second edition of this book, it was noted that "the delivery method has become part of the total reference environment" and, at the turn of the millennium, this is more true than ever.

Information Strategies

In the first and second editions of this guide, it was noted that reference strategies varied according the problem to be explored, the sophistication of the researcher, and the resources within the person's reach. Previous volumes discussed differences among "laypeople," undergraduate students, graduate students, faculty, and professional researchers. Many of these distinctions are beginning to blur. Library users once thought of as laypeople are beginning to take undergraduate and graduate level courses, often at a distance from the academic institution with which they are registered, connecting with their own computers. Computers that can provide access to e-mail and the Web are being marketed to students and their families. Resources within reach extend around the world. "Traditional" undergraduate students may come to their university libraries with inadequate preparation for writing research papers, having discovered the wealth of information available at their fingertips on the Internet but not having mastered the tools for critical analysis of those resources. Graduate students may be returning to the research environment after many years away at a time when only a few months away may drastically change resources available at their libraries. Thus, it is more reasonable to define information strategies by the type of problem rather than the type of library user.

Some library users need to find information about real-life issues that concern them. This can range from a need to find information about immigration and naturalization, to whether a news story is real or a hoax or "urban legend," to the types of decorations associated with Mardi Gras. Library users looking for this type of information may have limited time to spend looking for it in a library. They may phone the library to get advice on how to search for this information on the Internet or ask that it be mailed, e-mailed, or faxed to them. They may be best served by references to government Web sites, online almanacs, online encyclopedias, or general periodical indexes that include full-text articles that can be printed out quickly, downloaded, or e-mailed. Library users looking for this type of information especially appreciate electronic resources because they often provide information that is immediately accessible, rather than having to decipher and round up a list of sources from a bibliographic database. Many popular magazines include columns on Internet resources, and publications such as *Wired* (1993-) and *Yahoo Internet Life* (1996-) are devoted to the Internet. In the second edition of this guide we mentioned that *Newsweek* had a regular feature on the "Net;" now the *New Yorker* has a regular Web column and *Martha Stewart Living* includes references to Web sites.

Undergraduate research supporting term papers and coursework is often similar to the information needs described above in its urgency and the desire of undergraduate researchers for full-text and immediately usable information rather than a list of sources. An additional characteristic of undergraduate research is that material retrieved usually must be scholarly in nature, and undergraduates' professors often require—with good intentions—that a certain number of resources be in print rather than Internet resources. This last criterion is often the result of faculty members having received too many papers citing only Internet resources or looking suspiciously as though they had been downloaded from the Internet. Individuals researching undergraduate papers or projects still need to identify important books and articles in their disciplines and critically evaluate what they find, whether or not they acquired their articles full text on the Internet. They may need an electronic or print source that will help them choose a topic or design a research project. Undergraduate students may also be faced with designing a research project for the first time. They will also need to identify measures, tests, and scales used in social science research. They will require clear and concise discussions of abstract concepts, such as postmodernism, semiotics, existentialism, or teleology, that they may hear in class or find in their readings but not completely understand.

Undergraduate researchers need to find discussions of major thinkers in their fields—Foucault is popular in the social sciences these days—definitions of specialized or technical terms, and statistics to reinforce their arguments. The second edition of this guide noted that undergraduates' use of the electronic sources consisted of "online public access catalogs and general periodical indexes." Five years later, undergraduates use the Web search engines more than public access catalogs and almost certainly use public access catalogs on the Web. Students doing undergraduate research should be encouraged to become more familiar with specialized resources in their fields—both electronic and print—and critically evaluate what they find on the Internet. They can increase the quality of Internet sites they use by applying standards for evaluating resources and becoming familiar with portals that exercise some control over the Web sites they include, such as the *Scout Report for the Social Sciences*, or the library's own refereed lists of Web resources.

Graduate students, university faculty, and practitioners such as psychologists, social workers, economists, and those working in public policy or criminal justice are usually involved in very specialized research. Like people researching real-life problems or involved in undergraduate coursework, this user group seeks to locate articles, facts, books, and specialized Web sites on their topics, but intense professional networking, resource-sharing behavior, and the practice of identifying materials through lists of references in articles rather than indexes or abstracts often cause them to come to the library already knowing what materials they need to support their research. Some may feel little need for "finding" tools and may not be aware of indexing and abstracting sources in their fields. Some enjoy conducting research themselves and make an effort to discover all ways of finding information, including electronically.

Others may be suspicious of information available on the Internet, especially if it dominates their students' papers. On the other hand, professional practitioners are usually problem-oriented and generally prefer the Internet or database searching to searches of print indexes to save time when pursuing information on elusive, specialized topics. Practitioners with corporate libraries may rely completely on fee-based electronic database searches. Because social sciences research often involves scientific method, including controlling the variability of human behavior, graduate students, university faculty, and practitioners often need access to information about research design and social measurement. They need detailed information about various research options (surveys, questionnaires, and the like) and test and scale construction more than do the undergraduate or the practitioner. Graduate students, faculty, and practitioners may all need data of the type that can be found on the Internet and in commercial electronic sources.

All types of users may be interested in electronic subject-oriented discussion groups, but such groups have revolutionized the communication of academic and professional researchers. News of archaeological discoveries often appears on the archaeology discussion list (ARCH-L) before it appears anywhere in print. Novices can post questions on discussion lists or Ask-a-Librarian sites and receive advice from the top experts in the field within days, if not hours. Web sites such as *Government Documents in the News*[5] or *Anthropology in the News* make news and discoveries even easier to find.

The type of information needed to satisfy these types of research activities varies according to the specific problem, the discipline, and the level of research required to satisfy the information need. The needs of the social science researcher will further depend on whether the problem requires current or retrospective information, whether there are other disciplines within or outside the social sciences that should be considered, and the geographic and chronological parameters of the problem. The reference interview can uncover these parameters, help the researcher define questions that need to be answered, and match reference sources to individual questions.

Many libraries subscribe to suites of licensed databases that their users have access to within the library and remotely from home. The growth of distance education—students completing coursework via interactive television or courses on the Web—has created a demand for licenses for even more full-text databases.

Area Studies

In an article in the *International Encyclopedia of Education*, P. Foster defined area studies as "academic programs of study focusing upon particular nation-states or clusters of states characterized by contiguous geographic location and usually exhibiting common characteristics in terms of social structure, culture, or linguistic and historical traditions."[6] During the 1930s, U.S. colleges and universities began to develop academic programs around the study of particular regions of the world. These programs came to be known as "area studies" in course catalogs and bulletins and were often linked to disciplines in the social sciences as well as studies of language, culture, and humanities. During World War II and the postwar period, wariness toward other countries and a heightened demand for information about distant places lent urgency to the development of area studies programs. Bryce Wood, in his article on area studies in the *International Encyclopedia of the Social Sciences* (A-55), wrote that area studies programs in U.S. universities were "largely created on a `know-your-enemy' basis."[7] The phrase "area studies" was first used in a military intelligence context.[8] Western governments, including that of the United States, felt that the expertise was not available to inform international relations policymakers and military personnel about the languages, ethnic groups, cultures, and geographic characteristics of areas about which important military, political, and economic decisions would have to be made, especially Soviet bloc countries and developing nations, such as those in Latin America, Asia, and Africa.[9] At first, individuals were trained in language programs within the armed forces, then academe provided expertise through faculty specialists who focused on specific regions of the world. After World War II, grants from the Carnegie Corporation of New York and the

Rockefeller Foundation funded Russian studies centers at Harvard and Columbia Universities, which served as models for area studies centers at other academic institutions, many of which were supported by the Ford Foundation.[10] The National Defense Education Act, Fulbright-Hayes Act, Foreign Area Fellowship Program, and private foundation awards provided for expansion of area studies programs.[11]

Although sometimes called a discipline, area studies can be more accurately described as an interdisciplinary program that takes advantage of the expertise of faculty in a wide range of programs in the humanities, social sciences, and sciences. The Committee on World Area Research listed the most desirable features of area programs as intensive language instruction; joint seminars; group research; combined study in humanities and social sciences; participation of foreign students and faculty members; and the availability of specialized materials such as newspapers, official records, maps, and other sources.[12] Research and publication in area studies began to increase steadily, and by the 1960s three research councils—the American Council of Learned Societies, the National Research Council, and the Social Science Research Council—were all providing leadership in some aspects of area studies. Implications for college and research libraries increased substantially as the proliferation of publications emerging from world presses and world organizations skyrocketed. This geometric growth brought new problems for libraries associated with institutions that were trying valiantly to collect comprehensively in all areas. This challenge was heightened by staggering new printing costs, changing world alliances, and diverse user populations with more complex information needs.

The American Library Association's focus on area studies began as a project conceived and developed by the Collection Management and Development Committee, Resources and Technical Services Division. Its first volume, *Selection of Library Materials in the Humanities, Social Sciences and Sciences* (American Library Association) was published in 1985. From that publication grew the idea for a series of three volumes, the second of which was titled *Selection of Library Materials in Applied and Interdisciplinary Fields* (American Library Association, 1987). The third and final volume of the series was devoted exclusively to area studies, covering the entire world except for North America. Because of scheduling difficulties and potential manuscript length, it was decided to issue this volume in two parts, with Asia, the Iberian Peninsula, the Caribbean and Latin America, Eastern Europe and the Soviet Union, and the South Pacific grouped together in the first part and Australia, Canada, and New Zealand making up the second part of the publication, titled *Selection of Library Materials for Area Studies* (1990–1994). Other scholars, including members of learned societies and area studies departments, defined the world (excluding North America) in the following seven geographic regions: Africa, Latin America, South Asia, the Middle East, the Far East, the Slavic and East European countries, and Western Europe. All helped to define a structure for the literature and access to it.

Cecily Johns noted that while academic institutions and research centers developed area studies programs, public, school, and academic libraries are also interested in collecting materials in area studies. All types of libraries now serve diverse communities, including Spanish-speaking users and immigrants from Asia and former Soviet countries.[13] In their introduction to a collection of essays about area studies in U.S. libraries, Marianna Tax Choldin et al. wrote that "this nation's ability to deal successfully in strategic, political, economic, and cultural spheres with important parts of the world depends to a significant extent on our ability to provide access to information from and about those parts of the world."[14]

In the reference environment, area studies resources present additional challenges because of time lags in obtaining information, erratic indexing, and bibliographic control. The Internet has eased research in areas studies because many resources are now available on the Web that would have been impossible to gain access to even a few years ago. National organizations and national libraries have Web site and Web-publishing initiatives, such as Unesco's directory of social science institutions, that make communication and networking easier than ever.

Selection of Sources

The sources listed in this section were chosen for their relevance to the social sciences, regardless of whether they are considered "social sciences sources." Therefore, general sources like the *Encyclopedia of Associations* (A-67, A-68, A-69) are included if they are "the best there is" for the social sciences. Familiarity with the most general reference sources, such as *Books in Print* (R. R. Bowker) or the *WorldCat* (Library of Congress), is assumed. Because of the increasingly interdisciplinary and international nature of social sciences literature, sources have been chosen that respond to those concerns. To be considered for this section, a source had to cover social science disciplines broadly. Those concentrating only on one or two disciplines are listed in the individual chapters. Sources generally considered outside the social sciences, such as the *Humanities Index* (A-25), are mentioned if they cover several social science disciplines. Except for classics, up-to-date sources were preferred for this list.

New editions were examined and evaluated for their current relevance. Some older publications that were not included in the first edition of this book, such as *CQ Researcher* (A-26), are included in this edition because their usefulness for social science research has become more evident over the years. The final criterion is usefulness in the reference environment. Sources defined as reference tools include those that supply information within themselves (e.g., an address, a definition), that lead the user to other sources of information (e.g., a periodical index, a bibliography), and that combine these two features (e.g., an encyclopedia that provides a definition and includes a list for further reading). Textbooks and other sources more suitable for reading cover-to-cover were excluded, as were those intended primarily for juvenile audiences. Electronic sources have been included along with print sources because it is no longer feasible to separate sources by format, especially when sources are often available in multiple formats.

GUIDES AND HANDBOOKS

Guides to the Literature

A-1   Hoselitz, Bert F. **A Reader's Guide to the Social Sciences**. 2d ed. New York: Free Press, 1970.

This older book is still valuable for its examination of "differences in literary output in the major disciplines and the nature of available tools." It consists of chapters on sociology, anthropology, psychology, political science, economics, and geography, each written by a different contributor and each highly individual in organization and approach. Each chapter contains an essay on the development and nature of the discipline as a whole and subdisciplines, research methods, contemporary issues, theory and applications, and a bibliographic essay. Books discussed were not selected because they were the "worthiest titles in a field" but because they presented "certain peculiarities worth discussion." A general bibliography arranged by subject field concludes the work

A-2   Li, Tze-chung. **Social Science Reference Sources: A Practical Guide**. 3d ed. Westport, CT: Greenwood Press, 2000.

The third edition of Li's classic guide is limited to "basic, important reference sources in the social sciences." It eliminates the previous editions' chapters on the nature of the social sciences, patterns of information usage, and bibliographical needs of social scientists. The guide is divided into two sections. The first section, on social sciences in general, includes chapters on reference sources in the electronic age (databases, Web sites, search engines), research resources, access to resources (guides, reviews, bibliographies, indexes, selective dissemination of information, contents reproduction), sources of information (encyclopedias, dictionaries, directories), statistical sources, and government publications.

The second section includes reference materials in cultural anthropology, business, economics, education, geography, history, law, political science, psychology, and sociology. In all, Li discusses approximately 1,600 reference sources, of which more than 200 are Web sites. He groups comparable reference sources, discussing their similarities and differences. Because Li excludes from this edition most titles published after 1980, ceased serial publications, and sections on "additional reference sources," the second edition of this work and Webb's guide (A-3) may prove useful for older information. Li's chapter on reference sources in the electronic age is a good, concise summary of developments during the last twenty years or so. His discussion of database providers, search engines, and Web sites is as useful as is feasible for a print guide to electronic sources.

A-3 Webb, William. **Sources of Information in the Social Sciences: A Guide to the Literature**. 3d ed. Chicago: American Library Association, 1986.

This is the most recent edition of a classic guide originally compiled by Carl M. White and based on work with library science graduate students at Columbia University in the 1950s. Its purpose is to provide a systematic guide to the literature of social science fields. It covers history, geography, economics and business administration, sociology, anthropology, psychology, education, and political science. The guide also includes chapters on general social science literature: its evolution and uses and the structure of its information system. Each discipline chapter provides annotated citations to sources arranged by type. Although it is now out of print and predates the extensive use of the Internet in social sciences librarianship, Webb's guide remains valuable because it is the most comprehensive of those listed here. More than 8,000 items are discussed, including classic monographs, important journals, and databases in each field as well as reference books.

A-4 Schutt, Russell K. **Investigating the Social World: The Process and Practice of Research**. 2d ed. Thousand Oaks, CA: Pine Forge Press, 1999.

This comprehensive guide is a combination of a textbook and reference guide, introducing readers to social science research from the very beginning of the research process, ranging from "Reasoning about the Social World" and "Questions and Answers About the Social World" to theories, research strategies, scientific and ethical guidelines, measures, research design, sampling, survey research, qualitative methods, historical and comparative methods, examples of case studies using multiple methods, data analysis, and reporting research results. Appendixes include summaries of frequently cited research articles, questions to ask about research articles, finding information, using statistical packages, a table of random numbers, and a helpful list of Web sites.

Research Methodology

A-5 Bouma, Gary D., and G. B. Atkinson. **A Handbook of Social Science Research**. 2d ed. New York: Oxford University Press, 1995.

An introductory handbook to social sciences research for students and others in need of basic information about research, this book examines problem identification and definition, hypothesis development, identification of variables and their measurement, research design, qualitative research, and sampling. The second edition of this guide incorporates new information about the use of computers in social sciences research.

A-6 Miller, Delvert C. **Handbook of Research Design and Social Measurement**. 5th ed. New York: Longman, 1991.

This is an indispensable guide to the design of a social science research project, from defining a problem and turning an idea into a hypothesis to identifying outlets for publishing the results of an investigation. The handbook includes sections on research design and sampling; research methods; applied and evaluation research; methods and techniques of data collection (in the library, the field, the laboratory, and social science data and research centers); statistical analysis and computer resources; selected sociometric scales and indexes; and research proposals, funding, costing, reporting, and career utilization. The section on data collection covers literature searches, databases, and government information. It includes a bibliography of reference books and a list of data archives. Information is provided on sampling, scale construction, the return rates and costs of mail questionnaires, instructions for telephone interviewing, and other practical matters, and Miller addresses the more recent practice of social scientists to devise their own item scales.

Some of the chapters are specifically intended for the sociologist, but most are broad enough to be useful to researchers in other social science disciplines. The section on applied and evaluation research is new to this edition, added to respond to the growth of employment opportunities for social scientists in government, private industry, public policy, or other nonuniversity settings. This edition of Miller's handbook was published ten years ago and predates extensive use of the Internet (particularly the Web) in social sciences research. The reference value of the book is hampered by the lack of a thorough subject index.

A-7 Vogt, Paul. **Dictionary of Statistics and Methodology: A Nontechnical Guide for the Social Sciences**. 2d ed. Thousand Oaks, CA: Sage, 1999.

This compendium of quick definitions of statistical terms is intended to "lower the jargon barrier" by providing nontechnical definitions of statistical and methodological terms used in the social and behavioral sciences. This dictionary does not explain how to devise statistical measures or compute statistics and does not include algebraic equations in its definitions. For information on designing a research project, social scientists should consult Delvert Miller's *Handbook of Research Design and Social Measurement* (A-6). The strengths of *Dictionary of Statistics and Methodology* are its provision of examples that illustrate the verbal definitions and make them understandable to students in introductory statistics courses and social scientists who are not statistics experts or are familiar with only certain types of statistics, and its identification of the "bottom line"—why the topic is important. A standard error of the mean, for example, "gives an answer to the question: how good an estimate of the population mean is the sample mean?" A lurking variable "is a third variable that causes a correlation between the two others—sometimes, like the troll under the bridge, an unpleasant surprise when discovered."

BIBLIOGRAPHIES

A-8 Bibliographic Index: A Cumulative Bibliography of Bibliographies. Bronx, NY: H. W. Wilson, 1937- . Quarterly with annual cumulations.

Bibliographic Index is a subject index to bibliographies in all disciplines published separately, as parts of books or pamphlets, and in periodical articles. Approximately 10,000 bibliographies in books and 5,000 in periodicals are indexed annually. Bibliographies with more than fifty citations are included. Bibliographies with fewer citations are included for works by or about a person or on a specialized topic. Concentration is on citations in English, other Germanic languages, and the Romance languages. Material is selected from about 2,800 periodicals and 50,000 books scanned annually for bibliographies. *Bibliographic Index* is searchable by subject, keyword, or personal name. It enables the user to locate bibliographies on very specialized topics, including those published more recently than Theodore Besterman's *World Bibliography of Bibliographies* (Societas Bibliographia, 1965–1966) or its supplement compiled by Alice Toomey, *A World Bibliography of Bibliographies, 1964–1974* (Rowman and Littlefield, 1977). Recent issues list bibliographies on teenage girls, reality television programs, and social aspects of technology and the Internet.

A-9 **A London Bibliography of the Social Sciences**. 4 vols. London: School of Economics and Political Science, 1931–1932.

A London Bibliography of the Social Sciences. Supplement. London: British Library of Political and Economic Science, 1934–1968; Mansell, 1970–1989.

The first four-volume compilation of the *London Bibliography of the Social Sciences*, published in 1931–1932, was a union catalog of the holdings of the British Library of Political and Economic Science (BLPES) plus nine other libraries, including the National Institute of Industrial Psychology, the Royal Anthropological Institute, and the Royal Institute on International Affairs. The *London Bibliography* remains a critical source for social sciences researchers because of its historical scope. As a union catalog, the first compilation includes references to items dating back to at least the seventeenth century. The first supplement also consisted of additions to these libraries, but since then additions have represented only the collections of the BLPES and the Edward Fry Library of International Law (EFLIL). The BLPES collections are not restricted to economics, as the library collects extensively in all areas of the social sciences (with its greatest strength, in economics, political science, and law). Subjects covered in the bibliography include the whole range of social science topics. For example, the 1989 supplement included items on subjects as diverse as the 700 Club, Anglo-Saxons, body image, language acquisition, and traffic violations. Types of materials covered include books; discussion papers; occasional papers; and publications of governmental, intergovernmental, and private organizations. Periodical articles are not included. In 1990, the *London Bibliography of the Social Sciences* was absorbed by the *International Bibliography of the Social Sciences*, issued annually in four parts: *Sociology* (H-56), *Political Science* (B-15), *Economics* (C-17), and *Social and Cultural Anthropology* (G-50).

INDEXES AND ABSTRACTS

In this section, availability in electronic format is indicated at the end of each annotation. Annotations focus on the features of electronic versions, when they are available and widely used. In these cases, descriptions of the arrangement of the print formats of the indexes have been eliminated or abbreviated from previous editions of this guide.

General Periodical Indexes

A-10 **Academic Search FullTEXT**. Birmingham, AL: Ebsco, 1984- . Updated daily. Online format.

Academic Search FullTEXT indexes approximately 2,930 popular and academic journals in all areas, including the social sciences, plus the *New York Times*, *Wall Street Journal*, and *Christian Science Monitor*. It is available in Premier, Elite, and Select editions, varying by the number of journals indexed for which full text is provided. In the Elite edition, full text is included for approximately 1,380 journals. More than 1,780 periodicals are peer reviewed; of these, full text of approximately 700 is available. Full-text backfiles go as far back as January 1990, while indexing and abstract backfiles go as far back as January 1984. In some cases, full text is available as scanned pdf files, including graphics and illustrations, in addition to plain text.

Electronic access: Available online through EBSCO Host and on CD-ROM.

A-11 **access: The Supplementary Index to Periodicals**. Evanston, IL: John Gordon Burke, 1975- .

access is designed to complement the *Readers' Guide to Periodical Literature* (A-16) by indexing magazines not covered by the *Readers' Guide*, new national magazines, and regional publications as well as general interest publications. Author and subject indexes allow users to find articles on crop circles and Marfa mystery lights in *Fate* magazine, women's shoes in *W* and *Elle*, and tattooing in *Penthouse*; Mardi Gras traditions in *Louisiana Life*; and snowboarding in *Outside. access* is especially good for popular topics within the social sciences or popular treatments of a variety of topics.

Electronic access: Online access is available through the publisher.

A-12 Alternative Press Index. College Park, MD: Alternative Press Center, 1969- . Quarterly with annual cumulation. Online format. URL: http://www.altpress.org/api.html.

The Alternative Press Center, founded in 1969, is a "non-profit collective dedicated to providing access to and increasing public awareness of the alternative press." *Alternative Press Index* (API) was created to "provide access to the practices and theories of radical social change." It provides access to approximately 250 popular and scholarly "alternative, radical, and left" English-language periodicals for readers who want to locate articles on special issues or viewpoints not usually addressed in the mainstream publications indexed in *Readers' Guide* (A-16) or general electronic indexes such as *Expanded Academic Index ASAP* (A-15). Far from being restricted to underground publications, API indexes many highly regarded periodicals that appear on newsstands and in public and academic libraries but that may not be indexed elsewhere. It is international and interdisciplinary,"with its central focus on the practice and theory of socialism, national liberation, labor, indigenous peoples, gays/lesbians, feminism, ecology, democracy, and anarchism." Journals indexed include *Animals' Agenda*, *Progressive Librarian*, and *Journal of Prisoners on Prisons*. Each issue contains a list of periodicals indexed, with a note about the viewpoint of each. Standard bibliographic citations to articles of five paragraphs or more, bibliographies, directories and lists of resources, editorials, reviews, interviews, obituaries, speeches, poems, fiction, songs, recipes, and regular columns are arranged by subject. In addition to articles of fewer than five paragraphs, some of the items excluded are comic strips. The APC Web site includes the Alternative Press Center's Online Directory of periodicals (http://www.altpress.org/direct.html) with links to Web sites for periodicals such as *Lambda Book Report*, *Teen Voices*, and *Journal of Prisoners on Prisons*.

Electronic access: CD-ROM through NISCDiscover (National Information Services Corporation); online through BiblioLine.

A-13 ArticleFirst. Dublin, OH: OCLC Online Computer Library Center, 1990- . Updated daily. Online format. URL: http://www.oclc.org/servers/databases.

A-14 ContentsFirst. Dublin, OH: OCLC Online Computer Library Center, 1990- . Updated daily. Online format.

These online databases index a wide range of popular and scholarly periodicals in social sciences as well as medicine, technology, humanities, and popular culture. *ArticleFirst* provides indexing by author, subject, or title keyword for more than 12,500 journals. *ContentsFirst* provides table of contents access to the same journals.

Electronic access: Available online through OCLC's FirstSearch program.

A-15 Expanded Academic Index ASAP. Detroit: GaleGroup, 1976- . Daily. Electronic format.

Before online access became the norm, *Expanded Academic Index* and other databases produced by Information access Corporation (IAC) were issued on computer-output microfilm (COM), then on laser disc. The CD-ROM versions, known as *InfoTrac*, were offered on their own workstations and included several years of indexing. *InfoTrac* was the first periodical index issued on optical laser disc. *Expanded Academic Index* covers approximately 2,600 general-interest and scholarly publications in the humanities, social sciences, general sciences, and current events, with 1,400 full-text titles and 1,400 refereed journals. GaleGroup also offers *Academic ASAP*, which provides full text for 600 journals across all disciplines. Full text once available on accompanying microfilm cartridges is now included on the Web version.

Electronic access: Online and CD-ROM (1985-) from GaleGroup.

A-16 **Readers' Guide to Periodical Literature**. Bronx, NY: H. W. Wilson, 1900/1904- . Semimonthly. Online format. URL: http://www.wilsonweb.hwwilson.com.

Before the advent of electronic periodical indexes, *Readers' Guide* was almost every beginning library user's first periodical index. It still performs this function in libraries without electronic resources. For libraries with electronic periodical indexes, *Readers' Guide* is still useful as the only index that covers articles published in general interest periodicals before the mid-1980s, when most electronic indexes begin their coverage. It also has advantages over electronic indexes for users who wish to scan Wilson's excellent subject headings and lists of articles quickly rather than reading references to the articles on a computer screen or taking the time to make a long printout. *Readers' Guide* covers primarily popular, nontechnical periodicals published in the United States.

Having begun in 1901 with 15 magazines, it now indexes 204 general interest periodicals such as *Time*, *Newsweek*, *Sports Illustrated*, *Consumer Reports*, *Ms.*, and *National Geographic*, but it also covers *Foreign Affairs*, *Science*, *Monthly Labor Review*, and *Omni*. Use of *Readers' Guide* is not limited to general readers. Specialists can consult it to find out how their discipline is presented to the general public. Also, current events and research breakthroughs of public interest are often reported in newsweeklies before they are analyzed in more specialized scholarly journals. Articles in the newsweeklies identify researchers and research institutions, enabling readers to find more scholarly publications. Cumulative indexes are issued annually and in compilations of two to five years. Entries with standard bibliographic citations are arranged in one alphabet by author and controlled subject headings with topical and geographical subdivisions. Book reviews are listed separately by author at the end of each issue.

Nineteenth Century Readers' Guide to Periodical Literature (H. W. Wilson, 1944) is a two-volume set providing indexing for fifty periodicals from 1890 to 1899, with supplementary indexing for 1900 to 1922. *Poole's Index to Periodical Literature* and its five supplements (P. Smith, 1963) cover 1802 through 1907. *Readers' Guide Abstracts* provides 125-word abstracts for articles in 272 journals indexed in *Readers' Guide*. The service on microfiche (1986-) includes abstracts for all 60,000 articles indexed per year,[15] while the paper version (1988-) includes 25,000 abstracts per year selected for their lasting research significance. *Readers' Guide Full Text* (1994-) offers Mega (137 journals full text; 272 indexed) and Mini (85 full text; 160 indexed) versions.

Electronic access: Available online through WilsonWeb.

A-17 **UnCover**. Denver, CO: CARL Corporation, 1988- . Updated daily. Online format. URL: unweb.carl.org.

UnCover was originally based on the serial holdings of the Colorado Alliance of Research Libraries (CARL). Information was input from the tables of contents of more than 18,000 periodicals. *UnCover* now includes access by author, personal name (as a subject), and title keyword. Subject headings are not assigned to the articles. This practice enables the records to be added to the database within a short time. *UnCover* claims that articles appear there at the same time the periodical issues are delivered, which makes it the most up-to-date index anywhere. It also means that users must exercise some creativity in subject searching. *UnCover* also provides a table of contents search and the UnCover Reveal automated alerting service. Document delivery through fax and electronic image downloading to desktops is available through *UnCover*. A list of the social sciences indexed is available through the Web site. *Uncover* lists the most diverse range of periodicals of any periodical database included here. Titles include *Modern Bride*, *Sheriff: The Magazine of the National Sheriff's Association*, and *Journal of Social Distress and the Homeless*. Because of its origin in the Colorado Alliance of Research Libraries, *UnCover* remains an exceptionally strong index for Western periodicals (e.g., *Western Folklore*, *Colorado Miner*).

Social Sciences Indexes

A-18 **Applied Social Sciences Index and Abstracts (ASSIA)**. London: Library Association, 1987- . Bimonthly.

Until the debut of *Applied Social Sciences Index and Abstracts* in 1987, the only interdisciplinary abstracting service for the general social sciences was *Social Sciences Abstracts: A Comprehensive Indexing Journal of the World's Periodical Literature in the Social Sciences* (Columbia University, 1929–1933). Users seeking abstracts of periodical articles published after that date had to rely on general print or electronic periodical indexes, which were probably too general to cover the desired periodicals, or the abstracting services affiliated with their specific disciplines, such as *Psychological Abstracts* or *Abstracts in Anthropology* (see chapters on specific disciplines to identify abstracts in particular fields).

Applied Social Sciences Index and Abstracts is international in scope, covering more than 650 English-language journals and newspapers from sixteen countries, with more than 80 percent originating in the United States or the United Kingdom. It concentrates more on the "caring services" such as social welfare, prison services, and geriatrics, than on business, industry, history, international affairs, or theoretical approaches to social science disciplines. All articles in a core list of journals are indexed. Twenty percent of the journals indexed represent "fringe" disciplines like medicine, from which only relevant material is indexed.

Each citation includes standard bibliographic information plus an abstract of approximately 150 words. Full text is included for articles from approximately ninety journals.

Approximately 65 percent of the periodicals indexed in *Applied Social Science Index and Abstracts* are covered by either *Social Sciences Citation Index* or *Social Sciences Index*.[16] The print versions of these indexes do not provide abstracts, although the electronic versions do. Those not covered in these sources are frequently British or other foreign publications, such as *Indian Journal of Social Research* or *New Zealand Journal of Industrial Relations*.

Electronic access: CD-ROM and online (Dialog; Datastar).

A-19 **Current Contents: Arts and Humanities**. Philadelphia: Institute for Scientific Information (ISI), 1979- . Semiweekly. Electronic format. URL: http://connect.isihost.com.

A-20 **Current Contents: Social and Behavioral Sciences**. Philadelphia: Institute for Scientific Information (ISI), 1969- . Weekly. Electronic format (Current Contents Connect). URL: http://connect.isihost.com.

These contents reproduction tools from the publisher best known for citation indexes (see *Social Sciences Citation Index* [A-23]) enable readers to keep abreast of the contents of journals and multiauthored books in their fields without actually handling the books and journals themselves, and sometimes even before subscribers receive them. *Social and Behavioral Sciences* reproduces the tables of contents of multiauthored books and approximately 1,600 journals worldwide. *Arts and Humanities* covers more than 1,100 journals in disciplines of interest to social science researchers, including history, religion, archaeology, language, and linguistics.

Each issue contains a title word index to articles listed that week. An index by the name of the first author includes the address of the author or the person to whom reprint requests should be sent, if it was given in the article. Articles are also available by fax or mail through the ISI's "Document Solution" document delivery service. Researchers may elect to use ISI's "Discovery Agent" alerting service. Journals are listed in each *Current Contents* issue in which they are covered, as well as on ISI's Web page. A complete list of journals and books covered is issued twice a year, and is also available on ISI's Web site. An index to the issues of *Current Contents* in which they appear is published three times a year. *Current Contents* is valuable for pinning down very recent articles that academic library users have heard about when the articles have not yet been indexed and the library may not own the journals in which they appear. *UnCover* (A-17), *Academic Search FullTEXT* (A-10), and FirstSearch's *ContentsFirst* (A-14) provide table of contents information. *Academic Index* and

ContentsFirst cover fewer specialized social science periodicals, but *UnCover* indexes many of those covered by *Current Contents. UnCover* also has a table of contents alert service and an option for document delivery by fax.

> ***Electronic access:*** *Current Contents* is available on CD-ROM, tape, and diskettes and on the Web from Datastar, Dialog, GaleGroup, SilverPlatter, and Ovid.

A-21 PAIS International in Print. New York: PAIS, 1915- . Weekly.

Far from being strictly a periodical index, *PAIS International in Print* provides access to types of materials that are often difficult to find "on all subjects that bear on contemporary public issues and the making and evaluation of public policy, irrespective of source or traditional disciplinary boundaries." Rather than covering the social sciences comprehensively, *PAIS* concentrates on factual, statistical, and policy-oriented literature in economics, political science, international relations, public administration, law, environment, sociology, and demography. It is intended to be used by legislative and policy researchers, administrators, the business and financial community, and students.

PAIS indexes a wide variety of publication types, and it is especially good for tracking down material from governmental bodies (national, state, local, foreign, and international), pamphlets, reports, and conference proceedings. Books and articles from more than 951 periodicals that are selectively indexed are also included. Publications from all areas of the world are within its scope. *PAIS International in Print* continues the *Public Affairs Information Service Bulletin* (PAIS, 1915–1990) and *PAIS Foreign Language Index* (PAIS, 1972-). Items to be included are selected by the editors from a pool of new materials received directly by PAIS and in the Economic and Public Affairs Division of the New York Public Library, which houses one of the world's strongest collections on public affairs.

Entries are arranged by subjects drawn from standardized, controlled vocabulary outlined in *PAIS Subject Headings*, 2d ed. (PAIS, 1990). In addition to standard bibliographic information, descriptions of monographs include price, and many entries have short, descriptive annotations. Each year's annual bound volume includes an author index. A key to periodicals lists frequency, International Standard Serial Number (ISSN), address, and price for the periodicals scanned, and a directory of publishers and organizations includes addresses.

> ***Electronic access:*** CD-ROM and Web from 1972 to present from SilverPlatter, Ebsco, Internet Database Services (IDS), Ovid, FirstSearch, and Dialog.

A-22 Arts and Humanities Citation Index. Philadelphia: Institute for Scientific Information, 1976- . Biennial.

A-23 Social Sciences Citation Index. Philadelphia: Institute for Scientific Information ISI), 1969- . Triannual.

Arts and Humanities Citation Index (*AHCI*) and *Social Sciences Citation Index* (*SSCI*) each consists of three major components: the *Permuterm Subject Index*, the *Source Index*, and the *Citation Index*. Of these three indexes, the *Citation Index* is the revolutionary concept introduced by ISI when it first published the *Science Citation Index* in 1961. In the *Citation Index*, a researcher can look for any publication (by author, then date and source title) regardless of publication date and format (e.g., periodical article, book, unpublished paper, musical piece, artwork) and discover whether other authors cited that publication in their work during the period covered by the *Citation Index*. For example, a researcher could obtain a list of publications citing Darwin's *Origin of Species* for any given year by checking the *Citation Index* for that year under "Darwin C" followed by the date [1859] and title [*Origin of Species*]. This technique is especially useful for researchers who have a "perfect" article that is somewhat dated and would like to find an article on the same topic published more recently but have had no luck using conventional indexes. By using the citation to the first article as an access point in the *Citation Index*, the researcher may discover more recent articles on the same subject. In this way the citation to the first article functions as a very specific subject entry: Any later article citing the first article would be likely to address the same specialized concerns.

The *Permuterm Subject Index* is an alphabetical list of significant words from the titles of articles indexed, paired with every other significant word in the title. Because there is no controlled vocabulary and indexing is dependent on the publication title, users should check as many synonyms as possible in the electronic as well as print versions of the citation indexes.

Full citations to citing articles listed in the *Citation Index* and publications in the *Permuterm Subject Index* are arranged by author in the *Source Index*. The *Citation* and *Permuterm Subject* indexes offer brief citations (usually author's name, abbreviation of journal or book title, year, volume, and page), but the *Source Index* provides a more complete citation, including titles of journal articles. The *Citation Index* uses a system of coding to designate type of publication. The user can tell from a code letter if a publication is a book review, editorial, meeting abstract, review article, or other special publication. A *Corporate Index* arranged by country, city, organization, and academic department allows the researcher to discover what research is being conducted in specific institutions or to identify articles for which only the author's institution is known. The *Corporate Index* provides brief citations.

ISI's citation indexes are valuable for their comprehensive and interdisciplinary nature. *SSCI* indexes about 1,700 social sciences journals fully—more than any other social science index listed here—and an additional 5,700 journals from other disciplines selectively for material relevant to the social sciences. Thus, an article on therapy dogs in a veterinary journal may be indexed in *SSCI*, although the journal itself would not be fully indexed in *SSCI* but in *Science Citation Index (SCI)*. *SSCI* also provides cross-references to additional citations that appear in *SCI*. Users researching topics in linguistics, folklore, philosophy, religion, or history should also consult the *Arts and Humanities Citation Index*. *AHCI* indexes approximately 1,400 journals fully and 7,000 selectively. The selectively indexed journals are those indexed by *SSCI* and *SCI* that are reviewed for material relevant to the arts and humanities. Journal lists are available on Isis's Web site, arranged by category.

Like *Current Contents: Arts and Humanities* (A-19), *AHCI* covers disciplines of interest to social science researchers, such as archaeology, folklore, Asian studies, philosophy, linguistics, religious studies, film, television, and radio. Fully indexed sources include *American Antiquity, Historical Archaeology, William and Mary Quarterly, Film Quarterly, Journal of American Ethnic History*, and *Historical Journal of Film, Radio, and Television*. Those researching psychology, psychiatry, public health, anthropology, environmental issues, and any other topics that might touch on the life, physical, or earth sciences should also consult *SCI* (1961–).

In the reference environment, citation indexes can often help verify problematic citations. If a library user has a citation to a publication that has proven erroneous, a citation index can sometimes provide a reference to a source that has cited the publication correctly. This is especially useful for verifying citations to book chapters or older publications that may not be covered in electronic (or sometimes paper) periodical indexes or in standard bibliographies.

Most people prefer to search the citation indexes electronically, when available, to avoid tedious checking of each annual set for citations or several keywords. The older the cited article, the more the annual volumes must be checked. Furthermore, the small type in the print volumes has often provided the first definitive evidence of a librarian's need for bifocals. Electronic versions of these indexes can perform the same search more quickly and display or print out results in a clearer format.

Electronic access: Available on CD-ROM and the Web through ISI, Dialog, Datastar, Ovid, and First Search.

A-24 Social Sciences Index. Bronx, NY: H. W. Wilson, 1974- . Quarterly.

A-25 Humanities Index. Bronx, NY: H. W. Wilson, 1974- . Quarterly.

Both *Humanities Index* (HI) and *Social Sciences Index* (SSI) are subject and author indexes to English-language periodicals that are more scholarly and specialized than those indexed by *Readers' Guide to Periodical Literature* (A-16). H. W. Wilson, publisher of *Readers' Guide*, also publishes these indexes. Both index cover-to-cover the periodicals listed in the front pages of their issues, including review articles, scholarly replies, interviews, obituaries, and biographies, but excluding cartoons, editorials, and other ephemera. Periodicals indexed vary over the years, but at present *SSI* covers 460 periodicals in anthropology, area studies, community health and medical care, criminal justice and criminology, economics, family studies, geography, gerontology, international relations, law, minority studies, planning and public administration, policy studies, political science, psychiatry, psychology, social work and public welfare, sociology, urban studies, and other related subjects. *Humanities Index* covers 400 periodicals, some from disciplines often considered social sciences, such as archaeology and classical studies, folklore, history, language and literature, philosophy, and religion and theology. The periodicals that the indexes cover are determined by subscriber vote from lists prepared by the Committee on Wilson Indexes (a committee of the American Library Association's Reference and Adult Services Division).

Arrangement of both print indexes is by author and subject within one alphabet, with historical, form, and topical subdivisions. Subjects are assigned from each index's own subject authority file derived from the literature, reference works, other Wilson indexes, and *Library of Congress List of Subject Headings*. Since 1974, both indexes have included citations to book reviews.

Earlier periodical articles in the social sciences and humanities are included in other H. W. Wilson indexes: *Social Sciences and Humanities Index* (1965–1973/1974), *International Index* (1955–1965), *The International Index to Periodicals* (1920–1955), and *Readers' Guide to Periodical Literature Supplement* (1907–1919).

Electronic access: Both indexes are available online from Wilsonline, Epic, and FirstSearch, as well as on CD-ROM and magnetic tape.

News and Contemporary Issues Sources

A-26 **CQ Researcher**. Washington, DC: Congressional Quarterly, 1968- . Weekly.

Each issue of this weekly publication (titled *Editorial Research Reports* from 1968 to 1986) addresses a different "current topic of widespread interest." Recent issues have covered copyright and the Internet, the Electoral College, and hunger in America. Designed as a starting point for research, each issue provides an overview of the topic, a chronology of events, statistical tables and charts, a summary of current developments, and a "pro and con" discussion by experts on different sides of the issue. *CQ Researcher* is very popular with students beginning to work on term papers and others who want to find a variety of facts in one place. Despite its prepackaged appearance, *CQ Researcher* can be valuable for introducing students to research and encouraging exploration of all sides of issues. Especially useful are its bibliographies and lists of organizations that can be contacted for further information. All charts and statistical material provide citations to sources. Some issues of *CQ Researcher* have tangled with the difficulty of discovering the "true facts" of certain situations, such as determining the number of homeless people in the United States.

Electronic access: Available on the Web through CQ.com OnCongress.

A-27 **Editorials on File**. New York: Facts on File, 1970- . Biweekly.

Each issue of *Editorials on File* reprints approximately 200 editorials and editorial cartoons, arranged by topic, from about 150 newspapers in Canada and the United States. Newspapers covered are listed at the beginning of each issue and on Facts on File's Web site. Newspapers selected represent more than 50 percent of the total daily newspaper circulation in the United States and Canada. Editorials included represent a range of viewpoints on a wide variety of topics, many controversial. Each issue focuses on several topics of current interest. Recent issues have included many topics relating to the November 2000 elections, Hillary Clinton's election as a New York senator, and wildfires in Western states. The topics vary from issue to issue. Thus, *Editorials on File* can acquaint users with different perspectives on contemporary issues. Indexes to the subjects of editorials cumulate periodically.

Electronic access: Selected opinions are included on the *World News* CD-ROM from Facts on File.

A-28 **Facts on File World News Digest**. New York: Facts on File, 1940- . Weekly.

Each weekly issue of this looseleaf service provides a summary of newsworthy items as reported in more than 75 foreign and U.S. magazines, newspapers, press releases, and government publications and online sources. Issues also include maps and photos, statistics, biographies, and primary sources such as transcripts and speeches. Topics are arranged according to international, U.S., European, and other world news; a "miscellaneous" section includes news about finance, sports, awards, celebrities, deaths, film releases, music, television, medicine, and science. The top government officials are listed twice each year (e.g., "Leaders of the 107th Congress"). Year-end surveys list top stories, best-sellers, awards, and deaths. The index cumulates at three-, six-, and nine-month intervals, annually, and every five years. *Facts on File* is an ideal source for users seeking information about news events since 1940 that is concise yet more thorough than the brief abstracts offered by the *New York Times Index* (A-33) or *National Newspaper Index* (A-29).

Each year, Facts on File publishes an atlas that can be filed with the weekly issues. Because this atlas is frequently more up-to-date than the major world atlases, it can be very useful to those who want the most recent maps available in a size that can be easily photocopied.

Electronic access: Facts on File is also available on CD-ROM as *Facts on File News Digest* and online through Facts.com (1980-).

A-29 **Gale Group National Newspaper Index**. Foster City, CA: Gale Group, 1979- . Weekly. Online format.

This index covers the *Wall Street Journal*, the *New York Times*, the *Christian Science Monitor*, the *Los Angeles Times*, and the *Washington Post. National Newspaper Index* is available online through Dialog from 1979 to the present (1982 for *Washington Post* and *Los Angeles Times*). *Newsearch* (also available through Dialog) contains daily updates of *National Newspaper Index* plus eight other Gale Group databases: *Magazine Database, Business A.R.T.S. File, Newswire, Health and Wellness Database, Legal Resource Index, Trade and Industry Database, Management Contents,* and *Computer Database*. Records are kept in *Newsearch* for two to six weeks and then transferred to the other databases.

Electronic access: Online through Gale Group (current and past three years) and Dialog (1979-).

A-30 **Keesing's Record of World Events**. London: Longman, 1931- . Monthly.

Formerly known as *Keesing's Contemporary Archives* (1931–1986), *Keesing's Record of World Events*, like *Facts on File World News Digest* (A-28), offers summaries of news events. Issued monthly, rather than weekly like *Facts on File*, it concentrates more on political affairs, international relations, and economic issues than its American counterpart and less on human interest items, the arts, and celebrities. It does include items on social issues such as crime, public welfare, and strikes. *Keesing's* contains approximately 100 concise articles per issue. Articles are arranged geographically, and each issue includes an index by country name, followed by topic and by subjects not linked to particular countries (e.g., drugs, United Nations). Political and economic data for each country and for major international organizations are updated each year and published in a reference supplement. *Keesing's* publishes results of elections and rosters of new government officials when changes have resulted from elections, coups, or shakeups. Outline indexes are included in each issue, and cumulative subject indexes are issued periodically through the year. Full name and subject indexes are included in the annual volume.

Electronic access: Available online from 1960 to present from Keesing's (www.keesings.com).

A-31 **Newspaper Source**. Ebsco, 1995- . Updated daily. Electronic format.

Provides full text for 128 regional U.S. newspapers, 15 international newspapers, 6 newswires, and 9 newspaper columns, plus indexing and abstracting for four national newspaper, including the *New York Times, Wall Street Journal, Christian Science Monitor*, and *USA Today*.

Electronic access: Available online and on CD-ROM from Ebsco.

A-32 **Newsbank NewsFile Collection**. New Canaan, CT: Newsbank, 1986- . Quarterly.

Newsbank indexes articles of regional interest in approximately 500 newspapers in the United States, such as the *Atlanta Constitution*, the *New Orleans Times-Picayune*, and the *Bangor Daily News*. An accompanying microfiche "clipping file" of articles, keyed to references in the online database, can be purchased. Dialog offers the full text of approximately 50 regional newspapers, searchable as separate databases. *Global Newsbank* includes articles, news summaries, broadcasts, and transcripts from hundreds of international sources. *Newsbank* is also available with *Newsbank Popular Periodicals Premier*, which contains 120 full-text magazines.

Electronic access: Available on online and on CD-ROM through Newsbank.

A-33 **New York Times Index**. New York: New York Times, 1913- . Semimonthly.

The *New York Times*, published since 1851, is known as the "newspaper of record" for the United States because of its comprehensive news coverage and its inclusion of the full texts of a large number of source documents and speeches. *New York Times Index* provides detailed subject access to all *Times* articles, including book and movie reviews and obituaries. Under each topical subject heading, entries for individual articles are listed chronologically, with entries of unusual interest in boldface type. Each entry includes the date, section, page, and column of the article.

Abstracts, provided for significant news, editorial matter, and special features, includes information on photos, maps, graphs, inclusion of text or transcript, and length of article. The index provides cross-references from the names of persons, organizations, and places to the appropriate topical entries. The *Personal Name Index* to the *New York Times Index 1851–1974* by Byron A. Falk, Jr. and Valerie R. Falk (Roxbury Data Interface, 1976) and its supplement for 1975–1989 (Roxbury Data Interface, 1991) bring together all personal names for the years covered. Citations refer to the *New York Times Index* by year and page. Although this index is not authorized by the *New York Times*, it saves times when locating references to individuals whose fame spans a number of years. For example, it lists references to Ralph Nader for all years covered back to 1969.

Because of its detailed subject indexing and its provision of abstracts, *New York Times Index* can function as a ready-reference source in its own right as well as a newspaper index. If all that is needed is brief information about a particular event, such as the date and signatories of a treaty, the abstract included in the index may suffice. Because the citations are arranged chronologically under topics, the index can also serve as a day-by-day record of the development of a particular event. Also, because indexes for most local newspapers are not widely available, a date for a locally important event that might also be mentioned in the *New York Times* (e.g., a strike or a disaster) can often be pinpointed in *New York Times Index* and can serve as an access point for a fuller description in the local paper. Users who need more extensive coverage of current events but do not want to read the original newspaper articles may find that *Facts on File World News Digest* (A-28) or *Keesing's Record of World Events* (A-30) provides the necessary balance of brevity and detail. Those who need more up-to-date information than the *New York Times Index* offers (it is usually published three to four months after the dates of the newspapers indexed) can try indexes such as *National Newspaper Index* and *Newsearch* or search current issues and archives on the *New York Times* Web site (http://www.nytimes.com). access is free, but users must register and there is a charge for retrieving articles from the archive. Searchers can also use electronic indexes such as *National Newspaper Index* (A-29) or *Newsearch* online. For a more detailed analysis, consult *Guide to the Incomparable New York Times Index* by Grant W. Morse (Fleet Academic Editions, 1980).

A-34 **World News Connection**. Springfield, VA: National Technical Information Service, 1994- . Daily. Online format. URL: http://wnc.fedworld.gov/.

World News Connection is an online news source from Foreign Broadcast Information Service (FBIS), an agency of the U.S. Central Intelligence Agency. FBIS analysts monitor, translate, and publish foreign broadcasts, news agency transmissions, newspaper articles, periodical articles, conference proceedings, and other nonclassified reports. Since July 1979, FBIS has also distributed translations done by the Joint Publications Research Service (JPRS), which focused more on print media. FBIS distributes its reports to government agencies directly through a restricted Web site but to the public through *World News Connection*. Translations are usually posted on the Web site within twenty-four to seventy-two hours of the time of the original broadcast or publication. Regional coverage is in eight editions: East Asia, Central Eurasia, China, East Europe, Near East and South Asia, Sub-Saharan Africa, West Europe, and Latin America. Topics covered are mostly political issues but also include agriculture, economic conditions, education, finance, law, religion, transportation, and other topics of interest to social scientists.

Reports earlier than 1994 were distributed to depository libraries on microfiche and indexed by the *Index to the Foreign Broadcasts Information Service Daily Reports* (Newsbank, [dates vary]) and the JPRS reports by *Transdex Index* (Bell and Howell, 1974–1996). With the advent of *World News Connection*, depository libraries no longer received the microfiche. Previous editions of this book provide greater detail about access to earlier reports.

Electronic access: Available only online from National Technical Information Services (NTIS).

Indexes to Book Reviews

A-35 Book Review Digest (BRD). Bronx, NY: H. W. Wilson, 1905- . Annual.

Book Review Digest provides citations to and excerpts from book reviews published in approximately ninety English-language general interest, social sciences, humanities, and general science periodicals from the United States, Canada, and Great Britain. Periodicals covered include magazines such as *Atlantic Monthly and The New Republic*, scholarly periodicals, and periodicals for the library profession such as *Library Journal* and *Booklist*. To be included, books must have been published or distributed in the United States or Canada. Nonfiction books usually must have been reviewed in at least two of the periodicals covered, with the exception of *Reference Books Bulletin* within *Booklist*, for which one review is sufficient. Works of fiction must have been reviewed in three of the periodicals.

Textbooks, technical books, and government publications are excluded. Arrangement is by author or title main entry, with subject and title indexes. Each entry includes standard bibliographic information plus price, Dewey Decimal Classification, Sears subject heading, and excerpts from up to four reviews, and sometimes more for controversial books or those of unusual interest. Although *BRD* is useful for its excerpts, it indexes a relatively small number of periodicals. It includes some social science sources, such as *American Journal of Sociology and Archaeology*, but excludes others, such as *American Journal of Psychology* and *American Journal of Archaeology*. Those conducting comprehensive searches for book reviews in the social sciences should also consult *Book Review Index* (A-36) and the book review sections of *Social Sciences Index* (A-24) and *Humanities Index* (A-25), check codes for book reviews in *Social Sciences Citation Index* (A-23) or *Arts and Humanities Citation Index* (A-22), and search online periodical indexes and Internet review sites such as H-NET reviews.

Electronic access: Book Review Digest is available on CD-ROM, magnetic tape, and WilsonWeb, OCLC's EPIC, and FirstSearch.

A-36 Book Review Index (BRI). Detroit: Gale, 1965- . Bimonthly.

Book Review Index provides access by author, corporate author, or title main entry to standard bibliographic citations for reviews of books at least fifty pages long, including textbooks, novels, reference books, publications of small presses, works in foreign languages, and books on tape and in electronic media. *BRI* indexes all reviews in more than 600 publications, including general interest periodicals, scholarly publications in specialized disciplines (e.g., *American Anthropologist*, *Social Work*), general review publications (e.g., *New York Review of Books*), several newspapers (e.g., *Christian Science Monitor*), and British and Canadian publications. Unlike *Book Review Digest* (A-35), *BRI* does not require a minimum number of reviews for inclusion. *BRI* indexes a larger number of publications than *Book Review Digest*, including many of social sciences interest such as *American Journal of Archaeology*, *Africa Today*, and *Government Publications Review*, but does not provide excerpts from reviews.

Electronic access: Book Review Index is available online through DIALOG (1969-).

A-37 **H-NET Reviews in the Humanities and Social Sciences**. Lansing, MI: University of Michigan, 1998- . Irregular. Online format. URL: http://www2.h-net .msu.edu/reviews/.

H-NET Reviews is an online, scholarly review journal within H-NET, "an international inter-disciplinary organization of scholars teachers dedicated to developing the enormous educational potential of the Internet and the World Wide Web." H-NET resides on computers at MATRIX: The Center for Humane Arts, Letters, and Social Sciences OnLine at Michigan State University, but scholars worldwide participate in its intellectual activity, which includes e-mail discussion lists, a job guide, announce-ments of upcoming conferences and workshops, calls for papers, funding opportunities, and publica-tions. *H-NET Reviews* editors solicit reviews from scholars who have registered as reviewers. The reviews have no print equivalent. Because they reside on the Web, *H-NET Reviews* can be published more quickly than print reviews; can be more substantive because they do not have to adhere to page budgets; and can be interactive, with authors invited to submit comments on reviews. Forty-four reviews were published in January 2001; most of these were of books published in either 2000 or 1999, and a few earlier than that. Books reviewed were on fishing in the Great Lakes, the Electoral College, and the Parchman prison farm in Mississippi. The audience and writers come from an international community; both books reviewed and the reviews themselves include some written in German and French.

Dissertations

A-38 **Comprehensive Dissertation Index (CDI)**. Ann Arbor, MI: Xerox Uni-versity Microfilms, 1973- . Annual.

CDI is the only source providing author and keyword access to virtually every doctoral dissertation accepted in North America since the first three U.S. doctorates were conferred by Yale University in 1861. Whereas *Dissertation Abstracts International* (*DAI*) (A-39) provides access to dissertations from 550 schools, *CDI* indexes dissertations from approximately 700 schools, also including those listed in *American Doctoral Dissertations, Doctoral Dissertations Accepted by American Universities* (1933/1934–1954/1955), and a number of other sources, mostly lists from individual institutions. The first compilation of *CDI*, a thirty-seven-volume set covering 1861–1972, arranged more than 417,000 dissertations by keyword and contained a separate author index.

The following ten-year cumulation (1973–1982) cited 351,000 dissertations in a thirty-eight-volume set, and the most recent five-year cumulation (1983–1987) cited 162,000 dissertations in twenty-two volumes. Annual five-volume supplements have been issued since 1982, including all North American doctoral dissertations accepted for degrees during the preceding year. Lists of schools are included in each compilation and supplement. The subject index groups entries first by sciences or social sciences/humanities, then by broad discipline (e.g., education), and then by title keyword; there is a subject cross-reference list, and additional keywords are added if the title keywords are not sufficiently descriptive. The subject index also provides access by keyword to works other than dissertations required for doctorates, such as compositions or performances. Each entry includes author, title with keywords highlighted, degree, institution, date awarded, citation to *DAI* (if included there), and UMI order number, if microfilmed by and available from University Microfilms. *CDI* is also available on microfiche.

A-39 **Dissertation Abstracts International (DAI). A: The Humanities and Social Sciences**. Ann Arbor, MI: University Microfilms, 1938- . Monthly.

DAI provides more information than *CDI* (A-38) about each dissertation it indexes. Each year, *DAI* indexes approximately 47,000 doctoral dissertations submitted to University Microfilms (UMI) by nearly 550 participating institutions worldwide. Despite the large number of dissertations it indexes, *DAI* is not comprehensive; it covers only dissertations from those universities that participate in its microfilming program. Paper, microfiche, or electronic copies of dissertations can be ordered from UMI. Many universities do not lend dissertations through interlibrary loan, so some dissertations must be purchased from UMI by individuals who need access to them or by the library serving the researcher. Each monthly issue includes a list of participating institutions and the date their participation began. *CDI* provides coverage of more institutions, albeit without abstracts. In each issue of *DAI*, entries for dissertations are arranged first by broad subject category and then by subcategories. An outline of categories is included in the beginning of each volume.

Since 1966, *DAI* has been divided into three sections. *A* contains dissertations in the humanities and social sciences; *B* covers the sciences and engineering (including psychology and aspects of health sciences of interest to social scientists, such as occupational therapy and human development); and *C*, called "Worldwide," covers dissertations in all subject categories completed at institutions throughout the world. Each entry includes title, author, degree, date earned, and institution granting the degree; UMI order number; and author-prepared abstracts of up to 350 words in length. Each issue contains an author index and a keyword index of each significant word in the dissertation title. The last issue of each volume includes a cumulative author index. Because the authors determine the dissertations' titles and there is no controlled vocabulary list, it may be necessary to search under several different terms to find dissertations on a single subject.

Electronic searching of *DAI* is much more efficient than manual searching and has become standard in most large and academic libraries. Online or CD-ROM searching of the 1.6 million *Dissertation Abstracts* database permits the searcher to search under terms that might be found in the abstract as well as the title. The full text of some recent dissertations is available electronically in pdf format. These copies are available within minutes and at a lower cost than print formats, if an electronic copy is available and acceptable.

Electronic access: *Dissertation Abstracts* is available online through UMI's ProQuest online service, Dialog, and Data-Star. UMI offers several specialized electronic products, including a CD-ROM version.

Proceedings

In the reference environment, the first method of identifying proceedings, after checking one's own online catalog and perhaps a subject-specific database or WorldCat, is to identify the Web page of the sponsoring organization and check to see if the proceedings are available electronically or are at least identified online. When this is the case—and it often is—librarians bypass specialized directories of proceedings. If the conference and its proceedings cannot be identified on the Web, librarians can sometimes locate the presenter in question and e-mail the person to inquire about copies of the paper. There is no doubt that use of published indexes to proceedings has decreased with the increase of a Web presence for conferences and organization. Proceedings can still be elusive, however, and librarians should be aware of standard sources for pinning them down when the information highway reaches a dead end.

A-40 Directory of Published Proceedings. Series SSH—Social Sciences/ Humanities. Harrison, NY: Interdok, 1968- . Quarterly.

This quarterly index to preprints and published proceedings of conferences, congresses, symposia, meetings, and seminars worldwide is arranged chronologically by year and month. Most of the conferences were held in the United States, but the directory is international in scope and includes conferences held in other countries and in languages other than English. Each citation provides date, name, and location of conference; conference theme; sponsoring organization; and standard bibliographic information about the published record of the proceedings, including price and distributor. The last quarterly issue of the year is cumulative. Before this series began in 1968, information on social science and humanities proceedings was combined with the companion science series, *Series SEMT* (1965-). Publishers' addresses are listed in the directory, but publications can also be ordered through Interdok's Acquisition Service. Unlike *Index to Social Science and Humanities Proceedings* (A-41), *Directory of Published Proceedings* does not provide access to individual papers, but it does offer coverage of earlier proceedings.

Electronic access: Available online through Interdok.

A-41 **Index to Social Sciences and Humanities Proceedings (ISSHP)**. Philadelphia: Institute for Scientific Information, 1979- . Quarterly. Electronic format.

By far the most detailed and comprehensive index to proceedings, *ISSHP* provides access to published proceedings and to individual papers included in them. It covers "the most significant" proceedings published each year in all countries, in English and other languages, and in all areas of the social sciences and humanities. Each quarterly index covers approximately 6,200 papers from 700 conferences.

The index is produced on CD-ROM, online, and through ftp by the Institute for Scientific Information (ISI), the publisher of citation indexes (see *Social Sciences Citation Index* [A-23]), and parallels the comprehensiveness and numerous access points that distinguish those indexes. The index provides access by author, Permuterm key word, sponsor, meeting location, subject categories such as economics or history, and corporate or academic affiliation. Some papers are available through ISI's document delivery service, "Document Solution."

Electronic access: Available from ISI on CD-ROM, online through ISI Web of Science, and via ftp through Index to Social Sciences & Humanities Proceedings Search.

A-42 **Inside Conference**. London: British Library, 1993- . Daily. Online format. URL: http://www.bl.uk/services/bsds/dsc/infoserv.html#inside_conf.

The British Library maintains a file of all papers presented at every conference, symposium, workshop, congress, and meeting received at the British Library's Document Supply Center (BLDSC) since October 1993. Approximately 500,000 papers within 16,000 conference proceedings are added to the collection each year. Information available includes the first four authors of each paper; subject, key words; publisher; and conference venue, date, and sponsor. All subject areas are covered, including environment, psychology, social sciences, social work, and women's studies. Document delivery is available through mail, electronic delivery (pdf), or Ariel fax.

Electronic access: Available from the British Library's Inside Web service and through Dialog.

A-43 **Proceedings in Print**. Halifax, MA: Proceedings in Print, 1964- . Bimonthly.

Unlike the more specialized *Directory of Published Proceedings, Series SSH* (A-40) and *Index to Social Sciences and Humanities Proceedings* (*ISSHP*) (A-41), *Proceedings in Print* provides access to proceedings in all subject areas. Like these sources, it includes conferences, symposia, lecture series, congresses, colloquia, seminars, and meetings in all geographic areas and in all languages. The main body of the work is arranged alphabetically by name of conference, and each citation includes the place, date, sponsoring agencies, title of published proceedings, and standard bibliographic and ordering information. Corporate author, sponsoring agency, editor, and subject indexes are included. Unlike *Index to Social Sciences and Humanities Proceedings*, this index does not list individual papers. It does, however, list conferences for which proceedings have not been and probably will not be published—a useful piece of information for a researcher who is trying to verify whether a published record of a particular conference exists.

A-44 **World Meetings: Social and Behavioral Sciences, Human Services, and Management**. New York: Macmillan Reference Library, 1971- . Quarterly.

World Meetings is a two-year registry of future meetings, revised and updated quarterly. The main section of each index lists meetings by a registry number and includes the title of the meeting, location, date, name and acronym of the sponsor, description of content (e.g., number of papers to be presented), language and translation facilities, estimated number of attendees, restrictions, availability of papers or proceedings, number and kind of exhibits, and contact person for further information. There are indexes by keyword, date, deadline date for submission of papers, location, and sponsor. Each index provides the registry number under which entries are listed in the main section. This registry number remains constant for the same meeting throughout the issues, enabling the user to trace changes for any particular meeting.

Reports and Documents

A-45   **Catalog of U.S. Government Publications (CGP)**. Washington, DC: Government Printing Office, 1895- . Daily. Online format. URL: www.access.gpo .gov/su_docs/locators/cgp/index.html.

The Printing Act of 1895 created the *Catalogue of Public Documents of the . . . Congress and of All Departments of the Government of the United States* (called the *Document Catalogue*) and the *Monthly Catalog of U.S. Government Publications* (called the *Monthly Catalog* or MoCat). The *Document Catalogue* was a "comprehensive index of public documents" to be prepared "at the close of each regular session of Congress." Until it was discontinued with the 1940 volume, it was the definitive bibliography of government publications. After its discontinuation, the *Monthly Catalog* served that function. The electronic *CGP*, available free through GPO access, includes bibliographic records generated beginning with January 1994. It bears little resemblance to the print version, which served librarians, students, and researchers for more than 100 years. Still, there are remarkable similarities in the materials indexed.

Publications of Congress, executive departments, and independent agencies and commissions of the federal government cover all subjects in which the federal government is involved—almost everything. Documents indexed by the print and electronic versions include the expected congressional hearings and reports, environmental impact statements, and statistical publications, but also seafood cookbooks, the Army recipe file that includes creamed chipped beef for 100, a document on fingerprinting aliens, comic books, coloring books, publications about duck stamps, campaign finance information, and accident statistics from the Federal Highway Administration. An average of 20,000 titles per year have been indexed in the *Monthly Catalog*.[17] The *CGP* exploits the currency, strength, and flexibility of the Internet.

In addition to indexes by title, keyword, Superintendent of Documents (SuDocs) number, depository item number, GPO sales stock number, agency name, and date, it is also possible to limit a search to electronic titles by combining keyword searches with "http" or "PURL" (e.g., the search "http AND dog" retrieved an electronic government publication on using guard dogs to protect livestock). It is also possible to browse broad topics (e.g., animal welfare, nuclear power), find documents on "hot topics" (U.S. Census 2000, voting and elections), retrieve weekly lists of new electronic titles, and connect to agency Web sites and depository libraries. Each entry contains descriptive cataloging following AACR2, including standard bibliographic information, subject tracings, Library of Congress and Dewey classification, OCLC number, and GPO sales stock number if the item is for sale.

Electronic versions of the *Monthly Catalog* begin with 1976. Before that, the print version of the *Monthly Catalog* and its specialized indexes must be used to identify documents. The print version of the *Monthly Catalog* is arranged by SuDocs classification number and a catalog entry number found in the index. The SuDocs number is based on the department and subdivision publishing the document and the type of document; hence, documents from each issuing agency are listed together. Author, title, keyword, subject, and series/report number indexes also provide access. Indexes cumulate annually and semiannually. There are also decennial indexes (1941–1950 and 1951–1960) and quinquennial indexes (1961–1965, 1966–1970, 1971–1976, and 1976–1980). Oryx Press has published cumulative indexes for 1976–1980 and 1981–1986 (Oryx Press, 1987).

Access to the *Monthly Catalog*, spotty before thorough indexing began in July 1976 (for example, personal authors were not indexed between September 1946 and December 1962),[18] has been facilitated by several cumulative indexes. *Cumulative Title Index to United States Public Documents, 1789–1976* by Daniel W. Lester, Sandra K. Faull, and Lorraine E. Lester (United States Historical Documents Institute, 1979) is indispensable for identifying SuDocs numbers for earlier items if only the title is known. Subject access to earlier years is available through the *Cumulative Subject Index to the Monthly Catalog of U.S. Government Publications, 1895–1899* (Carrollton Press, 1977) and *Cumulative Subject Index to the Monthly Catalog of U.S. Government Publications, 1900–1971* (Carrollton Press, 1973–1975). The problem of access by personal author was addressed by *Cumulative Personal Author Indexes to the Monthly Catalog of U.S. Government Publications, 1941–1975* (Pierian Press, 1971–1979). John Andriot's *Annual Guide to U.S. Government Publications* (Documents Index, 1973-) is valuable for identifying hundreds of government publication series.

Although the *CGP* and the *Monthly Catalog* do index congressional publications and statistical materials, those publications can be found more efficiently in the *CIS Index to Publications of the United States Congress* (B-62) (Congressional Information Service, 1970-) (online as Congressional Universe) and *American Statistics Index* (online as Statistical Universe). Articles within periodicals that are U.S. government publications are not indexed in the *Monthly Catalog* or the *CGP* but in *Government Periodicals Universe* (formerly *U.S. Government Periodicals Index* [A-46]), and technical reports produced with government funding but not necessarily by federal agencies are indexed in the *NTIS Database* (A-48). The U.S. Government Online Bookstore (http://bookstore.gpo.gov/) functions as a "books in print" equivalent for federal publications available from the GPO. Some government publications that are not available from the GPO may be available for purchase or online from individual departments and agencies.

Several other publications facilitate the use of federal government documents, which can be complicated and intimidating to the novice. Joe Morehead's *Introduction to United States Government Information*, 6th ed. (Libraries Unlimited, 1999) is a standard, easily digested guide to the intricacies of the federal publication process. Frank W. Hoffman and Richard J. Wood's *Guide to Popular U.S. Government Publications*, 5th ed. (Libraries Unlimited, 1998) helps the reader figure out the "government" title for publications popularly known under other names, such as the Warren Report. An electronic current awareness source along the same lines is the Web site Government Documents in the News, from University of Michigan's Documents Center (http://www.lib.umich.edu /libhome/Documents.center/docnewsnew.html). Greg R. Notess's *Government Information on the Internet*, 3d ed. (Bernan Press, 2000) is as helpful as a print guide to Internet resources can be.

Electronic access: In addition to the CGP Web site, the *Monthly Catalog* is available on CD-ROM and online (1976-) from Dialog, Ovid, and FirstSearch.

A-46 Government Periodicals Universe. Washington, DC: Congressional Information Service, 1988- . Quarterly. Electronic format.

This publication continues Infordata's *Index to U.S. Government Periodicals* (1974–1987) as an index to articles with general interest or research value within periodicals published by U.S. government agencies. *Government Periodicals Universe* indexes 170 periodicals "with research value," such as *FDA Consumer, Survey of Current Business, Naval War College Review, FBI Law Enforcement Bulletin*, and *Morbidity and Mortality Weekly Report*.

Most of the periodicals included focus on U.S. history, government programs, public policy, technological activity, or activities and objectives of specific agencies. Because articles within government-published periodicals are not indexed in the *Catalog of U.S. Government Publications* (A-45) and *Readers' Guide to Periodical Literature* (A-16), and other social sciences indexes cover few of them, *Government Periodicals Universe* is the only access to many of them. It does not index statistical periodicals that are already indexed by *American Statistics Index* (C-31) or "documentary serials" such as *Weekly Compilation of Presidential Documents* or *Congressional Record* (B-58). *Government Periodicals Universe* may be searched by keywords, subject headings, title, author, Government Printing Office (GPO) item number, issuing agency, and Superintendent of Documents (SuDocs) number. Boolean searches allow users to combine terms like "disabled and handicapped persons" and "National Park Service" to find publications on the controversial issue of making national parks accessible to the disabled. A searchable and browsable list of periodicals indexed includes SuDocs numbers.

Electronic access: USGPI is also available on CD-ROM and may be licensed on magnetic tape.

A-47 Index to United Nations Documents and Publications. New York: Newsbank, 1956- . Monthly. Online format. URL: http://grc.ntis.gov/ntisdb.htm.

Before Newsbank made this index available on CD-ROM and on the Web through its access UN Web site, a series of print indexes provided access. They were *United Nations Document Index* (1950–1973), *UNDEX: United Nations Documents Index* (1973–1979), and *UNDOC: Current Index* (1979–1996). Readex is extending the *Index* back retrospectively five years every year; it will eventually cover 1945 to the present. The *Index* covers documents, publications, and official records issued by the United Nations and its organs (e.g., Security Council, Economic and Social Council) and related agencies (e.g., UNICEF) throughout the world on all topics with which the UN becomes involved: international relations, economic and social issues, trade, international law, statistics, human rights, population, education, and many other issues related to the social sciences. The *Index* allows researchers to identify articles on contemporary social issues such as terrorism, human rights, and children's issues. Many of the publications have a unique, international perspective. The *Index* is compiled from a list of documents and publications received by the Dag Hammarskjold Library at the United Nations in New York.

The *Index* may be searched by UN body, author, country, type of document (e.g., masthead, sales publication, official record, periodical), subject, title, words in text, document number, and date. Beginning with 1994, full text is available for UN resolutions and some other publications.

A-48   **NTIS Database**. Washington, DC: National Technical Information Service, 1964- . Weekly. Online format. URL: http://grc.ntis.gov/ntisdb.htm.

This indexing, abstracting, and sales service for "U.S. government-sponsored research, development, and engineering reports, . . . foreign technical reports, and other analyses prepared by national and local government agencies and their contractors or grantees" has had several titles: *Bibliography of Scientific and Industrial Reports* (1946–1949), *Bibliography of Technical Reports* (1949–1954), *U.S. Government Research Reports* (1954–1964), *U.S. Government Research and Development Reports* (1965–1971), *Government Reports Announcements* (1971–1975), and *Government Reports Announcements and Index* (1975–1996).[19] Informally, librarians may refer to it as simply "the NTIS index" after the National Technical Information Service, the agency of the Department of Commerce that is responsible for selling government-sponsored research to the public. Reports from more than 240 agencies are included. Seventy thousand items are added annually, including technical reports, computerized data files, databases, software, proceedings, guides, and manuals. The database included 2,112,000 records as of May 2000.[20] The NTIS database is most often associated with scientific reports, but also included are reports from the Department of Commerce, the Department of Transportation, the Department of Housing and Urban Development, and approximately 240 other agencies. Topics include communications, behavior and society, detection and countermeasures, health planning, administration and management, and information science. Most items are available to be ordered from NTIS. For those that are not, the entry indicates where the document may be obtained.

Electronic access: NTIS Database is available online through FedWorld.gov and Dialog.

A-49   **RAND Publications**. Santa Monica, CA: Rand Corporation, 1946- . Online format. URL: http://www.rand.org/PUBS/index.html.

The RAND Corporation is a private, nonprofit research organization. Founded immediately after World War II to address national security issues, Rand has since expanded its research to many other issues of domestic policy, including those in the social sciences such as education and public welfare. The diversity of RAND's supporting agencies—examples include the Rockefeller Foundation, the Russian Academy of Sciences, the National Science Foundation, and the National Institute of Child Health and Human Development—explains the broad range of topics covered in the reports. Recent reports address combating terrorism, reading comprehension, and anti-drug budgeting. The RAND Corporation publishes its findings in monographic reports, scholarly or professional journals, research briefs, issue papers, and books published by presses outside Rand. Recent RAND publications can be identified through RAND's Web site. They are searchable by keyword, publication type, and the Rand research center through which the project was done (Institute for Civil Justice, RAND in the Community). The amount of information about each report varies from a one-paragraph abstract to the entire publication. Other categories include "RAND Classics" (including a 1985 report on e-mail etiquette supported by the National Science Foundation), reports available on the Web, prepared subject bibliographies on a variety of topics (e.g., gaming and game theory, New York City, population, and television and communications policy), and "the best of the backlist." Indexes to earlier reports are *Selected RAND Abstracts* (1963-) and *Rand's Index of Selected Publications* (1946–1962).

DICTIONARIES AND ENCYCLOPEDIAS

A-50   **The Blackwell Dictionary of Twentieth Century Social Thought**. Edited by William Outhwaite and Tom Bottomore. Cambridge, MA: Blackwell, 1993.

This dictionary contains substantial articles on themes central to social science thought from the nineteenth century to the present. As such, it complements *Dictionary of the History of Ideas* (A-51) with its up-to-date, substantial articles on major concepts in social thought (e.g., alienation, everyday life), schools and movements (e.g., fascism, green movement), and institutions and organizations. The approach, like that of *Dictionary of the History of Ideas*, is interdisciplinary, encompassing philosophy, political theory, cultural ideas and movements, and natural science as well as the social sciences. Each entry has a brief bibliography. An appendix provides brief biographical information and a summary of the place in twentieth-century social thought of approximately eighty major figures (e.g., Bertrand Russell, Margaret Mead, Albert Einstein).

A-51   **Dictionary of the History of Ideas**. 5 vols. Edited by Philip P. Weiner. New York: Scribner's, 1973–1974.

This encyclopedia of "pivotal" ideas, many interdisciplinary and some of special importance to the social sciences, is "intended to exhibit the intriguing variety of ways in which ideas in one domain tend to migrate into other domains" across disciplines or time. It is useful for those wishing to discover the origin of fundamental concepts, such as work or the city, and study their relevance through history and within different disciplines. An analytical table of contents groups articles among seven categories, including "the history of ideas about human nature in anthropology, psychology, religion, and philosophy as well as literature and common sense" (e.g., behaviorism, imprinting, learning early in life); "[the] history of ideas about or attitudes to history, historiography, and historical criticism" (e.g., China in Western thought and culture, culture and civilization in modern times); "the historical development of economic, legal, and political ideas and institutions, ideologies, and movements" (e.g., social attitudes toward women, welfare state, vox populi); and "history of religious and philosophical ideas" (e.g., ritual in religion, ethics of peace).

The articles are broad, scholarly, and lengthy; the most likely audience is the specialist, advanced student, or serious lay reader. Each article is followed by a bibliography of important writings in English and other Western European languages. The last volume is a detailed index to the set that allows the user to locate treatment of specialized topics within the broad articles.

A-52   **Encyclopedia of the Social Sciences**. 15 vols. New York: Macmillan, 1930–1935.

The goal of attempting "a better analysis through a more comprehensive synthesis" of the social sciences led a committee composed of members of ten social sciences organizations to undertake this "comprehensive and unifying publication." This classic work, according to the introduction of its heir, *International Encyclopedia of the Social Sciences* (A-55), "summarized the achievements of the outgoing generation" of social scientists of the 1920s and 1930s.[21] Two boards of advisory editors, U.S. and foreign (and mostly European), attempted to include "all of the important topics" in politics, economics, law, anthropology, sociology, penology, and social work. History "is represented only to the extent that historical episodes or methods are of especial importance to the student of society."

Topics from the "semi-social sciences" (e.g., ethics, education, philosophy) and "the sciences with social implications" (e.g., biology, geography, medicine) were selected for the significance of their social aspects. Biographies of deceased persons are an important element of the encyclopedia; the 4,000 biographies included make up about 20 percent of the work. The first volume of the set contains a discussion of the development of social thought and institutions, "What Are the Social Sciences," including Greek culture and thought, Renaissance and Reformation, the individual and capitalism, and nationalism, followed by a discussion of the social sciences as disciplines within countries or geographic regions (e.g., Germany, Russia, Scandinavia, Latin America, Japan). The alphabetically arranged entries follow. The last volume is a "rigorously selected and annotated bibliography covering the works of primary importance in the development of the social sciences."

A-53 Gould, Julius, and William L. Kolb. **A Dictionary of the Social Sciences**. New York: Free Press, 1964.

The purpose of this dictionary, published under the auspices of UNESCO, is to provide the student or practitioner with a general introduction to the main problems and developments in the social sciences and to help specialists understand central concepts in fields outside their own. Approximately 1,000 basic concepts used in the social sciences (e.g., demography, collective behavior) are described and defined. Each entry is approximately one to two pages long and consists of several sections.

The first section (A) is "designed to set out concisely the core meaning(s) of the term as used in one or more of the social sciences," frequently employing quotations from the literature with the term in context; section B provides historical meaning and a more detailed discussion; sections C, D, E, and so forth supply further historical or analytical background, discuss convergence or divergence of opinion or differing usage among various social sciences disciplines, or provide other additional information. For example, section C of peyotism provides chemical and botanical information about peyote that supports the discussion of its use in ritual. Most of the entries are for major concepts in the social sciences, and the information provided is still valuable. Further reading indicated within entries includes classics written before 1960.

A-54 **International Encyclopedia of the Social and Behavioral Sciences (IESBS)**. 26 vols. Elsevier Science, October 2001. Online format. URL: www.iesbs.com.

The eagerly anticipated *IESBS* is the first major encyclopedia of the social sciences to be published since the *International Encyclopedia of the Social Sciences* was published in 1968. An enormous undertaking, it is available in print and electronically, includes 4,000 articles and 150 biographical entries, and will be kept current with annual updates. The *IESBS* Web site already provides information about the content, arrangement, and news about the encyclopedia. True to the interdisciplinary and collaborative nature of social sciences research that has only strengthened in the last thirty years, the *IESBS* includes "supersections" on overarching topics (e.g., biographies, ethics of research and applications, integrative concepts and issues), approximately forty sections on disciplines from anthropology to urban studies and planning, a list of the 4,500 contributors, some abstracts of hundreds of articles from "Academic Achievement, Cultural and Social Influences on" to "Youth Sports, Psychology of," plus several examples of full-text articles. Although the IESBS is still in press, librarians can use the Web site to check on its progress and content.

A-55 **International Encyclopedia of the Social Sciences**. 17 vols. New York: Macmillan, 1968.

International Encyclopedia of the Social Sciences, the most comprehensive subject encyclopedia for the field and still an essential tool for academic and public libraries, was designed to complement rather than replace its predecessor, *Encyclopedia of the Social Sciences* (A-52). Whereas that classic work approached the social sciences historically and included biographies of long-deceased persons, its successor includes less descriptive and historical and more analytical, methodological, and comparative information. For example, *Encyclopedia of the Social Sciences* contains an article on alcohol that covers the history of alcohol production and consumption and legal and biological aspects of alcohol. *International Encyclopedia of the Social Sciences* contains an article titled "Drinking and Alcoholism."

Intended for use by social scientists, students, professionals from other disciplines seeking information in the social sciences, and the public at large, the set includes signed articles on concepts, theories, and methods in anthropology, economics, geography, history, law, political science, psychiatry, psychology, sociology, and statistics. The goals of the editors are "to make the new encyclopedia as much a product of the current generation of social scientists as the earlier encyclopedia was of its generation" and to "make available to readers throughout the world the concepts, principles, theories, methods, and empirical regularities that characterize the social sciences today." The set is to "reflect and encourage the rapid development of the social sciences throughout the world." The geographic range of its editorial advisory board includes scholars from thirty countries, many of them non-Western (e.g., India, Sudan, Ghana, Thailand).

Encyclopedia of the Social Sciences contains 4,000 biographies, many of long-deceased persons such as Alcuin and Alexander the Great. *International Encyclopedia of the Social Sciences* includes longer biographies of approximately 600 persons, most of whom were not covered in the earlier encyclopedia, "whose research and writings have had an impact upon the social sciences." Biographies of living persons born before 1890 are included. Bibliographies at the ends of articles contain references for works cited in the text and suggestions for further reading, data sources, and titles of journals concerned predominantly with the topic of the article.

The last volume of the work contains a "Classification of Articles" in which topical and biographical article titles are listed under broad categories such as anthropology, education, religion, sociology, and statistics. Many articles are listed under several categories (e.g., ritual is under both anthropology and religion, supporting the interdisciplinary nature of the work).

The biographical supplement (volume 18) of the *International Encyclopedia of the Social Sciences* (Free Press, 1980) adds 215 biographies to the 4,000 in *Encyclopedia of the Social Sciences* and the 600 in *International Encyclopedia of the Social Sciences*. The editor intended to include eminent social scientists and persons from "marginal" areas, like philosophy and human biology, who were too young to qualify for inclusion in the mid-1960s when *International Encyclopedia of the Social Sciences* was prepared. Most of the people included meet the editor's criteria of death since the earlier volumes were published or birth rates of 1908 or earlier. Many of the people included in this volume were born around the same time—Margaret Mead (1901), Gregory Bateson (1904), B. F. Skinner (1904), Konrad Lorenz (1903), and Hannah Arendt (1906), as examples—reinforcing the editor's feeling that these people constitute a "generation whose members were the teachers of a substantial proportion of contemporary social scientists; . . . the generation that came between the nineteenth-century founders of the modern social sciences and the thousands of practicing social scientists today." Entries focus on the subjects' thought, contributions to the social sciences, and influence on colleagues and followers rather than on personal details. Articles are signed by contributors and include bibliographies of works by and about the biographee.

The most recent supplement, volume 19, *Social Science Quotations*, edited by David L. Sills and Robert K. Merton (Macmillan, 1991), reproduces in context "memorable ideas, memorably expressed" drawn from the writings from all periods that constitute the "historical core of the social sciences and social thought." Relevant quotations from figures in the physical sciences and humanities are included (e.g., Shakespeare, Einstein). Arrangement is by author, with a subject index. Placement of the quotation in context and provision of complete references make this supplement especially valuable for exploration of the social thought of major writers.

A-56 Miller, P. M. C., and M. J. Wilson. **Dictionary of Social Science Methods**. New York: John Wiley, 1983.

Unlike the other sources in this section that deal with history, concepts, and theories of the social sciences, this dictionary concentrates on explaining and putting into context research methods used in the empirical social sciences. Longer entries for terms of central importance (e.g., longitudinal study, experiment, census) place the term in context; discuss relevant vocabulary including references to some terms that may have their own entries; and assess the uses, limitations, advantages, and problems of the method. Entries for terms that can be found in standard dictionaries (e.g., *questionnaire*) are shorter but provide definitions and illustrative examples more relevant to social science research than most general dictionary definitions.

Although this dictionary explains the uses of specific tests and instruments (e.g., chi-square, two-tailed test), it does not explain construction of such tests in sufficient detail for the novice. Users wanting to not only identify a chi-square test or a Likert scale but also learn how to construct one should consult guides to research methodology such as Miller's *Handbook of Research Design and Social Measurement* (A-6).

A-57   Reading, Hugo. **A Dictionary of the Social Sciences**. London: Sociologia, 1976.

This dictionary provides very brief (usually one-line) definitions for more than 7,500 words and phrases used in all areas in the social sciences except economics and linguistics (terms from these areas are included if they are "frequently used in the social sciences"). Its strength lies in the large number of specialized terms it includes. The reader can identify, albeit briefly, very specialized words and phrases such as *armomancy* (divination from the shoulders of animals), *nosographical map* (a map showing the distribution of diseases), and more than fifty types of migration.

A-58   Social Science Encyclopedia. 2d ed. Edited by Adam Kuper and Jessica Kuper. New York: Routledge & Kegan Paul, 1996.

Social Science Encyclopedia contains approximately 600 articles covering the fields of anthropology, economics, political science and political theory, psychology, demography, development studies, linguistics, semiotics, and psychiatry, plus "intellectual traditions, professions, and problem areas" such as business studies and industrial relations, communication and media studies, geography, medicine, and women's studies. Areas new to this edition are post-modernism, material culture, cultural studies, discourse analysis, environmental economics, feminist practice, history of medicine, industrialization, and media and politics.[22] Five hundred scholars, mostly from the United States and the United Kingdom but also from European countries plus Australia, Canada, India, Israel, Japan, and South Africa, contributed articles. Articles range in length from less than one page (e.g., Prisoner's Dilemma, Privatization) to several pages (e.g., Energy, Mental Disorders). Even the shortest articles contain bibliographical references and suggestions for further reading. There is no subject index, and there are minimal cross-references (e.g., no cross-reference from Sects and Cults to Cargo Cults), but a section titled "Entries Grouped by Discipline and Subject" lists individual entries under broader headings such as "Demography" or "Psychology" in a manner similar to the "Classification of Articles" table in *International Encyclopedia of the Social Sciences* (A-55). Like the table in the earlier work, entries are listed under more than one heading (e.g., marriage under the headings for both "Anthropology" and "Sociology"), thus linking disciplines taking different approaches to the same phenomena.

Social Science Encyclopedia provides a much more thorough discussion of specialized terms than Reading's *Dictionary of the Social Sciences* (A-57), although Reading covers many more terms. *Social Science Encyclopedia* covers some newer or more specialized concepts that are too recent to be found in *International Encyclopedia of the Social Sciences* (e.g., post-modernism or discourse analysis) or that have changed since its publication (e.g., abortion, drug use) and can, therefore, be used to update the older work for topics in which timeliness is important.

ALMANACS

Almanacs are compilations of a wide range of statistical and factual information. Most are still published in annual print versions, but electronic almanacs and other electronic sources that provide information traditionally found in almanacs abound. They are usually more up-to-date and offer the advantages of interactivity and linking to external sources. The electronic version of the *Information Please Almanac*, for example, includes a "daily almanac" with weather, celebrity birthdays, and a link to a currency conversion table. Almanacs usually include important events of the preceding year, statistical information ranging from the unemployment rate to pet ownership, awards and prizes, facts about countries and states, sports information, forms of address, postal information, mileage tables, tax information, perpetual calendars, and innumerable other features. Sources of information are often cited. Frequently requested statistical information may be found more readily in an almanac than in more comprehensive compendia that require the user to sift through indexes and specialized tables before finding the desired information.

Although statistical information can also be found in specialized statistical sources such as *Statistical Abstract of the United States* (A-85), some items, like the lengths, locations, and types of bridges throughout the United States, may be difficult to identify in other sources. Almanacs are often the last resort (even after using a Web search engine like Google or AltaVista) for a librarian attempting to track down an elusive piece of information, such as the dates of Easter through the next century or the number of Cadillac Eldorados manufactured per year, and often they do answer the question. Familiarity with the contents of the various print and electronic almanacs will help librarians identify those instances in which an almanac should be consulted first, rather than last. Each almanac includes unique information, but they are inexpensive enough that even the smallest library can own several.

A-59 New York Times Almanac. New York: Penguin Group, 1997- . Annual.

This most recent entry into the almanac competition is comprehensive, packed with facts and statistics, and serious, with little emphasis on celebrities and entertainment, as befitting a publication of the "newspaper of record." It includes the "Almanac of the Year" (e.g., late-breaking news, prize winners, astronomical events), and sections on "The United States," "The World," "Science and Technology," "Awards and Prizes," "Sports," and maps. It is enlivened by feature articles such as "Sex in America" and "Religion in America."

A-60 The Time Almanac. Boston: Information Please, 1947- . Annual.

The *Time Almanac* was published as the *Information Please Almanac* for fifty years (1947–1998). Special features unique to *Time Almanac* include articles on hot topics from *Time* magazine writers ("The Genome Is Mapped: Now What?" and "For Dotcom Pioneers, the Gold Rush Is Over") ; a crossword puzzle guide; and "headline history," important events in chronological order from 5 billion B.C.E. (formation of the Earth) to the present. The electronic version has many features possible only on the Web: a daily almanac (e.g., this day in history, astronomical outlook, facts behind the news), links to breaking news, search features, encyclopedia articles with links to further sources, and a "fact monster" electronic almanac for children.

Electronic access: Available online at www.infoplease.com.

A-61 Whitaker's Almanack. London: J. Whitaker, 1869- . Annual.

A general almanac that reflects its British origins and place of publication, *Whitaker's* includes sections on the royal family (including their finances and order of succession), local government in the United Kingdom, British public holidays (e.g., Boxing Day), and parliamentary information such as lists of public acts and White Papers issued during the year. *Whitaker's* includes summaries of events of the year by region (e.g., Australasia and the Pacific, European Community) and by topic, with a British emphasis (e.g., the Value Added Tax, British television, conservation and heritage, archaeology, religion in the United Kingdom, tide tables for Liverpool and London Bridge). Recent editions cite Web sites such as the Queen's Household at Buckingham Palace (www.royal.gov.uk) and the Tower of London (www.hrp.org.uk). In the reference environment, *Whitaker's* is especially useful for the facts and data it provides on current activities in the United Kingdom.

A-62 The World Almanac and Book of Facts. New York: World Almanac, 1868- . Annual.

World Almanac is the most comprehensive of the almanacs listed here. It includes statistics and facts on economic, social, political, religious, financial, industrial, medical, and other topics. It also includes the year's top ten news stories, the year in photographs, a chronology of the year by month, consumer and health information, decisions of the Supreme Court, sports events, "off-beat news," quotes of the year, the year in color photographs, scientific achievements and discoveries, and the Internet and computers. There are a twenty-six-page synopsis of world history with a timeline (beginning with prehistory) and a twelve-page color atlas. *The World Almanac* began publication long before the other almanacs, making it a good source of factual information for the nineteenth century for libraries that own earlier volumes.

BIOGRAPHICAL SOURCES

Biographical information can also be found in other reference sources; see "Dictionaries and Encyclopedias."

A-63 Biography and Genealogy Master Index (BGMI/Bio-Base). Detroit: Gale, 1984- .

BGMI is a master index on microfiche to biographical dictionaries. *Bio-Base* was developed from the print *Biography and Genealogy Master Index (BGMI)* (Gale, 1980–1981) and its twenty-one annual and semiannual supplements. Because of the lack of any current, comprehensive biographical source for social scientists, it is often necessary to turn to other types of sources, including discipline-specific publications, those limited to certain geographic areas, or other specialized directories, to locate biographical information on social scientists. *BGMI* provides citations to specialized and general biographical sources such as *American Reform and Reformers*, *Notable Black American Women*, *Medal of Honor Recipients*, and *Current Biography*.

Each entry for a biographee provides life dates to aid in identification of people with similar names. Codes corresponding to the biographical works that contain information on the person are listed under the person's name; the full titles of the sources are listed in the users' guide that accompanies *Bio-Base*. The 2000 master compilation includes 12,700,000 citations to 1,250 biographical sources, including specialized publications like *A Popular Dictionary of Hinduism*, *Encyclopedia of American Comics*, and *Divining the Future: Prognosticators from Astrology to Zoomancy*. Living and deceased people from all areas of the world and all professions are included. Publications indexed are primarily U.S. ones but also include works published in other countries or those that are international in scope (e.g., *Who's Who*; *Biographical Dictionary of the Soviet Union, 1917–1988*).

BGMI is sometimes frustrating to use because the small amount of information given about each biographee can make identification difficult, especially for people with common names. Also, *BGMI* lists biographees under the form, spelling, and life dates given in each source. These often vary, resulting in multiple entries for the same person. Little information is provided about the length and nature of entries in each biographical source. Therefore, familiarity with the sources indexed will help the librarian determine whether the source contains fairly lengthy coverage of a person's personal life (e.g., *Current Biography*), very brief information (e.g., *Writers Directory*), or citations to biographical information in periodical articles, books, and collected works (e.g., *Biography Index* [A-64]).

Electronic access: Available online through GaleGroup and Dialog, and on CD-ROM.

A-64 Biography Index. Bronx, NY: H. W. Wilson, 1946- . Quarterly.

Biography Index provides access to biographical information contained in periodicals indexed by the other periodical indexes published by H. W. Wilson (e.g., *Readers' Guide* [A-16], *Social Sciences Index* [A-24], *Humanities Index* [A-25]), plus selected additional periodicals and books. Material covered by *Biography Index* is intended for both popular and scholarly audiences and includes obituaries, diaries, memoirs, book reviews, bibliographies, and collections of letters as well as periodical articles. Citations are arranged alphabetically under name of biographee. An index by profession or activity (e.g., financiers, feminists, explorers, Internet retailers) provides access to biographical information about people involved in those professions or activities even if the user does not know individual names.

Electronic access: Available on CD-ROM and online through WilsonWeb, Ofvid, EPIC, FirstSearch, and SilverPlatter.

A-65 International Encyclopedia of the Social Sciences. Vol. 1, Biographical Supplement. New York: Free Press, 1980.

This supplement is discussed under *International Encyclopedia of the Social Sciences* (A-55).

A-66 World Biographical Index. Munich: K. G. Saur, 1999- . Irregular. Online format. URL: http://www.saur-wbi.de/.

The *World Biographical Index* is an immense Internet database consisting of biographies originally published in separate reference works, and then cumulated in Saur's international biographical archive series. The series began in the German Biographical Archive; the online database now contains 2.8 million short biographical entries derived from 4,858 reference works in thirteen biographical archives added so far, including the African Biographical Archive, American Biographical Archive, and the British Biographical Archive, as well as the original German compilation. The *World Biographical Index* can be searched by personal name alone or in combination with other criteria, such as occupation, country, archive, or source. It is also possible to search by occupation and find, for example, all naval officers, museum specialists, or librarians in the database. Entries are slightly more extensive than those in *Biography and Genealogy Master Index* (A-63). They include name, occupation, birth and death dates, country, the reference source that includes the biography, and the Saur archive within which the reference source is included.

DIRECTORIES

A-67 Encyclopedia of Associations. Volume 1: National Organizations of the United States. Detroit: Gale, 1956- . Annual.

Encyclopedia of Associations is the single most valuable source available for finding information on nonprofit organizations, many of which are important to the social sciences. No specialized directory for the social sciences is as thorough. The addition of regional and international editions to this family of publications (see below) further enhances its usefulness. In this original set, 23,000 U.S. organizations and international associations with headquarters in the United States are arranged according to eighteen broad subject categories such as athletics and sports, labor, social welfare, culture, and education. The scope includes national nonprofit organizations, local and regional organizations if their concerns and objectives are of national importance, nonmembership organizations that disseminate information to the public, informational organizations, and inactive organizations (listed in the index as "defunct").

Entries include organization name, principal keyword, acronym, address, telephone number, e-mail address, Web site, name and title of chief official, number of members and staff, number of regional affiliates, a description of the organization with any computerized or telecommunication services, divisions of the organization, publications, and information about meetings. Alphabetical name and keyword, geographic, and executive indexes are included. The name and keyword index provides references to organizations in *Encyclopedia of Associations: International Organizations* (A-68) and seven other reference sources (e.g., *Research Centers Directory*, *Foundation Directory*). Much of the value of *Encyclopedia of Associations* lies in its usefulness in making referrals and identifying contact information that might be difficult to acquire otherwise. Librarians helping users find information on specialized topics can identify and contact or explore the Web sites of organizations dealing with those topics to find out what additional information they might compile and disseminate. Through contact with organizations, users may be able to identify people with similar interests and establish networks of communication, arrange to obtain information from electronic databases, receive information about professional accreditation, discover employment or education clearinghouses, get on mailing lists, and obtain other information that might not be available elsewhere.

Electronic access: Available online through GaleNet (as Associations Unlimited), Dialog, and Nexis/Lexis, and on CD-ROM from SilverPlatter and GaleNet.

A-68 Encyclopedia of Associations. Volume 4: International Organizations. Detroit: Gale, 1983- . Annual.

This international volume of *Encyclopedia of Associations* includes more than 20,000 international, multinational, binational, and national organizations. Included are UN-related organizations, multilateral treaty organizations, and international development banks. Like the volumes covering U.S. organizations, entries in this volume are arranged according to broad subject fields and include basic information about location, membership, and purpose. The 2000 edition includes 9,000 e-mail addresses and 5,500 Web sites. Brief listings are provided for organizations the editors were unable to contact directly for more detailed information. Name and keyword, geographic (country and city), and executive indexes are included. Cross-references to organizations included here are provided in the name and keyword index of the national *Encyclopedia of Associations*.

Electronic access: Available online through GaleNet (as Associations Unlimited), Dialog, and Nexis/Lexis, and on CD-ROM from SilverPlatter and GaleNet.

A-69 Encyclopedia of Associations: Regional, State, and Local Organizations. 5 vols. Detroit: Gale, 1988/1989- . Annual.

This member of the *Encyclopedia of Associations* family covers 115,000 associations and nonprofit corporations with interstate, state, intrastate, city, or local membership, and interest. Each volume covers a geographic region (e.g., Great Lakes states, South Central and Great Plains states), and associations are listed according to the location of their headquarters. Some local affiliates, branches, or chapters of national organizations listed in *Encyclopedia of Associations* are included here. Each volume is arranged geographically and then by association name. Entries are similar to those in *Encyclopedia of Associations* but are frequently briefer because of the difficulty in finding information on some local organizations. Name and keyword indexes are included, enabling the user to find information on, for example, VFW posts in a variety of cities or the Philadelphia Mummers Association.

Electronic access: Available online through GaleNet (as Associations Unlimited), Dialog, and Nexis/Lexis, and on CD-ROM from SilverPlatter and GaleNet.

A-70 Government Research Directory. Detroit: Gale, 1980- . Annual.

Government Research Directory, previously titled *Government Research Centers Directory* (1980–1982), includes entries for approximately 4,800 U.S. and Canadian government research programs, including some in other countries. Although most of the entries involve scientific and technical research, many social science areas are covered (e.g., education, gerontology, economics, business, geography, cartography). Programs include research and development centers, laboratories, test facilities, experiment stations, data collection and analysis centers, and research coordinating offices. Federal agencies that are themselves research organizations, as well as research facilities owned and operated by the federal government or by a contractor, are included. Entries are arranged by agency and sub-agency and include name, address, telephone number, e-mail address, date established, key contact people, description of research, special facilities such as computers or laboratories, and publications or information services. Information was derived from questionnaire responses. *Government Research Directory* includes subject and geographic indexes and a master keyword index to name of unit, parent agency, and subjects.

Electronic access: Available on CD-ROM, and online through GaleGroup and Dialog.

A-71 Research Centers Directory. 2 vols. Detroit: Gale, 1960- . Annual.

Research Centers Directory contains information on approximately 13,000 university-related and other permanent nonprofit research centers. The index volume includes broad sections relating to the social sciences: private and public policy and affairs, social and cultural studies, and multidisciplinary and research coordinating centers. These categories are further subdivided; for example, under the section "social and cultural studies" are found behavior and social sciences, education, humanities and religion, and regional and area studies. Centers are listed under these subdivisions; each entry includes institution and research center name and acronym, address, telephone and fax numbers, e-mail address and Web site, year founded, name and title of director, information on governance, sources of support, annual dollar volume of research when available, number of staff, research contact (including e-mail address if available), affiliated centers, institutional memberships, fields of research, special resources such as electronic resources or laboratories, publications, meetings, services to the public (e.g., consulting), and library collections. The directory is updated by *New Research Centers*, an intra-editional supplement. *International Research Centers Directory* (Gale, 1981-) contains similar information for 9,100 government, university, independent nonprofit, and commercial research centers in 150 countries, including some former Soviet republics.

> *Electronic access:* Both *Research Centers Directory* and *International Research Centers Directory* are available online through Dialog and Galenet and on CD-ROM through SilverPlatter.

A-72 Research Services Directory: A One-Stop Guide to Contract Research Firms and Laboratories. 8th ed. Lakeville, CT: Grey House Publishing, 2001.

Research Centers Directory (A-71) covers university-related and nonprofit research organizations, and *Government Research Directory* (A-70) covers government research programs. *Research Services Directory* lists approximately 6,200 commercial and corporate firms engaged in contract or fee-based research services. Listings include laboratories, research and development firms, and individual specialists and consultants. Services offered are advertising, artificial intelligence, market research, political research, product development, management consulting, social science research, and software development. Subjects covered include business, education, public affairs, social sciences, and the arts and humanities as well as the expected technological and scientific areas.

Entries are listed alphabetically and provide name, address, telephone and fax numbers, e-mail address, Web site, executives and contact people, company description, principal proprietary research fields and projects, special resources or equipment, publications, patents, principal clients, corporate memberships, affiliates, year founded, annual revenue, fees when available, and staff. The entries are based on the firms' responses to questionnaires. Executive, geographic, and subject indexes are included.

A-73 UNESCO. DARE: Directory in Social Sciences—Institutions, Specialists, Periodicals. Paris: Social and Human Sciences Documentation Center, UNESCO, 1991- . Updated continuously. Online format. URL: http://www.unesco.org/general /eng/infoserv/db/dare.html.

The DARE databank includes 11,000 directory entries for social science research and training institutions, specialists, documentation and information services, and social science periodicals. A search form allows users to search by type of entry (social science institution, peace institution, human rights institution, international law institution, information service, or periodical) combined with country name, keyword, geographical coverage, ISSN, or language of periodical. The last comprehensive print equivalent of this database was *World Directory of Social Science Institutions*, 5th ed. (Unesco Social and Human Sciences Documentation Center, 1990). Subject and regional spinoffs on CD-ROM have been published by Unesco Publishing. These include directories of social science institutions in Southeast Asia (1998), Latin America and the Caribbean (1996), the Arab Region (1996), Africa South of the Sahara (1995), and Central and Eastern Europe (1995).

A-74 Yearbook of International Organizations. Brussels: Union of International Associations, 1948- . Annual.

Much more comprehensive (29,495 organizations included in the index) than *Encyclopedia of Associations: International Organizations* (A-68), *Yearbook of International Organizations* is also more complex. The first volume, arranged alphabetically by the name of the organization, includes detailed information about organizations, including title in English (if available) and other languages, acronym, previous titles and abbreviations, officers' names, main and regional secretariat countries, address, electronic services such as e-mail and Web site addresses, date and place of foundation, sponsoring bodies, aims and activities, type of organization (e.g., research institute, commercial enterprise), membership countries, and publication titles. access is by a country index (i.e., by location of organization headquarters); a subject index, subjects called "Global Action Networks," in which organizations are classified by subject and region of concern (e.g., Africa, Caribbean, Nordic); a citation index listing international organizations cited as contacts by other international organizations; a publication title index; and an executive officer name index. Indexes include inactive organizations;

proposed, recently reported, or unconfirmed organizations; religious orders; fraternities; and multilateral treaties, but there are no entries for these organizations in the main section (hence the larger number of organizations listed in the indexes than in the main section). There is a separate quarterly International Congress Calendar listing future international meetings up to the year 2000, with cross-references to the yearbook entries and several separate specialized and regional directories: *African International Organization Directory, Arab/Islamic International Organization Directory, International Association Statute Series,* and *International Organization Abbreviations and Addresses.*

The yearbook was formerly published as *Annuaire de la vie internationale* (1908–1911), *Handbook of International Organizations (Repertoire des Organisations Internationales)* (1921–1939), and *Annuaire des Organisations Internationales/Yearbook of International Organizations* (1951–1980).

Electronic access: Available on CD-ROM.

AREA STUDIES

A-75 **Country Studies [Area Handbooks].** Federal Research Division of the Library of Congress. Washington, DC: Government Printing Office, 1988- . Irregular. Online format. URL: http://memory.loc.gov/frd/cs/cshome.html.

Country Studies consists of separate, individually titled, book-length studies of countries prepared by the Federal Research Division of the Library of Congress under the Country Studies/ Area Handbook Program of the Department of the Army. Previous editions were published in hard copy and were titled *Area Handbook for* [country name] (older editions), then [country name], *A Country Study* (newer editions). The *Country Studies* do not represent U.S. or Army opinions but are produced by multidisciplinary teams of social scientists. They are highly regarded for their objectivity. *Country Studies* published before 1987 were produced by the Foreign Area Studies Department of American University.

The Web site includes the full text of approximately 100 *Country Studies* published between 1988 and 1998. *Country Studies* may be identified by browsing a list of countries and retrieving tables of contents that, in turn, lead to full text of each chapter. Each *Country Study* includes chapters on the general characteristics of the country's society, physical environment, historical setting, population, ethnic geography, language and communication, social structure, living conditions, education, religion, national security, and social values. Appendixes include statistical tables on budgets, education, population, balance of payments, economics, and other topics such as crime and human rights issues. Maps are included in many *Country Studies,* and many of these are topical, illustrating issues such as transportation or economic activity. Images and charts are in pdf format. Some graphics not yet included in *Country Studies* have recently been added to the Web site. Each *Country Study* contains a bibliography for further reading. A recent *Country Study* can be the single most valuable source for a researcher who wants a comprehensive, thorough treatment of all aspects of a country's life.

A-76 **Background Notes.** Washington, DC: U.S. Department of State, Bureau of Public Affairs, 1964- . Irregular. Online format. URL: http://www.state.gov/www /background_notes/index.html.

Background Notes is a collection of approximately 190 brief profiles, previously published in paper pamphlets, on the history, culture, geography, government, politics, foreign relations, defense, economy, and business and travel information for countries of the world. *Background Notes* are updated on a staggered schedule; most of the profiles on the Web site include publication dates within the last few years. Most *Background Notes* include suggestions for further reading, information on travel, relations with the United States and other countries, principal government officials, and U.S. diplomatic representation. The Web version of *Background Notes* takes advantage of Web technology to provide links to electronic sources such as Department of State Travel Warnings and Consular Information Sheets (http://travel.state.gov). Because they are published more frequently, *Background Notes* can be used to update *Country Studies* (A-75) with the understanding that they represent official State Department views.

A-77 **CultureGrams: The Nations Around Us**. Orem,UT: CultureGrams, 1974- . Annual.

Readers seeking information about dining customs, dating and marriage, etiquette, greetings, contemporary and traditional clothing, and the meanings of gestures in various countries sometimes find that their search is more difficult than they thought it would be. These topics are not uniformly addressed in standard encyclopedias, and they are not within the scope of more scholarly publications such as *Europa Year Book* (A-78) and the CIA's *World Factbook* (A-80). *CultureGrams* (spelled *Culturgrams* from 1974 to 2000) offers brief discussions of all these topics plus more traditional data on land and climate, history, government, economy, and information for the traveler. *CultureGrams* was developed by the David M. Kennedy Center for International Studies at Brigham Young University. Brigham Young invited people from fifty countries to "spend fifteen minutes or so telling us what they think we most need to know about their country as a means of our better understanding each other." The project has continued, with *CultureGrams* now available as four-page reports for each of 177 countries, compiled in two volumes.

The 2001 edition includes *CultureGrams* for three new places: *Guam*, *Mozambique*, and *Uganda*. Country specialists check each *CultureGram* for accuracy. The kind of information included is valuable to teachers, health care workers, travelers, elementary and secondary students trying to capture the "flavor" of a country for a short paper, and language students. Examples of information included are the use of the formal *usted* rather than the informal *tu* in Honduras as well as the popularity in that country of frozen fruit juice sold in plastic bags called *topogios*, T-shirts with English slogans, and thong shoes. Although *CultureGrams* can be accused of generalization or even stereotyping countries and their citizens, it is produced by an authoritative institution, is a popular source among library users, and is the only one that offers this type of cultural information in one place. It is the best source to check if a library user is meeting a person from another country in a few minutes and wants a quick summary of greetings, appropriate gestures and those to avoid, and other lessons in etiquette. *CultureGrams* now offers *USA CultureGrams for International Visitors* (in ten languages) and a *Utah CultureGram*.

Electronic access: Available on CD-ROM.

A-78 **Europa World Year Book**. London: Europa, 1926- . Annual.

This annual guide (titled *Europa Year Book* from 1959 to 1988) includes information on international organizations and countries. The set begins with sections on the United Nations, UN-related organizations, and non-UN-related organizations. Each entry provides address, origins, members, organization, activities (including activities of divisions), publications, and statistics. Country chapters follow, with each including an introductory survey several pages in length covering general information such as location, climate, language, religion, flag, recent history, government, defense, economic affairs, social welfare, education, tourism, holidays, weights and measures, currency, and exchange rates. Statistical surveys follow, providing quantitative information on area and population, agriculture, forestry, fishing, mining, industry, finance, external trade, transport, tourism, communications, media, education, and other aspects of the country.

Each table indicates the source of the statistics. A section titled "Directory" discusses each country's constitution (but does not reprint it) and provides basic information, names, and addresses of relevant organizations and their directors in areas such as government, diplomatic representation, the judicial system, press, religion, government publishing, radio and television, trade and industry, transport, and tourism. Chapters are not as lengthy as those in *Worldmark Encyclopedia of the Nations* (A-81), but information and statistics are usually up-to-date. The regional publications in the Europa family are *Middle East and North Africa*; *Africa South of the Sahara*; *The Far East and Australasia*; *Central and South-Eastern Europe*; *Eastern Europe*; *Russia and Central Asia*; and *South America, Central America, and the Caribbean*; *The USA and Canada*; and *Western Europe*. The regional surveys provide considerably more detail than the parent volume. They include a review of current events in the region, essays on pertinent topics, status and activities of important regional organizations, and country chapters with essays and statistical tables. The *Europa Directory of International Organizations* (Europa, 1999- , annual) provides more detailed coverage of international organizations than is available in the *Europa World Year Book*.

A-79 Statesman's Year-Book: Statistical and Historical Annual of the States of the World. New York: St. Martin's Press, 1864- . Annual.

Like *Europa Year Book* (A-78), the *Statesman's Year-Book* offers chapters with background and statistical information on international organizations and countries of the world, but it is more concise. Each country chapter contains brief sections on history, area and population, climate, constitution and government, defense, international relations, economy, energy and natural resources, industry and trade, communications, justice, religion, education, and welfare. Diplomatic representatives in the United States and Great Britain are listed as well as U.S. and British diplomats in each country and UN representatives. Each chapter ends with a bibliography for further reading.

A-80 World Factbook. Washington, DC: Central Intelligence Agency, 1981- . Annual.

The *World Factbook* was first published in 1962 as an annual summary to update the CIA's National Intelligence Survey. The first unclassified edition was published in June 1971, and sales to the public began in 1976. Annual publication of the *Factbook* continued even after termination of the National Intelligence Survey. *Factbook* summarizes information on 266 political entities. Of these, 183 are UN members and 7 are not (e.g., Switzerland). Other categories are dependent areas (e.g., Isle of Man, Greenland), "miscellaneous" areas (e.g., Antarctica, Gaza Strip), four oceans, and the world. Each entity is compiled from information provided by the Census Bureau, Central Intelligence Agency, Department of State, Coast Guard, and other government agencies. This publication is produced for government officials, particularly those involved in international relations or defense, but much of the information is useful to social scientists. For each entity, there are one to three pages of facts and statistics on geography, people, government, economy, communication, natural hazards, political parties, and defense forces. For example, "People" includes net migration rate, ethnic divisions and their percentages, religion, language, and literacy rate. "Communication" includes mileage for railroads and highways and runway length for airports.

Appendixes include an atlas with some topical maps (e.g., ethnic groups in Eastern Europe, time zones). A listing of international organizations and groups includes informal names (e.g., "Four Dragons," "Group of Two," "Group of Eleven") as well as official names, aims, and members. Other appendixes include a guide to the UN system, abbreviations for international environmental agreements with popular names (e.g., "Nuclear Test Ban Treaty"), and international treaties with dates, objectives, and signatories.

The Internet version of the World Factbook allows users to compare descriptions of fields across countries. For example, selecting the field "terrain" brings together descriptions of terrain from Afghanistan to Zimbabwe. It also includes color jpg and pdf maps.

Electronic access: Available free on the Web at http://www.odci.gov/cia/publications/factbook /index.html.

A-81 Worldmark Encyclopedia of the Nations. 9th ed. Detroit: Gale, 1998.

This encyclopedia differs from other compendia such as *Europa Year Book* (A-78) and *Statesman's Year-Book* (A-79) in its editors' attempts to address issues such as economic development, social progress, and international cooperation.

The first volume of *Worldmark* includes articles on the UN system and the polar regions; tables on economic, demographic, and cultural indicators; a glossary of religious holidays; and abbreviations and acronyms used in the set. The remaining volumes contain country articles arranged by continent. Each country article begins with standard information that can be found in most general encyclopedias, such as a map; the country's capital, flag, monetary unit, national anthem, holidays; and weights and measures. Following this introduction are essays on approximately fifty additional topics, including topography, climate, flora and fauna, population, ethnic groups, religion, history, local government structures, migrations (e.g., between Gambia and Senegal in connection with the cultivation and harvest of peanuts), agriculture, animal husbandry, fishing, public finance, health, social welfare, housing, education, and tourism. Each country article also includes a list of famous people from the country and a bibliography of works for general readers, "classics," and other important works. A representative of the country or international organization examines each article, and the editors before publication critically assess the comments of these people. A glossary of special terms includes definitions for concepts such as fertility rate, life expectancy, and turnkey project.

STATISTICS

A-82 **Fedstats**. Updated continuously. URL: http://www.fedstats.gov /aboutfedstats.html.

Fedstats is a Web-based portal and search engine for statistical information available from federal agencies reporting expenditures of more than $500,000 per year in statistical activities (e.g., surveys, forecasts, data analysis). Users search for statistics through an A to Z topic list (from "Acute Conditions: Common Cold" to "Weekly Earnings"), through a list of agencies with statistical programs, statistics available by geographic areas, press releases (including links to agency press release sites), or a search across agency Web sites. Other features include links to kids' sites on agency Web pages and statistical profiles of states, counties, and congressional districts.

A-83 **Statistical Universe**. Washington, DC: Congressional Information Service, 1988- . Quarterly. Online format.

Government agencies and private sector organizations collect and disseminate enormous amounts of statistical information. It is difficult to identify publications that provide the exact statistical information needed using government issue indexes such as the *Catalog of U.S. Government Publications* (A-45), OPACs, periodical indexes, or general searches on Internet search engines. *Statistical Universe* provides several ways to search for statistics from various government agencies. It indexes publications from federal agencies such as the Census Bureau, the Bureau of Labor Statistics, the National Center for Educational Statistics, the National Center for Health Statistics, and the Bureau of Justice Statistics. Within *Statistical Universe*'s scope are federal publications in paper, CD-ROM, online, microfiche, or map format with primary data of research value or secondary data on specific topics, special studies, and analyses of statistical material. Congressional publications containing substantial statistical information are included. (See also *CIS Index to Publications of the United States Congress* [B-62].) Unlike *Monthly Catalog* (see A-45n), ASI includes publications not published for distribution. Excluded are highly scientific or technical data such as information disseminated by the National Technical Information Service (see *Government Reports Announcement and Index* [A-48n]) or the National Library of Medicine (NLM).

Statistical Universe incorporates the annual *American Statistics Index* and the *Statistical Reference Index*, both published by CIS. The dates statistics are available vary. Searches retrieve abstracts and often link to full-text sources. One of the most powerful features of *Statistical Universe* is its ability to search within tables of statistical publications for terms (e.g., prairie dogs) that might not be indexed. Content of each entry varies according to the agency that produced it, but federal publications include title, producing agency, date, length, report number, SuDocs number, and an abstract.

A-84 **A Matter of Fact: A Digest of Current Facts, with Citations to Sources**. Ann Arbor, MI: Pierian Press, 1985- . Semiannual.

A Matter of Fact indexes and provides full-text excerpts of statistical statements related to public policy, government, education, health, environment, economics, crime, and other social issues from congressional hearings and the *Congressional Record* plus 200 newspapers and periodicals. Arrangement is by Library of Congress subject heading. Each entry provides the statistic in context and a reference to the original source. Recent indexes have included statistics reported in the *AARP Bulletin, Christian Science Monitor, American Journal of Economics and Sociology, Families in Society*, and *Mother Jones*. As might be expected, statistics on the same subject from different sources reported by *A Matter of Fact* can be quite different.

A-85 **Statistical Abstract of the United States**. Washington, DC: Government Printing Office, 1879- . Annual.

Statistical Abstract is the "standard summary of statistics on the social, political, and economic organization of the United States." It reproduces tables drawn mostly from publications of the federal government (e.g., Census Bureau publications, *Digest of Education Statistics*, *Sourcebook of Criminal Justice Statistics*) and also nongovernmental organizations (e.g., statistics on religious preference from the National Council of Churches and the Princeton Religious Research Center; statistics on pet ownership from the American Veterinary Medical Association). Arrangement is by broad subject (e.g., "Population"), with introductory text describing the data collection environment for the subject. The source of each table is indicated, enabling *Statistical Abstract* to serve as an index to hundreds of statistical publications. For example, the table on pet ownership indicates that the figures come from the American Veterinary Medical Association's publication, *U.S. Pet Ownership and Demographics Sourcebook*.

Depending on resources available, users may be able to go to the original publication for more detailed data or to a more recent edition of the publication for the most recent statistics. Some tables cite the source of the statistics as "unpublished data" from a particular agency, an indication that a letter or telephone call to the agency may be the most efficient way to obtain additional information. Appendixes to *Statistical Abstract* include a guide to sources of statistics, a list of state and foreign statistical abstracts, a list of agencies that collect data by subject, and a section on statistical methodology and reliability. The *Statistical Abstract* is available on the Internet in pdf format, but this format is not easier to use than the print version. One of the *Statistical Abstract*'s best features is its browsability. If the table the index leads a user to isn't quite right, the one next to it might be. The pdf format of the electronic version hinders this type of quick browsing.

Electronic access: Available on the Web at http://www.census.gov/prod/www/statistical-abstract -us.html.

A-86 **Statistics Sources: A Subject Guide to Data on Industrial, Business, Social, Educational, Financial, and Other Topics for the United States and Internationally**. 18th ed. Edited by Jacqueline Wasserman O'Brien and Steven R. Wasserman. Detroit: Gale, 1962- . Annual.

Statistics Sources is a finding guide to statistics on 20,000 specific subjects collected by the U.S. government, international organizations, trade and professional associations, nonprofit organizations, and commercial publishers. Information is listed alphabetically by subject, with sources of statistics listed under each subject. In most cases, *Statistics Sources* refers the reader to a print or electronic source of information (e.g., *Economist Book of Vital World Statistics* [Times Books, 1990] for data on the labor force in Costa Rica) but sometimes cites an agency or organization as the source of information even if they do not publish the data they compile. The address and telephone number of the compiler of the statistics are provided. About 2,000 sources of published and unpublished statistical data are listed in an appendix. *Statistics Sources* also includes a bibliography of key statistical sources, a list of federal statistical telephone contacts, and a list of federal statistical databases.

GUIDES TO ELECTRONIC SOURCES

Zen and the Art of the Internet has reached the status of sacred text, rather than being an up-to-date how-to manual. Most print guides to the Internet are simply not current enough. To assist library users in the increasingly complex environment of electronic information, reference librarians must have a good command of the overall structure of the Internet, be able to decide when to turn to the Internet for information instead of a paper source, have at their command specific techniques for negotiating the Internet to find specific pieces of information, and be able to judge the quality of the information they retrieve. Depending on the educational philosophy of the library, librarians may also teach library users to use the Internet. The following guides, arranged from the most basic to the most detailed, can help librarians teach themselves about the Internet and also can be recommended to users. Most published guides to the Internet, no matter how up-to-date at the time of publication, have a limited shelf life. Fortunately, most are revised frequently and are also available for downloading on the Internet as well as being on the library or bookstore shelves.

A-87 Kovacs, Diane K., et al. **Directory of Scholarly and Professional E-Conferences**. 15th revision. Washington, DC: Diane Kovacs and the Directory Team, 1999. Online format. URL: http://www.KOVACS.com/directory.html.

Kovacs's directory was the first to list scholarly e-conferences. It now "screens, evaluates, and organizes discussion lists, newsgroups, MUDS, MOO'S, Muck's, Mushes, mailing lists, interactive Web chat groups, and e-conferences on topics of interest to scholars and professionals for use in their scholarly, pedagological professional activities." The directory is searchable by a global keyword search or by searches of words in the discussion list, an alphabetical list of 142 subjects (e.g., culture, ethnology, women's studies), and an alphabetical list of e-conferences from numerals (78-L, a discussion of pre-LP music and recordings) to Z (Zyoga, "a forum for the discussion of Yoga related to Zen Buddhist practice and philosophy"). Individual entries include title, description, subscription information, contact person, and broad (e.g., social sciences), middle (e.g., culture), and specific (e.g., Hawaii) subject descriptors. They also indicate whether the list is archived or moderated. The print edition of the list, *Directory of Electronic Journals, Newsletters and Academic Discussion Lists*, is published by the Association of Research Libraries.

A-88 **Gale Directory of Databases**. 2 vols. Detroit: Gale, 1993- . Annual with semiannual updates.

This directory is a merger and continuation of Gale's *Computer-Readable Databases, Directory of Online Databases*, and *Directory of Portable Databases*. The first volume of the set covers online databases and the second lists CD-ROM, diskette, magnetic tape, handheld, and batch access database products. It provides information on 13,854 databases, 4,000 producers, and 2,900 database producers and vendors. An introductory essay by Martha E. Williams, "The State of Databases Today," provides a concise overview, with many graphs and tables, of the enormous extent of database growth over the last twenty-five years (from 301 databases in 1975 to 11,605 in 2000). Each entry includes name, address, phone number, fax number, and e-mail address for the database producer; the type of database (e.g., bibliographic or directory); a description; subject coverage; language; geographic coverage; years covered; the year the database was first available; frequency of updating; vendor; system requirements; software; price; and availability of the database in other formats, print as well as electronic. Indexed by database producer, online service vendor (e.g., SilverPlatter), country, subject, and a master index of all database names, keywords within names, acronyms, alternate names, former names, and organization names.

Electronic access: Available online through Galenet, Datastar, and Dialog; available on diskette and magnetic tape.

A-89 **Librarians' Index to the Internet (LII)**. Maintained by Carole Leita. Sacramento, CA: Library of California, 1990- . Updated continuously; weekly e-mail updates. Online format.

The *Librarians' Index to the Internet* began in 1990 as librarian Carol Leita's gopher bookmark file. In 1993, it became the *Berkeley Public Library Index to the Internet*, mounted on the Berkeley Public Library's Web server. Leita added a search engine and subject index, and structured the LII so that other librarians could recommend entries. In 1997, the *Berkeley Public Library Index to the Internet* moved to Berkeley's SunSITE and became the *Librarian's Index to the Internet (LII)*. *LII* now consists of a searchable, annotated directory of 7,400 Internet resources, selected and evaluated by librarians. Other librarians can add entries to the *Index*. Every week, the *LII* distributes through e-mail a list of the top twenty resources added to the it.

In addition to its annotations and selectivity, one of the most useful aspects of the *LII* for social sciences librarians and researchers is its arrangement of Internet resources by topic, including most of the standard social science topics (e.g., economic, politics, business) but also world cultures, sports, media, collected biography, and recreation. It is also to possible to search by keywords, subject, titles, descriptions, or links.

A-90   **The Scout Report for Humanities and Social Science**. Madison, WI: Computer Sciences Department, University of Wisconsin-Madison, 1997- . Biweekly. Online format. URL: http://scout.cs.wisc.edu/report/socsci/current/index.html.

Scout Report is a free current awareness resource available through e-mail or the *Scout Report* Web site. Each *Scout Report* offers a selection of Internet resources chosen by librarians and other subject specialists. Each *Report* lists links to Web sites and brief explanations arranged according to the categories "Research," "Learning Resources," "New Data," "Current Awareness," and "In the News." A recent *Scout Report* listed links to pages for Internet Economy Indicators, a Web site on the Philadelphia Centennial Exhibit of 1876, and a glossary of political economy terms.

The *Scout Report* Web site includes a searchable archive of past reports. A search on the term "maritime," for example, retrieved Web sites on the Amistad, the Cape Cod Lighthouse Home Page, and the Network for Underwater Archaeology.

The *Humanities and Social Sciences Report* is part of the overall *Scout Report* Web site, which also includes the *Scout Report for Business and Economics* and the *Scout Report for Science and Engineering*, a *Weblog* of "interesting items that somehow don't fit our selection criteria" (e.g., *Toonopedia*, a "great hypertext encyclopedia of cartoons and comics"), and links to other resources.

NOTES

1. Edwin R. A. Seligman, "What Are the Social Sciences?" in *Encyclopedia of the Social Sciences* (New York: Macmillan, 1930–1934), 3.

2. Ibid., 4–7.

3. Ralf Dahrendorf, "Social Science," in Adam Kuper and Jessica Kuper, eds., *Social Science Encyclopedia*, 2d ed. (London: Routledge, 1996).

4. Kuper and Kuper, *Social Science Encyclopedia*, vii.

5. George H. Brett II, "Introduction," in Paul Gilster, *Finding It on the Internet: The Essential Guide to Archie, Veronica, Gopher, WAIS, WWW (Including Mosaic) and Other Search and Browsing Tools* (New York: John Wiley, 1994), xvi.

6. P. Foster, "Area Studies: Comparative and International Education," in *International Encyclopedia of Education*, 2d ed. (Oxford: Pergamon Press, 1994), 331.

7. Bryce Wood, "Area Studies," in *International Encyclopedia of the Social Sciences* (New York: Macmillan, 1968), 404.

8. Foster, "Area Studies," 31.

9. Wood, "Area Studies," 401.

10. Ibid.

11. Ibid., 403.

12. Ibid.

13. Cecily Johns, ed., *Selection of Library Materials for Area Studies. Part I.* (Chicago: American Library Association, 1990), xiv.

14. Marianna Tax Choldin et al., "Area Studies in the United States," *Advances in Librarianship* 15 (1991): 238.

15. *Reference Books Bulletin*, (January 15, 1987): 762–74 and (December 1, 1988): 620.

16. Comparison done by Lorraine Jean of The Pennsylvania State University Libraries (1987).

17. Tze-chung Li, *Social Science Reference Sources: A Practical Guide*, 2d ed. (Westport, CT: Greenwood Press, 1990), 135.

18. Joe Morehead, *Introduction to United States Public Documents*, 3d ed. (Littleton, CO: Libraries Unlimited, 1983), 62.

19. William Web, *Sources of Information in the Social Sciences* (Chicago: American Library Association, 1986), 27.

20. Dialog, NTIS: NationalTechnical Information Service [Bluesheet], http://library.dialog.com/blusheets /html/bl0006.html.

21. David Sills, "Foreword," in *The International Encyclopedia of the Social Sciences* (New York: Macmillan, 1968), xii.

22. *Reference Books Bulletin Annual Cumulation*, 1985–1986, 108.

Literature of the Established Disciplines of the Social Sciences

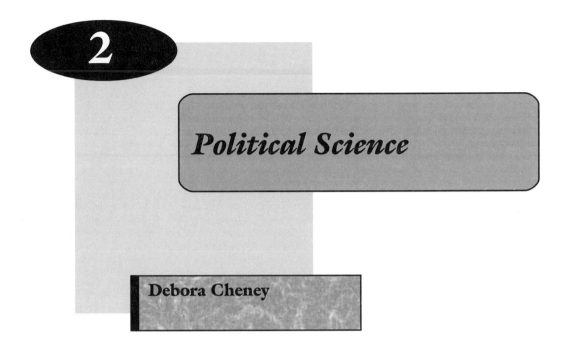

2

Political Science

Debora Cheney

ESSAY

Every day, newspapers, magazines, television, and radio bombard us with information dealing with political situations and developments. However, few of us think of this information as falling within the discipline of political science. Similarly, political science questions posed at library reference desks will frequently deal with current events and society, rather than with an analysis of a political theory or ideology. Yet all these questions fall into the arena of political science reference work.

One difficult aspect of categorizing political science questions is that they are dependent on both the type of library and the needs of patrons using that library. Each reference question can require different resources and different reference processes. In an academic setting, questions about the availability of foreign newspaper translations, articles about the impact of congressional redistricting on voter registration, and statements and voting records on a wide range of topics are likely to be posed. In addition, questions about political situations in other countries and the activities and publications of international and intergovernmental organizations are increasingly common. With the growing awareness of world events and the greater availability of information about these events, researchers are increasingly expanding their research to include non-U.S. sources. The breadth and complexity of many political science questions illustrate two facts about the discipline of political science: It lacks a clear definition and delineation of the subject from other social sciences, and the range of material covered in the field is very large.

Einstein once observed that politics was more difficult to understand than physics because of the number of relationships and factors involved.[1] This can be said also about the study of political science. Politics and the governance of human beings have, of course, been in existence since we first organized into societal groups. Yet the study of political science is a relatively new social science, born from the disciplines of history, economics, and government and nurtured by the fields of sociology, psychology, geography, and philosophy. Because of the field's interdisciplinary nature, political science reference questions often require sources and knowledge beyond those traditionally categorized as purely political science sources.

Evolution of Political Science

The birth of this new social science is usually placed at the turn of the twentieth century with the establishment of the American Political Science Association (APSA) in 1903. Before that time, most studies of politics took place within departments of history and economics. However, with the founding of the APSA, political science departments soon developed in colleges and universities across the country. The founding was also significant to the discipline, because it was a U.S. association and the discipline itself is a uniquely U.S. social science, with more than three-quarters of political scientists being American.[2] The predominance of Americans in the field focused most research in the area of U.S. politics, a bias that still exists today. However, this is changing not only because the end of the Cold War has placed the superpowers in a relationship of cooperation rather than competition, but also because information about other countries has become more available.

As the discipline developed, its lack of scientific principles was viewed by all as a primary deterrent in a field claiming the word *science*. Political scientists consciously tried to develop the principles and theories necessary for a scientific framework for this new field. However, the discipline continues to struggle with the need to define itself and its role.[3] The 1982 *International Handbook of Political Science,* edited by William G. Andrews (Greenwood Press, 1982), opens with the same sentence that the first article in the first issue of *Political Science Quarterly* (the first professional journal in the field) did in 1886: "The term *political science* is greatly in need of definition."[4] On the surface it would appear that U.S. efforts during the past century have done little to define the discipline of political science. Yet the profession has made a good deal of progress; it has produced a body of classic works, fostered specialization, developed a systematic theoretical structure, and developed models for analysis.

The discipline has passed through five developmental stages in the past 100 years. The first stage, the study of government, was an outgrowth of the marriage of history and economics. This period produced the great classics in political science, many of which stand up well even by today's standards of science[5] and were the basis for political organizational theory. However, the search for scientific rules for the discipline continued until after World War II, when the second stage, behaviorism, emerged. Behavioralists sought to scientifically learn why and how people react in political situations, and tried to predict occurrences and political actions. A third stage, the study of comparative politics, began to move political science out of its largely U.S. focus and to compare how nations and states operate. The fourth stage, the study of public administration, dealt with how governments and organizations (e.g., Congress, government agencies, political parties) operate. The final stage, the now-burgeoning field of public policy analysis, seeks ways to quantify and evaluate political decisions to maximize benefits for the public good. Each of these stages reflected the interest and themes of the historical periods in which it was born and effectively added new fields of specialization within the study of political science.

Fields of Specialization

Within political science there are many fields of research, each slightly different from the others and each borrowing from and overlapping to certain degrees with other social sciences. These fields can be grouped into seven broad areas: national governments, comparative politics, international politics, political theory, public law, public administration, and public policy analysis.

National Governments

The study of national governments is the oldest branch of political science, covering many topics and evolving out of the works of Plato and Aristotle. Originally this field dealt with the subjects of power, the state, and political institutions. Due to the U.S. dominance in political science, the field soon grew into the study of the powers and interactions of the legislative, executive, and judicial bodies at the national, state, and local levels. The study of the national governments branched out in the early twentieth century to include the study of voting and electoral patterns and the power of political parties within the U.S. political scene. Today, because of behaviorism and frequent forays into sociology and psychology, the key fields of study are the behavior and motivation of voters and the power of the media in the political process.

Comparative Politics

The study of comparative politics became an area of serious research after World War II with the emergence of behaviorism. Comparative politics research attempts to develop methodologies by which institutions and governments can be compared scientifically. Unfortunately, there has rarely been agreement on consistent methodologies, and, consequently, scientific cross-national comparisons rarely occur. Study in this branch of political science and the resulting literature tend to be primarily descriptive, occasionally crossing into the field of history, area studies, and economics.

International Politics

The study of international politics examines the interactions of independent political entities within an international sphere. These entities can be either separate nations or intergovernmental organizations (IGOs), such as the United Nations or the Organization of American States. Frequent topics of interest in this field are the foreign policies of countries or organizations, national defense policies, peace and military research, and diplomatic affairs. The literature of this field of study depends heavily on official government, organization, or intergovernmental documents, including proclamations, resolutions, reports, and policy statements.

Political Theory

The study of political theory seeks ways to explain and predict political phenomena through the philosophical and moral aspects of political ideologies. The field is divided into two major areas of study: normative and empirical. Normative theory concerns itself with analytical, moral, and philosophical issues. Empirical theory tries to predict behavior through established models and hypotheses.

Public Law

The study of public law is the counterpart to the legal profession. Whereas the attorney researches issues to know how best to represent a client in a court of law, a scholar studies the same material looking for patterns to describe how society places controls on the individual. Research, dominated by U.S. scholars, has focused primarily on the separation of powers, presidential power, and the powers of the courts. However, there is also extensive study of international law, covering the issues of accepted international legal behavior, both by individuals and nations. This field depends heavily on court decisions (including administrative and appellate courts) and on international agreements and treaties.

Public Administration

The study of public administration grew out of research since the 1880s on the daily operation of governments and bureaucracies and has developed a substantial body of classic literature to serve as a foundation.[6] The primary focus of public administration research is on governmental operations and the managerial processes associated with the successful operation of any organization, including budgeting, staffing, management, directing, analysis, and evaluation. Governments at all levels—national, state, and local—are studied. The field frequently approaches issues from a comparative politics standpoint, and an important area of recent study involves research on the governments of developing countries.

Public Policy Analysis

Public policy analysis, the newest field of study, combines economics, public administration, and national government as it delves into the decisions and actions of governments operating with limited resources. The field attempts to develop methodologies and models through which public policy decisions can be made. Despite its newness, the field has grown rapidly and is now considered a mature field of study.

Structure of the Literature

Information sources for political science fall into two categories: primary sources in either paper or machine-readable format from research or governmental bodies and secondary sources (e.g., accounts from monographs or serials). Each field within political science depends on these two information categories to differing degrees. For example, a study of legislative intent would require the publications of official bodies, such as the Congress or the United Nations General Assembly, to interpret legislative intent; a voting analysis study would require raw data of electoral results to develop a hypothesis concerning voting behavior; and a study of Chinese national economic policies would require government publications and monographic, serial, and newspaper accounts.

Reference service in political science is highly dependent on the nature of the question and the type of patron. It should be obvious that a firm grasp of other social science reference sources is requisite. A basic knowledge of current events and American history is also essential in conducting the reference interview. Familiarity with the structure of the United States and key intergovernmental organizations, such as the United Nations, is also essential. Finally, a working knowledge of the organization of government document collections and the characteristics of specific types of government publications, particularly congressional and judicial documents, is helpful. In short, to provide reference service to the field of political science one must be comfortable with the social sciences in general and with collections containing primary source materials.

The titles discussed in the remainder of the chapter represent the variety of political science reference resources available. The sources are arranged based on the subject and type of question that they could help to answer, in the following categories:

General Information

Public Administration and Public Policy—General Sources

U.S. Government—Executive Branch

U.S. Government—Congress

U.S. Government—The Presidency

U.S. Government—State and Local

National Governments—Worldwide

U.S. Politics—General

Elections and Political Parties—United States

Elections and Political Parties—The States

Elections and Political Parties—Worldwide

International Relations and Organizations

War and Peace; Terrorism

Human Rights

GENERAL INFORMATION

When faced with a reference question that does not neatly fall into one of the listed categories, the following titles should help to find the way through the numerous reference sources, journals, and monographs produced in the field of political science. This section covers only the most general indexes. Additional indexes and abstracts are covered in the specific sections below.

Guides to the Literature

B-1   Holler, Frederick L. **Information Sources of Political Science**. 4th ed. Santa Barbara, CA: ABC-Clio, 1986.

B-2   York, Henry E. **Political Science: A Guide to Reference and Information Sources**. Englewood, CO: Libraries Unlimited, 1990.

Holler is an excellent reference source describing more than 2,400 reference works and bibliographies in the area of political science. Although now dated, it still provides the most comprehensive overview of political science sources. Besides the concise annotations found in the text, Holler presents his theory of political science reference. Indexes are provided for author, subject, title, and type of reference source. York's work is a more recent title describing 805 major political science information sources.

B-3   Sears, Jean L., and Marilyn K. Moody. **Using Government Information Sources, Print and Electronic**. 3d ed. Phoenix, AZ: Oryx Press, 2000.

Research in political science often involves using primary source materials from congressional, judicial, or executive offices. Frequently, additional information about the availability and content of these primary sources is needed. The strength of this source is its focus on U.S. government publications. It provides an overview of subject searching, agency searching, statistical searching, and special techniques for searching in government publications. It also includes discussions of many electronic sources of information. It is well organized and well illustrated.

Handbooks

B-4   Robins, John P., et al., eds. **Measures of Political Attitudes**. (Measures of Social Psychological Attitudes). New York: Academic Press, 1999.

As political scientists move into the study of political behavior, the need to develop standardized scales has become increasingly more important. This volume, part of the Measures of Social Psychological Attitudes series, provides an overview of scale selection and evaluation and maximizing questionnaire quality, but also provides an excellent overview of the existing measures and scales measuring liberalism and conservatism, economic values and inequality, democratic values and political tolerance, racial attitudes, political alienation and efficacy, trust in government, international attitudes, political information, political agendas, political partisanship, and political participation. Each chapter is written by an expert and includes numerous bibliographic footnotes.

Dictionaries and Encyclopedias

B-5 Miller, David, ed. **Blackwell Encyclopaedia of Political Thought**. New York: Blackwell, 1996.

B-6 Benewick, Robert, and Philip Green, eds. **The Routledge Dictionary of Twentieth-Century Political Thinkers**. 2d ed. New York: Routledge, 1998.
As companion texts with some overlap, these volumes provide basic information on the leading political theorists, ideas, and political institutions in thirteen Western industrial countries, the former Soviet Union, and Eastern Europe. The texts have a decidedly British bias and cover only Western political traditions. The entries are arranged alphabetically; a subject index is provided. *The Routledge Dictionary of Twentieth-Century Political Thinkers* is less comprehensive than *Blackwell* but more up-to-date and broader in scope.

B-7 Hawkesworth, Mary, and Maurice Kogan, eds. **Encyclopedia of Government and Politics**. New York: Routledge, 1992.
This two-volume set has eighty-four articles that provide a sound introduction to the field of political study. The introductory essay reviews the evolution of political science, and entries are intended to provide a critical analysis rather than a descriptive capsule sketch. Entries are grouped in nine broad headings: political theory, central concepts; contemporary ideologies; contemporary political systems; political institutions; political forces and political processes; centripetal and centrifugal forces in the nation-state; policy making and politics; international relations; and major issues in contemporary world politics. Articles include references and further reading.

B-8 Bealey, Frank. **The Blackwell Dictionary of Political Science**. New York: Blackwell, 1999.

B-9 Comfort, Nicholas. **Brewer's Politics: A Phrase and Fable Dictionary**. London: Cassell, 1993.
A wide range of dictionaries focusing on political terms and definitions is available. The *Blackwell Dictionary* provides a valuable reference source for political science students not yet familiar with the unique vocabulary and context of political science terminology. It is more comprehensive in scope than many dictionaries and has been updated recently. Many entries also include related readings for students seeking greater understanding of terms and concepts. The scope of *Brewer's Politics* is wider. It seeks to include the "broad sweep of political language from technical and procedural terms through well-worn cliches to devastating insults," including those used by politicians and political journalists. As such it provides a unique entree into political language.

B-10 Plano, Jack C. **The Dictionary of Political Analysis**. (The Dictionary of Political Analysis). Santa Barbara, CA: ABC-Clio, 1982.
ABC-Clio has produced the series Clio Dictionaries in Political Science, which covers terms used within political science literature. *The Dictionary of Political Analysis,* one title in this series, is arranged in a typical dictionary format. Regardless of the format, dictionaries in the series always provide a discussion of the term and its significance. Many are now standards in the profession and, although somewhat out-of-date, serve as a useful starting point for students due to their format and the accessibility of their definitions.

Bibliographies

B-11 Dent, David W., ed. **Handbook of Political Science Research on Latin America: Trends from the 1960s to the 1990s**. Westport, CT: Greenwood Press, 1990.

B-12 Reich, Bernard, ed. **Handbook of Political Science Research on the Middle East and North Africa**. Westport, CT: Greenwood Press, 1998.

B-13 DeLancey, Mark W., ed. **Handbook of Political Science Research on Sub-Saharan Africa: Trends from the 1960s to the 1990s**. Westport, CT: Greenwood Press, 1992.

B-14 Taras, Raymond C., ed. **Handbook of Political Science Research on the USSR and Eastern Europe: Trends from the 1960's to the 1990's**. Westport, CT: Greenwood Press, 1992.
This series of works provides the researcher with an overview of the major trends and changes in political science research for the area and of the causes of those changes. Each title includes essays for each country in the region covered by the volume. The essays serve as extensive bibliographical introductions to the literature. Also included is an appendix containing a list of reference works and research centers. Name and subject indexes are included.

B-15 **International Bibliography of Political Science**. New York: Routledge, 1953- . Annual.
This standard bibliography merged with *The London Bibliography of the Social Sciences* in 1990. The bibliography is still highly selective, representing only "the most significant new material each year"; more than 2,500 journals are scanned for articles, as well as recent government publications and monographs. The bibliography is not current, being two to four years out-of-date. Since the merger, the focus has been on political science and international relations. Works included must be in one of the more prevalent languages of the world. Author and subject indexes are provided.

Indexes and Abstracts

Because much political science research requires primary source materials from government agencies and international organizations, researchers will need to locate these publications through a variety of sources. Large academic libraries are increasingly adding these publications to their electronic catalogs. However, because of the prevalence of microform collections containing primary sources, many sources are not yet accessible through a library's catalog. For this reason, it is extremely important to determine how each library makes these materials and microformatted collections accessible. Frequently it will be necessary to consult separate indexes and abstracts. Today, many of these indexes and abstracts are available in several formats. For example, the *Monthly Catalog of U.S. Government Publications* (A-45) is available as a CD, an online database, a computer tape to be loaded into a library's own catalog, and on the World Wide Web (1998-). In addition, a wider range of subject, organization, or format-specific indexes or abstracts is available to help locate relevant sources.

B-16 **C.R.I.S. Combined Retrospective Index to Journals in Political Science, 1886–1974**. 8 vols. Arlington, VA: Carrollton, 1978.

This eight-volume reference set indexes more than 115,000 articles in political science. Six of the volumes provide title keyword and author indexes. Most of the journals indexed are in English, mainly in the areas of political science, sociology, and history. Each entry lists the author's name, an abbreviated form of the article's title, the year, volume, journal number, and pagination for the article. This set is helpful in doing a quick historical search for information.

B-17 **International Political Science Abstracts**. Paris: International Political Science Association, 1952- . Annual.

This bimonthly publication abstracts annually more than 5,000 articles found in 600 journals and yearbooks produced worldwide. Some sources are covered in full, others selectively. Each supplement is broken down into six categories: political science, political thinkers and ideas, governmental and administrative institutions, political process, international relations, and national and area studies. English-language articles are abstracted in English, while all other article abstracts are provided in French. Subject, author, and periodical indexes are included.

Electronic access: Also available as a Web-based database and on CD-ROM.

PAIS International in Print. New York: Public Affairs Information Service, 1991- . Weekly. (See A-21)

Carrying the latest title change for *PAIS Index* (1914-), this index covers public and social policy materials, including periodicals, books, government publications, pamphlets, microfiche, and reports of public and private agencies. Selection is based on items' coverage of business, economic, and social conditions; public policy; administration; and international relations if published in English, French, German, Italian, Portuguese, or Spanish. Most entries include a brief note, updated monthly.

Electronic access: Available in several electronic formats: CD-ROM, WWW fee-based database, and computer tapes to be loaded into a library's online catalog.

B-18 **Political Science Abstracts**. New York, IFI/Plenum, c1981- . Annual.

This annual index adds 10,000 journals, major newspapers, public affairs magazines, and book entries to its database covering politics, public administration, public policy, and related fields since 1976. Because of its delay in availability, the print version is not useful for current search. The electronic version begins with 1975 and is updated quarterly. Cross-year searching gives it more flexibility for researchers, combined with the possibility for keyword and Boolean searches. Abstracts are succinct; author and descriptor term indexes available.

Electronic access: Also available as a fee-based Web database and on CD-ROM.

Reviews

B-19 **Annual Review of Political Science**. Palo Alto, CA: Annual Review, 1998- . Annual.

Provides a comprehensive literature review on major topics of interest to the profession. An excellent source for students to obtain a thorough overview of research in specific subject areas. Tables of contents can be viewed at http://www.annual reviews.org. Preceded by the *Annual Review of Political Science* (Ablex 1986–1990).

Electronic access: Available on the Web by subscription.

PUBLIC ADMINISTRATION AND PUBLIC POLICY—GENERAL SOURCES

Guides to the Literature

B-20   Simpson, Antony E. **Information-Finding and the Research Process: A Guide to Sources and Methods for Public Administration and the Policy Sciences**. Westport, CT: Greenwood Press, 1993.

Intended as a reference guide for conducting research in the policy sciences and public administration, this source provides an overview of research methods and search strategies, sources for an overview of theory and current developments, and sources for an overview of theory in applied contexts. Its strength is its focus on developing an information-finding strategy to identify the appropriate methodology and data to support the research question. It also focuses on the interdisciplinary nature of the policy sciences and public administration.

Dictionaries and Encyclopedias

B-21   Kruschke, Earl R. **The Public Policy Dictionary**. (Clio Dictionaries in Political Science). Santa Barbara, CA: ABC-Clio, 1987.

The Public Policy Dictionary is organized into broad subject chapters and terms. Each book in the series Clio Dictionaries in Political Science provides a discussion of each term and its significance. Although somewhat out-of-date, the dictionaries as a useful starting point for students due to their format and the accessibility of their definitions.

B-22   Shafritz, Jay M., ed. **International Encyclopedia of Public Policy and Administration**. 4 vols. New York: Westview Press, 1998.

This four-volume encyclopedia provides articles on more than 900 concepts relevant to the study of public policy and administration. The entries are written by over 400 contributors. Entries are well organized and provide a definition as well as sections providing discussion, illustrations, and nearly always a bibliography of related works.

Handbooks

B-23   DeSario, Jack Paul, ed. **International Public Policy Sourcebook**. 2 vols. Westport, CT: Greenwood Press, 1989.

The two volumes in this *Sourcebook* cover *Health and Social Welfare* and *Education and Environment*. Within each volume the subject area is divided by country. (Canada, Federal Republic of Germany, France, Israel, Japan, Sweden, United Kingdom, and the United States are included.) Each country chapter provides a study of public policy that can be used for comparative analysis with other countries. An excellent starting point for an understanding of each of these policy areas in a cross-national perspective.

B-24   Nagel, Stuart S., ed. **Encyclopedia of Policy Studies**. New York: Dekker, 1994.

B-25   Wholey, Joseph S., et al., eds. **Handbook of Practical Program Evalua-tion**. San Francisco: Jossey-Bass, 1994.

The *Encyclopedia of Policy Studies* provides a conceptual framework and overview of public policy studies. Each chapter is written by an expert and covers the conceptual challenges facing those in public policy analysis; also provided is an overview of specific policy problems—those with a political science, economic, sociological or psychological, urban and regional planning, and natural science or engineering emphasis. For guidance on the complex issues surrounding the analysis of program and policy analysis, consult the *Handbook of Practical Program Evaluation*. Chapters are written by individuals who cover topics ranging from evaluation design, practical data collection procedures, practical data analysis, and planning and managing evaluation for maximum effectiveness.

Indexes and Abstracts

B-26   **Sage Public Administration Abstracts**. Beverly Hills, CA: Sage, 1974- . Quarterly.

For topics in the area of public administration—U.S., international, state, and local—one would do well to begin a search in this bibliography. Produced quarterly, this service provides selective abstracts for approximately 200 scholarly journals on organizational behavior, budgeting, financing, personnel, and administration. Subject and author indexes are included and compiled annually.

U.S. GOVERNMENT—EXECUTIVE BRANCH

Directories and Handbooks

B-27   **Federal Agency Profiles for Students**. Detroit: Gale, 1999.

Federal Agency Profiles for Students provides an overview of the workings of U.S. government agencies that meets the curriculum needs of students and instructors. More than 175 agencies are profiled, and each description includes a statement of the agency's mission, its structure, primary functions, programs, budget information, history, current political issues, successes and failures, future directions, agency resources, agency publications, and a bibliography.

B-28   **Federal Regulatory Directory**. Washington, DC: Congressional Quarterly, 1979- . Biennial.

Less-detailed historical information, an overview of agency mission, and enabling legislation for the "Major Regulatory Agencies" are available in *Federal Regulatory Directory*. Congressional committees and regulatory responsibilities are included in these entries. Less complete information is provided for "Other Regulatory Agencies" and "Departmental Agencies" with a lesser regulatory role. The chapters on the "Reasons for Regulation" and "Early History and Growth of Regulation" provide excellent overviews. Although each of the above sources might be the first stop for compre-hensive information, Bruce Wettereau's *Desk Reference on American Government* (2d ed., Congres-sional Quarterly, 2000) provides a question and answer approach to frequently asked questions about the federal government. Chapters cover the government (in general), the presidency, Congress, campaigns and elections, and the Supreme Court. Most entries include supporting data.

B-29   Kurian, George. **A Historical Guide to the U.S. Government**. New York: Oxford University Press, 1998.

Kurian's *A Historical Guide to the U.S. Government* provides the researcher with a suc-cinct and composite historical profile of U.S. government agencies and departments. Each three- to five-page profile ends with a bibliography of related sources, and entries are signed by the authors.

Although a growing number of government agencies have been profiled in recent years in book-length histories, the wealth of information about government agency histories remains largely scattered, and this source provides a useful starting point for such information.

B-30 **United States Government Manual**. Washington, DC: Government Printing Office, 1935- . Biennial.

Formerly known as *U.S. Government Organization Manual*, the *United States Government Manual* is the classic historical and official source for general information about the U.S. government. Included in the text for each department, agency, and bureau are a mission statement for the body; a citation to its legislative authority; a discussion of the primary responsibilities and services provided; and names, addresses, and telephone numbers for key individuals and offices. Also included are organizational charts, maps delineating the federal regions for various departments, and addresses for these local contracts. Copies of the Declaration of Independence, the Constitution, and the Bill of Rights are located at the beginning of the volume. Indexing is by name of individual and agency/subject.

Electronic access: Now accessible via *GPO Access* (http://www.access.gpo.gov/nara/nara001 .html) from 1995/1996 to date.

B-31 **Federal Staff Directory**. Washington, DC: Congressional Quarterly, 1982- . 3 times/yr.

B-32 **Federal Directory, Executive, Legislative, Judicial**. Washington, DC: Carroll, 1980- . 6 times/yr.

B-33 **Federal Regional Executive Directory**. Washington, DC: Carroll, 1984- . Semiannual.

Each of these directories provides increasingly more detailed telephone directory information for government offices and executives. These sources go further into the organizational bureaucracy than *United States Government Manual* (B-30) and are particularly helpful in identifying individuals at the operational level. The only other telephone books that go to this level are agency telephone directories, which are available in many GPO depository libraries or at agency Web sites. This source is indexed by both personal and agency names. The *Federal Staff Directory* (also available at a fee-based Web site, http://fsd.cq.com) focuses on offices within the Washington beltway and is divided into four sections: the Executive Office of the President, the cabinet level departments, the independent agencies, and the quasi-official, international, and nongovernmental organizations.

A separate section includes brief biographies of key staff members. The *Federal Directory* is more streamlined and includes a listing of phone numbers; personal e-mail addresses; and executive branch, judiciary, and legislative staff. The *Federal Regional Executive Directory* is also produced for all federal regional offices and should be consulted when looking for addresses and telephone numbers of government offices outside the Washington area.

Electronic access: The Carroll directories are available on CD-ROM and as fee-based Web sites (http:///www.carrollpub.com), where they are updated more frequently.

B-34 **Washington Information Directory**. Washington, DC: Congressional Quarterly, 1976- . Biennial.

The *Washington Information Directory* provides a topic approach to the federal government agencies. Each topic area includes entries for federal government agencies, congressional committees, and nonprofit organizations instrumental in making and influencing policy. Each entry includes phone and fax numbers, contact name, and other directory information. It also provides a description of the work performed by the organization or government agency. This is the only directory that combines current information about government agencies, Congress, and the interest groups that reside within the beltway and seek to influence government. To locate historical information about cabinet heads, vice presidents and presidents of the Continental Congress, consult Robert Sobel, ed., *Biographical*

Directory of the United States Executive Branch, 1774–1989 (Greenwood Press, 1990). These brief biographies focus on the bureaucrat's government career and also provide references to book-length studies.

Indexes and Abstracts

B-35 CIS Index to U.S. Executive Branch Documents, 1789–1909: Guide to Documents Listed in the *Checklist of U.S. Public Documents, 1789–1909*, Not Printed in the Serial Set. Bethesda, MD: Congressional Information Service, 1990–95.

Together these two indexes provide access to government publications published by government agencies from 1789 to 1932, the period during which the United States developed into a major world and industrial power. Both indexes provide excellent indexing by subject, title, agency report numbers, and Superintendent of Documents (SuDocs) numbers. The arrangement is similar to the *CIS Index* (B-62). The main disadvantage is that both indexes are published in six parts, with each part covering a different group of departments/agencies, and no cumulative cross-agency index will be available. Most titles are available in an accompanying microfiche collection. Indispensable for historical research into government agencies, policies, and development, these titles complement the *CIS U.S. Serial Set Index* (B-62n) and the *Monthly Catalog* (A-45n).

U.S. GOVERNMENT—CONGRESS

Dictionaries and Encyclopedias

B-36 **Congressional Quarterly's Guide to Congress**. 5th ed. Washington, DC: Congressional Quarterly, 2000.

This is undoubtedly the best single volume for finding information about the history and operation of Congress and an excellent source for difficult questions about Congress. In seven sections it presents the origins and development of Congress, its powers, congressional procedures, housing and support, Congress and the electorate, pressures on Congress, and qualifications and conduct of members. A short biographical index is included, as well as an extensive bibliography.

B-37 **Congress A to Z**. 3d ed. Washington, DC: Congressional Quarterly, 1999.

For briefer information covering the history and operation of Congress, see *Congress A to Z*. An appendix contains historical lists (e.g., of floor leaders).

B-38 Silbey, Joel H. **Encyclopedia of the American Legislative System: Studies of the Principal Structures, Processes, and Policies of Congress and the State Legislatures Since the Colonial Era**. 3 vols. New York: Scribner's, 1994.

This three-volume encyclopedia focuses on the legislative processes more generally than *CQ's Guide to Congress* (B-36). It provides an important historical context for the role of legislative systems at the national, state, and local levels. Signed articles are included that cover the historical context, personnel and recruitment, structures and processes, legislative behavior, public policy, and legislatures within the political system. Chapters typically include extensive bibliographies.

Committees

B-39   Nelson, Garrison, and Clark H. Bensen. **Committees in the U.S. Congress, 1947–1992**. Washington, DC: Congressional Quarterly, 1993- . Quarterly.

For greater detail about committee membership, consult Nelson and Bensen's *Committees in the U.S. Congress, 1947–1992*. The first two volumes in a projected six-volume set document all of the assignments to congressional committees from 1789 to the present, including Senate and House standing committees and select and special committees. Each committee roster gives committee name and Congress, chairperson, members and service dates, majority and minority, and any changes to the committee. A very valuable historical source for documenting committees and their membership.

Directories

B-40   United States. Congress. **Official Congressional Directory**. Washington, DC: Government Printing Office, 1888- . Biennial.

This is an official historical reference source for information about the U.S. Congress, its members, committees, and operations. Because the directory is produced for the benefit of Congress, it also includes information about executive agencies, state government, international organizations, diplomatic corps, and the press assigned to cover Washington. A name index is available, as well as a collection of maps outlining congressional districts.

> *Electronic access:* Also available on the Web via *GPO Access* (http://www.access.gpo.gov/nara /nara001.html).

B-41   **Congressional Yellow Book**. Washington, DC: Washington Monitor, 1976- . Revised quarterly.

B-42   **Congressional Staff Directory**. Washington, DC: Congressional Quarterly, 1959- . Updated 3 times/yr.

Because there is a large amount of staff turnover and change within staff of members of Congress and of the congressional committees, a more current directory may be necessary to ensure accurate contacts. The *Congressional Yellow Book* presents directory-like information with quarterly revisions. *Congressional Staff Directory* provides contact information about each member of congress, committee assignments, and a list of both Washington and home staffs. There are lists of each committee and its staff, the staffs of the offices and agencies of Congress, and brief biographical data for selected, highly placed staffers. A large section is devoted to the states and congressional districts; it provides an overview of the district, recent election results, and a list of zip codes associated with the district. A subject and name index is provided; there are also personal name and subject keyword indexes.

> *Electronic access:* Also available at Congressional Quarterly's fee-based Web site (http://csd .cq.com).

Members of Congress

B-43   **Congressional Quarterly's Politics in America**. Washington, DC: Congressional Quarterly, 1981- . Biennial.

B-44   **The Almanac of American Politics**. Washington, DC: National Journal, 1989- . Biennial.

For reference questions requiring biographical information about members of Congress that can provide a political profile and overview of voting behavior and interest group support, consult *Politics in America*. This biennial publication presents an editorial biography of each legislator, including a photograph and a description of congressional district or home state. Information included exceeds that found in *Official Congressional Directory* (B-40), including a discussion of the legislator's activities while in Congress, an analysis of his or her legislative influence and political alliances, election data, and a brief campaign financing report. Of vital importance are the special interest group ratings provided for each legislator and a synopsis of key votes in the past year. A similar title, *The Almanac of American Politics*, also discusses each state's and district's political environment and provides a rating of every legislator's performance in Washington based on selected interest group ratings.

       Electronic access: *CQ's Politics in America* is available via a fee-based Web site (http://www.cq.com/). *Almanac of American* politics is also available via a fee-based Web site (http://www.nationaljournal.com) and on CD-ROM (1995-).

B-45   **Biographical Directory of the American Congress 1774–1996**. Washington, DC: CQ Staff Directories, 1997.

      The *Biographical Directory of the American Congress* is arranged alphabetically by name and is a key source for locating brief information about all people who have served in the U.S. Congress or its predecessors; it updates the *Biographical Directory of the United States Congress, 1774–1989*, formerly compiled by the Joint Committee on Printing (Government Printing Office, 1989; now available at http://bioguide.congress.gov/biosearch/biosearch1.asp). Each entry presents the dates of birth and death, place of birth, position within the government, education, and years in office.

B-46   **Members of Congress Since 1789**. 3d ed. Washington, DC: Congressional Quarterly, 1985.

      This work provides the same type of information as *Biographical Directory of the American Congress 1774–1996* (B-45), but in a much briefer format. (Appendix B of *Congressional Quarterly's Guide to Congress* [B-36] contains a list of "Members of Congress 1789–1999"). Entries include dates served and birth and death dates only. Karen Foerstel's *The Biographical Dictionary of Congressional Women* (Greenwood Press, 1999) and LaVerne McCain Gill's *African American Women in Congress* (Rutgers University Press, 1997) can provide more detailed and focused information, as well as photographs.

Vote Sources

B-47   Bosnich, Victor W., ed. **Congressional Voting Guide: A Ten-Year Compilation**. 5th ed. Bronx, NY: H. W. Wilson, 1994.

      This source provides an overview of how members have voted on selected major votes. A description of the selected legislation for each chamber and entries for each member of Congress are included. Each record includes a brief biography and presidential support score. Previous editions are useful for historical information outside the current ten-year period. Votes by member can also be found in *CQ Almanac* (Congressional Quarterly, 1945-), *CQ Weekly Report* (B-56), and *Congressional Universe* (B-60).

B-48   **Washington Representatives**. Washington, DC: Columbia Books, 1977- . Annual.

      A continuation of *Directory of Washington Representatives of American Associations and Industry*, *Washington Representatives* is a listing of lobbyists, foreign agents, consultants, and legal counsels working in the Washington area representing special interest groups. The directory provides the names, addresses, telephone numbers, and clients of all registered lobbyists. In addition to the alphabetical listing there is a subject/foreign interest/organizational names index.

B-49   Sharp, J. Michael. **Directory of Congressional Voting Scores and Interest Group Ratings**. 2d ed. 2 vols. Washington, DC: Congressional Quarterly, 1997.

One area of study of interest to political scientists is the relationship between the voting behavior of members of Congress and their interaction with and support from interest groups. Groups such as the Americans for Democratic Action have been ranking members of congress since 1947, although party voting and voting participation generally is available much farther back. This two-volume set provides a compilation of these rankings beginning in 1947 to allow cross-Congress comparisons. Each member profile provides the party voting scores (Conservative Coalition, Party Unity; Presidential Support) and also the group ratings from ten interest groups that rate members of Congress, including Americans for Democratic Action, the American Conservative Union, the American Civil Liberties Union, the American Security Council, the Chamber of Commerce of the United States, the Consumer Federation of America, the Committee on Political Education of the AFL-CIO, the League of Conservation Voters, the National Education Association, and the National Taxpayers Union.

Statistical Sources

B-50   Ornstein, Norman, et al. **Vital Statistics on Congress**. Washington, DC: AEI Press, 1980- . Biennial.

This is the most comprehensive biennial source for providing data and brief overviews of trends in Congress, including information about members of congress, elections, campaign finance, committees, congressional staff and operating expenses, workload, budgeting, and voting alignments. It is a standard source for the most frequently sought data about Congress and provides snapshots of hard-to-locate data frequently only available in a wide range of congressional reports or publications. It is complemented by data included in *Vital Statistics on American Politics* (B-128). Detailed information, data, and lists about the Senate and its members are available in volume 4 of Robert Byrd's historical study *The Senate, 1789–1989: Historical Statistics 1789–1992* (Government Printing Office, 1993).

Congressional Districts and Appointments

B-51   **Congressional Districts in the 1990s: A Portrait of America**. Washington, DC: Congressional Quarterly, 1993.

This is a useful descriptive and statistical profile of the 435 congressional districts, based on the 1990 Census and subsequent reapportionment. The volume is arranged by state; each entry provides a narrative description, including demographic, economic, social, and political changes since the 1980s; a map; and a statistical profile, including voting age, income and occupations, education, and housing patterns. Similar titles for historical information are *Congressional Districts in the 1980s* and *Congressional Districts in the 1970s* (Congressional Quarterly, 1983 and 1973). Additional historical information about congressional districts can be found in *United States Congressional Districts 1788–1841*, *United States Congressional Districts and Data, 1843–1883*, and *United States Congressional Districts, 1883–1913* (Greenwood Press, 1978, 1986, and 1990).

B-52   **Congressional District Atlas**. Washington, DC: Bureau of the Census, 1960- . Biennial.

Current congressional district maps can be located in *Congressional District Atlas*, which is produced for each Congress by the Census Bureau. Wall-sized maps of the most recent Congresses (beginning with the 104th Congress) showing congressional districts are also available in many map libraries and can be purchased from the Census Bureau. The Census Bureau's Web site *American FactFinder* can be used to create maps on-the-fly showing congressional district boundaries. Last produced in paper format for the 103d Congress.

Electronic access: Census data for congressional districts are available at http://www .census.gov/prod/www/abs/congprof.html. Produced on CD-ROM for the 105th Congress.

B-53 Martis, Kenneth C. **The Historical Atlas of United States Congressional Districts, 1789–1983**. New York: Free Press, 1982.

B-54 Martis, Kenneth C., and Ruth Anderson Rowles. **The Historical Atlas of Political Parties in the United States Congress, 1789–1989**. New York: Macmillan, 1989.

B-55 Martis, Kenneth C., and Gregory A. Elmes. **The Historical Atlas of State Power in Congress, 1790–1990**. Washington, DC: Congressional Quarterly, 1993.

Together, these three atlases provide some of the first historical mapping of congressional districts. Martis's works map all the congressional districts that have existed in the country through 1983, the development of political parties, and the development of state power in Congress as reflected in apportionment following each decennial census.

Periodicals

B-56 **Congressional Quarterly Weekly Report**. Washington, DC: Congressional Quarterly, 1943- . Weekly.

B-57 **National Journal**. Washington, DC: National Journal, 1969- . Weekly.

This is current information about legislative actions being undertaken in Congress, *CQ Weekly Report* is the best starting place. Produced as a news service for editors and commentators, this weekly service presents a quick factual account of what is happening on Capitol Hill, including legislative votes and presidential actions. The reports are indexed on a weekly, quarterly, and annual basis. A similar current awareness periodical is *National Journal*. This weekly publication tends to be more editorial in nature in its reporting but covers news items in greater detail than does *CQ Weekly Report* and typically focuses more on the executive branch. Congressional Quarterly takes the information used in producing *CQ Weekly Report* and reformats and condenses the information to present the annual *Congressional Quarterly Almanac* (1945-). These yearbooks highlight key actions, compile annual voting records, describe major legislation, and analyze Supreme Court decisions, citing back to the original *CQ Weekly Report* as appropriate. These almanacs are excellent starting places for information on congressional action in the past forty years. Recognizing a salable product, Congressional Quarterly also produces a further condensation of information in *Congress and the Nation* (1945-). Each volume in this quadrennial publication is arranged by a broad topical approach and is indexed by subject and personal name. The key value of this set is that it helps to pinpoint an issue through a number of years, thus providing an index into the companion volumes of *CQ Almanac* and *CQ Weekly Report*.

Electronic access: Weekly Report is available at CQ's fee-based Web site (http://www.cq.com). *National Journal* is also available at a fee-based Web site (http://www.nationaljournal.com).

Debate

B-58 United States. Congress. **Congressional Record**. Washington, DC: Government Printing Office, 1876- . Daily while Congress is in session.

Without a doubt any serious research into the operations and activities of the U.S. Congress is not complete without referring to *Congressional Record*. Produced daily while Congress is in session, the *Record* provides the closest thing to a verbatim account of what occurs on the floors of the House and Senate. It is indexed biweekly and annually by personal name and subject. The indexes include the "History of Bills and Resolutions" section, which summarizes the status of all bills and resolutions introduced in the current session.

Electronic access: The *Record* is now available from a wide variety of sources in electronic format, including *CQ.com on Congress* (http://www.cq.com), *Academic Universe* (F-15), *Congressional Universe* (B-60), *Thomas* (B-59), and *GPO Access* (F-14). These electronic versions can allow more sophisticated searching and very current access to this important source. *Thomas* and *GPO Access* are free services; *Academic Universe*, *Congressional Universe*, and *CQ.Com on Congress* are fee-based.

Legislative Status Sources

B-59 **Thomas: Bill Summary & Status Reports**

B-60 **Congressional Universe: Bill Tracking Reports**

B-61 **CQ.com on Congress**

Each of the major congressional information vendors provides bill status information. *Thomas* provides *Summary and Status Reports* going back to 1973. *Congressional Universe* and *Academic Universe*'s *Bill Tracking Reports* begin with 1989, and *GPO Access* begins with 1993. Each online vendor adds value to the basic status information by providing complementary information. *Congressional Universe* provides excellent legislative histories of major legislation that became public law and links to full-text sources, while *CQ.com* provides its editorial coverage in its flagship publication *CQ Weekly Report*. Overall, *Thomas* provides an excellent, well-developed status report whose historical coverage is not matched by either of the other vendors.

Prior to the advent of electronic access to congressional information, Commerce Clearing House's *Congressional Index* (Commerce Clearing House, 1937-) was the only way to accurately track all current federal legislation from inception to passage during the legislative calendar. While few researchers would use this source today for current information, given the wealth of other sources, it remains a valuable and succinct source for legislation going back to 1937. Similar information with far greater detail about a bill's content can be located in the now-defunct Library of Congress *Digest of Public General Bills and Resolutions* (Government Printing Office, 1936–1990).

Indexes and Abstracts

B-62 **CIS Index to Publications of the United States Congress**. Bethesda, MD: Congressional Information Service, 1970- . Monthly.

This is the preeminent reference source for locating all published hearings, documents, reports, and committee prints since 1970 and can be used to locate documents in either a Congressional Information Service (CIS) microfiche or a U.S. depository collection. This set indexes and provides detailed abstracts. CIS has also produced a number of titles to complement this initial set, and together these products provide remarkable access to the legislative actions and history of America. These companion titles are *CIS U.S. Serial Set Index*; *CIS Index to Unpublished U.S. Senate Committee Hearings, 1823–1968*; *U.S. Congressional Committee Hearings Index 1833–1969*; *CIS Index to Unpublished U.S. House of Representatives Committee Hearings, 1833–1954*; *CIS Index to U.S. Senate Executive Documents and Reports*; and *CIS U.S. Congressional Committee Prints Index, 1830–1969* (Congressional Information Service). All these titles can be searched at one time on *Congressional Universe* databases, which also provide keyword, Congress number, subject, and document type (e.g., hearing, report) access to the same records contained in all of the print indexes listed above. In addition, many of the entries now include full text. Libraries may also purchase access to the *CIS U.S. Serial Set Index* segment to make this a truly historical database to congressional materials. Many records will also contain full-text links to congressional hearings and committee reports after 1993. For those users who do not have access to this expensive resource, *Thomas* (B-59) provides access to the same materials since 1993. What will be missing is the excellent indexing (by subject or witness name, for example) that is the hallmark of the CIS publication.

B-63 **Congressional Member Organizations and Caucuses**. Bethesda, MD: Congressional Information Service, 1992- . Annual.

Since the 1970s, congressional member organizations and caucuses have played an increasingly important role in defining issues and legislation. These groups vary widely in their spheres of influence, models of organization, and amounts of material published. However, little of this material was available in libraries until this index and its accompanying microfiche collection became available. The index volume is a typical CIS product; entries are well described with subject and name indexes. The index and microfiche collection are updated annually.

B-64 Major Studies and Issues Briefs of the Congressional Research Service. Bethesda, MD: University Publications 1916- . Quarterly.

The Congressional Research Service (CRS) is the department within the Library of Congress that works exclusively as a reference and research arm for Congress. In addition to answering reference questions, the subject specialists on staff produce in-depth policy analysis and research on topics requested by members of Congress, their staffs, and committees. These reports are not issued to depository libraries unless appended to a committee report. They can be obtained in this microfilm collection (also available in microfiche) and its accompanying index. The index provides subject, name, title, and report number access. A base volume and collection cover reports from 1916 to 1989. The collection and index are updated quarterly.

The General Accounting Office also conducts audits, surveys, investigations, and evaluations of federal programs. These reports are indexed in *Abstracts of Reports and Testimony* and its *Index* (Government Printing Office, 1992-) and are now available on the Web at http://www.gao.gov/. The full text of these reports is also available via *GPO Access* (F-14).

Electronic access: The *Major Studies of America* index is also available on CD-ROM under the title *Congressional Research Service Index,* updated annually.

U.S. GOVERNMENT—THE PRESIDENCY

Dictionaries and Encyclopedias

B-65 **Guide to the Presidency**. 2d ed. 2 vols. Washington, DC: Congressional Quarterly, 1996.

Like all the CQ guides, this two-volume source provides an excellent overview of the origins, evolution, history, and present operation of the presidency. It is divided into seven sections: origins and development, selection and removal, powers, the president and the public, the White House and the executive branch, the chief executive and the federal government, and the president and the vice president. Each chapter includes footnotes and a selected bibliography. The appendix includes statistics, lists (e.g., of cabinet members), and charts relating to the presidency.

B-66 **The Presidency A to Z: A Ready Reference Encyclopedia**. 2d ed. Washington, DC: Congressional Quarterly, 1998.

B-67 Elliot, Jeffrey M., and Sheikh R. Ali. **Presidential-Congressional Political Dictionary**. Santa Barbara, CA: ABC-Clio, 1984.

For briefer information and definitions related to the presidency see *The Presidency A to Z: A Ready Reference Encyclopedia* or Elliot and Ali's *Presidential-Congressional Political Dictionary*. The advantage of *Presidential-Congressional Political Dictionary* is that it explains the significance of each term as well as giving a definition.

B-68 Levy, Leonard W., and Louis Fisher. **Encyclopedia of the American Presidency**. 4 vols. New York: Simon & Schuster, 1994.

This four-volume encyclopedia is the most comprehensive, detailed, and multidisciplinary encyclopedia available on the subject of the American presidency. Signed essays on 1,011 topics vary in length. Bibliography references are included with each entry. Authors were encouraged to include opinions and judgments in their essays. Appendixes include lists of presidents and their cabinet offices, as well as presidential elections. An index of legal cases and a general index are also included.

B-69 Kane, Joseph Nathan. **Facts About the Presidents**. 6th ed. Bronx, NY: H. W. Wilson, 1993.

This title is a quick, indispensable source for information about the presidents of the United States. The volume is divided into two parts. The first provides biographical information for each president, and the second presents comparative data about these men. Biographical information in this source includes genealogical background, highlights of each life and administration, presidential appointments to the Supreme Court and the cabinet, vice-presidential information, and electoral results. To balance out the factual information supplied by Kane, consult Charles F. Faber and Richard B. Faber, *The American Presidents Ranked by Performance* (McFarland, 2000) for rankings of performance in foreign relations, domestic programs, administration, leadership, personal qualities, and an overall assessment.

Statistical Sources

B-70 Ragsdale, Lyn. **Vital Statistics on the Presidency: Washington to Clinton**. rev. ed. Washington, DC: Congressional Quarterly, 1998.

This single volume provides an excellent summary of presidential selection, elections, appearances, public opinion, organization and the executive branch, policy making, congressional relations, and the judiciary from the perspective of the office of the president. The introduction by Lyn Ragsdale provides an excellent summary of presidential research and statistical patterns of the presidency.

Textual Sources

B-71 **Public Papers of the Presidents**. Washington, DC: Office of the Federal Register, 1957- . Irregular.

For the text of presidential papers and messages from 1929 to 1933 and 1945 to date, this source is absolutely necessary. Presidential papers and messages prior to compilation in these bound volumes are found in *Weekly Compilation of Presidential Documents* (Office of the Federal Register, 1965-). For messages and papers prior to 1929, see the ten-volume set *A Compilation of the Messages and Papers of the Presidents 1789–1897* (Government Printing Office, 1896–1899, Serial Set 3265-1 to -10). Franklin Roosevelt's papers have been collected in the thirteen-volume set *The Public Papers and Addresses of Franklin D. Roosevelt* (Random House, 1938–1950).

Electronic access: The *Weekly Compilation* is available via *GPO Access* (official version), *Academic Universe, Congressional Universe, Westlaw* (West), and the White House Web site (www.whitehouse.gov), as well as many other full-text bibliographic databases. The official version of the *Public Papers of the President* beginning with the Clinton 1995 administration is also available via *GPO Access* (http://www.access.gpo.gov/nara/pubpaps/srchpaps.html).

For multi-year searching, KTO and Bernan Presses created cumulative indexes to the public papers of Truman, Johnson, Nixon, Ford, Bush, and Reagan, entitled *Cumulated Indexes to the Public Papers of the Presidents* (Bernan Press, 1978-1995). A number of electronic projects are placing historical texts of presidential materials on the Web—most notably Yale's *Avalon Project* (http://www.yale.edu/lawweb/avalon/presiden/presiden.htm), and the Library of Congress *American Memory Project* is beginning with the papers, diaries,

and other manuscript materials for Presidents Lincoln and Theodore Roosevelt (http://lcweb2
.loc.gov/ammem/presprvw/prsprvw.html) as part of its presidential papers project.

U.S. GOVERNMENT—STATE AND LOCAL

The World Wide Web has greatly changed the accessibility of state and local government
information to researchers. Today state and local government Web sites provide access to a wide
range of information previously difficult to locate. For example, many state legislatures provide access
to legislative status, bill texts, information about legislators, and campaign expense information for
state legislators. Publications produced by agencies, tax forms, and a wide range of state-produced
statistics are now being distributed via the Web. Researchers will find that content, quality, and ease
of use will vary greatly from state-to-state. Although no single source provides access to all state
Web sites; the following sites are useful starting points for state-related information:

National Association of State Information Resource Executives—http://www.nasire.org
/stateSearch/index.cfm

State and local government on the World Wide Web—http://www.piperinfo.com/state
/index.cfm

Dictionaries

B-72   Elliot, Jeffrey M. **The State and Local Government Political Dictionary**.
(Clio Dictionaries in Political Science). Santa Barbara, CA: ABC-Clio, 1988.

This volume has the standard Clio dictionary arrangement of broad categories, and within
each chapter an alphabetical arrangement by topic. Each entry is defined, and cross-references are
made to related topics. A bibliography and subject index are also provided. For urban political terms,
consult another title in the same series, John William Smith, *Urban Politics Dictionary* (ABC-Clio,
1990). Entries are arranged alphabetically with definitions and significance of 600 terms relating to
twentieth-century urban politics and life.

Directories and Handbooks

B-73   **State Legislative Manuals on Microfiche**. Boulder, CO: Numbers and
Concepts, 1990- . Annual.

Researchers seeking historical information about states, their organizational structure, and
members of the legislature or heads of agencies will still need to use library materials. Frequently it
will be necessary to determine what publications were produced. Legislative manuals, for example,
frequently produced by the state governments and referred to as "blue books," actually come in all
colors and occasionally were produced by private concerns and not by the state governments. Just as
there is no standard publisher or color, these reference works varied greatly in content from state to
state and may include information about the state, just as state Web sites do today. Some simply provide a description of the government and biographical information concerning the legislature and the
governor's office. Sometimes a blue book and a state statistical abstract will be one and the same.
Blue books from those states still producing a print volume are reproduced as part of the collection.
The *State Legislative Manuals on Microfiche* collection is updated annually, although individual titles
in the set are not always updated annually due to publication patterns of individual manuals. For libraries
where this microfiche collection is unavailable, it may be necessary to determine the title and content of
a state's blue book by consulting Lynn Hellebust's annual *State Legislative Sourcebook: A Resource
Guide to Legislative Information in the 50 States* (Government Research Services, 1999-).

Statistical Sources

B-74 **Book of the States**. Lexington, KY: Council of State Governments, 1935- . Biennial.

The *Book of the States* is a standard directory, statistical compendium, and handbook about the operation and activities of state governments. This key source includes descriptions of state services, finances, elections, and constitutional changes considered in the previous two years. It is an excellent source for comparative information about states. The *Book of the States* is supplemented by the *CSG State Directory* in three parts (the title has varied over the years): *Elective Offices (Directory 1), Legislative Leadership and Staffs (Directory II),* and *Administrative Officials (Directory III).* This reference set presents basic directory information on each state's executive, judicial, and legislative branches, personnel, and key contacts. Bruce Wettereau's *Desk Reference on the States* (Congressional Quarterly, 1999) provides a different approach to some of the same information by asking and answering those frequently asked questions (FAQs) that arise during research related to the states. The answers often provide data. The Q&A format covers the states (generally), governorship, legislatures, campaigns and elections, state courts, and the state of the states.

B-75 **The Municipal Yearbook**. Washington, DC: International City Management Association, 1934- . Annual.

This publication is an excellent source for comparative statistical data and a broad discussion of the current trends in local government. The volume covers both city and county information gathered from through annual survey. The volume is arranged into broad topics discussing staffing, salary, finance, and legislative, judicial, and administrative concerns; lengthy statistical tables are also provided. There is a directory of county and selected city officials. There are geographic and subject indexes and an extensive bibliography of the current literature concerning local government issues that includes listings of database resources of interest to researchers dealing with local issues.

B-76 **State Directory: Executive, Legislative, Judicial**. Washington, DC: Carroll, 1980- . 3 times/yr.

This is an extremely valuable source for locating current names, telephone numbers, and addresses. Arranged like the *Federal Executive Directory* (B-32), it covers all state agencies. Two companion titles from the same publisher, *County Directory* and *Municipal Directory* (1984-) provide similar information for all counties and all municipalities larger than 15,000 population; both are updated semiannually.

Electronic access: All directories are available in CD-ROM and Web formats, where they are updated continuously.

Statistical Sources—The States

B-77 **County and City Databook**. Washington, DC: Government Printing Office, 1949- .

This is the official source and an excellent compilation of statistical data from government sources. This volume comes out every five years. It provides census data summary statistics, education, crime, labor, employment, and other data for all fifty states and their counties.

The County and City Extra (Bernan Press, 1992-) is an annual publication that imitates the layout and content of the official original volume. However, because it is updated more frequently, more current data can be included and updated in many of the categories. Both publications are complemented by the *State and Metropolitan Databook* (Government Printing Office, 1980- ; available on the Web at *http://www.fedstats.gov/fast.html*), last published in 1997/1998, and the annual *Places, Towns, and Townships* (Bernan Press, 1993-). Again the more frequent updating and the focus on smaller towns makes the Bernan Press publication a useful addition for most reference collections, although the content of data items is similar. Users should be aware that some data are not available on an annual basis, and annual editions may not contain as much new information as volumes in alternating years would.

> *Electronic access:* The Census Bureau has developed an electronic product, *USA Counties* (Government Printing Office, 1992-), that is available on CD-ROM and on the Web at http:// tier2.census.gov/cgi-win/usac/compare.exe. It is updated annually and provides 5,000 data items down to the county level. It is the most comprehensive statistical compendium of data for all U.S. counties.

B-78 Dodd, Donald B., comp. **Historical Statistics of the States of the United States: Two Centuries of the Census, 1790–1990**. 2 vols. Westport, CT: Greenwood Press, 1993.

This set provides a summary of Census data down to the state level. It is a useful compilation and snapshot of the United States across the decades from its beginnings to the most recent Census. An excellent source for beginning researchers who are less familiar with Census reports, but the complete Census reports will be needed for more detail and insight.

B-79 **CQ's State Fact Finder: Rankings Across America**. Washington, DC: Congressional Quarterly, 1993- . Irregular.

A wealth of tables providing percentages, rates, and per capita data on business, health, population, and education are included in this source devoted to comparative data of the fifty states. Each ranked subject provides one list of the states based on ranking and a second alphabetical list of the states giving their rank within the subject list. A subject index is included.

B-80 **State Profiles: The Population and Economy of Each U.S. State**. 1st ed. Lanham, MD: Bernan Press, 1999.

Each state profile provides population and labor force, household and personal income, economic structure, housing, agriculture, education, health, and government data to complement the textual description and analysis also provided. This volume provides a useful overview of the fifty states by pulling together data from a wide range of government sources to provide researchers with detailed comparisons and snapshots. An index of the specific data contained in each profile is included, as well as an overview profile of the United States for comparative purposes.

Statistical Sources—Local

B-81 Schmittroth, Linda, ed. **Cities of the United States**. 3d ed. 4 vols. Detroit: Gale, 1998.

The need for information about cities for a wide range of business, research, and personal purposes is unrelenting. Users may consult the Decennial Censuses for the most detailed data for very small communities and even for neighborhood level data (provided by tracts and block groups). However, frequently users want to begin with a broad-based "snapshot" of a community or city. The subtitle of the four-volume Schmittroth set, "A Compilation of Current Information on Economic, Cultural, Geographic, and Social Conditions," provides an overview of this set's content. The cities of several states have been profiled in the Municipal Reference Guide series (National Resource Directories; also available in CD-ROM format), which provides a two-page profile of cities by compiling data from the Decennial Census and the Economic Censuses. For city rankings consult two works by David Garoogian. His four-volume *America's Top-Rated Smaller Cities: A Statistical Handbook* (4th ed., Grey House, 1999) and *America's Top Rated Cities: A Statistical Profile* (Grey House, 2000) will provide current and concise information on top U.S. cities based on rankings in surveys published in a wide range of secondary sources. These volumes provide an excellent starting point for fast access to city rankings on business and living environment in major American cities that would require considerable searching to locate in the secondary literature.

Indexes and Abstracts

B-82 **Index to Current Urban Documents**. Westport, CT: Greenwood Press, 1972- . Quarterly.

This index/abstract and its accompanying fiche collection are an excellent place to find information about the operation of the major cities and counties in the United States. Included are local planning documents, budgets, demographic accounts of areas, environmental impact statements, annual reports, and zoning documents. The scope is primarily standard metropolitan statistical areas (SMSAs). This collection can be extremely useful for answering reference questions about local politics and areas for which the library has no newspaper collection.

Electronic access: Now available on the Web, where full-text pdf files or zipped pdf files are linked to index entries.

NATIONAL GOVERNMENTS—WORLDWIDE

Locating information about the political activities of governments other than the United States can require in-depth reference work, depending on the question posed. Just as the United States has organizational manuals and directories, so too do other countries. Often these are difficult to locate in a library's catalog. Consult *Guide to Official Publications of Foreign Countries* (B-83) to identify exact guides to publications of other countries, national bibliographies and catalogs, government directories and organization manuals, statistical yearbooks, laws and regulations, legislative sources, sources for statements of government policy, sources for economic affairs information, the budget, census data, health sources, labor sources, education sources, and court reports.

Two valuable resources for information about the political activities in a nation are the translations by the Joint Publications Research Service (JPRS) and the Foreign Broadcast Information Service (FBIS), both research units within the Central Intelligence Agency. These two agencies translate media reports from throughout the world. The press translations tend to be from major national newspapers, and the radio and television reports are collected from twelve worldwide listening stations maintained by the government. These translations are no longer distributed on microfiche to GPO depository libraries. There are two privately produced indexes that help in identifying specific topics: *Transdex Index* and *Index to the Foreign Broadcast Information Service Daily Reports* (B-190), now available from NTIS as *World News Connection*, which also provides the full text of the translations. Texts of radio broadcasts from Voice of America, the British Broadcasting Corporation, and similar services from other countries are also increasingly available via the Internet.

B-83 **Guide to Official Publications of Foreign Countries**. 2d ed. Chicago: American Library Association, Government Documents Round Table, 1997.

Dictionaries and Encyclopedias

B-84 Phillips, Claude S. **The African Political Dictionary**. Santa Barbara, CA: ABC-Clio, 1984.

B-85 Ziring, Lawrence. **The Asian Political Dictionary**. Santa Barbara, CA: ABC-Clio, 1985.

B-86 Rossi, Ernest E. **The European Political Dictionary**. Santa Barbara, CA: ABC-Clio, 1985.

B-87 Rossi, Ernest E., and Jack C. Plano. **Latin America, A Political Dictionary**. rev. ed. Santa Barbara, CA: ABC-Clio, 1992.

B-88   Ziring, Lawrence. **The Middle East, A Political Dictionary**. rev. ed. Santa Barbara, CA: ABC-Clio, 1992.

B-89   McCrea, Barbara P. **The Soviet and East European Political Dictionary**. Santa Barbara, CA: ABC-Clio, 1984.

B-90   Fry, Gerald. **The International Development Dictionary**. Santa Barbara, CA: ABC-Clio, 1991.

B-91   Plano, Jack. **The International Relations Dictionary**. 4th ed. Santa Barbara, CA: ABC-Clio, 1988.

When primary sources from a country are difficult to locate or briefer information may be appropriate, these titles in the Clio Dictionaries in Political Science series may provide information. Although many are now out-of-date, they are still useful for historical context of political events and persons within a region. They may help solve reference questions on the politics of a country and international relations. Like all dictionaries in this series, whether they are arranged in typical dictionary format or in subject chapters, they also provide the significance of the term defined.

Directories

B-92   **Worldwide Government Directory, with International Organizations**. Washington, DC: Keesing's Worldwide, 1987/1988- . Annual.

Worldwide Government Directory is an excellent directory for fast facts about country officials in the executive, legislative, and judicial branches. Entries include phone numbers, fax numbers, and addresses. Each entry provides the names and titles of the department's highest level executives. Also included are state enterprises, central banks, defense forces, and international and regional memberships. Similar information with less frequent publication is the *International Directory of Government* (3d ed., Europa Publications, 1999).

Encyclopedias and Handbooks

B-93   Banks, Arthur. **Political Handbook of the World**. Binghamton, NY: CSA Publications, 1927- . Annual.

Arthur Banks's *Political Handbook of the World*, like the *Europa Year Book: A World Survey* (A-78), provides excellent overviews in two- to five-page entries on the government and politics, political parties, and the legislature, as well as a list of cabinet members, news media, and intergovernmental representatives. *Europa World Year Book* also provides a statistical section of frequently requested data items and thus is an excellent starting point for many researchers. A wide range of encyclopedias focuses on a smaller number of countries or regions; the most notable is the Europa regional survey volumes. Separate volumes cover *Africa South of the Sahara, Eastern Europe and the Commonwealth of Independent States, The Far East and Australasia, The Middle East and North Africa, South America, Central America and the Caribbean, The USA and Canada, Western Europe, Central and South Eastern Europe,* and *Eastern Europe, Russia and Central Asia.* Some of these are new titles; most are updated annually. Briefer information about countries can also be found in the irregularly updated Department of State *Background Notes* (A-76) (http://dosfan.lib.uic.edu/ERC/bgnotes/index.html) and the Central Intelligence Agency's *World Factbook* (A80) (http://www.odci.gov/cia/publications /factbook/index.html). Book length, yet not always current, studies of countries are available in the Area Handbook series.

B-94 Freedom in the World: The Annual Survey of Political and Civil
Rights. New York: Freedom House, 1978- . Annual.

This volume seeks to monitor the progress and decline of political rights and civil liberties
in 192 nations and 60 related and disputed territories. These year-end reviews of freedom began in
1955, when they were called the Balance Sheet of Freedom. Each edition includes tables and charts
ranking countries on comparative measures of freedom, as well as an individual overview and ranking
on a scale from 1 to 7 in political rights and civil rights. Each edition includes an introductory essay
comparing freedom across the world; regional essays covering the United States, Latin America and
the Caribbean, Africa, the Middle East, Western Europe, Russia, and East Central Europe; an essay
surveying press freedom; maps of freedom; country reports; and statistical tables for comparing
countries.

B-95 Law, Gwillim. **Administrative Subdivisions of Countries: A Comprehensive World Reference, 1900 Through 1998**. Jefferson, NC: McFarland,
1999.

Understanding the internal administrative organization and structure of a country is frequently crucial to locating information about it. The names of these administrative divisions, their
populations, capitals, and changes to country boundaries and administrative organization. Additional
information supplied includes meanings of names, territorial extent, international ISO and FIPS
codes for countries, total population, area, language, and time zone. This is an excellent resource that
can help researchers locate country information more effectively. The information in Law's book can
be used with the Internal Revenue Service's *Sources of Information from Abroad,* Rev 2-93 (Internal
Revenue Service, 1993), which provides information about the accessibility of public records such as
court records; wills; patents; trademarks; company records; foreign tax returns; marriage, birth, and
death records; and the location of these records and how they can be obtained.

B-96 Truhart, Peter. **Regents of Nations: Systematic Chronology of States and
Their Political Representatives in Past and Present: A Biographic Reference
Book**. 3 vols. Munchen, Germany: K. G. Saur, 1984.

For historical information about "individuals whose activities decisively contributed toward
establishing, changing or largely sustaining the political structures of a country during specific
historical periods," consult this three-volume set compiled by Peter Truhart. For heads of state specifically,
consult the two volumes by Harris M. Lentz, *Heads of States and Governments: A Worldwide Encyclopedia of Over 2,300 Leaders, 1945 Through 1992* and *Encyclopedia of Heads of States and Governments
1900 Through 1945* (McFarland, 1994 and 1999).

B-97 **Political Risk Yearbook**. Syracuse, NY: Political Risk Services, 1991- .
Annual.

For probability forecasts on political and economic matters as well as political, economic,
and social data for each country of the world, consult the *Political Risk Yearbook*. The *Yearbook* is issued
in its print format in volumes covering different regions of the world: North and Central America,
Middle East and North Africa, Sub-Saharan Africa, East Asia and the Pacific, East Europe, West Europe,
and South America. Each country report provides an overview of the country and its stability, level of
turmoil, international investment restrictions, trade restrictions, economic policies, and a five-year
political and economic forecast projecting three possible scenarios.

Those libraries that can afford the Economist Intelligence Unit (EIU) publications or access
to their subscription-based Web site (http://www.eiu.com/) will find both data and analysis of current
events and developments in countries around the world. EIU is well-respected for its unbiased coverage
of countries and world events by the business community.

Electronic access: CD-ROM available. Web version available from the PRS Group at http://
www.prsgroup.com.

Constitutions and Parliaments

B-98 Blausten, Albert P., and Gilbert H. Franz, eds. **Constitutions of the Countries of the World**. Dobbs Ferry, NY: Oceana, 1971- .

This multivolume looseleaf set includes texts of constitutions, chronologies, and annotated bibliographies. Constitutions of all independent nations are included in English (translated if necessary). The volumes are updated as needed. Copies of constitutions can be found on the Web with the help of the *Constitution Finder* (http://www.urich.edu/~jpjones/confinder/). To focus specifically on the parliamentary body of each state and its function and procedures, consult George Thomas Kurian, *World Encyclopedia of Parliaments and Legislatures* (Congressional Quarterly, 1998). Each entry provides an historical background and describes structure and function of the parliament, constitutional provisions, and the legislative process. Entries are arranged by country and allow researchers to better understand how evolved parliaments differ from imposed (weak) parliaments. Each entry also provides a bibliography of additional resources about each country. The four-volume *Encyclopedia of Democracy* (Congressional Quarterly, 1995) covers people, events, and countries, focusing is on the elements that have made up the subject of democracy. Each entry includes a bibliography, frequent maps, tables, and photographs.

Statistical Sources

Researchers frequently need statistical information about individual countries, their governments, and their citizens. However, statistical information can be among the most difficult to locate because it requires knowledge of data collection methods and the political changes within a country. The following sources provide general summary information about countries gleaned from a wide range of sources. Most can be used as the first stop for statistics, and when they are not detailed enough the footnotes to the original source can lead the researcher to the original source. Whenever statistical information about a country is proving difficult to locate, the *Index to International Statistics* (*IIS*) (C-45) can be used to locate hard-to-find statistics. *IIS* is now also a commercially available electronic database, *Statistical Universe*.

B-99 Kurian, George Thomas. **Fitzroy Dearborn Book of World Rankings**. 5th ed. Chicago: Fitzroy Dearborn, 2000.

B-100 **Statistical Abstract of the World**. 3d ed. Detroit: Gale, 1997.

This statistical summary of about six pages per country provides statistics on human factors, such as demographics, health indicators, women and children, and religion; on education; on science and technology; on government and law, including elections, government budget, military affairs, human rights, and crime; on the labor force; on production sectors; and on the manufacturing sector. Overall this is an excellent source to complement the statistical sections included in the *Europa Yearbooks* (A-78) and for summation of data from a wide range of UN and other intergovernmental agency publications. When more detailed data are needed, the original sources (always footnoted) will need to be consulted.

B-101 Mitchell, B. R. **International Historical Statistics: [All Regions], 1750–1993**. New York: Stockton Press, date varies by volume.

This multivolume series provides historical time series for some of the most frequently requested data at the country level. Each volume includes population and vital statistics, labor force, agriculture, industry, external trade, transport and communications, finance, prices, education, and national accounts statistics. Separate volumes are *The Americas, Africa, Asia & Oceania, Europe, the Americas and Australasia*. An additional advantage of this source is that it will often provide insight into when statistical time series begin (due to wars, country name changes, etc.). In many cases, the original source may need to be consulted, and this will include the countries' national censuses, national statistical compendium, the United Nations, and other intergovernmental organization sources. Mitchell does provide information about these original sources for researchers seeking additional detail.

U.S. POLITICS—GENERAL

Dictionaries and Encyclopedias

B-102   Plano, Jack. **The American Political Dictionary**. 10th ed. Fort Worth, TX: Harcourt, Brace College, 1997.
Plano provides a fine outline of American politics in a dictionary format. The volume is divided into fourteen chapters, each covering specific topics (e.g., finance and taxation), important agencies, cases, issues, and statutes dealing with the chapter topic. A definition of each term, and a discussion of its significance within the American political scene, are included.

B-103   Safire, William. **Safire's New Political Dictionary**. 3d ed. rev. and enlarged. New York: Random House, 1993.
Safire's dictionary defines terms heard within the U.S. political arena. His goal is to provide information on unusual political terms and phrases that have worked successfully in the political process but are not defined in standard dictionaries. Safire gives not only the meaning of the word but also its origin. The dictionary format is augmented by an index and copious cross-references. The book is an excellent source for unusual political phrases or words. Complemented by *Brewer's Politics* (B-9), which focuses on similar content with emphasis on European terms.

B-104   Green, Jack P., ed. **Encyclopedia of American Political History: Studies of the Principal Movements and Ideas**. 3 vols. New York: Scribner's, 1984.
This three-volume set gives an overview of American politics for the last 200 years in standard encyclopedia fashion. The topics covered are exceedingly broad, covering societal and political issues (e.g., women's rights). At the end of each article is a bibliography to other sources on the topic. The articles are indexed by subject and personal name. An excellent source for a scholarly overview of an issue.

B-105   **Encyclopedia of Minorities in American Politics**. 2 vols. Phoenix, AZ: Oryx Press, 2000.

B-106   **Encyclopedia of Women in American Politics**. Phoenix, AZ: Oryx Press, 1999.

B-107   **Encyclopedia of Religion in American Politics**. Phoenix, AZ: Oryx Press, 2000.
These encyclopedias, part of the American Political Landscape series, seek to bring together overviews of significant events, biographical entries, court cases, and concepts in a single source. The two-volume *Encyclopedia of Minorities in American Politics* covers African Americans, Asian Americans, Hispanic Americans, and Native Americans. Each book includes appendixes containing reprints of important primary source materials and a timeline of important events.

Biographical Sources

B-108   **Who's Who in American Politics**. New Providence, NJ: R. R. Bowker, 1967- . Biennial.

Who's Who in American Politics presents biographical information concerning Americans active in politics. Each set covers nearly 30,000 individuals, including presidents, cabinet members, governors, state delegations to Washington, state legislatures, state officials, and mayors of cities larger than 50,000 people. Arranged alphabetically by state and then individual name, this reference source gives party affiliation, place and date of birth, family information, educational record, past and present government service, military service, honors, publications, religious affiliation, and legal and mailing addresses. A personal name index is also provided.

B-109   **Political Profiles**. 5 vols. New York: Facts on File, 1976–1979.

This excellent set presents detailed biographical data of the people who dominated public and political affairs in the United States between World War II and 1976. One volume is devoted to each of the five presidential administrations from Truman through the Nixon/Ford years. Inclusion in a volume is not based solely on having held a political office but rather on the political impact an individual had during that administration. Because a person's influence may extend beyond a presidential term of office, some individuals are included in a number of volumes. The information is presented in an essay format. Each volume begins with a description of the political environment of that presidency and concludes with a chronology and an extensive bibliography covering the people and times.

ELECTIONS AND POLITICAL PARTIES— UNITED STATES

The ability to use election data and demographic data by congressional district has resulted in a growing interest in and ability to analyze election results, candidates, and the performance of elected officials. The Web has greatly increased access to current information, yet researchers will need some guidance on what resources are available and reliable. For researchers Fenton S. Marton and Robert U. Goehlert, in *How to Research Elections* (CQ Press, 2000), provide an excellent summary of print and Internet resources. Data archives and historical sources are also included.

Dictionaries and Encyclopedias

B-110   **Congressional Quarterly's Guide to U.S. Elections**. 3d ed. Washington, DC: Congressional Quarterly, 1994.

For quick answers concerning most elections in the United States, this *CQ Guide* is the best place to start. Arranged in topical chapters, the book covers political parties and their development in America, presidential elections, gubernatorial elections, elections to the U.S. Congress, and southern primaries and their importance in the electoral process. The volume also provides basic statistical data on past elections. Indexing is provided by subject and personal name.

B-111   Maisel, L. Sandy. **Political Parties & Elections in the United States: An Encyclopedia**. 2 vols. Hamden, CT: Garland, 1991.

This two-volume encyclopedia covers 1,200 terms, political parties, organizations, and individuals in signed articles. Bibliographical references are included with each entry. An index locates information within entries. Appendixes include lists of women in Congress, major party convention sites and dates, and speakers of the House.

B-112 Kurian, George Thomas, ed. **Encyclopedia of the Democratic Party**. 2 vols. Armonk, NY: Sharpe, 1997.

B-113 Kurian, George Thomas, ed. **Encyclopedia of the Republican Party**. 2 vols. Armonk, NY: Sharpe, 1997.

B-114 Ness, Immanuel, and James Ciment, eds. **Encyclopedia of Third Parties in America**. 3 vols. Armonk, NY: Sharpe, 2000.

Together, these three encyclopedias cover the bulk of political party history in the United States. They are a welcome aid in finding information that previously was only scantily covered or was dispersed throughout a number of resources. The *Republican* and *Democratic* volumes are arranged to provide a history; overviews of party positions; and a discussion of ideology on topics such as abortion, the media, tort reform, and welfare. The lists are the same in each volume, so users can compare party positions on each topic. Each topic is authored by a scholar.

In addition, biographies of major figures within each party, and a summary of conventions, platforms, and election results, are also provided. Each set has separate subject and biography indexes. The *Third Parties* volumes include a history of third parties in history, third-party maps, detailed histories of each party, and biographies of key figures in the third parties. Each entry is written by a scholar and includes bibliographic references. An index by subject and biography name is included. As comprehensive as this set is, it does not include some entries found in Edward L. Schapsmeier's *Political Parties and Civic Action Groups* (Greenwood Press, 1981); this single-volume reference work still provides useful information for selected entries.

B-115 Havel, James T. **U.S. Presidential Candidates and the Elections: A Biographical and Historical Guide**. 2 vols. New York: Macmillan, 1996.

This set provides historical coverage for all presidential candidates, not just those who won the presidential race. The first volume provides biographical information about all presidential candidates and the second volume provides a summary of each election, including highlights, candidates of every party, and votes for nomination within each party. This is an excellent source for information that is difficult to locate in a single place.

Interest Group Influence and Campaign Spending

B-116 Fritz, Sara, and Dwight Morris. **Handbook of Campaign Spending: Money in the 1992 Congressional Races**. Washington, DC: Congressional Quarterly, 1994.

The *Handbook of Campaign Spending* details how each candidate spends money received. The data are derived from FEC reports. Money spent on overhead (office furniture, travel, salaries, etc.), fund-raising, polling, advertising, and donations is detailed for each member of Congress. Part 1 is devoted to a background on raising and spending money. A volume was also published covering the 1990 congressional races.

B-117 Ness, Immanuel. **Encyclopedia of Interest Groups and Lobbyists in the United States**. 2 vols. Armonk, NY: Sharpe Reference, 2000.

The profiles in this source cover 197 specific groups divided into larger subject categories, such as banking, finance, insurance and real estate, media and entertainment and information, health and medical, environment, political, and religious or ideological. Each entry provides an overview, a history, current and future activities, financial facts, and a bibliography of resources about the group. The second volume of the set includes a wide range of tables and figures and provides lists of political action committees (PAC) showing the top PACs in a wide range of categories such as defense, agriculture, and health. The final section in this volume also provides graphs and charts on expenditures for lobbying activities by category grouping. The bibliography included is also extensive and provides an excellent resource for researchers.

The information in this set complements *Open Secrets* (B-118), providing more detailed descriptions of the groups. Information about interest groups from their own perspective is also widely available on the Web. A fee-based search engine, *PolicyFile* (http://policyfile.com/) and a free site, *Policy.com* (http://www.policy.com/), provide researchers with search engines specifically focusing on organizations that seek to influence policy, their publications, and information available on their Web sties. *Policy.com* also provides overviews of topics that can be useful for gaining a quick understanding of the policy issues, with links to key policy influencers.

B-118 Makinson, Larry. **Open Secrets: The Encyclopedia of Congressional Money & Politics**. 4th ed. Washington, DC: Congressional Quarterly, 1996.

This source focuses on the candidates who receive PAC money. It is derived from official campaign contribution reports filed with the Federal Election Commission (FEC). It profiles the 535 members of Congress in two pages each, providing details about the industries, companies, labor unions, and other organizations that contributed to each congressperson's election campaign. It also profiles the 37 standing committees of the House and Senate and identifies which industries and interest groups contributed most heavily to the members of the committees. Two additional sections provide industry profiles and an overview of the source of election money. Each edition covers a different election. The fourth edition covers the 1994 election.

Electronic access: Available on the Web at http://www.opensecrets.org/ (Center for Responsive Politics).

B-119 **Special Interest Group Profiles for Students**. Detroit: Gale, 1999.

This volume provides profiles of special interest groups in the following categories: economic groups, single-issue groups, and social action groups. Each profile provides background information about the group, its employees, and its members; PACs; mission; structure; functions; programs; budget; history; and political issues, focusing on current concerns and controversies. Successes and failures, future directions, group resources, and publications are also covered, and there is a bibliography of resources for additional information.

B-120 Zuckerman, Edward. **Almanac of Federal PACs**. Ashburn, VA: Amward, 1986- . Biennial.

This source focuses on PACs themselves. The 1994 edition is arranged in two parts: The first is about major PACs and their sponsoring organizations that contributed at least $50,000 to congressional candidates in 1992 elections, and the second is about federally registered PACs that raised or spent at least $1,000 during the 1991–1992 election cycle. Part 1 provides information about the sponsoring organization, as well as a historical summary going back to 1983–1984, providing receipts, expenditures, and contributions to Democrats and Republicans for each PAC. Within each part, PACs are grouped by the sponsoring business, lobbying and law firms, labor unions, and interest groups. See also the Washington Representatives in the Vote Sources section, on page 18 of the almanac.

Statistical Sources

B-121 **America Votes: A Handbook of Contemporary American Election Statistics**. Washington, DC: Congressional Quarterly, 1956- . Biennial.

This is the classic reference source for statistical data about U.S. elections since 1950. The text gives election results for presidential, congressional, and gubernatorial races. Data are presented down to the city/township/county level, depending on the manner in which the state gathers the information. Each volume presents total votes per candidate, political party, voting population within the area, and pluralities and percentages of the vote won. For a snapshot of the 1992 elections, consult Kimball W. Brace, *The Election Data Book: A Statistical Portrait of Voting in America 1992* (Bernan

Press, 1993) for an overview of both the states (tables provide population, race, voter population, voter turnout, and voter registration) and the actual voting statistics for presidential and congressional candidates. This volume provides both an historical and election-specific viewpoint, while also allowing the researcher to place the data within the context of census and other voter-related data.

B-122 Dubin, Michael J. **United States Congressional Elections, 1788-1997: The Official Results of the Elections of the 1st Through 105th Congresses**. Jefferson, NC: McFarland, 1998.

Until this volume, no single source documented the election results for members of Congress beginning with the 1st Congress. This volume represents significant work locating data from state sources, books, articles, almanacs, election compilations, and newspapers. Sources for all data are well documented for each Congress. Included are the names of candidates, election results Congress-by-Congress and state-by-state, party affiliation, and a statistical summary of election results. Runoff elections are also documented. This volume is indispensable for its historical coverage.

B-123 McGillivray, Alice V. **Congressional and Gubernatorial Primaries, 1991–1992: A Handbook of Election Statistics**. Washington, DC: Congressional Quarterly, 1992.

B-124 McGillivray, Alice V. **Congressional and Gubernatorial Primaries, 1993–1994: A Handbook of Election Statistics**. Washington, DC: Congressional Quarterly, 1995.

B-125 McGillivray, Alice V. **Presidential Primaries and Caucuses, 1992: A Handbook of Election Statistics**. Washington, DC: Congressional Quarterly, 1992.

B-126 Cook, Rhodes, and Alice V. McGillivray, eds. **U.S. Primary Elections 1995–1996: President, Congress, Governors: A Handbook of Election Statistics**. Washington, DC: Congressional Quarterly, 1997.

B-127 Cook, Rhodes, and Alice V. McGillivray, eds. **U.S. Primary Elections 1997–1998: Congress, Governors: A Handbook of Election Statistics**. Washington, DC: Congressional Quarterly, 1999.

For data about the primary elections and caucuses, Alice McGillivray and her co-editors have continued to issue a series of volumes that provide complete coverage beginning with 1992 elections that covers presidential and congressional races. These volumes are companions to *America Votes*. Researchers who want to focus solely on the presidential elections and want historical coverage beginning in 1920 should consult these companion volumes by Alice V. McGillivray, et al.: *America at the Polls, 1920–1956* and *America at the Polls, 1960–1996* (Congressional Quarterly, 1994 and 1998). Data are presented for each state down to the county level.

B-128 Stanley, Harold W., and Richard G. Niemi. **Vital Statistics on American Politics**. Washington, DC: Congressional Quarterly, 1988- . Biennial.

This is the most comprehensive biennial source for providing data and brief overviews of trends in American politics, including elections and political parties, campaign finance and political action committees, public opinion and voting, the media, Congress, the presidency and executive branch, the judiciary, federalism, foreign and military policy, social policy, and economic policy. It is a standard source for the most frequently sought data about American politics and often provides snapshots of hard-to-locate data.

ELECTIONS AND POLITICAL PARTIES— THE STATES

Information about state elections is becoming more widely available as computer technology makes it possible to generate maps and statistical tables more easily. State government Web sites also provide additional information about election results, political parties, and candidates. Research in this area has frequently focused on a single state or on making a comparative analysis of a small group of states. The following sources provide comparisons of all fifty states.

Handbooks

B-129   Appleton, Andrew M., and Daniel S. Ward, eds. **State Party Profiles: A 50 State Guide to Development, Organization, and Resources**. Washington, DC: Congressional Quarterly, 1997.

B-130   Thompson, Joel A., and Gary F. Moncrierf. **Campaign Finance in State Legislative Elections**. Washington, DC: Congressional Quarterly, 1998.

State Party Profiles provides a succinct overview of each state's Republican and Democratic parties in a single volume. Each signed entry covers party history, organization development, current party organization, and a resource guide. Entries are well documented with source materials from the secondary literature. *Campaign Finance in State Legislative Elections* is based on a series of studies by the comparative State Legislative Campaign Finance Project. The work includes chapters on spending patterns, contribution patterns (gender, race, and financing), and an overview of campaign finance in the states. Many data tables and figures to illustrate findings are included. This book is as much a reference book as a monograph.

Statistical Sources

B-131   Barone, Michael, William Lilley, and Laurence J. DeFranco. **State Legislative Elections: Voting Patterns and Demographics**. Washington, DC: Congressional Quarterly, 1998.

This volume provides the most complete data for all fifty states and their legislative districts on voting patterns and their relation to state demographics. Each state chapter provides an overview, maps of state senate districts and house districts, and tables showing election and demographic data by district. Election results for three elections are included when available, beginning with 1992; demographic and race data are based on the 1990 Decennial Census.

B-132   Lilley, William, Laurence J. DeFranco, and Mark F. Bernstein. **The Almanac of State Legislatures: Changing Patterns, 1990–1997**. 2d ed. (State Data Atlas). Washington, DC: Congressional Quarterly, 1998.

This volume updates the information provided in *The Almanac of State Legislatures* by William Lilley, Laurence J. DeFranco, and William M. Diefenderfer (Congressional Quarterly, 1994), which established the content and format. This volume now provides historical data for race and demographic variables by district. Together these volumes illustrate through maps of state senate districts and house districts, combined with data tables, the changing demographics of state legislative districts. Based on 1990 Decennial Census data, the tables provide the most detailed snapshots of state legislative districts available in any single source and demonstrate the considerable amount of work needed to rationalize state legislative districts to correlate with 1990 Decennial Census data.

B-133 Lilley, William, Laurence J. DeFranco, and William M. Diefenderfoer. **The State Atlas of Political and Cultural Diversity**. Washington, DC: Congressional Quarterly, 1997.

Using 1990 Decennial Census data, the authors of this volume provide an overview of racial group distribution through state legislative districts. As race becomes increasingly more important in state politics, these maps and data tables highlight the relationship between race and state house and state senate races across the United States.

ELECTIONS AND POLITICAL PARTIES— WORLDWIDE

Dictionaries and Encyclopedias

B-134 Delury, George E. **World Encyclopedia of Political Systems and Parties**. 3d ed. 3 vols. New York: Facts on File, 1999.

This definitive source on political systems has recently been updated to include changes in Eastern Europe, the Soviet Union, and Africa. Some entries, such as those for China, Taiwan, and South Africa, have been entirely revised to include changes in those countries. Covering 170 countries and 8 territories, this three-volume encyclopedia is an excellent source for general information about the politics of a country, political systems, heads of states, and some statistical data. Each chapter is written by a different contributor. Arranged alphabetically by the country's name, each entry includes a description of the government of the country, an electoral history, a description of all parties active within the system, and a bibliography concerning the politics of the state. To allow researchers to locate comparative information about parliaments by the structure or function, the International Centre for Parliamentary Documentation of the Inter-Parliamentary Union gathered data directly from national parliaments about powers and procedures. *Parliaments of the World: A Comparative Reference Compendium* (2d ed., Facts on File, 1986) allows researchers to determine which parliaments publish their debates, which use committees (and what type) for their work sessions, what volume of legislation is enacted each session, and whether the media are allowed to telecast debates.

B-135 **Greenwood Historical Encyclopedia of the World's Political Parties** [series]. Westport, CT: Greenwood Press, 1982- .

B-136 **Longman Current Affairs Series**. Detroit: Gale, 1991- .

Similar information can also be found in the series Greenwood Historical Encyclopedia of the World's Political Parties. The volumes in the Greenwood series take an historical approach, and each volumes covers a different region of the world: the Americas (Canada, Latin America, and the West Indies), Asia and the Pacific, Europe, and the Middle East and North Africa. Volumes in the Longman Current Affairs series are more current and also cover the Americas and the Caribbean, Africa and the Middle East, Asia and the Pacific, the European Community, pressure groups, and Islam and Islamic groups.

B-137 Katz, Richard S. **Party Organizations: A Data Handbook on Party Organizations in Western Democracies, 1960–90**. London: Sage, 1992.

Party Organizations provides comparative time series data and information about the structure of political parties. This first volume in a series of three omits countries such as France, Portugal, Spain, and Greece. Information on the internal organization is provided in "organigrams," in addition to data derived from party rules; statutes; official records covering membership, staff, representation of women, income, and expenditures; and election records.

B-138 Rose, Richard, ed. **International Encyclopedia of Elections**. Washington, DC: Congressional Quarterly Press, 2000.

This single-volume encyclopedia includes entries written by experts from around the world. The entries cover countries and election-related concepts and terms. Entries focus on current events, but bibliographical entries provide sources for historical context. The appendix includes a table of "basic features of parliamentary elections" and "basic features of presidential elections."

Election Statistics

A growing number of statistical volumes provide access to election statistics for regions and countries. These statistical compendia make it possible in many cases to compare election results down to the local level and are increasingly making it easier to conduct historical research on changing parties, governments, and candidates. The following list of selected resources represents the wealth of data now available.

B-139 **Britain Parliamentary Elections Results, [years]**. Aldershot, England: Ashgate, 1997- . (publisher varies).

Data are provided down to the constituency level by party and candidate for elections since 1832. Separate volumes, compiled by Fred Craig, cover 1832–1885, 1885–1918, 1918–1949, 1950–1973, and 1974–1983; Colin Rallings and Michael Thrasher have compiled and edited the recent volumes covering 1983–1997. Interim volumes have been published since 1983 as *Britain Votes*. The most recent volume includes election year, total electors, turnout, candidates, party, vote, share of total vote, and change in vote for the party. For additional information about British elections, consult *British General Elections* (separate volumes cover each general election since 1931; publisher varies; 1997 edition published by Macmillan). Additional information is available about the electorate from the British Election Study in Ivor Crew et al., *The British Electorate, 1963–1992* (Cambridge University Press, 1995). For a list of election studies in Europe, consult Ekkehard Mochmann et al., *Inventory of National Election Studies in Europe, 1945–1995* (E. Ferger, 1998).

B-140 Feigert, Frank. **Canada Votes, 1935–1988**. Durham, NC: Duke University Press, 1989.

Data are provided down to the riding level in each province, by party, and gleaned from a wide number of government sources. For candidate information and more recent elections, consult the annual *Canadian Parliamentary Guide: Parlementaire Canadien* (Gale Canada, 1909-).

B-141 Nohlen, Dieter, et al., eds. **Elections in Africa: A Data Handbook**. New York: Oxford University Press, 1999.

This is an excellent summary of electoral systems and political developments in African countries. The data result from a research project at the Institute of Political Sciences of the University of Heidelberg that began in the 1960s. The introductory chapter covers "Elections and Electoral Systems in Africa," and succeeding chapters for each country summarize election outcomes by party, by referendums, and for parliaments (or their equivalents). Each chapter also includes extensive footnotes for data sources.

B-142 Singh, V. B. **Elections in India: Data Handbook on Lok Sabha Elections**. New Delhi: Sage, 1986- .

Two volumes cover 1952–1985 (pub. 1986) and 1986–1991 (pub. 1994). The volumes contain detailed election data for the Lok Sabha elections since 1952 and the thirteen Lok Sabha constituencies of Punja, where elections were held in 1992. Lists of winner and runner-up candidates, party affiliation, and votes polled are included. Data are derived from many sources, including the Election Commission of India.

B-143 Caramani, Daniele. **The Societies of Europe: Elections in Western Europe Since 1815, Electoral Results by Constituencies**. New York: Groves Dictionaries, 2000.

This is projected as a series of volumes to improve "comparative-historical analysis" of European elections. The introductory chapter covers "Electoral Laws and Systems, the Institutional Development of Elections in Europe, and the Territorial Structuring of the Vote in Europe." Succeeding country chapters provide data for each country. The volume is accompanied by a CD-ROM containing the data included in the print volume.

INTERNATIONAL RELATIONS AND ORGANIZATIONS

The growing interest in international relations is evident in the number of publications on this topic, the growing periodical literature, and the increased use of the publications of international organizations such as the United Nations and European Union. The number of international organizations and intergovernmental organizations (IGOs) continues to grow. This makes it a challenge for researchers to locate information related to their research from these sources. However, as libraries maintain standing orders for the publications of organizations such as the United Nations and its member organizations, it has become easier to locate many of their publications. In addition, organizations such as the European Union have developed a network of depository libraries that receive their publications. Since 1990 a growing number of indexes and other sources also have been made available, frequently in electronic format and via the Web. This section provides resources for research related to international relations, generally, and also includes separate sections on the United Nations and European Union, the two largest organizations with the most sophisticated and broad-based methods for distributing publications and the information they generate.

General

B-144 American Library Association. Government Documents Roundtable. **Guide to Country Information in International Governmental Organization Publications**. Bethesda, MD: Congressional Information Service, 1996.

This guide is intended as a research tool to acquaint readers with principle series and publications that contain information on countries published by international governmental organizations. The entries are arranged by worldwide and regional areas, subarranged by broad subject categories. Regions include Worldwide, Africa, Asia/Pacific, Europe, Latin America/Caribbean, Middle East, and North America. The directory will be useful for locating comparative data for many countries in a region or to locate information about smaller, less well-covered countries that are members of many international and intergovernmental organizations.

B-145 Hajnal, Peter I. **International Information: Documents, Publications, and Electronic Information of International Governmental Organizations**. 2d ed. Englewood, CO: Libraries Unlimited, 1997.

For an overview of international organization publishing, consult *International Information*. Individual chapters provide an overview of publishing patterns, arrangement of collections, reference and information works, citation forms, and computerized information systems in international organizations. The focus is largely on the United Nations and the European Community, but the overview is useful for other organizations as well.

B-146 Williams, Robert V. **The Information Systems of International Inter-Governmental Organizations: A Reference Guide**. Stamford, CT: Ablex, 1998.

Until recently the information produced by many IGOs was difficult to locate because methods for publishing and providing access to this information varied dramatically. As the importance of these organizations has grown, so has the sophistication of their distribution methods. This volume seeks to provide an overview of the types of information published by IGOs and how to access that information. Not all IGOs are covered, but those of the United Nations, UN Specialized Agencies, and a selection of other IGOs are included. This guide will allow researchers to determine the most effective way to obtain information generated by the IGOs.

Dictionaries and Encyclopedias

B-147 **Historical Dictionaries of International Organizations Series**. Metuchen, NJ: Scarecrow Press, 1993- .

This series includes volumes on the European Community, the International Monetary Fund, international organizations in sub-Saharan Africa, European organizations, international tribunals, international food agencies, and refugee and disaster relief organizations. Each volume may have slight differences in arrangement to accommodate the organizations covered; however, each provides basic maps, a chronology, an overview of basic documents and members, a dictionary, and a bibliography of sources about the organizations included.

B-148 Jentleson, Bruce W., and Thomas G. Paterson. **Encyclopedia of U.S. Foreign Relations**. 4 vols. New York: Oxford University Press, 1997.

Prepared under the auspices of the Council on Foreign Relations, this encyclopedia provides historical context and coverage of the concepts, defining events and people. Entries include bibliographical references to related materials, and the appendix includes a "Chronology of U.S. Foreign Relations," a "Table of National Data," and a classified "Bibliography of Reference Works."

B-149 Ziring, Lawrence, et al. **International Relations: A Political Dictionary**. 5th ed. (Clio Dictionaries in Political Science). Santa Barbara, CA: ABC-Clio, 1995.

Entries provide definitions as well as significance of terms and events related to international relations.

Directories

B-150 **Yearbook of International Organizations**. 3 vols. Munchen: K. G. Saur, 1948- . Annual.

This work is similar to *Encyclopedia of Associations: International Organizations* (A-68) in concept and format but provides information about international organizations. Compiled by the Union of International Associations, volume 1 provides organization descriptions that include historical background, aims, activities, publications, and membership. Volume 2 lists international organization participation by country. Volume 3 is a subject index.

B-151 **International Information Directory**. Washington, DC: Congressional Quarterly Press, 2000.

Use this directory for quick facts about international organizations, arranged in broad subject areas such as agriculture and nutrition, communications and the media, crime and drug control, culture and recreation, education, employment, and labor. This single volume mixes international organizations, U.S. agencies, U.S. congressional committees, and nonprofit organizations related to these international issues and located in Washington, DC. Each entry includes Web address for the agency, a key contact, address, phone and fax numbers, and a brief description of the agency. Chapters are "Resources by Country," "Intergovernmental Organizations," "Resources in the States," and the "United Nations." This directory is useful for locating the U.S. offices and locations of many international organizations and for understanding the interplay of U.S. government agencies and international organizations and nonprofit organizations in Washington.

World Wide Web Databases

B-152 **CIAO (Columbia International Affairs Online)**. New York: Columbia University, 1997- .

CIAO is fee-based resource designed to be a comprehensive resource for theory and research in international affairs. It publishes and provides access to the full text of a wide range of scholarship from 1991 on, including working papers from university research institutes, occasional papers series from nongovernmental organizations, foundation-funded research projects, and proceedings from conferences. It also has more than 160 links to international affairs centers, institutes, and resources; U.S., international, and foreign government sites; environmental studies Web pages; and news media services.

Electronic access: Available on the Web at http://www.ciaonet.org/.

Bibliographies

B-153 **International Organizations Series**. New Brunswick, NJ: Transaction, 1992- .

Each volume in this series is devoted to a specific organization or to a particular region's organizations. Each includes a selective, annotated, critical bibliography of the organization that includes books, articles, databases, theses, and the like. The materials selected must be about the organization rather than by the organization, although the organization's most important official publications will be included. Volumes in the series cover the European Communities, the Arab Regional Organizations, COMECON, the International Monetary Fund, the Commonwealth (British), the French Secret Services, the North Atlantic Treaty Organization, the Organization of African Unity, the Organization of American States, the Israeli Secret Services, and the World Bank.

Indexes

B-154 **American Foreign Policy and Treaty Index**. Bethesda, MD: CIS, 1993–1999.

This index is no longer published, but it provided access to primary and secondary source publications related to U.S. foreign policy. It gave researchers a single source for periodicals such as the *U.S. Department of State Dispatch* (Government Printing Office, 1990–1999; available at http://www.state.gov/www/publications/dispatch/index.html); congressional hearings, reports, and documents related to foreign policy issues; legislation; and funding, while also providing access to statements "hidden" in a wide range of government sources. The index was accompanied by a microfiche collection containing copies of materials included in the *Index*.

United Nations and Member Organizations

The role the United Nations plays in international politics, peacekeeping, development, and human rights continues to make it of vital interest to researchers. The following sources provide excellent access to the United Nations, its organization, and its publications. For additional insight and resources also consult the following two sources.

B-155 United Nations. Dag Hammarskjöld Library. **United Nations Documentation: A Research Guide, 2002**. URL: http://www.un.org/Depts/dhl/resguide/.

B-156 **A Guide to Information at the United Nations**. New York: United Nations, 1995.

Directories and Handbooks

B-157 Osmanczyk, Edmund Jan. **Encyclopedia of the United Nations and International Relations**. 2d ed. New York: Taylor & Francis, 1990.
This is a compendium of political, economic, and social information related to the United Nations and the many specialized agencies and intergovernmental and nongovernmental organizations that cooperate with the United Nations. The work is organized in alphabetical order. Many entries conclude with bibliographical references and have extensive cross-references.

B-158 **Basic Facts About the United Nations**. New York: United Nations, 1998.
For an overview of the United Nations that is not in encyclopedia format, consult this guide compiled by the United Nations. Entries provide an overview of UN organization as well as separate chapters on broad subject areas, and a variety of appendixes provide basic documents, charts, and maps.

B-159 Gorman, Robert F. **Great Debates at the United Nations: An Encyclopedia of Fifty Key Issues, 1945–2000**. Westport, CT: Greenwood Press, 2000.

B-160 **Yearbook of the United Nations**. New York: United Nations, 1947- . Annual.
This source is an annual summary of the activities of the United Nations and its related intergovernmental organs for the previous twelve months. The volume has a broad topical approach and includes a subject, name, and resolution/decisions index. The appendix includes the annual agenda of each organ. Because of UN publishing practices, the *Yearbook* has often been as many as three years behind; however, since 1992, efforts have been made to keep it more current. This publication does provide useful historical information and a summary of UN activities.

B-161 **Annual Review of United Nations Affairs**. Dobbs Ferry, NY: Oceana, 1949- . Annual.

B-162 **U.N. Chronicle**. New York: United Nations, 1964- . 11 times/yr.
Annual Review of United Nations Affairs contains reprints of documentation, resolutions, decisions, addresses, and statements that document the development of six major UN bodies: the General Assembly, the Security Council, the Economic and Social Council, the Trusteeship Council, the International Court of Justice, and the Secretariat. For a more recent summary of UN activities, *U.N. Chronicle* should be consulted.
Electronic access: U.N. Chronicle is available full text in a number of sources such as *ProQuest* (F-67) and *Dow Jones Interactive* (D-49).

B-163 **A Global Agenda**. Lanham, MD: University Press, 1991- . Annual.
This work was formerly titled *Issues Before the . . . General Assembly of the United Nations*. This publication describes key topics of importance that will be discussed in a particular session of the General Assembly, the legislative body of the United Nations. The book is arranged in seven topical areas: making and keeping the peace, arms control and disarmament, economics and development, global resource management, human rights and social issues, legal issues, and finance and administration. Chapters are written by experts; extensive citations to resolutions, newspaper articles, press

releases, and reports are built into the text. Information gleaned from this source should be used to approach indexes for relevant documentation and other materials.

Statistics Sources

Comparative international statistics are now increasingly available in print and electronic formats, allowing researchers to locate data to support research projects more easily. Of the several annuals published by the United Nations, two of the most important are described below.

B-164   United Nations. Statistical Office. **Demographic Yearbook. Annuaire Demographic, 1948-** . Statistical Office of the United Nations. New York: United Nations, 1948- . Annual.
This standard reference work, in English and French, contains information about 220 countries and areas of the world. Part 1 consists of twenty-five basic annual tables presenting data on natality, mortality, marriage, and divorce, extracted from official statistics, using 1948 as a common year. Part 2 contains tables relating to the economically active populations, by age, sex, industry, occupation, and status of employment. Every reference collection should include this title among its holdings.
Electronic access: Also available on CD-ROM as the *Demographic Yearbook: Historical Supplement* (United Nations, 2000), covering the period 1948–1997.

B-165   United Nations. Statistical Office. **Statistical Yearbook. Annuaire Statistique, 1948-** . New York: United Nations, 1949- . Annual.
The *Statistical Yearbook* provides information about world regions compiled into summary tables with technical notes, population and social statistics, economic activity data, and international economic relations information. The *Statistical Yearbook* is kept up-to-date by the *Monthly Bulletin of Statistics* (United Nations, Department of Economic and Social Development, 1992-), available in print and also via a fee-based Web site from the United Nations Statistics Division (http://www.un.org/Depts/unsd/).

Indexes

B-166   **Access UN**. New Canaan, CT: NewsBank/Readex, 1997- . Monthly. Electronic format.
This index to provides access to United Nations documents, including official records, masthead documents, draft resolutions, meeting records, UN sales publications, and the UN Treaty Series citations. It is available as a fee-based index on the Web and on CD-ROM (*Index to United Nations Documents and Publications*). The Web index covers publications from 1956 to date and also includes the full text of several thousand UN documents and links to sources available at UN Web sites as direct links with each record. Searching is by keyword in author, title, and series fields, as well as searches by session and document number. The index is based on titles included in the Readex UN microfiche collection and thus may omit some sources that would be listed in *United Nations Documents Index* (A-47n) (formerly UNDOC).

European Union

The changes in the European Union during the last decade of the twentieth century will have a far-reaching impact on Western Europe and its relationships with Eastern Europe, the United States, and other countries around the world. In many ways these changes typify the globalization of politics, economics, and social issues that are frequently of interest in political science research.

Dictionaries and Encyclopedias

B-167   Rosenberg, Jerry M. **The New Europe: An A to Z Compendium on the European Community**. Washington, DC: Bureau of National Affairs, 1991.

More than 2,500 entries answer questions about the European Community (EC), the Single European Act, the European Free Trade Association, and Eastern Europe from the EC's founding to fall 1990. Information is taken from contemporary practice, official documents, formal conferences, and news releases. An introduction provides an overview of the EC structure; a chronology of the EC since 1957 is also included. The work is arranged in alphabetical order; extensive cross-references are included.

B-168   **The European Communities Encyclopedia and Directory**. 2d ed. London: Europa, 1996.

This single-volume encyclopedia is arranged in four parts: an A–Z of the EC, essays on the EC, a statistical survey, and a directory. The A–Z section provides dictionary-type definitions of EC institutions, people, and events. The essay section has six essays describing the institutional, legal, social, and economic frameworks of the EC. The statistical survey section supplies an overview of demographic, agricultural, industrial, trade, and financial figures, and the directory section gives detailed information on principal officers with their addresses and telephone, telex, and fax numbers. Appendixes include treaties; measures involved in the implementation of the Internal Market; a list of Community-wide trade, industry, professional, and consumer organizations; and a list of EC databases.

B-169   Dinan, Desmond, ed. **Encyclopedia of the European Union**. Boulder, CO: Lynne Rienner, 1998.

This is a handy single-volume encyclopedia about the European Union. Entries are signed, and some include bibliographical entries for additional information. A series of appendixes cover "overview of institutional change, 1958–1998," "national representation in EU Institutions as of 1998," "special committees of the Council of the European Union," and so forth.

B-170   Roney, Alex, and Stanley Budd. **The European Union: A Guide Through the EC/EU Maze**. 6th ed. London: Kogan Page, 1998.

This is an excellent summary and overview of the European Union, the way it works, the Treaty of Rome, the single market, decision-making and its influences, individual policies, developing Europe, and international matters. Those who would like an official perspective should consult *European Union: A Guide for Americans* (Delegation of the European Commission to the United States, 2000).

Electronic access: Available on the Web at http://www.eurunion.org/infores/euguide /euguide.htm.

Directories and Handbooks

B-171   **Fact Sheets on the European Union**. 9th ed. Luxembourg: Office for Official Publications of the European Communities, 1999.

The *Fact Sheets* provide nonspecialists with a general introduction to European integration and Parliament's contribution to that process. Each fact sheet is a summary, outlining the main aspects in a clear and instructive approach.

Electronic access: Also available on CD-ROM, and on the Web http://www.europarl.eu.int /dg4/factsheets/en/default.htm.

B-172 **General Report on the Activities of the European Union**. Brussels: Office for Official Publications of the European Communities, 1995- . Annual.

This is a summary of each year's activities related to the single market, external relations, foreign and security policy, human rights, community institutes and financing, community law, and cooperation in justice and home affairs. An appendix includes a summary of the progress of legislation and a list of publications cited in the report. This source is an excellent place to begin research on a topic within the European Community. Formerly titled *General Report on the Activities of the European Communities* (1967–1994).

Periodicals

B-173 **Bulletin of the European Union**. Brussels: European Commission, 1994- . Bimonthly.

This bulletin reviews the work of the EU institutions and gives citations to major documents and publications.

B-174 **European Access**. Cambridge: Chadwyck-Healey, in association with the European Commission, 1989- . Bimonthly.

This bulletin provides an overview of EU institutions and activities and citations to major EU documents, periodicals, and newspaper articles.

Indexes

B-175 **Justis European References CD-ROM**. London: Context Electronic; distr. by Martinsville, NJ: Global Transactions, 1996- . Updated quarterly. Electronic format.

This CD-ROM, formerly titled *EC References*, provides access to CELEX, SCAD, the *Official Journal* (*C Series*), statutory instruments, and *Parliament and Weekly Law Reports* from the European Union (EU). The full text of documents is also included. Keyword and Boolean searching is permitted. The source effectively replaces the *SCAD Bulletin* (European Union, 1985-), a weekly publication listing EU documentation and articles from selected non-EC periodicals. The CELEX database and other EU databases are also available online directly from the EU (http://europa.eu.int/geninfo /info-en.htm). *Westlaw*, a full text service (St. Paul, Minnesota), and *Academic Universe* (F-15) also provide access to most EU databases. All EU databases contain documents in English, French, and German.

WAR AND PEACE; TERRORISM

Research related to war, nuclear disarmament, and the peaceful settlement of disputes has grown dramatically in recent years. Researchers now study specific conflicts and the growth of the military in countries around the world, and theorize about the most effective methods for settling disputes. The following section focuses primarily on the subjects of war and peace in general; however, a growing number of resources focus on specific disputes. (Information on the Arab-Israeli conflict, the Vietnam War, and the situation and conditions in Bosnia and Herzegovina, for example, is available to those researchers seeking to focus on the specific.) Literature in this area also covers acts of terrorism—another area of growing interest to political science researchers.

Dictionaries and Encyclopedias

B-176   Ali, Sheikh R. **The Peace and Nuclear War Dictionary**. (Clio Dictionaries in Political Science). Santa Barbara, CA: ABC-Clio, 1989.
Arranged in typical dictionary format. As always, the significance of each term is provided.

B-177   Burns, Richard Dean. **Encyclopedia of Arms Control and Disarmament**. 3 vols. New York: Scribner's, 1993.
This encyclopedia is intended to provide an overview of current arms control and disarmament scholarship. The three volumes are divided into five topics: national and regional dimensions, themes and institutions, historical dimensions to 1945, arms control activities since 1945, and treaties. Articles are lengthy and include extensive bibliographical references. The volume includes a subject index to locate information on topics spread throughout the book.

B-178   Ciment, James, ed. **Encyclopedia of Conflicts Since World War II**. 4 vols. Armonk, NY: Sharpe, 1999.
This encyclopedia focuses on war and conflicts since World War II. Entries are by country and cover internal as well as international conflicts. For example, Cambodia is divided into three sections: Civil Wars, 1968–1998; U.S. Interventions, 1969–1973; and the Vietnamese Invasion, 1978–1979. Entries on conflicts such as the Canadian Quebec Separatist Movement, 1960–1987, are also included. Entries vary in length from three to five pages and include maps, photographs, and a bibliography.

B-179   Dupuy, Trevor N., ed. **International Military and Defense Encyclopedia**. 6 vols. Washington, DC: Brassey's, 1993.
This six-volume set provides a comprehensive overview of war, defense, the military, budgets, force structures, external threats, arms control, and peace. Chapters are written by subject experts. The encyclopedia is divided into 786 articles in seventeen subject areas: aerospace forces and warfare; combat theory and operations; leadership, command, and management; countries, regions, and organizations; armed forces and society; history and biography; land forces and warfare; logistics; manpower and personnel; materiel and weapons; naval forces and warfare; technology, research, and development; military theory and operations research; defense and international security policy; military and international security law; military intelligence; and the general military. An extensive subject index is included, as are statistics and bibliographies.

B-180   Kurtz, Lester, ed. **Encyclopedia of Violence, Peace, and Conflict**. 3 vols. New York: Academic Press, 1999.
By providing a cross-disciplinary approach to violence, this three-volume encyclopedia provides researchers with a view of violence, peace, and conflict from perspectives ranging from anthropological to ethical studies to sociological studies. The entries consist of lengthy chapters that provide a research summary and review, including a glossary and extensive bibliographical citations. The chapters are written and signed by scholars.

B-181   Macksey, Kenneth, and William Woodhouse. **Penguin Encyclopedia of Modern Warfare: 1850 to the Present Day**. New York: Penguin, 1991.
Consult this encyclopedia for coverage of wars prior to World War II.

B-182   Ramsbotham, Oliver, and Tom Woodhouse. **Encyclopedia of International Peacekeeping Operations**. Santa Barbara, CA: ABC-Clio, 1999.
For a focus specifically on peacekeeping missions and forces, consult this single-volume encyclopedia. Most entries are signed and include related bibliographical entries for further study.

Directories and Handbooks

B-183 **World Armaments and Disarmament: The SIPRI Yearbook**. New York: Humanities Press, 1969- . Annual.

B-184 **United Nations Disarmament Yearbook**. New York: United Nations, 1976- . Annual.

Produced by the Stockholm International Peace Research Institute, *The SIPRI Yearbook* presents broad subject essays on arms control and weapons development, as well as statistical tables, lists (e.g., of the UN Peacekeeping Forces), and selected texts (e.g., the Rio Declaration). Topics include weapons and technology, military expenditures, recent developments in arms control, the use of weapons in space and the oceans, and the control of nuclear weapons. This yearbook tends to be more current than *United Nations Disarmament Yearbook*, the focus of which is the activities of the UN in the disarmament process.

B-185 **Patterns of Global Terrorism**. Washington, DC: Department of State, 1983- . Annual.

B-186 Jessup, John E. **A Chronology of Conflict and Resolution, 1945–1985**. Westport, CT: Greenwood Press, 1989.

For an annual summary and overview of worldwide terrorist activities, consult the Department of State's *Patterns of Global Terrorism*. Overviews of terrorism in world regions, state-sponsored terrorism, a chronology of significant terrorist incidents, background information on major terrorist groups, statistics, and a map showing the location of major terrorist incidents are included. For a historical overview of events relating to conflict and resolutions, *A Chronology of Conflict and Resolution* is extremely useful. For a quick overview of defense data for each country, *Defense and Foreign Affairs Handbook* (International Media Corporation, 1977-) is helpful.

Electronic access: *Patterns of Global Terrorism* is also available on the Web at http//www .state.gov/www/global/terrorism/gt_index.html.

B-187 **Defense and Foreign Affairs Handbook**. Washington, DC: Copley and Associates (for the International Strategic Studies Association), 1976- . Annual.

This volume provides a country-by-country summary of the military forces within the context of the economic, technological, and social structure of each country. Each entry could be used to enhance the *Europa Yearbook* entry for each country (A-78) and to provide a historical, political, and defense perspective on each country's position within the world community. Terrorist organizations, major news media, a summary of the defense infrastructure and position, a description of military forces, insurgency groups, and intelligence services are also covered.

Statistics

B-188 **The Military Balance**. London: International Institute for Strategic Studies, 1963- . Annual.

This work provides an annual update of military forces and defense expenditure for more than 160 countries. The first part provides country-specific information within regional groupings. Information about the strategic issues facing the region, the significant changes in defense postures, economic status, and military aid arrangements is included. The second part provides tables and analyses covering defense expenditures, military manpower, strategic nuclear forces, and conventional forces in Europe. A third section provides maps of world regions.

B-189 **Arms Control Reporter**. Brookline, MA: Institute for Defense and Disarmament Studies, 1982- . Monthly.

Produced monthly in looseleaf, floppy disk, and CD-ROM formats, this valuable reference service is the most current source for information dealing with arms control developments and negotiations. The service acts as a digest on various arms topics, culling a description of the status of a negotiation, the chronology of its talks, an analysis of its terms, and excerpts from essential documents. The digest also indexes key newspaper accounts (foreign and domestic) and Foreign Broadcast Information Service translations (see B-190).

B-190 **Index to the Foreign Broadcast Information Service Daily Reports**. NTIS Database. Washington, DC: National Technical Information Service, 1964- . Weekly. (See A-48)

B-191 **Peace Research Abstracts Journal**. Thousand Oaks, CA: Sage in association with the Dundas, ONT, Peace Research Institute, 1964- . Bimonthly.

Formerly titled *Peace Research Abstracts* and produced by Quaker scientists, this bimonthly indexing service is a major source for locating journal articles and monographs dealing with peace. Entries are arranged in broad subject categories; author and subject indexes are included.

HUMAN RIGHTS

Answering human rights questions can be difficult because activities in which an organization is involved may not be labeled or described as human rights activities, despite having the ultimate goal of achieving human equity. In 1993 the United Nations sponsored the World Conference on Human Rights (June 14–25). This conference, the first sponsored by the UN in twenty-five years, helped to focus attention on human rights issues. In addition, the end of the Cold War and an increasing number of civil wars across the world have brought greater attention to this important topic. Three organizations known for their work on human rights are Amnesty International, Human Rights Watch, and Human Rights Internet. These organizations put out a wide range of publications, annual reports, and periodicals related to human rights issues and practices around the world. In addition, international organizations, such as the UN, produce a wide range of information related to human rights. The following sources focus on sources devoted solely to human rights issues; additional sources can be located using *Access UN* (B-166), *Justis European References* (B-175), and any library's catalog.

Dictionaries and Encyclopedias

B-192 Langley, Winston E. **Encyclopedia of Human Rights Issues Since 1945**. Westport, CT: Greenwood Press, 1999.

B-193 Lawson, Edward. **Encyclopedia of Human Rights**. 2d ed. New York: Taylor & Francis, 1996.

B-194 Maddex, Robert L. **International Encyclopedia of Human Rights: Freedoms, Abuses, and Remedies**. Washington, DC: Congressional Quarterly Press, 2000.

These three encyclopedias provide differing levels of detail related to human rights issues. Edward Lawson's encyclopedia is the single most comprehensive compendium on the topic. This work brings together material about international, regional, and national activities undertaken between 1945 and 1990 to promote human rights. Entries are arranged in alphabetical order and provide an overview of international documents and organizations that affect human rights. Each entry provides extensive references to UN documents and the complete text of important documents and instruments (e.g., the Program of Action Against Apartheid adopted by the General Assembly). Cross-references are included in articles, and a subject index is included to help locate entries or related topics. Appendixes provide a selected bibliography, a glossary, status of international human rights conventions, a chronological list of international instruments concerned with human rights, the International Labor Code, an organigram for the UN Centre for Human Rights, a list of UN studies and reports on human rights issues, a membership list of intergovernmental organizations concerned with human rights, and a list of national institutions concerned with human rights. The briefer entries in the *Encyclopedia of Human Rights Issues Since 1945* are useful for quicker definitions of concepts, terms, people, and events.

The *International Encyclopedia of Human Rights* pulls together definitions of 150 important concepts and terms, 100 documents significant to the historical development and the current state of human rights, descriptions of agencies and organizations, and biographies. The text includes many illustrations. Entries include telephone and fax numbers, e-mail addresses, Web sites, further reading, references to court decisions and other legal judgments, and references to documents not included in the volume.

Directories and Handbooks

B-195 **Amnesty International Report**. London: Amnesty International Publications, 1976- . Annual.

B-196 **Human Rights Watch World Report**. New York: Human Rights Watch, 1991- . Annual.

B-197 United States. Department of State. **Country Reports on Human Rights Practices**. Washington, DC: Government Printing Office, 1979- . Annual.

Together, these three sources provide an overview of human rights violations in countries of the world. *Amnesty International Report* (formerly titled *Amnesty International Annual Report*) is arranged by country and provides a one- to two-page summary of human rights-related activities and violations. *Human Rights Watch World Report* is divided into regions (Africa, Americas Watch, Asia Europe and Central Asia, Middle East and North Africa, United States), and each section provides a regional overview and country-specific summaries. Chapters on subjects such as children's rights, women's rights, and special issues such as academic freedom, lesbian and gay rights, and prisons are also included. *Country Reports on Human Rights Practices* (formerly titled *Report on Human Rights Practices in Countries Receiving U.S. Aid*) provides a brief overview for each country, followed by a summary of the year's events related to human rights, civil liberties, and government attitudes and actions related to discrimination and respect for political rights. (The source is submitted to the Senate Committee on Foreign Relations and the House Committee on Foreign Affairs by the Department of State.)

Electronic access: *Amnesty International Report* is available on the Web at http://www.web.amnesty.org. *Human Rights Watch World Report* is available on the Web at http://www.hrw.org. *Country Reports* is available on the Web at http://www.state.gov /www/global /human_rights/hrp_reports_mainhp.html.

B-198 **Yearbook on Human Rights**. New York: United Nations, 1946–1993.

B-199 **Yearbook of the European Convention on Human Rights**. The Hague/ The Council of Europe: Nijhoff, 1955- . Annual.

The *Yearbook on Human Rights* provided a summary of international developments related to human rights, an overview of activities of UN supervisory bodies, and an overview of national developments in selected countries from year to year. Unfortunately, the yearbook is not current, the last volume covers 1988 (appeared in late 1993). The Council of Europe's *Yearbook of the European Convention on Human Rights* covers 1996.

Electronic access: The United Nations Office for the Commission on Human Rights now maintains an extensive Web page (http://www.unhchr.ch/), which provides access to current information and developments. The Council of Europe also maintains a Web site for access to current information (http://www.dhdirhr.coe.fr/).

Bibliographies

B-200 **Human Rights Internet Reporter**. Washington, DC: Human Rights Internet, 1980- . Annual.

B-201 **Human Rights Bibliography: United Nations Documents and Publications, 1980–1990**. 5 vols. New York: United Nations, 1993.
The *Reporter* contains the most comprehensive review of human rights literature available from nongovernmental sources. Each *Reporter* issue has a theme (e.g., ethnic, religious, and racial conflict [1994]; women's rights as human rights [1995]). Entries included in the *Reporter* are usually well annotated and include citations to journals and monographs. For a bibliography limited to UN materials related to human rights, consult *Human Rights Bibliography*. This set was compiled on the occasion of the World Conference on Human Rights.
Electronic access: The HRI Web site (http://www.hri.ca/) provides access to its fee-based databases, including a directory of human rights organizations, and its publications database. The site also serves as a useful starting point for links to human rights resources on the Web. The *Human Rights Bibliography* database with full-text documents included is also available on CD-ROM.

NOTES

1. Robert B. Harmon, *Developing the Library Collection in Political Science* (Metuchen, NJ: Scarecrow Press, 1976), 12.

2. William G. Andrews, ed., *International Handbook of Political Science* (Westport, CT: Greenwood Press, 1982), 3.

3. Theodore J. Lowi, "The State in Political Science: How We Become What We Study," *American Political Science Review* 86 (March 1992): 1–7.

4. Frederick L. Holler, *Information Sources in Political Science* (Santa Barbara, CA: ABC-Clio, 1986), 1.

5. Lowi, "State in Political Science," 2.

6. Jay M. Shafritz and Albert C. Hyde, *Classics of Public Administration,* 3d ed. (Pacific Grove, CA: Brooks/ Cole, 1992).

3

Economics

Kristi Jensen

ESSAY

Because the term *economics* has so many connotations, it would be misleading to present a single, rigid definition. Adam Smith, often referred to as the father of economics, defined economics as the "science of wealth." Alfred Marshall, founder of the Cambridge School of Economics, defined it as the "study of men in the ordinary business of life." Any undergraduate student taking an introductory economics course would define economics as a study of supply and demand. The scope of economics is also important, because it concerns the supply and demand of goods and services at the individual and institutional level as well as on a national and international basis. A consumer deciding what vegetables to buy at the supermarket and a nation making policy decisions about the flow of imports into its markets are both engaging in economic behavior.

Economics can be subdivided into three major subfields: economic theory, applied economics, and economic history. *Economic theory*, also called *pure or basic economics*, is concerned with the relationships between variables in the economic system (e.g., if "A" rises, then what will happen to "B"?). An economic theorist will study data, attempt generalizations, and then build these generalizations into theories. The theorist also develops economic principles by constructing a hypothetical situation to determine what would be the consequences of a course of action. Some of the greatest names in economics—Smith, Marshall, Ricardo, Mill, and Marx—were theorists whose ideas are still studied today. Once largely speculative, economic theory is now based on a priori reasoning and, increasingly, on mathematical models and measurements.

In *applied economics*, economic theories are applied to Marshall's "everyday business of life" by public and private policy makers. Policy decisions based on economic knowledge or reasoning are designed to bring about positive results, such as high profits or low taxes. Among applied fields are banking, public finance, labor and industrial relations, land and agricultural economics, and transportation. Some of these applied fields constitute areas of study that can stand alone. For instance, agricultural economics usually commands a separate department in most universities. Agricultural economists have their own professional associations and have amassed an enormous amount of literature and data that nearly exceeds that of all other fields of economics combined.

Economic history is the study of economic institutions in varying cultures and time periods. Often regarded as a branch of economics with little relationship to economic theory and applied economics, economic history had slipped into benign neglect in recent years. However, economic historians have discovered that the economic behavior of the past has implications for today. In addition, some of the statistical and mathematical procedures developed for economics have been successfully applied to historical problems.

There are two main branches of economics: microeconomics and macroeconomics. *Microeconomics* is concerned with the small economic unit, such as the household, a commodity, or an industry. It is dedicated to the study of resource allocation, which in its simplest form relates to the "making ends meet" of the budget-conscious household or corporation. Macroeconomics examines economic relationships on the large scale, such as looking at how the change in an economic variable affects the economy of a nation. An economist examining the impact of a plant closing on the buying behavior of employees' households would be doing a microeconomic study; a thesis on the effect of plant closings on the unemployment rate of a state or country would be a macroeconomic study.

Brief History of Economics

Obviously, economics has been around since the beginning of civilization, or since humans wanted something and had to choose from limited resources. Both Plato and Aristotle were students of economics, although to the ancient Greeks economics pertained to the management of the household. The Greek philosophers supported the notion of an exchange economy as a way for humans to build up their property or material possessions.

The genesis of modern economic thought paralleled the growth of trade during the Middle Ages. Monarchs, attempting to diminish the power of the nobility, extended trade privileges to towns. Guilds, the forerunners of today's trade unions, developed as people became free to pursue livelihoods other than farming. As towns and guilds competed for business with other towns and guilds, the regulation of trade became an issue. Therefore, most early economic thinking revolved around issues relating to money, interest, revenues, and taxation. Slowly, intellectuals realized that financial concerns were related to other problems, such as population and natural resources. Early economic writings tended to be very moralistic and persuasive in tone because their authors were generally spokespeople for a guild, a church, a town, or a class with a cause to promote.

In the seventeenth and eighteenth centuries, two powerful schools of thought developed in Europe. In Great Britain, the mercantilist school grew in favor. Mercantilists, reacting to the growth of nationalism, advocated active government influence on the balance of trade and payments. They encouraged the export of goods in exchange for full employment and rapid economic growth. In France, a competing school developed that championed a "physiocratic" system. Followers of the physiocratic school were called "economistes," and they advocated a laissez-faire, or "natural," economic system in which land, and not trade, would be the major source of wealth.

Adam Smith's publication of *The Wealth of Nations* in 1776[1] established the classical school of economics that would flourish for more than 100 years. Heavily influenced by the physiocrats and their laissez-faire philosophy, Smith established the doctrine of free enterprise and attacked the mercantilists. Because he wrote about the economic aspects of particular political decisions, Smith established the school of political economy—the early name for contemporary economics. Other prominent political economists were David Ricardo, John Stuart Mill, Jean Baptiste Say, and Thomas Malthus. These classical economists were convinced that production, income, and consumption were based on economic laws, lending credence to the notion that economics was an empirical science.

A neoclassical school developed in the late nineteenth century. Led by Alfred Marshall, it promoted the concept of demand as integral to economic relationships. An excellent mathematician, Marshall was influential in establishing the use of mathematical formulas to explain economic theories.

This growing fascination with economics in Europe did not immediately translate into comparable activity in the newly formed United States. Although Adam Smith's theories of free enterprise and laissez-faire would seem attractive to a citizenry recovering from a revolution, his ideas were not widely discussed in academic circles. American higher education was still heavily influenced by religious groups and clerics, who were suspicious of Smith's ideas on religious doctrine and were not anxious to change the status quo.

The United States was in its honeymoon period, and the British influence in economics was found objectionable. British economists seemed to have a disdain for the service sectors (of which U.S. clerics and educators were a part), and they were too interested in the promotion of free trade among countries. America preferred to suppress foreign competition so that it could develop its domestic industries. Economics had to be adapted to U.S. audiences and philosophies. Not until the turn of the twentieth century was economics firmly established as an academic discipline, although the courses were usually taught under the auspices of political science. Economists were still not secure in teaching positions in higher education; this contributed to their leading the fight for academic freedom and the establishment of tenure in U.S. universities.

The Industrial Revolution radically changed society. Suddenly there were new economic concerns, such as the growth of railroads, high government expenditures, the influence of powerful unions, and the dire social conditions of many cities. At the height of the Revolution, a new school called "institutional economics" developed. This school championed the study of institutions—corporations, unions, interest groups—and their thirst for power and property. Led by Thorstein Veblen, more a social satirist than an economist, the institutional school for the first time examined the social role played by economic institutions.

The devastation of the Great Depression, which began in October 1929, emphasized the shortcomings of economic theory: It was inadequate for dealing with the real problems of employment and income. John Maynard Keynes, perhaps the greatest economist of the twentieth century, ushered in the "Keynesian Revolution" with his publication of *The General Theory of Employment, Interest and Money*.[2] This seminal work advanced the macroeconomic approach to economic theory: It suggested that a government could establish policies leading to full employment and stable prices. Keynes advocated better government use of fiscal and monetary policy, and his policies are still promoted and widely discussed today, although not with the same fervor they once were.

Economics Today

Economics has undergone tremendous growth since World War II. An understanding of basic economics is now integral to nearly every academic discipline, and the employment of economists in business, industry, and government is at an all-time high. Economics has become quite specialized and is now characterized by many subfields (e.g., consumer economics, health economics, behavioral economics, environmental economics).

Two things distinguish modern economics. First, economics has become a mathematically based discipline. Research is approached empirically, theories are expressed mathematically, and economists are finding that a grounding in statistical and mathematical techniques has become essential for almost any study of economics. The proliferation of computers, now accessible to most researchers, has enabled the processing of large datasets to prove and disprove economic hypotheses. The application of statistics to economics is called *econometrics*, and it constitutes the most rapidly growing field of economics. Despite an increase in the number of dissenting voices who believe the field should focus less on the "rational man" and mathematics, no viable alternative approach has risen to replace the status quo. An increase in dissent, however, may account for some of the increase in specialized subfields, including feminist, institutional, and post-Keynesian economics.

Second, we have moved into what is called the *global economy*, which has tremendous implications for economic research and policy decisions. The consequences of the Great Depression in the 1930s and World War II in the 1940s dramatically demonstrated that economic problems have worldwide impact. Nations no longer operate as autonomous economic institutions but are linked by a strong bond of interdependence. Recognition of this is demonstrated by international collaborations, such as the economic summits of world leaders, by the amount of economic research generated by international agencies, and by the growing exchange of scholars at international conferences. Other manifestations are the expansion of development economics, which pertains to the study of the economic growth of low-income nations, and the growing interest in the application of economics to the information revolution. This combination of information and high technology is revolutionizing how we function and interrelate with each other. Economics continues to play a pivotal role in addressing many of the questions and concerns raised by the networked information revolution.

Is Economics a Social Science?

Economists now proceed in their research efforts by using the scientific method. They test theories by relating them to empirically observable data. Because economists cannot duplicate their data in a laboratory, they must use the empirical methods of social scientists, not scientists. Like any other social science, economics is subject to the vagaries of human nature; therefore, its theories cannot be totally reliable and accurate, as the following story illustrates.

In the spring of 1973, the U.S. consumer was shocked by a rapid escalation in meat prices. Government economists calculated that the price of meat would drop by the end of the year, as high prices would diminish the demand for meat and ranchers would loosen up supplies. Based on its research, the government established special policies to bring control to meat prices. However, the economic experts and their carefully calculated theories were unable to predict the behavior of U.S. homemakers. Angered by high prices, the homemakers demonstrated their power by quickly organizing a massive national boycott of meat, causing an immediate decrease in meat prices.

Economics cannot exist as an isolated science, because the understanding of many economic problems is related to an understanding of our social and political system. For example, a study of women in the labor force would not be complete without knowledge of the changing social mores that have supported the move of mothers and married women into the workforce. Like other social sciences, economics has policy implications. Desirable economic policy decisions must consist of both scientific economic analysis and socially ethical value judgments.

Nobel Laureate Robert Solow of the Massachusetts Institute of Technology wrote, "Modern economics tries hard not to be a social science, but it can't help itself. Social institutions and relationships help shape the production and distribution of wealth. The power of wealth is sometimes reflected in social institutions."[3] He would find a supporter in Douglass North, winner of the 1993 Nobel Prize in Economics, who believes that traditional economics focuses too much on mathematics and not enough on human behavior. He finds that the beliefs a society has in common are not analyzed enough in traditional economics, and that the irrationality of people's behavior contributes to the success or failure of economies.[4]

The Literature of Economics

The literature of economics has evolved as the discipline has grown in breadth and complexity. Early economic works were either pamphlets that protested or advocated a cause or, beginning in the eighteenth century, full-length studies of economic theories. Economists have drawn from monograph literature for centuries: When Adam Smith wrote *The Wealth of Nations* in 1776, he cited nearly 100 authors. Early economists seriously studied existing literature to make sure that their "original" theories had not been expounded earlier. They borrowed heavily from the business world, using materials such as journals of mining and banking, annual reports of railroads, and the histories of industries.

Early theorists such as Smith, Marshall, and Marx became prominent through their monographs. Their works generated a flood of secondary works that questioned, interpreted, and modified their ideas. Even today, monographs continue to be published that discuss the theories of these economists.

As the discipline grew more scientific, the literature of economics changed. Professional economics associations, such as the Royal Economic Society (1890), were organized, and they founded journals. These journals grew in importance as timely channels of economics communication became necessary. The first economics journal was the *Quarterly Journal of Economics*, founded by Harvard University in 1886. Soon professional journals supplanted monographs as the most popular research tools for the burgeoning number of economic faculties, researchers, and students.

As economists began to explore econometrics and built theories that required analysis of data, access to statistics became critical. Government publications, which expanded rapidly in the twentieth century, now supply much of the statistical data necessary for manipulation. International organizations, especially those affiliated with the United Nations, also provide economic data and sponsor specialized research. The advent of computerization meant that these statistical data could be easily processed and disseminated.

The urgency to publish research before it becomes obsolete has led to the development of another form of literature, the working paper or "gray" literature. Working papers are semipublished papers or preprints, in that they are not yet available through official channels such as journals or books. Instead, they are inexpensively produced and distributed by the author, a department, or an organization, such as the National Bureau of Economic Research. Many organizations now provide access to the full text of their working papers via the Internet. In addition, several resources have been developed that allow scholars to search the content of the working papers made available by many of these organizations at once. The dissemination of working papers, particularly in electronic form, overcomes the problem of publishing lags so common with journals in the social sciences. Another advantage of working papers is that they often elicit informal feedback for their authors. Those papers with special merit may eventually find their way into print, but by that time the information will have already been received by the researchers who need it.

As economics has expanded in size and influence, a tremendous body of literature has grown correspondingly. Economics researchers must wade through this labyrinth of material and statistics. Trends in recent economic literature reveal both an increasing global emphasis and the interdisciplinary nature of economics. Economics is viewed as being integral to many of the sweeping concerns of the new millennium, such as environmentalism, internationalism, and the growth of the networked information society. Each new subfield established has necessitated the development of new journals and other forms of publication. This means that not only must economists be familiar with the literature of their own specialty, they also must stay abreast of techniques and theories being developed in other specialties that could be of value to them.

The American Economic Association's subject classification scheme, which is used to organize economics literature, is continuously reviewed and modified to reflect these trends. New classifications recently added include information and Internet services, trade and environment, alternative energy sources, technological change, choices and consequences, and economics of gender.

Following is a selective and, of necessity, subjective list of economics reference works that could form the core of a reference collection. Because many of these sources are scholarly or heavily statistical in nature, they would be most appropriate for an academic library reference collection. They are representative of the types and variety of reference sources that today's economists use to satisfy their information needs.

HANDBOOKS

For many basic economic questions, many of which are statistical in nature, a simple reference book such as *The World Almanac* (A-62) or the *Time Almanac* (A-60) may be all that is needed. Two other reference tools, described in more detail in Chapter 1, are worth noting here because they offer users an easy and convenient way of locating general economic information and statistics.

Europa World Year Book. London: Europa, 1926- . (See A-78)

The Statesman's Year-Book: Statistical and Historical Annual of the States of the World. New York: St. Martin's, 1864- . Annual. (See A-79)

The most useful annual is the *Europa Year Book*. For each country there is an essay on economic affairs, plus current statistics culled from major statistical sources. In addition, the first volume contains detailed information on major international organizations, many of which play critical roles in the world economy. One advantage of this work is the easy access it provides to information originally contained in a wide variety of resources, such as *International Trade Statistics Yearbook* (C-49) and *Year Book of Labour Statistics* (C-52). The disadvantage, however, is the datedness of the information when compared to the most recent publication of the original data source.

The Statesman's Year-Book provides a limited amount of economic information. Brief paragraphs cover topics ranging from economic policy to industry (output and labour) and international trade (imports and exports) for each country.

DICTIONARIES AND ENCYCLOPEDIAS

Dictionaries and encyclopedias are crucial for helping patrons and librarians to understand the plethora of terminology that has developed in contemporary economics. Many of these terms are not in common use—"bounded rationality," "zero sum game," "crawling peg"—and the following sources all can be helpful in defining them and putting them into proper context. There are many fine dictionaries and encyclopedias on the market; this list is a sampling of the best.

C-1 **Encyclopedia of American Economic History: Studies of the Principal Movements and Ideas**. 3 vols. Edited by Glenn Porter. New York: Scribner's, 1980.

This three-volume work is the only reference source solely devoted to the subject of economic history. The word "encyclopedia" in the title is a bit of a misnomer, as this is really a collection of essays set in a framework designed to give the reader an overview of the economic history of the United States. The encyclopedia opens with a discussion of the historiography of U.S. economic history and follows with essays emphasizing its chronology. Much of the encyclopedia relates to the economic sectors and institutions and the roles they played in the expansion of the economy. The final section on the social framework of economics stresses the human consequences of economic change. The editors of this encyclopedia wanted it designed for the educated layperson, and they achieved their objective. The text is supplemented by lengthy bibliographies and charts, and the appearance of the pages, with wide double columns and large print, enhances the readability of the text.

C-2 **Encyclopedia of Political Economy**. Edited by Phillip O'Hara. New York: Routledge, 1999.

With the rising voice of dissent arguing that economists must move beyond the "rational man" and maximized utility, this work is a useful tool for scholars and students wanting to explore some dissenting concepts. Entries cover concepts, principles, and theories; the fields of political economy; and major figures in the field of political economy. Although the focus is on political economy, terms are often defined from a variety of economic perspectives in an attempt to bridge the communication gap created by an increase in specialization within the field of economics and the number of economic subfields.

The work is intended for scholars and students and provides clear and easily understandable entries. References are provided at the end of some entries to allow for further exploration. The work is arranged alphabetically; however, twenty subject lists guide users to information on particular topics in three broad categories: institutional spheres, subject areas, and schools of thought. Users interested in diversity topics might explore the family and gender (institutional sphere) or race and ethnicity (subject areas) subtopics.

C-3 **Fortune Encyclopedia of Economics**. Edited by David R. Henderson. New York: Warner, 1993.

According to the preface, this encyclopedia is designed to "emphasize areas where economists agree, while also specifying where and why they disagree." The result is a very readable encyclopedia that can be used by everyone, from undergraduates with no background in economics to faculty. The readability of this work is due not only to the writing style but also to a large print font and essays that are punctuated with interesting sidebars, charts, and anecdotes. A biographical section emphasizes individuals of historical importance or who have won the Nobel Prize.

International Encyclopedia of the Social Sciences. 17 vols. Edited by David S. Sills. New York: Macmillan, 1968–1979. (See A-55)

Encyclopedia of the Social Sciences. Edwin R. A. Seligman, ed.-in-chief. New York: Macmillan, 1930-1935. (See A-52)

International Encyclopedia of the Social Sciences and its predecessor, *Encyclopedia of the Social Sciences*, show up on every list of social science reference sources, and for good reason. Both are effective reference sources when one is searching for information on economics, perhaps reflecting the fact that the original editor, Edwin Seligman, was a noted economist who made sure that the subject was adequately covered. Seligman authored an introductory essay on the social sciences in the original encyclopedia; in this essay he exalted economics by naming it the second social science after political science (with due credit given to the ancient Greeks).

C-4 **The McGraw-Hill Dictionary of Modern Economics: A Handbook of Terms and Organizations**. 3d ed. New York: McGraw-Hill, 1983.

Now in its third edition, this dictionary has been a mainstay of reference collections and often the first choice of librarians. All definitions are written in a concise and understandable style and are often supplemented by references to current and original sources to which one can refer a patron for elaboration of a term. Charts and diagrams are used to clarify definitions. A nice feature is a separate section that describes more than 200 public, private, and nonprofit groups active in economics. This dictionary does not provide any biographical information.

C-5 **McGraw-Hill Encyclopedia of Economics**. rev. ed. Edited by Douglas Greenwald. New York: McGraw-Hill, 1994.

This encyclopedia was written as an extension of the popular *McGraw-Hill Dictionary of Modern Economics* (C-4). In a unique approach to compiling a reference book, the editor solicited input from prominent economists, who compiled the list of subjects and also nominated the experts to write the articles. The result is a one-volume encyclopedia of great utility and clarity, although it is most appropriate for upper-division students and faculty. This revision dropped thirty subjects from the first edition and added thirty-seven new ones (e.g., an article on the collapse of the Soviet Union). The articles include bibliographical references and extensive cross-references. A detailed subject index helps users locate concise information within the essays. A nice feature is the inclusion of a chronology of economic events.

C-6 **The MIT Dictionary of Modern Economics**. 4th ed. Edited by David W. Pearce. Cambridge: MIT Press, 1992.

This dictionary was written for the undergraduate with a need to define the words, phrases, and concepts of economics. The definitions are concise, most consisting of a paragraph, and make liberal use of cross-references. There are few bibliographical references. Each edition of this work is extensively revised to reflect the current state of economics. This edition has 2,800 entries. Recommended for all levels.

C-7   **The New Palgrave: A Dictionary of Economics**. Edited by John Eatwell, Murray Milgate, and Peter Newman. Reprinted with corrections. New York: Stockton Press, 1991.

This is the long-awaited edition of the classic *Dictionary of Political Economy*, originally edited by Inglis Palgrave in the 1890s and reprinted in 1910, 1923–1926, 1963, and 1976. The original dictionary's objective was to enable the student to "understand the position of economic thought at the present time" (preface), and its emphasis was on the English-speaking world. It was written by recognized scholars and is still valuable for the quality of its essays and the historical perspectives it contributes.

This new edition is designed to reflect the growth and influence of economics in the twentieth century. It is the most comprehensive reference work available on economics, with more than 2,000 entries by 900 contributors. *The New Palgrave* includes more than 700 biographies, some from the first edition. An economist included in *Palgrave* must have either been dead or born before 1916. While the editors had to set some sort of limit, this means that economists such as Nobel Prize winners Herbert Simon and Robert Solow are not included because of their relative youth.

The articles in *Palgrave* are signed, authoritative, and lengthy and include cross-references and bibliographies. They also tend to be quite technical and may presuppose some knowledge of economic theory. Some articles in *Palgrave* will be too esoteric for ordinary laypeople and many undergraduate students. This is a scholarly work and does not always reflect contemporary economics; for example, "Reaganomics" and "trickle-down theory" are not listed in the index. The contributors were asked to write a personal account of a topic, which means that some articles only present one side of a controversy as opposed to a balanced account.

An important work, *The New Palgrave* will be a standard in most academic and large public reference sections. However, librarians should be aware that it is not appropriate for all audiences and that for basic definitions a simple economics dictionary will probably be adequate.

BIOGRAPHICAL SOURCES

Biographical sources are important to economics because the study of economic theory is closely tied to the individuals who developed the theories. If one desires to know more about Keynesian economics or has merely heard the name of John Stuart Mill dropped in class, the following sources would be helpful.

C-8   Polkinghorn, Bette, and Dorothy Lampen Thomson. **Adam Smith's Daughters: Eight Prominent Women Economists from the Eighteenth Century to the Present**. Northampton, MA: Edward Elgar, 1998.

A revised, expanded edition of the original 1973 work by Thomson, this work is made up of eight "brief intellectual histories of women who have been active in economics". Each essay is between ten and twenty pages long and contains brief biographical information that often explains how each woman became involved in the field of economics. A discussion or summary of major written works is also provided. Extensive bibliographic notes allow for additional in-depth research on the lives and works of these often overlooked scholars. An increased interest in feminist economics and diversity issues make this a worthwhile introductory resource for any reference collection.

C-9   American Economic Association. **Directory of Members**. Evanston, IL: American Economic Association, 1880- . Irregular. Online format. URL: http://www .eco.utexas.edu/AEA.

This directory originally was issued every few years as a special issue of the *American Economic Review*. It contained most of the elements found in standard biographical directories, including activities, fields of concentration, doctoral dissertation titles, and publications. However, its irregularity detracted from its usefulness.

The directory is now available online as a cooperative service of the American Economics Association and the Department of Economics at the University of Texas. *The American Economic Association Online Directory of Members* currently provides access to three searchable databases: the 1993 and 1997 Surveys of Members and the current Membership List The surveys contain more detailed information including fields of research and educational background but are more likely to be outdated. The membership list has basic information, e.g., mailing address, telephone numbers, e-mail address, etc. and is updated on a monthly basis. (See figure 3.1.)

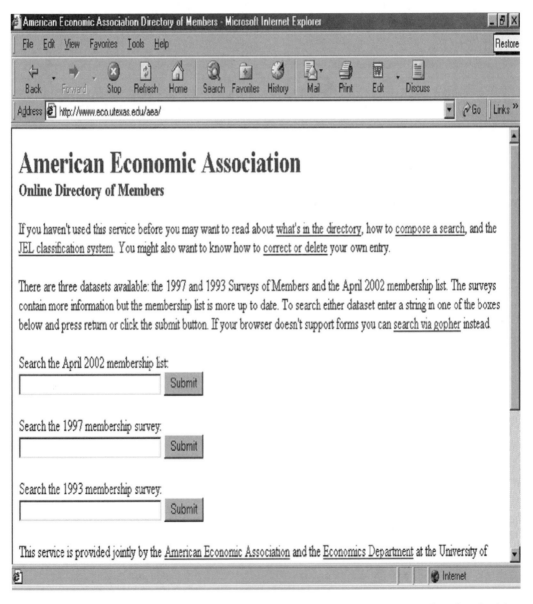

Figure 3.1. American Economic Association, Online Directory of Members. Reprinted with permission of the American Economic Association.

C-10 Pressman, Steven. **Fifty Major Economists**. New York: Routledge, 1999.

In his introduction Pressman asserts, "All the key economic figures from the past are contained in this volume." Some might debate his claim, but most would agree that the fifty figures included in this work did contribute important ideas to the field of economics and are "worthy of continued study." As one might expect, this work is made up of fifty essays arranged by the date of birth of each economist, from the earliest to the most recent.

Each three- to five-page essay includes a necessarily short biography and a summary of the important ideas disseminated by each economist. Pressman also provides a narrative explanation of the importance of each economist from his perspective, as well as what he believes is or has been the perspective of most economists. Each essay ends with a bibliography of the most important writings by and about this economic figure. A brief glossary, which defines key terms used frequently throughout the work, is also included.

C-11 Blaug, Mark. **Great Economists Before Keynes: An Introduction to the Lives & Works of One Hundred Great Economists of the Past**. Atlantic Highlands, NJ: Humanities Press, 1986.

C-12 Blaug, Mark. **Great Economists Since Keynes: An Introduction to the Lives & Works of One Hundred Modern Economists**. 2d ed. Northampton, MA: Edward Elgar Publishing, 1998.

Blaug is a distinguished British economist who must have enjoyed writing these books. Each essay is two to five pages long and is designed to be read more as a chapter in a book than as a reference book of facts. The biographical information is present—birth date, schools, residences, and the like—but so are the economist's theories, ideas, and major works. The essays are very readable, and the early economists are listed in chronological order so that one can read the volume straight through to better understand the history of economics. Blaug includes interesting facts (e.g., Adam Smith burned almost all of his unpublished manuscripts before his death) and his own editorial comments (e.g., Marshall's life "was relatively uneventful even for an academic").

A nice feature is that a portrait or photograph is included for each economist, who on the whole seem to be a rather stuffy group. It is interesting to note that the volume on modern economists includes only one woman, and unlike her male counterparts, who have formal photographs included with their biographies, she was photographed seated at a meal. *Great Economists Since Keynes* was revised in 1998 and includes the same 100 entries with updated information. Blaug considered revising his list of 100 great economists based on recent awards and developments but decided to "stick with" his initial choices.

C-13 **Nobel Laureates in Economic Sciences: A Biographical Dictionary**. Edited by Bernard Katz. Hamden, CT: Garland, 1989.

This work presents readable and informative biographical essays on Nobel Prize laureates. Each essay includes a selected bibliography. This information is readily available elsewhere, but this volume presents the information in a convenient format. Nobel Prize winner Samuelson wrote the introduction.

C-14 Blaug, Mark. **Who's Who in Economics**. 3d ed. Northampton, MA: Edward Elgar Publishing, 1999.

This work includes brief bio-bibliographical blurbs on 500 deceased and 1,100 living economists who lived from 1700 to 1996. The criterion for inclusion was that an economist must publish, or have published, regularly in learned journals of economics or else be cited often in the leading histories of economic thought. The biographies of the 500 deceased economists were written by Blaug or provided by the deceased before their deaths. The living economists included in this work provided the relevant information themselves. Included with the biographical blurbs are statements (300 words or less) written by the economists that present their principal contribution to economics;

these can be very revealing. Special indexes include listings by field of interest, country of birth, and country of residence.

BIBLIOGRAPHIES

Besides being used for reference, the following resources can be useful for collection development activities. Librarians involved in such activities also will find many excellent reviews in economics journals. Most important is the *Journal of Economic Literature* (C-26), which provides reviews or descriptive information on nearly all worthwhile books. Other important journals are the *American Economic Review*, the *Southern Economic Journal* (Southern Economic Association), and the *Journal Economical* (Royal Economic Society).

As the field of economics becomes more specialized, it is important to note that many focused bibliographies are available covering specific areas, for example, agriculture or post-Keynesian economics. Although the resources listed here are more encompassing of the field as a whole and might be used in any academic collection, more specialized resources might be acquired depending on the research interests of the faculty at a particular institution.

C-15 **Bibliographic Guide to Business and Economics**. New York: G. K. Hall/ Macmillan, 1974- . Annual.

This source includes cataloging information for business and economics titles acquired and cataloged by the Research Libraries of the New York Public Library. Books, nonbooks, and serials are included with their authors, titles, subjects, and series combined into one alphabetical sequence. This source does not have much reference value except for verification purposes but can be useful for collection development activities. There is a three-year time lag between the date of the volume and its publication date.

C-16 **Business Library Review**. New York: Gordon and Breach Science, 1984- . Quarterly.

Formed by a merger of *Economics and Business* and the *Wall Street Review of Books,* this source is designed to be a comprehensive survey of materials—books, computer software, films, and videos—recently published in the areas of business and economics. The reviews include in-depth discussions of single titles and an annotated bibliography of other works. All reviews are invited. Materials are selected for inclusion for both their timeliness and content; unfortunately, *Economics and Business* has suffered from publication delays, which negates some of its usefulness as a selection tool.

C-17 **International Bibliography of Economics** [*Bibliographie Internationale de Science Economique*]. Paris: UNESCO, 1952- . Annual.

This is part of UNESCO's four annual volumes in the *International Bibliography of the Social Sciences* (the other three are in sociology [H-56], political science [B-15], and social and cultural anthropology [G-49, G-50]). Because it attempts to cover materials in all languages and from all countries, it is a significant work for researchers in this new era of the global economy. Although each volume includes about 8,000 citations and indexes 1,500 journals, it is not a comprehensive work. Users should examine the prefatory material, which explains what has been included and what is excluded. There are a classified subject index and an alphabetical subject index in both French and English. Titles are in their original language, but if they are other than French or English, they are also translated into English. A major drawback is the twelve- to thirty-month delay between the publication date of the materials and their inclusion in the bibliography. *International Bibliography of the Social Sciences* sponsors a monthly current awareness service called the International Current Awareness Service in Economics.

C-18   **University Research in Business and Economics**. Morgantown, WV: Bureau of Business Research, College of Business and Economics, West Virginia University, for Association for University Business and Economics Research, 1982- . Annual.

The previous title of this work was *AUBER Bibliography* (1957–1982). This bibliography of materials is produced by members of the American Assembly of Collegiate Schools of Business (AACSB) and the Association for University Business and Economic Research (AUBER). Included are periodicals, bulletins, working papers, and conference proceedings, many of which do not appear in standard indexes and abstracts yet are critical to adequately assess the volume and scope of economic research in academic institutions. It is especially good for locating regional information. Publications are arranged by a classified subject listing, by the name of the sponsoring institution, and by author. The usefulness of this source is diminished by a publishing time lag of several years.

C-19   University of London Library. **Catalogue of the Goldsmiths' Library of Economic Literature**. Compiled by Margaret Canney and David Knot. New York: Cambridge University Press for the University of London Library, 1970–1983.

C-20   Harvard University. Graduate School of Business Administration. **The Kress Library of Business and Economics. Catalogue, Covering Material Published Through 1776 with Data Upon Cognate Items in Other Harvard Libraries**. Boston: Baker Library, 1940.

C-21   Harvard University. Graduate School of Business Administration. **The Kress Library of Business and Economics. Catalogue, 1777–1817**. London: Bailey Bros. & Swinfen on behalf of Baker Library, 1957.

C-22   Harvard University. Graduate School of Business Administration. **The Kress Library of Business and Economics. Catalogue, 1818–1848**. Boston: Baker Library, 1964.

C-23   Harvard University. Graduate School of Business Administration. **The Kress Library of Business and Economics. Catalogue, 1473–1848**. Boston: Baker Library, 1967.

C-24   **Goldsmiths'-Kress Library of Economic Literature: A Consolidated Guide**. Follows Detailed, Subject Approach to the Catalogue of the Goldsmiths' Library. Woodbridge, CT: Research Publications, 1976.

Herbert Somerton Foxwell, professor of economics at Cambridge University and later at the University of London, was a passionate bibliophile. For years he haunted book shops and perused used book catalogs, eventually amassing one of the world's greatest book collections in economics. In 1901, he sold much of this collection to The Goldsmiths' Company, who then presented the collection to the University of London. Later, a second collection, many of its books duplicates of the first library, was compiled and sold to Harvard University's Kress Library of Business and Economics in 1929.

Together these two libraries constitute an outstanding historical collection not only in economics but also in the political sciences, transportation, commerce and business, sociology, and other social sciences. Both collections have been supplemented with additional works, although the Foxwell collection remains their core.

Both catalogs are arranged chronologically. The Kress volumes are alphabetical by main entry within each chronological division; the Goldsmiths' volumes have broad subject subdivisions (e.g., agriculture, population, finance) within each chronological division. Both sets have title and author indexes. A joint collection of these outstanding libraries has been produced on microfiche, along with a consolidated guide. This is a rich resource for students of economics and social history.

INDEXES AND ABSTRACTS

Because of the expansion of the field of economics, its diversification, and its scientific orientation, journals and serials have become one of the most critical tools to the economics researcher because they are current. In addition to the formal journal literature, economics researchers also rely heavily on the distribution of working papers to access current research. With the advent of the Internet, several large databases have appeared that support the dissemination of cutting edge research via these working papers. The following tools supply access to most economic journals and help researchers locate the more ephemeral working paper literature.

Indexes produced by H. W. Wilson should never be overlooked because of their ease of use, familiarity to library patrons, and availability in most libraries. Together the *Social Sciences Index* (A-24) and the *Business Periodicals Index* (D-42) adequately cover the major economic journals. Because economics is interdisciplinary, these indexes allow users to find economic literature published in journals of business, political science, sociology, and so forth.

Another excellent general index is the *PAIS International in Print* (A-21). One of its strengths is its orientation toward literature on public policy, which is, of course, profoundly interrelated with economic conditions. Formerly known as the *PAIS Bulletin*, this resource covers a wide range of literature, including journals, monographs, international and federal documents, and reports of private and public organizations. Easy to use, *PAIS* is especially effective when searching for information on the economics of particular geographic areas. *PAIS International* is also available online from a variety of database providers and in CD-ROM format.

C-25 **Index of Economic Articles in Journals and Collective Volumes**. Homewood, IL: R. D. Irwin, 1961- . Annual.

This is the major index of economic literature. Almost 300 journals are indexed selectively (articles indexed must have authors and economic content) along with festschriften, conference proceedings, collected essays, and books of readings. All materials included in the index must either be in English or have an English summary. Articles are arranged by a classification system developed by the American Economic Association (see figure 3.2). This classification system includes more than 300 subject categories, which are regularly updated to reflect changes in the field, and is specifically designed for the economics researcher. The noneconomist or student might find this classified index cumbersome or intimidating; happily, the editors have included an alphabetical subject guide to the classification scheme. A particularly useful aspect of this index is that articles containing geographic information or data are identified by a geographic description code. There are two major drawbacks to this index: There is no cumulative index, and there is a publication lag of three to six years. This timeliness problem is fortunately obviated by the *Journal of Economic Literature* (C-26).

C-26 **Journal of Economic Literature**. Menasha, WI: American Economic Association, 1963- . Quarterly.

Journal of Economic Literature attempts to maintain communication within the broad economics profession. Published quarterly, it functions as the profession's current awareness journal and updates *Index of Economic Articles* (C-25). Each issue has several key components: two or three long survey articles, lengthy book reviews arranged by subject, a nonevaluative annotated list of new books and journals, a content listing of current journals, a classified subject index of English-language articles in 400 current journals, and a selection of author's abstracts of journal articles. The classified subject index is cumulated annually and becomes the *Index of Economic Articles*.

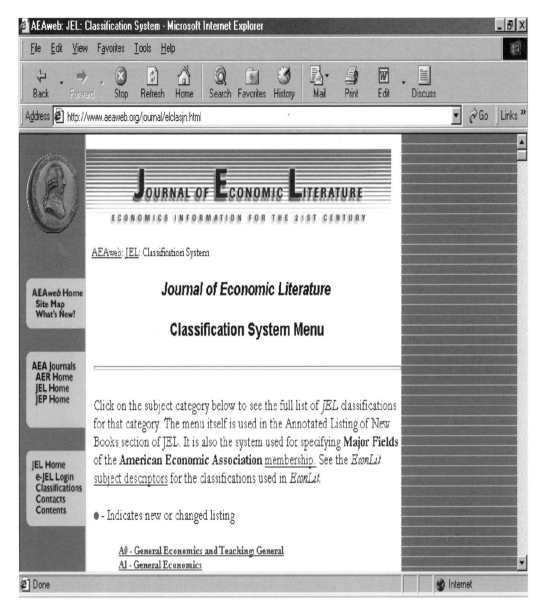

Figure 3.2. *Journal of Economic Literature*, **Classification System Menu. Reprinted with permission of the American Economic Association.**

Electronic Versions

C-27 **Abstracts of Working Papers in Economics**. New York: Cambridge University Press, 1986- . Formerly published 8 times/yr. Since 1994, published 6 times/yr.

Each issue of *AWPE* covers 400 recent papers procured from more than seventy research centers around the world. Each paper is indexed by author and issuing institution, and access to these items is also facilitated through a keyword/permuted title index.

Electronic access: The electronic version of this resource, made available through *EconLit* (C-28), offers several advantages over the print version. *EconLit* is a more inclusive index because it contains working papers and dissertations as well as additional abstracts. Author affiliations are also included for post-1990 citations. This version also offers many more search options, as users can search by geographic descriptors, document type, and named person.

C-28 **EconLit**. Nashville, TN: American Economic Association. 1969- . Monthly. Online format. URL: http://www.econlit.org/econlit/access.html.

This resource is produced by the American Economic Association and distributed to libraries online or in CD-ROM format through a number of service providers identified on the *EconLit* Web site. *EconLit* includes citations to articles indexed in *Journal of Economic Literature* (C-26) since 1969 and the annual volumes of *Index of Economic Articles* (C-25). Abstracts are provided, including those that do not appear in *Journal of Economic Literature*. Subject indexing and abstracting of books (1987) and indexing of dissertations (1987) have been added. In 1994, *Abstracts of Working Papers in Economics* was added to the database.

C-29 **IDEAS. Research Papers in Economics**. 6 times/wk. Online format. URL: http://ideas.uqam.ca/.

In an effort to enhance the dissemination of economics research, the *IDEAS* database continues to grow thanks to the cooperative efforts of more than 100 volunteers in twenty-five countries. It currently provides access to over 77,000 abstracts of working papers, 33,000 journal articles, and 600 software components. The *IDEAS* search mechanism allows searching of each area (working papers, journal articles, etc.) or of all areas at once. Abstracts can also be browsed by JEL Classification category, author name, or working paper series title. Some papers may be downloaded directly to the user's computer; others must be acquired from the author or issuing institution.

C-30 **Social Science Research Network (SSRN) Electronic Library**. Social Science Electronic Publishing, 2000- . Continually. Online format. URL: http://papers .ssrn.com.

The goal of the *SSRN Electronic Library* is to encourage "the early distribution of research results by reviewing and publishing submitted abstracts and by soliciting abstracts of top quality research papers around the world." To achieve its goal, SSRN has partnered with a wide variety of publishers, academic institutions or departments, and governmental entities to provide access to working papers in a variety of fields including economics. The database currently contains almost 24,000 abstracts and 10,500 full-text papers. Contact information is provided for papers that cannot be downloaded.

Multiple points of access can be utilized to locate an appropriate abstract. The traditional Web database searching options are provided, with a quick search box and advanced search options appearing on the opening Web page (see figure 3.3). In addition, several browse options are provided. Users can browse for titles by the *Journal of Economic Literature Classification System*, an important means for categorizing economic literature. An advance browse option also provides access to abstracts from a particular journal or about a particular topic.

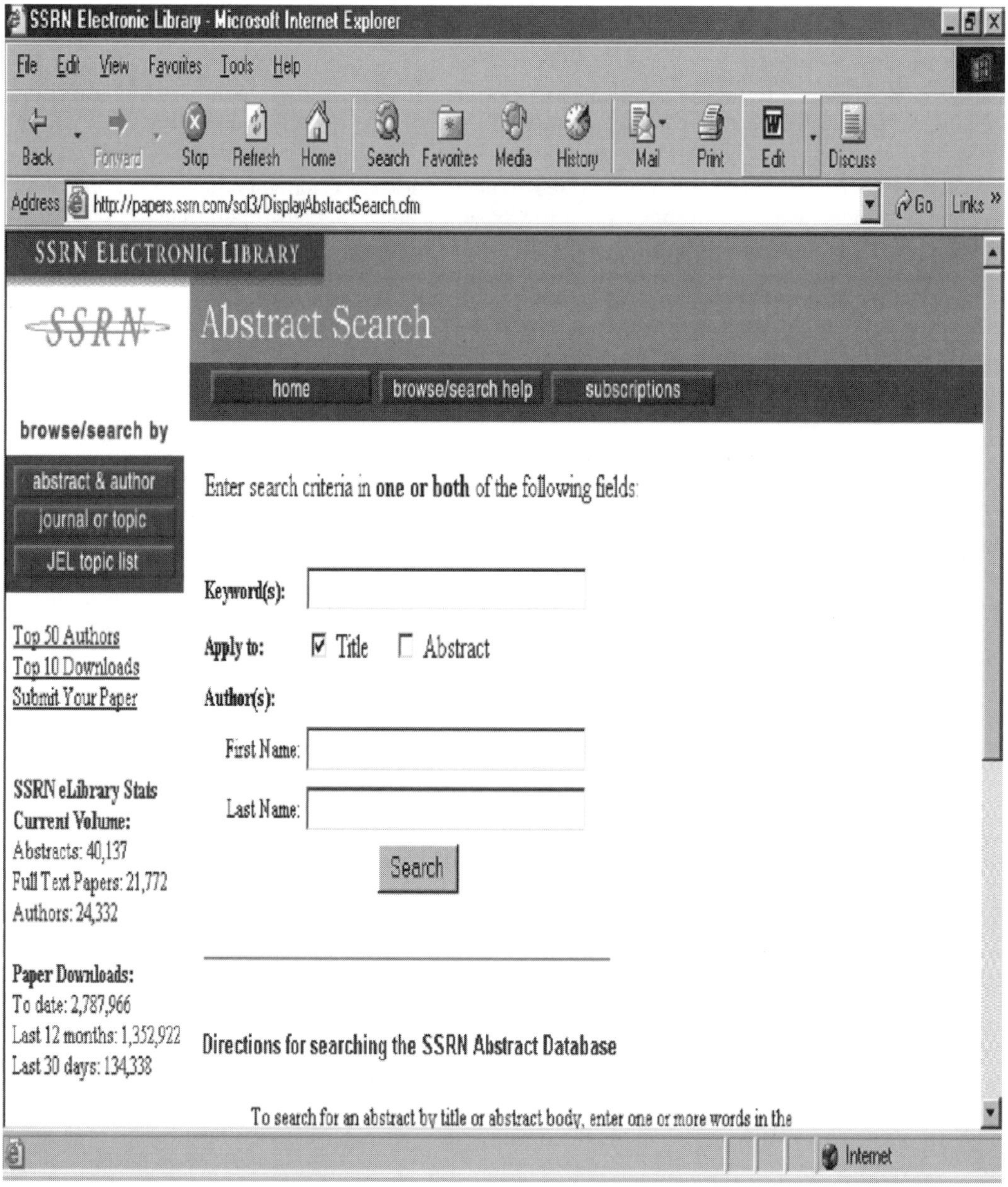

Figure 3.3. SSRN Electronic Library Abstract Search. Reprinted with permission from SSRN (http://search.ssrn.com).

STATISTICAL SOURCES

Statistics are so essential to the study of economics that they merit more detailed explanation. Reference librarians testify to an overwhelming number of statistical questions. These can be frustrating because they are difficult to interpret, and too often locating the correct answers is not easy.

As economics has grown as a mathematically based science, the need for quantitative data on which to base hypotheses has become critical. Economic statistics are generated from a variety of sources: governmental, international or intergovernmental groups, and private organizations.

Governmental Sources

The federal government is the major producer and supplier of economic statistics. Most of the statistics it publishes, it also collects; however, it also compiles statistics from nongovernmental groups.

The macroeconomic data collected by government agencies are needed to develop fiscal, monetary, and wage-price policies to further the Keynesian goals of full employment and low inflation. These goals were codified in the United States by the Employment Act of 1946 and by the Full Employment and Balanced Growth Act of 1978. The major users of these statistics are the Council of Economic Advisors, the Federal Reserve Board, the Department of the Treasury, the Office of Management and Budget, the Congressional Budget Office, and the Joint Economic Committee. All these statistics are made readily available to anyone, and the private sector uses them for activities such as labor-management wage negotiations and corporate market and investment analyses.

Until the 1920s the federal government did not systematically produce detailed measures of the nation's economic performance. The Great Depression prompted the study of business cycles and impressed upon the government the need to develop economic indicators to forecast the state of the economy. In 1937 a nonprofit research group, the National Bureau of Economic Research (NBER), was charged with developing a series of statistical indicators that could be used to measure the nation's economic health. These indicators were designed to gauge production, consumption, prices, and financial markets and, as such, to indicate downturns and upturns in the business cycle. Now formally referred to as the economic indicators, these twelve macroeconomic measures have become the darlings of broadcasters and politicians, who announce them with great fervor.

The federal government's statistical collection efforts have grown into a massive and complex bureaucracy. Unlike most countries, whose statistics are compiled by a centralized agency, the United States diffuses this activity among more than 100 agencies. This has resulted in bewilderment for the researcher trying to determine the proper sources for data. The Office of Statistical Policy in the U.S. Office of Management and Budget nominally supervises the collection of statistics and is charged with approving new statistical series and monitoring for waste and duplication. Unfortunately, its coordination has not always been effective, and it lacks the authority to make many positive changes.

It is important that moneys be allocated to research and funding that support the development of new statistical methodologies designed to measure the rapidly changing economy. The following illustration demonstrates the importance of having statistical methodologies that allow for change. The Consumer Price Index (CPI) is probably the best known of the economic indicators and is used to estimate the rate of inflation. It is determined by the cost of a "market basket of goods and services" that a typical consumer might purchase. For too many years, the government used a "market basket" determined by 1972 buying habits. Until 1987, it did not include any electronic equipment—microwave ovens, VCRs, compact discs, personal computers—yet Americans spent billions on these products in the 1980s. This negated the reliability of the Consumer Price Index as a measure of the cost of living.

Robert Eisner, author of *The Misunderstood Economy: What Counts and How to Count It,*[5] has long argued that our unreliable and misinterpreted statistics have distorted how we perceive our economy and result in ineffective and inappropriate policies. He explains that too many economic activities are not taken into account, such as the value of a homemaker's work. Recent changes in the way economic census data are collected reflect the need to be more inclusive of all economic sectors and activities. For example, the North American Industry Classification System (NAICS) used by the 1997 *Economic Census* identifies over 350 new industries previously excluded. (See C-36 for a further description of these changes.)

It is critical that reference librarians who handle economics questions stay abreast of changes in how statistics are collected, distributed, and manipulated. These changes affect how statistical comparisons are made and interpreted, and also librarians' selection of appropriate reference sources. Since the first edition of this book, several notable changes have taken place in the way the government uses statistics as a measure of the country's health. In 1991, the Bureau of Economic Analysis announced that the GNP, or gross national product, would no longer be the principal measure of our economy. It was replaced with gross domestic product (GDP), which does not include income produced by Americans abroad. At the same time, all statistics were moved from a 1982 to a 1987 base. This was a major development, because it affected how comparisons and contrasts had to be done between pre-1991 and post-1991 data. Another development took place in 1994, when the Bureau of Labor Statistics changed its principal measure of joblessness. How does a librarian discover these changes? It isn't easy, although serious librarians will want to regularly browse standard sources such as *Survey of Current Business* (C-38), where such announcements often appear.

There are other concerns besides understanding how economic data are compiled. Librarians should know how the compilers of statistical data define certain terms; many governmental statistical works include a glossary and a detailed preface. Timeliness is always a concern. Many government agencies, under pressure to release statistics as soon as possible, release preliminary figures that are then revised in subsequent months. Because of the lag between the time a statistical indicator is announced and its publication, reference librarians sometimes have to rely on nongovernmental sources during the interim. *The Wall Street Journal* and *Business Week*, and other media such as the television show *Wall Street Week*, can be helpful.

One of the most important developments for the economics researcher is the expansion of the Internet. It is the ideal medium for disseminating statistics and other information for which timeliness is essential, and it has the potential to revolutionize how research is conducted. The World Wide Web allows access to a wide variety of statistical resources including *EconData*, a program for statistical manipulation compiled by the University of Maryland Department of Economics. The National Performance Review (also known as Reinventing Government), conducted by Vice President Al Gore in 1994, mandated that more government information be made available online. The move toward a comprehensive economics and business Internet node was partially fulfilled when the Department of Commerce first released 300,000 public documents on the Internet in the summer of 1994. Many of these items or updated versions are available through the *National Trade Data Bank* (C-33) and *State of the Nation* (C-34), described in more detail below.

Indexes

C-31 **American Statistics Index**. Bethesda, MD: Congressional Information Service, 1973- . Annual with monthly supplements.

This source merits mention here because of its importance in locating economic statistics. Reference librarians familiar with this tool probably use it as their second source (after the *Statistical Abstract of the United States* [C-32]) for all statistical questions relating to economics. Its inclusiveness, reliability, and high standards of quality allow a user to find data without the hassle of wading through scores of government publications.

Electronic access: Also available in CD-ROM format as the *Statistical Masterfile*, on Dialog as *ASI Online*, and in the online database known as *Statistical Universe*.

General Sources

C-32 United States. Department of Commerce. **Statistical Abstract of the United States**. Washington, DC: Government Printing Office, 1894- . Annual. Online format. URL: http://purl.access.gpo.gov/GPO/LPS2878 or http://www.census .gov/prod/www/statistical-abstract-us.html.

For inclusiveness and ease of use, there isn't a better source. This all-purpose resource can answer most basic reference questions while also serving as a guide to further research. An indispensable guide for anyone interested in government information, it is now available on CD-ROM and online.

The online resource provides access to the full text of the 1995 to date volumes. Each section of the annual publication is available in pdf format. The print volume is actually easier to use when trying to browse this resource to identify a useful table. The advantage of the online version, however, is its accessibility. Users can access this resource anywhere they can access the Web (not just in the library).

C-33 United States. Department of Commerce. Bureau of Economic Analysis. **National Trade Data Bank**. Washington, DC: Department of Commerce, Economics and Statistics Administration, Office of Business Analysis, 1990- . Monthly. Online format. URL: http://www.stat-usa.gov.

The *NTDB*, as it is popularly known, is geared to those involved in international business, whether they need information on foreign labor trends or a report on fast food in Saudi Arabia. Included are *Country Reports on Economic Policy and Trade Practices*, a series of market research reports, and the *Handbook of International Economic Statistics*. It is the counterpart to the *National Economic, Social, and Environmental Data Bank*. It is available on CD-ROM and via STAT-USA, an online statistical service available through depository libraries.

C-34 United States. Department of Commerce. **State of the Nation**. Washington, DC: Department of Commerce, 1994- . Daily. Online format. URL: http://www .stat-usa.gov.

State of the Nation (*SOTN*) contains current and historical U.S. economic data and news releases related to the U.S. economy. Use the SOTN Library to access the most up-to-date information from governmental agencies covering the National Income and Product Accounts, economics indicators, and employment or unemployment. Data are often provided in formats that can be downloaded and easily imported into spreadsheets or databases. It is important to watch for separate readme.txt files that contain important documentation related to each dataset.

Specific Publications of Government Agencies

C-35 **Economic Indicators**. Prepared for the Joint Committee on the Economic Report by Council of Economic Advisers. Washington, DC: Government Printing Office, 1948- . Monthly. Online format. URL: http://www.access.gpo.gov/congress /cong002.html.

Economic Indicators is an update to the *Economic Report of the President* (C-39). It summarizes current statistics on income and spending, employment and wages, production and business activity, prices, credit, financial markets, and federal finances. These economic measures were designated by the National Bureau of Economic Research at the request of Congress in 1947. The *Economic Indicators* Web site provides access to the full text in both text and pdf formats from 1995 forward. Access to all files is available via a search engine. Full text since 1998 can also be browsed on a monthly basis by utilizing a table of contents list.

C-36 United States. Department of Commerce. Bureau of the Census. **Economic Census of the United States**. Washington, DC: Department of Commerce, Bureau of the Census, 1997- . Quinquennial. Online format. URL: http://www.census.gov /epcd/www/econ97.html.

With the advent of the Internet, the means of accessing government publications has changed dramatically. The 1997 *Economic Census* is a clear example of this change. As the 1997 *Economic Census* data and reports are compiled, they are being made freely available online (and later on CD-ROM); only highlights of the census are published in paper reports.

Another major change in the collection of economic census information was the move from the Standard Industrial Classification (SIC) system to the new North American Industry Classification System (NAICS). With a change in the way the data are being presented, a comparable change has been made in the way we "talk about" the census. The "Economic Census" terminology has now been used to refer to all data and reports, that is, publications are no longer titled as if they were part of a separate census for each sector of the economy, e.g., the census of manufactures. *Economic Census* still provides "counts" on U.S. agriculture and industry in the same way that the government counts people every ten years. However, the census reports are not broken down into the same subject areas used in the past (Agriculture, Construction Industries, Manufacturers, Mineral Industries, Retail Trade, Service Industries, Transportation, and Wholesale Trade).

NAICS groups the economy into twenty broad sectors, an increase from the ten divisions of the SIC system. Each of these sectors is listed on the *Economic Census* Web site and links to the available reports for that area. (Note: The Census of Agriculture is available on a separate Web site at http://www.nass.usda.gov/census/.) Although these changes allow a more detailed understanding of the U.S. economy, they also cause a profound break in the time series data available to researchers. Be prepared to read the online guides to understand these changes and how data from the most recent economic census can be compared to those of previous years.

The American Statistics Index (C-31) is an ideal way to locate specific data within the censuses. For assistance in using the censuses, librarians also may want to consult the specialized guides available in the following series.

C-37 United States. Bureau of the Census. **Factfinder for the Nation** (various titles). Washington, DC: Government Printing Office, 1977- . Irregular.

This series contains brief and concise guides to the various census titles and related information. Each guide discusses the history of a census, its content, possible use, and other useful sources and aids. Some full-text content of this resource is available in pdf format at the address provided above.

Electronic access: Some reports available online at http://www.census.gov/prod/www/abs /factfind.html.

C-38 United States. U.S. Department of Commerce. Bureau of Economic Analysis. **Survey of Current Business**. Washington, DC: Government Printing Office, 1921- . Monthly. Online format. URL: http://www.bea.doc.gov/bea/pubs.htm.

The primary source for economic information relating to business, the *Survey* analyzes current domestic economic activity and identifies and tracks trends. Each issue opens with "The Business Situation," an overview of the economic environment, followed by feature articles on subjects ranging from international travel fares to expenditures by foreign affiliates of U.S. corporations. Nearly half of each issue is devoted to statistical tables and charts containing economic series culled from public and private sources. Included is a special section on business cycle indicators.

Electronic access: Full-text online access to the content of this resource, primarily in pdf format with some files also available in html format, is provided from the BEA Web site, 1998–date. Online annual subject guides are also provided and separate the articles and tables found in this work into general, international, national, and regional categories for every year since 1995.

C-39   United States. President. **Economic Report of the President**. Washington, DC: Government Printing Office, 1947- . Annual. Online format. URL: http://www .access.gpo.gov/eop/.

This easy-to-use, convenient, and authoritative source on the U.S. economy is an essential reference work for every library. Required by the Employment Act of 1946, this report on the state of the economy is prepared by the executive branch for Congress. It details the current administration's economic programs and reviews the economy's past performance and outlook. The annual report of the Council of Economic Advisers is also included. Because it reflects the policies of the executive branch, the *Report* is also a political document. Two-thirds of the *Report* is narrative; the remaining third consists of 100 statistical tables covering the major economic indicators, with many series going back to 1929.

Online access to this report allows viewing of the entire report for any year since 1997. Spreadsheet files containing the statistics from Appendix B of the report are also available for these years. The contents of the *Report* from 1996 forward may also be searched for words and phrases through the same Web site.

C-40   United States. Department of Commerce. Bureau of Economic Analysis. **The National Income and Product Accounts of the United States, 1929–1997**. Washington, DC: Government Printing Office, 1992- . Irregularly updated.

This reference work represents the accounting system of the U.S. government as it includes data on the gross domestic product, personal income, government receipts and outlays, foreign trade, savings and investment, and business income. It presents a historical view of the finances of the United States. This is an essential tool for anyone researching the U.S. economy and should be used in tandem with the *Survey of Current Business* (C-38), which updates the accounts monthly with annual July revisions.

> *Electronic access:* Much of the *NIPA* data can also be downloaded from the *State of the Nation Library* (C-34). Articles, data, and press releases associated with the most recent revision of the National Income and Product Accounts are also available online at the Bureau of Economic Activity Web site (http://www.bea.doc.gov/bea/an1.htm).

C-41   United States. Bureau of Labor Statistics. **Employment and Earnings**. Washington, DC: Government Printing Office, 1895- . Monthly.

This statistical journal is devoted to employment data collected from both federal sources and states' unemployment insurance offices. Hours and earnings are given for major industry groups, and employment data are broken down by demographics such as age, sex, race, and Vietnam veterans. An appendix explains the survey tables and the methodologies used to collect the data. The historical compilations are entitled Employment, Hours and Earnings.

> *Electronic access:* Some of the tables printed in this publication can also be viewed online at http://www.bls.gov/cesee.htm.

C-42   United States. Board of Governors of the Federal Reserve System. **Federal Reserve Bulletin**. Washington, DC: Government Printing Office, 1915- . Monthly.

This is the official publication of the Federal Reserve Board and therefore includes material on new regulations, staff members, directory information, and tracking of monetary policies handled by the Federal Reserve Board. Most of the statistics pertain to banking and finance, such as money supplies, interest rates, foreign exchange rates, mortgage markets, and government finances. Most statistics are culled from reports made to the Federal Reserve Board or from the Treasury Department. *Federal Reserve Bulletin* is more technical than some other government publications, such as *Monthly Labor Review* (C-43). The District Federal Reserve Boards (of which there are eleven) all publish at least one periodical pertinent to the economy of their region.

> *Electronic access:* Examples of articles contained in the *Bulletin* can be found at http:// www.federalreserve.gov/pubs/bulletin/default.htm.

C-43 United States. Bureau of Labor Statistics. **Monthly Labor Review**. Washington, DC: Government Printing Office, 1915- . Monthly. Online format. URL: http://www.bls.gov/opub/mlr/mlrhome.htm.

Monthly Labor Review is the official organ of the Bureau of Labor Statistics, and each issue contains information on bureau activities and research, developments in labor relations, book reviews, and a list of recent Bureau publications. The *Review* regularly publishes about forty statistical series on employment and unemployment, wages, productivity, work stoppages, and the results of wage increases bargained by the unions. Many series are "seasonally adjusted" for variables such as climate changes and holiday retail periods. The articles in the *Review* are written for the layperson and therefore are very readable; the *Review* is even indexed in *Readers' Guide to Periodical Literature* (A-16).

The Bureau of Labor Statistics (BLS) Data Web page (http://www.bls.gov/datahome.htm) allows users to view and download a wide variety of data without accessing a particular BLS publication. Users can view the most requested data series, fill out forms to get to a particular data series, or view the *Economy at a Glance*. Some of the forms to request a series of data are rather convoluted and require persistence and the use of multiple help screens. The print publications might be easier to use for the one-time user; the forms would be useful for someone who frequently accesses these data or needs a large set of data to import into a spreadsheet or database. Ftp access is another alternative for users requiring a large volume of data.

C-44 United States. Bureau of Labor Statistics. **Handbook of U.S. Labor Statistics: Employment, Earnings, Prices, and Productivity and Other Labor Data**. 3d ed. Lanham, MD: Bernan Press, 1997- . Annual. Formerly United States. Bureau of Labor Statistics. *Handbook of Labor Statistics*. Washington, DC: Government Printing Office, 1924–1926–1989. Annual.

Now published by Bernan Press, this resource contains a compilation of the statistical series regularly published in *Monthly Labor Review*. In addition, the new publisher uses current population survey data to create tables that have not been routinely available in the past. New additions include tables covering labor force and employment characteristics of women by education or by family type (indicating the number of children in the family). Data tables are grouped together in chapters by their subject matter, for example, employment or prices. Historical data are provided, but the beginning date varies depending on the subject matter covered.

International Sources

Another important source of statistics is international organizations, most of which are intergovernmental groups (those whose memberships consist of governments). Among the most important are the United Nations, the European Economic Community (formerly the Common Market), the World Bank and the International Monetary Fund (IMF), and the Organisation for Economic Co-operation and Development (OECD). These organizations play important roles in disseminating the economic data needed for the smooth functioning of the world economy. They do not create statistics but instead gather them from various governments, often members of the organization.

Governments provide statistics to these organizations voluntarily. In general, the statistics of the poorer, undeveloped countries are less reliable and less skillfully presented than those of the more economically advanced countries. Timeliness is a major problem. Fortunately, more countries now have the ability to feed data via telecommunication lines into a centralized computer at an organization's headquarters. International agencies, such as the United Nations, experience greater time lags between the date the statistics are generated and their release than does the U.S. government. Timeliness and reliability also vary with the political situation of a country; those undergoing political upheaval might not release statistics for years. Also, as countries do not employ uniform methods of collecting data, comparability of international statistics is limited.

Sometimes librarians and other users searching for statistics on the United States turn to international sources. Not only might the data be in a convenient format, but often the international bodies issuing statistics will manipulate the data, including that of the United States, to enable statistical comparisons among countries. One category of resources that should not be overlooked is statistical abstracts produced by foreign governments (e.g., *Statistical Abstract of Ireland*). These are fundamental sources for economic statistics. Many international organizations use these statistical abstracts to compile statistics for their own publications. Although sometimes difficult to obtain, these abstracts offer unique information, particularly to those doing regional research.

C-45 **Index to International Statistics: IIS**. Washington, DC: Congressional Information Service, 1983- . Monthly with annual cumulations.

International statistics are a major headache for researchers and librarians, who must wade through the hundreds of publications produced by a myriad of organizations. Those fortunate enough to have the above source no longer need to be intimidated by reference queries requiring international statistics. *Index to International Statistics* is another exceptional index published by Congressional Information Service (CIS). Like its sibling indexes *American Statistics Index* (C-31) and *Statistical Reference Index* (C-63), it maintains the high quality standards for which CIS is known. This is the master guide to English-language statistics found in the publications of major intergovernmental organizations such as the United Nations, the World Bank, and the European Economic Community. Statistics can be located by subject, and there is a special heading for "Projections and Forecasts" that the economist will find especially useful. It is possible to look in the subject index under the name of a country or region. Subscribers have the option of purchasing both the index and a corresponding microfiche collection of international publications.

> *Electronic access:* The work is available on CD-ROM as part of *Statistical Masterfile* and as part of the online resource *Statistical Universe*.

United Nations

Established in 1945, the United Nations is the largest and most complex international organization in the world. Its charter calls for the development of friendly relations among nations and the solving of international problems through cooperation. The United Nations and its many affiliate organizations publish numerous research reports and statistical publications and constitute the primary source for international statistics of interest to economists. The best guide to UN statistical publications is the *Index to International Statistics* (C-45), but because many libraries do not own this invaluable source, some of the most popular UN publications are noted below.

C-46 **National Account Statistics: Main Aggregates and Detailed Tables**. New York: United Nations, 1985- . Irregular. Previous titles: *National Income Statistics of Various Countries* (1938–1947), *Statistics of National Income* and *Expenditures* (1952–1957), *Yearbook of National Account Statistics* (1958–1982).

National accounts are the accounting system of a nation: They are a collection of statistics on wages and profits (income), investment and savings (outputs produced), and consumption. These ingredients are often necessary to explain the behavior of a nation's economy. The *National Account Statistics of the United Nations* presents a condensed set of accounts designed to meet the needs of the general user. Each year the Statistical Office of the United Nations sends a national accounts questionnaire to its member countries. Data from these questionnaires are supplemented with data from other national and international sources. Aggregate account data and more detailed data by country are given in U.S. dollars.

C-47 United Nations. Department of International Economic and Social Affairs. **Industrial Commodity Statistics Yearbook**. New York: United Nations, 1967- . Annual.

C-48 United Nations. Department of International Economic and Social Affairs. **International Yearbook of Industrial Statistics**. New York: United Nations, 1995- . Annual. Previous titles: *The Growth of World Industry* (1967–1973), *Yearbook of Industrial Statistics* (1974–1984), *Industrial Statistics Yearbook* (1985–1991).

These two yearbooks present trends on world industrial activity. The *International Yearbook of Industrial Statistics* contains the content of what was formerly known as Volume 1 of the *Industrial Statistics Yearbook: General Industrial Statistics*. It provides information on industrial activity by country, encompassing data on number of establishments, employment, wages, investments, and the like. Production and employment indexes have been compiled by geographic regions and categories of countries. The *Industrial Commodity Statistics Yearbook*, formerly Volume 2, *Commodity Production Statistics*, presents production information by country and world region.

C-49 United Nations. Department of International Economic and Social Affairs. **International Trade Statistics Yearbook**. 2 vols. New York: United Nations, 1950- . Annual.

This is probably the most complete source available on international trade, which is of major importance to the world economy. The first volume, *Trade by Country*, presents trade data for nearly 160 countries and regions. Included are summary statistics, many covering twenty-five years, plus statistics on imports and exports by commodity and principal trading countries. Special tables are included in each annual on topics such as trends in international trade and trade among developing nations. Volume 2, *Trade by Commodity*, is devoted to tables showing total world trade of certain commodities arranged by country and region. Also included are price indexes for various commodities. All statistics are arranged by the Standard International Trade Classification (SITC). This title is also available as a machine-readable file.

C-50 United Nations. Department of International Economic and Social Affairs. **World Economic and Social Survey**. New York: United Nations, 1994- . Annual. Previous titles: *World Economic Report* (1947–1954), *World Economic Survey* (1955–1993).

One of the first sources to provide a comprehensive overview of the world economy, *World Economic and Social Survey's* objective is to identify economic issues that require attention and action by the world community. It is one the oldest publications of the United Nations and was the result of a General Assembly resolution that directed the Secretary General to "provide factual surveys and analyses of world economic conditions and trends." Each annual issue includes statistical charts and tables, plus chapters that analyze topics at the forefront of international discussions. The text is clearly written and will be of interest to nearly everyone in the social sciences.

Food and Agriculture Organization (FAO)

Established in 1945, the FAO became the first specialized agency of the United Nations after its founding. The FAO's mandate is to fight hunger and malnutrition. It does this by improving the production and distribution of food and other agricultural commodities, especially in developing nations. The data collected by this agency are especially important to economists, as agriculture still constitutes a major sector of the national product of most nations.

C-51 United Nations. Food and Agricultural Organization. **FAO Yearbook**. Vol. 1: **Production**. Vol. 2: **Commerce**. Rome: Food and Agriculture Organization, 1946- . Annual.

Production is a statistical summary of world and regional agricultural production. It has tables on crop and livestock production, land use, food supply, and use of farm machinery and pesticides for 158 countries. Special indexes of food production have been designed for comparability among countries. A special section on worldwide agricultural prices is in U.S. dollars. The text is in French,

Spanish, and English. *Commerce* (formerly known as the *Trade Yearbook*) is a worldwide summary of agricultural trade. Import and export statistics by country are provided for 128 agricultural commodities. The value of agricultural trade is included for selected countries. Special trade indexes allow comparability among economic regions. A nice feature is a ten-year chart of exchange rates in equivalent U.S. dollars.

> *Electronic access:* FAOSTAT provides online access to time series data from the various yearbook volumes. Small amounts of data are freely available, but a subscription is required for larger downloads. Data can also be downloaded as a comma delimited file (compatible with Excel and other spreadsheet programs).

International Labour Organization (ILO)

The ILO has been a specialized agency of the United Nations since 1946, although it was originally founded in 1919. Winner of the 1969 Nobel Peace Prize, the ILO has a mandate to promote satisfactory work and pay conditions and adequate employment opportunities. To meet this end, the ILO is active in research and in publishing on social and labor matters.

C-52 International Labour Organization. **Year Book of Labour Statistics**. Geneva: International Labour Office, 1935- . Annual.

The primary source for basic labor statistics for more than 180 countries, this publication includes data on active populations (i.e., those actively contributing to an economy by the production of goods and services), hours, wages, occupational injuries, industrial disputes, and consumer prices. Most charts are broken down by specific industries and occupational groups, and when available, cover ten years of data. The text is in English, French, and Spanish. The monthly *Bulletin of Labor Statistics* provides quarterly, monthly, and semiannual updates to the *Year Book*. Occasionally, special articles relating to labor statistics and their methodologies are published in the *Bulletin*.

International Monetary Fund (IMF)

Established in 1945, the IMF is affiliated with the United Nations and provides funds to member nations as needed. One of its major objectives is to assure free trade in the world, and it often offers credit to nations with balance of payment problems. Approximately 175 nations belong, and those that are the most economically stable contribute the most support and also have the most decision-making power. The reference sources produced by the IMF are noted for their timeliness, accuracy, and detail. The data collected usually come from member countries, supplemented by data from other published sources. To allow for comparisons, the data are sometimes rearranged to make them conform to the data of other countries. Sources published by the IMF are not for the novice, as they require specialized knowledge of economic statistics and terminology. Users should consult the extensive introductory material in the front of each source for additional information. The following IMP publications are also available in digital format.

C-53 **International Financial Statistics**. Washington, DC: International Monetary Fund, 1948- . Monthly with *Yearbook*.

International Financial Statistics is the principal publication of the IMF. Several pages of major economic measures are provided for member countries plus some other countries and territories. The first part of each issue is devoted to world and regional tables, compiled from data drawn from the country pages. For each country, seven years of data are given for exchange rates, liquidity, banking and money, interest, prices and production, imports and exports, and national accounts. This is a detailed, complex work. Users should be reminded to consult the introduction and the explanatory notes found on the country pages. The annual *Yearbook* provides the same data, but summarized over a thirty-five-year period. All information is in French, Spanish, and English.

Electronic access: Also available in CD-ROM and tape formats.

C-54 **Balance of Payments Statistics**. Washington, DC: International Monetary Fund, 1947- . Monthly with *Yearbook*.

"Balance of payments" means, quite simply, the amount of money flowing in and out of a country. These transactions can be based on the movements of goods and services, currency, gold shipments, investments, and the like. A country's handling of its debits and credits is an indicator of its economic health. For this publication, the IMF collects data from its member countries, supplemented by other sources. The monthly issues include aggregate data for countries reporting revised or additional data, which means that the countries included in the monthly issues vary from month to month. The *Yearbook* contains eight years of aggregate data for each of the 140 nations. Included is information on the sources of the data and an explanation of terminology. The second part of the *Yearbook* gives aggregate data for regions, such as the Middle East, and for categories, such as developing or industrialized nations. The first page of each monthly issue is a guide to the latest data available for each country, which can differ widely.

C-55 **Direction of Trade Statistics**. Washington, DC: International Monetary Fund, 1981- . Monthly with *Yearbook*.

This source provides import and export data for more than 135 countries. The data are listed by trading partners, so one can look up the volume of trade between, for example, Gabon and Italy. This reference tool only gives information on the dollar values of trade, not on the commodities traded. The countries represented account for 80 to 85 percent of the world's imports and exports. Import-export data are also aggregated by geographical divisions and categories of countries (e.g., industrial, developing). All trade volume is given in U.S. dollars. The *Yearbook* provides detailed data on 160 countries for the most recent seven years.

C-56 **Government Finance Statistics Yearbook**. Washington, DC: International Monetary Fund, 1977- . Annual.

This yearbook supplies detailed data on the financial operations of the central and consolidated governments of IMF member nations. Data on revenue, expenditure, lending, financing, and debt are provided for each country's central governments and for its consolidated government, which includes its central, state, and local governments and supranational authorities. To facilitate comparisons among countries, world tables by subject are provided in the front of each volume. An example of a comparison that can be made from the world tables is the percentage of a country's budget that is spent on health versus education.

C-57 **World Economic Outlook: A Survey by the Staff of the International Monetary Fund**. Washington, DC: International Monetary Fund, 1980- . Biannual.

Economists and policy makers are consistently concerned with economic trends and projections. Because of the volatility of economics in the world economy, projections are rarely available for more than five years. This source, which provides both short-term (one-year) and medium-term (four-year) forecasts, is widely used and is based on the respected research activities of the IMF. Most of the survey is narrative, with integrated statistical charts and graphs; a statistical appendix incorporates the projections.

Organisation for Economic Co-operation and Development (OECD)

The Organisation for European Economic Cooperation (OEEC) was established in 1948 to assist the Marshall Plan with the European Recovery Program. It changed its name to the Organisation for Economic Co-operation and Development in 1961. There are twenty-four members of OECD, all industrialized democracies, including the United States, France, Great Britain, Australia, and Canada. The mission of the OECD is to coordinate the economic, trade, and social policies of its member nations and to promote the development of the world economy. Increasingly, the OECD is playing a role in providing economic assistance to developing nations. Economists carefully watch the OECD; its members countries are economically powerful, and developments in these countries often determine the course of the world economy.

An online resource that will provide access to the periodicals and statistics produced by the OECD is currently under development. Monitor the *Source OECD* Web site at http://www.sourceoecd.org for online access to these useful publications.

C-58 Organisation for Economic Co-operation and Development. **OECD Economic Outlook**. Paris: OECD, 1967- . Semiannual.

This popular source provides the economic trends and short-term projections for the economies of OECD countries. Many charts and graphs are included, and the title sometimes includes special studies of interest to economists. An annex titled "Reference Statistics" supplies up to twenty years of economic indicators.

C-59 Organisation for Economic Co-operation and Development. **Main Economic Indicators**. Paris: OECD, 1962- . Monthly.

Economic and financial statistics are given in both tabular and graphical form for OECD countries. A companion publication, *Sources and Methods*, contains descriptive notes on how each country compiles its economic indicators and indicates to what extent comparisons can be made among member countries. Periodically, the statistics are summarized in *Main Economic Indicators: Historical Statistics*.

C-60 Organisation for Economic Co-operation and Development. **National Accounts**. Paris: OECD, 1950- . Annual.

This information is compiled according to the joint United Nations-OECD System of National Accounts. Provided are data on production and public and private consumption for each OECD country, plus aggregate information that allows for comparisons.

C-61 Organisation for Economic Co-operation and Development. **OECD Economic Surveys**. Paris: OECD, 1953- . Annual.

Each year, a separate economic review is produced for each country that is a member of the OECD. These handy guides cover trends, economic policies, and short-term forecasts for industry and finance. Each volume concludes with a statistical annex and a chronology of major economic events for the preceding year. Of note is a foldout insert in each volume that facilitates comparisons of basic economic indicators among the member nations.

World Bank

The countries that are members of the World Bank (which is officially the union of the International Bank for Reconstruction and Development and the International Development Association) are also members of the International Monetary Fund. The World Bank was originally concerned with the reconstruction of Europe after World War II but has now turned its efforts to the economic development of nations, especially those in the Third World. Its primary purpose is to make loans to government and private enterprises to foster development.

C-62 **World Development Report**. New York: Oxford University Press for World Bank, 1978- . Annual.

This has become a very popular source, especially as there is an increased emphasis on development studies. Much of the *World Development Report* is a discussion of the state of the world economy and the prospects for the next decade. Recent volumes are devoted to important discussion issues: The 1992 volume covers environmental issues, and the 1993 volume explores investing in health. An invaluable appendix, "World Development Indicators," allows researchers to compare the economies of low-income, middle-income, and high-income economies. *World Development Report* and other World Bank publications are notable for their readability and successful integration of text, graphics, and statistics.

State and Private Sources

For years the U.S. federal government advocated having the private sector assume some of the statistical tasks originally handled by the federal government. Although this might sound good in theory, it did not work well because the private sector does not have the resources necessary to design surveys and mount nationwide campaigns to collect statistics. Only the federal government has the money, the network, and the legal clout to attempt this type of work.

There are a few good private groups that collect, publish, and manipulate economic data, although on a more limited scope than the government and international organizations. Three of the best are the National Conference Board, the Survey Research Center at the University of Michigan, and the National Bureau of Economic Research. Two other prestigious groups that issue forecasts and projections on various aspects of the economy are the National Planning Association and the Wharton Econometric Model. Some of the private sources take readily available information and manipulate and display it in unique and convenient ways.

In addition, state governments, like the federal government, also collect and publish economic statistics. Some are sent to the federal government to be aggregated; others are published under separate titles.

C-63 **Statistical Reference Index**. Bethesda, MD: Congressional Information Service, 1980- . Monthly with annual cumulations.

A sibling of *American Statistics Index* (C-31) and the *Index to International Statistics* (C-45), this is an excellent guide to statistics published by states and by private and independent groups. Much of the information is not indexed elsewhere.

Electronic access: This title is available on CD-ROM as part of the *Statistical Masterfile*.

C-64 United States. Department of Commerce. Bureau of the Census. **Guide to State Statistical Abstracts**. 2000- . Online format. URL: http://www.census.gov /statab/www/stateabs.html.

This online bibliography lists the most recent statistical abstract (or its equivalent) for each state. Publisher contact information is provided, as well as links to Web sites often containing statistical tables from the abstracts. The availability of online content varies by state.

NOTES

1. Adam Smith, *An Inquiry into the Nature and Causes of the Wealth of Nations* (London: W. Strahan and T. Cadell, 1776).

2. John Maynard Keynes, *The General Theory of Employment, Interest and Money* (New York: Harcourt, Brace, 1936).

3. Robert M. Solow, "Review of *The New Palgrave*, edited by John Eatwell et al.," *New York Times Book Review,* March 20, 1988, 25.

4. Amanda Bennett, "An Economist Investigates the Irrationality of People," *Wall Street Journal,* July 29, 1994, 1(B).

5. Robert Eisner, *The Misunderstood Economy: What Counts and How to Count It* (Boston: Harvard Business School Press, 1994).

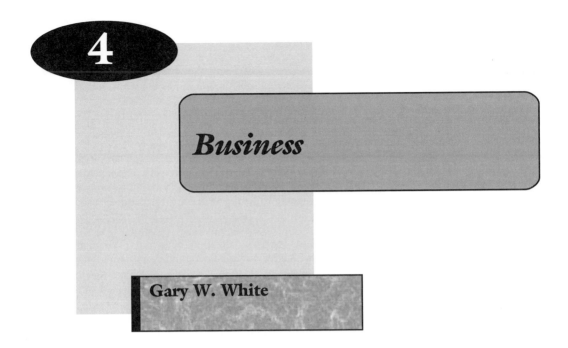

4

Business

Gary W. White

ESSAY

Business administration and closely related disciplines probably generate more information sources that any other area in the social sciences. The demand by the business community for an array of types of information has driven the publication of print and electronic business resources to an all-time high. There are several recent trends that contribute to the need for data for a variety of purposes.

The United States experienced an unprecedented economic boom during the last ten years. Beginning in 1991, the U.S. economy enjoyed continued economic growth, lower inflation, and lower unemployment. In fact, consumer inflation in 1999 was only 1.9 percent, the lowest in thirty-four years,[1] and unemployment in November 2000 was below 4 percent.[2] The tremendous stock market boom was at the same time a significant cause of this prosperity as well as a reflection of the economic strength of the United States. As of spring 2000, Federal Reserve data showed that nearly 50 million households, roughly one-half of the United States, now have investments in the stock market. The corresponding growth of online trading and day trading is also significant. A recent report by Forrester Research showed that 26 percent of Americans trade stock online.[3] There has been a correspondingly high demand for information related to investing and other areas of business, such as company or industry information and news, as more and more Americans entered the stock market.

The business downturn that began in late 2000 and has extended into 2002 has brought a new urgency to the demand for business information, economic intelligence, and new paradigms of management.

The rise of the Internet during the 1990 revolutionized the world. In libraries, it changed the very core of information delivery. Business-related informational sites constitute a huge portion of the Internet. In addition to "democratizing investing,"[4] because information is now readily accessible to everyone, the Internet also allows users unlimited potential in the search for information. The myriad of resources can, however, make these searches difficult. Other technological developments, especially those dealing with networking and communicating, further change how businesses operate and the nature of the informational needs of those seeking business information. The other impact of the Internet is the rise of Web-based businesses, or electronic commerce. E-commerce related ventures have contributed to the huge increases in the stock market as well as fundamentally changing how businesses operate and generate revenues. These trends, again, affect the need for informational resources in a variety of formats, especially electronic. To illustrate the impact of the Internet, one writer suggests that things are changing so fast that one business calendar year equals seven Internet business years.[5]

The other major trend of the last decade is the globalization of business. The breakdown of political systems in some countries, coupled with advances in telecommunications and the Internet, have allowed companies to enter new markets at an unforeseen pace. The downside is that the United States is now affected by events in other countries, such as the Asian financial crisis of 1997–1998.[6] In terms of business information needs, globalization of business has created a growing demand for country information, market research, political and economic risk, and demographic data. An awareness of these ongoing trends is important in using and interpreting business information resources. In addition, the value of information is readily apparent to companies operating in today's global environment. The ability to obtain and apply current information is directly tied to the ability to survive and succeed. The rapid growth and changing nature of business information products reflect this demand.

Functional Areas of Business

A basic understanding of the major functional areas of business is important in the provision of effective business reference services. The more knowledge one has about each of these areas, the more one increases the understanding of reference queries as well as the ability to locate appropriate sources of information. A summary of the scope of each function, including examples of typical information, follows.

Accounting is the basic system used to record and report data related to the operations and events that affect a company. Accounting data can be used by the management of an organization to plan, make strategic decisions, budget, and track performance. Accounting data are also useful to outside parties, including investors, creditors, and regulatory agencies. The financial data reported by a company provide a measure of the profitability as exemplified by the *income statement*, which describes earnings or profits, and the *balance sheet*, which summarizes assets, liabilities, and shareholder equity. *Financial accounting* is sometimes referred to as the branch of accounting that provides those outside the organization with information, while *managerial accounting* refers to accounting data used by the owners and employees of a business.

Generally Accepted Accounting Principles (GAAP) are the rules and procedures used to record and report financial information. The Financial Accounting Standards Board (FASB) is an independent, nonprofit organization that is the primary body determining financial accounting standards in the United States through the creation of new or modification of existing accounting principles. The main purpose of GAAP is to ensure that financial reporting is a uniform process allowing fair evaluation of financial activities over time. Reference works related to GAAP and FASB are covered in this chapter.

Finance is the field of business concerned with maximizing shareholder wealth through the effective management and use of various competing financial resources. Finance encompasses several basic components. *Capital budgeting* is an area of finance concerned with the cost of capital and the valuation of assets. The second area is *corporate finance*, which involves the study of finance as it relates to the individual firm. Included are such topics as making investments, acquiring capital, and managing daily cash flow. *Money, banking and financial instruments*, including stocks, bonds, and treasury securities, make up the third branch of finance.

Management refers to the coordination of all of an organization's resources, including fixed assets such as property, financial, information resources, and human resources to meet the goals of the organization. Coordination of resources is achieved through planning, acquiring resources, organizing or allocating resources, and controlling. Over the years there have been numerous schools of thought and theories related to management. The most comprehensive definition views management as the integrative process by which individuals create, maintain, and operate an organization through the selection of a set of goals. The discipline is firmly grounded in the behavioral and social sciences, and information seeking in management reflects interest in research on topics such as strategic planning, motivation, job satisfaction, leadership, and knowledge management.

Marketing is the business function concerned with getting the firm's goods or services into the hands of the customer. It includes such activities as product life cycle decisions (including new product information), consumer behavior, pricing, distribution, branding, selling, advertising, and public relations. The four variables that a company can control are known as the four Ps: product, place, promotion, and price. Market research may be the most information-intensive activity of the organization because it is the attempt to uncover critical factors related to new product development, target markets, competitor activities, size and characteristics of the market, pricing, and advertising. Most good market researchers are familiar with standard business reference materials that may provide information on topics ranging from the disposable income of households in a particular geographic location to the amount of money a competitor is spending on advertising. The section of this chapter entitled "Marketing, Demographics, and Advertising" covers the standard marketing reference materials.

Information is a key commodity that is crucial to the success of a company. However, it typically is not segmented into the various functional areas described above. Rather, information from these areas is integrated and viewed as a strategic resource essential to the entire organization. A single piece of information may be of use to those in various departments and levels of the organization. For example, demographic or economic data will be of interest to managers as well as those in product development and advertising.

Primary Versus Secondary Information

We have already discussed the concept of information as a central, strategic commodity. Information can be further classified as either primary or secondary. Primary data are collected to fill a specific research need. For example, to solve a particular problem or answer some specific questions, a company may decide to collect data through a market research survey or by conducting an experiment. Secondary data consist of information that is collected for purposes other than the research need at hand. Internal secondary data are available within the organization in such sources as accounting statements, sales records, or other information on a company's intranet. External secondary data are gathered from sources outside the organization, such as suppliers, competitors, customers, and libraries. If a company examines its sales records to gather demographic data about its customers, it is engaged in an examination of internal secondary information. If the same firm decided to conduct a literature search for information on consumers of products similar to their own, this material would also constitute external secondary data. The company is making use of data gathered by someone outside the company for reasons that are related to the company's information need but were not specifically gathered for that company. This chapter deals exclusively with external secondary data sources available in business libraries.

Key Business Research Concepts

Public and Private Companies

All companies are classified as either public or private. The differences between private and public companies have an enormous impact on the types of information that a company is required to disclose and that which is made available to the public. Privately owned companies are established either by an individual (single proprietorship), a small group of individuals (partnership), or a larger group of investors (closely held). The funds that are used to establish and operate private companies have been invested by individuals who hope to gain some profit from their investment. Because the company is wholly owned by these individuals, there are limited legal disclosure requirements. Laws governing corporations vary from state to state. Therefore, it is very difficult or impossible to find out what the earned income of the local corner store or gas station has been for the past year. The privately owned firm is simply not required to disclose any financial information to the public, so it usually does not.

Publicly owned firms are companies that are owned by shareholders. The Securities Act of 1933 and the Securities and Exchange Act of 1934 were enacted to oversee the formation and operations of publicly traded corporations, to protect the public from investor fraud, and to require that vital information be provided for public inspection. Public companies therefore publish annual and quarterly reports (among others) that contain financial statements that have been verified for accuracy by major accounting firms. The U.S. Securities and Exchange Commission (SEC) was established to provide oversight and to ensure that disclosure standards are followed by each publicly owned firm. Information from publicly traded companies is available to the general public and is therefore far easier to locate. Information supplied to the SEC is used to create many standard business reference sources.

When conducting company research, the first step must always be to establish whether a firm is public or private. If it is public and traded on one of the stock exchanges or over-the-counter (a computerized network of security dealers), it will always be possible to gather financial information about that company. The major stock exchange in the United States is the New York Stock Exchange and the major over-the-counter is the NASDAQ (National Association of Securities Dealers Automated Quotation system). There is also likely to be considerable commentary on the company's prospects or performance provided by analysts and the business press. Researchers can thus find information through annual reports and other SEC filings or through indexing and abstracting services covering the business literature. Sources are described more fully in this chapter under the "Company Information" and "Indexing, Abstracting, and Full-Text" sections.

On the other hand, finding information on the privately owned local company will require completely different tactics. It may be necessary to interview suppliers, competitors, or customers to begin to assess its financial health. Frequently one must rely on industry data as the only reliable secondary-source information available in published format. One other point to bear in mind is that some companies (e.g., banks, public utilities, insurance companies) belong to industries that are regulated by state or federal government agencies. Sometimes these companies are private or subsidiaries of other companies and are not selling stock on the open market. However, they are still required to disclose financial information. A number of the standard business directories listed in this chapter enable the researcher to determine the legal status of a company.

Corporate Parents, Subsidiaries, and Affiliates

Research on public companies can be confusing because a large company can be a parent company (a company that owns or controls another company); a subsidiary (a company owned or controlled by another company, i.e., the parent company); or an affiliate (a company that has an owner at less than 50 percent). Sometimes researchers are also interested in specific divisions or internal units of a company, or joint ventures, which are businesses in which two or more companies share ownership.

The huge number of mergers and acquisitions over the past decade has had a major impact on the strategy a researcher must use to locate information on a firm. The concept of parent and subsidiary is important with regard to public companies because such companies are legally required to disclose financial information at the parent level. This means that it is sometimes difficult to determine the exact financial status of a subsidiary corporation or to determine how subsidiary performance is affecting the corporation's overall performance.

Although parent companies are not required to report the segment income of their subsidiaries, many frequently do. The important point to bear in mind is that the information search must initially focus on the parent company if one is attempting to find information about a company that is a subsidiary of another. This chapter presents a number of reference tools that can assist in determining parent and subsidiary relationships as well as other business relationships between companies.

Industries

An industry is a group of companies that are involved in the same type of business. For example, American Airlines and United Airlines are both companies that operate in the air transportation industry. When conducting research on a company, it is also important to gather information on the industry in which it operates. Industry research provides insight into the performance of the specific company in relation to the other companies in the industry. Until recently, industries were classified by a system known as the Standard Industrial Classification (SIC) system. This system, developed by the Office of Management and Budget of the U.S. federal government, assigns four-digit codes to each industry. This system, in place for over fifty years, has recently been replaced with the North American Industrial Classification System (NAICS). The six-digit NAICS code will provide more specific industry classifications. In addition, NAICS includes over 350 industries, including many service and technology industries, not classified by SIC. The "Industry" section of this chapter covers the SIC and NAICS systems in more detail and covers the standard reference sources for conducting industry research.

Business Periodical Literature

For those conducting research, it is critical to have an understanding of the distinctions among trade, popular, and scholarly journals. *Trade* journals are typically published for a specific industry and are produced primarily for practitioners in that industry. Many trade journals are published by professional trade associations for a particular industry. Examples are *Advertising Age*, *Air Transport World*, *Supermarket News*, and *Chemical Week*. Many of these journals publish important information about the industry that may be difficult to locate elsewhere.

Popular business titles are those titles available at newsstands. They are aimed at a mass audience and are typically distributed on a national basis. These titles provide coverage of the major events and trends affecting businesses, as well as articles on specific companies or individuals. Examples are *Business Week*, *Forbes*, *Fortune*, *Inc.*, and *Money*. Many of these titles publish reference information, such as the *Fortune 500* or *Business Week*'s ranking of business schools.

Scholarly publications contain articles that report on the findings of researchers typically affiliated with universities, colleges, or research centers. The articles in these journals tend to be used more by academic researchers than by practitioners, although the findings often have an impact on the business world. Examples of some well-known scholarly titles are *Academy of Management Journal*, *Administrative Science Quarterly*, *California Management Review*, *Harvard Business Review*, *Sloan Management Review*, *Journal of Accountancy*, *Journal of Marketing Research*, *Journal of Finance*, and *Management Review*. Several sources included in this chapter provide descriptions of titles as well as core titles for business collections.

Timeliness of information is essential to meet the needs of researchers and those in the business community. An awareness of the scope and structure of the business periodical literature is necessary to have a good overview of how to conduct research and find information. The indexing and abstracting services section of this chapter are important tools to navigate the business periodical literature.

In organizing and outlining the most important guides, handbooks, encyclopedias, directories, and other reference sources, arrangement can be either by format (e.g., handbook) or by type (e.g., company information). However, business information sources generally fall into both types of categories. Thus, this chapter is arranged in a dual fashion. The result is that users will have a good overview of major business reference sources by type and by format. However, sources are not duplicated.

The sources presented in this chapter will provide the business researcher with a good overview of the basic business reference sources that are found in most libraries. A familiarity with these sources and the information they provide will aid any librarian serving those with business-related questions.

GUIDES AND HANDBOOKS

There are a number of useful reference guides and handbooks that can be used to guide researchers to appropriate business reference sources to find information on specific topics. These guides and handbooks typically provide descriptions of appropriate resources that can be used to obtain answers to specific business reference questions. The following titles are representative of the tremendous number of business reference tools available.

D-1 Woy, James, ed. **Encyclopedia of Business Information Sources**. 15th ed. Detroit: Gale, 2002.

This work contains information on over 31,000 resources outlined under more than 1,100 business topics. It includes topical subjects as well as industry-specific subjects. Each subject entry includes sources grouped according to various subheadings as applicable (e.g., general works, almanacs and yearbooks, CD-ROM databases, directories, online databases, Internet databases, statistics sources, trade associations, and periodicals and newsletters). The subject arrangement is the strongest feature of this work, providing a quick list of resources to address business questions. The fifteenth edition is scheduled to be published in 2001. A "Sources Cited" section provides pricing and ordering information. There is also a companion volume (D-2).

D-2 Balachandran, M., ed. **Encyclopedia of Business Information Sources— Europe.** Detroit: Gale, 1994.

D-3 Lavin, Michael R. **Business Information: How to Find It, How to Use It**. 2d ed. Phoenix, AZ: Oryx Press, 1992.

Although the first and second editions were written before the rise in popularity of Web-based resources, this reference source remains an excellent guide to business information sources. Lavin combines descriptive information on the major reference works and databases with well-written explanations of key business concepts. The book contains five sections: an introduction to business information; finding tools such as directories and indexes; information about companies; statistical information (including economic and industry statistics); and special topics, including taxation and accounting, business law, and marketing. Lavin also includes useful title and subject indexes. This book belongs on the bookshelf of every library providing business reference.

D-4 Daniells, Lorna M. **Business Information Sources**. 3d ed. Berkeley: University of California Press, 1993.

Like Lavin's work (see D-3), Daniells's book remains one of the major guides to business reference resources. The third edition (a major revision over the second edition written in 1985) provides a well-written introduction to general business reference works as well as to the major reference texts and journals in the various business disciplines. The book contains twenty-one chapters covering such areas as U.S. business and economic trends, foreign and domestic statistics and economic trends, industry statistics, investment sources, insurance and real estate, and international management. There are also author/title and subject indexes. Daniells's work is more encyclopedic than Lavin's book, but each complements the other. This title should be a standard in all libraries providing business reference service.

D-5 Butler, F. Patrick. **Business Research Sources: A Reference Navigator**. Boston: McGraw-Hill, 1999.

Butler, a professor of international business, has selected 100 top business reference resources in this ready reference guide. The book has fifty chapters with titles consisting of the names of specific reference works or a topical name with a sample reference source. Butler includes traditional business reference sources, reputable business journals, business periodicals and trade publications, and international sources. He also provides sample pages from print resources and lists electronic availability (including CD-ROM) and Web address for the producer of the resource. Although the list of resources is relatively small, this work serves as an up-to-date guide for business ready reference questions. The inclusion of electronic formats and Web addresses is particularly valuable.

D-6 Rasie, Lawrence. **Directory of Business Information**. New York: John Wiley, 1995.

Rasie's work is similar in structure to Gale's *Encyclopedia of Business Information Sources* (D-1), except with a subject rather than an alphabetical arrangement. It is arranged in four major parts: general business sources; the economy, industries, and companies; sources for specific business topics; and states and regions. There is also a listing of larger business libraries. This work is primarily a listing of resources that are available to find information on the given topic. Included are books, reference sources, newspapers and periodicals, electronic resources, and professional associations. Rasie lists addresses and telephone numbers of companies, governmental bodies, and publications. He also provides indexing information for periodicals.

D-7 Schlessinger, Bernard S. **The Basic Business Library: Core Resources**. 3d ed. Phoenix, AZ: Oryz Press, 1995.

This book is divided into three major sections: a core list of printed business reference sources, the literature of business reference and business libraries, and essays on business reference services and sources. The first section includes 200 titles, along with bibliographic information, ordering information, an overview of the authority and scope of the work, and an evaluation. Included are standard indexes, various handbooks and directories, standard packages including Moody's and Standard & Poor's, and newspapers and periodicals. Part two is an annotated bibliography, primarily derived from the library literature. Part three, entitled "Essays," actually contains lists of "best resources" in such areas as online databases and investment resources. This book is invaluable for the nonbusiness librarian or someone just entering the field.

D-8 Pagell, Ruth A., and Michael Halperin. **International Business Information: How to Find It, How to Use It**. 2d ed. Phoenix, AZ: Oryx Press, 1998.

This book is structured very similarly to Lavin's work (D-3). The value of both of these sources is their coverage of the subject background, which is often necessary to fully understand the sources being discussed. There are five parts, including an introductory chapter; seven chapters devoted to finding company information, which includes chapters on accounting standards and practices, directory sources, and international credit information and rankings; four chapters on marketing, marketing research, advertising, and exporting and importing; a section on industrial and economic statistics; and a section on international transactions. This is the definitive guide for international business information.

Each of these titles deserves a place in any library providing business reference services. The *Encyclopedia of Business Information Sources* provides detailed subject access to information, especially industry-specific topics. *Business Information Sources* is a comprehensive work providing information for a wide range of uses. *Business Information: How to Find It, How to Use It* has fewer entries than the *Encyclopedia of Business Information Sources* or *Business Information Sources*, but its explanation of business research methods and concepts is the most comprehensive of the three works. This is similarly true of *International Business Information: How to Find It, How to Use It*. *Business Research Sources* is the most recently published title in this category, and the only title that includes detailed electronic and Web information. Finally, *The Basic Business Library* is valuable as both a descriptive guide and a collection development tool.

ENCYCLOPEDIAS AND DICTIONARIES

Encyclopedias and dictionaries included in this section are meant to supplement those mentioned in previous editions of this book. Except for classics, such as the *New Palgrave Dictionary of Money and Finance*, this section consists primarily of recently published titles. Every basic business library should contain adequate subject dictionaries and encyclopedias for use in handling business ready reference questions.

D-9   Cooper, Cary L., and Chris Argyris, eds. **The Blackwell Encyclopedia of Management**. 12 vols. Cambridge, MA: Blackwell, 1997.

> **The Blackwell Encyclopedic Dictionary of Accounting** (Vol. 1). Edited by Rashad Abdel-Khalik.
>
> **The Blackwell Encyclopedic Dictionary of Strategic Management** (Vol. 2). Edited by Derek F. Channon.
>
> **The Blackwell Encyclopedic Dictionary of Management Information Systems** (Vol. 3). Edited by Gordon B. Davis.
>
> **The Blackwell Encyclopedic Dictionary of Marketing** (Vol. 4). Edited by Barbara R. Lewis and Dale Littler.
>
> **The Blackwell Encyclopedic Dictionary of Managerial Economics** (Vol. 5). Edited by Robert McAuliffe.
>
> **The Blackwell Encyclopedic Dictionary of Organizational Behavior** (Vol. 6). Edited by Nigel Nicholson.
>
> **The Blackwell Encyclopedic Dictionary of International Management** (Vol. 7). Edited by John O'Connell.
>
> **The Blackwell Encyclopedic Dictionary of Finance** (Vol. 8). Edited by Dean Paxson and Douglas Wood.
>
> **The Blackwell Encyclopedic Dictionary of Human Resource Management** (Vol. 9). Edited by Lawrence H. Peters, Charles R. Greer, and Stuart A. Youngblood.
>
> **The Blackwell Encyclopedic Dictionary of Operations Management** (Vol. 10). Edited by Nigel Slack.
>
> **The Blackwell Encyclopedic Dictionary of Business Ethics** (Vol. 11). Edited by Patricia H. Werhane and R. Edward Freeman.
>
> **Index** (Vol. 12). Edited and compiled by Meg Davies, with assistance from Liz Granger and Zeb Korycinski.

The *Blackwell Encyclopedia of Management* provides a comprehensive overview of business concepts. Each entry is typically one to three paragraphs long, although some entries are over a page in length. Each entry also includes a bibliography (when applicable) and author. The index volume contains a listing of entries, cross-references, and author information. The set originally cost about $1,200, but individual volumes can also be purchased. The entries are much shorter than those in the *International Encyclopedia of Business and Management* (D-10), but there are substantially more entries.

D-10   Warner, Malcolm, ed. **International Encyclopedia of Business and Management**. 6 vols. New York: Routledge, 1996.

Unlike the *Blackwell Encyclopedia of Management*, this six-volume set is arranged in a single alphabet across the first five volumes, and the final volume serves as the index. The set contains

500 entries, each of which is about five to eight pages long. Each listing contains a preliminary summary so that users can either get a quick summary or choose to read the entire entry. Each entry also has a bibliography and cross-references. The index volume contains a listing of all entries, cross-reference, authors, and authors' institutional affiliation. Originally the set cost about $1,300. Thomson Financial (which plans a second edition in 2001) offers a similar version in single volumes by topic.

Libraries with a high number of business clients should opt for at least one of the sets described above. They are complementary, but cost may be a prohibitive factor in obtaining both. The need for an encyclopedia with fewer but more extensive entries should be weighed against the need for a set with more terms but shorter definitions.

D-11 Warner, Malcolm, ed. **Regional Encyclopedia of Business and Management**. 4 vols. London: Thomson Learning, 2000.
The four volumes in this set (one each for the Americas, Asia Pacific, Emerging Countries, and Europe) are arranged in three parts. The first is "General Themes," which contains narrative sections on management in the particular geographic region. The second section consists of "Specialized Themes," including information on regional accounting, banking and finance, management, marketing, human resource management, and manufacturing (i.e., "Accounting in Europe"). The final section is "Country Profiles," entitled "Management in . . . (name of country)." Each of these is typically seven to eleven pages long. This set is ideal for those needing international business management information.

D-12 Malonis, Jane A., ed. **Encyclopedia of Business**. 2d ed. 2 vols. Detroit: Gale Group, 2000.
The Gale *Encyclopedia of Business* contains about 700 entries, most of which are one to two pages in length. Each entry contains an overview of the concept, "See also" references, and a bibliography for further reading. Bolded terms within the essays refer to other entries. This two-volume set contains traditional (i.e., accounting, management, marketing) as well as more recent (i.e., Y2K compliance, electronic commerce) concepts. The first volume contains an alphabetical listing of all terms as well as a biographical listing of contributors. The second volume contains an extensive index. At about $400, this set, which is over 2,000 pages in length, is much more affordable than the *Blackwell Encyclopedia of Management* (D-9) or *International Encyclopedia of Business and Management* (D-10).

D-13 Helms, Marilyn M., ed. **Encyclopedia of Management**. 4th ed. Detroit: Gale Group, 2000.
The Gale *Encyclopedia of Management* is presented in exactly the same format as the *Encyclopedia of Business*, except that it consists of 348 entries and is published in a single volume. There are a number of entries on the same topic in both the *Encyclopedia of Business* and *Encyclopedia of Management*, such as "Electronic Commerce," "Balance Sheet," and "Human Resource Management," but each work has a different list of contributors and thus different essays. Librarians should, however, analyze individual needs and resources before purchasing these and similar forthcoming Gale business encyclopedias.

D-14 Cross, Wilbur. **Prentice Hall Encyclopedic Dictionary of Business Terms**. Englewood Cliffs, NJ: Prentice Hall, 1995.
This work consists of two sections: an A to Z section and an essay section. The A to Z section contains over 500 terms with entries ranging in length from a single sentence to a page. The essay section is divided into subject areas: management, resources, procedures and regulations, money, and communications. Each consists of a five- to six-page narrative and a list of key topics that relate to that subject. There are eighteen appendixes, consisting of such items as "Investment Terms and Phrases," "Largest Commercial Banks in the United States," and "Foreign Words and Phrases." A reprint was published in 1999 under the title *Dictionary of Business Terms*.

D-15 Sheimo, Michael, ed. **International Encyclopedia of the Stock Market**. 2 vols. Chicago: Fitzroy Dearborn Publishers, 1999.

This two-volume work contains more than 2,000 entries about regional and world stock markets, including information on the economies of specific countries, individuals, related institutions (brokerage houses, banks), events, historical information, and slang terms. Entries vary in length from a paragraph to several pages and include "See also" references. Volume 1 contains a complete list of entries, and volume 2 contains a narrative appendix on emerging stock markets; a listing of world currencies by country; a country-by-country listing of finance, trade, and banking organizations; and an index. The 2000 Reference Sources Committee of the Collection Development and Evaluation Section of the Reference and User Services Association of ALA selected this as an outstanding reference source for the year.

D-16 Siegel, Joel G. **International Encyclopedia of Technical Analysis**. New York: AMACOM, 2000.

Technical analysis refers to the analysis of data, coupled with personal experience, to predict stock and other securities prices. Its underlying premise is that the past is the best predictor of the future. Entries are arranged alphabetically and range in length from a single sentence to several pages. There is an abundance of graphs and charts as well as an introductory section discussing the topic of technical analysis. There are also appendixes for sources of technical data and subscription charting services. This work is a good resource for difficult reference questions related to the securities markets.

D-17 Madlem, Peter, and Thomas K. Sykes. **International Encyclopedia of Mutual Funds, Closed-End Funds, and REITs**. New York: AMACOM, 2000.

This reference book consists of three separate sections, one each for mutual funds, closed-end funds, and real estate investment trusts. Each contains an introductory section that defines the topic as well as a section on how to invest in each. The sections are not alphabetical but rather have a subject arrangement. Each section also has listings of specific funds or trusts, including information such as telephone numbers, performance over time, and symbols. This guide is useful as a ready reference tool for these securities.

D-18 Newman, Peter, Murray Milgate, and John Eatwell, eds. **New Palgrave Dictionary of Money and Finance**. 3 vols. New York: Stockton Press, 1992.

The *New Palgrave Dictionary of Money and Finance* contains 1,008 entries in three volumes. It is encyclopedic in nature, with each listing typically three to five pages in length. Each entry contains an overview of the topic, a bibliography, and "See also" references. A listing of all entries and a listing of acronyms are given in the first volume. A companion set on economics and law was published in 1998. This work is the definitive source for terminology related to banking and finance.

D-19 Clark, John. **International Dictionary of Insurance and Finance**. Chicago: Fitzroy Dearborn Publishers, 1999.

The preface to this dictionary states that it is intended to provide access to the specialist terms of insurance and general finance. Included are established terms as well as slang terms, acronyms, and newly adopted terms. Most entries are one or two sentences long, and there are some "See" and "See also" references. This is a companion volume to D-20.

D-20 Clark, John. **International Dictionary of Banking and Finance**. Chicago: Fitzroy Dearborn Publishers, 1999.

The preface to this work states that it is intended to provide access to the specialist terms of banking and general finance. The scope and arrangement are identical to its companion volume, the *International Dictionary of Insurance and Finance*. Many of the entries are exactly the same in the two volumes, so buying both volumes may not be necessary for many libraries.

D-21   Collin, P. H., ed. **Dictionary of Business**. 2d ed. Chicago: Fitzroy Dearborn Publishers, 1998.

This dictionary, originally published in 1985 in Great Britain, looks more like a traditional standard dictionary than any other in this section. It is the only one to provide pronunciations, word usage (i.e., adjective, noun), and examples of the term in a sentence. There are several appendixes containing such items as world currency information, sample business letters, and geographic information.

D-22   Statt, David A. **Concise Dictionary of Business Management**. 2d ed. New York: Routledge, 1999.

This work, first published in 1991 as the *Concise Dictionary of Management*, is arranged in a standard A to Z format. Each entry is one sentence to one paragraph long, and there are ample "See" and "See also" references. Although the preface states that up-to-date terms have been added, there are still some obvious omissions, such as "knowledge management," "Y2K," and "electronic commerce."

D-23   Scott, David L. **Wall Street Words: An Essential A to Z Guide for Today's Investor**. rev. ed. Boston: Houghton Mifflin, 1997.

This book, first published in 1988, has been updated with 300 new entries for a total of about 3,900 entries. In this edition, newer investment areas such as derivatives have been addressed. Each entry is typically one to three sentences long, and there are ample examples. Scott also includes "See" and "See also" references where appropriate. There are also eighty-seven tips, written by financial experts, dispersed throughout the book.

D-24   **Elsevier's Dictionary of Financial Terms in English, German, Spanish, French, Italian, and Dutch**. 2d ed. Amsterdam: Elsevier, 1997.

There has been a proliferation of business foreign-language dictionaries over the past few years. This work is a one-stop guide to business terms in six languages. The second edition, containing over 2,800 terms, uses an abbreviation system to denote language under each term. There are also abbreviations for terms that are used in specific countries and for word forms, including abbreviations for masculine, feminine, and neuter words; adverbs; adjectives; and verbs. This work is written from an English perspective, and there are sections for each of the other languages referring back to the main body. This is a useful edition for libraries that may not need individual dictionaries for each of these languages.

D-25   Hussey, R., ed. **Oxford Dictionary of Accounting**. 2d ed. New York: Oxford University Press, 1999.

This pocket dictionary is a great source for those interested in accounting terminology. This work is international in scope, although there is a slant toward the United Kingdom in terms of examples (typically in pounds) and symbols. There are more than 3,500 entries covering all areas of accounting, including financial accounting, management accounting, taxation, corporate finance, and auditing. This inexpensive dictionary is a bargain for those serving accounting clientele.

D-26   Bennett, Peter D., ed. **Dictionary of Marketing Terms**. 2d ed. Chicago: American Marketing Association, 1995.

This work, produced by faculty who are members of the American Marketing Association, is considered the primary dictionary for marketing. There is a list of contributors showing the areas for which they wrote definitions. Each entry indicates the author, and many contain "See also" references. The book also contains an abundance of "See" references and an extensive bibliography. This work is considered the authoritative dictionary for marketing and should be included in reference collections serving clients interested in marketing.

D-27 Gastineau, Gary L., and Mark P. Kritzman. **The Dictionary of Financial Risk Management**. New York: Frank J. Fabozzi Associates, 1999.

Financial risk management refers to the trade-off between risk taking and rewards. This work contains both an overview of the topic as well as an A to Z listing of terms. Each listing is one sentence to a paragraph in length, and there are ample "See" and "See also" references. This specialized dictionary is great for finance, but many of the terms are also covered in more general business dictionaries.

DIRECTORIES

Directories are perhaps the most popular type of ready reference tools for business collections. Various directories serve to provide company information; information about individuals, private organizations, government agencies, and industries; and a variety of other types of business information.

D-28 DesJardins, Dawn Conzett, ed. **Directories in Print**. 18th ed. 2 vols. Detroit: Gale, 2000.

Formerly known as *The Directory of Directories*, this is the most comprehensive reference work for locating directories. This edition contains more than 15,400 entries arranged in twenty-six categories, including such subjects as management, employment, and labor; banking, insurance, and financial services; advertising, marketing, and public relations; and telecommunications and computer science. The directories are all listed in Volume 1; Volume 2 provides several indexes, including alternative formats, subject, and title and keyword. Supplements typically appear between editions. Each entry contains such information as directory title; author or editor; publisher's name, address, and contact information; e-mail and Web addresses; content description; price; and availability in alternative format. This standard and unique source has a place in all reference collections.

D-29 Sheets, Tara E., ed. **Encyclopedia of Associations**. 36th ed. 3 vols. Detroit: Gale, 2000.

The *Encyclopedia of Associations* is the most comprehensive resource for finding information on nearly 23,000 trade and professional organizations. Volume 1, published in three parts, contains the entries themselves as well as a keyword index. Volume 2 contains geographic and executive indexes, and Volume 3 is the supplement. Each entry contains such information as name, address, telephone and fax numbers, e-mail and Web addresses, executives, description, number of members, membership dues, number of staff members, publications, year founded, and meeting dates. There are two companion sets: *Encyclopedia of Associations: International Organizations* and *Encyclopedia of Associations: Regional, State, and Local Organizations*. The *Encyclopedia of Associations* is an invaluable business ready reference tool that should be a part of any reference collection.

Electronic access: All of these publications are available on *Associations Unlimited* in either Web or CD-ROM format.

D-30 **National Trade and Professional Associations of the United States**. 35th ed. New York: Columbia Books, 2000.

The *National Trade and Professional Organizations of the United States* directory is smaller in scope than the *Encyclopedia of Associations* (D-29), listing approximately 7,600 organizations. However, it is more focused because it includes only active, professional associations, and eliminates many categories included in the *Encyclopedia of Associations*, such as fan clubs, sporting, or hobby organizations. This work is arranged alphabetically, and each entry includes name, address, and telephone and fax numbers; Web site; number of members; number of staff; budget; executives; publications; and a historical note. Cross-references are included to track name changes. There are also subject, geographic, budget, executive, and acronym indexes.

D-31 **Ward's Business Directory of U.S. Private and Public Companies**. 8 vols. Detroit: Gale, 2000.

Ward's Business Directory lists approximately 90,000 U.S. companies, about 90 percent of which are private. Volumes 1 through 3 provide company information in a single alphabetical arrangement. Each entry includes company name; address; telephone and fax numbers; sales (or gross billings or operating revenues); whether the company is public, private, a division, a subsidiary, etc.; number of employees; ticker symbol and stock exchange if publicly traded; Web address; SIC (Standard Industrial Classification) and NAICS (North American Industrial Classification System) codes; brief description; and officers' names. Volume 4 is a "special features" and geographic listings volume. Special features include the 1,000 largest publicly and privately held companies, 1,000 largest employers, an analysis of private and public companies by both state and SIC and NAICS codes, and an analysis by revenue per employee of the top 1,000 companies. Volume 5 ranks sales within four-digit SIC codes. Volumes 6 and 7 are state rankings within four-digit SIC codes. Volume 8 is one of the first reference works to include NAICS by providing a national listing by sales within six-digit NAICS codes. There is also a supplement volume.

Electronic access: Ward's Business Directory is available on magnetic tape or diskette, and on the Web as part of Gale's *Business & Company Resource Center*.

D-32 **D&B Million Dollar Directory: America's Leading Public and Private Companies**. 5 vols. Bethlehem, PA: Dun & Bradstreet, 2000.

Dun & Bradstreet has been publishing this authoritative source on company information for more than thirty-five years. Companies listed must meet one of two criteria: either having over $9 million in sales or having 180 or more employees total at a headquarters or single location or 900 or more employees at a location if the company is a branch. The first three volumes of the set list companies in alphabetical order by name. Each listing includes address and telephone number, indication of public or private ownership, SIC code, annual sales volume (if available), number of employees (if available), names and titles of officers, names of directors, and founded/ownership date. Dun & Bradstreet has also begun placing a triangle symbol before publicly held companies and a square symbol before privately held companies, although not all entries contain these symbols. There are two cross-reference volumes: a geographic cross-reference (yellow pages) and an industry cross-reference (blue pages).

Electronic access: The *Million Dollar Directory* is available on CD-ROM and electronically.

D-33 **Standard & Poor's Register of Corporations, Directors, and Executives**. 3 vols. New York: Standard & Poor's, 2000.

Standard & Poor's has been publishing this standard business reference source annually since 1928. The 2000 edition contains information on over 55,000 companies and 70,000 top executives. Volume 1, the corporate listing volume, provides company name, address, telephone number, officers and titles, stock exchange, SIC codes and description of their business, assets or sales, and number of employees. The individual listings volume contains biographical information on directors, officers, and other executives. The index volume contains indexes by SIC, geographic location, corporate family (i.e., subsidiaries, divisions, and affiliates), and obituaries.

Electronic access: The work is available in electronic format, CD-ROM, or on the Web in *Standard & Poor's NetAdvantage*.

D-34 **Directory of Corporate Affiliations**. 5 vols. New Providence, NJ: National Register Publishing, 2000.

The *Directory of Corporate Affiliations* is the most useful directory for quickly determining the divisions, subsidiaries, and joint ventures of a company. Criteria for inclusion of information for U.S. companies are that their revenue must exceed $10 million, they must have substantial assets/ net worth, or they must have more than 300 employees. International companies must have revenues over $50 million. Volumes 1 and 2 are the *Master Index* volumes. Volume 1 contains indexes by company name, brand name, U.S. geographic location, and non-U.S. geographic location. Volume 2 contains indexes by

SIC and by "corporate responsibilities," which is a personnel index. Volume 3 is U.S. public companies; Volume 4 is U.S. private companies; and Volume 5 combines international public and private companies. There are more than 118,000 entries, over 43,000 of which are located outside of the Unites States. Most entries lists name, address, telephone and fax numbers, URL, year founded, stock symbol and exchange (publicly traded companies), revenues, assets and liabilities, net worth, earnings, number of employees, fiscal year ending date, a business description, personnel, directors, and legal agents. Parent companies are followed by listings of divisions, subsidiaries, and joint ventures. Non-U.S. subsidiaries are listed separately. Each subsidiary includes ownership percentages and reporting line.

> *Electronic access:* The *Directory of Corporate Affiliations* is also available in electronic format.

D-35 America's Corporate Families. 3 vols. Bethlehem, PA: Dun & Bradstreet, 2000.

Similar in scope to *Directory of Corporate Affiliations* (D-34) is Dun & Bradstreet's *America's Corporate Families*. The set includes 12,700 "ultimate parent" listings along with information on approximately 75,000 of their subsidiaries, divisions, and affiliates. Volume 1 is an alphabetical listing by ultimate parent. Information includes address, telephone and fax numbers, annual sales, number of employees, ticker symbol and stock exchange, SIC code, description of their business, net worth, number of sites, year founded, officer information, fiscal year end date, and a listing of divisions and subsidiaries. Volume 2 consists of three indexes: an index cross-referencing ultimate parent and subsidiary, division, and branch names; a city and state geographic listing; and an SIC (industry) listing. Volume 3 is a companion volume for international companies. This volume consists of several sections. Section one is an alphabetical cross-reference by ultimate parent, branches, subsidiaries, and divisions. It has two parts, one with U.S. ultimate parent companies and their foreign subsidiaries, and one with foreign ultimate parent companies and their U.S. subsidiaries. Section two is a geographic index, and section three is an industry (SIC) index. This is slightly smaller in scope than *Directory of Corporate Affiliations*, but Dun & Bradstreet provides more indexing.

D-36 Thomas Register of American Manufacturers. 33 vols. New York: Thomas, 2000.

The *Thomas Register*, published annually since 1905/1906, is one of the best-known reference sources. It differs from other directories in that instead of being arranged by company name, it is arranged by the types of products or services offered by the companies included. The 2000 (90th) edition consists of thirty-three volumes covering more than 156,000 companies and including over 62,500 product and service categories. Volumes 1 through 24 consist of an alphabetical arrangement by product or service. Volume 24 also contains a product index and a trademark and brand index. Volumes 25, 26, and 27 are company profiles, and most listings include company address, telephone and fax numbers, e-mail and URL, asset ratings, and company officials' names. Volumes 28 through 33 consist of reproduced catalogs from over 2,000 companies.

> *Electronic access:* The *Thomas Register* is available in electronic format, on CD-ROM, and is available free on the Web with registration.

D-37 CorpTech Directory of Technology Companies. 4 vols. Concord, MA: OneSource Information Services, 2000.

The *CorpTech Directory* contains information on more than 42,000 technology companies in the United States. It covers private companies, emerging companies, and technology-related branches of large companies. Volume 1 is an index volume containing indexes for company name, geographic location, and technology product. There is also a "Who Makes What" index, providing a list of companies that produce certain products. Volumes 2 through 4 contain company profiles. Entries typically include company name, address, telephone and fax numbers, URL, descriptions, sales, percentage of international sales, number of employees, executive names and titles, and SIC and product descriptions. *CorpTech* also indicates whether the number of employees is projected to grow, drop, or remain stable.

> *Electronic access: CorpTech* is available in electronic format, and the Web version is available free with registration.

D-38 **Directory of Multinationals: The World's Top 500 Companies**. 5th ed. 2 vols. London: Waterlow Specialist Information Publishing, 1998.

The *Directory of Multinationals* profiles 500 of the world's largest corporations. Criteria for inclusion are that U.S. sales must exceed $1 billion and overseas sales must exceed $500 million. Data are gathered from annual reports and other company reports. Volume 1 provides a ranking listing company name and sales in U.S. dollars. The remainder of Volume 1 and all of Volume 2 are the company profiles themselves, arranged in alphabetical order by company name. Each entry is about three pages long, and includes address, telephone number, Web site, directors, products and descriptions, corporate history and current situation, a listing of major shareholders, principal subsidiaries and affiliates, and the date the financial year ends. There are also two tables, one a geographical analysis that outlines sales, operating profit, and assets by region (U.S. and non-U.S.) and the other a product analysis table, providing net sales and net profit by product.

D-39 **Directory of Foreign Firms Operating in the United States**. 10th ed. New York: Uniworld Business Publications, 2000.

The latest edition of the *Directory of Foreign Firms Operating in the United States*, the companion to the *Directory of American Firms Operating in Foreign Countries* (D-40), lists over 2,000 foreign firms in sixty-nine countries and more than 4,000 businesses they own in the United States. Part one of the book is an alphabetical listing of firms by country (also listed alphabetically). Each entry includes address, telephone and fax numbers, type of business, CEO name, and number of employees. Part two is an alphabetical listing of all of the foreign firms in part one, providing the country name and page number. Part three is an alphabetical listing of all the American affiliates listed in part one, giving the name, the country in which the parent company is located, and the page number.

D-40 **Directory of American Firms Operating in Foreign Countries**. 15th ed. 3 vols. New York: Uniworld Business Publications, 1999.

This is the companion to the *Directory of Foreign Firms Operating in the United States* (D-39). This edition includes 2,450 U.S. companies, with 30,000 branches, subsidiaries, and affiliates in 190 countries. Volume 1 includes an alphabetical listing of U.S. corporations. Entries include name, address, telephone and fax numbers, CEO name, foreign operations officer, URL, number of employees, description of their business, and a listing of the countries in which they operate. The remainder of Volume 1 and Volumes 2 and 3 consist of an alphabetical index by country name. Entries under each country include the name of the company, address, telephone and fax numbers, URL, and a description of what the company does.

D-41 **American Big Business Directory**. 3 vols. Omaha, NE: American Business Directories, 1999.

The *American Big Business Directory* provides entries on nearly 200,000 companies with 100 or more employees. Volumes 1 and 2 consist of an alphabetical listing of companies. Each entry includes name, address, telephone and fax numbers, primary and secondary SIC, number of employees (within a range), sales figures (within a range), executives' names and titles, number of years in operation (over ten years is indicated with an asterisk), and credit rating. Volume 3 contains several different parts, including an alphabetical listing by state and city; an alphabetical listing by SIC code; a section listing top executives alphabetically by last name; and a "market planning statistics" section, which provides a table of the number of companies with certain numbers of employees (listed in ranges) in each state and employee number ranges within SIC code.

INDEXING, ABSTRACTING, AND FULL-TEXT SERVICES

D-42   **Business Periodicals Index**. New York: H. W. Wilson, 1958- . Monthly, with quarterly and annual updates.

Business Periodicals Index is the first indexing service devoted to business periodical literature. It currently indexes 527 scholarly and trade business titles and is arranged alphabetically by subject, including subject subdivisions. Each listing contains article title, author, periodical title, volume, issue number, page number, and date. A complete list of journals indexed is in the front of each volume. There are different versions of this resource, including *Wilson Business Abstracts* and *Wilson Business Full-Text*. This standard work was the primary source for business information before the rise of full-text electronic resources.

D-43   **ABI/Inform**. Detroit: Bell & Howell, 1971- . Daily. Electronic format.

ABI/Inform is perhaps the largest and best-known business indexing service. It has been published in various electronic formats for approximately twenty years. Currently *ABI/Inform* is available through Bell & Howell's *ProQuest Direct* and various other database aggregators in several varieties, including *ABI/Inform Global*, *ABI/Inform Research*, and *ABI/Inform Select*. The *Global* version currently indexes over 1,500 scholarly and trade titles, the *Research* version has over 1,250 scholarly and trade titles, and the *Select* version has 375 scholarly titles. *ABI/Inform* contains full-text versions of many of the articles included in the database, and *ProQuest Direct* offers some in pdf format. Dates of full-text availability vary title by title. This is the definitive electronic resource for business periodical literature.

D-44   **Business & Industry**. Detroit: Gale Group, 1994- . Daily. Online format.

Business & Industry is produced by Responsive Data Services (now part of the Gale Group). It indexes over 1,000 trade publications and is international in scope. About 60 percent of the articles are available as full text. *TableBase* is a related product, providing tabular data drawn from articles appearing primarily in trade publications. Ninety percent of the articles in *TableBase* are also full text. Responsive Data Services offers packages combining their electronic products.

D-45   **Business Source Premier**. Birmingham, AL: EBSCO, 1990- . Daily. Online format.

Business Source Premier is EBSCO's full-text business database. It includes the full text of more than 1,100 business titles, about 250 of which are currently not available in other databases. Most titles begin in 1990. *Business Source Premier* also includes a company directory of over 200,000 companies.

D-46   **General Business File ASAP**. Detroit: Gale Group, 1980- . Daily. Online format.

Gale offers this database, which is a combination of abstracting/full-text business and trade publications, company information, and investment analysts' reports. The database goes back to 1982, with full text becoming available in the 1990s. Gale also produces an international version.

D-47   **Wall Street Journal Index**. 2 vols. Ann Arbor, MI: University Microfilm International, 1958- . Monthly, with quarterly and annual cumulations. Online format.

The *Wall Street Journal Index* covers the 3-Star Eastern Edition of the *Wall Street Journal*. Published in two parts, which are two separate volumes annually, the *Index* has a corporate news section (*Barron's Index*), which is an index by company and organization name, and a *General News Index*, which indexes by subject. The *Wall Street Journal Index* includes over 8,000 subject headings. Beginning in 1958, the *Index* was published by Dow Jones & Company until 1989. UMI began producing it in 1990.

D-48 **Business NewsBank**. Naples, FL: NewsBank, 1970- . Daily. Online format.
Business NewsBank provides electronic access to over 400 business newspapers. It was available on CD-ROM from 1985 to 1994, and is currently accessed through the Internet. A microfiche set provides access to articles appearing before 1993. *NewsBank* also offers newspaper access for other subject areas.

D-49 **Dow Jones Interactive/Factiva**. New York: Dow Jones/Factiva, dates vary. Continually. Online format.
Dow Jones Interactive, now also known as *Factiva*, is a Web product that contains a full-text library of over 6,000 publications. These include hard-to-find copies of local and regional business publications and global publications. Users can search the entire database or select publications by title, region, or industry. The full-text archive of the *Wall Street Journal* is also available from 1984 to the present. *Dow Jones Interactive* also provides historical market information, including stock prices, and company and industry news and reports. *Factiva* reflects a combination of *Dow Jones Interactive* with *Reuters*.

Lexis-Nexis. **Academic Universe**. Dayton, OH: Lexis-Nexis, dates vary. Continually. Online format. (See F-15)
Academic Universe is Lexis-Nexis's Web database for academic institutions. The business section contains full-text company and industry news, reports, SEC filings, and accounting information. The news section provides full-text access to thousands of regional, national, and international newspapers, magazines, journals, and newswire reports. The legal section has segments on tax, corporate, and labor law as well as patents.

D-50 **PROMPT–Predicasts Overview of Markets & Technology**. Detroit: Gale Group, 1977- . Daily. Online format.
PROMPT has been available in various formats for over twenty years. The database includes comprehensive coverage of companies, products, markets, and technologies from business journals, trade publications, newspapers, and newsletters. It is currently available through InfoTrac Web from Gale.

D-51 **EconLit**. Nashville, TN: American Economics Association, 1969- . Monthly. Online format.
EconLit is the premier electronic indexing service for economic literature. It provides indexing and abstracting for over 400 economics journals as well as articles in collective volumes, books, book reviews, dissertations, and working papers. Coverage is from 1969 to the present, with abstracts from 1987 to the present. The *Journal of Economic Literature*, published by the American Economics Association since 1963, and *Index of Economic Articles in Journals and Collective Volumes*, published by the American Economics Association since 1886, are print counterparts providing indexing services.

D-52 **Accounting & Tax Index**. Ann Arbor, MI: Bell & Howell, 1921- . Quarterly with annual cumulations.
Formerly published as the *Accountants' Index* beginning in 1921 by the American Institute of Accountants (later the AICPA), the *Accounting & Tax Index* is now produced by UMI. The *Accounting & Tax Index* covers more than 1,000 publications. It is available electronically and is part of *ProQuest Direct* from Bell & Howell.

D-53 **Personnel Management Abstracts**. Chelsea, MI: Personnel Management Abstracts, 1955- . Quarterly with annual cumulations.
Personnel Management Abstracts, published since 1955, describes itself as a "guide to the literature of management, human resources, and personnel." It indexes about 100 titles, and arrangement is alphabetical by subject.

COMPANY RESOURCES

Company information is among the most frequently requested business reference questions. Finding current, accurate information about companies, including financial data and personnel information, is important to a wide variety of users, including students, job-seekers, and consumers. This section includes resources that are both popular and of high quality.

D-54 Securities and Exchange Commission (SEC) and EDGAR (Electronic Data Gathering, Analysis, and Retrieval System).

The U.S. Securities and Exchange Commission (SEC) was formed in 1934 as a result of two acts passed by Congress, the Securities Act of 1933 and the Securities Exchange Act of 1934. The SEC was essentially created to monitor the securities industry, to ensure that companies provide truthful information to investors, and to ensure that securities traders treat investors fairly. To fulfill this mission, the SEC requires that publicly traded companies submit filings at regular intervals. These include such well-known filings as annual reports, 10-Ks, 10-Qs (quarterly reports), and proxy statements. The SEC is thus the official repository of company information. SEC filings are also the basis for many business reference publications providing company information. Historically, these filings have only been available through microfiche sets, directly from the SEC, or in modified format from other publishers. *EDGAR* (*Electronic Data Gathering and Retrieval System*) revolutionized the availability and dissemination of SEC filings to the general public.

EDGAR "performs automated collection, validation, indexing, acceptance, and forwarding of submissions by companies and others who are required by law to file forms with the SEC." Companies were phased into *EDGAR* over a three-year period ending May 6, 1996. Beginning in 1994 for selected companies, and for all publicly traded companies after May 1996, users can search and retrieve SEC filings on the Web by logging onto *EDGAR* at http://www.sec.gov. Although *EDGAR* is the most authoritative resource, other companies repackage information into easier-to-use formats. *EDGAR* has also spawned other related sites such as *FreeEDGAR* (http://www.freeedgar.com).

D-55 Moody's (Mergent) Manuals. New York: Mergent FIS.

Moody's (now known as *Mergent FIS*) is, along with *Standard & Poor's*, the most widely recognized source for company information. The *Moody's* service consists of the following:

> *Moody's Bank and Finance Manual*, 1928-
>
> *Moody's Industrial Manual*, 1920-
>
> *Moody's International Manual*, 1981-
>
> *Moody's Municipal and Government Manual*, 1918-
>
> *Moody's OTC Industrial Manual*, 1970-
>
> *Moody's OTC Unlisted Manual*, 1986-
>
> *Moody's Public Utilities Manual*, 1914-
>
> *Moody's Transportation Manual*, 1909-

These eight manuals include information on more than 40,000 U.S. and international corporations; federal, state, and local governments; and financial institutions. Each listing includes a company history (including key dates for mergers and acquisitions), a business description, listing of officers, financial and stock data, income statement, and balance sheet. Arrangement varies somewhat between volumes. For example, the *International Manual* is arranged by country name, the *Municipal and Government Manual* is arranged by state, and the *Bank and Finance Manual* has a subject arrangement. Each of these volumes has an accompanying *News Reports* volume, which is updated weekly. These include items such as dates of earnings reports or SEC filings dates. Each manual is updated annually.

Mergent publishes the *Moody's Complete Corporate Index* to assist users in finding a particular company in one of the eight manuals. This annual index provides a single alphabetical index that lists the manual, volume number, and page number for the listing. Moody's is a great resource for historical company information. Mergent also offers the complete sets on microfiche.

Electronic access: Moody's is also available on CD-ROM and on the Internet through its *FIS Online* product.

D-56 Standard & Poor's Corporation Records. New York: Standard & Poor's, 1915- . 6 vols. Looseleaf with quarterly updates and daily news.

Standard & Poor's (along with *Moody's/Mergent*) is perhaps the best-known company information provider. *Standard & Poor's Corporation Records* are arranged in a single alphabet and are not divided by type as are the *Mergent Manuals*. The set consists of six volumes plus a daily news volume. Each of the six main volumes includes a subsidiary to parent cross-reference section. Although *Standard & Poor's Corporation Records* includes fewer companies than *Mergent*, it is updated on a quarterly rather than an annual basis (as are *Mergent's Manuals*). The news section is updated daily on regular business days. Each listing typically includes a company background, stock data, earnings and finance information (at least three years of data are given for most items), and market capitalization information. Bond descriptions are also listed.

A related volume is *Standard & Poor's Corporation Descriptions* (1941-), a monthly publication. This publication includes earnings report dates, bond ratings, company background, stock data and earnings, and finances.

Electronic access: Standard & Poor's Corporation Records is available in electronic format, on CD-ROM, and on the Internet as part of *Standard & Poor's NetAdvantage*.

D-57 Hoover's Handbooks. Austin, TX: Hoover's Business Press.

Hoover's Handbooks series consists of four titles (outlined below) and an index volume. Although Hoover's Handbooks are less than ten years old, they have quickly become a standard and well-known company information resource. These are handy and inexpensive ready reference guides for basic company information.

Electronic access: Hoover's is also available on CD-ROM and on the Web.

D-58 Hoover's Handbook of American Business. 2 vols. Austin, TX: Hoover's Business Press, 2000.

Hoover's Handbook of American Business, published since 1992, is the oldest component of Hoover's four-part series. The 2000 edition contains profiles of 750 companies, arranged alphabetically in a two-volume set. Each entry is two pages long and includes a company overview, history, a list of officer's names and titles, a list of major locations and sales figures in each, a list of products and operations, a list of competitors, ten years' worth of financials, and ten years of stock prices (in chart format). The first sixty pages of Volume 1 contain numerous ranking lists, such as "300 Most Profitable Companies," "300 Largest Employers," "Top 25 Tax and Accounting Firms," and "Top 20 in CEO Compensation." Volume 2 also contains indexes by industry; headquarters location; and brands, companies, and people named in the profiles.

D-59 Hoover's Handbook of World Business. Austin, TX: Hoover's Business Press, 2000.

This single-volume work contains profiles 300 of the largest non-U.S. based companies. The format is identical to *Hoover's Handbook of American Business* (D-58). There are slightly fewer ranking lists (fifty-six pages), but they are still quite comprehensive and useful. This volume also contains the same indexes listed in D-58.

D-60 **Hoover's Handbook of Private Companies**. Austin, TX: Hoover's Business Press, 2000.

This book is arranged slightly differently than the previous two titles. The majority of the book consists of the two-page entry described in D-59, for 250 privately held companies. In addition, basic information is provided for an additional 520 private companies that have revenues of $650 million or more. These summaries consist of company name, address, and telephone and fax numbers; Web site; major officers; sales; number of employees; a one-paragraph overview; and a list of top three key competitors. There are also twenty-three pages of ranking lists and the same indexes as in D-58 and D-59.

D-61 **Hoover's Handbook of Emerging Companies**. Austin, TX: Hoover's Business Press, 2000.

This final volume in the series is also the smallest. The book consists of 100 profiles, on a single page rather than on two pages as in the other volumes in this series. An additional 400 companies are listed, giving the same basic information that is used in *Hoover's Handbook of Private Companies* (D-60). Companies are selected based on growth (of sales and/or market value). Among the additional 400 companies, all had sales of at least $10 million and have reported at least three years of sales with a sustained growth of at least 100 percent. All of the companies are publicly traded or are projected to soon go public. This volume also contains thirty-one pages of ranking lists and the same indexes as the other volumes.

D-62 **Hoover's Handbook Index**. Austin, TX: Hoover's Business Press, 2000.

Although not part of the four-part series, this is an index to the more than 2,000 companies included in the series. This is essentially a master index by industry type; headquarters location; and brands, company name, and people named in the profiles.

D-63 **International Directory of Company Histories**. 35 vols. Farmington Hills, MI: St. James Press, 1988- . Irregular.

The *International Directory of Company Histories* began publication in 1988 and had grown to thirty-five volumes by 2000. To date, the directory has covered more than 4,550 companies. Companies included in the directory must have at least $50 million in annual sales and be influential in their industries or geographic locations. Ten percent of the entries are for nonprofit or private companies. Each volume profiles approximately 125 companies, and there are updates on approximately 45 companies per volume. Each entry consists of the company's name, address, telephone and fax numbers, URL, whether it's public or private, earliest incorporation date, number of employees, most recent sales figures, and SIC or NAICS (in recent volumes). Ticker symbol and stock exchange are given for publicly traded companies. The narrative text for each entry typically runs from three to five pages in length and is drawn from a variety of sources, including periodicals, books, Internet resources, and annual and other company reports. Each entry in recent volumes also lists a "Company Perspectives" box, which provides a statement of the company's mission and goals, and a "Key Dates" box, which includes important events in the company's history including such items as start date, major acquisitions, dates of product development, and date the company went public. Each entry also provides a bibliography for further reading. This unique and valuable reference source will be useful to anyone seeking company information.

D-64 **Corporate Yellow Book: Who's Who at Leading U.S. Companies**. New York: Leadership Directories, 1992- . Quarterly.

The *Corporate Yellow Book* (this description is based on the summer 2000 edition) profiles more than 1,000 companies and provides details on over 41,000 executives, 9,000 board members, and 6,000 subsidiaries and divisions. The directory is arranged alphabetically by company name. Each listing includes name, address, telephone and fax numbers, URL, number of employees, stock exchange, and ticker symbol. Most entries have a picture of the CEO and include name, title, educational background, and date of birth. Also listed are officers and their education, e-mail address, telephone number, as well as the name, telephone number, and e-mail address of their administrative assistants when available. There is a section for major subsidiaries, divisions, and affiliates that includes the name and contact information for the presidents. Each entry also includes a list of the board of directors and their titles. The company's auditor is also listed. There are indexes for company names and individual names. This is a useful ready reference source for background information on company executives and also a convenient source for finding a company's board of directors and human resource personnel.

Electronic access: The *Corporate Yellow Book* is available on the Internet as part of the *Leadership Library on the Internet.*

D-65 **Disclosure.** New York: Thomson Financial, 1977- . Weekly. Online format.

Disclosure, a Primark/Thomson Financial product, is a well-known electronic company financial and management information resource that offers information derived from SEC filings. The database includes coverage of over 12,000 companies and has been produced in various iterations for many years. Its counterpart, *Worldscope*, provides information on more than 15,000 companies. Both are available in electronic formats, including *Compact D*, *Disclosure Select*, and on the Internet through Primark's *Global Access* product (see "Electronic Databases"). These databases are valuable because users can build queries by entering parameters to retrieve a list of companies that meet the desired characteristics.

INDUSTRY RESOURCES

Industry research is an important corollary to company research. Industry research helps users identify competing firms and find comparative financial data from other firms or to find composite industry data. It also assists in the identification of major trends and serves to assist a wide range of users, including entrepreneurs, investors, and those engaged in strategic planning. Although industry information is also available in some sources covered elsewhere in this chapter (e.g., indexing, abstracting, and full-text sources), this section covers some other basic sources for industry research.

D-66 **Standard Industrial Classification (SIC) Manual.** rev. ed. Washington, DC: Office of Management and Budget, 1987.

The *SIC Manual* provides the foundation for the gathering and dissemination of industry data. The manual provides a numerical classification system by industry type. The classification system was initially developed to allow for the uniform presentation of industry data gathered from various sources. The 1987 edition supersedes the 1972/1977 edition. The SIC is arranged in a hierarchical format, using two-, three-, and four-digit codes, with each level becoming more specific. Each two-digit code represents a major industry group, a three-digit code is an industry-group number, and a four-digit code is the particular type of industry. For example:

Major Group 57—Home Furniture, Furnishings, and Equipment Stores

Industry Group 571—Home Furniture and Furnishings Stores

Industry Group 572—Household and Appliance Stores

Industry Group 573—Radio, Television, Consumer Electronics, and Music Stores

Industry number 5712—Furniture Stores

Industry number 5713—Floor Covering Stores

Industry number 5714—Drapery, Curtain, and Upholstery Stores

SIC Codes have been used for years as a standard coding system by the federal government, including the *Economic Census*, and by numerous business reference sources. The Standard Industrial Classification system has recently been replaced with a new classification system, the North American Industry Classification System (NAICS), although a dual-reporting system is still often used.

D-67 **North American Industry Classification System (NAICS).** Washington, DC: Office of Management and Budget, 1997.

The North American Industrial Classification System (NAICS) replaces the industrial classification systems previously used by the United States, Canada, and Mexico. The need for a revised system was also recognized for several other reasons: new and emerging technologies not reflected in the *SIC Manual*; service industries, a growth area since the 1987 publication of the *SIC Manual* (NAICS includes a sector containing thirty-five industries for professional, scientific, and technical Services); and industries involved with the production of advanced technologies, such as computer hardware and software and telecommunications. There are also new sectors for arts, entertainment, and recreation and for health care and social assistance. NAICS is also a numeric, hierarchical structure, but the final NAICS number is six digits long. The first two digits represent the industry sector, the third designates the subsector, the fourth designates the industry group, the fifth represents the NAICS industry, and the sixth digit designates the national industry (a zero means that the NAICS and U.S. industry are the same). The following example is based on that used in entry D-66:

Sector 44-45—Retail Trade

Subsector 442—Furniture and Home Furnishings Stores

Industry 4422—Home Furnishing Stores

NAICS Industry 44221—Floor Covering Stores

NAICS 442210—Floor Covering Stores

NAICS is used in the 1997 *Economic Census* and is emerging in various business reference sources.

D-68 **U.S. Industry and Trade Outlook.** New York: McGraw-Hill; Washington, DC: U.S. Department of Commerce/International Trade Administration, 2000.

The *U.S. Industry and Trade Outlook*, published annually since 1998, was formerly known as the *U.S. Industrial Outlook*, which was published from 1960 through 1994. This edition includes chapters on fifty-four industries grouped under the following categories: Natural Resources and Energy; Construction and Related Industries; Industrial Materials and Components; Production and Manufacturing Equipment; Information and Communications; the Consumer Economy; Health Care; Financial, Business, and Education Services; and Transportation. Each chapter includes information on industry trends, data, and an industry forecast. Global information is often included. The book also spotlights new technologies and contains general economic data and information. Historically, this is the authoritative source of industry information. The outlook section for each industry is particularly useful.

D-69 **Standard & Poor's Industry Surveys.** New York: Standard & Poor's, July 2000. Weekly or quarterly updates.

Standard & Poor's Industry Surveys, published since 1966, is updated weekly although many libraries receive it in quarterly updates. The July 2000 edition covers fifty-two industries and is published in three volumes. Each of the fifty-two industries is updated twice annually. Arranged alphabetically by name of the industry, each section contains four segments: Current Environment; Industry Profile (includes Industry Trends; How the Industry Works; Key Industry Ratios and Statistics; and How to Analyze a . . . Company); Industry References; and a Comparative Company Analysis. Most reports are over twenty-five pages in length. This publication is one of the best-known and respected sources of industry information.

Electronic access: *Standard & Poor's Industry Surveys* is available on CD-ROM and on the Web through *Standard & Poor's NetAdvantage*.

D-70 **Mergent's (Moody's) Industry Review.** New York: Mergent FIS, 1989- . Biweekly.

Mergent's Industry Review (formerly *Moody's*) is published every two weeks on Friday by FIS (Financial Information Services). More than 130 industries are included, arranged alphabetically by industry name. The information is primarily numerical and includes comparative company statistics and financial data, growth rates, and ratio comparisons. Over 3,500 companies are covered. The lack of narrative industry information makes this somewhat less useful than *Standard & Poor's Industry Surveys* (D-69) or the *U.S. Industry and Trade Outlook* (D-68).

D-71 **Dun & Bradstreet/Gale Industry Reference Handbooks**. Farmington Hills, MI: Gale Group, Volumes 1-7, 1998 to 2000.

Each of these volumes is devoted to specific industries, including computers and software, chemicals and pharmaceuticals, entertainment, hospitality, health and medical services, insurance, and telecommunications/broadcasting. Each contains chapters providing an industry overview, industry statistics, financial norms and ratios, company listings, rankings, mergers and acquisitions, associations, and consultants. These are also appendixes for SIC and NAICS conversions. Much of the content is derived from other Gale and Dun & Bradstreet products.

D-72 Tardiff, Joseph C., ed. **U.S. Industry Profiles: The Leading 100**. 2d ed. Detroit: Gale, 1998.

This reference guide contains profiles of 100 industries or industry groups in the United States, arranged alphabetically by title. Each section contains an industry snapshot; industry outlook; organization and structure of the industry; workforce information; "America and the World," which discusses the industry in the global marketplace; associations and societies; periodicals and newsletters; databases; general print sources; and suggestions for further reading. There are also a variety of graphics and rankings lists throughout the work. The narrative sections of this work are the most useful.

D-73 deJong, Andrea L., ed. **U.S. Market Trends & Forecasts**. Farmington Hills, MI: Gale Group, 1999.

U.S. Market Trends & Forecasts includes coverage of nearly 400 markets arranged by broad categories such as "Apparel," "Computers," and "Food." Each entry includes SIC code, market value and growth rates, information on market segments, market share data, and market forecasts. There are abundant bar and pie charts as well as tables of data. This work does not include a narrative description of the industries.

D-74 Cremeans, John E., ed. **Handbook of North American Industry**. 2d ed. Washington, DC: Bernan Press, 1999.

This is a reference source for industry information in the United States, Mexico, and Canada. Part one focuses on the North American Free Trade Agreement (NAFTA) and the events and policies that led to its implementation. It also contains industry summary data on North America as a whole as well as the individual countries. There are also industry rankings for each of the three countries. Part two contains industry information as defined by SIC codes. Coverage begins with "Products and Processes" and "What's New in . . ." narrative sections. There are also twelve standard tables and four standard figures in each section. Data are derived from governmental sources in the three countries. This important source is valuable in the way it pulls information together from various sources and presents it in an easy-to-use format.

D-75 Marlow-Ferguson, Rebecca, ed. **Encyclopedia of American Industries**. 3d ed. Farmington Hills, MI: Gale Research, 2001.

This two-volume set consists of a volume each devoted to manufacturing and service industries. Volume 1 covers 459 manufacturing industries and volume 2 covers 545 service industries, both of which are arranged by SIC code. Each entry in the third edition contains a description of the industry, NAICS code, an industry snapshot, organization and structure of the industry, historical background and development of the industry, current conditions, industry leaders, number and description of employees, a description of the industry in a global context, and a bibliography of further readings. The volumes also contain both a SIC to NAICS and a NAICS to SIC conversion guide and an index. There are also descriptions of both the SIC and NAICS systems. Each volume contains a foreword outlining both manufacturing and service industries within the U.S. and global economies.

D-76 Heil, Scott, ed. **Encyclopedia of Global Industries**. 2d ed. Farmington Hills, MI: Gale Research, 1999.
The second edition of this work contains coverage of 125 industries with global significance. Organization is under broad categories, which are arranged alphabetically. Each section contains the SIC code, industry snapshot, industry segment information, organization and structure, background and development of the industry, the current condition of the industry, major countries in the industry, and suggestions for further reading. Each section also contains information presented in a graphical format.

D-77 Cindric, Susan J., ed. **Encyclopedia of Emerging Industries**. 3d ed. Farmington Hills, MI: Gale Group, 2000.
This work is similar in format to both the *Encyclopedia of American Industries* and the *Encyclopedia of Global Industries*. Included are 118 growth industries, including 19 new additions to the second edition. Industries are arranged alphabetically, and each contains sections providing an industry snapshot, organization and structure, background and development, pioneers, current conditions, industry leaders, workforce characteristics, information on the global marketplace, research and technology, and suggestions for further reading. This volume has less graphical information than its two counterparts (D-75 and D-76).

INDUSTRY FINANCIAL RATIOS

A key method to analyze a company's performance is to compare its financial information with other companies in the same industry. Although several sources provide direct comparisons between specific companies (e.g., *Standard & Poor's Industry Surveys*), there are also several standard reference sources providing industry-wide financial ratios. These sources allow users to compare the financial information of a specific company to the industry as a whole.

D-78 Troy, Leo. **Almanac of Business & Industrial Financial Ratios**. 32d ed. Englewood Cliffs, NJ: Prentice-Hall, 2000.
Also popularly known as the "Troy Almanac," the *Almanac of Business & Financial Ratios* is arranged by industry name under sixteen broad categories, closely following descriptions used in the *Standard Industrial Classification Manual*. Each industry contains fifty data items arranged into two tables. Table 1 consists of financial information for all corporations with or without net income; Table 2 consists of financial information for corporations with net income. All data are grouped into thirteen categories of asset size, allowing for users to compare a specific company with the industry averages of companies with similar assets. One of these is the total for the entire industry. Data are gathered from tax returns filed with the U.S. Internal Revenue Service. The introductory section contains a listing and description of each item and ratio covered in the work.

D-79 **Industry Norms and Key Business Ratios**. Desk-Top ed. Murray Hill, NJ: Dun & Bradstreet, 1999–2000.
Industry Norms and Key Business Ratios includes over 800 different industries arranged numerically by SIC code. Dun & Bradstreet maintains an internal database of financial information, including public and private companies. Each page contains four columns arranged numerically by SIC. Each column lists the number of establishments from which the averages were derived, balance sheet averages, and ratios. Ratios are divided into three categories: solvency ratios (including quick and current ratios), efficiency ratios (including assets to sales and sales to inventories), and profitability ratios (including return on sales and return on assets). The ratios for each category are listed by

median, upper quartile, and lower quartile. The introduction contains definitions for each ratio and describes how they are calculated. There is also an extremely useful section on how the data should be analyzed and ways to apply the information.

D-80 **RMA Annual Statement Studies**. 1999–2000 ed. Philadelphia: Robert Morris Associates, 1999.

Robert Morris Associates, established in 1914, has published this work in various forms for over 80 years. The 1999–2000 edition includes data on over 575 industries arranged by SIC code. Each industry listing consists of two pages broken into three broad categories: current data sorted by assets, current data sorted by sales, and comparative historical data. The current data categories are broken down into six sections by sales/asset size to allow for better comparisons between similarly sized companies. Data are arranged by balance sheet and income statement items, followed by sixteen financial ratios. Each ratio lists upper quartile, median, and lower quartile. The introductory section explains the layout of the book, provides an explanation of the ratios and how they are computed, and provides a listing of SIC codes included. Robert Morris Associates gathers its data from financial statements provided to its member institutions, consisting primarily of banks and credit institutions. It claims that its data are more current than the information gathered from IRS tax returns.

STATISTICS

This section consists of sources providing statistical information that is primarily business/ economic in nature or has broad application in the business world. More general sources, such as the *Statistical Reference Index* (C-63), *American Statistics Index* (C-31), *Statistics Sources* (A-86), or *Statistical Universe* (A-83), are not included. Also, much of the information contained in print publications produced by the U.S. government is available on the Internet.

D-81 **Census of Population and Housing**. Washington, DC: U.S. Bureau of the Census, 1798- . Decennial.

The information gathered from the *Census of Population and Housing* is too large in scope to be covered adequately in this publication. Therefore, this summary will serve to highlight key pieces of information gathered in the decennial *Census of Population and Housing*. Among the types of data collected are demographic information (age, sex, marital status, etc.), income information, areas of population growth and characteristics of populations by geographic location, household characteristics, and ethnic origin. This information can be used in a variety of business applications, such as targeting market segments, identifying growing areas, finding areas with certain demographics such as income or age, site location decisions, and so forth. As previously mentioned, the *Census* provides information that is used as the basis for many business reference sources. The 2000 *Census of Population and Housing* data will be distributed primarily on the Web. The Bureau of the Census home page is http://www.census.gov.

D-82 **Economic Census**. Washington, DC: U.S. Bureau of the Census, 1954- .

The *Economic Census* is conducted every five years (in years ending in 2 and 7) to collect data on U.S. industries. The 1992 *Economic Census* was issued in seven parts: *Census of Construction Industries, Census of Manufactures, Census of Mineral Industries, Census of Retail Trade, Census of Service Industries, Census of Transportation,* and *Census of Wholesale Trade.* The 1997 *Economic Census* is based on NAICS code (see D-67) with release dates in fall 2000. Data are broken down into eighteen areas, including new areas such as "Information" and "Arts, Entertainment, and Recreation." Each segment contains detailed information on the industry covered, including geographic breakdowns. The 1997 *Economic Census* is available through the Internet (http://www.census.gov/epcd /www/econ97.html) or on CD-ROM. Only summary information will be available in print. The *Economic Census* is the most authoritative source for industry information, and it serves as the basis for many business reference sources, which repackage its data.

D-83 **CenStats**. Washington, DC: U.S. Bureau of the Census, 1990- . Updates vary by database. Online format. URL: http://tier2.census.gov/dbappweb.htm.

CenStats provides Web access to a number of *Census* publications and data items, including the *Annual Survey of Manufactures; Building Permit Data; Census Tract Street Locator; Consolidated Federal Funds Report*; *County Business Patterns*; *International Trade Data*; *Detailed Occupation by Race, Hispanic Origin and Sex; USA Counties*; and *Zip Code Business Patterns*.

Statistical Abstract of the United States. Washington, DC: U.S. Bureau of the Census, 1878- . Annual.

The *Statistical Abstract* is perhaps the most important statistical source. Each volume provides current and some historical data. Arrangement is under broad categories such as "Population," "Labor Force, Employment, and Earnings;" and "Business Enterprise." Although the *Statistical Abstract* covers all subject areas, information related to business makes up a large portion of the work. Tables of data are given a number, which is used in the subject index in the rear of the book. This inexpensive work is one title that belongs on every reference bookshelf. Users interested in longer time series of data can consult *Business Statistics of the United States* (D-84).

Electronic access: It is available on CD-ROM; a limited edition is available free on the Web at http://www.census.gov/prod/www/statistical-abstract-us.html.

D-84 **Business Statistics of the United States**. Lanham, MD: Bernan Press, 1951- . Annual.

Business Statistics originally was published by the U.S. Commerce Department's Bureau of Economic Analysis as a biennial supplement to the *Survey of Current Business*. From 1951 through 1992, it appeared in twenty-seven editions. In 1995, Bernan started publishing it annually. The current format contains more than 2,000 data time series. The 1999 edition contains annual data from 1970 to the present, quarterly data from 1990 through 1998, and monthly data from 1995 to 1998. Data are grouped into four major sections: U.S. economic data, industry profiles, historical data, and state and regional data. The first category includes statistics on income, spending, industrial production and capacity utilization, savings and investment, consumer and producer prices, employment and earnings, energy, money and financial markets, and international comparisons. The industry profiles are divided in a similar fashion as those in the *Economic Census*: construction; manufacturing (with separate sections for durable and nondurable goods); transportation; retail and wholesale trade; finance, insurance, and real estate; and government. Earlier editions contain data going back to the 1920s. This desk reference belongs in every business reference collection.

D-85 **STAT-USA/Internet**. Washington, DC: U.S. Department of Commerce, 1994- . Daily.

STAT-USA is an agency in the Economics and Statistics Administration, U.S. Department of Commerce. However, *STAT-USA* is not funded by taxpayers and is therefore a premium service for most users. Government depositories receive free access to this resource. *STAT-USA Internet* contains the *National Trade Data Bank*; market and country research, trade statistics (exports and imports), country reports, and current and historical trade leads. This is a particularly valuable resource for those researching international trade or seeking importing or exporting information.

D-86 **County and City Extra**. Lanham, MD: Bernan Press, 2000.

This annual edition provides up to date information on every state, county, metropolitan area, and cities with 1990 populations over 25,000. Data are also included from the most recent (in this case 1997) *Economic Census*. The bulk of the work is divided into five parts, one each for data on states, information for states and counties, data on metropolitan areas, information on cities, and data on congressional districts. Data appear in a format very similar to that of print *Census* data.

D-87 **Survey of Current Business**. Washington, DC: U.S. Bureau of Economic Analysis, 1921- . Monthly.

The *Survey of Current Business* is the major monthly periodical outlining the current economic situation in the United States. The "Business Situation" section at the beginning of each issue gives an economic overview and is a quick way to find current gross domestic product. Section D-1, "BEA Current and Historical Data," is what used to be published as blue pages. These pages contain a wealth of current and some historical data. Each issue also contains articles on special topics. The old yellow pages, "Business Cycle Indicators," were separated out and formed a new publication in February 1996 called *Business Cycle Indicators* (D-88). This title is essential for any business collection.

D-88 **Business Cycle Indicators**. New York: Conference Board, 1996- . Monthly.

Business Cycle Indicators, formerly a section in the *Survey of Current Business* (D-87), began publication as a new title by the Conference Board. The publication consists primarily of graphs of cyclical indicators, including BEA's composite indexes; employment; sales and orders; durable goods orders; fixed capital investment; prices and profits; money, credit, and interest rates; and several other indicators. Some information is available for thirty years.

D-89 **Federal Reserve Bulletin**. Washington, DC: Board of Governors of the Federal Reserve System, 1915- . Monthly.

The *Federal Reserve Bulletin* is the official monthly publication of the Federal Reserve Board. Each issue contains articles, staff studies, and legislative information. The bulk of each issue is typically "Financial and Business Statistics," which contain nearly eighty pages of statistical data. Sample headings are "Federal Finance," "Financial Markets," and "Consumer Credit." Each issue also has an index to the statistical tables; a list of the board of governors and staff; maps of the Federal Reserve system; and a listing of federal reserve banks, branches, and offices. This resource is particularly useful for its statistics related to banking and economics, and it serves as a staple for business reference questions.

D-90 **Monthly Labor Review**. Washington, DC: Bureau of Labor Statistics, 1915- . Monthly.

The *Monthly Labor Review* is the official publication of the Bureau of Labor Statistics. Each issue begins with several narrative articles on labor topics. There is also a "month in review" column, outlining recent events and book reviews. The bulk of each issue is "Current Labor Statistics," which has about fifty pages of labor data, collective bargaining data, price data, productivity data, and injury and illness data, among other topics.

D-91 **Employment and Earnings**. Washington, DC: Bureau of Labor Statistics, 1969- . Monthly.

Employment and Earnings, unlike the *Monthly Labor Review*, is strictly statistical. Current data are derived from a number of sources, including the *Current Population Survey*, *Current Employment Statistics*, and *Establishment Reports*. Data include current and historical earnings and hours information. Data are given at the local, state, and nationwide levels. This is the most authoritative source for income and employment data.

D-92 **CPI Detailed Report**. Washington, DC: Bureau of Labor Statistics, 1974- . Monthly.

The *CPI Detailed Report* is the monthly report on consumer prices. It includes statistical tables and covers two main indexes, the CPI-U (Consumer Price Index for All Urban Consumers) and the CPI-W (Consumer Price Index for Wage and Clerical Workers). This publication is strictly statistical; that is, there are no narrative articles. It contains historical and current data at both nationwide and city levels.

D-93 **PPI Detailed Report**. Washington, DC: Bureau of Labor Statistics, 1985- . Monthly.

This report, similar in structure to the *CPI Detailed Report* (D-92), focuses on producer price information. Arrangement is primarily by industry and product type. An annual supplement contains monthly data for the calendar year, annual averages, and information on weights.

D-94 **International Financial Statistics**. Washington, DC: International Monetary Fund, 1948- . Monthly.

This monthly publication by the IMF (also on CD-ROM) is a standard source for U.S. and international financial data. Coverage includes exchange rates, interest rates, gross national product, prices, and productions. Historical data are available on CD-ROM back to the 1940s. Beginning in 1975, separate Spanish, English, and French versions are available. The IMF also publishes an annual *International Financial Statistics Yearbook*. This is an invaluable source for those seeking international business data.

D-95 **Direction of Trade Statistics**. Washington, DC: International Monetary Fund, 1981- . Quarterly.

This publication contains import and export data for over 150 countries. In addition to individual country pages, there are also world-wide aggregate pages. The IMF also publishes an annual *Direction of Trade Statistics Yearbook*.

D-96 **International Trade Statistics Yearbook**. 2 vols. New York: United Nations, 1950- . Annual.

International Trade Statistics Yearbook, published annually by the United Nations for nearly fifty years, is produced in two volumes. Volume 1 contains detailed data by country, including data on imports and exports and percentage breakdowns of imports by broad economic category and exports by industrial origin. Also given are quantity and value (in U.S. dollars) of imports and exports. Volume 2 contains commodity tables by region and country. Most data are at least two years old when appearing in print.

D-97 **Standard & Poor's Statistical Service**. New York: Standard & Poor's, 1978- . Monthly.

Standard & Poor's Statistical Service includes a monthly "Current Statistics" and a series of "Basic Statistics." "Current Statistics" consists of approximately forty pages of data grouped under the headings "Agricultural," "Banking & Finance," "Building," "Electric Power & Fuels," "Income & Trade," "Metals," "Price Indexes," "Production and Labor," "Textiles, Chemicals, & Paper," and "Transportation." There is also a section providing great detail on Standard & Poor's indexes. "Basic Statistics" provides detailed data on each of the categories above. Also included is an annual *Security Price Index Record* primarily providing weekly and monthly averages for S&P's stock price indexes.

INVESTMENTS

The demand for investment information has grown exponentially over the past ten years as more and more individual investors have entered into the securities markets. The tremendous growth of the stock markets during the late 1990s spawned a desire for fast and accurate information, as well as leads into potential money-making stocks and other securities. This section covers primarily print resources; Web-based and other forms of investment information are addressed in other sections.

Journals and Newspapers

Trade journals and newspapers provide specialized business information in a format that is typically less expensive than other media. Although this section focuses on investments, thousands of trade journals exist for all different types of businesses. The listings below include only very prominent titles; many others are omitted because of space limitations.

D-98 **Wall Street Journal**. New York: Dow Jones, 1889- . Daily.

The *Wall Street Journal* is probably the oldest and most respected business publication. Published on every business day since its inception in 1889, it provides reliable business news and data. The front page has a two-column "What's News" section that provides highlights of the day's news. Section A contains headlines and general news stories; Section B is the "Marketplace" section, and Section C, the "Money & Investing" section, provides data from the securities markets. The *Wall Street Journal* contains a number of other types of information, including IPO announcements, book reviews, economic data, and politics. This is a standard source for any sizable library.

D-99 **Barron's: The Dow Jones Business & Financial Weekly**. New York: Dow Jones, 1921- . Weekly.

Barron's also ranks highly among investment publications. Published every Monday since 1921, Barron's provides a detailed overview of the previous week's activities. Included is information on stocks, mutual funds (including money market and closed-end funds), and commodities. A "Market Laboratory" section contains summary information in an easy-to-read format. "Up and Down Wall Street" contains commentary on current events affecting the financial markets. There are also research reports, insider transactions, dividend reports, and general business news stories. The data sections of this newspaper are particularly useful.

D-100 **Investor's Business Daily**. Los Angeles: Investor's Business Daily, 1984- . Daily.

Originally launched in 1984 as *Investor's Daily*, this publication consists primarily of investment data and financial tables. There are some news stories, but they tend to be brief and more focused on investments compared to articles in the *Wall Street Journal*. The tables in *Investor's Business Daily* are very detailed, and there is an index published at the end of each week. *Investor's Business Daily* is generally regarded as a complement to, not a replacement for, the *Wall Street Journal*.

D-101 **Money**. New York: Time, 1972- . Monthly.

Money, published monthly since 1972 by Time, Inc., is aimed at the individual investor. Issues tend to highlight mutual funds, but individual stocks are also included. There are also regular articles offering educational information, articles on savings and retirement planning, and several of "Best of" articles. The February issue is a guide to the best mutual funds. *Money* also provides some content at its Web site (http://www.money.com).

D-102 **Kiplinger's Personal Finance Magazine**. Washington, DC: Kiplinger Washington Editors, 1991- . Monthly.

Kiplinger's is another publication targeting the individual investor. Published since the late 1940s (its previous title was *Changing Times*), *Kiplinger's* offers investment advice, stock tips, educational columns, and other personal finance information. The Web site (http://www.kiplinger.com) also contains information from the magazine.

D-103 **Value Line Investment Survey**. New York, Value Line, 1936- . Weekly.

The *Value Line Investment Survey* is probably the most popular investment advisory service. It now appears in the traditional edition and, since 1995, an *Expanded Edition*. The traditional edition, in its present format since the 1960s, covers 1,700 stocks and has three sections. Part I is the

"Summary and Index"; Part II is "Selection and Opinion," a weekly newsletter containing forecasting articles and data; and Part III is "Ratings and Reports," which consist of one-page reports for each of the companies covered. Each company is updated four times per year. Reports contain company information, ten years of financial data, recent stock price, price projections, and, most important, ratings for timeliness and safety as well as a technical ranking. *Value Line* also computes a beta for most stocks. The *Expanded Edition* contains information on 1,800 smallcap stocks. Value Line also publishes surveys on options and mutual funds.

> *Electronic access:* Also available on CD-ROM and on the Internet.

Standard & Poor's Corporation Publications

In addition to its company information publications, Standard & Poor's publishes several works for investors. Many of these are available in print as well as through *Standard & Poor's NetAdvantage* on the Web or on CD-ROM.

D-104 **Standard & Poor's Bond Guide**. New York: Standard & Poor's, 1971- . Monthly.

Standard & Poor's Bond Guide provides summary data on corporate bonds. The arrangement is alphabetical by company name in a one-page format. However, there are two groups of headings for each company: one for the company as a whole and one or more for individual corporate bonds that the company has issued. Each entry includes interest dates, S&P rating, price, price range, current yield, yield to maturity, and redemption provisions. The *Bond Guide* is published once monthly (delivery date is approximately the twentieth of each month) and contains data through the last business day of the prior month. This title and *Mergent Bond Record* (D-121) are the two standard bond reference sources.

D-105 **Standard & Poor's Security Owner's Stock Guide**. New York: Standard & Poor's, 1947- . Monthly.

The *Stock Guide* is very similar in appearance and arrangement to the *Bond Guide*, except that data for each company appear on a single line that spans two pages. Information includes the ticker symbol, stock exchange(s) where it is traded, a rating for preferred stocks, short description of the business, price ranges, shares sold and price ranges for the previous month, ratios and return data, dividend information, balance sheet totals (cash and equivalents, current assets, current liabilities), and earnings information. Each issue also includes a "Preferred Stock Summary" and a "Mutual Fund Summary" at the end. The *Stock Guide* provides a quick snapshot of a company's performance and serves as an easy ready reference tool for information such as ticker symbol or stock ratings.

D-106 **Standard & Poor's Earnings Guide**. New York: Standard & Poor's, 1991- . Monthly.

The *Earnings Guide* provides earnings estimates gathered from over 2,300 financial analysts from more than 200 brokerage firms. Each issue provides earning expectations on over 5,500 stocks. Very similar in appearance to the *Stock Guide* and *Bond Guide*; each stock is listed on a single line on one page. Included are the stock rankings; high, mean, and low street estimates for the next quarter, along with number of estimates; projections for the following year; five-year earnings estimates; and recent stock prices.

D-107 **Standard & Poor's Stock Reports**. New York: Standard & Poor's, 1998- . Quarterly.

Once issued in three separate sections for the New York Stock Exchange, American Stock Exchange, and the NASDAQ, since 1998 *Standard & Poor's Stock Reports* has been published in a single series. Each company is listed on two pages, and includes a summary, current outlook, S&P

rating, ten years of financial information, "Important Developments," and information from the balance sheet and income statement.

D-108 **Standard & Poor's 500 Guide**. New York: Standard & Poor's, 1994- . Annual.

D-109 **Standard & Poor's Midcap 400 Guide**. New York: Standard & Poor's, 1994- . Annual.

D-110 **Standard & Poor's Smallcap 600 Guide**. New York: Standard & Poor's, 1995- . Annual.

These three directories contain coverage of the stocks that constitute each of these indexes. Each company is listed on two pages, the format being nearly identical to that of the *Stock Reports*. The *500 Guide* covers the stocks making up the S&P 500 index, the *Midcap 400* covers the 400 mid-capitalization stocks that make up the S&P Midcap 400 index, and the *Smallcap 600* covers the 600 stocks making up the S&P Smallcap 600 index. Each volume contains a valuable introductory section outlining the development of the index, a glossary of terms, an explanation of S&P ratings, and coverage of the financial data contained in the works. These are relatively inexpensive guides, and the *500 Guide* is especially useful for any library with a business clientele.

D-111 **Standard & Poor's Stock Market Encyclopedia**. New York: Standard & Poor's, 1985- . Quarterly.

The *Stock Market Encyclopedia* essentially reproduces the pages for the S&P 500 stocks from *Stock Reports*. The introductory sections contain some useful information, such as a list of companies with five consecutive years of earnings increases, a list of rapid growth stocks, and a list of stocks with A+ rankings.

D-112 **Outlook**. New York: Standard and Poor's, 1987- . Weekly.

The *Outlook* is Standard & Poor's weekly investment advisory publication. Each issue is now a standard twelve pages in length. Each contains a headline feature, usually highlighting the economy or the stock market outlook. Also included is an "In the Limelight" feature, which showcases several promising stocks. S&P uses a star rating system in the *Outlook*, with one star being the lowest and five stars the highest. "Sell" and "Buy" recommendations are regular features, and there is a quarterly index to the companies that are rated. Articles vary, but there is an ongoing "Master List Stocks" feature.

D-113 **Standard & Poor's Emerging & Special Situations**. New York: Standard & Poor's, 1984- . Monthly.

Emerging & Special Situations "is designed to serve aggressive investors who seek maximum capital gains through equity investments in emerging growth companies, new issues and special situations." A special situation is defined as a stock whose performance may benefit from some type of announcement or event. Each issue is twenty pages long and contains news stories, listings of new issues along with price and ratings, "spotlight" recommendations, and a "roster of upcoming offerings."

D-114 **Standard & Poor's Security Dealers of North America**. New York: Standard & Poor's, 1975- . Semiannual.

This directory contains a state-by-state listing of securities dealers, listed by city. Information includes types of businesses, branch locations, officers' names, number of employees, number of accounts, and division department heads. Also included are the names, addresses, Web sites (when available), and telephone and fax numbers of exchanges in North America as well as major foreign stock exchanges and associations.

D-115   CreditWeek. New York: Standard & Poor's, 1981- . Weekly.

CreditWeek is Standard & Poor's weekly publication analyzing the creditworthiness of companies, that is, bond issues. Each issue has several feature stories along with standard columns: "In the News," "New Ratings," "Revised Ratings," "CreditWatch List," and "Removed from CreditWatch." There is also a country arrangement to find information on foreign corporations. The "CreditWatch" section is an alphabetical listing of companies along with the *CreditWeek* issue date in which the company appeared. The purpose of this section is to highlight companies that have events that catch the attention of the S&P analytical staff.

D-116   Standard & Poor's Dividend Record. New York: Standard & Poor's, 1982- . Daily/Weekly.

Standard & Poor's Dividend Record is published daily Monday through Thursday, but subscribers can also subscribe to a weekly edition. Each issue contains a list of companies paying dividends, the amount of the dividend, and the date payable. It also lists stock splits, reverse splits, stocks beginning to pay dividends, and stocks increasing dividends. Mutual funds are also included.

D-117   Daily Stock Price Record. New York: Standard & Poor's, 1961- . Quarterly.

The *Daily Stock Price Record* is published in three editions, one each for the New York, American, and NASDAQ stock exchanges. These volumes provide historical stock prices, including high, low, closing price, and volume. Stocks are listed alphabetically and ticker symbols are also given. Dates are located down the left side and company names appear five or six to a page, across the top. At the end of each week are three data items: total volume in shares traded that week, a ratio comparing the stock's performance to the Dow Jones Industrial Average, and the "30 week moving average."

D-118   Emerging Stock Markets Factbook. New York: Standard & Poor's, 1986- . Annual.

Originally published by the International Finance Corporation, the 2000 edition of this work is the first published by Standard & Poor's. The book is divided into seven chapters and includes an introductory section (containing explanations and a background of the data collection) and several appendixes. Chapter one has data on the world markets and emerging market characteristics. Chapter two contains details of the performance and characteristics of the world stock markets since 1990. Chapters three through five contain detailed statistics on global indexes. Chapter six contains country-by-country stock market information, and chapter seven contains data summaries for emerging markets not covered in chapters three through five.

Mergent (Moody's) FIS Publications

D-119   Mergent Bond Record. New York: Mergent/FIS, 1936- . Monthly.

D-120   Mergent . . . Annual Bond Record. New York: Mergent/FIS, 1989- . Annual.

The monthly *Mergent Bond Record* includes Moody's Ratings, interest dates, call price and date, current price, yield to maturity, high/low prices, amount outstanding, and date issued for corporate bonds, and also includes ratings in a section on international corporate and convertible bonds. Ratings are also given for convertible bonds (U.S.), government, municipal, money markets, and bond funds. Information on equipment trusts, commercial paper, insurance, preferred stock, and industrial development and revenue bonds is also included. The annual volume provides an overview of the previous year's corporate and municipal bond ratings activity, including preferred stock ratings. This source is the most comprehensive print reference for bonds.

D-121 **Handbook of Common Stocks**. New York: Mergent/FIS, 1965- . Quarterly.

The *Handbook of Common Stocks* provides one-page summary information on more than 950 stocks. Similar to Standard & Poor's *Stock Reports*, although less expensive and smaller in the number of companies included, the *Handbook of Common Stocks* provides a business overview, recent developments, prospects, a chart outlining trading volume, ten years of financial data, earnings per share, and dividend information. Each volume also highlights a particular industry; the information appears to be drawn directly from *Mergent's Industry Review* (D-70). In 1999, Mergent began publishing a companion volume, *Handbook of Internet Stocks*, which includes profiles of 200 Internet companies.

D-122 **Mergent Dividend Record**. New York: Mergent/FIS, 1930- . Semiweekly.

Arranged alphabetically by company name, each issue lists the dividends paid since the previous issue. Dividends paid by mutual funds are listed in a separate section. Total dividend for the year and the previous year, amount paid at each dividend payment (typically quarterly), and date paid are provided under each company listing. Also included are companies paying new dividends, stock splits and their effects on dividends, and a list of companies offering dividend reinvestment plans. A cumulative volume is produced each year.

Additional Fact Books and Directories

D-123 **Morningstar Mutual Funds**. Chicago: Morningstar, 1991- . Biweekly.

Morningstar Mutual Funds contains one-page reports on more than 1,700 mutual funds. Reports include overall ratings; fund objective, manager profile, a narrative analysis, a box indicating current investment style, a twelve-year performance history; and an overview of the fund portfolio. Information about investing in the fund is also given, including address, telephone number, minimum investment, and fees. Morningstar has grown into one of the most prominent providers of mutual funds information.

Electronic access: Also available on CD-ROM and the Internet.

D-124 **Morningstar Mutual Fund 500**. Chicago: Morningstar, 2000.

Morningstar publishes this annual volume to highlight promising mutual funds, including both new and existing funds, that will lead to a well-diversified portfolio. The pages are identical to those in the biweekly publication. Also included are performance summaries of top funds for different time periods and for fund objectives. The volume includes a user's guide, a glossary of investment terms, and an index of fund managers.

D-125 **Mutual Funds Update**. Rockville, MD: Wiesenberger, 1992- . Monthly.

Wiesenberger, now owned by Thomson Financial, is the major competitor to Morningstar. Each monthly edition contains a "Mutual Fund Report" that outlines the previous month, provides a performance summary, and lists top funds. The bulk of the publication is a listing of mutual fund performance by investment category. Information for each fund is listed on a single line and includes a monthly and yearly ranking; annualized total returns for three, five, and ten years; market cycle rankings; and Wiesenberger's rating.

D-126 **New York Stock Exchange Fact Book**. New York: New York Stock Exchange, 2000.

The *Fact Book* provides very detailed information on the year's activities, including data for volume, block transactions, stock price trends, member data, stock splits, and off-hours trading. There is also an historical data section.

D-127 **Mutual Fund Fact Book**. Washington, DC: Investment Company Institute, 2000.

The Investment Company Institute is the national association of the investment company industry and, as of March 2000, includes more than 8,000 mutual funds. The *Fact Book* contains great details on the mutual fund industry, including the year in review, information about mutual funds in general, fees and expenses, mutual fund ownership and shareholder characteristics, retirement planning, and taxes.

D-128 **Stocks, Bonds, Bills, and Inflation Yearbook**. Chicago: Ibbotson Associates, 2000.

SBBI Yearbook provides historical data on stock markets, treasury bills, government and corporate bonds, and inflation. Data are presented per month, with most tables going back to 1926. This book is a terrific source of historical data, which can be used for many different purposes including identifying trends and predicting future changes.

ACCOUNTING AND TAXATION

FASB Publications

The Financial Accounting Standards Board (FASB) is the accounting profession's official organization, charged with creating new accounting standards and modifying existing standards. To disseminate information, FASB publishes a number of print publications. Publications can be ordered directly from FASB or through its Web site (http://www.fasb.org). Established in 1973, FASB has been officially recognized by both the Securities and Exchange Commission (SEC) and the American Institute of Certified Public Accountants (AICPA).

D-129 **Statement of Financial Accounting Standards**. Norwalk, CT: Financial Accounting Standards Board, 1973- . Irregular.

This is FASB's primary publication. Each new rule or modification of a previous rule is issued as a new statement. There are currently 139 authoritative statements. The frequency of publication varies.

D-130 **Statement of Financial Accounting Concepts**. Norwalk, CT: Financial Accounting Standards Board, 1978- . Irregular.

In 1973, FASB started a project to develop a conceptual framework for financial reporting and accounting. Since that time, FASB has published a number of *Discussion Memorandums*, *Research Reports*, *Exposure Drafts*, and these final *Concept Statements*. *Concept Statements* are "intended to serve the public interest by setting the objectives, qualitative characteristics, and other concepts that guide selection of economic events to be recognized and measured for financial reporting and their display in financial statements." Unlike the *Statement of Financial Accounting Standards* (D-131), these do not establish generally accepted accounting procedures.

D-131 **Accounting Standards. Current Text**. 2 vols. Norwalk, CT: Financial Accounting Standards Board, 1982- . Irregular.

This two-volume looseleaf service contains one volume each covering general standards and industry standards. It is arranged alphabetically and is updated irregularly. Citations are given for source materials, which can include FASB *Statements* and AICPA publications (see below).

FASB also publishes *Interpretations*, *Technical Bulletins*, *Implementation Guides*, *Special Reports*, and a monthly *Status Report*.

AICPA Publications

Established in 1887, the American Institute of Certified Public Accountants (AICPA) is the official national association for CPAs, with a membership that currently numbers over 30,000. It publishes several important publications, primarily the monthly *Journal of Accountancy*, as well as several newsletters and magazines, including the *Tax Advisor, CPA Letter*, and the *Practicing CPA*. Information about AICPA and its publications is available at its Web site, *AICPA Online* (http://www.aicpa.org).

D-132 **Statement of Auditing Standards**. New York: American Institute of Certified Public Accountants, 1973- . Irregular.

The Auditing Standards Board of the AICPA issues authoritative standards statements to guide auditing procedures. There are currently ninety statements.

D-133 **AICPA Professional Standards**. 2 vols. New York: American Institute of Certified Public Accountants, 1976- . Irregular.

This two-volume looseleaf service covers professional pronouncements issued by the AICPA, the International Accounting Standards Board (IASC), and the International Auditing Practices Committee (IAPC). Volume one contains statements on auditing standards and related auditing interpretations. Volume two provides statements on standards for accounting and review services, such as the Code of Professional Conduct and Code of Ethics. Coverage is international.

D-134 **AICPA Technical Practice Aids**. 2 vols. New York: American Institute of Certified Public Accountants, 1978- . Irregular.

This two-volume looseleaf service has a topical arrangement, which is outlined in the front of each volume. Volume one contains inquiries submitted to AICPA's Technical Information Service and responses. Volume two has four sections: statements of position of the Accounting Standards Division, statements of position of the Auditing Standards Division, Practice Bulletins, and a listing of issues papers of the Accounting Standards Division. An annual bound volume is also available.

D-135 **Accounting Trends and Techniques**. New York: American Institute of Certified Public Accountants, 1947- . Annual.

The AICPA conducts an annual examination of annual reports of 600 publicly traded corporations in order to analyze the accounting information included. This volume presents their findings. The work focuses on significant accounting trends, which are "revealed by a comparison of current survey findings with those of prior years." There are several sections covering the balance sheet, income statement, comprehensive income, stockholders' equity, statement of cash flows, and independent auditors' report.

GASB Publications

The Governmental Accounting Standards Board (GASB) was founded in 1984 to establish financial accounting standards for state and local governments. Its mission and publications are similar in structure to the Financial Accounting Standards Board. Publications can be obtained from GASB or at its Web site (http://www.gasb.org).

D-136 **Statement of Governmental Accounting Standards**. Norwalk, CT: Governmental Accounting Standards Board, 1984- . Irregular.

This is the primary publication of GASB. There are currently thirty-five official standards statements.

GASB also publishes *Exposure Drafts, Discussion Documents, Final Pronouncements*, and *Research Reports*.

Accounting Practices

Several commercial publications serve as unofficial guides to the official standards.

D-137 GAAP: Interpretation and Application of Generally Accepted Accounting Principles. New York: John Wiley, 2000.

This annual reference work is designed to make accounting standards (as outlined in FASB's *Current Text*) easier to understand. Whereas the *Current Text* is arranged alphabetically, *Wiley GAAP* is arranged like a balance sheet/income statement. Separate sections exist for some topics, such as inventories, accounting for pensions, and investments. Each section outlines the perspective and issues; provides a glossary of terms; and provides concepts, rules, and examples. There are also summaries from FASB's Emerging Issues Task Force.

D-138 Miller GAAP Guide: Restatement and Analysis of Current FASB Standards. San Diego, CA: Harcourt Brace, 2000.

The *Miller GAAP Guide* differs from the *Wiley GAAP* in that the arrangement is alphabetical by topic, similar to FASB's *Current Text*. Each chapter contains an overview and background; cross-references to other sections; detailed explanations; "practice pointers," which are tips for specific points; and abundant illustrations. The work also includes a list of Web resources, a topical index, a disclosure index, and information about specialized industry accounting principles. Miller publishes this work annually.

D-139 Miller Not-for-Profit Reporting: GAAP Plus Tax, Financial, and Regulatory Requirements. San Diego, CA: Harcourt Brace, 2000.

Miller also publishes this companion volume to the *Miller GAAP Guide* (D-138), aimed specifically at not-for-profit organizations. The format is very similar to the *Miller GAAP Guide*, but topics focus on FASB standards for not-for-profits. The work includes an introduction, which provides a good overview and definitions of not-for-profits, as well as a section on regulatory financial reporting, which covers topics such as tax reporting requirements and payroll requirements. This work is also published annually.

D-140 Miller GAAS Guide: A Comprehensive Restatement of Standards for Auditing, Attestation, Compilation, and Review. San Diego, CA: Harcourt Brace, 2000.

The *Miller GAAS Guide* closely follows the arrangement of the AICPA's *Professional Standards* (D-133), using the same numbering system used by AICPA. Each section contains an overview of the topic, cross-references, authoritative pronouncements, a procedures checklist, an analysis and application of procedures section, and practitioner's aids. There are also tips throughout the book, including "Planning Aid Reminders" and "Risk Assessment Points." The work contains an extensive cross-reference section and a list of relevant Web sites.

CPA Examination Guides

D-141 AICPA's Uniform CPA Exam. New York: American Institute of Certified Public Accountants, 1999.

This annual reference work is prepared by the Board of Examiners of the AICPA and is intended as a study guide for those preparing for the Uniform Certified Public Accountant examination. All jurisdictions in the United States require new CPAs to have passed this examination. The book, offering selected questions and unofficial answers, is divided into the areas of business law and professional responsibilities, auditing, accounting and reporting (taxation, managerial, governmental, and not-for-profit), and financial accounting and reporting. There is also a content specification outline section, which details coverage of content in the examination.

D-142 **Wiley CPA Examination Review**. 26th ed. 2 vols. New York: John Wiley, 1999–2000.

This annual work, previously published in four topical volumes, is now published in two volumes. This is its twenty-sixth annual edition. Volume 1 is titled "Outlines and Study Guide," and has modules for auditing, business law, intermediate financial accounting, advanced financial accounting, managerial accounting, governmental/not-for-profit accounting, individual taxation, and advanced taxation (corporate/partnership). Volume 2, arranged with the same modules, provides specific problems and solutions. There are also appendixes containing complete sample tests and real questions released by the AICPA.

International Accounting

D-143 **International Accounting Standards**. London: International Accounting Standards Committee, 2000.

The International Accounting Standard Committee (IASC) was formed in 1973 to formulate accounting standards and promote them worldwide and to improve the harmonization of accounting standards. Published annually, this work is arranged by standard number. Currently there are thirty-nine standards. The Standards Interpretations Committee (SIC) of the IASC writes interpretations of international accounting standards. Eighteen of these interpretations are included in the 2000 edition.

D-144 **TRANSACC: Transnational Accounting**. 3 vols. New York: Groves, 2000.

TRANSACC outlines in great detail the financial accounting rules of countries in the European Union, the United States, Canada, Japan, and Australia, as well as the standards adopted by the International Accounting Standards Committee (IASC). Arrangement is alphabetical by country name, and each country has both "individual" and "group" accounts sections. There is also a reference matrix by topic and country name at the beginning of Volume 1.

D-145 Arthur Andersen. **International GAAP Analysis**. North Vancouver, British Columbia: STP Specialty Technical Publishers, 1988- . Looseleaf with quarterly updates.

International GAAP Analysis covers eighteen countries and includes the international accounting standards. Under each country, arrangement is alphabetical by topic. All topics are covered under every country, allowing for easy comparison between countries. This work includes some countries not covered by *TRANSACC,* including Italy, Mexico, Norway, and South Africa. However, it omits Belgium, a country that is included in *TRANSACC.*

D-146 **Miller European Accounting Guide**. 3d ed. San Diego, CA: Harcourt Brace, 1998.

This work covers accounting practices in European countries. It contains more narrative than the other works in this section. Arrangement is by country name, and each section includes a background, form and content of published financial statements, accounting valuation, and future developments. Some countries are found here that aren't in the other works, including Ireland, Greece, Luxembourg, Portugal, Iceland, Turkey, the Baltic States, Czech Republic, Hungary, Poland, Belarus, and the Russian Federation.

Additional Accounting Resources

D-147 **Emerson's Directory of Leading U.S. Accounting Firms**. Bellevue, WA: Emerson Company, 2000–2001.

The 2000–2001 edition of this work covers 500 of the top accounting firms in the United States. Listings include firm name, address, telephone number, fax number, Internet address, approximate number of employees, CEO/managing partner, audit/accounting leader, tax leader, consulting leader, HR/recruiting leader, marketing leader, finance/administration leader, primary industries served, primary consulting services offered, and year founded. A limited edition is available free on the Web.

D-148 **Who Audits America**. 43d ed. Menlo Park, CA: Data Financial Press, 2000.

The first part of this book, taking up more than half the volume, is an alphabetical listing of companies that contains the names of their auditors, plus basic company information including ticker symbol, SIC, number of employees, sales, and assets. The second part is an "Auditor Summary," providing sales figures and number of clients. The third section covers companies audited by each of the "Big 5" accounting firms. Part four is non-"Big 5" accounting firms and their clients, and part five is a state-by-state auditor list.

Tax Guides

D-149 **U.S. Master Tax Guide**. Chicago: Commerce Clearing House, 2000.

This book, published annually for eighty-three years, is designed as a one-stop guide to answering popular individual and company tax questions. The 2000 edition has twenty-nine chapters covering such areas as exclusions from income, tax credits, retirement plans, and capital gains. There are also tax tables and a topical index. This handy guide will prove invaluable at tax time.

D-150 **Ernst & Young Tax Guide**. New York: John Wiley, 2000.

This guide, published annually since 1992, is divided into six major sections. Part one, "The Income Tax Return," contains information on filing, dependents, filing status, personal exemptions, and estimated taxes. Part two is "Income," containing chapters on wages and salaries, tip income, interest income, dividends, selling your home, etc. Part three is "Standard Deduction and Itemized Deductions," containing chapters covering such topics as medical/dental expenses, interest expenses, charitable contributions, and theft losses. Part four, "Figuring Your Taxes and Credits," contains chapters on child care credit, child tax credit, and education credits. Part five examines "Special Situations and Tax Planning," covering such areas as mutual funds, gift taxes, self-employment, and U.S. citizens living abroad. The final part, "Filling Out Your Tax Return," contains tax forms and schedules, tax tables, and tax rate schedules. The book also contains a glossary of tax and financial terms and introductory pages with information such as "50 of the Most Easily Overlooked Deductions" and "How to Avoid 25 Common Errors."

D-151 **J. K. Lasser's Your Income Tax**. New York: Simon & Schuster, 2000.

This annual guide is one of the more popular tax preparation guides. The 2000 edition is over 800 pages in length and contains tax forms that users can pull out, a tax planning section written by taxation experts at Arthur Andersen consulting, a guide to recent tax changes, an index for special situations such as divorce or working abroad; and a checklist to go through before submitting forms. There is an abundant use of examples, and nearly every page contains reminders, tips, or warnings. This reliable guide is invaluable to those preparing their own taxes.

Tax Services

D-152 **Standard Federal Tax Reporter**. Chicago: Commerce Clearing House, 1913- . Weekly updates.

Commerce Clearing House (CCH) began publishing this work in 1913. This set follows the Internal Revenue Code, and currently consists of nineteen volumes, with additional volumes for excise, gift, and estate taxes. There are also two volumes outlining the Internal Revenue Code, a volume for checklists and tax tables, and two citator volumes. The main volumes include the text of the

Code section, committee reports, regulations, proposed regulations, CCH's explanation, and listing of relevant cases and revenue rulings. Additional volumes contain U.S. tax cases, which are published twice per year.

Electronic access: Available on both CD-ROM and the Web.

D-153 Federal Tax Coordinator. New York: Research Institute of America, 1947- . Weekly updates.

RIA's *Federal Tax Coordinator* follows a subject arrangement rather than the Code itself. It consists of twenty-eight topical volumes, a topic index volume, and volumes with finding tables and practice aids. The finding tables are useful if a Code or regulation number or a case or revenue ruling number is known. The topic index is an alphabetical listing of all topics covered. Because related subjects are found near each other in the same volume, users are able to browse nearby sections. There are footnotes under each section listing relevant cases, revenue rulings, and so forth. Each volume also contains Code sections and recent developments.

Electronic access: RIA Checkpoint is the Web version of this service.

MARKETING, DEMOGRAPHICS, AND ADVERTISING

D-154 U.S. Census of Population and Housing and U.S. Economic Census. Washington, DC: U.S. Bureau of the Census, 1970- .

Data contained in many business reference books are derived from either the *Census of Population and Housing* (conducted every ten years) or the *Economic Census* (conducted every five years). The *Census of Population and Housing* compiles demographic data on every person in the United States; the *Economic Census* compiles the most complete information on industries. Data from these two sources serve as the backbone of market and demographic research. Data from the 1997 *Economic Census* and the 2000 *Census of Population and Housing* will be available electronically. A further description of each of these sources is provided under the "Statistics" section (see D-81 and D-82).

D-155 Market Share Reporter. 10th ed. Farmington Hills, MI: Gale, 2000.

The *Market Share Reporter* is an annual compilation of market share information derived from articles in print journals and newspapers. This edition has over 2,000 entries arranged by two-digit SIC code. Each entry has a table number, market share data (usually percentages or a ranking by sales), and the source. Most of the data in this edition are derived from 1998 and 1999 articles. There are company and brand name indexes as well as an SIC index and a listing of publications included. Coverage is for North America.

D-156 World Market Share Reporter. 4th ed. Farmington Hills, MI: Gale, 1999.

The *World Market Share Reporter* is arranged the same way as the *Market Share Reporter* (D-155), except that coverage is global. This edition contains 1,600 entries, some of which include International SIC and Harmonized Code classifications.

D-157 Choices II. [CD-ROM]. Tampa, FL: Simmons Market Research Bureau, 1998.

This CD-ROM product replaces the print *Simmons . . . Study of Media and Markets*, which ceased as a print publication in 1994. The market research data are compiled from an annual survey of approximately 20,000 households. The survey gathers product user data, demographic data, and media (television, newspaper, radio, etc.) use. The data can be cross-tabulated so that users can obtain information on demographics of consumers and the media that they use. This work, like *MediaMark* (D-158), is produced twice per year, and libraries can purchase the previous year's data at a significantly reduced price.

D-158 MediaMark. New York: MediaMark Research, 1998.

MediaMark is similar in structure to the print *Simmons . . . Study of Media and Markets*. These market research reports are compiled from interviews of over 22,000 households. Designed as a source for the advertising industry, these reports contain detailed demographic and marketing segmentations of media audiences. *MediaMark* is published in twenty volumes by product or service, such as "Beverages," "Travel, Insurance, Real Estate," and "Meat and Prepared Meals." *MediaMark* is published twice yearly, and the previous year's editions are available at a greatly discounted price.

D-159 **Standard Rate & Data Service**. Des Plaines, IL: Standard Rate & Data Service, 1919- .

> **Business Publication Advertising Source**. 1993- .
>
> **Circulation**. 1996- .
>
> **Community Publication Advertising Source**. 1995- .
>
> **Consumer Magazine Advertising Source**. 1995- .
>
> **Direct Marketing List Source**. 1993- .
>
> **Hispanic Media and Market Source**. 1993- .
>
> **Interactive Advertising Source**. 1996- .
>
> **Newspaper Advertising Source**. 1995- .
>
> **Out of Home Advertising Source**. 1995- .
>
> **Print Media Production Source**. 1995- .
>
> **Radio Advertising Source**. 1993- .
>
> **Technology Media Source**. 1995- .
>
> **TV & Cable Source**. 1994- .

Standard Rate & Data Service publishes the directories listed above, along with a host of international counterparts. Each directory provides information for advertising in the directory-specific medium, with arrangement being primarily geographic. Information typically includes address, telephone number, fax number, key personnel, service areas, and subscriber data (if available). SRDS publications at one time listed rates, but now primarily serve to provide contact information. Updates vary, but are typically monthly or quarterly. A Web version of some products is available at http://www.srds.com.

D-160 **Lifestyle Market Analyst**. Des Plaines, IL: Standard Rate & Data Service, 2000.

The *Lifestyle Market Analyst* is an affordable market research tool providing information at the local, regional, and national levels. There are four main sections. Part one contains market profiles of designated market areas (DMA) arranged alphabetically by geographic name. Each listing consists of two pages, the first containing demographic information and the second containing lifestyle information. Section two consists of "Lifestyle Profiles," an alphabetical listing of seventy-six interests and activities. Each profile is a two-page entry arranged alphabetically by DMA. The third part contains "Consumer Segment Profiles," which provide demographic and lifestyle information by demographic characteristics. The final section is "Consumer Magazines and Direct Marketing Lists," which are arranged alphabetically by interests and activities. This is an invaluable, and relatively inexpensive, tool for basic lifestyle information.

D-161   **Demographics USA**. New York: Market Statistics, 2000.

Demographics USA is published in two annual editions, a ZIP code and a county edition. The ZIP code edition is divided into six parts, among which are "Basic Demographics," "Detailed Demographics," and "Business Characteristics." The county edition has sixteen sections, including maps, demographic summaries, rankings, "Basic Demographics," household data, consumer expenditures, establishments, and employment data. The information appears to be derived primarily from *Census* data.

D-162   **Survey of Buying Power**. New York: Bill Communications, 2000.

Bill Communications has published this work for over seventy years. The 2000 edition begins with a section of "Metro and Media Market Ranking Tables." Among other rankings, two measures are a "Buying Power Index," which is a measure of spending power for which the *Survey* is best known, and "Effective Buying Income (EBI)," which is a measure of disposable household income. Section two contains "Metro and Media Market Totals," geographic breakdowns of population, EBI, retail sales, and Buying Power Index. Section three provides a five-year projection of the data in section two. Section four contains sales figures for ten broad categories, broken down by geographic location. The final section is a reference chapter containing a glossary and alphabetical listings of metro and media markets.

D-163   **Rand McNally Commercial Atlas and Marketing Guide**. 131st ed. Chicago: Rand McNally, 2000.

This atlas is one of the overall best, and certainly the premier atlas for marketing data. It is divided into five sections: metropolitan area maps, transportation/communications, economy, population, and state maps. There is a wealth of information. Illustrative examples are a map of AMTRAK, retail sales figures by state, a list of college enrollments, U.S. population trends, maps containing manufacturing data, and a list of area and zip codes. Data are derived from the most recent *Census,* and updates and current estimates come from a variety of other sources. This should be the one atlas in every business reference collection.

D-164   **Sourcebook of Zip Code Demographics**. 14th ed. Arlington, VA: CACI Marketing Systems, 1999.

This desktop guide provides a wealth of demographic data for every ZIP code in the United States. This edition contains 1998 data, consisting of over seventy demographic characteristics arranged by ZIP code. There is also a section in which the demographics are arranged into profiles of "Population Change," "Population Composition," "Income," and "Spending Potential." Another valuable section is the ACORN (*A Classification Of Residential Neighborhoods*) system, which identifies the top consumer groups in each ZIP code.

D-165   **Standard Directory of Advertisers**. 2 vols. New Providence, NJ: National Register Publishing, 2000.

Also known as the "Advertiser Red Book," this source covers advertising practices of over 25,000 companies. There are two editions, a business classification and a geographic edition. Volume 1 provides company listings. Each section provides contact information, personnel, advertising expenditures, media used, level and method of distribution, and date when the advertising budget is set. Volume 2 is an index volume providing product categories by state, brand names, SIC, and personnel indexes. This work fills a unique need and has been published for over eighty-five years. Each edition is updated by supplements in April, July, and October.

D-166   **Standard Directory of Advertising Agencies**. New Providence, NJ: National Register Publishing, July 2000.

This companion volume to the *Standard Directory of Advertisers* (D-165) is a directory of advertising companies. Arrangement is alphabetical by company name. Each entry includes contact information, number of employees, year founded, advertising specializations, annual billings, a breakdown of gross billings by media type, and personnel. This work has been published for over eighty years, and is currently published every January and July, with supplements in April and October.

D-167 **Brands and Their Companies**. Farmington Hills, MI: Gale, 2000.
This annual reference work contains information on over 22,000 brands and trademarks. There are two sections, one each for listings by brands and by company name. There is minimal information included. Each brand listing contains only the company name. The company name section contains address, telephone number, and, in some cases, Web addresses. The companion volume is *Companies and Their Brands* (D-168).

D-168 **Companies and Their Brands**. 2 vols. Farmington Hills, MI: Gale, 2000.
This two-volume work serves as a companion to *Brands and Their Companies* (D-167). Arrangement is alphabetical by company name. Each entry includes address, telephone and fax numbers, and an alphabetical list of brand names. Each brand name also has a descriptor. Gale has produced these works in such a way that complete information is not available unless both sets are purchased. This set does not have an index, and *Brands and Their Companies* does not have brand descriptors.

D-169 **Broadcasting and Cable Yearbook**. New York: R. R. Bowker, 2000.
This annual publication provides a wide range of information on the television, cable, and radio industries. It is divided into ten sections: an industry overview; television; cable; radio; satellites and other carriers; programming services; technological services; brokers and professional services; associations, events; education and awards; and law and regulation and government agencies. This is a convenient source for locating television and radio stations and cable television providers.

D-170 **LNA/Mediawatch Multi-Media Service**. New York: Competitive Media Reporting, 2000.
This service contains information on corporate advertising expenditures in newspapers, consumer magazines, television, cable, and outdoor advertising. The set consists of three titles: *Ad $ Summary*, *Company/Brand $*, and *Class/Brand $*. *Ad $ Summary* lists brand names alphabetically and shows total media expenditures, media used (using a coding system), and parent company. *Company/Brand $* is an alphabetical listing by company name providing active brands and year-to-date expenditures in each medium used. *Class/Brand $* provides brand name grouped by type of company and quarterly and year-to-date expenditures for each medium used.

D-171 **Direct Marketing Market Place**. New Providence, NJ: National Register Publishing, 2000.
This work is the primary reference source for the direct marketing industry. Arrangement is in five main chapters covering direct marketers; service firms and suppliers; creative services; associations, courses, and events; and a bibliography. The first three sections contain entries with firm name, address, telephone and fax numbers; e-mail and Web addresses if available; business description; number of employees; primary market served; advertising budget; and year founded. There is also a geographic index and a company and individual name index.

D-172 **Major Marketing Campaigns Annual**. Detroit: Gale Group, 1999.
This annual work profiles 100 major marketing campaigns of the previous calendar year. Each entry averages 4,000 words in length and includes an overview, historical background, target market, expected outcomes, marketing strategy, and so forth. There are also references to competitors and a bibliography. This is a companion volume to the *Encyclopedia of Major Marketing Campaigns* (D-173).

D-173   **Encyclopedia of Major Marketing Campaigns**. Detroit: Gale Group, 2000.

This work compiles 500 major marketing campaigns from the twentieth century. Each article is approximately 2,000 words in length and includes an historical overview, expectations of the campaign, and outcome. There is also an abundance of photographs. Each entry also lists company contact information, including Web site when available, and a list of further readings. *Major Marketing Campaigns Annual* (D-172) is a companion to this volume.

D-174   **Euromonitor Publications**. London: Euromonitor Plc.

Euromonitor publishes a series of reference works containing a wealth of international marketing data. Examples of titles are *International Marketing Data and Statistics*; *International Marketing Forecasts*; *European Marketing Data and Statistics*; *World Consumer Income & Expenditure Patterns*; *Consumer International*; *Consumer Asia*; *Consumer Europe*; *Consumer Latin America*; *Consumer Middle East*; and *World Retail Data and Statistics*. These volumes are somewhat expensive, but provide very detailed data that are difficult to acquire elsewhere.

ADDITIONAL REFERENCE SOURCES

D-175   **Official Guide for GMAT Review**. Princeton, NJ: Educational Testing Service, 1986- . Biennial.

Although there are numerous preparation guides for the Graduate Management Admission Test (GMAT), the *Official Guide for GMAT Review* is the standard reference work. The tenth edition, published in 2000, contains over 1,400 actual test questions; 200 analytical writing assessment topics, a math review section that includes algebra and geometry, test-taking tips, and a chapter summarizing the content of test tutorials. This is a popular work that belongs in the reference collection of any college or university offering business programs.

D-176   **Peterson's MBA Programs**. Princeton, NJ: Peterson's, 2001.

This is the definitive guide for current information on more than 2,900 Master of Business Administration (MBA) programs. Each in-depth profile contains the institution's name and location, followed by an overview of the program, degrees offered, costs, financial aid, resources and services, information for and about international students, application information, and additional information. There are also capsule profiles that are broken down into two major parts: programs located in the United States and U.S. territories and those located outside of the United States. "MBA Programs at a Glance" provides information arranged in tabular format for easy comparison. The book begins with several narrative sections, including "Why an MBA? Future Trends and Opportunities in the Twenty-First Century"; "The New MBA: What to Look for in Today's Reinvented Programs"; "Choosing the Right Program for Your Career Needs"; and "Getting Admitted to MBA Programs." There is also information on "GradAdvantage," a Web site where prospective students can apply to MBA programs. This is an invaluable source for anyone considering graduate education in business.

D-177   **Research and Information Guides in Business, Industry, and Economic Institutions [series]**. New York: Garland.

Labaree, Robert V. **Federal Trade Commission: A Guide to Sources**. 2000.

Schreiber, Mae N. **International Trade Sources: A Research Guide**. 1997.

Barbuto, Domenica M. **International Financial Statistics Locator: A Research and Information Guide**. 1995.

Womack, Carol Z., and Alice Littlejohn. **The American Stock Exchange: A Guide to Information Resources**. 1995.

Graham, John W. **The U.S. Securities and Exchange Commission: A Research and Information Guide**. 1993.

Johnson, Mary Elizabeth. **The International Monetary Fund, 1944-1992: A Research Guide**. 1993.

Heckman, Lucy. **The New York Stock Exchange: A Guide to Information Sources**. 1992.

Wilson, Carol R. **The World Bank Group: A Guide to Information Sources**. 1991.

Heckman, Lucy. **Franchising in Business: A Guide to Information Sources**. 1989.

This series, edited by Wahib Nasrallah, is designed "to bridge the gap between classical forms of literature and new alternative formats." The books in this series are primarily annotated bibliographies or descriptions of specific reference sources. Arrangement varies by topic, but the general tendency, especially for those dealing with specific organizations, is toward a chronological format. Each has an introductory section, although they vary greatly in length. Each also has a keyword index.

D-178   Manufacturing & Distribution USA. Detroit: Gale Group, 2000.

This edition updates two previous Gale publications: *Manufacturing USA* and *Wholesale & Retail Trade USA*. This edition provides statistics using more than 500 SIC and NAICS classifications in manufacturing, wholesaling, and retail industries. Gale plans to publish this biannually.

D-179   Information, Finance and Services USA. Detroit: Gale Group, 2000.

This work is an update and reorganization of two previous works, *Service Industries USA* and *Finance, Insurance, and Real Estate USA*. It presents, by SIC and NAICS, historical data, projections, national and state data, and leading companies in the information, finance, and service industries. Gale plans to publish this biannually.

D-180   Infrastructure Industries USA. Detroit: Gale Group, 2000.

This edition updates and reorganizes the information in two previous Gale publications, *Agriculture, Mining, and Construction USA* and *Transportation and Public Utilities USA*. Arranged by SIC and NAICS, most of this work consists of governmental data on shipping, employment, and establishments, and other data on agricultural, transportation, and utility industries. Gale plans to publish this biannually.

D-181   Small Business Sourcebook. 14th ed. 2 vols. Detroit: Gale Group, 2001.

This work has grown to be an indispensable source of information for small business start-ups. The two-volume set contains a listing, by topic, of small business profiles. Each entry contains start-up information, including articles, books, manuals, and other sources; professional associations and organizations; reference works; trade periodicals; Internet databases; computerized databases; and research centers. There are also sections on general business topics and a glossary of small business terms.

D-182   Business Plans Handbook. Detroit: Gale Group, 1995- .

This set has grown to seven volumes as of 2000. Each volume contains approximately twenty-five actual small business plans arranged alphabetically by name of the type of business. There are also several appendixes, including a business plan template; a listing of organizations, agencies, and consultants to aid the small business start-up process; a glossary of small business terms; and a bibliography. This is a great resource for individuals working on business plans.

D-183   Hamilton, Neil A. **American Business Leaders: From Colonial Times to the Present**. 2 vols. Santa Barbara, CA: ABC-Clio, 1999.

American Business Leaders contains profiles on more than 400 prominent men and women who have built businesses in the United States. Arranged alphabetically by last name, this two-volume set contains a wealth of biographical information. Each entry begins with birth and death dates and occupation, followed by the narrative listing. Profiles are one or two pages in length, and a bibliography of sources is included. Many listings also contain photographs.

ELECTRONIC DATABASES

Most traditional print indexing and abstracting services now have some electronic counterpart (i.e., Web, CD-ROM), but there are a number of other electronic resources available that those working with business reference materials should be aware of. Items included below are not indexing and abstracting services but provide access to other information via electronic delivery. This section covers some of the more popular electronic business resources but should not be considered comprehensive.

D-184   **Compustat**. New York: Standard & Poor's, dates vary. Daily. Online format.

Compustat is the premier source of company financial data. Produced for over thirty-five years, this database provides access to time-series of data that are especially useful for academic researchers. The North American database contains detailed data on more than 10,000 active companies and 9,000 inactive companies. The Global database covers over 12,000 companies, and includes data for more than twelve years. *Compustat* also provides access to a number of other financial files. Traditionally, *Compustat* has been available through mainframe computers. During the late 1990s and early 2000, *Compustat* moved to ftp delivery and Web-based access through several providers.

D-185   **Center for Research in Security Prices (CRSP)**. Chicago: University of Chicago, 1960- . Daily. Online format.

CRSP is a comprehensive database containing files with securities price information. Data included are files for daily stock prices from 1962 for New York and American Stock Exchange stocks as of 1972 for NASDAQ stocks. Files for other securities are also available. Like *Compustat*, *CRSP* was, until recently, available through the mainframe environment. However, it can now be accessed though other providers.

D-186   **Datastream**. New York: Thomson Financial/Primark, dates vary. Continually. Online format.

Datastream, a Thomas Financial/Primark company, is a popular provider of historical financial information. Included are equities and index data for over twenty-five years. Global in scope, *Datastream* also includes historical macroeconomic data, foreign exchange rates, interest rates, bonds, commodities, futures, options, and warrants. It is accessible via the Web.

D-187   **I/B/E/S**. New York: Thomson Financial/Primark, 1971- . Daily. Online format.

I/B/E/S 1971, is the leading information provider of analyst estimates (forecast data) and research for institutional investors. The database includes over 18,000 companies in sixty countries, providing estimates to over 2,000 institutional investors and 450 academic institutions. Most U.S. data are available 1976 to the present, and 1987 to the present for international data.

D-188 **Investext (Research Bank Web)**. New York: Thomson Financial/ Primark, 1987- . Continually. Online format.

Also known as *Thomson Financial Securities Data (TFSD)*, *Research Bank Web* (formerly *Investext*), is the most comprehensive collection of full-text investment analyst research reports. The database contains over 2.5 million reports on more than 40,000 companies from around the world. Sources include over 800 investment banks, market research firms, and professional associations. Users can access the database directly through Thomson Financial or through a number of third-party providers.

D-189 **Global Access (Disclosure)**. New York: Thomson Financial/Primark, 1985- . Daily. Electronic format.

Disclosure is perhaps one of the best-known company information databases. It has been available through various online sources, such as Dialog, and on CD-ROM for many years. Subscribers may select various usage levels with *Global Access*, but the basic *Global Access* includes company information and SEC filings plus Web access to *SEC* (U.S. Company Database, also called Compact D, with financial data on over 25,000 companies), *Worldscope* (database with financial data on over 17,000 global companies), and several other optional databases.

D-190 **Bloomberg**. New York: Bloomberg, 1981- . Continually. Online format.

Bloomberg is one of the best-known information providers for the securities markets. Until recently, *Bloomberg* required the installation of a special terminal. Now, the *Bloomberg Professional* service provides access to the *Bloomberg* database via the Web or through a computer supplied by Bloomberg. *Bloomberg* provides real time and historical data on the securities markets, as well as analytics. Other features include alerts and tools for creating portfolios. *Bloomberg* covers all types of financial instruments, including stocks, bonds, commodities, money market instruments, currencies, and derivatives. There is also a wealth of information available free at the Web site (http://www.bloomberg.com).

D-191 **Standard & Poor's NetAdvantage**. New York: Standard & Poor's, 1998- . Daily. Online format.

Standard & Poor's NetAdvantage is the Web version of the S&P print library package. It contains many of the print publications discussed elsewhere in this chapter, including the *Bond Guide* (D-104), *Stock Guide* (D-105), *Corporation Records* (D-56), *Industry Surveys* (D-69), *Dividend Record* (D-116), *Earnings Guide* (D-106), *Register of Corporations* (D-33), *Stock Reports* (D-107), and the *Outlook* (D-112).

D-192 **FISOnline**. New York: Mergent (Moody's) FIS, 1987- . Daily. Online format.

FISOnline (http://www.fisonline.com) is the Web equivalent to the Mergent (formerly Moody's Investors Service) print collections. *FISOnline* contains information on companies as found in its cornerstone manuals, as well as information on bonds and dividends.

D-193 **Hoover's Online**. Austin, TX: Hoover's, 1996- . Daily. Online format.

Hoover's Online (http://www.hoovers.com) provides an abundance of free company information that is very similar in scope to that found in its print manuals. There is also an optional premium service for more detailed information about the company such as key competitors, products and operations by segment, and in-depth financials.

D-194 **Business & Company Resource Center**. Detroit: Gale, 2000- . Daily. Online format.

Business & Company Resource Center, released in mid-2000, contains a comprehensive coverage of company and industry information. Integrating many of its print resources into this single platform, Gale complements the database by adding select *Investext* reports. This product supersedes *Gale Business Resources*, Gale's previous business information Web product.

INTERNET RESOURCES

The number of Web sites devoted to business is phenomenal. Keeping current with what is available is a daunting task for any librarian. Suggestions include perusing journals such as *EContent* or *Online* that frequently cover business-related Web sites. In addition to Web directories such as Yahoo!, there are also a number of print directories available. Some examples follow:

D-195   Wasny, Garrett. **World Business Resources.com: A Directory of 8,000+ Business Resources on the Internet**. New York: McGraw-Hill, 2000.

D-196   **The Prentice Hall Directory of Online Business Information**. Englewood Cliffs, NJ: Prentice-Hall, 1998.

D-197   Liu, Lewis-Guodo. **Internet Resources and Services for International Business: A Global Guide**. Phoenix: Oryx Press, 1998.

D-198   **Plunkett's On-Line Trading, Finance & Investment Web Sites Almanac**. Houston: Plunkett Research, 2000.

This section provides an overview of some of the major types of business Web sites, along with some illustrative examples of some of the best sites. There are obviously too many business Web sites to include in one section of a chapter on business sources.

Governmental

Web sites from the federal and state governments provide some of the most useful business-related information. Many of the federal government sites have been mentioned throughout this chapter, including the Census Bureau (http://www.census.gov) and the Small Business Administration (http://www.sbaonline.sba.gov). One of the most important federal sites is *EDGAR* (http://www.sec.gov) (see D-54).

D-199   **Bureau of the Public Debt Online**. URL: http://www.publicdebt.treas.gov.
The Bureau of the Public Debt Online allows users to directly purchase treasury bills, notes, and savings bonds.

Economic data are also important. Two government sites providing a wealth of business and economic data are *FRED* and the *Bureau of Economic Analysis*. Libraries with clients seeking business or economic data should be familiar with the information available at both of these sites.

D-200   **FRED—Federal Reserve Economic Data**. URL: http://www.stls.frb .org/fred/.
FRED, available at the Web site of the Federal Reserve Bank of St. Louis, offers a wealth of economic data, both current and historical. It is the definitive site for time-series data on a range of economic issues, including interest rates, gross domestic product, consumer price indexes, producer price indexes, employment, population, federal debt, productivity, housing starts, retail sales, industrial production, banking, and reserves.

D-201   **Bureau of Economic Analysis**. URL: http://www.bea.doc.gov.
The Web site for the Department of Commerce's Bureau of Economic Analysis provides a wide range of economic data and related information. Information includes state and local data, including gross domestic product and personal income; international data, including balance of payments, exports

and imports, and foreign direct investment; and U.S. nationwide data, including gross domestic product, personal income, and price indexes. There are also links to articles containing state and local, national, and international economic data. The *Survey of Current Business* is also available in pdf format.

Investment Portals

As mentioned previously, the number of investment sites is very large. However, there are several investments "portals" that provide good starting places for the individual investor.

D-202 Yahoo! Finance. URL: http://quote.yahoo.com.
Yahoo! Finance is consistently rated as one of the best and most heavily used investment sites. This portal provides a huge amount of free information, including delaying stock quotes, company and business news, free historical quotes, international information, portfolios (with free registration), market summaries, a mutual funds section, a foreign exchange converter, broker reports, analyst recommendations, stock screening tools, discussion forums, and links to SEC files. *Yahoo! Finance* is available for many countries around the world.

D-203 Microsoft MoneyCentral Investor. URL: http://investor.msn.com.
Microsoft's site is very similar in content to *Yahoo! Finance* (D-202). It offers free delayed quotes, real-time quotes with free registration, portfolio manager, a 401(k) planner, company and mutual fund reports, investments finder and matcher services, insider trading information, market reports, and SEC filings, among other information.

D-204 Invest-o-Rama. URL: http://www.investorama.com.
This site has received a lot of publicity in the business press and is generally considered a good place to determine how many investment sites are available on the Web. Currently its "Best of the Web" categorization of investments sites has over 14,000 listings. Sites are arranged by subject in a similar format to *Yahoo!*'s main site, http://www.yahoo.com. Registration is required.

Brokerage Firms

Many of the major brokerage firms have Web sites providing a variety of business information resources. Although they are primarily geared to their own customers (including individual investors), most offer quotes and company information, news, and online tutorials. Some of the major brokerage firms are listed here.

Merrill Lynch (http://www.ml.com)

J. P. Morgan (http://www.jpmorgan.com)

Charles Schwab (http://www.schwab.com)

In addition, there are many sites devoted to individual trading (day trading). Members can access real-time quotes, company news and reports, and so forth. Examples are

Ameritrade (http://www.ameritrade.com)

E*Trade (http://www.etrade.com)

Exchanges

The Web sites for securities exchanges contain a wealth of data about the exchanges and the types of securities traded on them. Virtually every major securities exchange has its own Web site. Following are four popular U.S. sites encompassing the primary markets.

D-205 **New York Stock Exchange**. URL: http://www.nyse.com.
The New York Stock Exchange Web site contains a list of all of the companies (over 3,000) on the exchange, searchable either alphabetically, by industry, through a search engine, or by clicking on a map of the world. There are also "Market Summary" and "Fact Book" links as well as index quotes and press releases. There is also some historical information under the "Data Library" link.

D-206 **NASDAQ**. URL: http://www.nasdaq.com.
The NASDAQ Web site is much like a portal site. Users can find stock quotes, company news, analyst recommendations, market news and activities, information on global markets, recent initial public offerings, earnings, and tools such as stock screening and portfolio tracking.

D-207 **Chicago Board of Trade**. URL: http://www.cbot.com.
The Chicago Board of Trade is the leading futures exchange in the world. The Web site offers a tremendous amount of information, especially under the "Market Information" and "Quotes and Data" links. These include information about and analysis of the products traded on the exchange as well as delayed quotes and other data. The CBOT offers an inexpensive real-time quote system as well.

D-208 **Chicago Board Options Exchange**. URL: http://www.cboe.com.
The CBOE is the primary options exchange in the world. There is a lot of free information at the site, including delayed quotes and market news, symbols directory, and an options calculator under the "Trader's Tool" link. Real-time quotes are fee-based.

Business News

The Web is also a timely medium for the dissemination of breaking news stories. There are a number of major business news sites, including some that are offshoots of major news sites, such as the following.

ABC News-MoneyScope (http://abcnews.go.com/sections/business/)

CNBC (http://www.cnbe.com)

CBS Marketwatch (http://cbs.marketwatch.com)

These sites typically offer a combination of news stories, which tend to be the focus of the site, with additional business information, such as stock quotes.

D-209 **CNNfn—The Financial Network**. URL: http://www.cnnfn.com.
CNNfn is notable for several reasons. It was one of the earliest, and most popular, Web sites by a media entity devoted to business news. It is also one of the best in providing company and investment information, including stock quotes, portfolios, mutual funds, currencies, and commodities. Its "Bond Center" has also received attention in the media.

D-210 **Bloomberg**. URL: http://www.bloomberg.com.
The Bloomberg site (see D-190) is also a source for business news and other investment information. "TV" and "Radio" links provide access to video and audio streams of business news stories.

Magazines/Newspapers

Many popular business magazines and newspapers offer select stories and other business information on the Web. Others offer a combination of premium and free information.

D-211 **Wall Street Journal Interactive**. URL: http://interactive.wsj.com.

The *Wall Street Journal Interactive* edition is available to subscribers for a modest fee. The site is divided into free versus subscriber services. Free information tends to be educational links, delayed quotes, and select business news. Subscribers to the premium service can access the top market and business news.

D-212 **Fortune.com**. URL: http://www.fortune.com.

Fortune provides this convenient Web site containing news stories, investor information, and company links. There are also lists of the Fortune 500 and Global 500 companies.

D-213 **Money**. URL: http://www.money.com.

The Web site for *Money* magazine functions as a source for business news. This site also contains a wealth of free investment sources; quotes; market information; educational links; portfolios; earnings releases; and personal financial tools including retirement, automobile, and insurance information.

International Business

D-214 **OECD Online**. URL: http://www.oecd.org.

The Organisation for Economic Co-operation and Development (OECD) consists of twenty-nine member countries who come together to discuss and implement social and economic policies. It publishes a wide range of business and economic reference sources, including the *OECD Economic Outlook* (C-58), *OECD Economic Surveys* (C-61), and OECD working papers. *OECD Online* contains a broad range of information, including country information and summaries of the *OECD Economic Surveys*; a "Financial and Investments" section containing information on international trading, investing, and related areas including trade regulations, international taxation, and disclosure requirements; a "Corporate Affairs" section containing information on corporate governance and privatization, among others; sections on e-commerce, economics, emerging economies; links to country Web sites; and an array of additional business-related materials. This site is one of the most important related to international business.

D-215 **United Nations**. URL: http://www.un.org.

The United Nations was established in 1945 to promote world peace through international cooperation. There are now 189 member countries. The UN Web site contains, among many other resources, a major section, "Economic and Social Development." Here users can find trade statistics, demographics of member countries, information on sustainable development, and a variety of related statistics.

D-216 **International Monetary Fund**. URL: http://www.imf.org.

The International Monetary Fund (IMF), established in 1945, consists of 182 member countries who come together "to promote international monetary cooperation, exchange stability, and orderly exchange arrangements; to foster economic growth and high levels of employment; and to provide temporary financial assistance to countries under adequate safeguards to help ease balance of payments adjustment." The Web site contains an abundance of country information, arranged alphabetically by country name. *World Economic Outlook* (C-57) is available in full text, as are several other publications and news releases. Users can also find international standards and codes adopted by the IMF.

D-217 **World Trade Organization**. URL: http://www.wto.org.

The World Trade Organization is the only international organization that addresses the rules of trading between different countries. Based in Geneva, it is member-governed. The Web site contains the full text of trade reports, the WTO annual report, and other publications; a statistics section containing current and historical trade statistics; and the full text of WTO's legal documents.

D-218 **International Organization for Standardization—ISO Online**. URL: http://www.iso.ch.

ISO, established in 1947, consists of 130 member countries with the mission of establishing standards that could be applied worldwide to promote international trade and to develop cooperation in all endeavors between countries. ISO (which means "equal"; it is not an acronym) publishes its agreements as *ISO Standards*. Although access is limited to members, the site contains a lot of good resources about the standards, and especially ISO 9000, which deals with quality management, and ISO 14000, which deals with environmental management. Both of these series of standards have a significant impact on businesses around the world.

D-219 **Kompass**. URL: http://www.kompass.com.

Kompass is a well-known international company directory publisher. The Web version contains two levels of service, free and subscribers. Users can conduct free searches for companies by product or service or by company name. Limits can also be placed for companies in specific geographic locations. Subscribers can obtain full-company listings.

D-220 **World Bank**. URL: http://www.worldbank.org.

The World Bank produces a number of useful print publications, including *World Bank Atlas*, *Global Development Finance*, and *World Development Indicators*. The Web site contains a number of useful data sections, mostly garnered from the print publications. There is a "Data" link that allows users to search data by topic, find country data, or query the data with search commands. There are also quick reference tables for economic information such as gross domestic product. The site also provides links to news stories, special reports, and the World Bank annual report.

Additional Resources

Two important areas for business information are often overlooked: "company home pages" and the Web sites for "professional associations and organizations." Company home pages can contain much useful information, such as links to public filings, a description of products, sales and marketing information, and personnel and contact information.

Professional associations and organizations often are charged with collecting data and other information about their given profession or organizational mission. Many of these Web sites contain such data, which can be difficult or expensive to find otherwise. Directories, such as the *Encyclopedia of Associations* (D-29), often provide home page URLs.

NOTES

1. Michael J. Mandel, "The New Economy," *Business Week* no. 3666 (January 31, 2000): 73–77.

2. Donald L. Schunk, "Quarterly Outlook," *Business and Economic Review* 47, no. 1 (October-December 2000): 31.

3. Roger O. Crockett, "Netting Those Investors," *Business Week* no. 3699 (September 18, 2000): EB26.

4. Nancy Opiela, "Client Online Trading: Opportunity or Obstacle?" *Journal of Financial Planning* 13, no. 7 (July 2000): 54–60.

5. John T. Chambers, "The Future of Business," *Executive Excellence* 17, no. 2 (February 2000): 3–4.

6. "Globalization: Lessons Learned," *Business Week* no. 3706 (November 6, 2000): 228.

5

History

Daniel C. Mack

ESSAY

History has always been difficult both to define and to classify. In general, history can be said to be the study of humanity's past. This definition is broad and unfocused, and for those very reasons is perhaps the best possible definition, as it reflects the range and scope of history as a discipline. This goes hand in hand with the difficulty in classifying history as a discipline. In this book we are classifying history as one of the social sciences, along with business, economics, and psychology. Such classification is valid but is not universal. Many texts, institutions, and scholars consider history to be one of the humanities. This viewpoint approaches history as being methodologically similar to the study of literature or philosophy. Both points of view have merit, and the researcher should keep both in mind when researching historical topics.

As an academic discipline, history is rapidly changing, for a number of reasons. Advances in technology have greatly increased both the discovery and the transmission of historical sources, while methodological paradigms continue to challenge the various interpretations of those sources. At the heart of these changes stands the very meaning of "history" as a field of inquiry. Now more than ever, librarians who deal with history need a firm understanding not only of the sources available to the historian but also of the practice of historical research and of the methodological processes by which historical materials are examined.

Historiography, or "the history of history," deals with the way in which history has been treated as a field of inquiry in the past. Since there exist a number of good, general introductions to the development of history, we trace here only some general, overall patterns in the progress of historical thought from antiquity to the present. For a more comprehensive discussion of the development of historical thought, an excellent introduction to the topic can be found in Alun Munslow's *The Routledge Companion to Historical Studies* (Routledge, 2000).

History as it is generally understood in contemporary Western society is a relatively recent discipline. Most ancient civilizations did not write what we would define as history. The Egyptians, Sumerians, Babylonians, and other peoples of the ancient Mediterranean and Near East kept such records as king lists and temple records. These documents, however, did not include the analysis that distinguishes modern historical practice. The Greeks were the first to write history as we know it. In the fifth century b.c.e., Herodotus and Thucydides wrote histories that are still read and studied today. Other Greek and Roman authors wrote historical texts as well, including such figures as Julius Caesar, Livy, and Tacitus.

For the Greek and Latin historians, history was a form of literature rather than a discipline in its own right. The tone of these authors is usually didactic; they tell a story to prove a point or to teach a lesson. The purpose might be political, as it was for Caesar; or moral, as it was for Livy. The purpose of writing history, therefore, was similar to that of writing drama, poetry, or philosophy: to use past events to learn about the human condition.

Medieval historians continued the traditions of their predecessors. The Catholic Church often became the guardian of historical records throughout the Western world, and members of its clergy, such as Bede and Einhard, were some of the major historians of the Middle Ages. The ancient practice of keeping annals, or yearly lists of important events, sometimes expanded to the writing of true historical chronicles, in which events were not merely listed but were examined within the context of the writer's social and cultural order. In the Renaissance, the recovery of Greek and Latin texts, both historical and otherwise, influenced historians such as Guiccardini and Machiavelli. Renewed interest in classical antiquity also influenced the development of the auxiliary sciences of history, such as archaeology, epigraphy, and numismatics. Scholars such as Biondo and Francini recorded the material culture of the past as it was brought to light.

It was during the Enlightenment and the nineteenth century that history, as we generally use the term today, developed as an academic pursuit in its own right. The humanism of the Renaissance collided with the rising nationalism of Western Europe and the naturalism of the newly developing physical sciences. Historians sought to duplicate within their discipline the sense of causality found in physics, chemistry, and other new fields of inquiry. Besides writing narrative history, scholars began to publish works analyzing specific problems in historical research. Along with this came increasing specialization, as historians focused on the history of specific peoples, geographic areas, disciplines, and groups. During the nineteenth and twentieth centuries, especially, individual schools of historical research came into prominence. For example, the *annales* historians of early- and mid-twentieth century France were heavily influenced by the dialectical materialism of Marx, focusing on the economic and social aspects of history. In the later twentieth century, feminist and gender studies had a great impact on historical research.

The most recent phenomenon to have an impact on historical research is postmodernism. Appearing initially in studies of art and architecture, during the second half of the twentieth century postmodernism invaded literary theory, the humanities, and the social sciences, and can now be found in nearly every area of academic inquiry. Definitions of the term and its scope differ, and there exist many forms of postmodern thought. In general, however, the postmodern view can be characterized by several traits: a rejection of objectivity, the denial of the existence of eternal truth, and the refutation of a reality external to the individual. For some historians, such as Keith Windschuttle, postmodern theory is completely destroying history as an academic discipline.[1] For other scholars, including Alun Munslow, postmodern theory is a valid methodological tool, and a natural progression from the schools of thought of the past.[2]

For students, librarians, and historians in the twenty-first century, a number of developments are important when practicing historical research. First, one must be aware of the ever-increasing interdisciplinary trend that is occurring in all of the social sciences, and the humanities as well. Second, specialization in historical research continues to evolve. Whether by time period; geographical area; ethnic, racial, or social group; or some other focus, historical writing continues its trend toward specialization. Along with this goes the history of various identity groups, such as gay, lesbian, bisexual, and transgendered people. Third, recent developments in theory and method require the researcher to have a basic understanding of these new trends. Postmodernism, feminist theory, and other intellectual trends will continue to have an enormous impact on historical research and writing. Finally, and perhaps most important of all in the long run, are the new technologies available to the historian. Computers and the Internet provide both research tools and venues for the dissemination of research. The World

Wide Web makes available huge collections of primary sources that were once accessible only to those who could afford to spend the time and money required to travel to the location of such sources. E-mail and discussion groups allow rapid scholarly communication. Emerging trends in digital publication offer exciting new avenues of multimedia publication that can reach worldwide audiences.

GUIDES AND HANDBOOKS

Guides and handbooks offer both the historian and the librarian a valuable introduction to historical research. They can provide a basic understanding of the field, they offer practical advice regarding methodology, and they place the field within the broader context of general academic scholarship. The best handbooks are not simply bibliographies of resources but also present information about their use. Some handbooks stand as classics in the field, and new ones regularly appear. Following are a number of outstanding handbooks for both historical research in general and specific areas of historical inquiry.

E-1 Barzun, Jacques, and Henry F. Graff. **The Modern Researcher**. 5th ed. Fort Worth, TX: Harcourt Brace Jovanovich, 1992.

This work has long been considered a classic for historical research and is extremely useful for research in other disciplines of the social sciences as well. The authors describe in detail the process of research, from gathering primary sources, to locating secondary literature, to analyzing information and presenting it for readers. The hypothetical as well as practical aspects of historical research are addressed. The work includes bibliographies, charts, diagrams, and other material that supports the written text. A list of recommended works for further reading and a large index make this work especially valuable.

The authors have updated the fifth edition to include discussions on recent changes in the field, including new areas of inquiry as well as changes in methodology and focus. Also presented is a discussion of the use of technology in research, including the use of personal computers for accessing information as well as for writing.

E-2 Bengtson, Hermann. **Introduction to Ancient History**. Translated from the 6th ed. by R. I. Frank and Frank D. Gilliard. Berkeley: University of California Press, 1970.

Bengtson's work has long been a standard for scholars of the ancient world. This series of essays addresses a number of issues of especial importance to the study of historical antiquities. This work discusses the auxiliary sciences of history, as applicable to ancient history, including the study of epigraphy, numismatics, and papyrology. Bengtson also indicates some of the specialized types of primary sources that are important to the ancient historian, including the use of literature, mythology, and archaeological resources.

A valuable bibliography discusses some of the most important reference works and periodicals for the study of ancient history. The first section of the bibliography discusses general works; the second concentrates on specific resources by topic and area. A personal name and topic index complete the handbook.

E-3 Blazek, Ron, and Anna H. Perrault. **United States History: A Selective Guide to Information Sources**. Englewood, CO: Libraries Unlimited, 1994.

This handbook is probably the most comprehensive guide for the study of U.S. history. It covers all periods of American history from the colonial era to the present and discusses resources for historical research written from the nineteenth century to the present. The first chapter discusses general reference works, including guides, indexes and abstracting services, and dictionaries and encyclopedias. Subsequent chapters address individual subjects, including politics and government, military history, social history, and history of individual regions and states.

Rather than merely presenting a bibliography of resources, Blazek and Perrault offer useful and descriptive annotations, which often include guidelines for using individual sources. Indexes for author, title, and subjects make this work an especially significant tool for those researching U.S. history.

E-4   van Caenegem, R. C. **Guide to the Sources of Medieval History**. (Europe in the Middle Ages Selected Studies, vol. 2). Amsterdam: North Holland Publishing, 1978.

Van Caenegem's guide, although slightly dated, is still the best English-language introduction to the special problems faced by the student of medieval history. This revised English translation of earlier German and Dutch editions discusses works published before 1976. The primary focus of van Caenegem is to direct researchers to medieval texts, which he does by discussing the tools used for locating information within such texts, as well as where they are located.

Five main sections make up the body of the guide. These deal with the typology of primary sources; libraries and archives of sources; major collections of texts; reference resources; and the auxiliary sciences of history, including epigraphy, genealogy, and numismatics. Each section is divided into chapters that treat individual fields within the section and discuss the sources and methods used in each field. Both English- and foreign-language works are cited. An index allows access by author, title, and subject.

E-5   Fritze, Ronald H., et al. **Reference Sources in History: An Introductory Guide**. Santa Barbara, CA: ABC-Clio, 1990.

This handbook is a fine introduction to the types of resources used in historical research. The twelve chapters that constitute this work give a schematic arrangement of resources by material type, including bibliographies, periodical indexes, statistical sources, and guides to archives. It is this arrangement that makes this work particularly helpful for persons new to historical research. By organizing the work by resource type, the scholar is presented with an orderly and systematic view of the types of resources used by the historian.

The primary focus of this work is on American and European history and English-language resources, although some foreign-language material is included as well, and much of the information is applicable to other fields of history as well. An index allows access by author, title, and subject.

E-6   Slavens, Thomas P. **Sources of Information for Historical Research**. New York: Neal-Schuman, 1994.

Slavens's work, although useful for students and historians, will be especially appreciated by librarians because of its arrangement by Library of Congress classification number. This unique scheme has the added advantage of covering many types of interdisciplinary resources not found in other handbooks to historical research. These include works on individual world regions, ethnic groups, and specialized topics such as gender studies and international law.

In addition to annotations, Slavens includes Library of Congress Subject Headings for each source. This is very handy for locating other, similar resources. The distinctive arrangement of the resource makes it especially effective for librarians who may not be very familiar with the basics of historical research.

E-7   Trinkle, Dennis A., and Scott A. Merriman. **The History Highway 2000: A Guide to Internet Resources**. 2d ed. Armonk, NY: M. E. Sharpe, 2000.

The Internet offers both vast riches and grave perils to the historical researcher. Collections of primary sources with scholarly commentary reside side-by-side on the World Wide Web with information that is biased, inaccurate, or invented. This guide is an outstanding tool for learning to distinguish between the two. An introductory chapter gives solid practical advice on the use of e-mail, newsgroups and browsing the World Wide Web. The authors then present a fine list of Web sites of primary and secondary sources for historical research. These are arranged by time period and by region. They are followed by additional sites for special topics in history, such as women's history;

history of science; the Jewish Holocaust; civil rights history; and collections of images, maps, teaching resources, libraries, and archives.

Entries list the URL of each site. Descriptive annotations discuss the content, source, and authority of each site. These annotations help the researcher evaluate the reliability of information found on the Web.

BIBLIOGRAPHIES

Bibliography publishing in many disciplines has increased dramatically during the last few years, and history is no exception. As historical research continues to encompass both new fields of inquiry and new methodologies, the researcher faces a vast array of bibliographies of various types. For specific time periods, geographic regions, or special topics or populations, one would do well to consult one of the handbooks listed in the section above. For general research, following are a few important titles for both retrospective and current bibliographies.

E-8   **Guide to Reference Books**. 11th ed. Edited by Robert Balay. Chicago: American Library Association, 1996.

This is the single best current bibliography for the researcher. This comprehensive resource provides annotations for reference sources in all fields of inquiry. The twelfth edition, edited by Robert Kieft, is scheduled for publication in 2004.

Retrospective Bibliographies

E-9   Beers, Henry Putney. **Bibliographies in American History: Guide to Materials for Research**. Bronx, NY: H. W. Wilson, 1942.

E-10   **Bibliographies in American History, 1942–1978: Guide to Materials for Research**. Woodbridge, CT: Research Publications, 1982.

These companion works present the researcher with a comprehensive listing of bibliographic materials in U.S. history from the nineteenth century through 1978. Material coverage includes monographs; individual articles as well as periodical indexes; U.S. and foreign government documents; and guides to serials, archives, and manuscript collections. All periods of history are included. Individual subjects covered include cultural, diplomatic, military, and social history, as well as works dealing with special topics such as race, religion, and genealogy. Regional and local history of individual states, possessions, and territories are covered in both publications. Although there are no annotations, there are indexes in each work that allow access to individual titles.

E-11   Paetow, Louis John. **A Guide to the Study of Medieval History**. rev. and corrected ed. Millwood, NY: Kraus Reprint, 1980. (1st ed. 1917, 2d ed. 1931).

E-12   **Literature of Medieval History, 1930–1975: A Supplement to Louis John Paetow's** *A Guide to the Study of Medieval History*. 5 vols. Edited by Gray C. Boyce. Millwood, CT: Kraus International Publications, 1981.

These two works offer the medievalist much the same type of information as the two preceding works do for the Americanist. Paetow presents a huge amount of information organized into three major parts. Part I comprises bibliographies, general reference works, treatments of the auxiliary sciences of history, and major collections of primary sources. The second and third parts are subdivided by time period, geographic areas, and subjects.

Individual chapters are extremely useful because of Paetow's arrangement. After presenting an outline of the chapter, he then provides both readings for those new to research in medieval studies and a bibliography of resources for the advanced scholar. Coverage includes monographs and articles in English, French, German, Italian, and Spanish. An index allows access by author, subject, and title. The 1981 supplement follows a similar arrangement and brings coverage forward to 1975.

Current Bibliographies

E-13 **The American Historical Association's Guide to Historical Literature**. 3d ed. Mary Beth Norton, general ed. New York: Oxford University Press, 1995.

Another classic for historical research, this work is published by the primary professional society for historians in the United States. Arranged in forty-eight sections, it lists thousands of sources with annotations for historical research in every area of the discipline. Geographic coverage is worldwide, and time periods extend from prehistory and antiquity though the late twentieth century. Publications issued from 1961 through 1992 are included.

The primary emphasis in this resource is on works in English, although some foreign-language material is included. Separate author and subject indexes complete the guide.

E-14 **L'Annee Philologique: Bibliographie Critique et Analytique de l'Antiquite Greco-Latine**. Paris: Societe d'Editions "Les Belles Lettres," 1926- . Annual.

Contrary to its title, this bibliography is of interest not only to students of classical literature but to the ancient historian as well. This annual publication includes books, articles, and dissertations on ancient Greek and Roman civilization from prehistory until 800 C.E. The bibliography is divided into two parts. The first part, as the title of the entire work indicates, deals with classical literature and lists materials on ancient authors, works, and genres. The second part is arranged by subjects and deals with such topics as epigraphy, numismatics, and religion. A separate section indexes festschriften.

Language coverage is broad but primarily focuses on publications in English, French, German, and Italian. Some entries include annotations in the language of the publication. Access is provided by several indexes. These include indexes of classical names, a geographical index, an author index, and an index of scholars from the Renaissance to the twentieth century who were influenced by classical antiquity.

Electronic access: An electronic version, *Database of Classical Bibliography: DCB* (Scholars Press, 1995) on CD-ROM, offers access to volumes 45–60.

E-15 **Annual Bulletin of Historical Literature**. London: Historical Association, 1911- . Annual.

This resource offers bibliographic essays on historical topics published within the previous year. An introductory chapter on general sources is followed by essays on individual time periods. The focus is primarily British and European but does include some material from American and world history. Likewise, most of the sources covered are in English, but a certain amount of foreign-language material is included as well.

E-16 **International Medieval Bibliography**. Leeds, UK: Department of History, University of Leeds, 1968- . Semiannual.

Covering the period from 500 to 1500 C.E., this work includes material from periodicals, collections of essays, colloquia, and festschriften dealing with all areas of medieval studies. Geographic coverage includes Britain, Europe, Russia, and the territories ruled by the Byzantine Empire. Both English- and foreign-language materials are included.

This bibliography is arranged by general subjects, which are further subdivided geographically, then alphabetically by author. Citations are not annotated but do indicate the type of material, and they include cross-references to other entries. Each volume provides access by a general index as well as an individual author index.

INDEXES AND ABSTRACTS

For those researching historical topics, a huge array of indexing and abstracting services may be useful, depending on the specific subject. Most subject-specific indexes will lead the scholar to information on the history of a particular discipline, such as art, education, or music. General interest and multidisciplinary tools are also helpful for those doing historical research. However, there exist only a few indexes that target historical journals as their primary content.

The widespread use of the World Wide Web for the delivery of indexing and abstracting services has led to the development of digital versions of some of these research tools. These resources, and their relationship to their print equivalents, are discussed below.

Print Indexes and Abstracts

E-17 America: History and Life. Santa Barbara, CA: ABC-Clio, 1964- . 5 issues/yr.

This is the primary resource for locating secondary literature in American history. Coverage ranges from prehistory and pre-Columbian history to the present, and the geographic scope includes both the United States and Canada. Subject coverage includes political, social, and cultural history, as well as area studies and contemporary events.

Each of the five issues per year consists of six sections. The first five sections are "North America"; "Canada"; "Unites States: National History to 1945"; "United States: 1945 to Present"; and "United States: Regional, State, and Local History." Each section includes citations, often with English-language abstracts, for articles from over 2,000 journals in over forty languages; book and audiovisual reviews; and dissertations from *Dissertation Abstracts International* (A-39). These parts are listed individually by subject headings and author name. The sixth section, "History, The Humanities, and Social Sciences," lists archives and libraries, proceedings, organizations, and meetings. The first four issues of each year include indexes by author, title, reviewer, and subject. Subject listings are divided by time period. The last issue of each year cumulates the first four.

Electronic access: This work is available both on CD-ROM and via the World Wide Web.

E-18 C.R.I.S.: The Combined Retrospective Index Set to Journals in History, 1838–1974. 11 vols. Washington, DC: Carrollton, 1977–1978.

This important tool offers the researcher the opportunity to search for secondary literature in all areas of history from the early nineteenth century to the third quarter of the twentieth century. The work indexes articles from journals in history and associated fields by subject, keyword, and chronologically. The first four volumes include world history, and the next five cover U.S. history. The final two volumes form an author index. The machine-generated entries are short, and include a keyword, abbreviated article title, author, year, volume, code number corresponding to journal title, and page numbers. The endpapers of each volume reproduce the key to the journal code numbers, and each volume also has an individual table of contents.

C.R.I.S. is not the easiest index to use, and it may be of use primarily to doctoral candidates or other researchers who need to perform an exhaustive literature review of secondary sources in history back into the nineteenth century. It will, however, uncover much information that is otherwise not indexed elsewhere.

E-19 Historical Abstracts. Santa Barbara, CA: ABC-Clio, 1955- . Quarterly.

This title forms a companion to *America: History and Life* (E-20), providing similar coverage for non-American history. Currently, *Historical Abstracts* consists of two sections: "Modern History Abstracts, 1450–1914" and "Twentieth Century Abstracts, 1914–Present." The historical coverage of this work ranges from the mid-fifteenth century to the start of the First World War. Geographic coverage includes the entire world except for the United States and Canada. Articles from over 2,000 journals from more than eighty nations and in over forty languages are indexed, as well as books and dissertations.

Each of the sections described above is issued quarterly. Citations are arranged in three categories. These include General (only for "Modern History Abstracts"), dealing with works on pedagogy, bibliography, and historical method; Topics, which covers broad subject areas such as military history or international relations; and Area or Country, which focuses on works dealing with historical topics by region. All entries are arranged chronologically and then by author. An annual index analyzes both sections.

Electronic access: Like *America: History and Life*, this work is also available on CD-ROM and via the World Wide Web.

Online Indexes and Abstracts

E-20 America: History and Life. Santa Barbara, CA: ABC-Clio, 1964- . Monthly updates. Online format.

This digital, Web-based version of *America: History and Life* is the preeminent electronic tool for locating secondary literature in American history. With a single search, the researcher can explore the contents of the print version of the index from its inception in 1964.

The easy-to-use search form allows researchers to enter any combination of keyword, subject term, author or editor name, title, language, document type, journal name, publication name, time period, or entry number. The search results list displays brief records with document type, author, title, citation, and ISSN. The full-record display includes the language of the work; a brief, English-language abstract; time period; and subject headings. Records can be tagged on the search results list for output via ASCII display for printing or for e-mail to the researcher's account. Searches can be modified without having to re-enter data.

E-21 Historical Abstracts. Santa Barbara, CA: ABC-Clio, 1955- . Monthly updates. Online format.

This is the Web-based version of the print index. Updated monthly, it shares the same search and output features as the electronic version of *America: History and Life* (E-20).

DICTIONARIES AND ENCYCLOPEDIAS

During the past several years there has been an explosion in the publication of specialized dictionaries and encyclopedias. This has been especially true in the field of history. The very nature of the discipline encourages specialization by time period, geographic location, and special topic. A complete survey of these resources is well beyond the scope of the present work. Following are several recent, well-written single- and multiple-volume dictionaries and encyclopedias for various periods. For more specialized works, consult a handbook or bibliography such as the *Guide to Reference Books* (E-8).

Dictionaries and encyclopedias can assist the historical researcher in several ways. These works can provide a general historical overview of a place, period, or subject; they can supply background information on an unfamiliar topic; and they often include bibliographies, which can lead to other important sources of information.

World History

There is a large number of single- and multiple-volume reference works on world history; these can be found in *Sources of Information for Historical Research* (E-6).

E-22 **Encyclopedia of World History**. New York: Oxford University Press, 1998.

This single-volume work is an outstanding ready reference source for general topics in the history of the world. The geographical coverage is worldwide, and time periods span from prehistory to the present. The content, derived from the *Oxford Illustrated Encyclopedia*, covers political, social, cultural, and military history.

Besides being useful, this volume is also handsome. Colored illustrations and maps contribute to the information in the text, which itself is well written and straightforward. An index allows access to information within individual articles.

Ancient History

Classicists still use the exhaustive *Paulys Real-Encyclopädie der Classischen Altertumswissenschaft*, begun by August Friedrich von Pauly (Metler, 1894–1967). The scope of ancient history in recent times has expanded beyond the traditional emphasis on the political, military, and literary history of the Greco-Roman world to include the civilizations of ancient Egypt, the Middle and Far East, and the Americas. Following are a few titles of interest to those researching ancient history.

E-23 **A Dictionary of Ancient History**. Edited by Graham Speake. Cambridge, MA: Blackwell Reference, 1994.

This work contains articles on the history and civilization of the ancient Mediterranean world, with an emphasis on Greece, the Hellenistic world, and the Roman Empire. Subject coverage includes social, cultural, political, and military topics. Illustrations, diagrams, and maps supplement the text.

E-24 **The Oxford Classical Dictionary**. 3d ed. Edited by Simon Hornblower and Antony Spawfort. New York: Oxford University Press, 1996.

The latest edition of this standard work provides signed articles on the Greek and Roman worlds. Geographic coverage includes all areas permeated by Greek and Roman civilization, and subject coverage consists of art, archaeology, geography, language and literature, science, technology, and religion. Political, military, social, and cultural history are all addressed. Entries include names of persons, institutions, and groups, as well as places, terms, and customs.

Many of the articles, which range in length from a short paragraph to several pages, include bibliographies. These can be especially valuable to the researcher, because they include both modern and ancient sources, and so form a helpful link to primary source material. A general bibliography lists additional reading.

E-25 **The Oxford Encyclopedia of Ancient Egypt**. Donald B. Redford, ed.-in-chief. New York: Oxford University Press, 2001.

This outstanding three-volume resource will serve as an exceptional example of the fine specialized historical encyclopedias currently available. Redford, himself a preeminent scholar of ancient Egypt, has assembled a board of contributors that reads like a "Who's Who" of Egyptology. Colored photographs, illustrations, maps, and bibliographies supplement the signed articles. The final volume includes a comprehensive index.

E-26 **The Penguin Encyclopedia of Classical Civilizations**. Edited by Arthur Cotterell. New York: Viking, 1993.

Another single-volume work, this encyclopedia covers not only the Greco-Roman world but also Persia, India, and early China. Historical coverage ranges from 550 B.C.E. to 600 C.E. Articles are signed and are supplemented by maps and illustrations.

E-27 The Encyclopedia of Ancient Civilizations. Edited by Arthur Cotterell. New York: Mayflower Books, 1980.

Related in format to Cotterell's previous work (E-26), *The Encyclopedia of Ancient Civilizations* includes information on ancient Africa and North and South America.

The Middle Ages and the Renaissance

E-28 Dictionary of the Middle Ages. Joseph R. Strayer, ed.-in-chief. New York: Scribner's, 1982–1989.

This huge project, comprising thirteen volumes of research on the medieval world, was produced under the sponsorship of the American Council of Learned Societies. Geographic coverage includes Europe, most of the Mediterranean world, and the Muslim Near East. The time period covers 500 to 1500 C.E. Topics include the arts, customs, society, culture, politics, and religion. Religion is especially well treated in the dictionary, which is not surprising for a work covering what is often referred to as the "Age of Faith." Although the Catholic Church in the West predominates, the Eastern Church, Judaism, and Islam are not neglected, nor are heretical movements within these faiths.

The editors of the dictionary state that novices, college students, and specialized researchers will all benefit from this work. Detailed bibliographies, maps, and illustrations accompany many articles, and a vast index with cross-references completes this important resource.

E-29 Encyclopedia of the Middle Ages. Norman F. Cantor, general ed. New York: Viking, 1999.

For those librarians and historians seeking a single-volume reference work on the Middle Ages, this encyclopedia will serve well. Covering the period from about 400 to about 1450 C.E., this work includes information on the medieval civilizations of Europe and the Muslim Near East and northern Africa. Maps as well as color and black-and-white illustrations highlight the text.

E-30 Encyclopedia of the Renaissance. 6 vols. Paul F. Grendler, ed.-in-chief. New York: Scribner's, 1999.

This encyclopedia covers the period from about 1300 to 1600 C.E. Geographic coverage emphasizes Europe but occasionally addresses Asia and the New World when applicable. Signed articles deal with the arts, customs, society, culture, politics, and religion of the Renaissance world. The influence of the fine arts and of humanistic scholarship on society, and vice versa, is especially well documented. Illustrations, some in color, accompany the text, as do maps. Bibliographical references and a very thorough index complete the work.

Modern History

E-31 The Facts on File Encyclopedia of the Twentieth Century. John Drex, general ed. New York: Facts on File, 1991.

This large, single-volume reference work covers the period from the turn of the century through the end of the 1980s. Geographic coverage is worldwide, with an emphasis on the United States and other developed nations. The content emphasizes not only political history and international relations but also social issues and movements, such as racism and the role of women.

The encyclopedia is illustrated and contains a comprehensive index. Bibliographical material directs the researcher to primary and secondary literature on individual topics. This is a fine work for researchers wanting a single-volume, ready reference tool for modern history.

American History

A huge number of new reference works on all aspects of American history have been published in the past ten years. These cover specific time periods, such as the Civil War or the 1960s; the history of specific groups, such as Hispanic Americans or American women; and various trends in American society and culture. Following are a few of the best dictionaries and encyclopedias available; the advanced researcher will find more in the *Guide to Reference Books* (E-8) or *Sources of Information for Historical Research* (E-6).

General American History

E-32 **The American Heritage Encyclopedia of American History**. John Mack Faragher, general ed. New York: Henry Holt, 1998.

Another fine single-volume reference work, this collection of essays covers all periods of American history from the pre-Columbian to the last part of the twentieth century. Although the primary focus is on political and social developments in the United States, the encyclopedia also addresses issues such as American arts and culture, international relations, and the development of science and technology.

The text is accompanied by illustrations and maps. Bibliographical references and a comprehensive index make this a handy work for both students and more advanced scholars.

Special Topics in American History

The following resources are some of the best works dealing with specific periods, groups, and special topics in American history.

E-33 **Encyclopedia of African-American Culture and History**. 6 vols. Edited by Jack Salzman, David Lionel Smith, and Cornel West. New York: Macmillan Library Reference, 1996.

This important work offers essays on all aspects of the African-American experience, from the arrival of the first slaves in the seventeenth century through the twentieth century. Many of the entries are biographical. The role of African Americans in art, literature, law, sports, science, and technology is emphasized, along with the political, social, and cultural movements that influenced the position of African Americans in American life.

The encyclopedia is arranged by subject. Entries are frequently accompanied by illustrations, photographs, charts, and tables. Bibliographical references and a comprehensive index complete the work.

E-34 **Encyclopedia of the American Civil War: A Political, Social, and Military History**. Edited by David S. Heidler and Jeanne T. Heidler. Santa Barbara, CA: ABC-Clio, 2000.

The American Civil War continues to be a favorite topic for both professional and amateur historians. This essential work, consisting of five volumes of essays, will be invaluable to both. Every aspect of the war is discussed, including the social, cultural, political, and legal issues that preceded and followed it.

Illustrations and detailed maps accompany the text in this encyclopedia. Besides bibliographic material and indexing, the work offers useful primary source material in the final volume, which consists of documents and appendixes.

E-35 **Gale Encyclopedia of Multicultural America**. 2d ed. 3 vols. Jeffrey Lehman, ed.; Robert von Dassanowsky, contributing ed. Detroit: Gale, 2000.

This reference tool offers information on over 150 ethnic and religious groups in the United States. The encyclopedia is especially useful for researchers trying to quickly locate historical and cultural information on Native American groups.

Heavily illustrated with photographs, drawings, and maps, the entries usually include bibliographies of both primary and secondary source material. A complete index concludes the work.

E-36 Mays, Terry M. **Historical Dictionary of the American Revolution**. Lanham, MD: Scarecrow Press, 1999.

This dictionary includes information on the military, political, social, and economic background of the America Revolution. Entries are found on the people, places, organizations, groups, and battles of the period, and include illustrations, maps, and bibliographical material for further reading.

DIRECTORIES

Directories are an often-neglected, but valuable, resource for the historical researcher. By providing contact information such as addresses, telephone and fax numbers, e-mail addresses, URLs, and institutional affiliation, directories can often direct the researcher to helpful persons, institutions, or organizations.

E-37 **Directory of Historical Organizations in the United States and Canada**. 14th ed. Nashville, TN: American Association for State and Local History, 1990.

Although somewhat out-of-date, this is the most recent edition of the most comprehensive directory of historical organizations in North America. More than 13,000 entries are included under four main categories: historical organizations in the United States, a quick reference guide to state history offices, organizations in Canada, and vendors of products and services in North America. Entries include full contact information, comprising addresses and phone numbers. Staffing information and organizational charts are offered for organizations when relevant. The final section, really a business directory, is largely out-of-date now. This still-valuable resource would be much improved by a new edition that included e-mail addresses and URLs for relevant entries, as well as vendors for computer-related products and resources.

E-38 **Directory of History Departments and Organizations in the United States and Canada**. Washington, DC: American Historical Association, Institutional Services Program, 1975- . Annual.

The twenty-fifth edition of this annual directory (1999/2000) lists various historical organizations in North America. Leaning heavily toward academia, the bulk of the entries consists of departments of history at colleges, universities, and research institutions in Canada and the United States. These entries are especially valuable to students in search of advanced degrees. Entries list names and addresses of contact faculty, degrees and areas of specialization, and data on enrollment and cost of tuition.

State and local historical associations are also included, with entries providing the relevant contact information. Several indexes allow researchers to search by name of institution, geographic area, and subject.

E-39 **Grants, Fellowships, and Prizes of Interest to Historians**. Washington, DC: American Historical Association, Institutional Services Program, 1987- . Annual.

The most recent edition of this directory, for the years 2000/2001, continues to provide historians with information for funding research. Awards are categorized under three headings: grants to individual persons for pre-dissertation, dissertation, postdoctoral, and independent research; grants to groups, including research teams, scholarly societies, and organizations; and prizes for monographs, dissertations, articles, and edited works. The entries are quite useful and give contact information including name of sponsoring organization, description of research areas that are funded, monetary amount of award, criteria for judging, and detailed information on application procedures. An index and bibliography to other sources of grant funding make this an especially handy work for the scholar in need of financial support for historical research.

ARCHIVES, MANUSCRIPTS, AND ORAL HISTORIES

Historians, perhaps more than scholars in any other field of inquiry, rely profoundly on archives and manuscripts. These form the foundation of primary source material upon which scholarly research in history is based. Although some oral history was preserved in writing in the past, with the proliferation of easy methods to produce and archive sound recordings, oral history became an important field of research over the course of the twentieth century.

The Internet has greatly facilitated historians' access to these collections. The World Wide Web offers the capability to go far beyond merely indexing a collection, to even offer remote users the ability to view facsimiles of their content. Many of the major directories to archives, manuscripts, and oral histories have ceased publication in print and are now offered only on the Web.

E-40 **ArchivesUSA**. Arlington, VA: Chadwyck-Healey, 1997- . Regularly. Online format.

This Web-based resource is one of the most outstanding sources available for researchers seeking primary resource material. Continuously updated, this cumulates the information previously found in the *National Union Catalog of Manuscript Collections*, the *National Inventory of Documentary Resources in the United States*, and the *Directory of Archives and Manuscript Repositories in the United States*. The database lists the holdings and contact information of over 4,000 repositories, and indexes nearly 100,000 special collections. These include archives and special collections at colleges, universities, and other academic institutions; holdings of government agencies, corporations, and organizations; and some private collections.

The search engine allows the researcher to search collections or repositories by name, keyword, geographic location, collection dates, NIDS Fiche Number, and NUCMC Number. The power and speed of searching makes this a primary resource for historians and librarians.

E-41 **Oral History Collections**. Compiled and edited by Alan M. Meckler and Ruth McMullin. New York: R. R. Bowker, 1975.

Although a new edition of this work would be useful, the 1975 edition still offers much for the historian investigating oral history. The bulk of the information deals with United States collections, but there are some foreign collections included as well. Time coverage goes to 1974. The work is divided into two parts. The first part provides name and subject access to individual oral histories, including such information as the interviewee's title or position, number of pages of material transcribed in each history, conditions of use, language of interview if not in English, length of the interview, and dates of interview. The second part lists information on the various centers of oral history in which the works in part one are located. These entries include the name, address, and telephone number of the repository; information on use of the collections; mission of the organization; and some of the major collections at each research center. This section is arranged geographically, by state or province and city.

E-42 **Oral History Index: An International Guide to Oral History Interviews**. Edited by Ellen Wasserman. Westport, CT: Meckler, 1990.

With a more international scope than the preceding work, this index lists more than 30,000 oral histories held by 400 institutions in the United States, Canada, the United Kingdom, and Israel.

Histories are listed by the name of the interviewee or of the collection. Entries include the date, place, and language of the interview; a short abstract; and a code for the institution at which the transcript is held. An index matches these codes with the name of the center; the organization with which it is affiliated, if applicable; and the address, telephone number, and other contact information.

CHRONOLOGIES

Chronologies offer the historian and the librarian perspective. By placing persons and events within their historical context, chronologies allow the researcher to see the "big picture."

E-43 Mellersh, H. E. L. **The Chronology of World History**. 4 vols. Santa Barbara, CA: ABC-Clio, 1999.

This large work covers the entire world from prehistory to 1998. As with many chronologies, coverage becomes more detailed as one comes forward in time. Volume one covers the ancient and medieval world, prehistory to 1491 C.E.; volume two, *The Expanding World*, covers 1492–1775; volume three, *The Changing World*, includes the years 1776–1900; and the final volume, *The Modern World*, covers 1901–1998.

Mellersh includes events of significance in all areas of human activity, including the arts, science, technology, and scholarship, as well as in political, social, cultural, and military history. Detailed bibliographic references and several indexes make this an especially useful work for librarians, historians, and researchers at all levels.

E-44 Carruth, Gorton. **The Encyclopedia of World Facts and Dates**. 9th ed. New York: HarperCollins, 1993.

The most recent edition of this popular work covers the whole world, indeed the entire universe, from 18 billion years ago to the end of 1992 C.E. Coverage is more detailed for more recent years, and the time spans for each period become progressively shorter; prehistoric periods cover millions of years, until we reach the twentieth century, at which point the chronology proceeds annually.

Time periods after the prehistoric period are arranged under nine headings: vital statistics and demographics; disasters; exploration and colonization; politics and war; economy and trade; religion and philosophy; science, education, and technology; arts and leisure; and sports, games, and society. Cross-references and a complete index make this a very convenient, single-volume reference tool.

E-45 Carruth, Gorton. **The Encyclopedia of American Facts and Dates**. 10th ed. New York: HarperCollins, 1997.

Similar to Carruth's *Encyclopedia of World Facts and Dates* (E-44), this resource covers North American events from 986 C.E. to 1996. Events are listed under four headings: exploration, war, politics and government, and statistics; arts and media; business, philosophy, religion, science and technology, and education; and crime, sports, and social events. Again, coverage is more detailed for more recent years.

E-46 Grun, Bernard. **The Timetables of History**. 3d ed. rev. New York: Simon & Schuster, 1993.

Grun's edition includes much material translated from Werner Stein's *Kulturfahrplan* of 1946 and is updated to include events from 5000 B.C.E. to 1990 C.E. Grun classifies events under seven categories: history and politics; literature and theater; religion, philosophy, and learning; visual arts; music; science, technology, and growth; and daily life. Especially useful for the researcher is the comprehensive index, which allows one to search for the names of persons, groups, creative works, and historical events. Geographical coverage is worldwide but does emphasize the industrialized West in later periods.

ATLASES

The disciplines of geography and history have always been intertwined; indeed, historical works are often classified along with area studies. Historical atlases are excellent resources for researchers to see, visually, how historical events have changed the face of the Earth. The enormous number of fine historical atlases prevents the listing of more than a handful of the best ones available. Historians and librarians should check *Sources of Information for Historical Research* (E-6) for atlases of specific regions, peoples, events, or time periods.

E-47 **Rand McNally Atlas of American History**. Skokie, IL: Rand McNally, 1999.

Of the several atlases of American history, this one is perhaps the most useful. Covering the historical geography of North America from the pre-Columbian period through the twentieth century, this atlas presents colored maps showing the migrations of peoples; the political expansion of the United States; and the progress of various political, military, social, and cultural movements. An index allows the researcher to locate specific information.

E-48 **The Times Atlas of World History**. 4th ed. Edited by Geoffrey Parker. Maplewood, NJ: Hammond Incorporated, 1993.

This excellent atlas contains hundreds of colored maps illustrating the geographical influence of historical events from prehistory to the present. Every geographical area of the world is covered, and included are natural, social, political, and cultural movements from prehistory through most of the twentieth century. Maps appear in various scales and use color keys and symbols to demonstrate their subjects. Colored illustrations, a world chronology, a glossary, and an index make this work especially useful for researchers.

E-49 Haywood, John, with Charles Freeman, Paul Garwood, and Judith Toms; cartographer, Nathalie Johns. **The Cassell Atlas of the Ancient World: 4,000,000– 500 BC**. London: Cassell, 1998.

Of the many atlases available for the various regions and periods of antiquity, this work is the most comprehensive. The detailed, colored maps are divided into the following sections: outline of world history, the Middle East, Africa, Europe and the Mediterranean, and Asia and the Americas. The maps trace the development of civilization in the arts, sciences, and intellectual thought as well as political, social, and military events. The researcher will find the encyclopedia of terms, the timelines, the table to the "Kings of Egypt," and the index especially useful.

GENERAL HISTORIES

Collectively known as the *Cambridge Histories*, the following works began as a project at Cambridge University in the late nineteenth century; the first editions were not completed until nearly halfway though the twentieth century. All of the works have undergone revision, and new editions are in various stages of publication. Generally, the *Cambridge Histories* are arranged chronologically and topically, with individual chapters authored by scholars specializing in the field under discussion. Although some of the prose is dense and makes heavy reading for students, these works still prove valuable for historians, librarians, and other researchers requiring a thorough and in-depth narrative historical discussion.

E-50 **The Cambridge Ancient History**. Cambridge: Cambridge University Press, 1922–1939.

The first edition was originally issued as twelve volumes, but the physical item consists of several more, due to some volumes being issued as second editions, and some in a new edition, edited by Johan Broadman and others, from 1982 to 1991. Geographic coverage includes most of the world, with an emphasis on the Mediterranean region, Europe, and the Middle East. Time periods covered range from prehistory to the fourth century C.E. Individual chapters are written by subject specialists.

Of particular value to researchers are the extensive bibliographies accompanying each chapter. The text is frequently accompanied by drawings, diagrams, maps, and charts, and plates depict archaeological artifacts and works of art.

Publication of new editions of individual volumes is unpredictable, and serious scholars should check all available editions for any given volume, as they may include different information and resources.

E-51 **The Cambridge Medieval History**. 8 vols. Cambridge: Cambridge University Press, 1911–1936.

E-52 **The New Cambridge Medieval History**. 7 vols. Cambridge: Cambridge University Press, 1995- .

The geographic coverage of these works includes Europe, the Byzantine Empire, and the Islamic Middle East and northern Africa. The time period covers the Christianization of the Roman Empire in the early fourth century C.E. to the end of the Middle Ages in the fifteenth century. As in the *Cambridge Ancient History* (E-50), specialists have contributed individual chapters. These sets contain no plates, but do include extremely detailed bibliographical references as well as maps in each volume. Various volumes have been edited and reprinted.

E-53 **The Cambridge Modern History**. 13 vols. Cambridge: Cambridge University Press, 1902–1926.

E-54 **The New Cambridge Modern History**. 14 vols. Cambridge: Cambridge University Press, 1957–1979.

As with the other *Cambridge Histories*, individual chapters of these works are authored by subject specialists. The new edition lacks many of the detailed bibliographic references found in the first edition, and is therefore favored by some scholars. Again, new editions of individual volumes appear sporadically, and some volumes have been reprinted. Scholars will want to consult all available editions.

BIOGRAPHICAL DICTIONARIES

Biographical resources are highly used reference tools in any collection, and the collection supporting historical research is no exception. For advanced research, or when trying to locate information on more obscure figures, historians and librarians have in the past been forced to rely on large, multivolume sets such as the *Dictionary of American Biography* (E-57n) and the *Dictionary of National Biography* (E-58). Unfortunately, these sets often are held only by larger libraries, they can be confusing and unwieldy to use, and they require scholars to check multiple sets and supplements. With the advent of electronic resources, this important biographical information is now much more accessible to researchers at all levels.

Single-Volume Biographical Dictionaries

E-55 **The Cambridge Biographical Encyclopedia**. 2d ed. Edited by David Crystal. New York: Cambridge University Press, 1998.

With over 15,000 entries and 22,000 cross-references, this is perhaps the most comprehensive single-volume biographical resource available. Most entries are short, but they give the vital facts and dates of the person discussed in each entry. Persons of all ethnic and racial background in politics and government, the arts, sports, science, technology, religion, literature, and other fields are included.

This work is especially useful because of the accompanying tables and charts, which list political figures, Nobel Prize winners, and leaders in other fields.

E-56 **Merriam-Webster's Biographical Dictionary**. Springfield, MA: Merriam-Webster, 1995.

Listing more than 30,000 persons deceased since 3000 b.c.e., this work is another convenient ready reference source of biographical information. Emphasis is on figures from American, Canadian, and European history, although there is coverage of people from Asia, Africa, and Oceania as well. Entries include full name, titles, degrees, birth and death dates or historical era, national or ethnic identity, and career highlights. Abundant cross-references are especially useful for non-Western names.

Multivolume Biographical Dictionaries

E-57 **American National Biography**. 24 vols. John A. Garraty and Mark C. Carnes, general eds. New York: Oxford University Press, 1999.

This vast resource includes biographical material on deceased Americans, defined as persons born in the United States or its original colonies; persons from territories later annexed to the United States; and naturalized citizens. Produced under the auspices of the American Council of Learned Societies, this work largely replaces the *Dictionary of American Biography* (Scribner's, 1928–1937) and its *Supplements* 1–10 (Scribner's, 1944–1994). The signed entries include full names, dates, titles, ethnicity, and detailed information of the person's career and relevance to American civilization.

E-58 **Dictionary of National Biography**. London: Oxford University Press, 1885–1901; reprinted 1921–1922 and 1937; supplements by Oxford University Press for 1901–1911, 1912–1921, 1922–1930, 1931–1940, 1941–1950, 1951–1960, 1961–1970, 1971–1980, and 1981–1985.

This is another huge biographical project, which gives biographical information for tens of thousands of men and women of British birth or decent, or famous in the British Isles. Like the *American National Biography* (E-57), this work gives detailed biographical information for well-known persons in all fields of human achievement. Entries are written by subject specialists and provide in-depth biographical information.

Electronic Resources

E-59 **Biography and Genealogy Master Index Online**. Detroit: Gale Research, 1997- . Continuously updated. Online format.

This amazing electronic resource indexes biographical information on over 10 million influential people worldwide, both contemporary and historical. The entries refer the researcher to hundreds of general and specialized biographical sources. The coverage is truly international in scope, and includes figures from all time periods.

Researchers have three search options: a simple search for any word in a person's name; an extended search, which allows for searching multiple terms, including words in name, birth and death date range, and source of information; and an expert search mode that allows complicated Boolean searching. Researchers will find this a valuable resource because of the large number of reference works it indexes.

CORE JOURNALS FOR HISTORICAL RESEARCH

As are other academic disciplines, history is well-provided with numerous journals for the dissemination of scholarship in the field. Journals offer the best way to find current information on specific topics. The growth of the Internet is radically changing academic publishing, and each day, more journals go online. To find out the indexing and availability of an individual journal title via the Internet, go to JAKE (Jointly Administered Knowledge Environment), hosted by the Cushing/Whitney Medical Library at the Yale University School of Medicine (http://jake.med.yale.edu/). Two important resources for full-text electronic journals in history, as well as in other social sciences and humanities disciplines, follow.

E-60 JSTOR. Online format. URL: http://www.jstor.org.
JSTOR is a nonprofit association for the archiving of digital periodicals, and is administered by a consortium of academic institutions.

E-61 **Project Muse**. Online format. URL: http://muse.jhu.edu.
Project Muse is an enterprise of the Johns Hopkins University Press, in collaboration with the Milton S. Eisenhower Library at Johns Hopkins University, and offers digital archiving of humanities and social science journals.

Because tens of thousands of journals are published, covering all areas and time periods of historical inquiry, we can only list a few of the most influential, important, and widely distributed titles for general history and for individual topics, regions, and eras. Detailed information on subject-specific journals can be found in *Sources of Information for Historical Research* (E-6).

General and Interdisciplinary History

E-62 **American Historical Review**. New York: Macmillan, 1896- . 5 issues/yr.
Published under the auspices of the American Historical Association, this journal publishes articles on both U.S. and world history, as well as on historiography, historical methodology, and the teaching of history. Entries include research articles, book and media reviews. The journal is indexed in numerous print and electronic resources.
Electronic access: Available full text via JSTOR (E-60) (http://www.jstor.org).

E-63 **Journal of Interdisciplinary History**. Cambridge, MA: MIT School of Humanities and Social Science, Autumn 1970- . Quarterly.
This title focuses on the use of multiple disciplines in the study of the past and encourages interdisciplinary research. The journal publishes research and review articles, research notes, and book reviews. Widely indexed.
Electronic access: Available full text via Project Muse (E-61) (http://muse.jhu.edu).

E-64 **Journal of Social History**. Pittsburgh, PA: Carnegie-Mellon University, 1967- . Quarterly.
Published by Carnegie-Mellon University, this journal focuses on social history from all geographical areas and time periods. Research articles and reviews include works on social movements, gender studies, ethno-history, and related topics. This journal is indexed in several print and online resources.
Electronic access: Available full text via Project Muse (E-61) (http://muse.jhu.edu).

E-65 **Journal of World History**. Honolulu, HI: University of Hawaii Press, 1990- . Semiannual.
The official journal of the World History Association, this publication features articles and reviews in all areas of world history and from all time periods. Emphasis is placed on cross-cultural studies and on historical developments that influence multiple civilizations and cultures. The journal is indexed in several print and digital works.
Electronic access: Available full text via Project Muse (E-61) (http://muse.jhu.edu).

E-66 **Social Science History**. Beverly Hills, CA: Sage, 1976- . Quarterly.

This journal is the official publication of the Social Science History Association. Its emphasis is on applying the methods of the social sciences to historical research and on analyzing events of the past in light of their influence on society and social movements. This journal is indexed in several print and online resources.

Electronic access: Available full text via Project Muse (E-61) (http://muse.jhu.edu).

United States History

The vast number of periodicals in all fields of American history does not permit a comprehensive examination of available titles. Researchers can locate specific titles for individual areas of U.S. history in *Sources of Information for Historical Research* (E-6). The following journals are highly respected and widely available.

E-67 **Journal of American History**. Bloomington, IN: Mississippi Valley Historical Association, 1964- [volume 51]. Quarterly.

This title began publication in 1907, and has been published by the Mississippi Valley Historical Association since 1964. The journal addresses all aspects of U.S. and reviews books, films, movie, television programs, museum exhibits, resource guides, microforms, oral history, archive and manuscript collections, and bibliographies of scholarship contained in recent periodicals and dissertations. The journal is indexed in various print and electronic resources.

Electronic access: Available full text via JSTOR (E-60) (http://www.jstor.org).

E-68 **Reviews in American History**. Westport, CT: Redgrave Information Resources, 1973- . Quarterly.

This excellent review journal covers all areas of U.S. history and provides in-depth reviews of the newest books in American history, retrospective essays that examine landmark works by major historians, and reviews of other media. This is another journal that is indexed by several print and electronic resources.

Electronic access: Available full text via JSTOR (E-60) (http://www.jstor.org).

INTERNET AND WORLD WIDE WEB RESOURCES

As in all subject areas, the last few years have seen an exponential growth in Internet and World Wide Web resources for history. And, as with most information on the Web, these resources vary enormously in content, format, and reliability. All researchers need to be aware of the dependability of the information they are accessing, and librarians and teachers of history have a special duty to teach students how to discern, distinguish, and evaluate these resources.

Online resources have various formats. In addition to some of the Web resources listed above, which are electronic versions of commercial print resources or of academic journals, there exist other types of material. Discussion lists and newsgroups allow historians to engage in scholarly communication and provide an informal venue for the dissemination of ideas. Web sites, especially, can take many forms, including meta sites, which function primarily as clearinghouses to other sites; search engines, which allow researchers to search the Web for specific words or phrases; and collections of primary and secondary historical material in electronic facsimile.

For a listing of discussion groups, go to *The Directory of Scholarly and Professional E-Conferences* (http://n2h2.com/KOVACS/). For Usenet newsgroups, go to the *Usenet Newsgroups Comprehensive Directory* (http://www.tile.net/tile/news/index.html).

Because of the huge amount of material on the Internet, only a few of the main resources for historical research are listed here. For more sites, see *The History Highway 2000: A Guide to Internet Resources* (E-7).

General, Interdisciplinary, and World History

E-69 **University History Departments Around the World**. URL: http://chnm .gmu.edu/history/depts/.
Maintained by the Center for History and New Media at George Mason University, this site is a collection of links to the Web sites of academic history departments from colleges, universities, and research institutions from around the world. It appears to be updated regularly.

E-70 **NM's Creative Impulse**. URL: http://history.evansville.net/.
This huge meta-site indexes Web sites on the history of various cultures and civilizations around the world and from every era. The content includes social, cultural, legal, political, and military history, as well as historical information on intellectual life and the fine and performing arts in various civilizations. There is a special emphasis on the fine arts. The site is maintained by the Harrison High School of Evansville, Illinois, and by the University of Evansville.

E-71 **World History Compass**. URL: http://www.WorldHistoryCompass.com /index.htm.
This meta-site offers links to many history-related sites, organized by geographic location, by time period, or by subject. The site is maintained by Schiller Computing of Stratford, Connecticut.

E-72 **World History Links**. URL: http://www.milan.k12.in.us/.
This meta-site indexes hundreds of other Web pages devoted to all periods and geographical locations of world history. This site is a production of the Milan, Indiana, Community School Corporation.

Ancient History

E-73 **Ancient World Web**. URL: http://www.julen.net/ancient/.
Maintained largely as a labor of love by Julia Hayden, this is one of the best meta-sites for ancient history. Not only does the site index Web pages by topic, such as religion, archaeology, daily life, and language and literature, it also includes a search feature and allows for submission of feedback.

E-74 **Argos: Limited Area Search Engine of the Ancient and Medieval Internet**. URL: http://argos.evansville.edu/.
Sponsored by the University of Evansville, Argos is one of the first and best peer-reviewed search engines on the World Wide Web. Coverage includes the Mediterranean world, the Roman Empire, and Europe from prehistory through about 1400 C.E.

E-75 **Diotima: Materials for the Study of Women and Gender in the Ancient World**. URL: http://www.stoa.org/diotima/.
Ross Scaife and Suzanne Bonefas began this project, hosted first by the University of Kentucky and then by The Stoa, to gather course materials, primary and secondary resources, and links for the study of women and gender in antiquity. Coverage includes the Mediterranean world and Europe from prehistory through about 500 C.E.

E-76 **University of Michigan Papyrus Collection**. URL: http://www.lib.umich .edu/pap/.

The University of Michigan houses one of the largest collections of papyri in the world, featuring over 10,000 papyri fragments. This excellent site features searching capabilities and facsimiles of papyri and provides much useful information placing these texts within their historical and cultural context.

Medieval and Renaissance History

E-77 **Centre for Reformation and Renaissance Studies**. URL: http://crrs .utoronto.ca/.

This research institution at the University of Toronto, Canada, offers a great deal of information on its Web site. Included are course-related materials, publications of the Centre, bibliographic materials, and a collection of diverse Web links dealing with the arts, culture, and religious thought of the Renaissance and Reformation in Europe from about 1300 to 1650.

E-78 **The International Medieval Institute**. URL: http://www.leeds.ac.uk/imi/.

Sponsored by the International Medieval Institute at the University of Leeds, United Kingdom, this site offers not only digital access to the *International Medieval Bibliography* but also links to numerous other sites dealing with all aspects of medieval culture.

E-79 **The Labyrinth: Resources for Medieval Studies**. URL: http://www .georgetown.edu/labyrinth/labyrinth-home.html.

This exceptional site, hosted and maintained by Georgetown University, provides admission to numerous resources for medieval studies. Primary resource materials, including both texts and images, are included, together with secondary and teaching resources. Access is provided by authors of primary texts; by national cultures; by subjects such as paleography, religious history, and music; and by special topics such as the Crusades, heraldry, and medieval women.

Modern History

There are too many Web sites for modern history to list them all here. For information on specific sites dealing with individual geographic regions, populations, or other topics in modern history, see *The History Highway 2000: A Guide to Internet Resources* (E-7). Following are two useful sites for various types of information available on modern history.

E-80 **Internet Modern History Sourcebook**. URL: http://www.fordham.edu /halsall/mod/modsbook.html.

Sponsored by Fordham University, this site is a fantastic resource for all fields of historical inquiry from about 1500 to the present. Indexed by subject, time period, and geographic location, this site provides access not only to primary and secondary sources but also to other subject-specific sites.

E-81 **Lecture List for Western Civilization II**. URL: http://mars.acnet.wnec .edu/~grempel/courses/wc2/lectures.html.

Developed and maintained by Professor Gerhard Rempel of Western New England College, this site offers the texts of lectures dealing with topics in modern history from Martin Luther though the late twentieth century.

United States History

Again, the plethora of available sites allows for only a few of the best ones to be listed here. For more sites, see *The History Highway 2000: A Guide to Internet Resources* (E-7).

E-82 **The Library of Congress**. URL: http://lcweb.loc.gov/.
This site is especially important to the researcher in the social, cultural, political, and legal history of the United States. From this site, one can search the Library of Congress's Online Catalog and special collections, the Thomas Legislative Information system, the American Memory Historical Collections, and link to numerous other sites.

E-83 **The Making of America**. URL: http://moa.umdl.umich.edu/index.html.
Hosted by the University of Michigan, this is a digital library of approximately 1,600 books and twenty journals, scanned from the University of Michigan Libraries. The time period covered ranges from the antebellum period through reconstruction, 1850–1877.

E-84 **National Archives and Records Administration**. URL: http://www.nara.gov/.
This official Web site of the federal agency provides information about the archives and records in its collection, searchable databases of its holdings, online access to important documents in U.S. history, and links to other sites.

E-85 **Smithsonian National Museum of American History**. URL: http://americanhistory.si.edu/.
This excellent Web site offers access to Smithsonian programs and collections, and describes resources available at the Museum for researchers. Historians can find collections of documents, artifacts, oral histories, and other resources for the study of American history and civilization.

NOTES

1. *The Killing of History: How Literary Critics and Social Theorists Are Murdering Our Past* (Paddington, Australia: Macleay Press, 1996).

2. *The Routledge Companion to Historical Studies* (London: Routledge, 2000).

6

Law and Justice

Kevin R. Harwell

ESSAY

We often think of law as certain binding practices that have been formally established for a community to follow. We all live with laws, happily or not, and bear the burden of obeying them or living with the consequences. Laws encourage certain behaviors and discourage certain others. Some laws always apply to us wherever and whoever we are. Others apply only within the context of place, relationships, possessions, and other factors.

Scholars study the influence of laws on individuals, organizations, and cultures, past and present. Law is a recognized topic of importance for many disciplines, including administration of justice, business, communications, economics, education, history, labor relations, political sciences, social work, and sociology. It is also a subject of study in its own right. Laws apply to researchers and students, both as private individuals and as members of an academic community. Laws may carefully regulate certain types of research, especially those involving human and animal subjects.

Most published writing about legal research deals with resources and methods for finding appropriate authorities: treaties, constitutions, statutes, regulations, cases, ordinances, and the like. A number of authors with law school students and faculty in mind have written good textbooks about finding authorities and secondary sources, such as law reviews and treatises. This chapter distills a large portion of that information into a discussion of resources and strategies that are most useful for undergraduate and non-law graduate students and faculty.

The key to successful legal reference service is in understanding how the corpus juris, the body of law, is organized. The complete corpus juris is actually an assemblage of all laws, reflecting multiple agencies and jurisdictions empowered to create law. The fact that laws come from many sources is a challenge to information seekers, who need to know what resources are important and how they interrelate.

The legal profession is very demanding of publishers and other information providers. Attorneys regularly serve clients who have much to gain or lose depending on the attorney's experience, knowledge, and access to information. The good news is that the delivery of legal information has been developed to accommodate quick access, timeliness, and accuracy. This large repertoire of materials is deliberately structured to help the researcher find the right information quickly. Special techniques are frequently used to provide up-to-date information. Timeliness has been advanced to a degree that has never before been possible because of electronic delivery of information. Since legal publishing is highly competitive, quality user support is readily available in the form of published guides, telephone assistance, and computerized training programs.

Structure of the Law: Forms of Authority

Several different types or forms of law exist that relate directly to the organization and function of government in the United States. The fundamental document that binds the entire system of law together is the Constitution of the United States. A state's constitution is similarly authoritative within the geographic and empowerment limits of the state. Treaties establish our relationships and procedures with other nations. Some researchers may be surprised to learn that specific provisions of treaties can prevail over the authority of state and federal laws. Only the federal government can enter into treaties and international agreements. The other forms relate more closely to the three branches of U.S. federal government. Statutory law is the law created by the U.S. Congress or other legislative bodies, such as the General Assembly of a state. Regulatory or administrative law is created by the executive branch of government and takes several forms: executive orders of the president or governor, regulations established by administrative agencies, rulings by agency-based adjudicatory boards, or rulings by attorney generals.

The last form of law is judicial or case law. This form is also known as common law and is established by the courts. Despite voluminous statutory and regulatory law, courts are frequently called upon to settle disputes in which these forms of law are inadequate or even silent. The tradition of common law originated in England. Historically, it was unwritten law, derived from general customs, practices, and rules passed from generation to generation. Although still regarded as a body of law distinct from statutes and administrative law, much of it has been set down in written judicial opinions. Opinions are lengthy essays written by judges to explain how appropriate law and reason was applied to the facts of an individual case to determine the decision.

The doctrine of precedent is fundamental to judicial decision making. Judges are obligated to apply existing, well-reasoned principles in deciding cases. They look for guidance in opinions from preceding cases involving similar facts and situational elements. By following precedents the courts promote uniformity and impartiality in the judicial system. However, with the passage of time, judges sometimes find that a long-standing principle has become outmoded. A new principle may become common law when a judge applies a new rule to specific case facts and situations. To determine whether the legal principles asserted in a case under study have become precedent, the researcher must find cases that refer to that case and affirm the principle. Case opinions in which the asserted legal principles have been followed in subsequent cases are said to have established precedent.

Specific common-law rules or principles relating to a legal issue may be binding or persuasive, reflecting the power of the information to influence a legal decision. If the rule of law in question is found to apply to the facts of a case at hand, it is binding. That is, the rule must be followed. Depending on the source of the rule and its content, it may apply only in part, or it may relate to the facts or situation only indirectly. In such an instance the rule may only be persuasive in that the court may choose whether to follow it. Judges must determine how closely the facts in a case resemble the facts or situation addressed in existing law. In some controversial cases, this condition may be unclear. Another characteristic of precedent is that it always follows jurisdiction. For example, U.S. district courts in the Third Federal Judicial Circuit must follow a case authority established by the U.S. Circuit Court of Appeals for the Third Circuit in cases involving similar facts. On the other hand, no case from California state courts is ever binding precedent in New York.

All law in the United States—statutory, administrative, and judicial—is established by jurisdiction or level of governmental authority. Coexisting with federal authority are the fifty state governments. Each state has its own lawmaking bodies and procedures. Federal law and the laws of each state embody discrete collections of primary sources. Within this array the researcher must determine which jurisdiction has the authority to make laws respective to a specific issue or problem. Since some lawmaking powers are shared between federal and state governments, determining the appropriate jurisdiction can be complex and involved. The researcher may have to investigate both state and federal sources to address a specific problem adequately.

Formulating Questions in Relation to Law

Legal questions generally reflect the needs and prior knowledge of the one who asks the question. A major misconception about legal research is that the question, "What is the law on . . . ?" has a definitive answer. Often it does not. Equally misconceived is the idea that the law is so complex that finding a reasonable answer is nearly impossible. The search may require diligence, but given the wide scope of statutes, regulations, and cases, one can almost always find an authority that addresses at least part of the issue at hand. Many questions require a fair amount of deliberation over ambiguous issues or sorting through a large collection of information. Three things will help the researcher to cope: knowing what to look for, knowing where to look, and knowing how to search. Most of this chapter is devoted to explaining where to look and how to search. Knowing what to look for depends on the researcher's needs. The following discussion is intended to help in that regard.

Many academic inquiries come with parameters that suggest places to start. The question, "How do state statutes relating to private militias compare between Montana and Texas?" anticipates that research will involve specific resources from the states mentioned in the question. "What laws apply to the operation of casino cruise ships in international waters?" suggests that the inquirer may need to make some preliminary determinations about casino cruise ships and consult a number of sources to formulate a complete answer.

Since many undergraduates, non-law graduates, and non-law faculty are unfamiliar with legal issues and resources, information needs vary considerably. The following examples are not at all exhaustive but illustrate the variety of needs that occur:

- Identify a legal citation and find the corresponding document.

- Find a summary of major laws relating to a broad social or business endeavor.

- Search for the reasons for a change in a certain law.

- Find several cases that support an argument in a legal brief.

Occasionally the researcher must sort out the elements of his or her question that pertain to law. The initial question is a starting point. The researcher will refine the question as he or she digs deeper into the resources and learns the breadth and depth of the legal issues involved. Researchers must establish the facts and legal issues that they will investigate. With regard to the subject matter under investigation, they should determine:

- Who is involved? Identify persons and parties, including corporate entities, in terms of roles and relationships. Race, nationality, gender, and age may or may not be important.

- What things are involved? Name the specific objects and events that are involved in the situation under investigation, such as a gun, an automobile, a contract, a slanderous statement, or an oil spill.

- Where and when? Location is often a key issue in the situation. Does the casino cruise ship operate in international waters, within territorial limits, or on an inland river? Timing is also an important element. Is the situation dependent on a specific time, or a time relative to another event?

• Legal theories: What is the anticipated cause of action? Is liability an issue? What relief is being sought? What specific procedures are at issue? Each of these questions is pertinent only some of the time. Identifying the potential legal issues and outcomes is vital, even though these may change as the researcher learns more about the law as it relates to the subject matter.

Some courses require students to write a legal brief, a lengthy essay in which they develop a well-reasoned argument, supported by primary legal authorities. They may be assigned specific cases from which to support their assertions, or they may have to search for cases. In the latter instance, students may need to read a number of cases addressing specific legal issues to choose the cases that support the position from which they will argue. This process can involve fairly sophisticated exploratory searching, selection of cases, and assimilation of information.

Organization of the Sources

Numerous government bodies are empowered to make law. Fortunately, the lawmaking units of our government are highly structured and closely integrated. Consequently, so are the sources. Legal resources may be the best-organized and most carefully tracked resources of all the social sciences, especially after a starting point has been established.

The ultimate goal of legal research is to determine what the primary authorities say about a particular topic or situation. This may require a synthesis of information from statutes, regulations, and cases, sometimes from more than one jurisdiction. Because of the huge volume of material found in primary sources, secondary sources and finding tools can provide a great deal of assistance toward reaching that goal.

Secondary sources include law reviews, treatises, restatements, legal encyclopedias, American Law Reports, and looseleaf services. This group of tools provides commentary, explanation, and summarization of the law by showing relationships between various forms of authority relative to specific legal issues. They provide excellent references to specific primary authorities pertinent to the topics at hand. Secondary sources are not authoritative in and of themselves, but they help the researcher find his or her way through the concepts and ideas found in primary authorities.

Finding tools are distinct from secondary sources because they refer users to appropriate sources without providing substantial legal information. Most non-law disciplines are replete with indexes and bibliographies. Law has these as well as specialized tools such as case digests, law finders, and citators, which help users to locate law in primary authorities and the analysis of law in secondary sources.

A good bit of legal activity happens in settings that do not receive much direct treatment in the traditionally recognized sources of legal information. This is particularly true of the operation of courts and the criminal justice system. Although case law is embodied in the written opinions of judges, researchers sometimes ask questions about the courts that can't be answered by utilizing case opinions or other authorities. Someone may need a trial transcript or a local court docket to complete an assignment. Others may want documentation that was submitted as evidence during litigation. Although these may be matters of public record, they are seldom part of the published record. Indeed, those that are published tend to relate to exceptional cases.

Finding an item in the public record that is not published is a challenge. Obviously, such resources are not usually indexed or found on the Internet. The researcher will have to contact the court where the information was filed, assuming that he or she can identify a specific case tried or heard in a specific court. Success depends on the researcher's resourcefulness, investigative skills, time constraints, and financial limitations.

Resources on the Internet

Over the last several years, many state and federal agencies have begun to use the Internet to disseminate official information, including statutes, regulations, other administrative law, and case opinions. By and large, recent informational output is already in place, to the point that experienced Internet searchers and scholars expect to find these things on the Internet before they think of looking elsewhere. Although the availability of information on the Internet appears to be boundless, it is far from all-encompassing. Some state governments have yet to place their statutory codes and other elements of law on the Web. These sources may be absent for several reasons. Some states have exclusive agreements with commercial publishers to disseminate the codes and court reporters as the official source for these authorities. By federal law, state and federal publications are in the public domain. However, commercial publishers have asserted copyright and license protection for their versions of official sources. More will be said about this debate elsewhere in this chapter. A lawmaking body or agency may not be able to put materials on the Web due to lack of supportive funding. For some agencies, the massive amount of material can be overwhelming. Interested parties may not have expressed the need or desire for Internet access.

The Internet environment for legal research presents two additional challenges. First, dissemination via the Internet is a recent phenomenon. With occasional exceptions, materials that are older than 1994, only exist in print or on commercial online services like Westlaw and LEXIS-NEXIS. The second challenge is that unless researchers use the commercial services, they may have to visit numerous Web sites to compile all of the pieces needed to complete the legal information puzzle. Consider the issue of legal ownership of firearms. Statutes, regulations, and court cases at state and federal jurisdictions bear on this issue. To find state and federal law pertaining to firearm ownership in Pennsylvania, the researcher may have to search a half-dozen or more separate Web sites. Even then, the search is likely to miss important state and federal court cases that are not on the Internet because of their age.

Fortunately, Web sites for legal research are not difficult to find. A number of no cost "portal" Web sites have been developed that compile and categorize existing sites to help minimize the effort needed to find and use legal information. Although there is some overlap among them, each service fills a particular niche. Commercial, for-fee legal information services, on the other hand, aggregate information from many sources into a single database or system of databases and serve it to subscribers through a Web interface. An example that is widely available at colleges and universities is Lexis-Nexis's *Academic Universe* (F-15).

The following pages serve as an introduction to numerous resources for legal research. New researchers may find the number and variety of titles daunting. However, the process is manageable if broken down into components, approaching legal research systematically, one resource at a time. The resources listed in this chapter are arranged according to their general functional types: general reference sources, primary authorities, secondary resources, and finding tools. A final section deals with researching the legal community itself, particularly the courts and the judicial process, special resources for the U.S. Supreme Court, and criminal justice information.

Legal research involves the use of many resources that provide information from the variety of agents that create law. Were it not for the fact that legal information is highly structured and systematic, legal research would be nearly impossible. Electronic information adds another layer to access mechanisms. The benefits of enhanced access far outweigh the challenges it presents. The rest of this chapter focuses on specific resources for legal research and addresses integrated approaches of using Internet resources with print and other materials to accomplish effective legal research for undergraduate students and non-law graduate students and faculty.

GENERAL REFERENCE SOURCES

Guides to Legal Information

F-1   Aker, James R., and Richard Irving. **Basic Legal Research for Criminal Justice and the Social Sciences**. Gaithersburg, MD: Aspe, 1998.

F-2   Cohen, Morris L. **Legal Research in a Nutshell**. 6th ed. St. Paul, MN: West Publishing, 1996.

F-3   Elias, Stephen, and Susan Levinkind. **Legal Research: How to Find and Understand the Law**. 7th ed. Berkeley, CA: Nolo Press, 1999.

F-4   Jacobstein, J. Myron, Roy M. Mersky, and Donald J. Dunn. **Fundamentals of Legal Research**. 7th ed. Westbury, NY: Foundation Press, 1998.

F-5   Kunz, Christina L., Deborah A. Schmedemann, Matthew P. Downs, and Ann Bateson. **The Process of Legal Research: Successful Strategies**. 5th ed. New York: Aspen, 2000.

Every discipline utilizes general reference sources—dictionaries, handbooks and directories, guides to research, and related materials—that provide information about the discipline but are not primary sources. Law is no different. Also, like many other disciplines, legal information is undergoing a long-term transformation from print to combinations of print and electronic formats. Comprehensive, timely research almost always requires use of materials in both formats. In recent years, traditional guides to legal information have evolved from research in a strictly print environment to a more integrated approach.

Of the titles listed above, Cohen, Jacobstein et al., and Kunz et al. are law school textbooks. Aker and Irving address their work to social sciences researchers who have little or no background in law. Elias and Levinkind's book is addressed to the layperson with no legal background. All of these books focus on finding legal authorities that support arguments and defend positions, as in a trial or hearing. Each deals with resources for American law in a comprehensive fashion. Each posits that the first step in legal research is to analyze the facts of the situation requiring research. Cohen and Jacobstein et al. describe resources by category: statutes, administrative law, cases, secondary sources, and so forth. Kunz et al. also describe the sources, but within the context of a recommended general strategy of (1) generating research vocabulary, (2) using secondary sources—law reviews, encyclopedias, and American Law Reports—to establish background information, (3) formulating the issues, (4) searching for authorities, and (5) reevaluating the issues.

Guides to Electronic Resources

F-6   Chandler, Yvonne J. **Neal-Schuman Guide to Finding Legal and Regulatory Information on the Internet**. New York: Neal-Schuman, 1998.

F-7   Evans, James. **Law on the Net**. 2d ed. Berkeley, CA: Nolo Press, 1997.

F-8   Halvorson, T. R. **Law of the Super Searchers, the Online Secrets of Top Legal Researchers**. Edited by Reva Bosch. Medford, NJ: CyberAge Books, 2000.

One of the demons of information seeking in the current Internet environment is that Web sites and their content are quite transitory. Yesterday's fabulous Web site for searching "ZYX" has been moved, taken down, bought out, or lost its funding. The generous business that provided the

Web space or content for free has had second thoughts. The agency that used the Internet to save funds has a different political appointee at the helm who has different ideas about fulfilling the agency's mission. Perhaps the visionary librarian or law professor who created the Web site has been promoted or moved on and no one has updated it. The result of all this is that what we recently knew was available may no longer be where we last saw it. Consequently, publishing information about the Internet, especially about specific Web sites and content, becomes outdated quickly. Fortunately, some legal sites have remained stable over the years, especially at certain law schools, federal agencies, and courts. They have been reliable enough that published guides to legal resources on the Internet can be helpful.

Chandler's *Neal Schuman Guide to Finding Legal and Regulatory Information on the Internet* describes and evaluates more than 900 Internet sites and organizes the discussion into seven chapters, based on the nature of the information: introduction, guides and meta-indexes, judicial law, government agencies, legislative sources, administrative law, and secondary sources. This manual covers federal and state sources, including official and unofficial Web sites. Most descriptions, especially the state-by-state listings, are rather brief, giving the name of the Web site, the URL, and a one-sentence or one-paragraph description. Many of the most useful sites are covered in detail and illustrated with screen captures. These details were most helpful when the book was first published. The value is diminishing as time goes by and Web site content changes. Each chapter concludes with "Chandler's Best Bets," a highly selective listing of Web sites described in the chapter.

Evans's *Law on the Net* is a publication of the well-known self-help publisher Nolo Press. This directory includes most of the categories of Chandler's work, but adds international law, law schools, legal practice, e-mail discussion groups, and newsgroups. Also helpful is an A to Z directory of Web sites by legal topic. Directory listings are more uniformly brief than Chandler's, but the brief listings provide more information about access, contacts, and content. Comments in each listing provide various supplemental information, such as frequent connection problems, reputation of the Web site owner, and other useful facts.

Halvorson's *Law of the Super Searchers, the Online Secrets of Top Legal Researchers* is unlike either of the previous guides. The author has transcribed interviews with eight legal researchers about their insights and practices using Internet and commercial sources. They talk about conceptualizing, planning, and carrying out their searches. Some talk about receiving search requests, dealing with clients, and general search tactics. They also compare use of fee-based services with free Internet resources and give examples of the free resources that occasionally surpass the usefulness of fee-based ones and vice versa. These "super searchers" work in intense, demanding environments in which speed, cost, and care matter. Their shared wisdom is valuable.

Internet Portals

F-9   Cornell Law School. **Legal Information Institute**. URL: http://www.law .cornell.edu. Accessed February 13, 2001.

F-10   **FindLaw**. URL: http://www.findlaw.com. Accessed February 13, 2001.

F-11   **Hieros Gamos, the Comprehensive Law and Government Portal**. URL: http://www.hg.org/. Accessed February 13, 2001.

F-12   **Internet Legal Resource Guide**. URL: http://www.ilrg.com/. Accessed February 13, 2001.

F-13   Library of Congress. **Global Legal Information Network**. URL: http:// memory.loc.gov/law/GLINv1/GLIN.html. Accessed February 13, 2001.

F-14 U.S. Government Printing Office. Superintendent of Documents. **GPO Access**. URL: http://www.access.gpo.gov/su_docs/index.html. Accessed February 13, 2001.

The *Legal Information Institute* (*LII*) is a nonprofit service of Cornell Law School supported by grants, the consulting work of its co-directors, and donations. Co-directors and Co-founders Peter W. Martin and Thomas R. Bruce set out, in 1992, to create key electronic collections of primary legal materials and commentary available to all users—students, teachers, and the general public—facilitated by also providing information retrieval and resource location tools. Of the no cost portal legal sites, Cornell's *Legal Information Institute* is one of the oldest and one of the best. Topical resources are logically organized, providing direct access to selected sections of federal statutes and regulations, and appropriate links to federal judicial decisions, state law materials, and other carefully selected materials on the Internet. *LII* also produces legal commentary to accompany first-, second-, and third-year law school courses. The course related materials are available through the Web site or for purchase on CD-ROM.

FindLaw is another leading Web portal that provides comprehensive access to legal information on the Internet. Coverage of resources overlaps the Cornell site in many respects. In addition to carefully described links to 25,000 other legal Web sites, it offers its own databases for searching state and federal case opinions and federal statutes. Users will find links to commercial information, such as stock quotes, consumer law, and entertainment information that the Cornell site does not have. *FindLaw* also provides numerous links to practice-related materials and law form Web sites. Additionally, the *FindLaw* search engine known as LawCrawler uses intelligent agents combined with the AltaVista search engine to search *FindLaw* and other legal databases and Web sites to create results lists tailored to legal research needs.

Hieros Gamos is also one of the original portals that continue to provide comprehensive hypertext access to legal information on the Internet, with more than 100,000 links to law and government sources. One of its remarkable features is a directory of worldwide government sources, which includes separate guides for each nation, the United Nations, the European Union, and other supra-national organizations. Each national guide includes links to official government Web sites, U.S. Central Intelligence Agency guides, Yahoo! Listings, and recent news stories.

The Internet Legal Resource Guide is a categorized index of over 4,000 selected Web sites of substance dealing with law and legal information for scholars, practitioners, and the general public. The focus of this guide is on American law, but foreign and international Web sites are included. Links to U.S. federal agencies, legislative materials and courts are logically organized and easy to use. Special features include links to resources for law students, potential law students, and a growing library of generic legal forms. This Web site is also the home of LawRunner, a query template collection for searching for legal Web sites using the AltaVista search engine.

Global Legal Information Network (*GLIN*) is a cooperative project in which governments of participating nations share original official texts of laws, regulations, and complementary legal sources that are maintained for public access. *GLIN* is an annotated hypertext guide to worldwide information about law and government. Useful and reliable links are made available for each of the world's nations.

GPO Access is the federal government's portal to agencies, documents, and legal materials on the Web, as provided directly by the agencies and branches of the federal government. Begun in 1993 and funded by the Federal Depository Library Program, this service is an outgrowth of the government's push to convert much of its publishing operations from print to Internet. Most resources accessible through the portal are available free of charge. Legal resources hosted directly at the Web site include public laws, the *United States Code* (F-38), *Code of Federal Regulations* (F-46, F-47), *Federal Register* (F-49, F-50), and U.S. Supreme Court cases. Agency and congressional information from *GPO Access* are described elsewhere in this book.

Commercial Aggregators of Legal Information

F-15 **Academic Universe**. LEXIS-NEXIS. Online format. URL: http://web.lexis-nexis.com/universe. Accessed February 13, 2001.

Academic Universe provides Internet access to virtually all full-text court cases ever published by federal courts and state appellate courts. Users will also find state and federal statutory codes, federal regulations and attorney general opinions, legal news, and law review articles. *Academic Universe* provides about 75 percent of the content of the complete LEXIS-NEXIS service to academic institutions. The flat-fee subscription is far less expensive than the cost of the full LEXIS-NEXIS service, and enables colleges and universities to offer in-house and remote access to students, faculty, and staff. In a technical sense, the information available through *Academic Universe* is not on the Internet, per se. Rather, it resides on electronic databases maintained by LEXIS-NEXIS. The information on the databases is made available through a Web-based interface. While the full LEXIS-NEXIS service is also available through a Web-based interface, as is its main competitor, Westlaw, the cost of these services is prohibitive to most academic institutions other than law schools. A number of more limited topical services that compile legal materials from a variety of sources are also available from law publishers and commercial information providers.

Handbooks and Manuals

F-16 **The Bluebook: A Uniform System of Citation**. 17th ed. Cambridge, MA: Harvard Law Review Association, 2000.

F-17 **Universal Citation Guide**. Madison: State Bar of Wisconsin, 1999.

F-18 Prince, Mary Miles. **Bieber's Dictionary of Legal Abbreviations: Reference Guide for Attorneys, Legal Secretaries, Paralegals and Law Students**. 4th ed. Buffalo, NY: William S. Hein, 1993.

F-19 Prince, Mary Miles. **Bieber's Dictionary of Legal Citations: Reference Guide for Attorneys, Legal Secretaries, Paralegals, and Law Students**. 5th ed. Buffalo, NY: William S. Hein, 1997.

Legal publishing is a highly specialized field within the publishing world. Unlike many disciplines where the primary literature consists of books and journal articles, recitation of author and title is not meaningful in references to statutes, regulations, cases, and so forth.[1] Official sources of primary authorities are numerous; however, they tend to be well established especially within their jurisdictions. As a result, law review publishers and legal scholars have developed a systematic standard that utilizes abbreviated but precise conventions to draft references to legal publications. The authoritative reference work for this standard is *The Bluebook: A Uniform System of Citation. The Bluebook*, now in its seventh edition, provides guidance on citing nearly every conceivable legal resource. A quick guide to commonly used resources is printed on the inside front cover. Half of the book is devoted to listing authorities by jurisdiction and secondary resources by type of publication. On these pages, printed on blue paper, authors will also find details of accepted abbreviations for each publication.

The Bluebook has been criticized for being too dependent on print resources. Indeed, the rules for citation direct the user to cite official print sources unless the only available access is electronic.[2] The strong tradition reflected in *The Bluebook* of citing print sources has recently been the center of controversy over copyright infringement. The federal judiciary, some state courts, and state legislatures have depended on commercial publishers, such as the West Publishing Company,[3] to publish official versions of primary authorities, such as reports of case opinions and statutory codes. The commercial publishers have asserted copyright protection for editorial enhancements, formatting, pagination, and citations to their products, even though the intellectual content created by state or federal government is public domain information. Such assertions have met mixed success in the courts. Most recently, West Publishing Company lost its battle to retain copyright of its page citations.[4]

In response to these developments, the American Association of Law Librarians[5] and the American Bar Association[6] have recommended a fundamental change to a "vendor neutral" citation. For example, a reference to a court opinion would show the name of the case, year of the case, identity of the court, opinion number, and paragraph number within the case, eliminating the need to identify the published source, page numbers, and other proprietary details consequential to commercial publishing. This effort has enjoyed a growing following, especially since it appears to be very workable with electronic resources, where page numbers are borrowed from print sources but are otherwise meaningless. Several states have adopted or are considering adopting vendor neutral citations as a choice for certain official filings.[7] The standard source for vendor neutral citations is the *Universal Citation Guide.*

Two problems that regularly occur while conducting legal research are identifying abbreviated references and determining an acceptable abbreviation to use in a properly drafted legal reference. Although many law books contain some kind of a table of abbreviations for the references they use, *Bieber's Dictionary of Legal Abbreviations* is a concise and comprehensive companion for all legal research. On the other hand, constructing a proper legal reference that will be recognizable and informative to a reader also requires some help. *Bieber's Dictionary of Legal Citations* includes the generally accepted abbreviation used for the titles of U.S. law books. Both citation guides are good companions to *The Bluebook.*

Dictionaries

F-20   Black, Henry Campbell. **Black's Law Dictionary**. Abridged 7th ed. St. Paul, MN: West Group, 1999.

F-21   Bouvier, John. **Bouvier's Law Dictionary and Concise Encyclopedia**. 8th ed. 3 vols. St. Paul, MN: West Publishing, 1914.

F-22   Garner, Bryan A. **A Dictionary of Modern Legal Usage**. 2d ed. New York: Oxford University Press, 1995.

F-23   **Words and Phrases**. 46 vols. St. Paul, MN: West Publishing, 1964- . Annual supplements.

Black's Law Dictionary is widely recognized as the standard dictionary for legal research. The first edition was published in 1891. The current edition includes about 25,000 legal terms. In addition to definitions of words in legal context, some encyclopedic information for some terms and concepts is also provided. The dictionary has easy-to-understand pronunciation symbols, etymologies, legal quotations, and maxims. This edition is an attempt to compile a complete collection of the terminology of law from original sources, including judicial decisions and writings of specialist scholars.

Bouvier's three-volume dictionary, while certainly out-of-date in many respects, is valuable for historical terms. It is a scholarly work with many lengthy articles and numerous references to cases, statutes, and other sources.

Even attorneys need to consult an authority on grammar and usage now and then. *A Dictionary of Modern Legal Usage* is not limited to legal terminology; however, it does provide definitions and usage recommendations for much legal jargon.

Dictionary-like in content and encyclopedic in size, *Words and Phrases* is a compendium of the "Words and Phrases" volumes originally published with each of the individual digest series published by West Group. It does not offer editor-crafted definitions of legal terms. Rather, it provides direct quotations from court cases in which the definition of a distinct word or phrase was critical. This extensive resource has great value as a case-finding tool. In it the researcher can usually locate a case by using a common word or term that normally would not appear in the more restrictive descriptive word indexes of many other legal sources. The forty-six-volume set is updated annually with "pocket part" supplements for each volume.

F-24 **Everybody's Legal Dictionary**. Nolo Press, 2001. Online format. URL: http://www.nolo.com/dictionary/wordindex.cfm. Accessed February 13, 2001.

F-25 **FindLaw Legal Dictionary**. Online format. URL: http://dictionary.lp .findlaw.com/. Accessed February 13, 2001.

F-26 **Law.com Dictionary**. U.S. Equity Partners, L.P., 2001. Online format. URL: http://dictionary.law.com/. Accessed February 13, 2001.

F-27 **Oran's Dictionary of Law**. West Group, 1998. Online format. URL: http:// www.wld.com/conbus/orans/Welcome.asp. Accessed February 13, 2001.

F-28 **Jurist, The Legal Education Network. Legal Dictionary**. University of Pittsburgh School of Law, 2001. Online format. URL: http://www.jurist.law.pitt .edu/dictionary.htm. Accessed February 13, 2001.

These law dictionaries are available on the Web without charge. Although they may be of some use in casual research, they provide no more depth than a pocket dictionary or glossary. Nonetheless, they are convenient and easy to use and understand. At least three of these are electronic versions of print dictionaries. The *FindLaw Legal Dictionary* is the Merriam-Webster's *Dictionary of Law*.[8] Other familiar print titles are *Oran's Dictionary of Law*[9] and *Real Life Dictionary of the Law*,[10] the basis for the *Law.com Dictionary*. In situations where the need is for careful scholarship, researchers wisely turn to *Black's Law Dictionary*.

PRIMARY RESOURCES

Constitutions

F-29 Cogan, Neil H. **The Complete Bill of Rights, the Drafts, Debates, Sources, and Origins**. New York: Oxford University Press, 1997.

F-30 Congressional Research Service, Library of Congress. **The Constitution of the United States of America, Analysis and Interpretation**. Online format. URL: http://www.access.gpo.gov/congress/senate/constitution/index.html. Accessed February 13, 2001.

F-31 National Archives and Records Administration. **The Constitution of the United States**. Online format. URL: http://www.nara.gov/exhall/charters/constitution /conmain.html. Accessed February 13, 2001.

F-32 Legal Information Institute, Cornell Law School. **The Constitution of the United States of America**. Online format. URL: http://www.law.cornell .edu/constitution/constitution.table.html. Accessed February 13, 2001.

F-33 **United States Code**. Washington, DC: Government Printing Office, 1926- .

Because all American law, ultimately, is predicated on the Constitution of the United States, researchers will find numerous resources that provide the text of the Constitution, including textbooks on law and civics, statutory codes, and various manuals offered as government publications. As indicated, above, the National Archives and Records Administration and the Legal Information Institute at Cornell Law School offer the Constitution on the Internet. It is always available in volume 1 of the United States Code.

Federal constitutional law is a common topic for treatises, law review articles, and other secondary sources. Annotated versions of the Constitution are helpful to scholars. *The Constitution of the United States of America, Analysis and Interpretation* (GPO) provides systematic analysis that is based on the use of the Constitution to decide court cases. *The Complete Bill of Rights, the Drafts, Debates, Sources, and Origins* attempts to provide a complete, accurate, accessible set of texts for interpreting the first ten amendments. To provide the reader with tools to determine the original meanings and intentions, the author provides proposed drafts and historical discussions that accompanied passage of each amendment, and treatment of the amendment in historically significant legal works.

Like the Constitution of the United States, state constitutions govern the establishment of state laws. State constitutions can be found in printed codifications of state statutes and at most official state government Web sites. On the Internet, researchers can find most state constitutions using one of the well-known Internet legal directories, such as *FindLaw* (F-10), *Hieros Gamos* (F-11), and Cornell's *Legal Information Institute* (F-9).

Session Laws and Codified Statutes

F-34 **Congressional Universe**. Online format. URL: http://web.lexis-nexis.com /congcomp. Accessed February 13, 2001.

F-35 **Public Laws. GPO Access**. Online format. URL: http://www.access.gpo .gov/nara/nara005.html. Accessed February 13, 2001.

F-36 **United States Code Congressional and Administrative News**. St. Paul, MN: West Publishing, 1945- . Annual.

F-37 **United States Statutes at Large**. Washington, DC: Government Printing Office, 1873- .

Congressional Universe offers the complete *U.S. Statutes at Large* delivered to subscribers via the Web. The public laws can be searched in full text from 1988 to present. Older public laws are searchable by public law number, enacted bill number, or by volume and page number in the *U.S. Statutes at Large*.

Statutes are enacted through the legislative process. The first time a series of statutes is published in an official capacity, they are published in the order in which they are passed. These are often referred to as session laws or public laws. When the U.S. Congress passes a bill, the resulting enactment is assigned a public law number and is published singly in pamphlet form as a slip law. At nearly the same time, GPO releases the text of the law on its *Public and Private Laws* Web site. The Web site provides the text of all public and private laws as plain ASCII text or as .pdf files, which can be read using the Adobe Acrobat Reader. Coverage for the Web site begins with the 104th Congress, which began in January 1995.

Public laws are then collated into a second publication, *United States Statutes at Large*, in the order in which they have been enacted. The relationship between these two publications is close. The pagination of the slip laws is such that when the text is republished in *United States Statutes at Large*, the page numbers remain the same.

United States Code Congressional and Administrative News (USCCAN) is an example of commercially published U.S. statutes. West Group is undeniably quicker than the GPO in bringing the statutes to press. While waiting until enough statutes are passed by Congress to produce the next bound volume of *USCCAN*, West publishes softbound *Advance Sheets*. Each *Advance Sheet* may contain one or more statutes. Users will also find committee reports relevant to individual statutes, as well as all executive orders and presidential proclamations, in *USCCAN*.

Codifications

F-38 **United States Code**. Washington, DC: Government Printing Office, 1926- .

F-39 **United States Code. GPO Access**. Online format. URL: http://www.access .gpo.gov/congress/cong013.html. Accessed February 13, 2001.

F-40 **United States Code Annotated**. St. Paul, MN: West Publishing, 1927- .

F-41 **United States Code Service. Lawyers Edition**. Rochester, NY: Lawyers Co-operative Publishing, 1972- .

F-42 **U.S. House of Representatives. Office of the Law Revision Counsel. Search the United States Code**. Online format. URL: http://uscode.house.gov /usc.htm. Accessed February 13, 2001.

Statutes are usually republished a second time in an official capacity in the form of a codification. Codifications provide the text of statutes in topical rather than chronological order. The text of the statutes is analyzed. Sections that have been repealed, superseded, and expired are removed. The remaining sections of statutes are reorganized by topic. Additionally, codifications include references needed to trace the legislative history and amendments of the statute. This is especially important for the researcher investigating laws that have been amended several times over the years. One need only imagine trying to make sense of the social security laws using only *United States Statutes at Large*. Since its original passage, the Social Security Act of 1935[11] has been amended almost annually. Typically, appropriations legislation and private laws, which relate to specific persons, are routinely excluded from codifications.

The process of codifying the statutes requires, at times, a few relatively minor changes to the text as found in the statutes. Usually, these are grammatical changes that have little effect on the understanding of the law or its interpretation, but not always. Whenever there is a discrepancy between the text of the codification and the text of the statutes, the statutes are the authority on which to rely. From time to time, the U.S. Congress has enacted entire titles of the *United States Code* into positive law, effectively eliminating such discrepancies until new enactments amend such titles.

The *United States Code* (*USC*) is the official codification of the federal statutes and is compiled by the U.S. House of Representatives Office of Law Revision Counsel. Its fifty titles are reissued every six years, with annual bound supplements between revisions. Accompanying tables list "Acts by Popular Name" and citations to sections of the Code[12] where specific statutes, executive orders and proclamations, and reorganization plans are found. Although it is the official version, use of the *USC* presents several challenges to researchers. Its main disadvantage is that complete revisions are made only once every six years. The annual supplements are usually distributed quite late. Also, it contains few notes and no references to related regulatory and case law materials. The general index to the *USC* is found in the main series and with a separate index published with each supplement.

Two commercial publications, *United States Code Annotated* (*USCA*) and *United States Code Service* (*USCS*), contain all of the elements of the *USC*, along with annotations referring to court cases in which individual sections of the code were a significant issue, references to administrative regulations relevant to the code section, and extensive notes on the section's legislative history. Moreover, each title is kept current with supplemental pamphlets that provide the text of new statutes and annotations reflecting the lawmaking that has occurred since the last revision of the bound *USCA* or *USCS* volumes. General indexes and tables for the commercial versions are more extensive and kept more current. Each of these features presents a distinct advantage over the official version.

In the past, competitors West Publishing Company and Lawyers Co-operative Publishing (LCP) published *USCA* and *USCS*. Since the merger of West with LCP's parent company, Thomson Corporation, the *USCS* has been sold to Lexis-Nexis Publishing. The main content difference between *USCA* and *USCS* is that *USCA* reprints the wording of the *USC*, whereas *USCS* follows that of *United States Statutes at Large* (F-37). Like the *USC*, both contain the U.S. Constitution, with *USCA* and *USCS* providing extensive references to related case law.

The *USCA* and *USCS* are both available on CD-ROM. The *USCA* is available online through Westlaw. The *USCS* is available online via LEXIS-NEXIS and *Academic Universe.* However, the *Academic Universe* system for accessing *USCS* treats each section of the *USCS* as a separate record. Unfortunately, *Academic Universe* offers no browse function, whereby the user can move from one section to the next in the order of the *USCS.* Researchers are limited to what they can find by doing keyword searches. Given the terse language of many statutory sections when read alone and out of context, the result of this format is that the researcher is never sure that he or she has found all of the consecutive sections of a portion of the statutes that need to be studied. Obviously, the usefulness of federal statutes in this environment is seriously restricted.

While the print version of the *United States Code* remains the only official version, the U.S. House of Representatives Office of Law Revision Counsel (LRC), which compiles the *United States Code,* also produces an unofficial Web version. On the LRC's page, researchers can view the most recent updating of the *Code* available. It is searchable by keywords, which can be used for free-text searching or in searching by fields. The page also provides "Classification Tables" that list *Code* sections affected by recent legislation, and a page listing all of the titles of the *Code* that are currently enacted as positive law. One can further update research by consulting sections added by new legislation but not yet incorporated into the *Code.* Unlike the version offered by *Academic Universe,* the LRC version sports a browse feature whereby one can view *Code* sections immediately before and after any section displayed.

GPO Access also offers the *United States Code* on the Web, using a database it acquires from the LRC. Although the site is not as friendly as the one offered by the LRC, it is the only site available for free that provides historical versions of the *Code* going back to 1994.

The Cornell *Legal Information Institute* offers the user-friendliest version of the *Code* available for free. Using the database acquired and updated from the LRC, the *Institute* is constantly adding new and useful features. Like the LRC and *GPO Access* sites, Cornell offers keyword searching. Users can also search by title and section, and by the *United States Code* Table of Contents. To search by table of contents, users are first offered a list of the *Code* titles. Choosing a title leads to a list of chapters, then a list of sections in a chapter. Finally, the full text of the section is displayed, with hypertext links to updating information, other sections of the *Code,* and notes, which give the effective date of the section, public law source, and amendment history. It also links to parts of the *Code of Federal Regulations* enabled by the *Code* section. The Cornell site also permits browsing and keyword searching within any given title. These combined features make the Cornell site relatively easy to use. Researchers should, however, verify any *Code* section upon which they must rely with the official, print version of the *United States Code.*

State Statutes

Each state publishes a state law equivalent of *United States Statutes at Large* (F-37), often referred to as session laws. Many also publish slip laws and codifications of statutes. For a list of statutory authorities for the states, consult table T1 of *The Bluebook: A Uniform System of Citation* (F-16). As mentioned previously in this chapter, not every state publishes its statutes on the Internet, but a number of them do. Some publish session laws; some publish codifications. A few publish both. *FindLaw* (F-10), *Hieros Gamos* (F-11), and Cornell's *Legal Information Institute* (F-9) provide directories of links to state statutes. State statutes are also found on Westlaw and LEXIS-NEXIS and *Academic Universe.* As with the federal statutes, *Academic Universe* does not provide a browse function, which limits the usefulness of the service.

F-43 **Subject Compilations of State Laws.** Westport, CT: Greenwood Press, 1981- .

This series of bibliographies should be on every reference shelf. Few libraries can afford to acquire session laws or codifications of all fifty states. Even those that do have patrons who need to know the statutes from several states on one topic or another. The Subject Compilations of State Laws series provides references to books, articles, government documents, looseleaf services, treatises, legal newspapers, and cases that contain compendia and compilations of state statutes on various topics. The first two volumes also contain research guides that provide the user with information needed to locate codes and compendia of state regulations. Tables include a list of looseleaf services containing state regulatory law and a list of regulatory codes by state with information on the issuing agency. These are excellent guides for finding the states that publish regulatory codes and those that do not. In addition, the bibliographies are indexed by author and contain directories of publishers. More recent issues present a comprehensive list of subjects for the entire series, with references under each subject heading to recent compilations of laws or to earlier issues of *Subject Compilations of State Laws*, whichever is more appropriate.

Regulations and Other Administrative Law

F-44 **Administrative Decisions. GPO Access**. Online format. URL: http://www .access.gpo.gov/su_docs/admin.html. Accessed February 13, 2001.

F-45 **CIS Federal Register Index**. Bethesda, MD: Congressional Information Service, 1984- .

F-46 **Code of Federal Regulations. GPO Access**. Online format. URL: http:// www.access.gpo.gov/nara/cfr/index.html. Accessed February 13, 2001.

F-47 **Code of Federal Regulations**. Washington, DC: Office of the Federal Register, National Archives and Records Administration; Government Printing Office, 1938- .

F-48 **Codification of Presidential Proclamations and Executive Orders. GPO Access**. Online format. URL: http://www.nara.gov/fedreg/codific/index.html. Accessed February 13, 2001.

F-49 **Federal Register. GPO Access**. URL: http://www.access.gpo.gov/su_docs /aces/aces140.html. Accessed February 13, 2001.

F-50 **Federal Register**. Washington, DC: Office of the Federal Register, National Archives and Records Administration; Government Printing Office, 1936- .
An additional component of administrative law consists of agency judgments regarding controversies arising out of violations or interpretations of the agency's regulations or statutes the agency is charged to enforce. A number of agencies are empowered with such quasi-judicial responsibilities. Decisions are frequently accompanied by published opinions in which an administrative law judge explains how appropriate law has been applied to the facts of the case to arrive at the decision. In this respect, they resemble the judicial opinions. The opinions are published by or by the authority of the agency. Their value lies in interpretation of law or clarification of an agency's role and procedures. Unfortunately, they tend to be irregularly published and poorly indexed. Fortunately, most agencies that make and publish decisions also utilize the Internet. *Administrative Decisions*—a service of the U.S. Government Printing Office through its *GPO Access* portal—is a linking service that provides access to decisions.
A number of federal administrative and independent agencies are empowered by the U.S. Congress to establish regulations, also referred to as rules. These statements carry the same force of law as the statutes. The agencies are required to follow certain procedures, which include publishing proposed rules and providing an opportunity for public comment, before establishing and publishing final rules. Proposed rules and final rules are published in the *Federal Register*. Final rules are codified in the *Code of Federal Regulations*.

State administrative agencies also establish rules and regulations, but publication is quite varied, with some states publishing complete codifications and others leaving the agencies to issue their own. Some commercial looseleaf services collect and publish regulations from all fifty states on certain topics.

The Code of Federal Regulations (*CFR*) is the codification of the general and permanent regulations of the executive agencies of the U.S. government. In print, it comprises about twenty-four linear feet of shelf space, organized in fifty titles arranged by agency. It is equipped with tables of contents, various finding aids, tables of statutory authority, lists of changes, and a general index. Each title is revised annually as groups of titles are updated during different quarters of the year. The commercial *CIS Federal Register Index* is much more extensive, more current, and far superior to the one published by the government as part of the *CFR*.

Federal administrative law also encompasses presidential proclamations and executive orders. Proclamations generally relate to celebrations and commemorative events. Executive orders direct and govern the activities of government officials and agencies. These documents are published in numerous places, including the *Federal Register* and *Code of Federal Regulations*. They are also found in the *Weekly Compilation of Presidential Documents, Public Papers of the Presidents of the United States*, and *Codifications of Presidential Proclamations and Executive Orders.*

The Federal Register is the daily register of rules and regulations issued by federal executive agencies. It is the historical, chronological source of federal regulations as well as the daily supplement to the *Code of Federal Regulations*. It also includes announcements of all proposed rules and regulations, public hearings, and presidential executive orders and proclamations. Each issue has a table of contents and is arranged by the executive agency that supplies the content for that day. Indexes, although not extensive, are cumulated monthly, quarterly, and annually.

Judicial Cases

West Group (West Publishing Company)

F-51 **National Reporter System** (various series). St. Paul, MN: West (now West Group), 1879- .

F-52 **American Digest System. Decennial Digests**. St. Paul, MN: West (now West Group), 1908- .

Having earlier established that the lawmaking activity of the judiciary comes in the form of published opinions, researchers should also understand that most court cases do not result in published opinions. At the trial court level—that is, the case heard in the court of original jurisdiction—opinions are written in only a small percentage of cases. As the case is appealed to higher and higher courts, the probability that an opinion will be written and published increases. Virtually all cases heard by the court of last resort, the U.S. Supreme Court, result in opinions that are published. "Reported cases" in the sense of legal research are cases that have resulted in published opinions. The principal publisher of general case reports in the United States is West Group, through *National Reporter System.*

West Group produces extensive legal libraries of publications that reprint the official text of the law. These publications provide extensive annotations, notes to the official text, general indexes, and law finding aids. West Group products interrelate all forms of law through the use of tables, indexes, and systems of classification and provide updating services that maintain the currency of publications better than that of the government sources. Some of the specific products are mentioned in this chapter, such as legal encyclopedias and the statutes.

West Group attempts comprehensive coverage of case law. They claim comprehensive coverage of all state appeals court cases and federal court cases in the United States. They are also the official publisher of many state court reporters. Other elements of the West library, including federal and state statutory codes and law encyclopedias, are heavily cross-referenced to case reports using case citations as well as a highly developed, detailed classification system characterized by standardized "Topics and Key Numbers."

National Reporter System (*NRS*) is an extensive, multiple component series of reporters covering state and federal case reports. Seven regional reporters cover state appellate court cases in all fifty states. Four reporters cover federal cases in general. Three topical reporters, *West's Bankruptcy Reporter*, *West's Education Law Reporter*, and *West's Military Justice Reporter*, complete the system. These reporters present cases in chronological order (see table 6.1).

Table 6.1. West Reporters and Digests

FEDERAL COURT CASES

Court	Reporter	Digest
U.S. Supreme Court	*Supreme Court Reporter* (1882-)	*Supreme Court Digest* and *Federal Practice Digests*
U.S. Courts of Appeals	*Federal Reporter* (1880-)	*Federal Practice Digests*
U.S. Court of Customs		
U.S. Court of Patent Appeals		
U.S. Court of Claims		
U.S. Claims Court	*U.S. Claims Court Reporter*	*Federal Practice Digests*
U.S. District Courts	*Federal Supplement* (1932-)	*Federal Practice Digests*
District Court of D.C.		
U.S. Customs Court		

STATE APPELLATE COURT CASES

State	Reporter	Digest
CT, DE, MD, ME, NH, NJ, PA, RI, VT, DC	*Atlantic Reporter* (1885-)	*Atlantic Digest*
IL, IN, MA, NY, OH	*Northeastern Reporter* (1885-)	*Northeastern Digest* (ceased 1968)
IA, MI, MN, ND, NE, SD, WI	*Northwestern Reporter* (1879-)	*North Western Digest*
AL, AZ, CO, HI, ID, KS, MT, NM, NV, OK, OR, UT, WA, WY, CA	*Pacific Reporter* (1883-)	*Pacific Digest* (through 1960)
GA, NC, SC, VA, WV	*Southeastern Reporter* (1887-)	*Southeastern Digest*
AL, FL, LA, MS	*Southern Reporter* (1887-)	*Southern Digest* (ceased 1988)
AR, KY, MO, TN, TX	*Southwestern Reporter* (1886-)	Not published. Use state digest or *Century Digests* and *Decennial Digests*.

West's *American Digest System,* sometimes simply referred to as the *American Digest,* enables users to identify cases by topic and is the only complete topical index to case law in the United States. It is composed of ten units plus an annual series of supplementary digests, each of which has its own index and tables of cases. Each unit is organized by West's Topic and Key Number classification scheme, except for *Century Digest*, which covers the period 1658–1896 and uses a different numbering system. The following is a list of *Decennial Digests* and their respective periods of coverage:

Century Digest	1658–1896
1st Decennial Digest	1897–1905
2d Decennial Digest	1906–1915
3d Decennial Digest	1916–1925
4th Decennial Digest	1926–1935
5th Decennial Digest	1936–1945
6th Decennial Digest	1946–1955
7th Decennial Digest	1956–1965
8th Decennial Digest	1966–1975
9th Decennial Digest, part 1	1976–1981
9th Decennial Digest, part 2	1982–1985
10th Decennial Digest, part 1	1986–1991
10th Decennial Digest, part 2	1991–1996
General Digest	1996–Date

The *National Reporter System* and the *American Digest System* are published in tandem to enable users to find cases that are on the right topic and in the right jurisdiction. West's process for compiling the *NRS* and the *American Digest* is informative for understanding how to use these tools.

When publishing case reports, the editors at West analyze each case opinion and write headnotes, brief statements describing each legal rule and issue addressed in the opinion. The headnotes are published with each case report, appearing just before the opinion. They are also published in the *American Digest*, which is actually a detailed outline of case law in the United States. To create the *American Digest*, the headnotes are first arranged in seven broad divisions: persons, property, contracts, torts, crimes, remedies, and government. The headnotes in each division are further subdivided by topics. More than 400 topics have been established in this way. The topics, rather than the broad divisions, are arranged alphabetically in the *American Digest*.

The headnotes in each topic are further arranged into a more detailed outline, with each outline point assigned a sequential key number. The result is that for any given point of law, a unique Topic and Key Number combination will lead the user to all headnotes for cases on that point of law. To bring this system full circle, users will note that in the case reports in the *National Reporter System*, each headnote is published in the reporter with the digest Topic and Key Number identified. West marks each reference to a Topic and Key Number with a miniature symbol of a key, to ensure that the user recognizes that this is an entry point into the *American Digest System*.

West extracts certain sets of headnotes from the *American Digest System* to create discrete digest sets that serve as companions to the reporters in the *National Reporter System*. For example, the companion digest to Supreme Court Reporter is *West's Supreme Court Digest*. There are companion digests to most regional reporters. Additionally, West publishes a state digest and reporter for nearly all fifty states and the District of Columbia.

Consequently, the digests perform three basic functions. They serve as case finding tools through their general indexes and topical outline, they abstract cases, and they provide the ability to cross-reference related cases within jurisdictions and from one jurisdiction to another. Researchers using the West reporters and digests will often be successful if they first identify a case that is on the desired point of law, either using the digests or an appropriate secondary source. The case can also be located in a *National Reporter System* reporter. Then, researchers can check the headnotes in the case report, particularly noting the Topics and Key Numbers identified with the headnotes. These Topics and Key Numbers can be used in virtually any West digest to find other cases that address the same point of law. West has been so successful in publishing case reports that many jurisdictions have adopted a West reporter as their official case reporter. In legal literature, more often than not, a reference to a court case will be a citation to a West reporter.

Court cases are also available through *Academic Universe* (F-15), which provides virtually every state appellate and federal case opinion that ever appeared in a standard case reporter. The cases are organized by federal court or by state and are searchable in full text. Many jurisdictions are also publishing current opinions on the Web. All of the Web portals listed previously in the chapter provide well-organized, direct links to Web pages for federal and state court cases.

Lawyer's Co-operative Publishing

F-53 **Digest of United States Supreme Court Reports. Lawyers' Edition**. Rochester, NY: Lawyer's Co-operative Publishing, 1927- .

F-54 **United States Supreme Court Reports. Lawyer's Edition**. Rochester, NY: Lawyer's Co-operative Publishing, 1926- .

Lawyers Co-operative Publishing (LCP),[13] which is discussed in depth with secondary sources, has often been described as a second principal publisher of general case reports. The company has experienced many changes as a result of becoming part of the Thomson Corporation, which now owns its historical competitor, West Publishing Company.

LCP has always stressed extensive analysis of selected "controlling" cases in its annotated case law reports. Comprehensive indexing provides sophisticated links to material in other LCP products, including *American Law Reports* (F-68), statutory law sources, practice formbooks, and *American Jurisprudence* (F-58). One LCP product deserves mention here. *United States Supreme Court Reports, Lawyer's Edition* (*LEd*), also provides complete U.S. Supreme Court opinions. Although it wasn't started until 1926, LCP has published every opinion rendered since 1789. Editorial enhancements include headnotes with references to subject headings in its own digest. In addition, it provides topical annotations similar to *American Law Reports* and summaries of briefs filed by attorneys in presenting cases before the U.S. Supreme Court. *LEd* is available through *Academic Universe* (F-15), complete with annotations and briefs.

Bureau of National Affairs

F-55 **United States Law Week**. 2 vols. Washington, DC: Bureau of National Affairs, 1947- .

United States Law Week has been widely and historically recognized as an excellent source for the full text of U.S. Supreme Court opinions. It provides weekly coverage of Supreme Court proceedings and is one of the most current print resources in existence. It is published in two looseleaf volumes, one containing a journal of Supreme Court proceedings with cases on the docket, summaries of recently filed cases, and the text of opinions reported; the other including summary and analysis of the decisions of lower federal courts and noteworthy federal statutes. Both have topical indexes and tables of cases.

Official Sources, U.S. Supreme Court

F-56 **Supreme Court of the United States**. URL: http://www.supremecourtus .gov/index.html. Accessed February 13, 2001.

F-57   **United States Reports**. Washington, DC: Government Printing Office, 1754- .

One final point about case reports for U.S. Supreme Court cases must be made. The official reporter of U.S. Supreme Court case opinions is not published by West Group or by Lawyers Co-operative Publishing, but by the federal government. Cases are first reported as slip opinions, then republished in paperbound collations as preliminary prints, and, finally, usually a few years later, as bound volumes of *United States Reports*. The Government Printing Office publishes case reports just as they are received from the court, with no editorial embellishment. Following the name of the case and certain necessary preliminary data such as the docket number, one will find a syllabus summarizing the facts and findings of law for the case, then the opinion of the court and any concurring or dissenting opinions that might have been written. Each bound volume of *United States Reports* includes a list of cases.

Shepard's Citations

Another key publisher in the realm of general case law does not publish case reports, digests, or annotations. The *Shepard's* citators enable a researcher to accomplish three important, related tasks. First, *Shepard's* citators help to find parallel citations—in other words, citations to various publications that give the same case reports. This service also helps in tracking citations of a case in question as it has progressed through the appeals, provided that the case has been reported at each step. Finally, *Shepard's* citators enable the researcher to determine whether the rules of law asserted in a reported case have been treated favorably or unfavorably by later cases. This last function of *Shepard's* citators has to do with determining whether the case has established precedent. If other courts that seek guidance to decide similar cases continue to refer to a rule of law asserted in the case in question, that rule is regarded as good authority in that it has established a precedent.

At first glance, the pages of *Shepard's* citators have all the glamour and pizzazz of a telephone book or actuarial tables. The presentation, if bland, is fairly simple to follow. The case to be investigated is referred to as the "cited" case. The cases that make reference to the cited case are the "citing" cases. Those who have used *Social Sciences Citation Index* will find that *Shepard's* citators perform the same function. In fact, *Shepard's* citators are the model on which the *Social Sciences Citation Index* (A-23) was originally based.

Lexis-Nexis publishes more than 100 different *Shepard's* citators covering statutes, regulations, case law, topical reporters, restatements, law reviews, popular name tables, and many other aspects of legal publishing. There is a separate citator series for each reporter in the *National Reporter System* (F-51) and a citator for each state reporter. Detailed instructions for using *Shepard's* citators are provided in many guides to legal literature, including each of the titles described in the beginning of this chapter. The use of electronic formats has greatly simplified use of *Shepard's* citators, although some libraries still maintain this service in print.

A few words of caution about *Shepard's* citators are necessary. They are comprehensive rather than selective about the references they publish. They collects all cases citing a decision and often give too many references to follow up effectively, even though they provide marginal notes to help the user select the more important references. Also, cases dealing with the same point of law but not citing one another are not listed in *Shepard's*. The converse is also true, of course. One case citing another may relate only in an extraneous way or on a single point that may not be the issue of interest to the researcher. West's digests are far superior tools for cross-referencing cases—which they were intended to be. *Shepard's* citators are intended for use in tracing the history of a case and determining the continuing validity of its legal holdings. In addition, the citators are an important link between West's and Lawyers Co-operative's systems because they provide references to case annotations appearing in the *American Law Reports* (F-68). In summary, *Shepard's* citators are used to determine the authority of a case and quickly expand a search to other relevant materials.

Shepard's for U.S. Supreme Court cases has recently been added to *Academic Universe*. Similar legal citators include the Auto-Cite service of LEXIS-NEXIS and the Insta-Cite service of Westlaw. Auto-Cite differs from Shepard's in that it is more selective, listing only citing cases and other citing references that have a significant impact on the strength of precedent in the case under study. Westlaw's Insta-Cite service is comprehensive, like *Shepard's*, and provides other features that aid in the evaluation of precedent.

Shepard's Citations are now produced in several formats: print, CD-ROM, as an online service of LEXIS-NEXIS, and as an Internet service of Matthew Bender Publishing.

SECONDARY RESOURCES

Encyclopedias

F-58 **American Jurisprudence**. 2d ed. Rochester, NY: Lawyers Co-operative Publishing Co., 1962- .

F-59 **Corpus Juris Secundum: A Complete Restatement of the Entire American Law As Developed By All Reported Cases**. St. Paul, MN: West Group, 1936- .

F-60 **West's Encyclopedia of American Law**. St. Paul, MN: West Group, 1998.

Law encyclopedias offer comprehensive subject coverage of the law. They may target a general audience, like *West's Encyclopedia of American Law*, or present more formal restatements of U.S. case law, such as *Corpus Juris Secundum* or *American Jurisprudence*, which are intended by their publishers to be comprehensive expositions of case law on formal legal constructs and topics. Regardless of type, however, they are good sources with which to start because they survey the law on a diverse range of topics and provide extensive references to cases. Therefore, the user will not only find substantial background information on a legal question but also numerous exact citations to the text of primary authorities on the topic.

American Jurisprudence, or "*Am Jur*," as it is popularly known, is based on the selective case reporting philosophy of Lawyers Co-operative, including only those cases most relevant to the topic being discussed. Therefore, it tends to provide fewer citations to cases but more analysis of case law. It cites relevant annotations in *American Law Reports* (F-68). A general, comprehensive index and a "Desk Book" volume that serves as a table of contents accompany the encyclopedia. *Am Jur* also provides a quick reference source containing legal forms, facts, tables, statistics, court organization, historical documents, and American Bar Association materials. It is updated by annual pocket supplements and revised volumes.

Corpus Juris Secundum (CJS) provides an extensive exposition of U.S. case law in encyclopedic form. Its articles contain extensive notes to cases on the points of discussion. Therein lies its forte. A good use of *CJS* is as a case-finding tool because the liberal number of footnotes draws the user to cases directly related to the most specific points in the articles. References to West Topics and Key Numbers are also included. The set is covered by a comprehensive general index and separate indexes for each title volume. The entire encyclopedia is updated by annual pocket supplements and revised volumes.

Compared to *Am Jur* and *CJS*, *West's Encyclopedia of American Law* is a layperson's law encyclopedia. It is the most complete reference source of its kind. The 4,000 general articles are informally written and richly illustrated with photographs and other visual aids. Nevertheless, it is an outstanding source on the history and organization of U.S. law and legal issues. Special features include "In Focus" pieces that supplement regular entries with additional details, facts, and arguments. "Milestones in the Law" provide a close look at selected landmark cases. Biographies of notable attorneys, judges, and other public figures usually include graphic timelines that provide a historical setting for the subject of the biography.

This is a terrific set of books to have at hand for quick reference and general background on legal topics.

Electronic access: *American Jurisprudence* is also available on CD-ROM, currently distributed by West Group.

Surveys of Law

F-61 **Annual Survey of American Law**. New York: New York University School of Law, 1942- .

F-62 **Martindale-Hubbell Law Digest**. New York: Reed Reference, 1991- .

F-63 **Martindale-Hubbell International Law Digest**. New York: Reed Reference, 1991- .

Unlike encyclopedias, surveys of law provide an abbreviated overview of the law, sometimes only relating changes that have been made to the law in the preceding year. *Annual Survey of American Law* is one of the oldest and continually most valuable reference tools tracing changes in law. It provides general discussions highlighting changes and developments in federal and state statutes, regulations, and case law. It is indexed by subject and contains tables of statutes and cases. Originally, the articles were first published in *New York University Law Review*. Since 1963, however, *Annual Survey* has been an original publisher of the work of legal scholars. Each volume of *Annual Survey* presents a series of articles by scholars and practitioners that survey yearly changes in the law and report on new legal developments. It is a good starting point for those researching current legal issues and issues of topical interest.

Martindale-Hubbell Law Digest is a compendium that summarizes the laws of each of the fifty states, the District of Columbia, Puerto Rico, and the Virgin Islands. The laws of each state are presented under almost 100 principal topics and numerous subtopics. The principal topics are carefully selected to represent those that have been found to be most useful to the legal profession. These topics are organized in a uniform arrangement, enabling the user to compare law between states quickly and easily. *Law Digest* also provides a digest of federal copyright, patent, and trademark laws; the federal courts; selected uniform codes; and rules of conduct set forth by the American Bar Association. *Martindale-Hubbell International Law Digest* summarizes laws of more than seventy-eight countries and the European Union. As in the *Law Digest*, topics are selected that are most likely to be of interest to attorneys and businesses. The digest also includes the annotated texts of several international conventions to which the United States is a party.

Periodicals and Journals

F-64 **Index to Legal Periodicals and Books**. Bronx, NY: H. W. Wilson, 1929- .

F-65 **Index to Periodical Articles Related to Law**. Dobbs Ferry, NY: Glanville Publications, 1958- .

F-66 **LegalTrac**. Foster City, CA: Information Access, 1980- .

F-67 Bell and Howell. **ProQuest Direct**. Online format. URL: http://proquest .umi.com/pqdweb. Accessed February 13, 2001.

Articles in law journals are usually a productive starting point for research. They provide scholarly analysis of the law, commentary on court decisions, discussion and news of changes in the law, surveys on topics of special interest, and other current legal issues. Like treatises, they contain extensive background information and references to the primary text of the law, so they can be used to find out what the law is, to find an argument about to what it should be, and to discover where it is located.

Law review and law journal articles vary considerably with respect to their usefulness to beginning or experienced researchers. Persons of nearly every level of experience and familiarity can find useful articles within an almost limitless selection of topics. Because publication cycles for periodicals tend to advance more quickly than some of the other types of literature, periodical articles address new issues and changing understandings much more quickly. Although all law publishers are concerned with providing up-to-date information, no other type of publication can match the breadth of topic selection and treatment found among legal periodical articles.

Many law review articles provide objective information, but law reviews also serve as a forum for discussion and debate. Researchers will find articles that are very critical of certain laws, court cases, or procedures. Other articles will push heavily for reform. Virtually all of the articles are scholarly, carefully researched, and referenced efforts, nonetheless. Law schools and other academic institutions, bar associations, other law-related organizations, and commercial publishers, all publish law reviews. Student editorial boards that are closely advised by law school faculty often edit law school law reviews. Law review articles identified as "Notes" or "Comment" are usually written by students. However, even student edited law reviews will include a few articles in each issue written by experienced scholars or practitioners.

Index to Legal Periodicals and Books indexes scholarly articles in law reviews and other legal periodicals. The American Association of Law Libraries began publishing the *Index* in 1929. Coverage of legal periodicals begins with 1908. Publication was taken over by H. W. Wilson in 1961, and since then its format has taken on the appearance of the other periodical indexes produced by that publisher. The print edition is issued monthly, except September, with quarterly, annual, and three-year cumulations. Article titles are arranged by subject and author/title. Subject headings represent a form of controlled vocabulary that is more standard to legal indexes generally than to the periodical indexes of other disciplines. Subject headings are listed at the front of each volume, along with a table of abbreviations for the titles indexed. Each volume contains a table of cases cited in the articles indexed and lists of cases by subject. A book review index is included. This index is one of the best places to start when searching for the development of law on a topic.

Index to Periodical Articles Related to Law covers articles on the law that appear in periodicals that are not law reviews—the journals of other disciplines, legal newspapers, and some popular magazines—or those periodicals that are not indexed in *Index to Legal Periodicals and Books.* Arranged by author/title and subject, it is published quarterly, cumulated annually in the October issue, and supplemented with ten-year cumulations.

LegalTrac is a cooperative effort between the publisher and the American Association of Law Libraries to index more than 800 titles on CD-ROM. Coverage consists of law reviews, legal journals, legal newspapers, and law specialty publications from English-speaking countries. The database also includes law-related articles from over 1,000 general interest newspapers, newsletters, and journals. Publications are searchable by name, subject, case, and statute.

Electronic access: *Index to Legal Periodicals and Books* is also available as a CD-ROM WILSONDISC from Wilson, and online through OCLC FirstSearch service, covering legal periodicals published since 1981. Recent years have seen more and more legal periodicals become available electronically, either as a second publishing venue for an established title, or as the original version. *FindLaw* (F-10) provides links to many law reviews published on the Internet. *ProQuest Direct*, mentioned elsewhere in this book, indexes more than 100 law reviews and provides most articles in full text. *Academic Universe* (F-15) makes about 300 law reviews available and searchable in full text.

F-68 American Law Reports. Rochester, NY: Lawyers Co-operative, 1919- .

Like West Group, Lawyers Co-operative Publishing (LCP) offers an integrated system of law books, incorporating many features that are similar to those used by West. LCP, however, has always operated under a more selective publishing philosophy. LCP attempts to identify those cases that add significantly to an understanding of the law. The result is a product that is less costly and requires far less shelf space.

The case report products of LCP include *American Law Reports* (*ALR*), consisting of six series (see table 6.2) plus *United States Supreme Court Reports, Lawyers' Edition* (*LEd*) (F-54). The case reports given in the several *ALR* series and the *LEd* are not nearly as significant, however, as the analytical essays, or annotations, that follow each case report. The scope of the annotations is never limited to the issues that come to play in deciding the case. The annotations are legal memoranda presenting all known established or developing dispositions on the issue. For example, in a recently published annotation, "Liability of Internet Service Provider for Internet or E-mail Defamation," the author described the scope of the issue and explained situations in which the courts have consistently held ISPs liable. He went on to discuss situations in which ISPs have always been held not liable and situations in which the courts have not established a reliable response.[14] Each annotation is heavily footnoted with references to cases and statutes on the same issue. For legal research, an *ALR* annotation on the topic at hand will provide a substantial amount of information on all aspects of the topic.

Table 6.2. American Law Reports Annotated

ALR	Vols. 1–175	1919–1948
ALR 2d	Vols. 1–100	1948–1965
ALR 3d	Vols. 1–100	1965–1980
ALR 4th	Vols. 1–90	1980–1991
ALR 5th	Vols. 1-	1992–Date
ALR FED	Vols. 1-	1969–Date

The several ALR series are indexed by topic in the *Index to Annotations* and the *Quick Index*, both of which are provided to subscribers. Topical access is also provided by four digests—one each for ALR and ALR 2d, a multivolume set that digests ALR 3d, 4th, and 5th and ALR Federal, and *Digest of the United States Supreme Court Reports, Lawyers' Edition* (F-53). As time goes on, changes in the law must be reflected in the annotations. LCP publishes new information in each volume of the *ALR*. An "Annotation History Table," found in the last volume of the *Index to Annotations*, lists all affected existing annotations, indicates whether an annotation was supplemented or superseded, and provides a reference to the new information in recent volumes of the *ALR*. *ALR*s are quite useful in print. They are also available online through LEXIS-NEXIS, but not through *Academic Universe* (F-15).

Treatises and Looseleaf Services

F-69 Commerce Clearing House. **CCH Internet Tax Research Network**. Online format. URL: http://tax.cch.com/. Accessed February 13, 2001.

F-70 **CCH Standard Federal Tax Reporter**. Chicago: Commerce Clearing House, 1913- .

F-71 Corbin, Arthur Linton. **Corbin on Contracts, a Comprehensive Treatise on the Rules of Contract Law**. 8 vols. St. Paul, MN: West Group, 1950- .

F-72 **Criminal Law Reporter**. Washington, DC: Bureau of National Affairs, 1967- .

F-73 Davis, Kenneth Culp, and Richard J. Pierce. **Administrative Law Treatise**. 3d ed. New York: Little, Brown, 1994.

F-74 Eis, Arlene L. **Legal Looseleafs in Print**. New York: Infosources, 1981- .

F-75 **Labor Relations Reporter**. Washington, DC: Bureau of National Affairs, 1937- .

Legal treatises attempt to provide a comprehensive discussion of individual topics or issues of law. A chief characteristic is that they provide well-referenced, scholarly commentary on the law. In their textbook on legal research, Jacobstein and Mersky identify five basic types of legal treatises:

1. critical, or those that critique and analyze the law;

2. interpretative, or those that attempt to provide a general understanding of the law;

3. expository, or less scholarly restatements of case law such as the articles in law encyclopedias;

4. textual, or textbooks for law students; and

5. educational handbooks and reference sources for law practitioners.

Any particular treatise may contain elements of more than one of these types.[15]

Most libraries have examples of treatises. Titles on a particular topic can be found easily in general bibliographies of legal materials. They can be identified in a library catalog by subject and call number. Law materials lie in the Library of Congress "K" classification schedule or the Dewey "340-349" range of classification numbers. Often a treatise is all a library patron requires to answer his or her legal question. There are literally thousands of legal treatises. Authors include highly reputable scholars. A few command considerable scholarly authority and have been persuasive influences in the courts. The two series of books described below contain some excellent examples of this type of legal source.

The Hornbook series of West Group is probably best known as a series of textbooks for law students. Named for the sixteenth-century practice of mounting a paper inscribed with a basic instructional lesson on a tablet with a handle and covering it with a thin sheet of translucent animal horn for protection, Hornbooks now are written by recognized legal scholars on specific areas of jurisprudence and legal study. The West series includes over forty titles on topics of legal study in such areas as administrative law, constitutional law, contracts, criminal law, evidence, labor law, torts, and urban planning.

As a companion to its Hornbooks, West publishes another series of titles that can be likened to condensed treatises. The Nutshell series includes over 100 individual titles by various authors covering specific areas of jurisprudence and legal practice. The titles in the series are written for the layperson rather than for the legal specialist. The series is published in the form of paperback pocketbooks. Each title is intended to provide a compact reference resource to which the student or lawyer can turn for "a succinct exposition of the law. . . ."[16]

Two examples of noteworthy treatises are Davis and Pierce's *Administrative Law Treatise* and *Corbin on Contracts*. Both are highly respected in the courts, the legal profession, and legal scholarship. *Administrative Law Treatise* is the definitive treatment of administrative law—the law of agency power and procedure, providing practical guidance and commentary on seminal cases as well as the latest developments. This treatise is also quite readable for nonspecialists in the law. Similarly, the eight-volume *Corbin on Contracts* is the work to consult regarding working rules applied in contract transactions.

Another good starting point is a looseleaf service that covers the legal area in question. These services are referred to as "looseleaf" because they are often published as loose pages to be filed in a ringed binder to permit frequent updating by interfiling revised individual pages or sections. This is a device used by a number of law publishers to keep materials up-to-date. They are often more current than the primary sources because of the speed and regularity with which they are updated. Looseleafs combine the text and elements of primary authorities, secondary sources, and finding tools in one place. Most looseleaf services integrate background and analysis of the law in a specialized subject. They provide the text of all the laws relevant to the subject covered: statutes, regulations, cases, etc. They also provide access to this information through comprehensive indexes and highly developed finding aids. For these reasons, the authors of *The Process of Legal Research* (F-5), a guide to legal literature, refer to looseleaf services as "mini" libraries.

Topics covered by looseleaf services—such as tax law, labor law, education law, and trade regulation—are multifaceted, important to business or the practice of law, and frequently changing. Looseleaf services tend to be expensive to purchase and maintain. Print versions require frequent filing as the publisher may send packets of updating pages every year, every month, or even every week. Several publishers now offer looseleaf titles online or on CD-ROM, which reduces the maintenance burden somewhat. However, delivering an electronic product with the same functionality, or better, than the print has proven to be a difficult task for some publishers.

Looseleaf services are not used in the same linear way as a novel, textbook, law review article, or treatise. For example, in a tax looseleaf service, a researcher may typically start with a subject index, go to a section of the Internal Revenue Code, select a case annotation, read the full text case opinion, consult the citator, and finally analyze the citing cases. Each of these steps is necessary to identify a case and check the validity of the law asserted in the case. To provide hypertext links to references within the text of a record is a relatively simple thing for an electronic product designer to do. To design the product to help researchers keep track of what they have seen and where they are in the service at any instant, while permitting the researcher to move fluidly throughout the service, is not so simple.

As with legal treatises, a complete list of looseleaf services would be impossible to include in this chapter. The closest thing to a complete list is *Legal Loose-leafs in Print*. Following is a discussion of three titles that are among the most commonly known of looseleaf sources and probably among the most useful in any library.

One type of looseleaf reporter is fundamentally a newsletter, published at regular intervals to be filed consecutively in a binder. An example is the *Criminal Law Reporter*, which provides summary and analysis of current developments in criminal law. It is supplemented weekly with information on court decisions, federal legislative action, reports, news briefs, and more. The researcher will find the full text of Supreme Court decisions, federal rules and procedures, a cumulative index, and a table of cases.

Another type of looseleaf service is essentially a treatise that is kept in a binder and updated with new pages—reflecting changes in the law, recent cases, or reformulated commentary—that replace existing pages that contain out-of-date information. This saves the cost of publishing complete new editions every year or so. *CCH Standard Federal Tax Reporter* is a nearly perfect example of this type of looseleaf reporting system. Sooner or later, the reference desk in almost every library gets a question on taxes. This service is one of the most extensive, covering the full text of federal statutes, federal regulations, summaries of court cases, and administrative decisions. It is published in sixteen individual binders and covers all aspects of federal tax law, providing the full text of the IRS Code and federal tax regulations. It also gives extensive analysis and commentary on the law. Material in the set is located through a series of indexes, finding aids, a table of cases, and a citator that provides access by name of a tax decision to historical records and later decisions. It is updated weekly. The *CCH Standard Federal Tax Reporter* is fully represented in the *CCH Internet Tax Research Network*, a well-executed service that preserves the content and the functionality of the print product, while adding features one might expect in an online service, such as full-text searching and fluid navigation throughout the service.

A comprehensive tool for researching the law of labor-management relations is found in BNA's *Labor Relations Reporter* and its many components. This service began in 1937 and now comprises twelve binders and six case reporters covering all manner of state and federal labor relations law, labor arbitration, wage and hour issues, fair employment practices, individual employment rights, and disabilities issues. Most of the information is provided in full text with the binders providing the current year's statutes and cases. The historical cases are found in the case reporters. The service is also available in an online, Internet version by separate subscription.

Secondary Sources and Search Strategy

Use of secondary sources depends entirely on what the researcher wants to accomplish. A good treatise or looseleaf service may provide all the information needed. However, these resources are a step away from the primary authorities. They represent the law, to be sure, but they are dependent on the author or editor's judgment, opinion, and other subjective determinations. Sometimes, using the primary authorities exclusively makes the most sense for research. When seeking support for a legal position, argument, or assertion, the researcher may have to consider many cases before finding the ones that suit the position best.

In other circumstances, the researcher wants to quickly identify the most significant cases, statutes, etc., on either a broad or narrow topic. Someone else's knowledge and experience with the topic may be greatly appreciated. The numerous secondary sources provide varying degrees of objectivity and evaluation. They also lean on conventional, established understandings of the law to differing degrees. The greatest variety will be found in law reviews, where readers will find the very latest in cutting-edge scholarship, but in some articles the author takes a position that is far from neutral. As mentioned before, law reviews serve as a forum for debate and give voice to those who seek reform. Nonetheless, in all law review articles, both reform-oriented and more objective, references to primary authorities are carefully evaluated and selected for analysis. An article on the researcher's topic may yield a treasure trove of useful references.

On the other end of the spectrum of secondary sources is the formal law encyclopedia, such as *Corpus Juris Secundum* (F-59) or *American Jurisprudence* (F-58), in which every notion has been solidly established in multiple jurisdictions. Encyclopedias reflect trends supported by many cases much better than they identify exceptional cases.

Annotations of *American Law Reports* (F-68) fall between law reviews and encyclopedias in that they cover recent developments and developing trends in the law but deliver them in reliably objective, thorough discussions. Authors of *ALR* annotations do not assert new ideas or criticism. They do not push for reform. Cases and statutes included in annotations are carefully evaluated before inclusion. When looking for the significant cases upon which important legal issues turn, *ALR*s can be very helpful.

BEYOND THE QUESTIONS OF LAW

Thus far, this chapter has discussed many standard resources necessary for researching questions of the law, with little regard for other investigations about the courts and the judicial process. The courts handle many thousands of cases each year. The processing of such a mass of cases, start to finish, is a phenomenon many researchers find worthy of study. A few basic resources are offered in this discussion that will serve as springboards for further investigation. Serious researchers will seek additional materials. More general reference sources will be helpful, including *Statistical Universe* (A-83) and *PAIS International in Print* (A-21), as will some of the social sciences indexes, such as *Social Sciences Abstracts* (H-50) and *Sociological Abstracts* (H-49).

The Courts in General

Handbooks, Manuals, and Guides

F-76 Carp, Robert A., and Ronald Stidham. **The Federal Courts**. 3d ed. Washington, DC: Congressional Quarterly Press, 1998.

F-77 Carp, Robert A., and Ronald Stidham. **Judicial Process in America**. 4th ed. Washington, DC: Congressional Quarterly Press, 1998.

F-78 Levy, Leonard W., ed. **Encyclopedia of the American Constitution**. 4 vols. New York: Macmillan, 1986.

F-79 Janosik, Robert J., ed. **Encyclopedia of the American Judicial System: Studies of the Principal Institutions and Processes of Law**. New York: Charles Scribner's Sons, 1987.

F-80 Vile, John R. **Encyclopedia of Constitutional Amendments, Proposed Amendments, and Amending Issues, 1789–1995**. Santa Barbara, CA: ABC-Clio, 1996.

The Federal Courts provides a comprehensive description of the federal judiciary. It discusses the history, organization, and powers of the federal courts and selection of judges. Researchers will also find comparisons of decision making at the trial and appellate courts. The guide also offers a discussion about policy making by American judges. This is a useful, objective, jargon-free introduction to the federal courts. As might be expected, with the same authors and publisher, *Judicial Process in America* offers a similar treatment of the topic. Here, the authors discuss the foundations of law in the United States, with coverage of the various actors in a case: lawyers, litigants, and interest groups. The criminal court process is described and compared to the civil court process. The roles of federal and state judges are also compared. With regard to the history and origins of the judicial system, as well as the decision making and policy making in the courts, the content of this book overlaps with the first guide.

The Encyclopedia of the American Constitution bridges history, law, and political science in four volumes. The 2,100 articles address doctrinal concepts of constitutional law, judicial decisions, public acts, biography, and historical periods. Most articles are approximately 6,000 words in length, with some topics being covered in several related articles. This work was written for general readers with little background in law. Finding aids include subject, name, and case indexes, and a chronology of constitutional history. Most articles include references to further reading.

Encyclopedia of the American Judicial System encompasses both substantive law and legal procedures. Categories include legal history, institutions and personnel, behavior, constitutional law, and research methodology.

The Constitution of the United States has stood the test of time and the onslaught of over 10,000 proposals to amend it. Vile's *Encyclopedia of Constitutional Amendments* is a complete source on the amendments in one volume. It provides the complete text of the Constitution as of the 27th Amendment (1992). Amendments are listed by date proposed and date ratified. The *Encyclopedia* also lists the number of proposed amendments, by decade, and the most popular amending proposals by year. Researchers will appreciate the bibliography and list of cases. Over 400 encyclopedic entries discuss the twenty-seven ratified amendments and many of the other proposed amendments, major constitutional reforms, biography, organizations, U.S. Supreme Court decisions, and unresolved issues.

Directories and Biographical Sources

F-81 American Bar Association and the Association of American Law Schools. **The Official Guide to U.S. Law Schools**. Newtown, PA: Law School Admission Council/Law School Admission Services, 1986- . Annual.

F-82 Administrative Office of the U.S. Courts. **Understanding the Federal Courts**. URL: http://www.uscourts.gov/UFC99.pdf. Accessed February 13, 2001.

F-83 **The American Bench**. Minneapolis, MN: Reginald Bishop Froster and Associates, 1977- .

F-84 **BNA's Directory of State and Federal Courts, Judges, and Clerks**. 2001 ed. Washington, DC: The Bureau of National Affairs, 2001.

F-85 **Martindale-Hubbell International Law Directory**. Summit, NJ: Martindale-Hubbell Law Directory, 1991- .

F-86 **Martindale-Hubbell Law Directory**. New York: Martindale-Hubbell Law Directory, 1931- . Annual.

F-87 Nelson, Stephen. **Almanac of the Federal Judiciary**. 2 vols. Englewood Cliffs, NJ: Prentice-Hall Law and Business, 1984- . Semiannual.

F-88 **United States Court Directory**. Washington, DC: Administrative Office of the Court of the United States, 1978- .

F-89 **West's Legal Directory on Lawoffice.com**. Eagan, MN: West Group, 1994- . Online format. URL: http://www.lawoffice.com/. Accessed February 13, 2001.

F-90 **Who's Who in American Law**. Chicago: Marquis Who's Who, 1977/1978- .

The Official Guide to U.S. Law Schools is published each year as an aid to students and others seeking admission to law school or planning a legal career. Prospective law students will find information about legal education, the law profession, and facts about ABA-approved law schools. The handbook presents information on admissions requirements, course programs, and degree requirements; library and physical facilities; expenses and financial aid; and so forth for more than 170 law schools accredited by the American Bar Association. Admission profiles of most of the schools listed cover Law School Admission Test (LSAT) scores and grade-point averages accepted by the schools. Information on the profession includes lawyers' salaries across the United States and minority opportunities in law. Needless to say, this is a heavily used source among prelaw students.

Understanding the Federal Courts is a pamphlet that describes the federal courts in common language. It includes sections on how the federal courts relate to other branches of government and to the public, the structure and jurisdiction of the federal judiciary, appointment of judges, steps in the judicial process, and administration of the federal courts. It concludes with a glossary of terms and contact information for Federal District Courts and Circuit Courts of Appeal.

The American Bench is a one-volume desk book containing biographical information on approximately 18,000 federal and state judges, along with the jurisdiction and organizational structure of their courts. Biographies are contributed by the judges themselves and cover such items as personal, educational, and legal background; current and previous judgeships; important decisions and publications; civic organizations; and personal interests. The volume is thumb-indexed and arranged by federal and state levels. It provides maps showing federal court districts and state court districts for each state. State entries cover descriptions of the courts by jurisdictional level and the judges in alphabetical order. The work includes a comprehensive name index.

BNA's Directory of State and Federal Courts, Judges, and Clerks is a basic directory providing contact information for courts, judges, and their staffs at the state and federal level. A large amount of information is publicly available at the courts but is not published. Some research requires such information and simply cannot be fulfilled without contacting the court directly. The directory provides an organizational chart for each court system and indexes for geographic areas and names.

For more than 100 years, the *Martindale-Hubbell Law Directory* has been an extensive directory for the legal profession. Listings in this multivolume, annual source are available to all lawyers who have been admitted to the American Bar Association. This is the most comprehensive law directory published. Arranged by state and city, information on each listed attorney includes date of birth, date of admission to the bar, college and law school attended, American Bar Association membership, specialty, and a "confidential" rating of legal ability. The directory also lists law firms by city. Users should be aware that attorneys elect whether to be included in this directory and pay a fee for the privilege. The *Martindale-Hubbell International Law Directory* is a spinoff of the *Law Directory*. It reflects the rapidly expanding interest in international law. The 2000 edition lists more than 900,000 lawyers practicing in 170 countries. The information is similar to that presented in the *Law Directory*. Additional components of the *Martindale-Hubbell Law Directory* are *Martindale-Hubbell Law Digest* (F-62) and *Martindale-Hubbell International Law Digest* (F-63).

Almanac of the Federal Judiciary is a two-volume, semiannual biographical directory that profiles all current judicial appointments to federal courts. For each judge the almanac provides general information, including current appointment, address, year the current appointment began, and president who made the appointment. Other information includes education, private practice and related professional experience, activities, appointments and positions, honors and awards, and noteworthy rulings. Also of interest are evaluative quotations from lawyers. Volume one provides profiles for each U.S. district judge and is organized by federal circuit and then by state and U.S. judicial district. Volume two has profiles for the U.S. Supreme Court justices followed by U.S. Circuit Court of Appeals judges, arranged by federal circuit.

United States Court Directory is the official directory of the federal courts, providing addresses, telephone numbers, names of justices, and key staff of virtually every federal court in the United States, including the U.S. Supreme Court, all of the U.S. Circuit Courts of Appeal, all of the U.S. District Courts, and all specialized federal courts and federal judicial agencies. This directory was originally published semiannually. It has been published annually since 1990.

West's Legal Directory on Lawoffice.com lists more than a million attorneys and firms worldwide. It is searchable by name, practice area, city, county, and state. Entries consist of basic contact information: name, address, phone, fax, E-mail, and Web site. The directory includes profiles of international counsel, corporate counsel, and U.S. government attorneys.

In its tenth edition, *Who's Who in American Law* is similar to other Marquis biographical guides. It provides biographical notes on thousands of living lawyers and "professionals in law-related areas," including judges, legal educators, scholars, librarians, legal historians, and social scientists. Upon invitation from the publisher, the legal professional usually submits information for the biographical sketches. The people listed are selected on the basis of "reference value," which is determined by either their position of responsibility or noteworthy achievement. As with its cousins, entries in this Who's Who include vital statistics, family information, education, certifications, writings, military experience, religion, legal interest, addresses, and so forth.

Special Resources for U.S. Supreme Court Research

F-91 Biskupic, Joan, and Elder Witt. **Guide to the U.S. Supreme Court**. 3d ed. 2 vols. Washington, DC: Congressional Quarterly Press, 1997.

F-92 Biskupic, Joan, and Elder Witt. **The Supreme Court and the Powers of the American Government**. Washington, DC: Congressional Quarterly Press, 1997.

F-93 Biskupic, Joan, and Elder Witt. **The Supreme Court and Individual Rights**. 3d ed. Washington, DC: Congressional Quarterly Press, 1997.

F-94 Biskupic, Joan, and Elder Witt. **The Supreme Court at Work**. 2d ed. Washington, DC: Congressional Quarterly Press, 1997.

F-95 Epstein, Lee, Jeffrey A. Segal, Harold J. Spaeth, and Thomas G. Walker. **The Supreme Court Compendium: Data, Decisions, and Developments**. 2d ed. Washington, DC: Congressional Quarterly Press, 1996.

F-96 Friedman, Leon, and Fred L. Israel, eds. **The Justices of the United States Supreme Court 1789-1978: Their Lives and Major Opinions**. New York: Chelsea House, 1995.

F-97 Martin, Fenton S., and Robert U. Goehlert. **How to Research the Supreme Court**. Washington, DC: Congressional Quarterly Press, 1992.

F-98 Irons, Peter, and Stephanie Guitton, eds. **May It Please the Court: Arguments on Abortion**. New York: The New Press, 1995.

F-99 Irons, Peter, and Stephanie Guitton, eds. **May It Please the Court, the Most Significant Oral Arguments Made Before the Supreme Court Since 1955**. New York: The New Press, 1993.

F-100   Irons, Peter, ed. **May It Please the Court: Courts, Kids, and the Constitution**. New York: The New Press, 2000.

F-101   Irons, Peter, ed. **May It Please the Court, the First Amendment, Transcripts of the Oral Arguments Made Before the Supreme Court in Sixteen Key First Amendment Cases**. New York: The New Press, 1997.

F-102   Hall, Kermit L., ed. **The Oxford Companion to the Supreme Court of the United States**. New York: Oxford University Press, 1992.

F-103   Hall, Kermit L., ed. **The Oxford Guide to United States Supreme Court Decisions**. New York: Oxford University Press, 1999.

F-104   Van Geel, T. R. **Understanding Supreme Court Opinions**. 2d ed. New York: Longman, 1997.

Few institutions evoke the prestige and mystique of the United States Supreme Court. Its power is a natural draw for researchers in law, history, politics, and other social science disciplines. Fortunately for them, resources for researching the Supreme Court are much more numerous than for any other court in the United States. This section focuses on resources useful to researchers who want to know more about the Court, its role, history, procedures, justices, and importance. The availability of opinions has been discussed in a previous section.

The most useful resource for learning about the Supreme Court is probably Congressional Quarterly's *Guide to the U.S. Supreme Court*, a two-volume title now in its third edition. This carefully researched, highly readable book tells the story of the Court's development, its people, and their decisions from the first time it convened with only three justices in 1790 to present. Illustrated chapters cover the origins of the Court's power, controversies, and new challenges. They explain the relationship of the Court to other branches of government, the states, and the individual. They also explore rights, freedoms, and due process.

Three works from CQ by the same authors are *The Supreme Court and Individual Rights*, *The Supreme Court and the Powers of the American Government*, and *The Supreme Court at Work*. Since each was meant to stand alone as a useful narration about the Court, a bit of duplication of material is to be expected. Together, they expound further on fundamental themes developed by the *Guide to the U.S. Supreme Court*. *The Supreme Court and Individual Rights* explores the Court's role as guardian of individual rights and liberties. Chapters start with meager beginnings that deal with the Bill of Rights, slavery, and the 13th through 15th Amendments. They continue through modern times with the controversies over affirmative action and rights of illegal immigrants. Those who investigate division of powers between branches of government, and between the Court and the states, will appreciate *The Supreme Court and the Powers of the American Government*. The Supreme Court has historically sought to define these relationships, from *Marbury v. Madison*[17] to the present. Congress and the president have asserted their own authority, often in conflict with each other and with the Court. The history of the Court is outlined in the first three chapters of *The Supreme Court at Work*, which also details its operations and traditions. This third book also explains the role of the chief justice, the associate justices, and supporting staff. Furthermore, it recounts the various places where the Court has met over the years and provides brief biographies of each of the justices through 1996. Appendixes provide significant documents and summarize over 400 significant cases decided by the Court.

Another significant reference work from Congressional Quarterly is *The Supreme Court Compendium: Data, Decisions, and Developments*, an effective recitation of an abundance of facts, figures, and gathered information. Separate chapters cover institutional aspects of the Court, processes and caseload statistics, trends in opinions and decisions, nominations and confirmations of justices, activities of the justices and their departures from the Court, voting behavior and opinions of the justices, the political and legal environment of the Court, public opinion, and impact. Each chapter begins with a brief essay, but most of the data are offered in tables.

Several titles have been mentioned that provide biographical information about the justices of the Supreme Court. In most instances, these provide fairly brief treatment with possibly a few references for further study. *The Justices of the United States Supreme Court 1789–1978: Their Lives and Major Opinions* provides a unique contribution in this regard. Each entry is fifteen to twenty pages, long, including a portrait or photograph, and gives the reader a fuller account of the life and significant work of each justice. Each biography has been contributed by a legal scholar and discusses basic facts of the justice's life, his or her background in the law, his or her distinctive path to the Supreme Court, major decisions, and underlying legal philosophy.

Unlike the other research guides described in this chapter, Martin and Goehlert's *How to Research the Supreme Court* is not focused on researching the law as such. This guide covers sources for finding and interpreting statutes, guides to government and legal research, and materials providing background information on the Supreme Court. The sources listed enable the researcher to study the Court as a political, historical, social, and economic player in American society. A significant portion of the book is devoted to two areas: a selected bibliography on the Court and a bibliography of works about individual justices.

Peter Irons, Director of the Earl Warren Bill of Rights Project at the University of California, San Diego, and a member of the Supreme Court Bar, found that hearings of the Court had been tape recorded since 1955. The recordings were kept at the National Archives and Records Administration. Few people had ever listened to a recorded hearing. Seeking to correct that problem, Irons set about to publish selective recordings and transcripts. The result has been a series of book and audiotape sets whose titles begin with the phrase, "May it Please the Court . . ." . Each set consists of two to six audiocassettes containing live recordings of selected oral arguments and a book with the transcripts of the arguments. The value of the four titles published to date is not so much in providing new words for research but in hearing the voices, tempo, and inflection of the justices and the attorneys as they deliberate significant cases in the highest court in the nation.

In the absence of the works by Biskupic and Witt, another good starting point is a one-volume handbook, *The Oxford Companion to the Supreme Court of the United States*. Although it is more concise, its useful features are significant and include the full text of the Constitution of the United States with all amendments through the 27th, a narration on the succession of judges, trivia and traditions of the Court, and indexes for finding cases and topical materials. A separate section discloses that the Court is a hybrid of political, social, economic, and cultural forces. The book provides a comprehensive guide to the current operation of the Court. It also discusses Court doctrine, day-to-day operations, and the history of the Court. Like other reference works on the Supreme Court, it provides brief biographies of the justices and lists historically significant cases.

Two noteworthy items address the problem of understanding the outcomes of the U.S. Supreme Court, that is, the decisions and opinions of the Court. *The Oxford Guide to United States Supreme Court Decisions* covers major issues that have confronted the Court, judicial matters, and legal terminology. This guide analyzes over 400 cases, illuminating changes in constitutional law, and maps the historical dynamics that have accompanied those changes. On the other hand, *Understanding Supreme Court Opinions* delves into the process of legal reasoning, analysis, and justification used by the justices. This book examines the Court's role as policy maker and teacher, and explores the problem of writing a Supreme Court opinion. Part two looks at the processes of making decisions and writing opinions, including the legal materials, standards of review, precedent, and justification. The summary chapter at the end clarifies how to understand a Supreme Court opinion.

The Supreme Court of the United States conveys much information, prestige, and influence in its work of deciding cases that could not be concluded by any other court or forum. The controversies brought to the Court are sometimes far reaching and touch on fundamental dilemmas brought about by our imperfect social, religious, and policy-making systems. The news media are often abuzz with the drama surrounding a case that will soon be argued in the Court, or one that was recently decided. Yet relatively few people have actually witnessed the proceedings of the Court. Most of the official public work of the Court consists of hearing scheduled arguments, rendering decisions, and releasing opinions that explain how the decisions were made. The justices, their staffs, and attorneys representing the litigants attend the hearings. Spectators, including members of the press, must fit within a relatively small gallery in the Court provided for them. Cameras are not permitted.

CRIMINAL JUSTICE

Criminal justice as a subject of study is by nature highly interdisciplinary. The social and behavioral aspects of criminology are multifaceted. The legal materials addressing criminal issues are voluminous. All court cases fall into two large genres: civil cases and criminal cases. Criminal justice research often extends into such a variety of sources and subject areas that no resource exists that can be considered comprehensive. Field researchers observe human behavior within police departments and in parking lots. Forensic scientists study medicine and entomology. The works described below focus on information sources that deal directly with criminal justice.

Guides to Research, Handbooks, and Encyclopedias

F-105 Benamati, Dennis C. **Criminal Justice Information: How to Find It, How to Use It**. Phoenix, AZ: Oryx Press, 1998.

F-106 The Criminal Justice Distance Learning Consortium. **The Definitive Guide to Criminal Justice and Criminology on the World Wide Web**. Upper Saddle River, NJ: Prentice Hall, 1999.

F-107 Durham, Jennifer L. **Crime in America: A Reference Handbook**. (Contemporary World Issues). Santa Barbara, CA: ABC-Clio, 1996.

F-108 **Encyclopedia of Crime and Justice**. Edited by Sanford H. Kadish. New York: Free Press, 1998.

F-109 **The Oxford Handbook of Criminology**. Edited by Mike Maguire, Rod Morgan, and Robert Reiner. 2d ed. New York: Oxford University Press, 1997.

Although much of Benamati's *Criminal Justice Information: How to Find It, How to Use It* is devoted to classic use of resources for legal research, it acknowledges that legal research is often conducted in the context of crime incidence, law enforcement practices, economic and environmental factors, and other issues. Chapters also discuss legal authorities, reference sources, statistical information, government publications, and international criminal justice information.

The Criminal Justice Distance Learning Consortium boldly labels their *Definitive Guide to Criminal Justice and Criminology on the World Wide Web*. The claim of "definitive guide" has some validity. This resource discusses Web sites, e-mail discussion lists, and search engines covering an extensive array of criminal justice, criminology, and career information and issues. It also gives very fundamental information about using the Internet, including what the Internet is, making a connection to the Internet, navigating across the Web, using e-mail, and security matters.

Crime in America does not provide the comprehensive treatment of an Oxford Handbook, but it does survey current challenges in criminal justice in the United States and provides a springboard for further research. Typical of ABC-Clio's Contemporary World Issues series, a variety of sections include a survey of the problem, a brief history of crime, biographical sketches, statistics, a directory of organizations, print resources, and selected nonprint resources.

Encyclopedia of Crime and Justice is one of the few scholarly encyclopedias available in a discipline full of popularly written reference works on heinous acts of crime, barbarous prisons, incorrigible gangs, and notorious gangsters. The *Encyclopedia* attempts comprehensive coverage of subjects dealing with the nature and causes of criminal behavior, crime prevention, punishment and treatment of offenders, institutions of criminal justice, and criminal law. Authors were allowed their own point of view so long as their treatment of diverse topics was evenhanded. Although subject matter and writing style were intended to emphasize stable, established notions and practices rather than transitory matters, this work is badly in need of updating.

Oxford Handbooks have a reputation for providing solid, objective information to introduce new subject matter to researchers. *The Oxford Handbook of Criminology* is no exception, providing a comprehensive, state-of-the-art orientation to criminological analysis and research with a British focus. The information is presented in twenty-five chapters by experienced specialists, organized into four broad areas: theory and history; forms of crime and criminality; crime control and justice; and social dimensions of crime, justice, and victimization.

Indexes

F-110   **Criminal Justice Abstracts**. Monsey, NY: Criminal Justice Press, 1968- .

F-111   **NCJRS Abstracts Database**. Rockville, MD: National Institute of Justice, National Criminal Justice Reference Service, 1972- . Online format. URL: http://www.ncjrs.org/search.html.

Although several indexes to criminal justice periodicals and other current information exist, *Criminal Justice Abstracts* is the service that covers the most scholarly and authoritative research. Begun in 1968, it indexes international journals, books, reports, dissertations and unpublished papers in disciplines closely related to criminology.

Casting a much wider net than *Criminal Justice Abstracts*, the National Criminal Justice Reference Service is a nationwide clearinghouse for justice research, much as ERIC is a clearinghouse for education research. The *NCJRS Document Database* is a bibliographic index to the research reports NCJRS has collected. Begun in the 1970s, the database provides access to more than 100,000 documents, with approximately 500 items added each month. It covers a wide variety of justice-related topics, including research and statistics on the courts, probation and parole, corrections, forensics, law enforcement, and many others. Resources indexed in the database include federal, state and local government reports; books; research reports; journal articles; and unpublished research. Some materials are not often covered in bibliographic databases, such as filmstrips and law enforcement product reviews. Many researchers have regarded the database as difficult to use because of its nonselective coverage of criminal justice topics. Availability of documents indexed in the database is quite variable. Books, journals, government documents, and technical reports are available from standard sources. Many unpublished reports and documents that have received little distribution otherwise may be available through direct links to the documents on the Internet. Prior to 1996, a fair percentage is available through the NCRJS or through interlibrary loan from libraries that purchased the NCJRS Microfiche Collection.

Statistical Sources

F-112   **Bureau of Justice Statistics**. Online format. URL: http://www.ojp.usdoj .gov/bjs/abstract/cvusst.htm. Accessed February 13, 2001.

F-113   U.S. Department of Justice, Bureau of Justice Statistics. **Criminal Victimization in the United States**. Washington, DC: National Criminal Justice Information and Statistics Service, 1973- . Online format. URL: http://www.ojp.usdoj .gov/bjs/abstract/cvusst.htm. Accessed February 13, 2001.

F-114   U.S. Department of Justice. Bureau of Justice Statistics. **Sourcebook of Criminal Justice Statistics**. Washington, DC: Government Printing Office, 1973- . Online format. URL: http://www.ojp.usdoj.gov/bjs/abstract/scjs99.htm. Accessed February 13, 2001.

F-115   United States Federal Bureau of Investigation. **Crime in the United States/ Uniform Crime Reports for the United States**. Washington, DC: Government Printing Office, 1930- .

F-116   United States Federal Bureau of Investigation. **Crime in the United States/ Uniform Crime Reports for the United States**. Washington, DC: Government Printing Office, 1995- . Online format. URL: http://www.fbi.gov/ucr.htm. Accessed February 13, 2001.

Criminal Victimization in the United States and *Sourcebook of Criminal Justice Statistics*, significant as they are, are only two of many publications and reports available from the Bureau of Justice Statistics (BJS) Web site. BJS is the primary U.S. source for criminal justice statistics of all types. The agency works in cooperation with other federal agencies and state agencies to collect, analyze, publish, and disseminate information on crime, criminal offenders, victims of crime, and the operation of justice systems at all levels of government.

The purpose of the *Sourcebook of Criminal Justice Statistics* is to compile reliable criminal justice and related statistics for use by criminal justice professionals and other researchers. The result is a rich, easy-to-use reference consisting of over 700 statistical tables, arranged in the following six sections:

- Characteristics of the criminal justice system

- Public attitudes toward crime and criminal justice topics

- The nature and distribution of known offenses

- Characteristics and distribution of persons arrested

- Judicial processing of defendants

- Persons under correctional supervision

Reliability of data is a key feature of the *Sourcebook*. Each source is carefully evaluated with regard to data collection and reporting methods prior to inclusion. Each table is annotated with the source of the data. A consolidated list of source publications is provided after the tables. The information provided in the *Sourcebook* is extensive, but the source references allow researchers to conduct even more in-depth investigations.

News media report regularly on current trends in crime data. They often relate the frequency with which certain crimes occur, such as auto theft, burglary, and rape. More than likely, the source of such information is *Crime in the United States/Uniform Crime Reports for the United States*. The *Uniform Reports* have been published for seventy years and are based on actual arrest and related data collected by law enforcement agencies in nearly every jurisdiction of any size in the nation. The original basis for the data was the Uniform Crime Reporting (UCR) Program established by Congress for collecting data. The Program established reportable crimes and reporting procedures so that law enforcement agencies could begin collecting data in a uniform manner. Jurisdictions vary somewhat in the legal definition and established severity of certain types of crime. UCR did not change the way various jurisdictions enforce law, but it did change they way crimes were reported for the sake of the Program. In more recent years, the National Incident-Based Reporting System (NIBRS) has expanded and modernized UCR to include twenty-two offenses on which extensive information is collected, and an additional eleven offenses for which only arrest data are gathered. The Program strives for highly reliable data. This objective is achieved to the degree that almost all law enforcement agencies are now reporting arrests according to guidelines.

Arrest data only tell part of the story of crime. Many crimes do not lead to arrests and, in fact, are not even reported to police. To compensate for the deficiency left by UCR, the National Crime Victimization Survey (NCVS) was developed in 1973. Since then, approximately 80,000 persons in 43,000 households have been surveyed each year to gather statistical information about the incidence of crime from the victim's point of view. The surveys are conducted by telephone by the

Census Bureau under the direction of the Bureau of Justice Statistics. In a single year, a selected household may be phoned several times to measure the incidence of recent crimes. The data are compiled, and projections for the entire nation are estimated. Interviews include questions about violent crimes, such as rape and sexual assault, robbery, aggravated assault, and simple assault. Homicide data are gathered from the FBI's UCR Program. Questions about property crimes, such as burglaries, motor vehicle thefts, and thefts of other property, are also included.

The Bureau of Justice Statistics does not publish a comprehensive report from the NCVS. Instead, it publishes a number of focused, topical reports. *Criminal Victimization in the United States* is an annual overview of the results of the survey. Just as arrest data reported in the *Uniform Crime Reports* is reliable, but has limitations, so do the victimization data from NCVS. Responses offered by telephone survey respondents are not verified and are often not verifiable. Some critics argue that the crime is over-reported in the NCVS. Others suggest situations in which survey respondents may under-report crime, even if their anonymity is assured. Researchers familiar with the UCR and the NCVS understand the limitations of both data gathering programs.

Criminal Justice Information on the Internet

F-117   Florida State University School of Criminology & Criminal Justice. **Links Criminal Justice**. Online format. URL: http://www.criminology.fsu.edu/cjlinks/. Accessed February 15, 2001.

F-118   Radzinowicz Library, Institute of Criminology, University of Cambridge. **Institute of Criminology**. Online format. URL: http://www.law.cam.ac.uk/crim /CRIMLINK.HTM. Accessed February 15, 2001.

F-119   **National Archive of Criminal Justice Data (NACJD)**. URL: http:// www.icpsr.umich.edu/NACJD/. Accessed February 15, 2001.

Criminal justice resources on the Internet are plentiful and diverse. All of the major subtopics are well represented: criminology, incidence of crime, victims of crime, crime prevention, law enforcement, criminal justice systems, corrections and punishment, and rehabilitation. The federal government is heavily involved in each of these areas, with various agencies responsible for different pieces of the puzzle. *GPO Access* (F-14) is a useful portal to agencies. The Department of Justice Web site provides access to the Federal Bureau of Investigation (FBI), U.S. Marshals Service, Immigration and Naturalization Service (INS), Drug Enforcement Administration (DEA), and Bureau of Justice Statistics. Through the U.S. Treasury Department researchers will find Web pages for the Bureau of Alcohol, Tobacco, and Firearms (BATF), U.S. Customs Service, and the Secret Service. Other federal agencies responsible for law enforcement and criminal justice are the Central Intelligence Agency (CIA), U.S. Coast Guard, and U.S. Sentencing Commission. State and local agencies also maintain Web sites useful for criminal justice information.

A large number of Internet portals provide direct links to numerous criminal justice Web sites. *Criminal Justice Links* Web page at the Florida State University School of Criminology and Criminal Justice is one of the most extensive directories of links to criminal justice on the Internet. The directory is logically arranged into a two-tiered hierarchy that leads to thousands of links. A novel and highly useful feature is the use of a schematic diagram of criminal justice processing that is hyperlinked to lists of Web sites that provide information about every step of the criminal justice process as it is known in the United States. Researchers simply identify the processing step on the chart, then click on it. The links direct them to a list of pertinent Web sites.

The *Institute of Criminology* at the University of Cambridge is an excellent directory of carefully selected Web sites maintained by one of the world's premier criminal justice research centers. This Web site is much less sophisticated in design than the Florida State Web site, but the collection of links provides a very good selection of mostly UK and European criminal justice Web sites.

The *National Archive of Criminal Justice Data (NACJD)* archive was established in 1978 as a division of the Intern-university Consortium for Political and Social Research (ICPSR) to acquire, archive, and process data from the Bureau of Justice Statistics, National Institute of Justice, the Office of Juvenile Justice and Delinquency Prevention, and the Federal Bureau of Investigation. Data from individual researchers, other government agencies, and international sources are also collected and made available. *NACJD* is an archive of primary data rather than one of published reports and statistics reflecting completed analysis. The service also provides technical assistance and training in quantitative methods for analysis of criminal justice data. Data sets are available for download from the *NACJD* Web site. Some sets are also available on CD-ROM.

Notable Trials

F-120   Knappman, Edward W., ed. **Great American Trials**. New York: Gale Research, 1994.

F-121   Knappman, Edward W., ed. **Great World Trials**. New York: Gale Research, 1997.

F-122   Lief, Michael S., H. Mitchell Caldwell, and Benjamin Bycel. **Ladies and Gentlemen of the Jury, Greatest Closing Arguments in Modern Law**. New York: Scribner's, 1998.

The "Great Trials" encyclopedic works by Gale Research look at notable trials as public events of social and historical significance. Such treatment is a departure from research into strictly legal issues and concerns. However, since cases do not arise apart from a social environment, examining the context of a case is an important endeavor for many students and other scholars. Both works summarize the events, deliberations, and findings of famous trials of history. Entries are written on a popular level, include illustrations, and offer suggestions for additional reading. Each entry is several pages in length and includes significant facts, such as the names of the defendants, charges, chief attorneys for the defense and prosecution, judges, location and dates of the trial, verdict, sentence, and a statement about the significance of the trial.

Great American Trials describes 100 of the most famous trials in American history, beginning with the Anne Hutchinson Trials of 1737 and 1738. Trials were selected on the basis of legal and historical significance, political controversy, public sensation, or literary fame, such as the trials of the Boston Massacre (1770), Lizzy Borden (1893), Joe Hill (1914), Teapot Dome (1926–30), *Brown v. Board of Education* (1954), Ernesto Miranda (1963 and 1967), *Roe v. Wade* (1973), *Falwell v. Flint* (1984), Pete Rose (1990), and John Gotti (1992).

Great World Trials summarizes 100 of the most famous trials in world history. Included are the trials of Jesus of Nazareth (33 C.E.), Socrates (399 B.C.E.), Mary, Queen of Scots (1586), Bounty Mutineers Court-Martial (1792), and the Nuremberg Trial (1945–1946). More recent trials are also summarized, including the Klaus Barbie Trial (1987) and the Tianenmen Square Dissidents Trial (1991).

Great American Trials and *Great World Trials* serve the academic community best as springboards for research. They provide enough information to spark the interest of the reader, with references that lead to additional material for those who care to continue. Careful researchers should note that although the title refers to "trials," some cases were also appealed to higher courts where they received hearings. A research impact is that trials with no appeals result in published legal opinions only infrequently. Furthermore, *Great World Trials* is about trials in a variety of cultures over a wide span of time. Primary authorities in the modern American sense of legal research may not be as apparent for follow-up research. In many of the historical cases, they may not exist at all. Rather, news sources and court records, when available, may be the only original records. Other writings, including historical and scholarly publications, will also help.

Ladies and Gentlemen of the Jury is an engaging book that presents a selection of transcripts of actual closing arguments delivered in court. Cases were selected for their historical significance and the eloquence of the closing argument. Included, among other, are Robert Jackson at the International Military Tribunal at Nuremberg, two closing arguments by Clarence Darrow, Gerry Spence at *The Estate of Karen Silkwood v. Kerr-McGee, Inc.*, and Bobby DeLaughter at the trial of Medgar Evers's assassin. Although modern readers can no longer experience the oral delivery of rhetoric that made history, they can appreciate persuasive word crafting within the world of the courtroom.

LAW AND OTHER DISCIPLINES

F-123   Newman, Peter, ed. **The New Palgrave Dictionary of Economics and the Law**. New York: Stockton Press, 1998.

F-124   Sarat, Austin. **Crossing Boundaries: Traditions and Transformations in Law and Society Research**. Edited by Marianne Constable, Valerie P. Hans, David M. Engel, and Susan Lawrence. Evanston, IL: Northwestern University Press, The American Bar Foundation, 1998.

A number of disciplines share an interest in law and legal institutions in a social context and endeavors to bring new valid investigative processes to the study of law. Scholars from history, political science, anthropology, psychology, and others are eager to share insights from their own disciplines to develop this scholarly venue. These efforts have given rise to theoretical frameworks and problem-solving skills that have generally been beyond the realm of legal scholarship. One of the oldest recognized interdisciplinary efforts is between law and economics. *The New Palgrave Dictionary of Economics and the Law* enables researchers to explore the economic analysis of the legal system and the influence of the legal system on the nation's economy. The 399 topics were chosen from among seven main subject areas: society, economy, polity, law in general, common law systems, regulation, and biography. The second edition is an entirely new work. Each essay is signed, averages about 5,000 words in length, and includes a bibliography for further reading and research. This work was developed as a companion to *The New Palgrave Dictionary of Money and Finance* (D-18) and *The New Palgrave: A Dictionary of Economics* (C-7), from the same publisher.

Crossing Boundaries: Traditions and Transformations in Law and Society Research discusses the continuing development of interdisciplinary theories and practices in law and society research. Race, religion, social class, gender, ethnicity, and nationality are adequately addressed, as are courts, juries, government agencies, mediators, and legal professionals. Although the law establishes numerous boundaries of jurisdiction, age, relationships, and so forth, actors in each of these categories bring customs, expectations, and knowledge that reflect boundaries that may be quite different from legal boundaries.

NOTES

1. *The Bluebook: A Uniform System of Citation*, 17th ed. (Cambridge: Harvard Law Review Association, 2000), 129.

2. West merged with Thomson Corporation and was renamed West Group. See Daniel Wise, "$3.4 Billion Merger of Legal Publishers Cleared by U.S. Judge," *New York Law Journal* (February 18, 1997): 1.

3. *West Publishing Co. v. Hyperlaw, Inc.*, 158 F.3d 674 (2d Cir. 1998).

4. "The Final Report of the Task Force on Citation Formats," *Law Library Journal* 87 (Summer 1995): 577–633.

5. American Bar Association, ABA Legal Technology Resource Center. *ABA Official Citation Resolutions*, http://www.abanet.org/citation/resolution.html.

6. Bobbi Cross and Michelle Ayers, "Emerging Electronic Citation Formats," *The Legal Intelligencer* (September 2, 1998): 5.

7. *Merriam-Webster's Dictionary of Law.* (Springfield, MA: Merriam-Webster, 1996).

8. Daniel Oran and Mark Tosti. *Oran's Dictionary of Law*, 3d ed. (St. Paul, MN: West Group, 2000).

9. Gerald N. Hill and Kathleen Hill. *Real Life Dictionary of the Law, Taking the Mystery out of Legal Language* (Los Angeles, CA: General Publishing Group, 1997).

10. The Social Security Act (Act of August 14, 1935, c. 531, 49 Stat. 620).

11. For the sake of this discussion, comments about the *Code* refer to the common content of *USC*, *USCA*, and *USCS*.

12. Lawyer's Co-operative Publishing was formerly a direct competitor of West Publishing Company, but now West's successor, West Group, and Lawyer's Co-operative Publishing are both subsidiaries of Thomson Corporation. See "The West-Thomson Megamerger: Boon or Monopoly?" *The Connecticut Law Tribune* (March 4, 1996): 1.

13. Jay M. Zitter, "Liability of Internet Service Provider for Internet or E-mail Defamation," *American Law Reports* 84 (2000): 169–190.

14. J. Myron Jacobstein, Roy M. Mersky, and Donald J. Dunn. *Fundamentals of Legal Research*, 7th ed. (Westbury, NY: Foundation Press, 1998).

15. The individual titles in this series are listed inside the cover of any book in the series.

16. *Marbury v. Madison*, 5 U.S. 137 (1803).

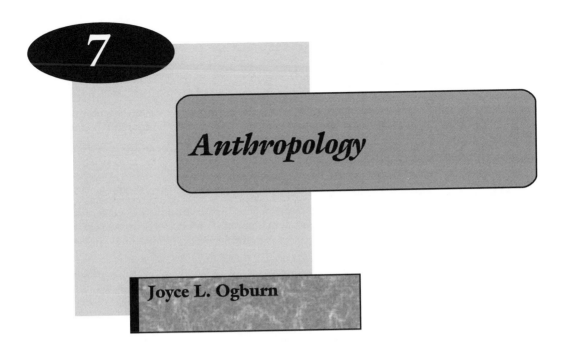

7

Anthropology

Joyce L. Ogburn

ESSAY

Nature of the Discipline

Anthropology holds a fascination for many people, and with good reason. It explores the entire spectrum of human experience: its past and present physical and cultural makeup, its history and evolution. As the study of humans, it encompasses the social, cultural, historical, and physical aspects of human life. This broad scope allows anthropologists to investigate the human experience from the perspective of the humanist, the social/behavioral scientist, and the natural scientist.

The field is usually considered a social science because of its unifying concern for human culture and life, and the dominance of cultural anthropology in the history of the discipline. Anthropologists conduct their studies as they relate to culture, for culture does not function separately from biology, behavior, language, social structure, and history. Anthropologists share a common concern for the evolution of the human species, which encompasses physical and social/cultural change over time. They also are united by their approach to the study of humans. Anthropologists employ the comparative method, which allows them to study behavior and biology across a wide array of traits and conditions. Anthropologists also maintain a relativistic view of human cultures. Under the relativistic approach anthropologists consider all peoples and cultures valuable to study and do not pass judgment on what they find. Anthropology is a holistic discipline, governed by the idea that all human groups are of one species, have a common history, and have culture and language. To obtain a full understanding of the human species, anthropologists study humans from all perspectives, often utilizing a cross-disciplinary approach.

As a social science, anthropology shares methodology and theory primarily with sociology, psychology, history, and geography. These disciplines emphasize fieldwork, surveys, behavior, and the social life of humans. But anthropology also has strong ties to the natural sciences, such as medicine, biology, and geology. These disciplines focus on fieldwork, laboratory studies, and measurement of natural phenomena. In addition, anthropologists who are interested in the arts, and the literary and oral traditions of societies study the humanistic disciplines.

Because of the need to study peoples and material remains in their native environment, anthropologists stress fieldwork as a method of investigation. Many anthropologists learn a variety of languages to understand and communicate with the peoples they study. Anthropologists also study ancient languages to interpret the culture of ancient peoples.

Anthropology, rooted in history and natural philosophy, developed as a distinct discipline both in Europe and the United States in the nineteenth century. Toward the end of the nineteenth century anthropology emerged as a recognized body of knowledge, theory, and professionals. By the twentieth century anthropology was well established as an academic discipline.

From its very beginnings anthropology has been associated with museums, academia, institutes, scientific associations, and governmental bodies. Many museums, such as the Peabody Museum of Archaeology and Ethnology (Harvard University), the American Museum of Natural History (New York), and the Field Museum of Natural History (Chicago), have departments of anthropology. A few libraries have significant collections of anthropological literature, with the Tozzer Library at Harvard University housing the premier anthropological collection in the United States. Anthropologists have worked in U.S. government agencies since the nineteenth century in such institutions as the Smithsonian, the Bureau of American Ethnology, and the Bureau of Indian Affairs. There are institutions and organizations devoted solely to anthropology (the Wenner-Gren Foundation for Anthropological Research, the Archaeological Institute of America) and laboratories for anthropology (the Glenn A. Black Laboratory of Archaeology at Indiana University). All major American academic institutions have a department of anthropology, some founded as early as the late nineteenth century. Anthropologists enjoy membership in large scientific associations (section H of the American Association for the Advancement of Science) and have had their own associations since anthropology's inception (the American Ethnological Society, the American Anthropological Association, the American Association of Physical Anthropologists). Anthropologists are also eligible for membership in the National Academy of Sciences.

Anthropology in the United States traditionally has comprised four subdisciplines: sociocultural anthropology, archaeology, physical anthropology, and linguistic anthropology. Each has its own distinct theory and methodology, but they overlap in many areas of study, such as mortuary studies (physical condition of the remains of the dead and funereal rituals and artifacts), medical anthropology (the place of medicine within a culture and biological aspects of health, disease, and nutrition), sociobiology and ethology (the convergence of studies of behavior and biology,) and culture change (how and why cultures, societies, material remains, and peoples have changed in historic and prehistoric times).

The emphasis on four subdisciplines in anthropology has a very long history. In recent years, however, a great amount of tension has arisen between the subdisciplines, leading to an extended discussion among anthropologists as to whether there are still four subfields. The perceived rift is primarily between sociocultural and physical anthropology. Some anthropologists argue that there are no longer any common elements in theory, method, or study between the two subdisciplines. Moreover, it has been suggested that since an increasing number of physical anthropologists are now working within biological or medical organizations and departments, they may indeed have more in common with natural scientists than with other anthropologists. Many anthropologists, however, still prefer to think of anthropology as a unified field and argue that the discipline is strengthened by its diversity.

The subdisciplines have developed their own literatures, based on their own specific data and research needs.

Sociocultural Anthropology

This subdiscipline maintains the closest relationship to other social sciences. Sociocultural anthropologists study social relationships, the structure of society, and the function of individuals and cultural variables within a society. Sociocultural anthropologists are concerned with such things as social organization, culture change, and acculturation.

The major methodologies of sociocultural anthropologists are ethnography, survey, and oral history. Key concepts and components of sociocultural anthropology include kinship studies, ethnology, ethnography, folklore, ethnomusicology, ethnohistory, comparative religion, area studies, ethnic studies, economic anthropology, cultural ecology, and educational anthropology.

Archaeology

Archaeologists investigate the history and development of an entire culture or groups of peoples over time and space. Archaeology can be perceived as a bridge between physical anthropology and sociocultural anthropology, as a link between physical characters, human behavior, and culture. Archaeologists seek an understanding of cultures based on their material and physical remains. To achieve this end, archaeologists describe and classify artifacts, study the relationships among sites, and build cultural chronologies. Archaeologists reconstruct the history of cultures, how they lived, and how or why they changed.

Archaeology relies primarily on the methods of excavation, survey, sampling, collection, and relative and chronometric dating. The field encompasses aspects such as historical archaeology, classical archaeology, ethnoarchaeology, archaeoastronomy, archaeozoology, prehistory, salvage archaeology, conservation and resource management, underwater archaeology, biblical archaeology, and amateur archaeology.

Physical Anthropology

Physical anthropology (sometimes called bioanthropology or biological anthropology) has the closest ties to the natural sciences, especially to primatology, human biology, and branches of medicine. Physical anthropology investigates the relationship of the human physical condition to human culture over time and space. Physical anthropologists analyze skeletal material collected from archaeological sites for age at death, cause of death, general health and nutrition, ethnic affiliation, and sex. Physical anthropologists also study other primates, the genetic relationships of human groups, health of historic and prehistoric populations, and change in human anatomy and behavior over time. Many physical anthropologists serve as advisors in forensic matters by determining the identification of human remains. They generally work most closely with archaeologists; indeed, often anthropologists specialize in both archaeology and physical anthropology.

Physical anthropologists use such methodologies as laboratory work, anthropometry, biochemical analysis, comparative anatomy, trace analysis, and taxonomy. Biological anthropology, medical anthropology, skeletal biology, paleopathology, forensic anthropology, dental anthropology, primatology, human variation, human adaptation, human evolution, and human ecology are fields of specialty within physical anthropology.

Linguistic Anthropology

This may be considered the more humanistic of the branches of anthropology. Linguistic anthropologists study the origins, evolution, and nature of language; relationships among human languages; and the history, development, and structure of languages. As it relates to anthropology, linguistics functions as a social science: the function of language within a society, culture as revealed through language, and the relationship of cultures through language. Fairly recent applications of linguistics involve the investigation of the capacity for language in other animals, particularly nonhuman primates.

The standard methodologies of linguistics are phonetics, phonemics, structural analysis, semantics, morphology, syntactics. Linguistic anthropology includes philology, psycholinguistics, sociolinguistics, lexicography, paralinguistics, cognitive anthropology, semiotics, symbolism, dialectology, and bilingualism.

Structure and Use of the Literature

Anthropology has a body of literature that includes scholarly and popular material. Scholarly literature includes all branches of anthropology, while most of the popular literature is written about archaeology, human evolution, and human cultures. In addition, anthropologists communicate their research through government reports, applied literature, and more recently, advocacy literature. Advocacy literature embraces the concept of working for the survival of cultures or nonhuman primates, not merely studying them.

The greatest sources of raw data for anthropologists are field notes and material collections. For cultural anthropologists, field notes include ethnographic observations, films, photographs, and artifacts. Archaeologists use artifact collections, site maps, GIS data, excavation notes, photographs, and drawings. Physical anthropologists rely on skeletal material, medical records, genetic data, and fossils. Linguists employ field notes, tape recordings, written historical records, and sound spectrograms. Increasingly, anthropological data are being encoded in electronic format and databases for analysis and synthesis. Some of these databases have been made available to other researchers.

Dissertations are primary sources of data that often do not get published elsewhere. Anthropological collections, usually housed in museums and laboratories, constitute a valuable resource for research. Descriptions or catalogs of some of these collections are accessible over the Internet, for example the *Collections at the Peabody Museum* of the Yale University Peabody Museum of Natural History (http://www.peabody.yale.edu/collections/).

The secondary literature, or the results of anthropological investigation, exists in several published forms. Although dissertations include valuable raw and synthesized data, the primary reporting of research results occurs in journal articles and reports issued by laboratories, museums, and departments of anthropology. Monographs are major vehicles for publishing syntheses of anthropological research and concepts; however, the journal literature is increasingly dominating the dissemination of anthropology research.

Some of the major journals for communicating research results are *American Anthropologist, Current Anthropology, American Journal of Physical Anthropology, Man, Anthropological Linguistics, American Antiquity, American Journal of Archaeology, American Ethnologist*, and *Anthropos*. Many more specialized journals exist. To understand current developments in their fields, anthropologists can turn to several sources, including newsletters such as *Anthropology Newsletter, Science News, History of Anthropology Newsletter, Physical Anthropology News*, and also major journals such as *Current Anthropology, Science and Nature*. One online source, *Anthropology in the News*, follows news stories about anthropology and stays current (http://www.tamu.edu/anthropology/news.html).

Anthropologists tend to rely on both current and older literature. Sometimes older literature offers the only source of data on cultures, collections, languages, and sites that have disappeared or changed over time. Early, seminal works still have much to offer to researchers in terms of data, synthesis, and theoretical approach.

More anthropology resources are appearing online, some freely available and some for fee only. The discipline has not made as many significant and innovative advances in the use of the Internet in delivering resources as it might. This said, the reference resources listed below demonstrate that a lot has happened in the past five years in terms of converting, duplicating, or presenting new information in electronic formats. Online full text of the journal literature lags behind other disciplines, but fortunately some key journals are available in various aggregator packages and in *JSTOR* (E-60). Some seminal monographic works are being reproduced online, but the growth in this area is slow. Online, digital exhibits are increasing in number, and intellectual access to special collections is growing through the conversion of finding aids to digital format.

The Reference Environment

Although the body of reference literature for anthropology has grown far richer in recent years, the eclectic nature of anthropology compels anthropologists to use the literature and reference sources from many other fields. Cultural and general anthropology has the greatest number of resources, however, relevant literature for the other subdisciplines of anthropology has improved and is also supported by reference sources for other disciplines. For example, physical anthropologists can use the medical and biological literatures, which have extremely good reference bases. Numerous bibliographies exist, primarily covering particular geographic areas; however, they are less useful in the general reference environment than other reference works. Because of the international scope of anthropology, researchers use published literature from all over the world. Finding or accessing this literature can be challenging because indexing of that material may not exist, may not be widely available, or may not be current.

Depending on the focus of an anthropologist's study, reference service must be prepared to cover the full spectrum of reference literature. Several indexes and abstracts are devoted to anthropology, but other subject literature should be consulted to cover all the relevant sources. Although *Anthropological Literature* (see G-46, G-47, and G-48) and *Anthropological Index* (G-45) are now available online, researchers may still need to consult other non-anthropology databases to be thorough. The reference librarian who serves anthropologists must be familiar with a wide range of reference tools.

The classification of anthropology in the Dewey Decimal System or Library of Congress schedules presents access challenges. In Dewey, anthropological material can be classed in the 300s (sociocultural anthropology), the 500s (physical anthropology), the 600s (medical anthropology, paleopathology), the 800s (linguistic anthropology), or the 900s (archaeology). The Library of Congress classification presents equal difficulty. Although primarily assigned to the GN classification, a great number of anthropological materials are also classed in CC (archaeology), D (cultures as a part of world history), E/F (history of the Americas, Native Americans), GR (folklore), P (linguistic anthropology), Q (human evolution and biology, primatology), and R (medical anthropology, paleopathology). Clearly this great spread of anthropology among so many classifications demonstrates both the breadth of anthropology and problems of access, reference, and bibliography.

Anthropology Bibliography

The subjects of anthropology bibliography and reference tools dominated the library literature in the late 1970s and 1980s, and reference publishing increased markedly in the 1990s. The anthropology bibliography literature addresses problems of information and access as well as the value of specific printed and online sources to some of the subdisciplines of anthropology. A review of these articles reveals that access to anthropological literature has improved in the last several decades. Several groups are trying to address the problems of anthropology bibliography and reference. Anthropologists and librarians concerned with the state of anthropology bibliography and reference sources founded the Library-Anthropology Resource Group in Chicago in 1971 and have published several important reference works. The Anthropology and Sociology Section (ANSS) of the Association of College and Research Libraries has a Bibliography Committee that works on problems of bibliography and gathers information on sources and developments in subject bibliography. ANSS (G-5) publishes a newsletter called *ANSS Currents*, manages an informational Web site called *ANSSWeb* (http://www.lib .odu.edu/anss/index.html), and sponsors a list service called ANSS-L (LISTSERV@UCI.EDU) that supports the exchange of information among its members and other interested parties. The Internet now supports numerous anthropology-related list services and a growing number of sophisticated World Wide Web sites that point to a variety of information sources.

Reference Sources

Sources included in this chapter represent the best reference literature available in anthropology. The list is slanted toward more recent titles, and in general bibliographies have been included only when they present the lone or main access to a body of literature. Electronic and CD-ROM databases are included among the titles. Older resources that have been superseded or are terribly dated have been excluded.

As mentioned previously, the reference literature for anthropology is not nearly as extensive as that for the other social sciences, although the reference base has improved tremendously since this chapter was first published in 1989. Several new and comprehensive encyclopedias have been published, and more guides, dictionaries, and biographical sources have appeared. The conversion of *Anthropological Literature* (G-46, G-47, G-48), *Anthropological Index* (G-45), and the *Human Relations Area Files* (see G-97n) to electronic formats signaled a major step forward in providing electronic access to anthropological research. Despite these advances, anthropologists will still want to consult the reference publications available in allied subjects.

ASSOCIATION AND SOCIETY INFORMATION

For the most part, associations and societies devoted to anthropology have developed a presence on the Internet. A few of the main sites are listed here. They share common characteristics of providing information for and about members and information about their publications and activities. When looking for a particular organization, consult the general Web portals for anthropology, as they often maintain current links to association and society Web sites. The American Anthropological Association remains one of the richest sources of information, both its printed *Guide* and its online resources. However, one should not overlook the sites and printed materials published by the other organizations when seeking information about specific subfields and specialties. Some prime examples are included in this section.

G-1 **AAA Guide**. Washington, DC: American Anthropological Society, 1989/ 1990- . Annual.

G-2 **Guide to Departments of Anthropology**. Washington, DC: American Anthropological Association, 1969/70–1988/89.

These works contain information on academic, museum, research, and government departments of anthropology in the United States and Canada. It provides statistics on enrollments, employment, and degrees granted. Included is a list of dissertations by author from 1954 on. The work also contains indexes of people and departments. The more recent publication added the AAA membership directory and membership by unit of AAA. The guide is most useful for finding names, addresses, and statistics. As the AAA site has expanded, much of this information has been incorporated there and may become accessible only to members.

G-3 **American Anthropological Association**. URL: http://www.aaanet.org/.

The home site of the AAA, this is one of the most extensive association sites and has links to many of the others. Information included covers the history, work, sections, meetings, and publications of the association; careers; and ethics. Under the section on government relations, it has links to important AAA position statements about race, human rights, evolution, race and intelligence, language rights, and so forth.

G-4 **American Association of Physical Anthropology**. URL: http://www.physanth.org/. Like many other association sites, this one for AAPA has information on its services, meetings, publications, careers, and position statements. The association newsletter, *Physical Anthropology*, is published online at http://www.physanth.org/newsletter/physanthnews.html.

G-5 **Association of College and Research Libraries, Anthropology and Sociology Section. ANSSWeb**. URL: http://www.lib.odu.edu/anss/index.html. *ANSSWeb* is home to information primarily for the use of its members. Of interest to others is the text of its newsletter, reviews of abstracts and indexes, a guide to essential resources, and links to sites with detailed information about reference sources or electronic journals. It concentrates on providing unique content rather than being a portal to numerous anthropology and sociology Web sites.

G-6 **Society for American Archaeology. SAA Web**. URL: http://www.saa.org /index.html. Much like the Web sites for associations and societies, *SAA Web* encompasses a variety of information on archaeology, careers, education, and government affairs. It maintains information limited to member-only access.

G-7 **Society for the Anthropology of Europe. Society for the Anthropology of Europe (SAE) Web Site at H-Net: H-SAE**. URL: http://www.h-net.msu.edu/~sae/. This society Web site serves its members and others by providing organization and access to, among other things, syllabi, discussion threads, photo galleries, bibliographies, the Society archive, and links to sites about Europe.

GUIDES AND HANDBOOKS

G-8 Cantrell, Karen. **Funding for Anthropological Research**. Phoenix, AZ: Oryx Press, 1986.
Funding programs are listed alphabetically. The entries discuss the profiles of the program and list relevant information for applying. The book includes subject and sponsor (divided by type) indexes. There are also a bibliography and a list of useful online databases. No update has been published, so the more current general sources should be consulted as well.

G-9 Cassell, Joan, and Sue-Ellen Jacobs, eds. **Handbook on Ethical Issues in Anthropology**. Washington, DC: American Anthropological Association, 1996. Online format. URL: http://www.aaanet.org/committees/ethics/toc.htm.
The handbook is the online version of the American Anthropological Association Special Publication No. 23. The handbook is designed for use in classes to teach about and communicate the complex issues of ethics in relation to the theory and practice of anthropology. It includes a brief history of the AAA Committee on Ethics, which guided the development of the handbook, and has useful case studies. References are embedded in the articles.

G-10 De Miller, Anna L. **Linguistics: A Guide to the Reference Literature**. 2d ed. Englewood, CO: Libraries Unlimited, 2000.
DeMiller's work is an exceptional and expansive guide to 1,039 resources essential to linguistics. Anthropological linguistics does not have its own reference literature, so one should consult this guide to find the best resources for linguistics in general. It is organized by general linguistics, allied areas (anthropological linguistics is listed as one of these), and languages. All entries receive annotations. Includes author, title, and subject indexes.

G-11 Folsom, Franklin. **America's Ancient Treasures: A Guide to Archaeological Sites and Museums in the United States and Canada**. 4th ed. Albuquerque: University of New Mexico Press, 1993.

Folsom arranges his information geographically, divided by state. The format is a bit confusing: It intersperses topical articles with the main articles, making it more like a travel guide with basic descriptive information. Included are a glossary, references, and an index.

G-12 Grimes, Barbara. **Ethnologue: Languages of the World**. 13th ed. 1996- . Online format. URL: http://www.sil.org/ethnologue/.

Ethnologue is an unusual online resource that replicates the printed version and also is available as a CD-ROM (with some differences in coverage). It comprises 112 language maps, 241 overviews of language situations by country, 682 bibliographic references, 6,703 language descriptions, a language name index with more than 39,000 alternate names and dialect names, a language family index with 99 language family trees, and 64,811 linked cross-references. The preface provides a good introduction to its use.

G-13 Kibbee, Josephine Z. **Cultural Anthropology: A Guide to Reference and Information Sources**. Englewood, CO: Libraries Unlimited, 1991.

Kibbee's work is a superior guide to general reference material in anthropology. Although the title suggests that only sociocultural anthropology is covered, liberal coverage is given to other subfields. There are 688 fully annotated sources. This work also lists major anthropological journals, organizations and institutions, libraries, archives, and publishers. The index includes authors, titles, and subject.

G-14 Levinson, David. **Ethnic Groups Worldwide: A Ready Reference Handbook**. Phoenix, AZ: Oryx Press, 1998.

Ethnic groups are described within their geographic context: Europe, Africa, Asia and the Pacific, and the Americas. Each geographic region opens with an introduction and bibliography. Descriptions of ethnic groups then follow in alphabetical order. The index helps the user find information about ethnic groups in multiple locations, such as the Albanians in Egypt or the Albanians in Germany.

G-15 McMillon, Bill. **The Archaeology Handbook: A Field Manual and Resource Guide**. New York: John Wiley, 1991.

A good guide for students, this book also serves as a good ready reference source because it lists addresses for museums, field schools, state archaeology offices, and archaeological organizations. The bulk of the work is devoted to the nature of archaeology and excavations. Included are suggested readings and an index.

G-16 Shapiro, Michael Steven. **The Museum: A Reference Guide**. New York: Greenwood Press, 1990.

Museums house major anthropological collections and primary source material. The chapter on natural history (including anthropology) provides a good overview and bibliography of the history and development of museums. Appendixes cover additional information on major museums and museum-related periodicals.

G-17 Van Willigen, John. **Becoming a Practicing Anthropologist: A Guide to Careers and Training Programs in Applied Anthropology**. Washington, DC: American Anthropological Association, 1987.

Van Willigen provides a short guide to the field of applied anthropology. He discusses the profession, skills and knowledge, and undergraduate and graduate programs. To help the student decide on a career in applied anthropology, the author employs task assignments designed to assess individual academic programs and student needs.

G-18 Weeks, John M. **Introduction to Library Research in Anthropology**. 2d ed. Boulder, CO: Westview Press, 1998.

Although it is extensive in coverage of numerous relevant international resources, many entries are unannotated in this work. It opens with general information on the use of libraries in conducting research in anthropology. The resources section is organized by type of resource. Appendixes comprise Library of Congress classifications, major anthropological collections in the United States and Canada, the arrangement of the HRAF *Outline of Cultural Materials*, and the HRAF *Outline of World Cultures*. The index is organized by authors, ethnic groups, and geographic areas. Although quite useful, this work contains numerous errors, and citations are not fully reliable.

G-19 Westerman, R. C. **Fieldwork in the Library: A Guide to Research in Anthropology and Related Area Studies**. Chicago: American Library Association, 1994.

This work is arranged by subdiscipline and by geographic area and then subdivided by type of literature to meet specific research needs. The early chapters discuss the literature and resources of related disciplines. It covers 1,591 sources, more than any other guide to anthropology resources; more than two-thirds cover area studies literature. Although the number of resources is extensive, the organization is confusing and difficult to use for all but veteran users of reference guides. It lacks subject indexing, and many references to key sources, cited often in comparison with related works, cannot be found in the index.

G-20 Williams, John T. **Anthropology Journals and Serials: An Analytical Guide**. New York: Greenwood Press, 1986.

This work describes a wide range of serials and includes helpful annotations about their scope. The work is divided by the four areas of archaeology, cultural anthropology, linguistics, and physical anthropology. Included also are a section on indexes and abstracts and three indexes for title, subject, and geographic area. Librarians and researchers will find this a useful guide to the serial literature of anthropology. Basic bibliographic information is listed, followed by annotations. Although the annotations are still relevant, entries include long out-of-date prices.

G-21 Woodhead, Peter. **Keyguide to Information Sources in Archaeology**. London: Mansell, 1985.

Woodhead's book covers the world of information on archaeology, including the literature, reference materials, and nontraditional sources of information. This title also gives the general historical development of archaeology and a section on organizations arranged by country. An index aids the researcher in using this work.

G-22 Woodhead, Peter. **Keyguide to Information Sources in Museum Studies**. London: Mansell, 1994.

Museums can be integral to anthropology, and this guide lists many resources on museum studies. Its coverage includes the history of museums and organizations, current and retrospective literature, and bibliographies. Indexed.

BIBLIOGRAPHIES

Anthropologists can turn to many specific bibliographies, especially for area studies, but this section discusses only very general bibliographies or ones that provide the primary access to a particular segment of the literature. For a more complete listing of bibliographies, consult chapter 1 on general social science sources. Many bibliographies of online resources, or so-called webliographies, are of varying quality, comprehensiveness, currency, or accuracy. Only those that are maintained and have wide coverage are included here. Obviously this is a volatile environment, and caution and good judgment should be exercised when consulting any Internet Web sites.

G-23 **Anthropology Internet Page**. URL: http://www.stjohns.edu/library
/staugustine/anthropo.html.
This site is organized by topics, which include but are not limited to general anthropology,
archaeology, ethnomusicology, indigenous peoples, linguistics, physical anthropology, postmodernism,
ethnic regions or groups, and sociocultural anthropology. It also provides links to related subject areas.

G-24 **Anthro.Net**. URL: http://www.anthro.net/
Regional, topical, and thematic areas are listed. Also provided are tools (such as glossaries) and
a useful search feature. This site claims to maintain "a database of over 40,000 reviewed web sites with
anthropological content built by the interests of its users. The system collects the search terms submitted
by its users and uses proprietary software to hunt down internet based journal articles, well developed
topical sites and bibliographic references for anthropology, archaeology and the other social sciences."
Despite these claims, some of the sites to which it points have questionable relevance to anthropology.

G-25 Department of Anthropology. University of California at Santa Barbara.
UCSB Department of Anthropology Links Directory. URL: http://www.anth.ucsb
.edu/links/pages/.
One of the first and best sites to compile links to Internet sites, this one still delivers. Some
590 Web sites of anthropological interest are organized into categories: topical, geographic, departments
and museums, upcoming conferences, and a list of several other portals. It has two useful features: it
lists the number of entries within the topics and provides a search engine.

G-26 Erickson, Paul A. **History of Anthropology Bibliography**. rev. ed. Halifax,
Nova Scotia: Department of Anthropology, St. Mary's University, 1998.
There are few resources devoted to the history of anthropology. Erickson's bibliography is a
compilation of titles published in this subject and in related areas. The main body is organized alphabetically. The revised edition incorporates all of the titles of the first edition and the supplements; it
also includes newer publications. The index guides the user to authors, subjects, geographic areas, and
individuals. There are some errors in the citations.

G-27 Heider, Karl G., and Carol Hermer. **Films for Anthropological Teaching**.
8th ed. Arlington, VA: American Anthropological Association, 1995.
Anthropologists rely heavily on film for data recording and for teaching. This source lists
many useful films for teaching, with emphasis on ethnography and archaeology. Films are listed first
by geographical area, then by topic. An alphabetical list then follows. Lists of distributors and publication codes are included. The work is completed by a personal name index.

G-28 Kemper, Robert V., and John F. S. Phinney. **The History of Anthropology:
A Research Bibliography**. New York: Garland, 1977.
Beginning researchers in the history of anthropology will find this source a good place to
start. Because of its date, many recent and important sources are not listed. Newer bibliographies
contain more sources, but no other is arranged topically.

G-29 Library-Anthropology Resource Group, comp. **Anthropological Bibliographies: A Selected Guide**. Edited by Margo L. Smith and Yvonne M. Damien.
South Salem, NY: Redgrave Publishing, 1981.
This serves as a guide to more than 3,200 bibliographies, filmographies, and discographies
relevant to anthropology. The authors arranged the work by geographical area, with a topical section
following. An extensive index is included. The book's format and print style discourage use, and it is
now fairly out-of-date. Plans to publish a more current edition were abandoned.

G-30 Library-Anthropology Resource Group, comp. **Serial Publications in Anthropology**. Edited by F. X. Grollig and Sol Tax. 1st ed.: Chicago: University of Chicago Press, 1973. 2d ed.: South Salem, NY: Redgrave Publishing, 1982.

Useful as a historical guide, this source details publishing information on serial titles. It includes an index. It is primarily helpful because it groups anthropological serials in one source. Its major drawbacks are that it lacks annotation and is extremely dated. Williams's *Anthropology Journals and Serials* (G-20), although also out-of-date, is more current and contains valuable annotations.

G-31 Archeology and Ethnography Program, National Park Service. **The National Archeological Database (NADB)**, n.d.- . Regularly. Online format. URL: http://www.cast.uark.edu/other/nps/nadb.

Maintained and operated by the Center for Advanced Spatial Technologies at the University of Arkansas, Fayetteville, on behalf of the National Park Service, *NADB* was created "to meet a congressional directive to improve access to information on archeological activities nationwide." It has two parts: the *NADB-Reports* and *NADB-MAPS*. *NADB-Reports* is an inventory of 240,000 archaeological reports and gray literature. *NADB-Reports* are searchable by state, county, worktype, cultural affiliation, keyword, material, year of publication, title, and author. *NADB-MAPS* (Multiple Attribute Presentation System) uses GIS maps to illustrate the distributions of cultural and environmental resources across the United States at the state and county levels.

G-32 Ogburn, Joyce L., comp. **Resources for Anthropology & Sociology Librarians & Information Specialists**, 1995- . Quarterly. Online format. URL: http://www.lib.odu.edu/anss/resources.htm.

Ogburn publishes a lengthy bibliographic guide to resources to assist librarians and information specialists in locating literature relevant to their needs. It is organized by the subjects anthropology, sociology, and general social science. Each of these major headings is further subdivided by topics such as bibliographic control, bibliometrics, guides to reference literature, information needs, online database searching, preservation, publishing, and writing. It is updated as new resources are published.

G-33 Library of Congress. American Folklife Center. **Resources in Ethnographic Studies**, n.d.- . Online format. URL: http://lcweb.loc.gov/folklife/other.html.

Folklife resources can be very useful to anthropologists. This resource focuses more on folk life and related areas than anthropology, but has a decided ethnographic slant. Although it is does not include as many entries as some sites, it provides access to a different set of links and resources than do the other anthropology-oriented Web sites and portals. Included among its topics are ethnomusicology and mythology.

G-34 **WWW Virtual Library: Anthropology**. URL: http://vlib.anthrotech.com/.

This site is extensive, and its topics include many narrow fields within anthropology, such as agricultural, business, cyber, environmental, and visual anthropology. Users can see when each site was added and modified, how many hits it has received, its rating (up to four stars), and the number of votes it received. It has basic and advanced search capabilities.

LIBRARY CATALOGS AND SPECIAL COLLECTIONS

Library catalogs have quickly moved online. Older, print versions are still listed here, although the online version may be the first place consulted. Some libraries have yet to convert all records for their older titles to their online catalogs, but these are becoming fewer in number. Access to special collections of archival and manuscript materials (including photographs, fieldnotes, artifacts, and the like) has also become digital. In many cases finding aids or brief descriptions of collections are online, and parts of collections may be present in digital format as a database of exhibit.

G-35 Dutton, Lee S., ed. **Anthropological Resources: A Guide to Archival, Library and Museum Collections**. New York: Garland, 1999.

There are no other resources that provide such broad coverage and description of so many archival, library, and museum collections (more than 150). Dutton enlisted the aid of archivists, curators, and librarians (mostly at the institutions described) to produce a work of this scope. It is organized by geographic area and then by institution. The United States has by far the most entries, with Canada following next. Other countries with good coverage are Great Britain, France, the Netherlands, and Australia. Each description includes addresses, contacts, and descriptions of the collections. Online access to finding aids, descriptions, and catalogs are noted, but the Internet addresses may be out-of-date.

G-36 **Haddon: The Online Catalogue of Ethnographic Footage 1895–1945**. Oxford University, Economic and Social Research Council. 1996- . Online format. URL: http://www.rsl.ox.ac.uk/isca/haddon/HADD_home.html.

Haddon is an online catalog of 1,571 films and film footage created between 1895 and 1945 and housed in institutions around the world. The site maintains a list of institutions that have collections. Searching can be done by predetermined regions, subregions, or countries, which quickly produces a list of all associated films. One has the option to search by free text or by person such as director, producer, photographer, or anthropologist. At present this is the only online catalog devoted to anthropology film.

G-37 Harvard University. **HOLLIS, Harvard Online Library Information System**. Online format. URL: http://hollisweb.harvard.edu/.

Harvard University. Peabody Museum of Archaeology and Ethnology. Library. **Catalogue: Authors**. Boston: G. K. Hall, 1963.

Harvard University. Peabody Museum of Archaeology and Ethnology. Library. **Catalogue: Authors. Supplement**. Boston: G. K. Hall, 1970–1979.

Harvard University. Peabody Museum of Archaeology and Ethnology. Library. **Catalogue: Subjects**. Boston: G. K. Hall, 1963.

Harvard University. Peabody Museum of Archaeology and Ethnology. Library. **Catalogue: Subjects. Supplement**. Boston: G. K. Hall, 1970–1979.

Harvard University. Peabody Museum of Archaeology and Ethnology. Library. **Index to Anthropological Subject Headings**. 1st ed.: Boston: G. K. Hall, 1963. rev. ed.: Boston: G. K. Hall, 1971. 2d rev. ed.: Boston: G. K. Hall, 1981.

Harvard University. Peabody Museum of Archaeology and Ethnology. Library. **Author and Subject Catalogues of the Tozzer Library**. 2d. enlarged ed. Boston: G. K. Hall, 1988.

Library catalogs include useful information that supplements bibliographies and indexing services. They prove especially beneficial to retrospective and historical research. Many are now online, and some have much older, printed counterparts. The holdings of the Tozzer Library at Harvard (previously the Peabody Museum of Archaeology and Ethnology Library) are among the most comprehensive and important. The printed catalogs are reproductions of library cataloging cards. The printed version contains retrospective literature and is fairly comprehensive. It can be used as an index source to periodical literature, pamphlets, and books.

The Tozzer collection emphasizes American archaeology and ethnology, including Mexico and Central America, but there are materials from all over the world. The catalogs have not included periodical literature since 1982. (*Anthropological Literature* [G-46, G47, G-48], which does cover periodicals, began publication in 1979.) The second edition of the printed catalogs is published as

1,116 microfiche and includes all the entries of the first edition and all new holdings added through June 1986. Printed catalogs from other major libraries and museums of anthropology, area studies, and natural history also should be consulted.

G-38 **Bibliographic Guide to Anthropology and Archaeology**. Boston: G. K. Hall, 1987- . Annual.

This annual publication supplements the Tozzer Library author and subject catalogs, covering monographs and serials added since 1988.

G-39 National Anthropological Archives. **Guide to the Collections of the National Anthropological Archives**. 1999- . Online format. URL: http://www.nmnh .si.edu/naa/guide/_toc.htm.

The National Anthropological Archives is an important repository of primary source material that documents the history of the discipline. Its collections encompass cultural anthropology, linguistics, archaeology, and physical anthropology among its stash of manuscripts, fieldnotes, correspondence, photographs, maps, sound recordings, film, and video. Many of the collections derive from those of eminent American anthropologists, also including the records of the American Anthropological Association. Like many guides to primary sources and special collections, this one provides good descriptive information and links to finding aids where available. See also *Guide to Anthropological Fieldnotes and Manuscripts in Other Archives* (G-41).

G-40 National Anthropological Archives. **Guide to the Collections of the Human Studies Film Archives**. 1999- . Online format. URL: http://www.nmnh .si.edu/naa/guide/film_toc.htm.

The Human Studies Film Archives collects, preserves, documents, and distributes ethnographic moving image materials. It also collects many other formats and types of materials that supplement its film and video collections. The guide is searchable by keyword and browseable by geographic region, but it also has ethnic group, subject, and political/geographic indexes.

G-41 National Anthropological Archives. **Guide to Anthropological Fieldnotes and Manuscripts in Other Archives**. 1999- . Online format. URL: http://www .nmnh.si.edu/naa/other_archives.htm.

Functioning in effect as a supplement to the *Guide to the Collections of the National Anthropological Archives* (G-39), this resource guides users to materials in collections other than the Smithsonian. It is an alphabetical list by name of anthropologist, with location of the holding institution. Also covered are the locations of the record of anthropological expeditions, field schools, conferences, and associations.

ABSTRACTS AND INDEXES

Anthropology

G-42 **Abstracts in Anthropology**. Westport, CT: Greenwood Press, 1970- . 8 times/yr.

Abstracts in Anthropology is a standard source to consult when doing a literature search. Included are books, articles, and papers from conferences. It is divided into four sections: archaeology, cultural anthropology, linguistics, and physical anthropology. It includes author and title indexes. Abstracts are usually 50 to 100 words in length. Unlike many other sources, there is no electronic version.

G-43 **Anthropological Index Online**. 1997- . Online format. URL: http://lucy .ukc.ac.uk/rai/AnthIndex.html or http://lucy.ukc.ac.uk/AIO.html.

G-44 **Anthropological Index to Current Periodicals in the Museum of Mankind Library**. London: Royal Anthropological Institute, 1977–1997.

G-45 **Anthropological Index to Current Periodicals in the Library of the Royal Anthropological Institute,** 1963–1976.

This index covers more than 750 periodicals received at the Library of the Museum of Mankind, by broad geographical area. The online version is at present available free, and also will be offered through RLG's CitaDel service. It has more extensive coverage of European literature than *Anthropological Literature* (G-46, G-48). The printed versions are subdivided by physical anthropology, archaeology, cultural anthropology, and linguistics. They contain an annual author index.

G-46 **Anthropological Literature**. [CitaDel file]. Mountain View, CA: Research Libraries Group, 1993- . Quarterly.

G-47 **Anthropological Literature on Disc**. [CD-ROM]. Boston: G. K. Hall, 1994- . Annual updates.

G-48 **Anthropological Literature**. Pleasantville, NY: Redgrave Publishing, 1979–1983; Cambridge, MA: Harvard University, Tozzer Library, 1984- . Quarterly.

This work is compiled at the Tozzer Library (Harvard University), formerly the Library of the Peabody Museum of Archaeology and Ethnology. It covers serials publications, symposia, collections of readings, and festschriften and is international in scope. Although both electronic versions started coverage from the year 1984, the editors added earlier coverage as retrospective conversion of the Tozzer Library holdings progressed. The electronic versions now have great time depth. The original publication switched from print to microfiche in 1984, and back again to print in 1988, complicating the use of the older materials. These versions are arranged by the four areas of anthropology in addition to a division on general works, theory, and method. They are extensively indexed by author, subject, and sources.

G-49 **International Bibliography of Anthropology**. London: Routledge, 1998- . Annual.

G-50 **International Bibliography of Social and Cultural Anthropology**. London: Routledge, 1958–1997. Annual.

Originally devoted primarily to sociocultural anthropology, this annual publication is a good international source, but volumes are several years behind in publication. It lists all written forms of information except unpublished theses. It includes author and subject indexes. In 1989 the subject guide, *Thematic List of Descriptors—Anthropology*, was published. In the late 1980s the coverage began expanding more heavily into physical anthropology. *IBSCA* dropped social and cultural anthropology from its title in 1998.

Electronic access: The electronic version is integrated into the *International Bibliography of the Social Sciences*, which is published over the Internet and as a CD-ROM.

Related Subjects

America: History and Life (AHL). Santa Barbara, CA: ABC-Clio, 1964- . 5 times/yr. (See E-17 and E-20)

Many American archaeologists work specifically in North America. *America, History and Life* provides them with access to a wealth of literature on archaeology, anthropology, Indians, paleontology, and ethnology in America. Its coverage extends over 2,000 journals published worldwide and also includes dissertations.

Electronic access: AHL is available online and as a CD-ROM.

G-51 **Art and Archaeology Technical Abstracts**. New York: Getty Conservation Institute, 1955- . Semiannual.

Researchers can use this abstracting service for information on the technical aspects of archaeology, including dating techniques, chemical analysis, conservation, and preservation. As of this writing there are plans to make all volumes accessible electronically by fall 2002.

G-52 **Biological Abstracts: A Comprehensive Abstracting and Indexing Journal of the World's Literature in Theoretical and Applied Biology, Exclusive of Clinical Medicine**. Philadelphia, PA: BIOSIS, 1926- . Semimonthly.

Biological Abstracts is an indispensable source for researchers in archaeozoology, human evolution, primatology, and anthropometry. Many of the source journals are not indexed by anthropological services. It has abstracted an enormous body of biological literature from journal and review articles, meetings, reports, and monographs.

> ***Electronic access:*** *Biological Abstracts* is also searchable online as *BIOSIS*. The database gives more expanded access points to the biological literature than the print version does and is updated monthly.

G-53 **Ethnic Newswatch**. Stamford, CT: Softline Information, 1992- . Quarterly. Electronic format.

An unusual resource, *Ethnic Newswatch* is a full-text electronic service that covers newspapers, journals, and magazines of the ethnic and native presses, resources not typically contained in other indexing or full-text databases or available in many libraries. Content covers a number of social science and humanities subjects with an international and regional flavor. Current coverage is from 1990 on, with selective coverage back to 1985. The search interface, available in both English and Spanish, makes it useful to a wider population than many other resources. Available over the Internet and as a CD-ROM.

G-54 **GeoRef**. Alexandria, VA: American Geological Institute, 1990- . Updated monthly. Electronic format.

GeoRef, an electronic database, comprises four major geological sources: *Bibliography of North American Geology* (Government Printing Office, 1906/1907–1970), *Bibliography and Index of Geology Exclusive of North America* (Geological Society of America, 1933–1968), *Bibliography and Index of Geology* (American Geological Institute, 1933-), and *Geophysical Abstracts* (U.S. Geological Survey, 1929–1971). Its covers from 1785 to date and at present has more than 2.2 million entries. It is a useful resource for the literature of archaeology, paleontology, and prehistory because of its subject coverage and historical depth. A very useful thesaurus and guides to searching are provided to assist in effective retrieval of results. *GeoRef* is available through several online service providers and as a CD-ROM.

G-55 **Index Medicus**. Bethesda, MD: National Library of Medicine, 1960- . Monthly.

Physical anthropology has long been associated with medicine, and some researchers rely heavily on medical literature. In addition to medical topics, this premier index covers subjects such as anthropometry, physical anthropology, genetics, and ethnopsychology.

> ***Electronic access:*** A major advantage to this index is its availability online as *PubMed*, which brings together *MEDLINE*, *PreMEDLINE*, *HealthSTAR*, and relevant material from other sources to create a database of more than 9 million citations. It provides the capability of linking to full-text sources listed in citations where access is permitted through library subscription.

G-56 Linguistics and Language Behavior Abstracts. San Diego, CA: Sociological Abstracts, 1985- . Quarterly.

G-57 Language and Language Behavior Abstracts. San Diego, CA: Sociological Abstracts, 1967–1984.

Although anthropological indexes and abstracts cover linguistic anthropology, researchers still need to turn to this source to perform a complete literature search on linguistics and language. Approximately 1,500 publications, both monograph and serial in nature, are reviewed for possible inclusion.

Electronic access: This source can be accessed online or acquired as a CD-ROM. The manual and thesaurus should be consulted for successful searching.

DICTIONARIES AND ENCYCLOPEDIAS

Many fine new dictionaries and encyclopedias were published in the 1990s. These new sources are more current than the older ones likely to be found in many library collections. The old ones still have value, because anthropological concepts and terms do not change as rapidly as some other fields; however, they are not listed in this edition. Obviously the more recently published sources are preferred for reference and generally are more comprehensive in treatment.

General Anthropology

G-58 **Anthromorphemics**. 1997- . Online format. URL: http://www.anth .ucsb.edu/glossary/index2.html.

One of the few online dictionaries, *Anthromorphemics* allows the user to view the entire list of definitions in the dictionary, search by term, or limit the search to terms specific to archaeology, cultural anthropology, or physical anthropology. It is quite serviceable for finding definitions quickly.

G-59 Barfield, Thomas. **The Dictionary of Anthropology**. Malden, MA: Blackwell, 1997.

This dictionary has more than 500 entries, including 42 fairly substantial biographies. Entries vary in length and depth, but many of the shorter entries are enhanced with cross-references. Historical and contemporary definitions are provided where appropriate. All the references are cumulated at the end of the volume. It gives minimal coverage of archaeology, biological, and linguistic anthropology, but it covers major religious traditions, geographical areas of the world, and regional anthropological traditions. It is a good source for ready reference.

G-60 De Laet, S. J., ed. **The History of Humanity**. New York: Routledge, 1994- .

Each of the seven volumes in this set is devoted to a period in human history. Although the entire set may be of interest, of particular note for anthropology are the earliest volumes, which cover prehistory and early civilization. Each volume has an introduction, followed by sections on themes (many of which are anthropological in nature, such as archaeology, linguistics, oral traditions, and religion) and regions (by place and period). Each volume has a bibliography and index.

G-61 Ingold, Tim, ed. **Companion Encyclopedia of Anthropology**. London: Routledge, 1994.

Ingold organizes topical articles into sections by humanity, culture, and social life. An international array of anthropologists wrote the thirty-eight articles, which the author intends to be read, not consulted for ready reference. Each article contains a bibliography. It serves as a good overall view of general subjects of anthropology. Indexed. See also *Companion Encyclopedia of Archaeology* (G-63).

Archaeology

G-62 Bahn, Paul. **Collins Dictionary of Archaeology**. Santa Barbara, CA: ABC-Clio, 1993.

This dictionary includes short definitions and biographies, with further readings provided by broad subject area. Appended are maps of geographic areas showing locations of major sites.

G-63 Barker, Graeme, ed. **Companion Encyclopedia of Archaeology**. 2 vols. New York and Oxford: Routledge, 1999.

Like the *Companion Encyclopedia of Anthropology* (G-61), this work is not a standard encyclopedia. Instead of many topical entries, it uses a relatively few long chapters on thematic issues. It attempts to give a systematic overview of archaeological theory, approach, and method. Chapters have references for further consultation. It concludes with a comprehensive index. Using it effectively requires devoting time to reading its chapters.

G-64 Cunliffe, Barry, ed. **The Oxford Illustrated Prehistory of Europe**. Oxford: Oxford University Press, 1994.

The articles in this encyclopedia are organized by time period rather than by an alphabetical or topical approach. Many photographs and figures accompany the text. Further readings, chronological tables, acknowledgments, and the index follow the article section.

G-65 Ellis, Linda, ed. **Archaeological Method and Theory: An Encyclopedia**. New York: Garland, 2000.

Archaeological method and theory are covered in other resources, but not as stand-alone subjects. Beginning with a useful subject guide that groups related entries, this work covers a wide range of methods and theory. Articles, written and signed by worldwide experts, are arranged alphabetically and indexed by subject and name. Each entry has further readings for each entry and cross-references. Biographies are included.

G-66 Fagan, Brian, ed. **The Oxford Companion to Archaeology**. New York and Oxford: Oxford University Press, 1996.

Fagan has compiled a work containing 700 entries that provide good coverage of human fossils; historical sites; geographical areas; and the people, history, theory, and substance of archaeology. Some entries are short or are missing a bibliography. The purpose of the maps and tables is not evident, nor are they referenced by their related entries. However, the work is authoritative, well written, and provides the very up-to-date information in an expanded dictionary format. It is indexed.

G-67 Jelks, Edward B., and Juliet C. Jelks, eds. **Historical Dictionary of North American Archaeology**. New York: Greenwood Press, 1988.

This work directs researchers to information on prehistoric Indian cultures, sites, and artifacts of North America. Most of the entries, contributed by experts, are short, and some include references to definitive works on the subject. Some of the references in the bibliography are incorrect. To use the dictionary one must rely on the index to find all relevant entries. The index, however, is poorly cross-referenced and not comprehensive. There are entries in the body that are not in the index.

G-68 Mignon, Molly Raymond. **Dictionary of Concepts in Archaeology**. New York: Greenwood Press, 1993.

One of three thematic concept dictionaries published about anthropology, this one is devoted to archaeology. The others cover cultural anthropology and physical anthropology. These concept dictionaries develop themes fully by imparting the current meaning and tracing the origins and context of concepts. In this work, seventy-two concepts receive lengthy treatment, including subjects such as adaptation, archaeoastronomy, culture, evolution, lithics, paleoanthropology, and stratigraphy. Each concept lists references and additional sources. The work is indexed by name and subject.

Physical Anthropology

G-69 Milner, Richard. **The Encyclopedia of Evolution: Humanity's Search for Its Origins**. New York: Facts on File, 1990.

A semi-popular treatment, this work makes the concepts of evolution and human origins very accessible to all levels of readers. Laced with biographies, fossil finds, and discussions of relevant subjects and controversies, it includes an index of names, places, and subjects.

G-70 Spencer, Frank. **The History of Physical Anthropology: An Encyclopedia**. 2 vols. New York: Garland, 1997.

Spencer has created a highly successful work in the history of physical anthropology. This encyclopedia is the only work of its scope on this subject and can serve the needs of a wide variety of scholars in the history of anthropology, science, and medicine. An international group of scholars and specialists contributed the biographies and essays on subjects such as sites, fossils, national traditions, theories, controversies, institutions, and museums. Entries include primary and secondary resources, and when known, where archival materials can be found. It uses cross-references, includes a bibliography, and concludes with an index.

G-71 Stevenson, Joan C. **Dictionary of Concepts in Physical Anthropology**. New York: Greenwood Press, 1991.

Much like the *Dictionary of Concepts in Archaeology* (G-68), this volume on physical anthropology concentrates on the major ideas in anthropology and develops their origin and context. Each of the seventy-five concepts receives lengthy and in-depth treatment and is accompanied by an extensive list of references and a bibliography. Some of the concepts covered are culture, eugenics, evolution, phylogeny, primates, and taxonomy. There are subject and name indexes.

G-72 Tattersall, Ian, Eric Delson, and John Van Couvering, eds. **Encyclopedia of Human Evolution and Prehistory**. 2d ed. New York: Garland, 2000.

This is a comprehensive, scholarly guide to the subject of human evolution. It includes an introduction to the subject that provides a good overview and entrée to the articles, a subject list by topic, and charts on the classification of primates and geologic periods. All of the approximately 800 articles are signed and contain further readings. In addition to subjects, the encyclopedia has biographies of major figures. Cross-references are included within the body of the encyclopedia, and it has a unified index.

Cultural Anthropology

G-73 Barnard, Alan, and Jonathan Spencer, eds. **Encyclopedia of Social and Cultural Anthropology**. New York: Routledge, 1996.

Barnard and Spencer have produced a good ready reference source that contains 231 entries, accompanied by further readings, along with 238 short biographies, five long biographies, and a glossary of more than 600 terms. It extensively cross-references the entries, biographies, and glossary terms. It traces the history, development, and current state of concepts, theories, and methods, while also covering subdisciplines, related fields, and geographic areas. Although all topics, biographies, authors of references, and terms are indexed, this is not the case for many of the personal names mentioned within the entries. The book includes a bibliography and index.

G-74 Gonen, Amiram. **The Encyclopedia of the Peoples of the World**. New York: Henry Holt, 1993.

In this volume the reader will find information on modern cultures and ethnic groups. Its focus is more on political and geographical history than on cultural and linguistic diversity. The peoples of the world are defined within nationalities. Articles include the common and indigenous names of groups and provide cross-references to related articles. Maps show the locations of lesser-known peoples. The book concludes with an index and bibliography.

G-75 Lee, Richard B., and Richard Daly, eds. **The Cambridge Encyclopedia of Hunters and Gatherers**. New York: Cambridge University Press, 1999.

Hunting and gathering has dominated the history of human existence. An encyclopedia of this nature adds to the reference literature in great measure. The first part relates case studies from seven regions, with each study amplified by a general introduction and an archaeological overview. The second part is organized into topical essays. The text of both parts includes reading lists and many black-and-white photographs and illustrations. The work concludes with a list of organizations and advocacy groups devoted to indigenous peoples and an index.

G-76 Levinson, David, ed. **Encyclopedia of World Cultures**. 10 vols. New York: G. K. Hall/Macmillan, 1991.

This source is the definitive guide to its subject and is without parallel in its comprehensive treatment. The arrangement is by geographic area (one per volume). Each entry has specific descriptive information on the culture, including, but not restricted to ethnonym, location, physical environment, demography, linguistic affiliation, economy, kinship, marriage and family, political organization, and religion. Each volume includes an ethnic names index, bibliographies, filmographies, maps, and a complete list of cultures. The final volume cumulates the indexes, bibliographies, and lists.

G-77 Levinson, David, and Melvin Ember, eds. **Encyclopedia of Cultural Anthropology**. 4 vols. New York: Henry Holt, 1996.

A wide range of anthropological subjects is covered in depth by this encyclopedia. With 340 lengthy entries accompanied by a bibliography and cross-references, the encyclopedia highlights the cross-cultural, holistic approach and use of fieldwork that are the hallmarks of cultural anthropology. Most entries are devoted to subjects, theoretical constructs, geographical/cultural areas, cultural groups, and major anthropological institutions and organizations. Unlike some reference works on cultural anthropology, this one treats relevant aspects of archaeology, biological anthropology, and linguistics, so it is useful for the entire discipline. Major anthropologists are discussed within the articles rather than as separate biographies. Indexed.

G-78 Winthrop, Robert H. **Dictionary of Concepts in Cultural Anthropology**. New York: Greenwood Press, 1991.

Like its counterparts in physical anthropology and archaeology, this dictionary covers major themes, in this case those that have shaped cultural anthropology. It includes definitions, origins, and developments of ideas, as well as references for eighty concepts such as adaptation, culture, diffusion, ethnicity, kinship, nature, race, religion, and symbolism. References and further sources are provided, and the dictionary is indexed by name and subject.

Linguistic Anthropology

G-79 Asher, R. E., ed. **The Encyclopedia of Language and Linguistics**. 10 vols. Oxford: Pergamon Press, 1994.

This set contains an impressive collection of articles and appendixes that include much information of use to anthropologists. In addition to nine volumes of alphabetically arranged topical entries and biographies, the tenth volume has a 100-page glossary, a list of the languages of the world, a classified list of entries (including anthropology and languages, and biographies arranged by category), and indexes for names and subjects. An excellent source for information on language and linguistics.

G-80 Bussmann, Hadumod. **Routledge Dictionary of Language and Linguistics**. New York: Routledge, 1996.

With coverage of both language and linguistics, this dictionary provides information on many concepts, theories, and terms of interest to anthropologists. Many entries have readings and cross-references.

G-81 Crystal, David. **The Cambridge Encyclopedia of Language**. 2d ed. New York: Cambridge University Press, 1997.

This encyclopedia presents the subject of language in an easy-to-use and understandable manner, making its content accessible to many audiences. It is organized into very broad themes subdivided by topics, with text accompanied by many colorful illustrations. It contains a glossary and an index.

G-82 Crystal, David. **An Encyclopedic Dictionary of Language and Languages**. Cambridge, MA: Blackwell, 1992.

Crystal has written a dictionary that serves as a good companion to the Asher encyclopedia (G-79), having longer, more detailed entries for topics and concepts. It includes only a few short biographies of major figures.

G-83 Trask, R. L. **A Student's Dictionary of Language and Linguistics**. New York: St. Martin's Press, 1997.

Because this is a resource for students, the definitions and biographies provided are concise and therefore useful for quick consultation. It includes further readings grouped by general subjects at the end.

BIOGRAPHICAL SOURCES

Specifically biographical sources are listed here. Biographical information can be found in many of the dictionaries and encyclopedias cited above, and they are indicated where appropriate. Biographies of anthropologists can be found in biographical sources of social science, science and medicine, and humanities.

G-84 Gacs, Ute, Aisha Khan, Jerrie McIntyre, and Ruth Weinberg, eds. **Women Anthropologists: A Biographical Dictionary**. New York: Greenwood Press, 1988.

This biographical source focuses on women of the twentieth century, some living, some deceased. The people covered represent broad coverage of the fields of anthropology. The book includes fifty-eight entries and two appendixes, one on field areas and one on chronology of birth dates. General references are listed, and the work is indexed.

G-85 Library-Anthropology Resource Group, comp. **Biographical Directory of Anthropologists Born Before 1920**. Edited by Thomas L. Mann. New York: Garland, 1988.

This work consists of very short biographical entries on people, born before 1920, who have made a contribution to anthropology. Entries include birth and death dates, place of birth, profession, contributions to anthropology, and citations to biographies. Entries vary in length, not necessarily in proportion to the person's importance to anthropology. Also, important anthropologists have been omitted. The work includes an index and additional tables with number of anthropologists by country, birth year, death year, and career.

G-86   Library-Anthropology Resource Group, comp. **International Dictionary of Anthropologists**. Edited by Christopher Winters. New York: Garland, 1991.

Written by anthropologists and librarians, this work provides lengthy biographical treatment for major figures. Biographies of 725 anthropologists born before 1920, both living and dead, are included. Entries range from several paragraphs to several pages and contain a list of major works and sources of additional biographical information. Includes a short glossary and an index of names, places, ethnic and institutional names, and major subjects.

G-87   Murray, Tim, ed. **Encyclopedia of Archaeology: The Great Archaeologists**. 2 vols. Santa Barbara, CA: ABC-Clio, 1999.

A good treatment of the history of archaeology, this work has lengthy and detailed biographies. It is organized by birth date and starts with William Camden (1551–1623) and concludes with David Clarke (1938–1976). Fifty-eight archeologists are covered, and each biography concludes with references to primary and secondary material. A glossary, substantial bibliography, and epilog on writing archaeological biography are additional features.

ATLASES

Anthropology is served by a number of good atlases. Some of those listed here are fairly current and well-done, well-illustrated, and contain scholarly articles. Older atlases may also prove useful for some purposes, especially if they have not been superseded. The general public and scholars will find atlases useful for concise information about anthropological topics.

G-88   Aston, Mick, and Tim Taylor. **The Atlas of Archaeology**. New York: DK Publishers, 1998.

This tool starts with a chronological approach to describing major archaeological sites. It also features an excellent gazetteer that places and describes sites within a geographical context, including topographic information. The text includes short topical essays on archaeological subjects such as stone tools. It contains color illustrations, maps, a glossary, and a bibliography.

G-89   **The Atlas of Mankind**. Chicago: Rand McNally, 1982.

This atlas includes major concepts of sociocultural anthropology, like kinship, marriage, and taboo, which are not limited by geographical area. It also covers the distribution of modern languages. The work is well-illustrated and contains a glossary, general index, and index of place names.

G-90   Constable, Nick. **The World Atlas of Archeology**. New York: Lyons Press, 2000.

This atlas encompasses both time and space, organized geographically. Coverage starts with early hominids and continues through historic times. Each geographic area has an introductory section followed by sections that highlight a site, find, topic, or culture. Each two-page section (seventy-seven in all) contains a timeline, photos, and a short descriptive text. Although it is global in coverage and comprehensive in time frame, this atlas is quite general, has no bibliography, and lacks detail. It is, however, indexed. It best serves a general, not scholarly, audience.

G-91   Price, David H. **Atlas of World Cultures: A Geographical Guide to Ethnological Literature**. New Berry Park, CA: Sage, 1989.

As with other resources produced by the Human Relations Area Files, this atlas employs a cross-cultural approach to assist the user in finding literature about more than 3,500 cultural groups. Forty maps illustrating the location of groups constitute the first part of the work. The second part is the bibliography. The concluding part is a culture index that links the culture to the maps and the relevant citations in the bibliography, along with other information, such as the HRAF code for the culture.

G-92 Whitehouse, David. **Archaeological Atlas of the World**. London: Thames & Hudson, 1975.

This atlas contains maps locating archaeological sites, but no site is discussed extensively. It is mainly useful as a tool for finding the specific locations of a large number of sites. It contains a few further readings and an index.

G-93 **The World Atlas of Archaeology**. Boston: G. K. Hall, 1985.

This atlas contains color pictures and excellent maps. Because the articles are long, general, and descriptive, this is not really a ready reference tool; however, the glossary could prove useful for that purpose. The work is arranged by regions of the world, subdivided by subjects. It covers early humans through historical times. It is copiously illustrated and has bibliographies and an index.

REVIEWS AND CURRENT LITERATURE

G-94 **Annual Review of Anthropology**. Palo Alto, CA: Annual Reviews, 1972- . Annual. (Continues *Biennial Review of Anthropology*, 1959–1971).

This reviewing source covers topics and problems of current interest and recent publications in anthropology. Review articles are written by specialists. Although it is international in scope, it is slanted toward English-language sources.

Electronic access: Annual Reviews publishes this source online as well as in print.

G-95 Association of College and Research Libraries, Anthropology and Sociology Section. **ANSS Reviews**. 1996- . Biannual. Online format. URL: http://www.lib.odu .edu/anss/reviews.htm.

The Bibliography Committee of the Anthropology and Sociology Section writes substantial and authoritative reviews of the abstracting and indexing literature that supports anthropology and sociology. The reviews are originally published in *ANSS Currents*, the section's newsletter, but are reproduced online on *ANSSWeb* and thereby made available to anyone. Approximately two new reviews are added per year.

G-96 **Reviews in Anthropology**. Philadelphia: Gordon & Breach, 1974- . Quarterly.

In contrast to the *Annual Review of Anthropology* (G-94), *Reviews in Anthropology* aims to review new books, not current topics. A unique feature is its inclusion of comments by the authors of the books in response to the critical reviews. Occasionally this source reviews nonbook materials.

HUMAN RELATIONS AREA FILES

G-97 **eHRAF Collection of Ethnography**. New Haven, CT: Human Relations Area Files, 1997- . Annual. Online format.

Human Relations Area Files (*HRAF*) includes primary source materials (more than 1,000,000 pages from books, articles unpublished material, and data tapes) by culture, geographic area, and cultural traits. *HRAF* is organized by culture files and subject files. More than half of the documents are included in full text. *HRAF* also includes translations of some materials. Beginning in 1995 *HRAF* has been produced solely as an electronic product, and over time has been incorporating previously published microfiche files.

    HRAF is touted as a tool for cross-cultural research and is designed to facilitate this goal. The *Outline of World Cultures*, originally developed by George Murdock and last printed in a sixth edition in 1983, serves as a classification of world cultures, arranged geographically, with alphanumeric classifications that form the basis of the classification for *HRAF* materials. It is included as a hypertext file with links to the corresponding cultures within *eHRAF*. Murdock's *Outline of Cultural Materials* (last published in print in a fifth edition in 1982) provides a classified system of subjects for the *HRAF* materials.

    The *HRAF* Web site (http://www.yale.edu/hraf/) is indispensable for understanding the relationship of all the *HRAF* materials and their contents. Other Web sites that provide extremely helpful guides to use are those at the University of Illinois (http://www.library.uiuc.edu/edx/hraf.htm), the University of Michigan (http://ets.umdl.umich.edu/e/ehraf/), and Boston University (http://www.bu .edu/library/research-guides/hrafhome.html). The *HRAF Source Bibliography* (Human Relations Area Files, 1976-) lists all books, articles, and manuscripts processed for HRAF, organized by culture units.

    Over the years researchers have prepared specialized printed bibliographies based on the *HRAF* resources. Parts of *HRAF* have been distributed as CD-ROM or online products, such as the *Cross-Cultural CD* (SilverPlatter, 1989–1994) and the *eHRAF Collection of Archaeology* (HRAF, 1998-). The *Bibliography of Native North Americans* has been produced as a CD-ROM and online by SilverPlatter. Both update and include earlier versions published in four print editions as the *Ethnographic Bibliography of North America*.

8

Sociology

Diane Zabel and Christine Avery

ESSAY

As its name clearly implies, the social nature of the human animal is the focus of sociology. Although such an interest has been a subject of philosophical contemplation since ancient times, the modern discipline of sociology emerged in the nineteenth century. The origin of the term is attributed to the nineteenth-century French philosopher Auguste Comte. Comte is generally regarded as the founder of modern sociology. Lee Braude's 1994 bibliographic essay on the emergence of sociology is a good choice for those who wish to know more about the development of sociology as a discipline.[1] This essay discusses some of the major developments in sociology from the mid-nineteenth century to 1930, with an emphasis on the development of American sociology. More than eighty works are cited in this essay, making it a valuable tool for any librarian needing a summary of the most seminal publications in the field. Braude's coverage concludes with 1930, because by that date American sociology had firmly established itself as a discipline. A symbol of this, according to Braude, was the 1929 construction of the Social Science Research Building at the University of Chicago. In 1999, Braude published a follow-up bibliographic essay in *Choice*, tracing developments in sociology since 1930.[2] The phenomenal growth in sociology since 1930 is evidenced by the increase in the number of works that Braude cites in his analysis of the discipline's progress. Braude's critical evaluation of key contemporary works is useful to librarians, graduate students, and others needing to become conversant with the core literature in sociology. *Choice* also publishes bibliographic essays on subfields of major disciplines. One example is Harry Gold's article on the development of political sociology, a subspecialty that emerged in the post-World War II era.[3] It is particularly important for academic librarians to browse this feature of *Choice* because these bibliographic essays are outstanding and provide an easy means of gaining familiarity with the literature of a discipline or subdiscipline.

Sociology is a social science, using empirical methods to study human group behavior. It is the broadest of the social sciences, overlapping with psychology, anthropology, education, political science, business, history, communication, statistics, law, and economics. Some subfields of sociology, notably the sociology of work, the sociology of law, political sociology, the sociology of welfare, the sociology of the environment, and the sociology of work conflict, illustrate this overlap.[4] Sociology has distinguished itself from these related fields by developing a unique perspective. Both psychology and sociology study behavior, but whereas psychology concentrates on individual behavior, sociology is concerned with collective behavior and how groups influence individual behavior. Historically, anthropologists have primarily studied tribal peoples and pre-industrialized societies. Consequently, anthropological methodologies were developed primarily for the study of non-Western societies. However, since World War II, anthropologists have increasingly studied urban societies in Western countries and in the Third World. Like sociologists, many anthropologists have researched many relevant contemporary topics ranging from drug abuse to unemployment. In contrast, sociological methodologies were developed primarily for the study of modern Western societies.

Sociology has affected other disciplines. For example, history traditionally studies prominent people and important events in the past. Historians have adopted a sociological perspective with their increased interest in the daily life of average people, the family, and work. Sociology has also had an impact on librarianship. Leigh Estabrook's 1984 study using citation analysis to measure library researchers' use of sociological materials found that 8 percent of library citations were sociological references.[5] She concluded that this was not insignificant and projected that in the future, library researchers would probably increase their use of sociological works, especially those publications relating to computing and technology issues.

Sociology has been applied to the study of society's problems. Topics under sociological investigation include alcohol and drug abuse, family violence, homelessness, crime, and racial discrimination. In 1994, Neil J. Smelser, a prominent sociologist, accurately predicted that in the future more research would focus on subjects such as step-parenting, dual-career couples, commuter marriages, telecommuting and home-based work, the economic and ethical consequences of medical technology, the social epidemiology of AIDS, and the social aspects of environmental threats.[6] These were important themes in the late 1990s and continue to be in the twenty-first century. Social work developed as a practical response to social problems and is based in sociology. Throughout its history, sociology has been closely allied to social reform movements. Along with teaching in universities, sociologists work in industry, government, human services, and private social agencies.

A range of research methods characterizes the discipline of sociology. Sociological conclusions are not based on common sense but are the product of systematically collected data. After developing a hypothesis, sociologists select a research method and collect data, which are interpreted, reviewed, and sometimes replicated. The most heavily used research method in sociology is survey research. Survey research uses questionnaires, interviews, or both to determine what people think, to predict behavior, or to measure public opinion. This technique uses a sample, a representative number of people from the population studied. Generalizations about large groups of people are based on these samples.

Sociology shares the tradition of fieldwork with anthropology. Fieldwork uses direct observation to collect data. Some sociological studies involve the participation of the observer, who becomes part of the group studied. Case studies analyze a community, a family, or an occupation. The collection and analysis of statistical data are important in sociology. Sociologists require statistics on the demographic and social characteristics of special groups. Instead of generating their own data, they may rely on statistics already collected. Sociologists in the United States make heavy use of data collected by the Census Bureau and other government agencies.

Many sociologists make use of machine-readable data files. There are several repositories for machine-readable social science data. The most well-known archive in this country is the Inter-University Consortium for Political and Social Research (ICPSR), which is centered at the University of Michigan. The Consortium receives, processes, distributes, and archives large datasets. It also sponsors workshops and training sessions that are useful to data users and data librarians.

A large number of scholarly books are published annually in the area of sociology. Approximately 4,100 academic titles in sociology were published or distributed in the United States and Canada in 1997 alone.[7] Only two other subject categories in the social sciences surpassed this publishing output: history and business/economics. However, this figure from *The Bowker Annual* excludes the number of popular titles published in sociology. Herbert Gans authored a fascinating study on fifty-six best-sellers written by American sociologists during the period 1950 through 1995.[8] Each of these titles sold more than 50,000 copies; included were the 1950 classic *The Lonely Crowd* (which topped 1 million in sales); Arlie Hochschild's groundbreaking study, *The Second Shift* (documenting the chore wars between men and women); and three works by Lillian Rubin (*World of Pain, Intimate Strangers*, and *Just Friends*). Gans's insights about these best-sellers suggest the impact that sociology has had on the general public. These best-sellers have addressed issues such as loneliness, poverty, racism, social injustice, and gender inequality, topics that obviously struck a chord with many Americans.

Collection development in sociology can be a challenge given the large volume of monographic output. Fortunately, there are selection tools that can help librarians evaluate new titles in sociology. Although it dates from the 1980s, Sharon Quist's article on the value of book reviews in sociology is still relevant reading for beginning sociology librarians.[9] Quist outlines the importance of reviews and lists journals in sociology where book reviews can be found. Another article that should be required reading for sociology selectors is Judith Fox's critical comparison of *Choice* and *Contemporary Sociology* as book selection tools.[10] This evaluative article reiterates the importance of not using *Choice* exclusively for collection development decisions given only moderate overlap between *Choice* and *Contemporary Sociology*, a premier scholarly review journal in sociology.

Citation analysis has been employed as a tool to study the literature of sociology. James Baughman conducted one of the earliest studies in 1974.[11] Baughman's research resulted in a list of most frequently cited sociology journals. A few years later, William Satariano conducted a readership analysis, examining journals that socialists reported reading.[12] Both of these early studies laid the foundation for subsequent studies of sociology literature by establishing core lists of journals relevant to sociologists. In 1984, Beth Shapiro examined several citation and readership studies in the social sciences in order to profile sociologists' use of book and journal material. Her reviews of the research found that sociologists make greater use of monographic literature than many other social scientists, and there is an emphasis on recent English-language material. A synthesis of Shapiro's findings indicates that

1. 50 to 62 percent of all citations from scholarly research in sociology are from nonserial publications (e.g., monographs, documents, reports);

2. 90 to 93 percent of all citations are from English-language sources; and

3. 50 to 70 percent of all citations are from sources less than ten years old.[13]

Blaise Cronin, Herbert Snyder, and Helen Atkins have conducted the most recent citation analysis in sociology.[14] These authors analyzed tens of thousands of references from scholarly monographs and academic journals for a nine-year period (1985–1993). Their findings suggest that there may be two distinct populations of highly cited authors: one in monographs and the other in journals.

The literature of sociology is widely dispersed across related disciplines and the numerous subfields of sociology. Major subfields include criminology, social work, marriage and the family, demography, gerontology, ethnicity, women's studies, and urban studies. *Sociological Abstracts*, the major database in the discipline, identifies approximately thirty broad subfields, ranging from group interactions to feminist/gender studies. Sociological research is highly interdisciplinary. There is only a small core of reference literature relating to general sociology. However, there are many specialized works relating to the numerous subfields of the discipline.

GUIDES

Guides explain the research process in a discipline. Some are bibliographies, listing the core literature in the discipline. Sociology has several basic research guides written primarily for undergraduates. Until the publication of *Sociology: A Guide to Reference and Information Resources*, there was no comprehensive guide to the literature.

H-1   Aby, Stephen H. **Sociology: A Guide to Reference and Information Resources**. 2d ed. Englewood, CO: Libraries Unlimited, 1997.

This annotated bibliography is well organized and inclusive, and represents a substantial revision of the first edition. Aby's guide provides undergraduates, graduate students, faculty, and other researchers with descriptions of 516 of the major reference sources in sociology and related areas. Most of the print and electronic resources listed date from 1985 through 1996. The sources cited are in English. Part 1 describes basic social science reference sources and their applicability to sociology. Sources in the related disciplines of education, economics, psychology, social work, anthropology, and history are cited in part 2. Parts 3 and 4 constitute the bulk of the book and include sources dealing specifically with sociology and more than twenty major subfields of the discipline, including social problems and race and ethnic relations. This guide is useful for reference and retrospective collection development purposes and is a core sociology title for academic and large public libraries.

H-2   Johnson, William A. [et al.]. **The Sociology Student Writer's Manual**. 3d ed. Upper Saddle River, NJ: Prentice Hall, 2002.

This is a "how to" book aimed at sociology students to help them learn how to do research in the library and write a variety of papers in sociology effectively. The third edition is substantially updated. There is a very basic introduction to the study of sociology. Part 1 serves as a style manual for sociology writing, providing instructions on writing, formatting, and citing sources using the guidelines established by the American Sociological Association. Part 2 focuses on research in sociology, with chapters on the research process, sources, and conducting social research. This section incorporates a substantially updated section on Internet resources and distance learning. Part 3 outlines how to write a range of papers: on social issues, critical reviews of sociological literature, quantitative research, and research. The chapters on writing a literature review and a qualitative research paper are both new to this edition and each includes a sample paper. This is an essential manual for students enrolled in beginning to upper level sociology courses via distance education. It will also help students improve their writing in general.

H-3   Strenski, Ellen, ed. **A Guide to Writing Sociology Papers**. 5th ed. New York: Worth Publishers, 2001.

Like previous editions, the fifth edition of this classic was written by a team of sociology and English teachers at the University of California, Los Angeles. After defining sociology and comparing it to other social science disciplines, undergraduates are offered detailed practical advice on preparing research papers in sociology. They are given advice on how to frame a research question, structure a writing assignment, and develop a logical argument in a paper. Writers counsel students on organizing their time, writing and revising drafts, learning footnote and bibliography formats (including the format for machine-readable data files), and submitting papers. There are detailed instructions on how to avoid plagiarism. Other chapters lead students through the preparation of papers requiring library research, ethnographic field research, and quantitative research. There is also a chapter on how to write textual analysis papers. Sample papers illustrate guidelines outlined in chapters. This part of the handbook incorporates extensive information on researching online, including tips on finding and evaluating online information. The general information contained in this excellent text could be used by students writing papers for other social science courses. No doubt the newest edition of this book will be as useful as previous editions.

H-4 Szuchman, Lenore T., and Barbara Thomlison. **Writing with Style: APA Style for Social Work**. Pacific Grove, CA: Brooks/Cole, 2000.

This is a guide to using the APA style in conjunction with social science papers. The examples and exercises used in the book are very helpful because they have been chosen within the social science context and aid students in learning to follow writing conventions somewhat unique to the social sciences. The authors provide advice about terminology and logical errors that should be avoided. The book includes chapters on topics social science students always struggle with, such as how to write a methods section in a paper, how to write an abstract, and how to prepare a poster session.

DICTIONARIES AND ENCYCLOPEDIAS

General

Practically every academic discipline has one or more specialized encyclopedias. Scholarly encyclopedia articles can provide an overview, present background information, help to define and narrow a topic, and suggest additional resources. Most articles will conclude with a bibliography, which is often substantial. Most disciplines also have specialized dictionaries that will help define terms and concepts relating to that discipline.

H-5 Bankston, Carl III, ed. **Sociology Basics**. 2 vols. Pasadena, CA: Salem Press, 2000.

This set has been primarily designed for high school and undergraduate level college students. However, it is also useful to general readers and nonspecialists needing basic information on sociological topics. The set brings together ninety articles on topics of broad interest such as bureaucracies, war and revolution, and workplace socialization. The articles have been derived from the *Survey of Social Science: Sociology Series*, a five-volume set published by Salem Press in 1994. Entries (which are uniform in length), follow a standard format that includes a concise explanation of the topic, a brief summary of the topic's significance, definitions of key terms, an overview, a description of how the topic relates to practice and everyday life, the historical and cultural context, cross-references to related articles, and an annotated bibliography. The illustrated set includes a glossary and a detailed subject index. High school and academic libraries (particularly those supporting undergraduate sociology and social science curricula) will want to consider this set for purchase if they do not have the set on which it is based.

H-6 Blau, Judith, ed. **The Blackwell Companion to Sociology**. (Blackwell Companions to Sociology). Malden, MA: Blackwell, 2001.

This volume has been designed to serve as a handbook for the twenty-first century as it includes chapters on topics that will be relevant in the next decade and beyond. Internationally renowned sociologists have contributed chapters. Essays cover traditional and emergent areas of sociology and are grouped into eight thematic sections: referencing globalization; relationships and meaning; economic inequalities; science, knowledge, and ideas; politics and political movements; structures: stratification, networks, and firms; individuals and their well-being; and social action. One particularly useful feature is the descriptive and detailed bibliography of data resources on the Internet relating to sociology. The volume concludes with an extensive bibliography of print resources referenced in each chapter.

H-7 Borgatta, Edgar F., ed.-in-chief. **Encyclopedia of Sociology**. 2d ed. 5 vols. New York: Macmillan Reference USA, 2000.

The much-anticipated second edition of this outstanding reference work has received rave reviews, including starred reviews in both *Library Journal* and *Booklist/Reference Books Bulletin*. Topical essays from the first edition have been updated and expanded, and new articles have been added. There are sixty-six new articles, and the encyclopedia has been expanded from four to five volumes. The new essays are cutting edge, covering important contemporary issues such as the Internet, privacy, and epidemiology. Those articles that have not been updated are identified, and although not revised, their bibliographies have been updated. Special attention has been paid to the indexing, which has been substantially expanded, resulting in an exhaustive index that is almost 200 pages long (more than double the length of the original index). The first edition of this multivolume encyclopedia was a landmark because it was the first inclusive encyclopedia of sociology. Like other Macmillan encyclopedias, the set was outstanding in content, organization, and design. It received the Dartmouth Medal, a prestigious award given by the American Library Association, in 1993. The second edition of this exceptional encyclopedia promises to also become a reference classic that will be found in most academic and large public libraries.

H-8   Boudon, Raymond, and Francois Bourricaud. **A Critical Dictionary of Sociology**. Chicago: University of Chicago Press, 1989.

This is an abridged translation of the first and second editions of *Dictionnaire Critique de la Sociologie*, which were published in Paris by the Presses Universitaires de France in 1982 and 1986. This work is almost encyclopedic in nature, providing lengthy essays on subjects such as bureaucracy, capitalism, family, Durkheim, power, social change, suicide, and utopia. Fewer than 100 topics are covered. Each essay concludes with ample cross-references and a core bibliography. Graduate students and researchers in sociology, history, political science, and philosophy will find this dictionary useful. However, any of the other encyclopedias listed in this section would be a better choice for most undergraduates needing a quick introduction to terms, concepts, and people in sociology.

H-9   Johnson, Allan G. **The Blackwell Dictionary of Sociology: A User's Guide to Sociological Language**. 2d ed. Malden, MA: Blackwell, 2000.

This dictionary covers the language and concepts of sociology concisely and in easily accessible language. It also includes brief biographical sketches of major figures in the development and practice of sociology. Explanations are accompanied by cross-references and suggested readings as appropriate. A comprehensive index is useful for tying many of the definitions together.

H-10   Lawson, Tony, and Joan Garrod, eds. **Dictionary of Sociology**. Chicago: Fitzroy Dearborn, 2001.

This title is based on the second edition of *The Complete A–Z Sociology Handbook*, which was first published in the United Kingdom by Hodder and Stoughton Educational in 2000. It has been designed as a basic glossary, defining terms in all fields of sociology. Each term is defined in a single sentence. Illustrative examples are used to help clarify concepts. Entries range in length from one or two lines to a long paragraph. The length of an entry is generally determined by the importance of a topic as well as the controversy surrounding it. Several features make it user friendly, including a simple A to Z arrangement and abundant cross-references.

H-11   Magill, Frank N., ed. **International Encyclopedia of Sociology**. 2 vols. London, Chicago: Fitzroy Dearborn, 1995.

This set is an exceptional reference work that every academic library should own. Designed for the general reader, it is broad in scope and includes 338 articles averaging four pages in length. The articles follow a standard format, beginning with an overview that introduces and explains the topic. This is followed by an "applications" section that explains how the topic has been explored in sociological studies and relates the topic to everyday life. Next is the "context" section, which examines the topic in relation to relevant historical and cultural themes and explores the implications of the topic. Finally, each article includes an annotated bibliography directing the reader to other sources that have been carefully selected for their usefulness to the nonspecialist. All articles are extensively cross-referenced. The index is quite detailed, and there is also a glossary of 450 sociological terms, followed by a general bibliography.

H-12   Marshall, Gordon, ed. **A Dictionary of Sociology**. New York: Oxford University Press, 1998.

This comprehensive source written by British sociologists is probably the best single-volume compilation of sociological terms and explanation of concepts. There are over 2,500 entries, and the authors do a good job of providing an international perspective in their coverage of terms, methods, and concepts. The dictionary includes biographies of sociologists who have influenced the history of sociology but excludes sociologists still living at the time the work was published. Readers are able to easily pursue the relevant literature on any given subject, as the text is generous in the provision of citations and suggestions for further reading. Examples and illustrations of points are well done.

H-13   Vogt, W. Paul. **Dictionary of Statistics and Methodology: A Nontechnical Guide for the Social Sciences**. 2d ed. Thousand Oaks, CA: Sage, 1999.

This dictionary is intended to be an easy-to-use reference work for statistical concepts and methodological terms in the social and behavioral sciences. It is aimed at readers of research with the stated goal of helping them to be critical readers of works that might otherwise be too technical. Definitions are written clearly and contain no formulas. It is an excellent source that contains approximately 2,000 definitions and illustrations. The author makes frequent use of examples and has assembled a well-chosen array of suggestions for further reading on major points.

Specialized

Sociology has far more specialized encyclopedias and dictionaries than general ones. In addition to the sources listed below, sociologists may want to consult encyclopedias and dictionaries relating to psychology, statistics, political science, economics, or the social sciences in general.

H-14   Bankston, Carl L., ed. **Encyclopedia of Family Life**. 5 vols. Pasadena, CA: Salem Press, 1999.

This encyclopedia set covers all aspects of American and Canadian family life. More than 200 authors, many of them academics, have contributed the 452 essays. The signed articles range in length from 250 to 4,000 words. There are long essays on broad topics. Among the core topics covered are aging and elderly care, child rearing, education of children, the concept and history of the family, love, marriage, parenting, religion, sexuality, and work. There are almost 100 other topical essays that are approximately 2,500 words in length, covering subjects such as adoption, child care, dating, death, fatherhood, grandparents, in-laws, poverty, retirement, siblings, tax laws, teen mothers, and weddings. Shorter entries define terms and cover people, laws, and organizations. Some examples of these more concise essays include entries as diverse as Mary Cassatt, Habit for Humanity International, Human Genome Project, Megan's Law, Parents Without Partners, Gail Sheehy, and *Wisconsin v. Yoder*.

More than half of the essays are substantial in length (at least 1,500 words) and conclude with bibliographies. Many of the articles are illustrated with tables, graphs, charts, and photographs. This set is distinguished by several helpful appendixes: a timeline from 451 through 1998, highlighting important changes in the family; a chronology from 1000 through 1996, listing important legislation and court decisions; a listing of support groups; a glossary; and a list of articles by category. Access to articles is also enhanced through extensive cross-referencing and a detailed index. The final volume also contains an annotated, selective bibliography. This informative and well-designed multidisciplinary set will be found in many high school, public, and academic libraries.

H-15   Barkan, Elliott Robert, ed. **A Nation of Peoples: A Sourcebook on America's Multicultural Heritage**. Westport, CT: Greenwood Press, 1999.

This collection of essays on more than twenty racial, religious, and ethnic groups in the United States fills an important gap in the literature since the *Harvard Encyclopedia of American Ethnic Groups*, the first scholarly English-language discussion of many ethnic groups, dates from 1980. Although not as comprehensive as the landmark Harvard publication or the more recent edition of the *Gale Encyclopedia of Multicultural America* (H-19), this work is marked by in-depth analytical essays written by leading scholars. The volume begins with a thoughtful overview on multiculturalism. Among the groups covered are African Americans, American Indians, Central and South Americans, Cubans, East Europeans, Japanese, Jews, Koreans, Middle Easterners, North Africans, Poles, and West Indians/Caribbeans. Each essay is similar in content, addressing issues relating to the group's arrival, adaptation, integration (economic, political, and cultural), current status, and impact on America's heritage. Each essay concludes with an extensive bibliography. In addition, there is a selective general bibliography. This important work on America's multicultural heritage will be found in many public and academic libraries.

H-16   Cayton, Mary Kupiec, Elliott J. Gorn, and Peter W. Williams, eds. **Encyclopedia of American Social History**. 3 vols. New York: Scribner's, 1993.

Since the 1960s, historians have become increasingly interested in the daily life of average people. Many have studied the family, work, and groups that have been underrepresented in standard texts (notably women and minorities). Many of the 180 thematic essays included in this extraordinary encyclopedia will be useful to sociologists as well as historians. For example, there are articles on social change, ethnicity and race, popular culture, social problems, and social protest. This encyclopedia quickly became the standard in its field. No other reference work is as comprehensive or inclusive in the area of American social history. It is not surprising that this outstanding work was a contender for the 1994 Dartmouth Medal, receiving Honorable Mention. It was also selected as one of 1994's "Outstanding Reference Sources" by the Reference Sources Committee of the American Library Association's Reference and Adult Services Division (now the Reference and User Services Association). In 1998, selections from the set were published under the title *Everyday Life: American Social History* by Macmillan Library Reference USA.

H-17   **Encyclopedia of Crime and Justice**. New York: Free Press, 1983.

Although this interdisciplinary encyclopedia is almost two decades old, it remains a core reference in criminology. It contains articles relating to the causes of crime; criminal behavior; criminal law; criminal procedures; criminal justice systems; and the prevention, punishment, and treatment of crime. Topics included are arraignment, careers in criminal justice, computer crime, regulation of guns, and white-collar crime. Most of the contributors were professors of law, sociology, criminology, and related disciplines or researchers affiliated with research centers. The encyclopedia is directed to a wide audience, and the clear writing style and superb organization make it understandable to the general reader as well as the specialist. Articles range from 1,000 to 10,000 words in length and conclude with substantial bibliographies. Extensive cross-referencing and a detailed general index contribute to the excellence of this work. There is also a legal index providing references to cited legal documents and a glossary of terms. Another particularly useful feature is the explanation of legal citations. This comprehensive work can be found in many high school, academic, and medium-sized to large public libraries.

H-18   **Encyclopedia of Social Work**. 19th ed. 3 vols. Washington, DC: National Association of Social Workers (NASW), 1995.

There were sweeping changes with the nineteenth edition of this well-respected reference work. The encyclopedia was expanded to three volumes and, for the first time ever; it became available in CD-ROM format. More than half of the topics included in this edition are new. In addition, virtually all of the articles that were retained from the previous edition were expanded, revised, or updated. The number of biographical entries increased from 99 to 142. This edition is essentially an all-new version of a reference classic. In addition, it made a conscious effort to address issues relating to diversity, including racism, homophobia, and age discrimination. The *1997 Supplement* includes articles on federal social legislation from 1995 to 1997, the Internet as a resource tool, managed care research findings, and recent developments surrounding legal issues such as confidentiality and privilege. Because the *Encyclopedia* contains substantive essays on timely social topics (such as adolescent pregnancy, alcohol abuse, anorexia, domestic violence, and homelessness) in addition to articles on social work practice, this set will be helpful to general users needing information on social problems.

H-19 Dassanowsky, Robert, and Jeffrey Lehman, eds. **Gale Encyclopedia of Multicultural America**. 2d ed. 3 vols. Detroit: Gale Group, 2000.

The American Library Association's Ethnic and Multicultural Information Exchange Round Table have endorsed this set. It assembles essays on approximately 150 cultural groups residing in the United States, including ethnic groups (such as Filipino Americans, Hawaiians, Polish Americans, and Welsh Americans), ethno-religious groups (including the Amish, the Druze, and Jewish Americans), and Native American cultures (such as the Blackfoot, Creeks, Hopis, Ojibwe, and Yupiet). The essays are significant, averaging 8,000 words in length. Each composition contains the following information about each group: history, acculturation, assimilation, language, religion, family and community dynamics, employment and economic traditions, politics and government, and the group's contributions to American society. Essays conclude with useful features such as listings of periodicals, broadcast (radio, television, and Internet) media, organizations, associations, museums, and research centers. Readers are also directed to additional sources of information.

More than 200 images complement the text. A general index provides access to personal names, events, organizations, topics, and keywords. There is also a bibliography (with brief annotations) listing books and periodicals. Gale has also published a two-volume companion work, the *Gale Encyclopedia of Multicultural America: Primary Documents* (1999), edited by Jeffrey Lehman, which brings together documents as varied as political cartoons and recipes.

H-20 Dressler, Joshua, ed. **Encyclopedia of Crime and Justice**. 2d ed. 4 vols. New York: Macmillan Reference USA, 2002.

This is the long-awaited revision of the classic encyclopedia on criminology (see H-17). Dressler is one of the nation's leading criminal law scholars. This set is a complete revision of the original work. It is interdisciplinary in scope, examining the sociological, psychological, historical, legal, and economic aspects of crime. Among the themes treated are social issues, types of crime, legal procedures, the legal system, and law enforcement. The 250 articles have been contributed by sociologists and legal scholars. Among the topics included are domestic violence, crime in developing countries, drinking and driving, gender and crime, rural crime, computer crime, obscenity and pornography, sex offenses, wiretapping and eavesdropping, arraignment, appeal, perjury, guilty pleas, competency to stand trial, sentencing, victim's rights, community policing, search and seizure, and the legal rights of prisoners. There are a general index, an index of cited cases, and a glossary of terms. This much-needed revision of a core reference work in criminology is an essential purchase for most high school, academic, and medium-sized to large public libraries.

H-21 Goreham, Gary, ed. **Encyclopedia of Rural America: The Land and the People**. 2 vols. Santa Barbara, CA: ABC-Clio, 1997.

Approximately one-quarter of Americans now live in rural areas, representing a rural revival. This encyclopedia focuses exclusively on life in rural America. Other standard reference works include articles on rural life, notably *The Encyclopedia of Sociology* (H-7) and the *Encyclopedia of American Social History* (H-16). The *Encyclopedia of Rural America* is unique, however, because no other reference work offers such a comprehensive treatment of rural topics. The result is an engaging, multidisciplinary, attractively designed encyclopedia that brings together more than 200 entries ranging from agricultural prices to stock car racing. The signed articles have been written by subject specialists and include references for further reading. The second volume pulls together these references in the form of an extensive bibliography. Abundant "see also" references and a thorough index lead readers to these highly readable and varied articles. This is a handsome set that will be found in many public and academic libraries.

H-22 Gottesman, Ronald, and Richard M. Brown, eds. **Violence in America: An Encyclopedia**. 3 vols. New York: Scribner's, 1999.

This award-winning multivolume encyclopedia examines all aspects of violence in America, from the role of biology in aggression to the historical aspects of violence. It also looks at the way violence is depicted in American culture, from painting to cinema. The encyclopedia is extensive in scope, including entries on broad issues, topics, movements, events, individuals, and organizations. It was named by

Library Journal as one of the "Best Reference Sources 1999." The work begins with a long essay providing an overview of the nature and history of violence in America. There are approximately thirty major essays ranging from 5,000 to 12,000 words in length that provide surveys of other far-reaching topics such as drugs, endocrinology, film, gun violence, literature, police, prisons, schools, television, theories of violence, war, weapons, and women. Roughly 200 shorter essays, ranging from 1,000 to 5,000 words in length, cover a wide range of topics, including hunting, the Ku Klux Klan, the My Lai Massacre, pornography, professional wrestling, and psychological violence. Shorter entries range from 500 to 1,000 words in length and cover topics as diverse as Pearl Harbor, the Pullman Strike, road rage, tarring and feathering, and the zoot-suit riot. The first volume includes a chronology of significant events, from riots to executions. Following the overview, volume 1 contains entries ranging from abolition to the Fugitive Slave Act. Volume 2 covers entries from John Wayne Gacy to the Pullman strike. Volume 3 picks up with the Quakers, ending with an entry on the zoot suit riot. This volume also includes a listing of organizations, publications, and Internet resources. Extensive cross-references and detailed indexing assure access to articles. The set is distinguished by excellent layout and design and the inclusion of interesting and illustrative sidebars. This is a set that will be found in many high school, public, and academic libraries.

H-23 Hawes, Joseph M., and Elizabeth F. Shores, eds. **The Family in America: An Encyclopedia**. 2 vols. Santa Barbara, CA: ABC-Clio, in press.

This encyclopedia is scheduled for release in summer 2002. It is one of six titles that will make up ABC-Clio's The American Family series. This encyclopedic series is being marketed as a comprehensive reference work for general readers, students, professionals, and scholars. The goal of the series is to provide multiple perspectives on the history and current state of the American family. Consequently, contributors have been recruited from a range of disciplines: sociology, psychology, health, anthropology, and history. Each title in the series has its own advisory board comprising distinguished researchers. The publisher promises that each title will be generously illustrated and amply indexed, with references for further reading. ABC-Clio also claims that the entries will be cogent, free of jargon, and unbiased, and that the volumes will offer a fresh approach to issues relating to the family. The publisher plans to make the series available on the World Wide Web following completion of the print series. This set is obviously aimed at high school, public, and academic libraries because it is described as a work between a how-to book and a specialized, scholarly text.

H-24 Kausler, Donald H., and Barry C. Kausler. **The Graying of America: An Encyclopedia of Aging, Health, Mind, and Behavior**. 2d ed. Urbana: University of Illinois Press, 2001.

This single-volume encyclopedia covers many dimensions of aging. There are almost 500 entries covering topics as diverse as age-associated memory impairment, the Alzheimer's Disease Support Center, creativity, falls, friendships, hip replacement, Medicaid, the nun study, and retirement planning. The scope includes the impact of aging on mental processes, diseases associated with aging, exercise and health, stress and coping, social relationships in later life, research findings, and organizations and services for the elderly. The second edition has been expanded to include more than 150 new entries. Many of the new articles cover new concerns among the elderly such as strain as a result of computer use. This encyclopedia has been designed for the nonspecialist and lay reader. This highly readable volume is a useful addition to any library collection needing basic and practical information on the biological, physical, and social aspects of aging.

H-25 Levinson, David, ed. **Encyclopedia of Marriage and the Family**. 2 vols. New York: Macmillan, 1995.

This encyclopedia summarizes research on topics relating to the family through more than 160 articulate essays on issues across the lifespan, from child care to grandparenthood. The scope is multidisciplinary, with articles on topics as varied as bankruptcy, eating disorders, family stories and myths, infertility, religion, and retirement. There are many eminent contributors, including leading family scholars, sociologists, psychologists, anthropologists, lawyers, and researchers from other disciplines. Entries include numerous cross-references and extensive bibliographies. The organization of the set is enhanced by a detailed subject index and functional layout. In addition, the layout is attractive and the binding is sturdy. The latter quality is important because this set receives heavy use in high school, public, and academic libraries. Special libraries serving practitioners working with families have also purchased this set.

H-26 Nash, Kate, and Alan Scott. **The Blackwell Companion to Political Sociology**. (Blackwell Companions to Sociology). Malden, MA: Blackwell, 2001.

This is one of several titles in the Blackwell Companions to Sociology series, designed for upper level undergraduate students, graduate students, and scholars. Other forthcoming titles in this series include *The Blackwell Companion to Organizations* (to be released in November 2002) and the *Blackwell Companion to the Sociology of the Family* and *The Blackwell Companion to Criminology* (both scheduled for publication in 2003). Information provided by the publisher indicates that this volume is a collection of thirty-eight essays in the subfield of political sociology.

The editors are eminently qualified, either having authored or edited other works in this interdisciplinary field of sociology. Nash and Scott provide a general introduction to the specialization of political sociology. Subsequent articles are grouped into four broad themes: "approaches to power and the political," "the state and governance," "the political and the social," and "political transformations". The result is a collection of essays on topics ranging from "developments in Marxist theory" to "gender and the state." Each chapter includes an abstract and reading list, features that make the volume especially useful to students. A detailed index leads users to concepts within essays.

H-27 Ness, Immanuel, and James Ciment. **The Encyclopedia of Global Population and Demographics**. 2 vols. Armonk, NY: Sharpe Reference/M. E. Sharpe, 1999.

Almost two decades have passed since the publication of the *International Encyclopedia of Population* (Free Press, 1982), John Ross's landmark encyclopedia that became a core work in demography. Ness and Ciment have filled a gap with this set that includes essays on ten broad topics in demography (such as migration, cultural identity, and the demography of health care and education) as well as population and demographic data for 194 countries. There is a companion CD-ROM. The essays complement the tabular data, outlining facts behind these statistics and demographic trends. Undergraduates and nonspecialists in particular will find the essays immensely readable and interesting. The tabular data make up two-thirds of the volume and all of the second volume. Data were gathered from reliable sources such as publications produced by the World Bank, the International Labour Organization, the Central Intelligence Agency, and agencies of the United Nations.

Data are presented for three time periods: 1965, 1980, and 1995, allowing users to discern important patterns or trends. Basic demographic data ranging from vital statistics to health indicators are presented for regions of the world and individual nations. An interesting feature is the inclusion of a chronology of important events for each country profiled. This well-designed compendium of global demographic data will be helpful to public and academic library users.

H-28 Roberts, Pamela, and Tracy Irons-Georges, eds. **Aging**. 2 vols. Pasadena, CA: Salem Press, 2000.

This encyclopedia treats the topic of aging from many perspectives. Aging has been defined to include the lifespan from middle age to old age. The 300 plus entries cover the biological, medical, social, cultural, financial, legal, legislative, and employment aspects of aging. Among the topics covered are age discrimination, cataracts, dual-income couples, durable power of attorney, elder abuse, hospice, life insurance, living wills, midlife crisis, nursing and convalescent homes, vacations and travel, volunteering, and wrinkles. There are also articles on programs, organizations, and people.

In addition, there are essays on the image of aging in books, plays, films, advertising, television programming, and other media. The alphabetically arranged essays range in length from 300 to 4,000 words. Longer entries (articles that are at least 1,500 words in length) conclude with a bibliography. Approximately 200 illustrations round out the set. The second volume includes several unique appendixes: a bibliography of nonfiction books (arranged by subject); a mediagraphy listing fictional works, plays, films, television shows, and even songs; a listing of resources relating to aging, including organizations and programs; and a listing of individuals who have studied aging as well as notable elderly individuals. A detailed index provides access to ideas, names, events, and organizations. This set will be useful to general readers, students enrolled in a range of courses, and professionals in the field of gerontology.

H-29 Shumsky, Neil Larry, ed. **Encyclopedia of Urban America: The Cities and Suburbs**. 2 vols. Santa Barbara, CA: ABC-Clio, 1998.

This set was selected as one of 1999's "Outstanding Reference Sources" by the Reference and User Services Association's (a division of the American Library Association) Reference Sources Committee. It complements ABC-Clio's 1997 encyclopedia on nonmetropolitan areas, the *Encyclopedia of Rural America*. The 574 entries are the work of more than 300 contributors from a range of disciplines: history, sociology, criminology, geography, political science, economics, urban planning, literature, American studies, and art and architecture. The result is a rich compendium that includes entries as diverse as ballparks, Tom Bradley, Charlie Chaplin, Chrysler Building, density, greenbelt towns, homelessness, Edward Hopper, Judaism, Jack Kerouac, Sinclair Lewis, Los Angeles, municipal bonds, organized crime, parades, prohibition, retirement communities, supermarkets, traffic, urban flora, violence, War on Poverty, and zoos.

Individual entries include cross-references and references for further reading, and an extensive bibliography (arranged by broad subject categories) can be found in volume 2. The second volume also contains lists of entries by subject as well as a thorough and comprehensive index. This major encyclopedia will be found in many large public and academic libraries.

H-30 Turner, Bryan S., ed. **The Blackwell Companion to Social Theory**. 2d ed. Malden, MA: Blackwell, 2000.

The editor, a professor of sociology at Cambridge University, is a renowned scholar in the area of sociological theory. This volume is an updated and expanded version of the well-received first edition. In particular, four new chapters address areas that were overlooked in the original: the foundations of social theory; anthropology; phenomenology; and the sociology of the body. There is also increased coverage of feminist topics. Although the first chapter presents an overview of the historical origins and foundations of social theory, the *Companion* focuses on contemporary approaches to social thought. The volume is organized by themes rather than by theorists. Access to concepts and the ideas of individual theorists are augmented through the detailed index. The *Companion* has been designed for upper level undergraduates, graduate students, and scholars.

HANDBOOKS

Handbooks are designed for graduate students, practitioners, and researchers. They are used for a quick consultation to find basic information about a field or to locate statistics, rules, and other factual information.

H-31 Bouma, Gary D., and G. B. Atkinson. **A Handbook of Social Science Research: A Comprehensive and Practical Guide for Students**. 2d ed. New York: Oxford University Press, 1995.

This handbook is written for social science students with little or no previous experience with social science research methods. It provides a general introduction to research methods, with well-placed examples. The book takes a nonstatistical, nonmathematical approach and presents the research process in an understandable manner. The handbook divides the research process into three phases. The first phase deals with selecting a problem and formalizing it as a research objective. This includes choosing and defining relevant variables, deciding on a research design, and organizing a sample. The second phase is concerned with data collection, and the third phase involves the analysis and interpretation of data. This volume is very useful to the general reader and offers a wealth of practical advice.

H-32 Chafetz, Janet Saltzman. **Handbook of the Sociology of Gender**. (Handbooks of Sociology and Social Research). New York: Kluwer Academic/Plenum, 1999.

This is part of the Handbooks of Sociology and Social Research series, started by the publisher in 1999. Chafetz is well-established in the sociology of gender field, having authored several books on gender equity. Several experts in the sociology of gender have contributed to the volume. More than twenty chapters address all aspects of gender analysis in sociology, including historical analysis; cross-cultural investigations; and studies of gender differences along cohorts such as age, race, and ethnicity. Among the topics covered are gender theories, gender and religion, the feminization of poverty, gender and criminal justice, race and gender in the workplace, international immigration, health care, education, gender and science, political involvement, and gender and the military. Essays conclude with substantive bibliographies. Chafetz's concluding chapter nicely summarizes the last three decades of research relating to gender sociology. A thorough index enhances the work's usefulness. This handbook will be in demand by all academic libraries supporting coursework in gender studies.

H-33 Denzen, Norman K., and Yvonna S. Lincoln, eds. **The Handbook of Qualitative Research**. 2d ed. Thousand Oaks, CA: Sage, 2000.

This is an invaluable handbook aimed at graduate students interested in qualitative research, faculty who wish to become better informed, and faculty who are expert researchers but want to be informed about the latest developments in the field of qualitative research methodology. This source represents a distillation of knowledge within the field of qualitative research. It has been used as a text in both undergraduate and graduate research methodology courses. Part I of the volume gives a history of the field of qualitative research, looks at research traditions, and discusses the politics and ethics of field research. Part II looks at the major historical and contemporary paradigms that have influenced and shaped qualitative research. Part III examines the methods that researchers can make use of in actual studies. It looks at the history and uses of specific methods. Part IV is concerned with collecting and analyzing qualitative data; Part V deals with interpreting qualitative data and discusses methods of evaluating the quality of data; Part VI takes a look at the future of qualitative research. The volume contains forty-one essays with extensive reference lists as well as a thorough subject index.

H-34 Dunlap, Riley E., and William M. Michelson, eds. **Handbook of Environmental Sociology**. Westport, CT: Greenwood Press, 2002.

Environmental sociology, the study of the social aspects of environmentalism, emerged as a unique specialty more than twenty-five years ago. In 1976, the American Sociological Association created a section for this field. This volume introduces readers to this discipline, providing background information and summarizing research findings on important topics such as the environmental movement, design of the built environment, natural and technological hazards and disasters, impact assessment, and rural environments. This handbook will also be important for students and scholars in related academic fields, especially urban and regional planning, social ecology, and environmental studies.

H-35 Fritz, Jan M. **The Clinical Sociology Handbook**. New York: Garland, 1985.

Clinical sociology broadly refers to the application of sociology to solve social problems. The field was defined in a seminal article dating from 1931. Fritz has documented the subsequent literature for the period 1931 to 1981. Journal articles, books, dissertations, and unpublished papers are annotated. Other chapters present information about professional associations, ethical standards, and education and training. This sourcebook is directed to graduate students and professionals.

H-36 Hawes, Joseph M., and Elizabeth I. Nybakken, eds. **American Families: A Research Guide and Historical Handbook**. Westport, CT: Greenwood Press, 1991.

This handbook serves as a guide to the field of American family history. Although nineteenth-century studies of the family exist, family history is a relatively new academic discipline. Eleven chapters synthesize the literature on the discipline itself, the range of methodologies employed by scholars, the family during specific historical periods (e.g., pre-industrial times, the Great Depression, World War II), and special topics in family history (specifically women and families, African-American families, Native American families, and immigrant working class families). These well-written and engaging bibliographic essays will help students enrolled in sociology, history, or women's studies courses where family history or social history is an important component.

H-37 Herron, Nancy L., and Diane Zabel, eds. **Bridging the Gap: Examining Polarity in America**. Englewood, CO: Libraries Unlimited, 1995.

This handbook brings together twelve bibliographic essays synthesizing the literature on contemporary social problems that are polarizing America. These issues are driving a wedge between generations, sexes, races, and ethnic groups. The social problems examined include media and popular culture; public policy and the government; law and the justice system; poverty, welfare, and unemployment; child care and elder care; hunger and nutrition; homelessness; children and learning; adults and literacy; substance abuse; the health care system; and the changing American family.

Chapters also outline strategies for locating additional information, such as useful Library of Congress subject headings; listings of indexes and databases; and, in some cases, specific periodicals, monographs, and nonprint materials. Listings of selected federal legislation and court cases are also included when relevant. This descriptive rather than prescriptive work can be used as a handbook for social workers, child care specialists, gerontologists, educators, and policy makers. It could also serve as a supplementary text for courses involving the study of contemporary social issues. It is an essential addition to all academic library collections and should also be considered for public and high school libraries.

H-38 Mohan, Raj P., and Arthur S. Wilke, eds. **International Handbook of Contemporary Developments in Sociology**. Westport, CT: Greenwood Press, 1994.

This handbook provides readers with an overview of major trends and literature dealing with sociology in various nations around the world. It is limited to developments in the field of sociology from roughly the mid-1970s through the early 1990s. The organization of the text is by continent, with each surveyed nation covered in a separate chapter (e.g., "Current Status of Sociology in Spain"). Each chapter includes a bibliography and an extensive list of references. The handbook is aimed at practicing sociologists and gives a snapshot of the work being conducted by sociologists of varying nationalities. This is a valuable source because most of the reference literature focuses on the work of sociologists in the United States.

H-39 Quah, Stella R., and Arnaud Sales, eds. **The International Handbook of Sociology**. London: Sage, 2000.

This handbook is the collaborative effort of more than twenty sociologists who are experts in their respective fields as well as leaders within the International Sociological Association. Each chapter summarizes the work of Western and non-Western sociologists on specific topics, grouped into six themes: conceptual perspectives; social and cultural differentiation; changing institutions and collective action; demography, cities, and housing; art and leisure; and social problems. This is an important handbook that brings together diverse schools of thought on specialized fields of sociology, including emerging areas such as the sociology of tourism, the sociology of art, and sociotechnics.

H-40 Padilla, Feçlix, ed. **Handbook of Hispanic Cultures in the United States: Sociology**. Houston, TX: Arte Publico Press, 1994.

This volume is part of a four-volume set on Latino culture in the United States. The remaining volumes cover history, literature and art, and anthropology. This work begins with an introductory essay on the sociology of Hispanic people. The signed essays that follow are very broad in scope. There are essays on religion, migration, education, politics, employment, marriage and the family, the role of women, and mass communication. Chapters range from "Cuban Women in the United States" to "Latinos in American Politics." Scholars of Hispanic origin wrote many of the essays. Each chapter concludes with a substantial bibliography listing both English- and Spanish-language materials. The publication of this set was significant because it was the first comprehensive work on Hispanic culture in the United States. Many academic libraries acquired it, and it was also purchased by some public libraries serving Latino communities.

H-41   Rea, Louis M., and Richard A. Parker. **Designing and Conducting Survey Research: A Comprehensive Guide**. 2d ed. San Francisco: Jossey-Bass, 1997.

Academic libraries should consider purchasing multiple copies of this handbook, based on our experience that this concise and clearly written book on the sample survey process is almost continuously checked out. In 250 pages, Rea and Parker do an excellent job of leading users through the process of designing, conducting, and analyzing sample survey research. The second edition incorporates much more information on statistical analysis. In addition, the practical examples and exercises have been expanded to include a larger range of subjects, making this handbook pertinent to students in various social and behavioral science disciplines. A new chapter covers the focus group process in detail. In addition to being an exceptional resource for students in a range of courses, this guide will be useful to many practitioners (e.g., sociologists, psychologists, urban planners, municipal managers, and political scientists) involved in data collection activities.

H-42   Rebach, Howard M., and John G. Bruhn, eds. **Handbook of Clinical Sociology**. 2d ed. New York: Kluwer Academic/Plenum, 2001.

The first edition of this work was published a decade previously. Although this handbook has been primarily designed for practitioners working with individuals, groups, and communities, it will also help inform students about the subfield of clinical sociology. The book is organized into four sections. Part 1 provides background information on the development and history of clinical sociology. Part 2 examines levels of intervention, including working with individuals, working in communities, and interventions in organizations such as public schools. Part 3 focuses on tools used by practitioners, ranging from mediation to preventive programming. Part 4 discusses how clinical sociologists approach specific social problems (e.g., health care equity, poverty, violence, domestic violence, and racism). The final section includes insights contributed by three clinical sociologists. This section is particularly interesting because there are few academic programs in clinical sociology, and consequently no single career path to the profession.

H-43   Rossi, Peter H., James D. Wright, and Andy B. Anderson, eds. **Handbook of Survey Research**. New York: Academic Press, 1983.

Survey research is common in sociology and other social sciences such as political science, psychology, education, and marketing. Although this title was published almost two decades ago, it still serves as a comprehensive handbook on survey design and analysis. Many advanced students and researchers in the applied social sciences still consider it a classic work. Although the chapter on computers in survey research is obviously dated, the chapters on sampling theory, measurement theory, applied sampling, questionnaire construction, response effects, data collection, mail and self-administered questionnaires, missing data, statistical tools for analyzing data, causal modeling, and trend studies are timeless. In fact, more than one copy of this standard handbook is still needed in many academic libraries, given the heavy demand for both theoretical and practical information on the methodology of sample survey research.

H-44   Smelser, Neil J., ed. **Handbook of Sociology**. Newbury Park, CA: Sage, 1988.

This was the first general handbook of sociology to be published in more than twenty years. Previous to this, the last general handbook, *Handbook of Modern Sociology*, edited by Robert E. Lee Faris (Rand McNally), was published in 1964. The twenty-two chapters of Smelser's handbook of contemporary sociology are organized under four broad sections: theoretical and methodological issues, bases of inequality in society, major institutional and organizational settings, and social process and change. Most subfields of sociology are covered except for social psychology and sociology of the economy. There are articles on classic areas in sociology such as quantitative methodology, race and ethnicity, social movements, deviance and control, and family sociology. Other articles address comparatively new subfields such as the sociology of science and the sociology of age. Each chapter has been written by a prominent authority and concludes with a lengthy bibliography. This comprehensive handbook has been designed for graduate students, faculty, and researchers. It remains an essential reference work.

H-45 Smelser, Neil J., and Richard Swedberg, eds. **The Handbook of Economic Sociology**. Princeton, NJ; New York: Princeton University Press, Sage Foundation, 1994.

This handbook has been designed for upper level undergraduate and graduate students, researchers, and scholars in the fields of economic sociology, economics, economic history, and economic anthropology. The first chapter introduces readers to the field of economic sociology, moving from its foundations as found in the works of Weber and Durkheim to more recent developments. Thirty essays follow, organized in three parts. Part I covers the topic generally, from multiple perspectives. Essays in part II focus on economic systems, economic institutions, and economic behaviors. The third part draws together diverse research, focusing on the intersection between economics and other topics, including education, religion, politics, leisure, gender, ethnicity, and the environment. Access to essays is enhanced through the detailed name and subject indexes.

H-46 Sussman, Marvin B., Suzanne K. Steinmetz, and G. W. Peterson. **Handbook of Marriage and the Family**. 2d ed. New York: Plenum, 1999.

The first edition of this handbook (edited by Sussman and Steinmetz) was published in 1987 and quickly became the bible for graduate students and scholars in the marriage and family field. In fact, this handbook has an illustrious history. The 1987 edition updated one of the field's classic reference works, Harold Christensen's *Handbook of Marriage and the Family* (Rand McNally, 1964). This edition differs substantially from the 1987 edition. The editorial team has been expanded to include Gary W. Peterson, and there is increased coverage of family therapy and mediation, in part because one of the other editors (Suzanne Steinmetz) recently obtained a master's degree in social work and certification in civil and family mediation.

New topics were added to the second edition as a result of new authors and growing interest and research in topics such as family communication, adolescence, and health. Family scholars, sociologists, social workers, psychologists, demographers, historians, and researchers in communication, economics, political science, medicine, and anthropology have contributed almost thirty articles. Among the topics covered are comparative perspectives on the family, the future of families, postmodernism and family theory, marital dissolution, qualitative family research, family relations in adulthood, families and work, family abuse and violence, marital and family therapy, human sexuality, and strengthening twenty-first-century families. The second edition of this important interdisciplinary handbook belongs on the shelves of all academic libraries and special libraries serving professionals in the field of marriage and family life.

REVIEWS OF RESEARCH

Reviews of research synthesize the literature in a discipline or subfields of a discipline. Although only the most important review publications in sociology are described in this section, topical reviews can be found in a number of publications. Some examples of specialized review publications are the *Annual Review of Gerontology and Geriatrics, Comparative Social Research, Current Perspectives in Social Theory, Research in Social Problems and Public Policy, Research in Social Stratification and Mobility, Research in the Sociology of Health Care*, and *Research in Race and Ethnic Relations*.

H-47 **Annual Review of Sociology**. Palo Alto, CA: Annual Reviews, 1975- . Annual.

In this publication, scholars critically review important research in the discipline. Topics vary from year to year, making this an excellent source for identifying current topics in the field. Recent essays have covered cohabitation, welfare reform, part-time and temporary employment, the relationship between ethnicity and sexuality, and the death penalty debate. Sociologists as well as other social scientists contribute essays, a reflection of the increasingly interdisciplinary nature of sociological research. This is a core journal in sociology.

Electronic access: The *JSTOR* database provides the full text of articles from this important journal for the period 1974 through 1994. See also H-43.

H-48 **Annual Review of Sociology Online**. n.d. Annual. Online format. URL: http://www.annualreviews.org/.

The Web version of this journal allows subscribers to browse the table of contents, search abstracts, and retrieve the full text of articles for given time periods. Abstracts and full text are searchable for the past five years only, but users may view tables of contents for the period 1984 to the present. Subscribers can also preview the content of forthcoming editions. One unique feature is the ability to view both the most frequently read and the most frequently cited articles.

INDEXES, ABSTRACTS, AND DATABASES

Sociology has many specialized print and electronic indexes. Basic indexes for general sociology and the major subfields of sociology are listed in this section. Sociological literature may also be found using databases from other disciplines: *PsycINFO* (J-75), *ERIC* (I-68), *EconLit* (C-28), *Anthropological Literature* (G-46 through G-48), *America: History and Life* (E-17), and *Historical Abstracts* (E-21). In addition, sociological literature can be found in the following multidisciplinary databases: *Social Sciences Abstracts* (H-50), *Web of Science*, *Dissertation Abstracts*, and *PAIS*.

H-49 **Sociological Abstracts**. Bethesda, MD: CSA, 1969- . Monthly. Online format.

Sociological Abstracts is the premier bibliographic database in the field of sociology. This international database begins coverage in 1963 and has a Web interface. Core journals in sociology are fully abstracted. Journals in related fields (e.g., anthropology, economics, education, statistics, political science) are selectively abstracted. Although abstracts are not evaluative, they provide substantial descriptions of articles. *Sociological Abstracts* is global in scope, abstracting articles without regard to their language of publication. All areas of sociology are represented. Subject coverage is broad, ranging from addictive compulsive behaviors to feminist/gender studies.

H-50 **Social Sciences Abstracts**. New York: H. W. Wilson, 1983- . Weekly. Online format.

Social Sciences Abstracts indexes core English-language periodicals in a wide range of social science disciplines, including sociology, political science, anthropology, geography, economics, and law. The database covers the period 1983 to the present. This Web-based database is an excellent starting point for undergraduate students and for students researching interdisciplinary topics.

H-51 **Criminal Justice Abstracts**. Monsey, NY: Willow Tree Press, 1968- . Quarterly.

This quarterly index is published in cooperation with the Criminal Justice Collection of Rutgers University Libraries. Each issue indexes and abstracts journal articles and books relating to courts and the legal process, policing, crime (both from the perspective of the offender and the victim), adult corrections, juvenile justice, delinquency, crime prevention, and crime control. The scope is international. Subject and geographical indexes are provided. This is a good source for students needing scholarly literature on criminology, corrections, criminal law, crime prevention, policing, and prison administration.

Electronic access: Electronic counterparts (both in CD-ROM and Internet format) are provided through Silver Platter.

NCJRS Web Site. URL: http://www.ncjrs.org/. (See F-111)

NCJRS is a national clearinghouse for information about criminal justice and law enforcement. It sponsors the *NCJRS Abstracts Database*, which contains abstracts of more than 160,000 criminal justice publications, including research reports, government publications, journal articles, books, and unpublished materials. It may be searched free of charge via the NCJRS Web site. Users can search by key words and link to full text if it is available. Print copies of many of the publications listed can be obtained for a nominal fee. In addition, contact information is provided for commercially produced information. This database is an excellent source for students, practitioners, and researchers needing information on topics relating to law enforcement, corrections, juvenile justice, delinquency prevention, drugs and crime, victims of crime, and the role of the courts in criminal justice. There is one caveat: Because NCJRS serves as a clearinghouse, publications are not refereed and information can range from scholarly articles to product announcements.

H-52 **Popline**. Baltimore, MD: National Information Services Corporation, 1970- . Monthly. Online format.

This is the premier database in population studies. It indexes and abstracts the scholarly literature in population studies and related topics including fertility, family planning, contraceptive methods, demography, population law, AIDS and other sexually transmitted diseases, maternal and child health, population and the environment, and population policy. It provides citations to journal articles, books, technical reports, and unpublished materials. The database covers the period 1970 to present and is updated monthly. It has a Web interface.

BIBLIOGRAPHIES

There are several bibliographic series in sociology. Many of these produce titles that are particularly useful for undergraduate researchers.

H-53 **Bibliographies and Indexes in Sociology**. Westport, CT: Greenwood Press, 1985- .

More than twenty titles have been published since this series began in the mid-1980s. Recent titles in this bibliographic series include *Work-Family Research: An Annotated Bibliography* (1997) and *Pro-Choice/Pro-Life Issues in the 1990s* (1996). This series has been designed for undergraduate and graduate students, researchers, and practitioners.

H-54 **Contemporary Social Issues**. Santa Cruz, CA: Reference and Research Services, 1986- .

This inexpensive series of bibliographies on current social problems is popular with undergraduate students. Bibliographies in this series assemble and categorize the popular, technical, and scholarly literature on a topic that has been published in books, pamphlets, journal articles, and government documents. Titles in this series also provide a listing of dictionaries, bibliographies, organizations, and periodicals on the topic. Among topics covered in this series are AIDS, animal rights, biotechnology, comparable worth, domestic violence, eating disorders, the feminization of poverty, food pollution, gay and lesbian families, the greenhouse effect, homelessness, labor abuses against women and children in the global economy, multiculturalism on campus, pornography and censorship, rape, reproductive rights, substance abuse, toxic waste, racism in the criminal justice system, and gender issues such as women and cyberspace. Many college and university libraries have placed a standing order for this series, which issues four bibliographies a year. Public libraries and high school libraries will want to selectively acquire titles in this series.

H-55 Contemporary World Issues. Santa Barbara, CA: ABC-Clio, 1988- .

This well-regarded series presents well-organized overviews on hot topics relating to society, health, education, and the environment. Some recent titles in the series are *Tobacco* (2001), *Privacy Rights* (2001), *World Population* (2001), *Work and Family in America* (2001), *Police Misconduct in America* (2001), *Nuclear Power* (2000), *Pornography in America* (2000), *Genetic Engineering* (1999), *Hate Crimes* (1999), *Affirmative Action* (1999), and *Prisons in America* (1999). All of the titles in the series share some similarity in format. They include well-written essays; chronologies; biographies; statistical data; annotated bibliographies; a listing of nonprint and Internet resources; and directories of relevant organizations, glossaries, and accurate and thorough indexes. Many of the titles in this series have been not only reference best-sellers but also award winners. This is an essential resource for high school, public, and academic libraries.

H-56 International Bibliography of Sociology. London: Routledge, 1951- . Annual.

Routledge publishes this work on behalf of the British Library of Political and Economic Science at the London School of Economics. It is a volume in the *International Bibliography of the Social Sciences*. Other volumes relate to economics, political science, and anthropology. *International Bibliography of Sociology* indexes the scholarly literature produced internationally in sociology, social psychology, and demography in a given year. Some publications missed in previous volumes are also listed. English- and foreign-language journal articles and books are included. Textbooks, popular magazine articles, newspaper articles, short articles, book reviews, and translations are excluded. Entries are organized under a classification scheme. Author, subject, and place-name indexes are provided. In the past, this series had a time lag of two to three years. Since the mid-1990s, this time lag has shortened, an important improvement because the purpose of this series is to provide bibliographic coverage of current literature.

Electronic access: Available through SilverPlatter's online versions (CD-ROM and Internet access) of the *International Bibliography of the Social Sciences*.

H-57 Opposing Viewpoints Series. San Diego, CA: Greenhaven Press, 1980- .

Titles in this outstanding series present contrasting views on important social issues. Recent titles have covered controversial issues such as abortion, addiction, euthanasia, gun control, health care, homosexuality, the death penalty, censorship, juvenile crime, race relations, the Internet, and the environment. Junior high and high school librarians have praised the series for its clarity, balance, insightful essays, and inclusion of useful supplementary material such as statistics and illustrations. Many public and academic libraries also acquire titles in the series. This series has long been regarded as an excellent resource for debates, papers, and other assignments requiring students to present both sides of an issue.

H-58 Social Theory: A Bibliographic Series. Santa Cruz, CA: Reference and Research Services, 1986- .

Undergraduate and graduate students in sociology, political science, anthropology, philosophy, and literature will value this bibliographic series on social theory. Although most of the titles in this series have focused on specific theorists (including Ernst Bloch, Georg Lukacs, Hannah Arendt, Herbert Marcuse, Jacques Derrida, Jacques Lacan, Jurgen Habermas, Max Weber, Michel Foucault, Simone de Beauvoir, Theodor Adorno, and Talcott Parsons), a few have looked at broader themes (e.g., deconstructionism, feminist theory, and women of color). Although the topics covered are complex, this series provides quick access to the major works by and about important social theorists. Some academic and large public libraries have a standing order for this inexpensive series.

H-59 **A World View of Social Issues**. Westport, CT: Greenwood Press, 2000- .
This new series published by Greenwood presents cross-cultural comparisons of social issues. *Crime and Crime Control* (2000) was the first title in the series. Other titles are *Child Abuse* (2000), *Teen Violence* (2001), *Women's Rights* (2001), *Domestic Violence* (2001), *Teenage Pregnancy* (2001), and *HIV and Aids* (2001). *Substance Abuse* is scheduled for publication in 2002. These resources will help high school and college students identify global differences and similarities and provide a broader view of how these social problems affect countries outside the United States. For example, *Crime and Crime Control* explores the problems of crime and crime control in fifteen countries, ranging from Iran to the United Kingdom.

BOOK REVIEWS

Book reviews are essential in sociology, given the publishing explosion in this area. Several databases can also be used to retrieve citations (and sometimes the full text) of reviews, notably *Sociological Abstracts* (H-49), *Social Sciences Abstracts* (H-50), and *ProQuest Direct*.

H-60 Clawson, Dan, ed. **Required Reading; Sociology's Most Influential Books**. Amherst: University of Massachusetts Press, 1998.
This work on sociology's most influential books published since 1972 began as a special issue of the journal *Contemporary Sociology*. That special issue was published in May 1996 to commemorate *Contemporary Sociology's* twenty-fifth anniversary. Because the issue generated much discussion and debate, Clawson (who had initiated the special issue) went forward with the idea of creating a longer list in monograph form. The result is a collection of essays on the impact that seventeen specific books have had in the field of sociology. Most of these books were originally reviewed in *Contemporary Sociology*, so there are excerpts from those reviews. Many of these books were also included in that 1996 special issue of *Contemporary Sociology*. Not only is *Required Reading* fascinating reading, it also can be a valuable training tool for librarians with liaison or selection responsibilities in sociology.

H-61 **Contemporary Sociology: A Journal of Reviews**. Washington, DC: American Sociological Association, 1972- . Bimonthly.
Predominantly English-language books in sociology and related disciplines are critically evaluated in this journal of reviews. Approximately fifty to sixty books are analyzed per issue in signed reviews of varying length. Important works are given more extensive treatment in feature review essays. Recently published books not reviewed in an issue are listed in a classified arrangement as publications received. *Contemporary Sociology* is indexed in *Book Review Index*. Librarians in medium-sized to large academic libraries will probably use this as a selection tool.
Electronic access: Full-text articles from this important journal are available through some databases such as *ProQuest Direct* and *JSTOR*.

DIRECTORIES

Sociology only has a handful of key directories. An increasing amount of directory information is being made available on the Internet.

H-62 **Directory of Departments of Sociology**. n.d. Irrregular. Online format. URL: http://www.asanet.org/pubs/dod.html.
This is an essential source of information on more than 2,000 departments of sociology. Information includes the name of the departmental chair, degrees or courses offered, and basic directory information, including e-mail address and URL for departmental home pages. This information is

provided free of charge. Members and nonmembers of the Association may obtain a hard copy for the minimal fee of $10 per copy.

H-63   **Directory of Members**. Washington, DC: American Sociological Association, 1950- . Annual.

This directory provides basic information for approximately 13,000 Association members. It can be used to find an individual's mailing address, office phone number, e-mail address, and section memberships. Data are taken from the Association's membership files. There is also a geographical listing of members.

H-64   **Guide to Graduate Departments of Sociology**. Washington, DC: American Sociological Association, 1965- . Annual.

This directory has been published for more than three decades. It lists over 250 graduate departments and is an essential source for anyone needing information on graduate programs in sociology in North American and abroad. It provides useful information such as tuition costs, student enrollment statistics, profiles of faculty members, number of degrees granted for the previous year, specialties, and listings of recent Ph.D.s awarded (including a listing of dissertation titles). Several indexes are provided, allowing users to easily compare various departments with particular programs.

H-65   **Opportunities for Research Support**. n.d. URL: http://www.asanet.org /student/oppresrc.html.

This Web site lists funding opportunities for sociologists. The name of a contact person, with complete directory information (including e-mail address and the URL for the organization's home page) is given for each foundation or organization listed. A description is provided (generally one or two paragraphs in length) of the research supported by each organization. Although this has not been designed as a comprehensive source of information about grant opportunities, the site directs users to sources of funding that are less widely known, such as the United States Institute of Peace and the Consortium of Social Science Associations.

BIOGRAPHICAL SOURCES

There is no biographical source that covers all of sociology. In addition to the following works, librarians will also have to use standard biographical sources to find information on sociologists.

H-66   Berger, Bennett M., ed. **Authors of Their Own Lives: Intellectual Autobiographies by Twenty American Sociologists**. Berkeley: University of California Press, 1990.

This is an interesting use of autobiography to trace in part the development of American sociology. Berger has assembled a collection of autobiographical essays by twenty prominent American sociologists. Many of the essays are very personal, including reminiscences about childhood and adolescence, not just the development of the subject's career and adult life. Among the sociologists contributing are David Riesman, Andrew Greeley, Nathan Glazer, Barbara Rosenbaum, Jessie Bernard, Pepper Schwartz, and Herbert Gans. This is a source that will be found in most college and university libraries supporting sociology and other social science curriculums.

H-67   Deegan, Mary Jo, ed. **Women in Sociology: A Bio-Bibliographical Sourcebook**. New York: Greenwood Press, 1991.

Deegan, a professor of sociology, has published widely on the history of sociology and on women in sociology. This interesting and valuable guide profiles fifty-one notable nineteenth- and twentieth-century women sociologists. The earliest woman included is Harriet Martineau, the nineteenth-century English writer who has been called "the first woman sociologist." The most contemporary woman included is Dorothy E. Smith, a prominent feminist theorist. Each profile includes a biographical sketch averaging three to four pages in length. A section discussing the major themes in the woman's work follows this. There is also a section outlining critiques and analyses of that work. A substantial bibliography rounds out each entry. Each bibliography contains a selective listing of an individual's publications and writings about her (including books, articles, dissertations, presented papers, archival materials, and other unpublished materials). Many of the women included in this volume extend beyond the field of sociology. For example, Alice Rossi co-founded the National Organization of Women. Consequently, this important reference work will be found on the shelves of many academic libraries and large public libraries.

H-68 McGuire, William, and Leslie Wheeler. **American Social Leaders**. Santa Barbara, CA: ABC-Clio, 1993.

Horatio Alger, Bruno Bettelheim, Helen Gurley Brown, and Marion Wright Edelman are among the 350 social reformers profiled in this exceptional biographical dictionary. The men and women represented in this single-volume sourcebook include leaders of reform movements, public intellectuals, journalists, photographers, cartoonists, publishers, inventors, and industrialists. The one-to two-page biographical sketches are readable and interesting. Some include a portrait, and all provide a brief bibliography. This reference work will be found in high school, public, and academic libraries.

Electronic access: In 1998, ABC-Clio released a CD-ROM version of this reference source.

H-69 Rappaport, Helen. **Encyclopedia of Women Social Reformers**. 2 vols. Santa Barbara, CA: ABC-Clio, 2001.

This encyclopedia was designated an "Outstanding Reference Source" for 2002 by the American Library Association's Reference and User Services Association. It is broad and international in scope, profiling women from around the world who have been influential in reform movements ranging from environmentalism to Third World human rights. Figures are both historical and contemporary; coverage is from the eighteenth century to the present. Many of the women are activists who have received no coverage in other biographical sources. This award-winning encyclopedia belongs on the shelves of high school, public, and academic libraries.

H-70 Ritzer, George, ed. **The Blackwell Companion to Major Social Theorists**. (Blackwell Companions to Sociology). Malden, MA: Blackwell, 2000.

This is a collection of essays on twenty-five leading social theorists. These thinkers include both classical and contemporary social theorists. The editor, a distinguished professor of sociology at the University of Maryland, is well known in the field of social theory, having published widely and having chaired the American Sociological Association's section on theoretical sociology. He has assembled an impressive list of contributors. Although the essays vary in style, there are similarities in terms of coverage. Among the classical theorists covered are Auguste Comte, Harriet Martineau, Karl Marx, Charlotte Perkins Gilman, and W .E. B. Du Bois. Some of the leading contemporary theorists included are Erving Goffman, Daniel Bell, Michael Foucault, Norbert Elias, and Judith Butler. This is an essential purchase for any academic library serving the social sciences as well as the humanities because many of these thinkers are covered in philosophy, religion, and history courses.

H-71 Slattery, Martin, ed. **Key Ideas in Sociology**. London: Fitzroy Dearborn, 2002.

This collection of essays on fifty leading nineteenth- and twentieth-century sociological thinkers is scheduled for publication in summer 2002. Information provided by Fitzroy Dearborn Publishers indicates that these articles will not only convey biographical information but will give readers a sense of the impact that these thinkers have had on the field. In addition, the essays will provide a history of the development of the discipline. Each article will include an annotated bibliography. There will also be a general bibliography.

STATISTICAL SOURCES

Sociologists rely heavily on secondary data—in particular, statistical data collected by government agencies. The U.S. government is the world's largest publisher. Government publications include census data, statistics, court opinions, congressional reports, patents, technical reports, and publications of government agencies. Some sociologists, especially demographers, use statistical publications issued by intergovernmental agencies, such as the World Bank, the World Health Organization, and the United Nations. Basic statistical compendia such as the *Statistical Abstract of the United States* (A-85), the *Statistical Yearbook* (B-165), and the *World Development Report* (C-62) will be useful to sociologists. The statistical compilations described in this section will also be valuable.

H-72 **American Men and Women: Demographics of the Sexes**. Ithaca, NY: New Strategist Publications, 2000.

This source describes American consumers, including their lifestyles, incomes, and attitudes. A wide range of variables associated with adults is examined. The strength of the book is that it brings together data from a variety of federal government sources and presents it in conjunction with attitudinal data from the General Social Survey (a widely used survey that has been administered for many years by the National Opinion Research Center in Ann Arbor, Michigan). This reference source differs from other compilations of data from federal sources in that the publisher went back to the original data to get summary statistics that would better illustrate certain trends. Each statistical table is accompanied by an explanation as well as an interpretation of what the data appear to indicate for the future. The publisher has included a list of contacts for additional information as well as a glossary and an index.

H-73 Chadwick, Bruce A., and Tim B. Heaton. **Statistical Handbook on the American Family**. 2d ed. Phoenix, AZ: Oryx Press, 1999.

This handbook brings together data from public domain national databases as well as two widely used surveys (the National Survey of Families and Households and the General Social Surveys). The handbook was designed to provide current information on a variety of variables related to the American family at the end of the twentieth century. There are 340 tables, charts, and illustrations documenting the substantial changes in some areas of family life over time, as well as areas of stability. A wide range of topics is covered, including quality of marriage and family life, divorce and separation, children, sexual attitudes and behaviors, living arrangements, working women, and child care arrangements.

H-74 **Data Resources for Sociologists**. n.d. URL: http://www.asanet.org/student /data.html.

This is a Web guide to publicly available datasets that are of particular interest to sociologists for primary and secondary data analysis. There is a description of each dataset, including information about content, access, and search and retrieval capability. Contact information is provided, including the name of a contact person, complete directory information for that individual, and the URL for the sponsoring organization's home page.

H-75 Exter, Thomas G. **Regional Markets: The Demographics of Growth and Decline: Volume 1: Population; Volume 2: Households**. Ithaca, NY: New Strategist Publications, 1999.

The author of this set of statistical resources looks at population change in the United States at regional, state, metropolitan, and county levels with projections to the year 2003. This source is a compilation of the kind of practical information needed by researchers with questions that have business implications. Areas with the fastest growth can be contrasted with areas that are the greatest population losers.

H-76   **Global Trends: The United Nations CyberSchoolBus**. n.d. Online format. URL: http://www.un.org/Pubs/CyberSchoolBus/special/globo/glotrend/index.html.

This is a wonderful source of global and regional information pertaining to population, health, food and agriculture, women, children, economic development, climate and environment, and social indicators. Information is portrayed graphically in the form of graphs and charts. The site allows users to download or print these graphs free of charge provided that they are being used as visual aids for educational purposes. This rich site allows users to find important data such as world population projections, charts relating to global hunger, estimated number of adult and children infected or living with HIV/AIDS, projected emissions of greenhouse gasses, and adult illiteracy rates.

H-77   Heaton, Tim B., Bruce A. Chadwick, and Cardell K. Jacobson. **Statistical Handbook on Racial Groups in the United States**. Phoenix, AZ: Oryx Press, 2000.

This handbook documents the similarities and differences between racial groups in the United States. The book's strength is that there are over 400 tables and figures that pull together information from providers of statistical information (such as the Bureau of the Census and the U.S. Department of Education) as well as data on attitudes and behavior from a variety of surveys (including the National Survey of Families and Households, the National Longitudinal Study of Adolescent Health, the National Survey of Family Growth, the General Social Survey, and the Gallup Poll Monthly). Sections cover demographic trends, education, economics, health, sexual issues, religion, crime, and political participation. Summary statistics describing attributes of members of groups are paired with attitudinal data. For example, data describing numbers of people employed and where they work are coupled with data on attitudes of people toward work and economic issues. This is an important reference source that aids in understanding the growing diversity of the U.S. population.

H-78   Kaul, Chandrika, and Valerie Tomaselli-Moschovitis. **Statistical Handbook on Poverty in the Developing World**. Phoenix, AZ: Oryx Press, 1999.

One-fourth of the world lives in poverty, according to a UN publication cited in this book. Poverty has far-reaching global implications. Although this volume examines poverty around the world, special emphasis is on poverty in developing nations, countries that the World Bank classifies as being low- and middle-income countries. The first part of this compilation presents key economic indicators for more than 190 countries. The remainder of the book presents data on developing countries, showing variations between these developing countries. Introductory comments before each section help users understand the data and the importance of each measurement. The sources of the data are clearly identified and originate from authoritative and reliable data producers such as the World Bank, the World Health Organization, and the Food and Agriculture Organization. There is a goldmine of data in this compendium. One can find data on people living below national poverty levels, population aged sixty and over, access to sanitation and clean water, access to health care, estimated AIDS cases, illiteracy rates, life expectancy of men compared with women, and the percentage of children in the labor force. This handbook will be useful to libraries serving high school, undergraduate, and graduate students.

H-79   Littman, Mark S., ed. **A Statistical Portrait of the United States: Social Conditions and Trends**. Lanham, MD: Bernan Press, 1998.

In his previous career, Littman was employed as a demographic statistician by the U.S. Bureau of the Census. He has almost thirty years of experience working with demographic data. His experience is reflected in this user-friendly and well-organized compendium of social and demographic data. Each of the chapters presents essays, graphs, charts, and trend data culled from a range of public and private sources on broad categories including population, living arrangements, education, health, housing, labor force participation, income, wealth, poverty, crime, and voting patterns. Of particular interest is the chapter covering leisure, volunteerism, and religiosity. The data depict changes over several decades. Chapters range in length from five to fifteen pages, all concluding with sources leading the user to additional information and a listing of Web sites. The visual presentation of the data is excellent, allowing for a quick overview and analysis of the information. Detailed tables in the appendix provide more in-depth data, such as tables showing U.S. threatened and endangered plants and animal groups for the period 1980–1995. This is a valuable compendium that will be an asset to all data collections.

H-80 Mitchell, Susan. **American Attitudes: Who Thinks What About the Issues That Shape Our Lives**. 3d ed. Ithaca, NY: New Strategist Publications, 2000.

New Strategist Publications' market niche is reference books on consumer demographics. Its publications are essential to librarians supporting marketing curricula as well as corporate and larger public libraries serving the business community. *American Attitudes* is a rich compendium of data on American attitudes and opinions. Marketers and other researchers can use it to find out what Americans think about work, sex, marriage, family, money, politics, government, and other subjects. Data are drawn from the General Social Survey, a well-known study conducted by the University of Chicago's National Opinion Research Center. The Survey conducts personal interviews with more than 1,000 English-speaking Americans. *American Attitudes* is a rich source of data on changing public opinion as well as the social and demographic factors behind shifts in opinion.

H-81 **Racial and Ethnic Diversity: Asians, Blacks, Hispanics, Native Americans, and Whites**. 3d ed. Ithaca, NY: New Strategist Publications, 2000.

Like other New Strategist publications, this is a rich source of information on consumer trends and consumer behavior. This particular title assembles and compares a range of data on whites, blacks, Hispanics, Asians, and Native Americans. Chapters analyze trends relating to education, health, housing, income, labor participation, living arrangements, population, spending, and wealth for each group. In addition to statistical data on these segments of the U.S. population, there is a chapter contrasting attitudes on a host of issues from immigration to affirmative action. Data are drawn from a range of federal government agencies as well as from particular sources such as the General Social Survey, a biennial survey coordinated by the University of Chicago's National Opinion Research Center. This compilation has far-reaching value beyond marketing. It will be useful to a range of students and researchers needing comparative social and economic data on racial and ethnic groups.

H-82 **Statistical Universe Database**. 1973- . Monthly. Online format.

This Web-based database indexes statistics and data found in documents published by federal governmental agencies. In essence, it duplicates the *American Statistics Index* (C-31). It also links to several hundred full-text documents published by federal agencies since 1994. There are also direct links to additional publications on individual federal agency Web sites. This database is regarded as the most comprehensive index to statistical data contained in federal government publications. Users needing a range of social and economic data can search summaries of federal statistical publications and then link to the full text of some of these publications via *Statistical Universe* (A-83) or its links to go evenues, crime data, data on federal government spending, and numerous demographics such as age, race, gender, educational attainment, income, marital status, and occupation. This database also indexes and abstracts statistical data contained in documents from state government agencies, private sources, and international organizations.

H-83 **U.S. Census Bureau Home Page**. Online format. URL: http://www. census.gov/.

The Census Bureau maintains a comprehensive and well-designed Web site that provides more than census data (which in itself is an important source for sociologists and social scientists). The site includes news reports, statistical reports on timely topics, and the latest economic indicators. The site has a detailed subject index and quick links to news about the most recent census data, population projections and estimates, housing data, poverty, statistics, and so forth. There is also a link to the Web version of the reference classic, the *Statistical Abstract of the United States* (A-85).

H-84 **The World Bank Group: Development Data**. Online format. URL: http:// www.worldbank.org/data/.

This Web site is the premier source of data on global development. It is a rich source of information on the world and its people. Data are drawn from a wide range of authoritative sources, including agencies such as the Food and Agricultural Organization, the International Labour Organization, the International Monetary Fund, the Organisation for Economic Co-operation and Development, the United Nations, the World Conservation Monitoring Centre, and the World Health Organization. Users can find country data for more than 200 nations and regions, data on development indicators ranging from life expectancy and mortality to land use and deforestation, and information on the development goals targeted by major international organizations. This site will be invaluable to anyone researching global issues relating to poverty, education, gender equality, mortality, access to health services, and sustainable development.

INTERNET RESOURCES

The discipline of sociology has strongly embraced the Internet as a dissemination tool. There are several excellent megasites that will lead users to some of the best Web resources.

H-85 **American Sociological Association**. URL: http://www.asanet.org.

This is the official Web site of the Association (ASA). Along with providing information for ASA members (such as information relating to upcoming conferences, recent publications, and calls for papers), it provides information for the public, defining sociology and providing information on careers in sociology. It is a rich source of information for students. The site includes a comprehensive directory of sociology departments, recent job postings, announcements of funding opportunities, and a listing of large-scale databases available for public use. This is an excellent source for undergraduates considering sociology as a major and for students pursuing graduate education in sociology.

H-86 **Inter-University Consortium for Political and Social Research**. URL: http://www.icpsr.umich.edu.

This is the official Web site of the Inter-university Consortium for Political and Social Research (ICPSR). ICPSR is a not-for-profit, membership-based organization that provides access to the world's largest archive of computerized social science data. In addition, ICPSR assists member colleges and universities by providing training in basic and advanced techniques in qualitative social analysis. This organization was founded in 1962 and serves more than 325 colleges and universities in North America. There are also several hundred members outside the United States and Canada. ICPSR has four general goals: to acquire social science data, to preserve the data, to provide open and equal access to the data, and to promote the effective use of social science data. Data relate to a wide range of social science disciplines: sociology, demography, political science, history, economics, criminal justice, public health, foreign policy, and law. This detailed Web site explains ICPSR's mission, provides information for members, and includes the searchable database of archived ICPSR data. There are also links to other data sites. This site is an essential source for all academic libraries with social science librarians.

H-87 **Social Sciences Information Gateway: Sociology**. URL: http://sosig .esrc.bris.ac.uk/sociology/.

The Social Sciences Information Gateway is a searchable Web site that describes and organizes thousands of Internet resources. There are categories for more than twenty disciplines, including sociology. The sociology guide is organized by subfield, allowing users to go to Internet resources relating to numerous categories, such as social movements, schools of thought, and sociology of the family. Users can also search the site by type of Internet resource (including collections of articles, papers and reports, data, educational materials, journals, mailing lists and discussion groups, organizations and societies, and research projects and centers). This site also provides good links to other megasites in sociology.

H-88 **The Socioweb: Your Independent Guide to Sociological Resources on the Internet**. URL: http://www.sonic.net/~markbl/socioweb/.

This extensive Web site, launched in 1995, links to other megasites in sociology, relevant commercial sites, sociological associations, sociology departments around the world, and news about upcoming conferences. Users can also join online discussions about issues in the field. One interesting feature is the section linking to Internet resources pertaining to key thinkers in sociology (e.g., Auguste Comte, George Herbert Mead, Marx, Lenin, Engels, Herbert Blumer, Paul Rosenfels, Robert K. Merton, and Emile Durkheim).

H-89 **WWW Virtual Library: Sociology**. URL: http://socserv2.mcmaster.ca /w3virtsoclib.

This site was established in 1995. This is the most thorough Internet resource in sociology, linking students, faculty, and researchers to associations, organizations, university departments, newsgroups, listservs, chat room discussions, research centers, electronic journals and newsletters, databases, curriculum resources, courses, and software. There is a sophisticated search engine and links to many other Internet sites of potential interest to sociology students and faculty, such as sites pertaining to demography and population studies, sustainable development, migration, and ethnic relations. This well designed and frequently updated Web site should be the starting point for all sociology students (undergraduate through graduate level) looking for Internet resources.

NOTES

1. Lee Braude, "The Emergence of Sociology," *Choice* 32, no.2 (October 1994): 237–248.

2. Lee Braude, "Promise Deferred: Sociology Since 1930," *Choice* 36, no 9 (February 1999): 999–1009.

3. Harry Gold, "Political Sociology: A Developing Field," *Choice* 27 (February 1900): 999–1099.

4. Neil J. Smelser, *Sociology* (Cambridge, MA: Blackwell, 1994), 14–15.

5. Leigh Estabrook, "Sociology and Library Research," *Library Trends* 32 (Spring 1984): 461–476.

6. Smelser, *Sociology*, 17.

7. David Bogart, ed., *The Bowker Annual*, 44th ed. (New Providence, NJ: R. R. Bowker, 1999), 508–509.

8. Herbert J. Gans, "Best-sellers by American Sociologists: An Exploratory Study," in Dan Clawson, ed., *Required Reading: Sociology's Most Influential Books* (Amherst: University of Massachusetts Press, 1998), 19–27.

9. Sharon Quist, "Book Reviews in Sociology," *The Reference Librarian* 15 (Fall 1986): 75–85.

10. Judith H. Fox, "*Choice* as a Book Selection Tool in Sociology: A Comparison with *Contemporary Sociology*," *Choice* 13, nos. 1–2 (1990): 35–152.

11. James C. Baughman, "A Structural Analysis of the Literature of Sociology," *Library Quarterly* 44 (October 1974): 293–308.

12. William A. Satariano, "Journal Use in Sociology: Citation Analysis vs. Readership Patterns," *Library Quarterly* 48 (July 1978): 293–300.

13. Beth J. Shapiro, "Sociology," in Patricia A. McClung, ed., *Selection of Library Materials in the Humanities, Social Sciences, and Sciences* (Chicago: American Library Association, 1985), 189.

14. Blaise Cronin, Herbert Snyder, and Helen Atkins, "Comparative Citation Rankings of Authors in Monographic and Journal Literature: A Study of Sociology," *Journal of Documentation* 53, no.3 (June 1997): 263–273.

Part 3

Those Disciplines with a Social Origin or That Have Acquired a Social Aspect

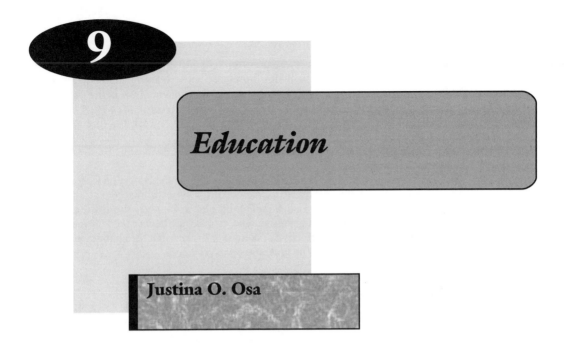

9

Education

Justina O. Osa

ESSAY

Nature of the Discipline

Education, broadly defined, involves the instruction and training by which people learn to use their physical, moral, and cognitive powers. It can also be described "as the deliberate, systematic and sustained effort to transmit, evoke, or acquire knowledge, attitudes, values, skills and sensibilities, and any learning that results from the effort, intended or unintended."[1] Although much of human learning occurs informally and even unconsciously, most societies have institutionalized some aspects of education. The discipline of education, as a profession and as a scholarly enterprise, is concerned primarily with formal human learning. In this light, Page and Thomas define education as the "process in which one achieves social competence and individual growth, carried on in a selected, controlled setting which can be institutionalized as a school or college."[2]

Each of the many participants involved in formalized education carries out different roles. Teachers used to practice the art and science of imparting "to each generation the organized knowledge of the past."[3] Today the passive acceptance of information that leads to knowledge is passé. Currently teachers are being called upon to go beyond the imparting of knowledge to package learning materials in such a way that students are stimulated to put their own personal stamp, as it were, on what they are learning. The voice of advocates of active, self-initiated learning is loud and clear. The theory of constructivism is gaining ground and is being applied to instructional activities.

Constructivism is a theory, based on research from cognitive psychology, that advocates that people learn by constructing their own knowledge through an active learning process, rather than by simply absorbing knowledge directly from another source.[4] Teachers are now being expected to assume the role of facilitator, coach, and guide in the teaching and learning process. In an effort to increase their knowledge, students make a serious study of subjects while actively constructing knowledge based on their individual personal context of prior knowledge, skills, dispositions, and feelings. Policy makers influence the conditions under which education occurs by being responsible for the authoritative educational decisions that guide other decisions.[5]

As a result of society demanding change and accountability in the educational arena, policy makers and leaders are faced with complex and multifaceted questions about educational policy making, finance, governance, and management. Scholars of education study the institutionalized process of education in its various settings. At the present time, scholars are being called upon to conduct research that will help devise creative and effective strategies to bring about the changes and reform that are desperately needed to create a fulfilling educational experience.

Education and the Social Sciences

Education comprises the formal and informal educational practices from infancy through adulthood, as well as all the knowledge from scholarly disciplines associated with education. A wide range of social science and humanities disciplines form the "foundations" of knowledge in education: psychology, sociology, history, philosophy, economics, anthropology, political science, and law.

Education is not, precisely speaking, a science but rather a profession that uses virtually all of the social science methods, concepts, and theories.[6] For this reason, educational research has a definite interdisciplinary flavor. For example, much research is done in the *history of education*. The *sociology of education* concentrates on education as a social enterprise, examining the behavior and processes of groups in social institutions. The *anthropology of education* studies educational functions within "primitive" societies and also applies anthropological methodologies such as ethnography to the study of education in modern settings.

Researchers in the *economics of education* study the production and utilization of resources in society, drawing on related concepts from business administration, political science, and management. *Educational policy* analysts study matters such as federal, state, and local influence on education; school and university governance; educational law; and other issues derived from the general area of political economy. As a final example, *educational psychology* studies individual students and teachers in educational settings, focusing on such aspects as human development, attitudes, values, learning theory, metacognition, and learning models.

Academic Subdisciplines of Education

Like most academic subjects, education is actually a loosely conjoined group of subspecialties. Although not all educational researchers would necessarily agree with the details of the discussion presented here, it is offered as one way to conceptualize the discipline of education. Another way to become familiar with educational specialties and methodological perspectives is to read relevant encyclopedia articles.[7]

Education As Rational Activity

The philosophy of education can be divided into two areas: *normative*, which is concerned with assessing educational aims and purposes, and *analytical*, which is concerned with explaining and clarifying basic educational terminology and concepts.[8] According to Watson, the philosophy of education tries to interpret the meaning of educational processes by showing its relationship to other human activities.[9] Philosophy of education specialists try to make educators aware of assumptions by asking questions such as, "Who should be educated?" "How should they be educated?" "To what extent does a particular educational system perpetrate injustice?" and "What is the proper way to teach ethical concepts?"[10] Philosophy of education also stimulates reflection on basic issues and concepts that are cardinal to education. Some of these include teaching, learning, knowledge, being educated, and the construct of the "good life." The major philosophies that have influenced education in America are realism, idealism, pragmatism, progressivism, perennialism, essentialism, and existentialism.

Educational research uses the same methods as researchers in the social, behavioral, biological, and physical sciences.[11] It is a systematic study of the field of education. The educational researcher uses many research methods and designs such as experimental, survey, historical, ethnographic, literary, and program evaluation. The literature of this academic area frequently addresses questions of validity and reliability.

Educational Specialties

Some educational practitioners and researchers specialize in a particular level of institutionalized education, roughly defined by age cohort. *Early childhood education* (birth to age eight) concentrates on the social, emotional, physical, and cognitive development of very young children. *Infant education* (birth to age three), a subset of early childhood education, has an added emphasis on parent/child relationships. These two fields draw heavily on the literatures of child psychology, developmental psychology, and human ecology (also known as family consumer sciences, child and family studies, or home economics).

Other level-based educational specialties include *elementary* (grades 1–8), *secondary* (grades 9–12), and *higher or postsecondary education*. Professional educators and scholars in all three areas can concentrate on different subspecialties, such as instruction and curriculum development; administration; program evaluation; educational psychology; educational technology; and bilingual, multicultural, or special education.

Educational inquiry also can center on nontraditional delivery systems—that is, institutionalized systems not necessarily associated with particular age cohorts. *Adult and continuing education*, sometimes referred to as "lifelong," "recurrent," or "informal" education, is an increasingly popular field. Education has become not just a period of formal schooling in students' lives but lifelong engagement. Many types of programs can be offered on a continuing education basis, such as literacy training, career development, vocational/technical training, equivalency education, professional development, and education for personal enhancement. *Distance education*, which includes independent study and correspondence or home study, is delivery of education for nontraditional students who are unable to attend in normal settings due to geographical isolation, job obligations, physical condition, or other limitations. Advances in new technologies now provide a broad range of technological options to those involved in distance education. Distance education increasingly uses such modern mass communication technology as interactive videoconferencing and electronic instructional audio tools, video tools, electronic data, computer-assisted instruction, computer-managed instruction, and computer-mediated education. Print materials are also used in distance learning. They include study guides, handouts, workbooks, textbooks, and course syllabi.

Management of Educational Systems

Educational administration "is concerned . . . with directing and managing human energy in order to accomplish educational objectives which have been formulated by governmental authority and expressed in written policies."[12] Most people in this field focus on the management or leadership of schools and school systems. Educational administrators often assume many roles in the discharge of their duties. They are leaders, managers, initiators, crisis managers, facilitators, coaches, guides, dispensers of rewards and punishments, mediators, judges, counselors, and comforters. For these activities they need to be well grounded in administrative theory and techniques, politics, school, school law, finance, personnel, psychology, human relations, and other related areas.

Teaching

Specialists in *curriculum and instruction* used to concentrate on the systematic transmission of information. The emphasis in teaching has moved away from a model of expert delivery of knowledge from the custodian of knowledge, the teacher, to the student, the empty glass coming to the class to be filled. Teaching has moved to a model in which the classroom becomes a community of learners. Those involved in curriculum and instruction analyze particular subjects—political science, economics, foreign language, science—to design developmentally appropriate instructional activities. *Educational media technologists* specialize in the creation of materials and procedures for individual students through the use of a variety of multimedia delivery systems, such as computer-assisted learning and interactive television. The marriage between teaching and technology is gaining increased attention as a current trend and issue in education. When one looks into the crystal ball that holds the future of technology in teaching, one finds that the image is clear in some places, cloudy in others, but surely a presence is observable. Many in the field of education would prefer that pedagogy drive the use of technology and that technology remain a tool to enhance teaching and learning.

Learning

Educational psychologists, interested in both cognitive and affective differences among individual students, design and administer tests that measure levels of achievement, aptitude, intelligence, and other personal characteristics. They also carry out research on the psychology of the learning process. The study of multiple intelligence is influencing the theory of how people learn. Howard Gardner, the father of multiple intelligence, asserts that there is not a single intelligence, but rather seven. His view is that multiple intelligences are seven different ways to demonstrate intellectual ability. The seven types of multiple intelligences are visual/spatial, verbal/linguistic, logical/mathematical, bodily/kinesthetic. musical/rhythmic, interpersonal, and intrapersonal.[13]

Guidance and counseling specialists use knowledge about normal human growth and development to help students solve personal problems or make career and educational choices. In recent years experts in the field have written extensively about redesigning school counseling programs into a comprehensive format. Integral to the Comprehensive School Counseling Model is the developmental approach. It is an attempt to identify certain life skills and experiences that students need to have as a part of going to school and preparing for adulthood. They learn more about themselves and others in advance of problem moments in their lives. The eight strands included in the Comprehensive Developmental Guidance Program (pre-K through 12) are (1) self-knowledge and acceptance, (2) interpersonal and communication skills, (3) responsible behavior, (4) conflict resolution, (5) decision making/problem solving, (6) motivation to achieve, (7) goal setting, and (8) career planning.[14]

Educational Occupations

Some educators concentrate on preparing students for particular occupations. *Professional pedagogies* (e.g., music education, art education, physical education) prepare students to teach in these areas. *Professional education* prepares students to be competent practitioners of specialized occupations such as medicine, nursing, or law. *Vocational, cooperative, or distributive education* is part of the secondary school curriculum designed to prepare students for those occupations that do not require a baccalaureate degree.[15] *Teacher education* transmits to future teachers the "body of knowledge and skills surrounding the processes of learning and teaching."[16] It also provides continuing educational training for practicing teachers and can be formal or informal courses, seminars, or workshops. The National Council for the Accreditation of Teacher Education (NCATE) monitors how effectively teacher education programs prepare students to teach. NCATE is the only national body charged with the responsibility for maintaining standards and ensuring accountability and continuous improvement in teacher preparation in all teacher education programs. NCATE develops standards and design strategies and processes to ensure and maintain quality in teacher preparation through the initial and continuing accreditation of teacher education professional units at all levels. The new NCATE standards are performance based and have moved from "know what" to "know how."

Special Cohorts

Other areas of educational practice and research focus on specific groups within society. "*Multicultural education* is an educational process or a strategy involving more than one culture, as defined by national, linguistic, ethnic, or racial criteria."[17] The aim of multicultural education is to recognize the integrity, contributions, strengths, and viability of people from different backgrounds, while helping students adjust to a modern pluralistic society.[18] The changing demographic characteristics of the American population, and consequently American schools, is a major ongoing phenomenon that characterizes the social fabric of American society and schools. Multicultural education aspires to help all students develop positive cross-cultural attitudes, values, dispositions, perceptions, and behaviors. Multicultural educators believe that identity and positive self-esteem are based on the pride that each child has in his or her cultural group's history, achievements, solidarity, and loyalty. This belief drives the mandate that the school curriculum, instructional materials and activities, school personnel and school services reflect the multicultural nature of the student body.

Special education provides educational services designed for exceptional students. Exceptional students are defined as those who have physical, mental, or behavioral disabilities. Special education laws and practices have greatly increased access to activities and opportunities that used to be withheld from these students. The inclusion movement promotes the integration of students with disabilities into the regular classroom as opposed to putting students with disabilities in separate schools or classes. Supporters of full inclusion argue that the practice of segregated education for students with disabilities is a violation of their rights to receive an education as good as that being offered to 'regular' students. Both advocates and opponents of inclusion use budgetary reasons to defend their stands. A genuine cooperation between the special education and general education teachers is a crucial variable in the success of inclusion policy. Gifted and talented students are often considered part of this population.

At-risk education is targeted for a more specific population than either urban or multicultural education and is designed to help students who are likely to fail or be failed by the educational system. It is designed for students who have a high probability of dropping out of school or not achieving in school. The issue of at-risk students has generated a major concern for educators. There is an increase in studies and development activities designed to improve the education of students at risk. Some of the predicaments of this group of learners are due to disadvantaged background, low socioeconomic status of their families, geographical location, and weak language and numerical skills. At-risk education includes *early intervention programs*, specialized curricula, and development of retention and reentry programs.[19]

Urban education is concerned primarily with education that occurs in, and is affected by, the various factors generated by an urban environment. Urban educational specialists can be challenged by having to deal with such problems as a diverse student population, racial segregation, violence, poor housing and living conditions, and significant teacher turnover. Diane Ravitch strongly believes that the new wave of school reform now underway rejects the idea that the failure of a huge proportion of poor children in the inner cities is inevitable. The rescue of urban schools entails dismantling entrenched and patronage-driven school board bureaucracies, holding schools accountable for their performance, and encouraging well-planned experimentation with charter and contract schools and vouchers.[20]

Comparative and International Education

As we move into the early part of the twenty-first century, we find a growing set of international economic and social imperatives that are stimulating the globalization of education. Because schooling serves as a strategic instrument for promoting national economic development, globalization of educational policy and reform leads to a significant increase in the emphasis on global awareness.[21] Arnove observed that comparative and international education is enjoying a renaissance. Globalization has infused the ever-present need to learn about each other with an unprecedented urgency and emphasis.[22]

Education and Technology

It is expected that a high proportion of jobs in our nation in the future will require some level of computing skills. Positions in education will certainly be affected by the use of computer technology. In educational situations, computers mediate the flow of information, communication, and instructional materials.[23] It is not surprising, therefore, to find that advances in electronic technology are transforming education, causing the educational process to be redesigned, and changing the way students, both young and old, are learning. Technology is promoting the effectiveness of school reform. It enhances the development of new methods of teaching and learning inside and outside the classroom. There are online resources such as lesson plans, simulations, course materials, and research sources to assist both students and teachers in the teaching and learning process. Data, picture, video, and sound bytes are used to revolutionize education. Technology is removing classroom walls as students and teachers interact with colleagues and experts through chat rooms, live video conference, e-mail, and fax machines. Students, teachers, administrators, educational researchers, educational psychologists, educational media technologists, educational specialists, and others involved in the educational process are finding dramatic changes occurring in how they define and carry out their roles.

In the computer-based learning environment, students are becoming more active learners and better prepared for the digital economy they will function in as adults, and teachers are becoming facilitators. Administrators at all levels are dealing with the cost of providing new resources, as well as using the capabilities of the technologies to improve their work environment. Educational researchers are finding that the Internet and e-mail are having a dramatic effect by facilitating cooperative efforts between participants who are widely separated geographically. Educational psychologists are seeing an effect on learner thinking and the entire learning process. Educational media technologists are facilitating the use of interactive videoconferencing, which is particularly useful in the delivery of distance education. The new technologies are opening up significantly increased educational possibilities for the at-risk student and the disabled.

Electronic formats will continue to expand and enrich learning experiences. The challenge to education is to integrate the new technology into the instructional programs and to use it to improve learning, reduce costs, and increase accessibility to information.

The Reference Environment

Many different types of people use the educational resources in the library. Members of the community are often involved on school boards or in parent-teacher organizations, or are simply concerned about current educational issues. High school students and their parents need information about colleges and the financing of a college education. Professional educators are interested in current developments in curriculum, educational technology, and management. These people may either be searching for how-to literature or need scholarly materials. Educational policy makers at all levels of government seek data and opinions on the current status and possible future directions of education. Finally, educational scholars need access to the full range of bibliographic sources and research literature.

As is always true in a reference situation, the librarian should identify resources appropriate to the needs of the individual in terms of subject, purpose, level of research, and format. For example, the needs of members of the community interested in current educational issues may well be met by popular, nonscholarly sources such as current magazines and newspapers. High school students and their parents, as well as undergraduates seeking information related to college selection, can find the answers to many of their questions in institutional and financial aid directories.

Professional educators need to ground their practice in the best theories of the day, but they do not always have time to read the primary literature. Therefore, professional or trade journals, handbooks, and other mediating sources may meet their needs. A good professional should be aware of the important periodicals and major organizations that produce practitioner-oriented literature in the field.[24] Two of the most important tools for the busy practitioner are *ERIC* (I-68), a vast database maintained by the Educational Resources Information Center, and *Education Index* (I-65).

The needs of policy makers and scholars, including education students, are more complex and involve the whole range of material from primary to tertiary and from popular to theoretical. One important source of primary information in education is a series of national data-gathering programs largely financed by federal funds, listed in the biography current edition of 2001 edition of *The Condition of Education* (I-147) as NCES surveys.[25] Examples of educational datasets generated by these programs are the Higher Education General Information Survey (HEGIS), a yearly survey of postsecondary educational institutions in the United States, and the National Longitudinal Study of the High School Class of 1972. These information-gathering programs result in large numerical databases that can be manipulated by the individual researcher.

Other sources of information potentially useful to the policy maker, scholar, student, or general citizen are listed in this chapter. Titles have been chosen according to their importance to the field. This list is necessarily selective and not comprehensive, and with the exception of a few retrospective titles and some classics in the field, titles included in this chapter represent basic education reference tools. Three books listed in the section on guides are particularly good sources for information on educational reference tools omitted from the present discussion: Nancy O'Brien's *Core List of Books and Journals in Education* (I-3), Dorothea Berry's *Bibliographic Guide to Educational Research* (I-4), and Peter Olevnik's *American Higher Education: A Guide to Reference Sources* (I-2).

Given education's close relationship to virtually all of the social sciences, the researcher must be cautioned not to limit inquiry to sources specifically identified as "educational." Education is by nature an interdisciplinary field, and researchers and librarians should keep in mind that there may be vital materials located in other areas of the library collection than in the obvious (Library of Congress) L class and the (Dewey) 300s.

The librarian must be prepared to draw on any source listed in this book when dealing with an educational reference question. A major case in point is educational psychology, where much of the primary source material is covered by sources identified as "psychological" rather than "educational." For this reason, only one educational psychology title is included in this chapter, *The Handbook of School Psychology* (J-66). Readers should refer to chapter 10 for important educational psychology sources, especially the "Works on Tests and Measurements" section.

GUIDES

I-1 American Reference Books Annual (ARBA). Bohdan S. Wynar, ed.-in-chief. Englewood, CO: Libraries Unlimited, 1970- . Annual.

Picking up where the *ARBA Guide to Education* (Libraries Unlimited, 1985) left off, each volume of *ARBA* now includes a chapter covering education. This general source for reviews of major English-language education reference books published in the United States and Canada during the previous year serves as a valuable tool for building or evaluating an education reference collection. *ARBA* is comprehensive in coverage and provides critical and evaluative annotated descriptions. Arrangement is by subject and subdivided by type of tool, such as bibliographies, encyclopedias, directories, handbooks and yearbooks, and indexes. Reviews are numbered consecutively throughout the volume and are indexed by author, title, and subject.

I-2 Olevnik, Peter P., et al. American Higher Education: A Guide to Reference Sources. Westport, CT: Greenwood Press, 1993.

Olevnik's annotated guide covers 790 higher-education reference sources between 1861 and 1992 and is the most thorough and up-to-date source of information on the subject. Included are guides to the literature, dictionaries and encyclopedias, directories, handbooks, manuals and other compendia, almanacs, statistical guides, yearbooks, abstracts, indexes, reports, bibliographical sources, and computerized databases. Arrangement is by type of reference work and then by general topics. Indexing is by author, title, and subject.

The major drawbacks are the poor print format, the omission of such subjects as distance education and special education, and the lack of newer sources for such subjects as urban education. Even so, the work is an impressive compilation of higher-education reference sources and a useful tool for collection management.

I-3 O'Brien, Nancy P. **Core List of Books and Journals in Education**. Phoenix, AZ: Oryx Press, 1991.

This annotated list represents a core collection of 979 English-language books and journals in the field of education. Most of the works are from the United States, with a few from Canada and Great Britain. Coverage is primarily from the late 1980s; however, a select number of classics still in print are included. The work also contains U.S. government documents and UNESCO monographs but excludes materials pertaining to children's literature.

Organization is based on eighteen subjects: comparative education, content areas, educational administration and law, educational psychology/guidance/counseling, educational reform, educational research/statistics, educational technology/media, elementary/secondary education, general sources, health/physical education, higher and continuing education, history and philosophy of education, measurement, multicultural education, resources for teaching, special education, teacher education, and vocation education. Indexing is provided for authors/editors, titles, and subjects.

Although this guide is limited by including only English-language titles, has some noticeable gaps, and is becoming dated, it is still useful for collection management purposes.

I-4 Berry, Dorothea M. **A Bibliographic Guide to Educational Research**. 3d ed. Metuchen, NJ: Scarecrow Press, 1990.

A Bibliographic Guide to Educational Research is annotated and is an enlarged and updated version of the 1980 edition. It lists some 1,050 annotated titles, primarily from the United States, with some from Great Britain, Canada, and Australia. Many works published between 1975 and 1980, as well as older titles that have historical value, have been retained, but most of the 585 new titles and 213 new editions included in the volume were published between 1980 and 1989. As in previous editions, annotations are descriptive rather than evaluative. Arrangement is by form of information, such as book catalogs and bibliographies; periodical directories, indexes, and abstract journals; research studies, including ERIC documents and an explanation of computer searching for ERIC materials; government publications; special types of materials; other types of reference materials; and research papers. Indexing is by author/editor/compiler, title, and subject.

I-5 Freed, Melvyn N. **The Educator's Desk Reference (EDR): A Sourcebook of Educational Information and Research**. New York: American Council on Education/Macmillan, 1989.

EDR is a useful, easy-to-use, one-volume sourcebook for major information sources in the academic field of education. Its six major sections include an annotated list of education reference materials, organized by type; leading publishers in the field of education and publishers' guidelines for authors; descriptions of major statistical and nonstatistical packages for microcomputer software used in educational research; profiles of standardized educational research tests and inventories; guidelines for educational research methodology and design; and a directory of selected regional and national educational organizations.

Although a number of the sources listed in this handbook are no longer current, the sections outlining procedures for submitting articles, manuscripts, or software programs to publishers, and the summary of research processes, are well-written and retain their usefulness.

I-6 Buttlar, Lois. **Education: A Guide to Reference and Information Sources**. Englewood, CO: Libraries Unlimited, 1989.

This annotated guide to primarily English-language sources describes and frequently assesses more than 900 general and specialized education reference titles, including major guides, bibliographies, indexes, abstracts, and other reference sources. In addition, it also indicates online databases, research centers and organizations, and significant periodical titles. Emphasis is on U.S. works published after 1980, with some coverage of titles published in Great Britain and a few multilingual sources sponsored by UNESCO or other international organizations.

The guide is divided by subject into twenty chapters, beginning with general education and selected social science disciplines relevant to education. This is followed by chapters with sources organized in fourteen categories representing specific aspects of education. In addition to the traditional areas, chapters cover such topics as distance education, bilingual and multicultural education, international and comparative education, and women's studies and feminist education. Indexing is provided by author, title, and subject.

Buttlar's work serves as a good companion to Marda Woodbury's *Guide to Sources of Educational Information* (2d ed. Information Resources Press, 1982). There is considerable overlap between the two works, and while Buttlar's guide provides many newer titles, each contains titles not found in the other. It should be noted, however, that Buttlar's work has some errors and omissions, and although it covers online database searching, there is no reference to CD-ROM technology. Both of these works are now dated, and readers should use them together with the newer guides to education sources, such as *ARBA* (I-1), Olevnik's *American Higher Education* (I-2), O'Brien's *Core List* (I-3), or Berry's *Bibliographic Guide* (I-4).

I-7 Collins, Mary Ellen. **Education Journals and Serials: An Analytical Guide**. Westport, CT: Greenwood Press, 1988.

This annotated bibliography covers journals and serials published one or more times per year. Even though it is limited to English-language titles, it is international, including titles from Canada, England, Ireland, Australia, New Zealand, South Africa, Nigeria, India, Pakistan, and Israel. Covered are magazines, journals, proceedings, almanacs, and association publications that meet the frequency criteria. Collins also lists selected significant newsletters and government documents. Serials from neighboring disciplines such as child welfare and psychology are listed if they relate to education in some way. The 803 entries are grouped within seventeen topical areas and are indexed by publisher, subject, title, and geographical location.

Bibliographical information is extensive, including such data as title changes, frequency, price, publisher, editor, circulation, availability of reprints, electronic analogs, indexing coverage, and target audience. Annotations, provided only for examined items, attempt to give general characterizations in terms of audience, topics covered, average number of articles in an issue, special features or columns, and the like.

This is supposed to be an analytical guide, but the entries and annotations are considerably more descriptive than evaluative, and there are no comparisons between titles. Although it is a good source for answering reference questions about education serials, and its accurate descriptive information will at least get the user started on the path toward evaluation and selection of education serials, it is somewhat dated. Users are advised to verify current publication status because a number of journals have ceased publication.

I-8 Loke, Wing Hong. **A Guide to Journals in Psychology and Education**. Metuchen, NJ: Scarecrow Press, 1990.

A Guide to Journals in Psychology and Education provides a detailed description of journals in the areas of education and psychology. The main audience of this product is authors. The information provided, especially under the subheading "Special Features," assists authors in the process of deciding which journals would most likely be interested in their articles, and how to submit their manuscripts. It is also useful for those seeking information about education and psychology journals for reading or subscription purposes. Despite being dated, it still contains valuable information for authors and scholars in the fields of education and psychology.

I-9   Berger, James L., ed. **Educators Guide to Free Videotapes**. 45th ed. Randolph, WI: Educators Progress Service, 1998.

Educators Guide to Free Videotapes is an annual publication from Educators Progress Service. It provides information on free videotapes that teachers could find useful. These videotapes are highly accessible because they are listed by topics, and there are title, subject, and source indexes. A sample request form and form for evaluating materials are provided.

I-10   **Comparative Guide to American Elementary & Secondary Schools**. Milpitas, CA: Toucan Valley Publications, 1998.

This guide assembles in a single volume relevant and significant evaluative and demographic statistics for each regular public school district in the United States with an enrollment of more than 2,500 students. The National Center for Education Statistics is the source of the data used, except for the Web address and the expenditures per student, to write the guide. The raw data for the school year 1995/1996, which was the most current in 1998, were used. The data for the expenditures per student figures were drawn from the U.S. Bureau of the Census Public Elementary-Secondary Finance Data.

The guide is arranged by state, and under each state qualifying school districts are arranged alphabetically by county; under each county, the districts are arranged alphabetically by city. Information provided under each entry includes address, telephone number, Web address, grade span, number and type of schools, student enrollment, number of full-time-equivalent teachers, student/classroom teacher ratio, expenditures per student, librarians, guidance counselors, ethnicity of student population, and national socioeconomic status indicator. The alphabetical city index is especially useful for identifying the name of a school district that operates schools in a particular city or town or for locating or verifying in which county a particular city or town is located.

I-11   Nehmer, Kathleen Suttles, ed. **Elementary Teachers Guide to Free Curriculum Materials 1998–1999**. 55th ed. Randolph, WI: Educators Progress Service, 1998.

Elementary Teachers Guide to Free Curriculum Materials is an annual publication from Educators Progress Service. It provides teachers with information on free materials considered appropriate for elementary classrooms. The guide provides a complete, current, annotated entry for the selected books, magazines, maps, bulletins, pamphlets, exhibits, and charts. Items are arranged by curricular area. Each entry has a brief description, grade level, and source information. Accessibility is further enhanced by separate title, subject, and source indexes. There is also another index that lists new items included in this edition. Feedback is solicited from teachers.

I-12   Brown, David. **Goldmine, 1995–96: Finding Free and Low-Cost Resources for Teaching**. 5th ed. Brookfield, VT: Ashgate, 1993.

This is a British-based annual publication. It is a valuable source of information for teachers, especially those in the United Kingdom, who are interested in free and low-priced classroom resources. The guide covers all subject areas. It is divided into three parts: entries, suppliers' addresses, and index. The sections on world geography and history are new in this edition.

I-13   **Educators Guide to Free Science Materials**. 39th ed. Randolph, WI: Educators Progress Service, 1998.

The guide serves as an awareness tool to free social studies classroom materials in various formats. It lists, classifies, and provides information on the nature, contents, type, purposes, and use of these resources. Each annotated entry includes suggested grade level, ordering information, URL, and fax numbers when available. The subject areas covered include aerospace education, biology, chemistry, environmental education, general science, and physics. Science teachers who are busy or/and have access to limited funding will find this guide of great use. The title, subject, and source indexes enhance the level of accessibility to the resources listed and make the guide easy to use. The guide also provides instructions and a sample letter for requesting the resources listed.

I-14 **Educators Guide to Free Social Studies Materials**. 38th ed. Randolph, WI: Educators Progress Service, 1998.

This annotated list of social studies materials in all formats provides a continuous medium for resources that are currently available free of cost. The materials are appropriate for K–12 classrooms. The resources listed are arranged by curriculum areas of citizenship, communication and transportation, famous people, U.S. geography, world geography, government, history, maps, social problems, and world affairs. Titles under each curriculum area are arranged alphabetically. Information under each entry includes a brief description, suggested grade level, full ordering information, and URL when available. The guide also provides instructions and a sample letter for requesting the resources listed. The title, subject, and source indexes make the guide easy to use and the materials readily accessible.

I-15 British Council, National Academic Recognition Information Centre for the United Kingdom (NARIC). **International Guide to Qualifications in Education**. 4th ed. London: Mansell Publishing, 1996.

This is a guide to educational credentials. It is intended to be used in making admission, training, and employment decisions. Although this guide was written for use in the United Kingdom, it will be useful in other countries because of its coverage. The guide covers 165 countries from which students come to the United Kingdom. Each country entry consists of a short introduction, a description of the educational system, marking systems, and a survey of the structure of education level by level. A guide to reading transcripts of educational certificates is included in this international guide. There are also ten appendixes, which provide information about degrees and certifications from specific geographic regions, such as European Baccalaureate, Caribbean Examinations Council, West African Examinations Council, South Pacific Board of Education Assessment, University of West Indies, and Roman Catholic Ecclesiastical Education System.

I-16 **Educators Guide to Free Films, Filmstrips and Slides**. 59th ed. Randolph, WI: Educators Progress Service, 1998.

According to the publisher, this is "the only complete GUIDE to all films, filmstrips, slides, and audiotapes that are available free of cost throughout the United States . . . even throughout the world." There are 881 titles in this edition; 141 of them are new. Educators are strongly advised to use only the most current edition of the work because some formerly listed titles are deleted and new titles are added. The title, subject, and source indexes make the guide easy to use and the materials listed easily accessible. The "What's New Index" is a new feature in this edition. Instructions on how to use the guide and a sample letter of request for resources are provided.

I-17 **Elementary Teachers Guide to Free Curriculum Materials**. 56th ed. Randolph, WI: Educators Progress Service, 1999.

This guide provides a comprehensive, current, annotated list of selected, maps, bulletins, pamphlets exhibits, charts, magazines, and books. The purpose of this guide is to assist teachers and librarians in selecting and using current and appropriate resources that would enhance effective and efficient teaching and learning. The items listed are free of charge and are intended to be used as supplementary teaching aids, especially in schools that are not adequately funded. Materials included in this guide are selected only after thorough and meticulous screening. Titles are arranged by general subject area. Each entry includes information on the nature, content, availability, distribution conditions, and instructional value of the item. There are title, subject, and source indexes that make the guide easy to use. There is also an index listing materials that are new to this edition. Feedback on the quality and relevance of the items is solicited from teachers.

I-18 Mitchell, Bruce M., and Robert E. Salsbury. **Multicultural Education: An International Guide to Research, Policies, and Programs**. Westport, CT: Greenwood Press, 1996.

This guide derived its information from an international study of multicultural education conducted by the authors. The main focus of this work is multicultural education and multicultural efforts around the globe. In an attempt to provide a good representation of the world's educational systems, countries that did not participate in the international study of multicultural education are included. A total of forty-two nations are included, with a chapter devoted to each. Each country profile includes the following segments: "History of the System," "Structure of the System." "Multicultural Education Efforts," and "Summary."

I-19 Compton, Carolyn. **A Guide to 100 Tests for Special Education**. New ed. Upper Saddle, NJ: Globe Fearon, 1996.

The goal of this guide is to inform teachers about specific tests that are used to assess academic strengths and weaknesses. It is a valuable guide to measuring instruments used to assess learning difficulties and other problems associated with learning. One hundred tests are profiled in the guide. Under each test is a description of it and information on its strengths and limitations. The introduction in the guide provides background information on testing, the uses and misuses of testing, interpreting test results, and communicating with parents.

I-20 **Educational Opportunity Guide: A Directory of Programs for the Gifted**. Durham, NC: Duke University Talent Identification Program, 1998.

This annual guide to programs for the gifted provides information on programs at schools, colleges, and at camps in the United States and abroad. The focus is on secondary school students, although programs are included for elementary school students. The listings are arranged by state. The indexes provide access by grade level, gender, format, and topic. There are sections that provide information on international programs, resources for the gifted, academic competitions, and advertising for specific programs.

I-21 **Educators Guide to Free Guidance Materials**. 36th ed. Randolph, WI: Educators Progress Service, 1997.

According to the publisher, this guide is indispensable for everyone involved in the field of guidance. It is designed to be an awareness tool for the guidance materials that are currently available free of cost. The listings are grouped by media formats and print guidance materials. Materials are supplied in four categories: career planning materials, social-personal materials, responsibility to self and to others, and use of leisure time. The title, subject, and source and availability indexes make the guide easy to use and the materials readily accessible. Instructions on how to use the guide and a sample letter of request for resources are provided.

BIBLIOGRAPHIES AND CATALOGS

I-22 **Dictionary Catalog of the Teachers College Library**. Boston: G. K. Hall, 1970.

Dictionary Catalog of the Teachers College Library. **1st Supplement**. Boston: G. K. Hall, 1971.

Dictionary Catalog of the Teachers College Library. **2d Supplement**. Boston: G. K. Hall, 1973.

Dictionary Catalog of the Teachers College Library. **3d Supplement**. Boston: G. K. Hall, 1977.

I-23 **Bibliographic Guide to Education**. Boston: G. K. Hall, 1979- . Annual.

Teachers College Library has one of the world's largest and most comprehensive collections of materials on education. It is an in-depth collection of books, serials, and audiovisual and other materials aimed at the needs of graduate students and advanced researchers. The library collects in all languages, levels, and aspects of education, including elementary and secondary education, higher and adult education, early childhood education, history and philosophy of education, applied pedagogy, international and comparative education, educational administration, education of the culturally disadvantaged and physically challenged, nursing education, and education of minorities and women. Because coverage is worldwide and includes administrative reports of local, regional, and national educational organizations and governmental units for various countries and for U.S. states and large cities, the library serves as an excellent source of material on comparative and international education.

Dictionary Catalog is a photoreproduction of the Teachers College Library author/title/subject card catalog of monographs, periodicals, audiovisual materials, and research reports. *Bibliographic Guide* serves as an annual update to *Dictionary Catalog* and its three supplements. The full spectrum of the field of education is reflected in its holdings, including information about home schooling, homeless youth, AIDS, distance education, aging, education of women and minorities, theses and nonbook materials, and selected educational materials in the New York Public Library. Complete LC cataloging information, ISBN, and identification of NYPL holdings are provided for each title. Together, the *Catalog* and *Guide* bring bibliographic control to a significant portion of the world's output of literature on education.

I-24 **National Information Center for Educational Media (NICEM)**. Albuquerque, NM: Access Innovations, 1964- . Quarterly. Electronic format.

NICEM maintains a 420,000-plus record database of nonprint educational materials produced in the United States. Media covered include 16mm films, 35mm filmstrips, 8mm motion picture cartridges, overhead transparencies, videotapes, slides, and audio recordings. Although much of the material is produced for K–12 instruction, some college- and graduate-level audiovisual sources are included. Entries in the database give author, title, producer, subjects, format, availability, and descriptive abstracts.

Information in the database is available in a variety of formats. It is available online through Dialog (file 46) under the name *A-V Online,* and after hours through CompuServe's *Knowledge Index* (K1046). Updating for *A-V Online* is quarterly. NICEM is also available on CD-ROM through SilverPlatter. Updating of the CD-ROM data is semiannual. In addition, NICEM A-V MARC is available on *BiblioFile* CD-ROM from the Library Corporation.

Since the mid-1960s a series of print and microfiche bibliographies has been issued, some devoted to a particular format. For example, *Film & Video Finder* (Plexus, 1987- ; annual), which provides information on educational AV materials; *Audiocassette & Compact Disc Finder* (Plexus, 1986- ; annual), which contains mostly educational audio materials; and *Filmstrip & Slide Set Finder* (Plexus, 1990- ; annual), are also available.

I-25 Maddux, Cleborne D. **Distance Education: A Selected Bibliography**. Englewood Cliffs, NJ: Educational Technology Publications, 1992.

This bibliography covers information relating to the delivery of education at remote sites and addresses issues relating to providing education for nontraditional students in rural and remote areas of the nation and the world. Articles are classified into six categories: general articles; problems and cautions; research; project descriptions: United States; project descriptions: international applications; and issues and trends. Some articles appear in more than one category. This is a good place to start, particularly when initiating a distance education program.

I-26 Sparks, Linda. **Institutions of Higher Education: An International Bibliography**. Westport, CT: Greenwood Press, 1990.

According to its preface, this international bibliography is an attempt to bring together in one comprehensive source citations of books, dissertations, theses, reports, and ERIC microfiche relating to the histories of institutions of higher education around the globe. Community colleges, universities, seminaries, colleges, and specialized postsecondary institutions are covered. Entries are arranged alphabetically by country, state, and geographic regions. Citations are put under the current names of institutions. Although the names of the institutions are in English, the references are in the original language in which they were published. Whenever available, entries include author or editor, title, place of publication, publisher, date, and number of pages. There are author and subject indexes. This international bibliography is a rich source of historical resources on institutions.

I-27 **El-Hi Textbooks and Serials in Print**. 2 vols. New York: R. R. Bowker, 1985- . Annual.

This bibliography was formerly known as *American Education Catalog*, *Textbooks in Print*, and *El-Hi Textbooks in Print*. It is very similar to *Books in Print*. It has become the only up-to-date, wide-ranging general education bibliography in the U.S. It serves as a useful source for identifying, locating, and verifying textbooks, textbook series, and related teaching materials. The scope covers currently available textbooks, teaching materials, periodicals, and other pedagogical materials appropriate for the elementary, junior and high schools. The 126th edition is in two volumes. Entries are published in volume 1, and volume 2 contains the title index, author index, series index, serials subject index, and serials title index. This edition lists 90,120 elementary, junior, and senior high school items, which are arranged under twenty-two broad subject areas. Each entry includes author, title, pagination, year of publication, cost, ISBN, and publisher.

I-28 **The Educational Software Selector**. Hampton Bays, NY: Educational Products Information Exchange (EPIE) Institute, 1984- . Semiannual. Electronic format.

Designed to provide information on software products for all grade levels by subject, this work describes software, contents of program packages, and summary listings by hardware and software suppliers. Each listing includes name, types, uses, scope, grouping, description, components, configurations, availability, and reviews. Appendixes consist of a glossary, EPIE courseware evaluations, and forms for selection and use of software.

REVIEWS

Book Reviews

I-29 **Educational Studies: A Journal in the Foundations of Education**. Charlottesville, VA: American Educational Studies Association, 1970- . Quarterly.

I-30 **The Review of Education**. Bedford Hills, NY: Redgrave, 1975- . Quarterly.

Both of these journals provide long, critical reviews of current monographs in education. *Educational Studies* concentrates on foundational areas: history, philosophy, comparative and international, social sciences, policy studies, and educational matters. Each issue typically contains one to three review essays, followed by shorter book reviews, lists of books received, and notices of forthcoming conferences. Most books reviewed seem to be university press publications. *The Review* has a similar approach, concentrating on English-language scholarly and professional books, with selected foreign-language publications. However, *The Review* is less pleasing in typography and layout than *Educational Studies*.

As review media go, the journals are relatively current, covering most books within one or two years of publication. Given even that modest time lag, however, the primary users would be professors of education and other educational researchers rather than collection development specialists. Both journals are covered by *Book Review Index* (A-36) and *Education Index* (I-65). A large university library will need both titles; a smaller collection could make do with one or the other, depending on the needs and preferences of local faculty.

Literature Reviews

I-31 **Review of Educational Research**. Washington, DC: American Educational Research Association, 1931- . Quarterly.

I-32 **Review of Research in Education**. Washington, DC: American Educational Research Association, 1973- . Annual.

The aim of the American Educational Research Association is to improve the practice of education by supporting and disseminating research. Both of these publications, as well as a long list of other titles, are produced by AERA or under its auspices to further that aim.

Review of Educational Research (*RER*) is devoted to critical state-of-the-art essays. Each issue contains four or five articles, some reporting original research but most presenting analyses of current educational research literature. *RER*'s scope is broad: It covers some natural science, social science, and humanistic issues in addition to purely educational concerns.

Review of Research in Education (*RRE*) attempts to synthesize current research on selected topics. Its main purpose is to help improve theoretical work in education by examining what has been done and what still needs to be done. *RRE* articles cover all substantive and methodological issues in educational research, although articles on learning and instruction predominate.

Both tools include extensive references and complement another AERA publication, *Encyclopedia of Educational Research* (I-54). Students beginning a research project with encyclopedia articles should also consult these two review sources for additional, more current information.

Media Reviews

I-33 **Media Review Digest**. Ann Arbor, MI: Pierian, 1974- . Annual.

This core media reference tool began in 1970 as *Multi Media Reviews Index*. It provides reviews and descriptions of films, videocassettes, video discs, filmstrips, audio records, tapes, compact discs, slides, transparencies, illustrations, kits, maps, anatomical models, games, and other miscellaneous media types. *Media Review Digest*, which is available both in print and on magnetic tape, covers some 40,000 citations and references taken from more than 135 periodicals and reviewing services. Primary emphasis is on educational and informational media, but feature films are also included, with Motion Picture Association of America film ratings listed as appropriate. Arrangement is by main entry within broad media categories. Descriptive information includes full bibliographical data along with sale or rental availability and price. Some entries are accompanied by extracts of reviews. The editorial staff assigns, as appropriate, audience-level indicators (e.g., primary, elementary, adult) and review ratings (good to excellent, average to good, fair to poor, descriptive only) based on their reading of the reviews.

In addition to the main entry listing, items are indexed by subject, geographical area, and reviewer. Subject access is by Library of Congress subject headings and "General Subject Indicators" (broad headings suggested by the content of the reviews). The *Digest* also has sections devoted to film awards and prizes, producers and distributors, and mediagraphies. Beginning in 1995, it includes a new section devoted to reviews of CD-ROMs.

I-34 Only the Best: The Cumulative Guide to Highest-Rated Educational Software, 1985–89, Preschool–Grade 12. 4 vols. New York: R. R. Bowker, 1989.

I-35 The Annual Guide to Highest-Rated Educational Software, Only the Best. New York: R. R. Bowker, 1990–1991.

These two publications have as their purpose to help educators, teachers, librarians, and parents sift through the mass of available education software programs. *The Annual Guide* served as an update to the master volume, *Only the Best*. More than 6,000 programs were evaluated by thirty-five editors/researchers from the United States and Canada, and 185 programs were identified as meeting the criteria for selection as "highest-rated software." In addition, 46 programs that received an "excellent" grade from at least one of the evaluation services used by *Only the Best* were listed in part II as an ALERT service to promising new programs that had not yet obtained the high level of agreement on excellence required by *Only the Best* programs. Arrangement is alphabetical by title, subject areas, and software and producers.

DICTIONARIES

I-36 **Dictionary of Education**. 3d ed. Edited by Carter Victor Good. New York: McGraw-Hill, 1973.

Even though it is now more than twenty years old, this comprehensive dictionary, compiled with the assistance of more than 100 recognized experts, continues to be *the* classic in the field of education. It contains approximately 33,000 entries and cross-references, covering technical and professional terms and concepts from the whole range of education and some related fields, such as psychology, sociology, and philosophy. Definitions cite the literature as appropriate. Foreign-language terms are excluded, but separate sections are provided for Canada, England, and Wales. Also excluded are personal names, school systems, institutions or organizations, places, and publications, except "where a movement, method, or plan is represented."

I-37 Shafritz, Jay M., Richard P. Koeppe, and Elizabeth W. Soper. **The Facts on File Dictionary of Education**. New York: Facts on File, 1988.

This dictionary serves as a supplement to Good's *Dictionary of Education* (I-36), primarily because it includes entries on significant persons, court cases, legislation, organizations, periodicals, government agencies, tests, and newer terms and areas not covered in Good. It contains more than 5,000 entries, has extensive cross-referencing covering education terms from kindergarten through grade 12, and has references at the end of some entries. Brief glossary definitions are given for peripheral items, and more detailed treatment is provided for significant educational concerns. It should be noted that approximately one-quarter of the terms have been borrowed almost verbatim from Shafritz's *Facts on File Dictionary of Public Administration* (Facts on File, 1988).

I-38 Barrow, Robin, and Geoffrey Milburn. **A Critical Dictionary of Educational Concepts: An Appraisal of Selected Ideas and Issues in Educational Theory and Practice**. 2d ed. New York: Teachers College Press, 1990.

Unlike most dictionaries, which primarily define and describe, the main "purpose of this book is to probe and critically assess some of the key concepts in education." It covers more than 120 main entries, consisting of words, ideas, and issues in education, and includes entries under such subjects as computer literacy, mainstreaming, multiculturalism, core curriculum, critical thinking, and ethnography. There are boldface cross-references and brief references at the end of each section. Full references are provided in the bibliography at the end of the volume. This is a valuable reference book for undergraduate and graduate libraries with programs in sociology, psychology, and education.

I-39 Hirsch, E. D., Jr., Joseph F. Kett, and James Trefil. **The Dictionary of Cultural Literacy**. 2d ed. rev. and updated. Boston: Houghton Mifflin, 1993.

The revised and updated *Dictionary* reflects current changes in U.S. culture, including multiculturalism; changes in world history and geography, such as the collapse of the Soviet empire; political upheavals in Eastern Europe; the Gulf War and other military conflicts; and advances in science and technology. It is divided into twenty-three subject categories ranging from a section on mythology and folklore to world geography, politics, and technology. Each entry consists of a concise definition and the current *cultural* sense of the term. Also included are cross-references, a pronunciation guide, a topical index, and illustrations.

I-40 Jarvis, Peter. **An International Dictionary of Adult and Continuing Education**. New York: Routledge, 1990.

This comprehensive reference source defines more than 5,000 terms in the international field of adult and continuing education. The main emphasis is on the United States, Canada, Europe, and Great Britain, with some coverage of the Far East, Africa, and South America. The book includes important people in the field, both historical and contemporary; agencies and organizations; terms and concepts; movements; and significant awards and studies. *International Dictionary* is a useful tool for the professional adult educator, adult learning organizations, and libraries.

I-41 Blake, David, and Vincent Hanley. **The Dictionary of Educational Terms**. Brookfield, VT: Ashgate, 1995.

This dictionary is a useful source for understanding British education and terminology. The definitions are distinctively slanted to the National Curriculum in Great Britain. The definitions, which are often in brief paragraphs, are clear. There are cross-references, which sometimes include addresses of relevant agencies or institutions for more information. There is a list of useful acronyms before the actual dictionary listings. The educational terms in the dictionary are applicable beyond Great Britain.

I-42 Lawton, Denis, and Peter Gordon. **Dictionary of Education**. 2d ed. London: Hodder & Stoughton, 1996.

This is a useful source of information on education and training in Britain and Wales. This work is made up of four sections, each with a distinctive focus. The first section contains essays on the background of education and the discussion of the core concepts in education. The second section is a dictionary with alphabetical listings of brief definitions. There are also cross-references to other terms in the first and second sections. The third section presents a chronology of key events in the history of English education from as far back as 1800. The fourth section is a list of acronyms. Scholars and practitioners will find this dictionary a valuable resource.

I-43 McBrien, J. Lynn, and Ronald S. Brandt. **The Language of Learning: A Guide to Education Terms**. Alexandria, VA: Association for Supervision and Curriculum Development, 1997.

This is a glossary of over 200 education terms sponsored by the Association for Supervision and Curriculum Development. The focus is on K–12 education. According to the foreword, the purpose of this work is to enlighten parents, school board members, business leaders, and other concerned citizens about educational jargon in an objective way, using everyday language. The explanations are of varying length ranging from a few sentences to a full page. Some of them include examples and resources both online and offline for additional information. The index by topic at the end of the book provides a list of key words related to that subject. This topic list is useful for locating and identifying terms and related terms that are cross-referenced for further searching and information. This work is valuable for rendering education rhetoric understandable, especially to those outside the education profession.

I-44   Palmer, James C., and Anita Y. Colby. **Dictionary of Educational Acro-nyms, Abbreviations, and Initialisms**. 2d ed. Phoenix, AZ: Oryx Press, 1985.

This dictionary serves as a source for locating the meaning of acronyms, abbreviation, and initialisms that proliferate in all types of educational writings. It will be a useful resource for scholars, educators, laypersons, and students who need to find the meaning for a particular set of letters. Most of the entries are the result of thorough review of a variety of literature and writings in the field of education. This second edition has 4,011 entries, of which 1,995 are new. The dictionary is arranged in two parts. Part I is the listing of acronyms, abbreviations, and initialisms, which are arranged alphabetically by acronym, and identical acronyms are arranged alphabetically by unabbreviated form. Part II is the reverse list of acronyms, abbreviations, and initialisms, which are arranged alphabetically by their unabbreviated forms. The reverse list is not intended to serve as an authority list for the acronyms. Although most entries consist of the acronyms and the terminologies they represent, some entries include modifiers in parentheses, which indicate a geographic location or identify a parent organization. The dictionary is by no means an authority list, nor is it exhaustive.

I-45   Ellington, Henry, and Duncan Harris. **Dictionary of Instructional Tech-nology**. London: Kogan Page, 1986.

This dictionary is a comprehensive glossary of the most widely used and important British and American instructional technology. The primary audience for the work is educational and train-ing technologists of all types and background. There are over 2,800 terms, which are briefly defined. The terms are drawn from the various branches of mainline instructional technology and from the main fields and disciplines that are related to or overlap with instructional technology. Some of the terms used in Anglophone countries other than Britain and America, and terms for assessment tech-niques and types of testing tools, are also included. The cross-referencing is clear.

I-46   Accardo, Pasquale J., and Barbara Y. Whitman. **Dictionary of Develop-mental Disabilities Terminology**. Baltimore, MD: Paul H. Brookes, 1996.

This is a multidisciplinary dictionary, which draws developmental disabilities terminology from several fields of study such as education, psychology, medicine, psychiatry, social work, family therapy, physical therapy, and speech/language pathology. There are over 3,000 terms defined in this dictionary. Selection of terms to be included was based on the likelihood that the terms would be used in writing assessment reports on individuals with developmental disabilities. The goal of this dictionary is to assist those who read and use such assessment reports who may not be conversant with terms from the different disciplines, which are often used in writing such reports. The definitions of terms are clear, simple, and explicit. Illustrations are provided to further enhance clarity.

I-47   **Dictionary of Special Education and Rehabilitation**. 4th ed. Edited by Glenn A. Vergason and M. L. Anderegg. Denver, CO: Love Publishing, 1997.

This dictionary is an excellent source for locating the meaning of special education and rehabilitation terminology. The terms included in this work are drawn from texts and professional books and reflect current use and practices in the fields of special education and rehabilitation. This dictionary provides a listing of main organizations, abbreviations and acronyms, periodicals and journals, legal terms, and sources of legal assistance that are useful to the discipline.

THESAURUSES

I-48   **Thesaurus of ERIC Descriptors**. Phoenix, AZ: Oryx Press, 1968- . Irregular.

Thesaurus of ERIC Descriptors is a controlled vocabulary used by the ERIC system (I-39) in indexing education literature. It was developed under the auspices of the Educational Resources Information Center (ERIC) of the Office of Educational Research and Improvement, U.S. Department of Education. The thirteenth edition, published in 1995, contains 10,363 vocabulary terms, of which 5,759 are main-entry descriptors. Major and minor "descriptors are assigned to identify subject content, educational level, age level, validation status of a program, research methodology employed, test utilized, form or type of document," and the target audience when specified by the author.

Descriptors appear in the thesaurus along with their syndetic apparatus (broader terms, narrower terms, cross-references, etc.), scope notes, and posting counts. The book contains four listings of terms used for indexing and searching: the main alphabetical display, the rotated display, the hierarchical display, and the descriptor groups. Introductory sections provide information on new, transferred, invalid, and deleted descriptors.

The thesaurus is easy to use and should be the first step in every ERIC search. Because it displays relationships among concepts, it is also useful for beginning a search on a topic with which one is unfamiliar, regardless of sources ultimately used.

I-49 Knapp, Sara D. **The Contemporary Thesaurus of Social Science Terms and Synonyms: A Guide for Natural Language Computer Searching**. Phoenix, AZ: Oryx Press, 1993.

This interdisciplinary thesaurus is intended for use by people performing natural-language computer searches and by writers and speakers looking for alternative expressions in the social and behavioral sciences. It includes synonyms and related terms for more than 6,000 concepts from many social science fields, ranging from anthropology to business, education, political science, public administration, psychology, sociology, and women's issues. Each of the groups of synonyms, near-synonyms, closely related terms, or specific examples that describe thousands of concepts is listed alphabetically under a concept title. Cross-references from other significant title words are provided. Concepts and terms were selected from actual search requests, newspapers, specialized thesauruses, databases, and subject dictionaries, or contributed by experts in the field. The book does not include words that do not have synonyms or closely related terms, proper names, names of tests, most technical terms, slang terms, or British spellings. There is, however, an index of British spelling in Appendix B.

Two particularly useful sections are "Basics of Computer Searching," which describes online and CD-ROM searching and explains the basic search process and how to analyze a topic search; and "Natural Language Searching," which explains what natural-language searching is and when and how to use it.

I-50 **Thesaurus: European Education Thesaurus**. 1991 ed. Luxembourg: Office for Official Publications of the European Communities, 1991.

This third edition of the EUDISED thesaurus, the new multilingual documentary language, was developed for managing multilingual information on education in Europe. It is "structured in hierarchical relations and associative relationships," and is available in all nine official languages of the European Community. Coverage includes a variety of subjects, from educational principles and systems to teaching curricula and subjects, psychology, sociology, economics of education, and public administration. The descriptors are grouped by forty-two microthesaurus semantic fields. Cross-references are provided from unofficial terms in each language. Similar to the *Thesaurus of ERIC Descriptors* (I-48) in many respects, it has descriptors; categories; occasional scope notes; listings of broader, narrower, or related terms; and a rotated listing of descriptors.

I-51 **ERIC Identifier Authority List (IAL)**. Edited by James E. Houston, Carolyn R. Weller, and Carol A. Patt. Phoenix, AZ: Oryx Press, 1995.

ERIC Identifier Authority List is published as a supplement to *Thesaurus of ERIC Descriptors* (I-48). It contains subject terms not included in the controlled vocabulary but considered by the indexer to be very relevant to the record. Thus it provides additional access points to materials in the *ERIC* database. The terms covered in the thesaurus include new terms, the names of projects, legislation, persons, places, organizations, tests, and groups. This thesaurus serves as an excellent source for searching the *ERIC* database for topics, which are identifiers and not descriptors. The number of occurrences of the term in the ERIC print indexes is listed along with the term. Identifiers are arranged alphabetically in categories.

ENCYCLOPEDIAS

General

I-52 **The Encyclopedia of Education**. 10 vols. Edited by Lee C. Deighton. New York: Macmillan, 1971.

This encyclopedia continues to be a classic in the field and is a good starting point for many inquiries. The 1,000-plus signed articles cover educational institutions, systems, history, philosophy, and research, plus related disciplines such as English, mathematics, and sociology. Although it concentrates on U.S. education, it also covers international education. However, it is recommended that users wanting more current information on educational systems in other countries consult the 1994 edition of *The International Encyclopedia of Education* (I-53).

Articles are grouped by broad topics in the main portion of the set. The index volume includes a detailed subject index and alphabetical guide that gives "see" and "see also" references for each article. Most articles have excellent bibliographies. There is a definite need for an updated and revised edition of this excellent reference tool.

I-53 **The International Encyclopedia of Education**. 2d ed. 12 vols. Edited by Torsten Husen and T. Neville Postlethwait. New York: Pergamon/Elsevier Science, 1994.

The new edition of *The International Encyclopedia of Education* presents an international overview of current educational problems, theories, practices, and institutions. The 1,266 signed entries have been subdivided into twenty-two "mega fields," ranging from adult education to comparative and international education, educational technology, girls and women in education, and technical and vocational education and training. *The International Encyclopedia* reflects the fact that more than 80 percent of empirical research is published in English and comes from the English-speaking countries, especially the United States. It includes cross-references between relevant entries, which facilitate quick and easy access to typical educational themes and topics, and bibliographies at the end of most entries. Volume 12 provides a three-level subject index, a classified list of entries, and a name index. Also included in the index volume are lists of abbreviations and acronyms, contributors, and major education journals.

I-54 **Encyclopedia of Educational Research**. 6th ed. Edited by Marvin C. Alkin. New York: Macmillan, 1992.

This new edition of one of the standards in the field fulfills its goal of summarizing relevant research on education theory and practice. It is published every ten years and is sponsored by the American Educational Research Association. About 44 percent of the topics are new and include such subjects as AIDS, critical thinking, parent choice (vouchers), peer counseling, education for teenage parents, and women's education in the Third World. A current bibliography and a "see also" notation are provided at the end of each article. The preface includes a section describing the organizing scheme, which is divided into sixteen broad topic headings with subheadings listed at either one or two levels of specificity.

The sixth edition of the encyclopedia consists of 257 new and revised, signed articles from 325 contributors. The last volume provides an extensive index to acronyms, proper names, and specific topics. Particularly interesting is a special appendix titled "Doing Library Research in Education," which provides the basic strategy and practical examples for pursuing additional library research in the field. Older editions of the encyclopedia should be retained for their retrospective coverage of the research literature.

I-55 Dejnozka, Edward L., and David E. Kapel. **American Educators' Encyclopedia**. Rev. ed. by David E. Kapel, Charles S. Gifford, and Marilyn B. Kapel. Hamden, CT: Greenwood Press, 1991.

This handy one-volume reference tool contains more than 2,000 concise articles in twenty-two broad subject areas. The updated entries in this 2d edition cover all levels of education and reflect the changes in U.S. education. The subjects addressed include attention deficit disorder, *A Nation at Risk*, the Odyssey of the Mind program, reading levels, statistical passages, and various computer languages. A short bibliography is provided at the end of each entry. There is a separate section for abbreviations and acronyms, and the twenty-seven appendixes provide a variety of information—from the Code of Ethics of the Education Profession to lists of award recipients and names and addresses for regional accrediting associations.

Specialized

I-56 **Encyclopedia of Higher Education**. 4 vols. Edited by Burton R. Clark and Guy R. Neave. Tarrytown, NY: Pergamon, 1992.

This set contains more than 300 well-written, informative articles on current international knowledge about higher education and will serve as a complement to *The International Encyclopedia of Education* (I-53). It improves on the older *International Encyclopedia of Higher Education* (Jossey-Bass, 1977) by grouping articles under significant topics and categories and by being considerably more readable. Volume 1 discusses the national systems of higher education in more than 130 countries and is divided into four main sections: "Higher Education and Society"; "The Institutional Fabric of the Higher Education System"; "Governance, Administration, and Finance"; and "Faculty and Students—Teaching, Learning and Research." Volumes 2 and 3 present analytical articles on such diverse topics as accreditation, distance education at postsecondary schools, equality and higher education, and promotion and tenure. The last volume has essays on individual academic disciplines, including their "development and structure, orientation and thought," and concludes with comprehensive author and subject indexes.

I-57 **Concise Encyclopedia of Special Education**. Edited by Cecil R. Reynolds and Elaine Fletcher-Janzen. New York: John Wiley, 1990.

This single-volume ready-reference tool is a revised and updated edition of the three-volume *Encyclopedia of Special Education: A Reference for the Education of the Handicapped and Other Exceptional Children and Adults* (John Wiley, 1987). About 90 percent of the more than 300 articles were condensed and streamlined, and most of the biographies of living individuals were deleted. Many articles were revised to reflect changes that have occurred over the last three years; some were entirely rewritten; and some, such as the AIDS article, are completely new. Unfortunately, a number of articles were abridged but not updated, even though newer information was available at the time. Each article is followed by a bibliography of additional information, as well as "see" and "see also" references.

I-58 **Encyclopedia of Early Childhood Education**. Edited by Leslie R. Williams and Doris Pronin Fromberg. New York: Garland, 1992.

The purpose of this reference work is to bring together the many perspectives relating to all aspects of early childhood education, the issues of child advocacy, and reflections on the current forces of change affecting the development of the field.

Following an introductory chapter, chapter 2 reviews the "historical, intellectual, and philosophical sources" used by early childhood theorists and practitioners. The sociocultural, political, and economic contexts of child care and early education are considered in chapter 3. Chapter 4 presents various points of view on the development of young children. Chapter 5 is devoted to describing early childhood curricula and programs, particularly in terms of the variations in form and content. The last chapter "discusses the knowledge base of early childhood teacher education and perspectives on early childhood educators, including how adults influence early childhood education."

I-59 **Encyclopedia of Multiculturalism**. 6 vols. Edited by Susan Auerbach. North Bellmore, NY: Marshall Cavendish, 1993.

This easy-to-use set is devoted to the large minority groups in the United States and provides a wealth of information supporting multicultural education. The intended audience is primarily middle school, high school, and public libraries. The set explores intergroup relations and the implications of significant events in our history, from the Pueblo Revolt of 1680 to the Los Angeles riots of 1992. There are brief biographical sketches of selected significant individuals. The encyclopedia's 1,438 entries take a broad view of diversity by covering a wide range of groups: Jewish Americans, European national groups, the Canadian population, and contemporary groups such as older Americans. Arrangement is alphabetical and includes entries on people, places, concepts, events, laws, and organizations. Volume 6 features a timeline highlighting important events in U.S. multiculturalism from 43,000 B.C.E. to 1993 C.E. There are also a filmography and a resource list with addresses of organization, government agencies, museums, and independent research centers. A comprehensive subject index, a general index, and a bibliography are provided at the end of the last volume.

I-60 **International Encyclopedia of Teaching and Teacher Education**. Edited by Lorin W. Anderson. 2d ed. New York: Elsevier Science, 1995.

The purpose of this international encyclopedia is to provide teachers, teacher educators, graduate students, and researchers with a quick and rich source of information that could guide and support their academic and pedagogical activities. This work draws articles from the popular *International Encyclopedia of Education*, second edition, revises some articles, and adds some new articles and essays relevant to teaching and teacher education. There are a total of 140 well-referenced articles with a list of suggested further reading in this second edition. *International Encyclopedia of Teaching and Teacher Education* is divided into two main parts.

Part A is on teaching and consists of eight sections on the nature and characteristics of teachers, theories and models of teaching, instructional programs and strategies, teaching skills and techniques, school and classroom factors, students and the teaching-learning process, teaching for specific objectives, and the study of teaching.

Part B is on teacher education and comprises three sections on concepts and issues in teacher education, generic initial teacher education, and continuing teacher education. As a result of the significant conceptual, theoretical, philosophical, and methodological changes in education since the first edition was published in 1987, this second edition incorporates a multidisciplinary perspective. There is are very extensive name and subject indexes, which enhance access to articles and essays.

I-61 **International Encyclopedia of the Sociology of Education**. Edited by Lawrence J. Saha. New York: Elsevier Science, 1997.

This one-volume encyclopedia is based on *The International Encyclopedia of Education, Second Edition* (I-53). Although some of the articles have been revised, others are new and fill the gap to catch up with new developments within the discipline of the sociology of education. This is a comprehensive and up-to-date overview of the sociology of education. The purpose for this encyclopedia is to provide a state-of-the-art resource for an audience of students, professors, researchers, educational practitioners, teachers, teacher educators, and policy makers. The scope is international, and as a result of the depth and the broad area of coverage of the entries the encyclopedia is useful in many subareas within the sociology of education, such as sociological theory, the study of the family, educational structures, and educational processes.

There are ten sections in this volume: "Social Theories in the Sociology of Education," "Sociological Fields in the Study of Education," "Research Traditions in the Sociology of Education," "The School as a Social System," "The Structure of Educational Systems," "School Processes," "Family and Schooling," "Teachers in Society," "Youth in Schools," and "Educational Policy and Change." At the end of the encyclopedia is a list of contributors, name index, and subject index. The articles are well referenced, and several of them provide a suggested list for further reading. Although the entries are research-based, a wide range of readers can understand them.

I-62 Baker, Colin, and Sylvia Prys Jones. **Encyclopedia of Bilingualism and Bilingual Education**. Clevedon, England: Multilingual Matters, 1998.

According to its preface, this encyclopedia is based on a celebration of the colorful diversity of languages in the world, and the goal is to raise awareness about language diversity, reduce the prejudice and stereotyping that surround language minorities, and communicate the beauty of bilingualism in a constructive and positive manner. It also aims at being academically sound and accessible to a wide range of audiences.

The encyclopedia is divided into four sections: "Individual Bilingualism," "Languages in Society," "Languages in Contact in the World: Language Maps of the World," and "Bilingual Education." The topics covered are presented in such a clear, simple, and comprehensible style that previous knowledge is not necessary. Illustrations, graphics, and photographs enhance the readability and comprehension of each topic. The topics are also supplemented and illustrated by text boxes and numerous examples. The treatment of the topics is well balanced because they are discussed from different perspectives representing the views of both language majorities and language minorities. At the end of most topics are references and a suggested list for further reading. The appendixes, consisting of a glossary, a bibliography, photographic credits, and author and subject indexes, further add to the usefulness and ease of use of this encyclopedia. Students, scholars, researchers, and educators will find the contents of this encyclopedia valuable.

I-63 **World Education Encyclopedia**. 3 vols. Edited by George Thomas Kurian. New York: Facts on File, 1988.

This encyclopedia is a descriptive survey of the actual working of the national educational systems in the world. It compares the systems but does not evaluate them, provides information on the systems without criticizing them, and analyzes the national education systems without passing judgment. The work is divided into five sections: "Global Education." "Major Countries," "Middle Countries," "Minor Countries," and "Appendixes." "Global Education" comprises two vital and highly informative introductory write-ups: "World History and World Education" and "Statistical Dimensions of Global Education." The amount of information found on the system of education in each of the countries is the criterion used to divide the countries into major, middle, and minor countries. Entries for each country include basic data, history and background, constitutional and legal foundations, an overview of the educational system, administration, finance and educational research, nonformal education and adult education, teaching profession, summary, glossary, and bibliography. Although this global report of the state of education in the late twentieth century is dated, the information it contains is still useful.

I-64 **The International Encyclopedia of Curriculum**. Edited by Arieh Lewy. Oxford: Pergamon, 1991.

This one-volume work is based on material from *The International Encyclopedia of Education* (I-53), which has been revised and updated. It is a comprehensive collection of essays, written by experts in the field of curriculum studies, which attempts to provide extensive and up-to date coverage of international curricula. The preface provides a summary of the history of curriculum studies. Issues and topics that are of concern and interest to students, scholars, and researchers as evidenced in the curriculum literature guide the structure of this encyclopedia. It consists of two main parts: "Curriculum as a Domain of Scholarly Inquiry" and "Specific Study Areas."

Part 1 contains articles representing scholarly inquiry that are cross-curricular. The four sections that make up Part 1 are "Conceptual Framework." "Curriculum Approaches and Methods," "Curriculum Processes," and "Curriculum Evaluation." Part 2 consists of entries that concentrate on subject and topical research in specific study areas. Both the hard core scholarly and less scholarly study areas are covered. Although most of the articles are applicative in nature, some deal with the development of theories and models. The scholarly disciplines covered in Part 2 are language arts, foreign language studies, humanities curricula, arts curricula, social studies, mathematics education, science education programs, physical education, and international curriculum. Section 13 provides information on international curriculum associations and journals. There are contributor, name, and subject indexes at the end of the international encyclopedia. Students, scholars, and researchers in the field of curriculum studies will find this international encyclopedia useful.

INDEXES AND ABSTRACTS

Major Tools

I-65 **Education Index**. Bronx, NY: H. W. Wilson, 1929/1930- . Monthly with quarterly and annual cumulations (print format).

The index covers approximately 400 English-language periodicals, yearbooks, and monographs in series. Subject coverage, which extends to all aspects of the field of education, is constantly expanding to include new areas and is structured according to Library of Congress subject headings. Arrangement is alphabetical in an integrated author and subject listing, with a separate section at the back for book review citations. As with other Wilson indexes, the list of periodicals indexed is decided by subscriber vote, collected under the auspices of the American Library Association's Committee on Wilson Indexes.

For the historian of education, *Education Literature, 1907–1932* (Garland, 1979) provides a comprehensive index of nearly 44,000 citations.

Electronic access: The WILSONDISC CD-ROM version of *Education Index*, which became available in 1984, is user-friendly and less expensive than SilverPlatter's ERIC (I-68); it has improved and expanded searching features, including new truncation characters and the ability to tag each periodical with a custom message. *Education Index* is available online through WILSONLINE, BRS Online, and OCLC. Both the CD-ROM and the online versions provide access by descriptor, subject, author, title keyword, publication type, language, and periodical title. *Education Abstracts*, considerably more expensive than *Education Index*, provides comprehensive abstracting and indexing for 400 core international periodicals, yearbooks, and monographic series. Abstracts range from 50 to 150 words, and the online database is updated twice a week.

I-66 **Current Index to Journals in Education**. Phoenix, AZ: Oryx Press, 1969- . Monthly with semiannual and annual cumulations (print format).

Operating under the auspices of the ERIC system (I-68), *CIJE* serves as an index to approximately 830 major educational and education-related journals and has a database of nearly 500,000 records. It is arranged by broad ERIC subjects and EJ numbers, and access is provided by author, title, and journal contents indexes. There are also lists of the ERIC Clearinghouses with addresses; source journals with frequency, subscription cost, publisher, and address, as well as recent thesaurus additions and changes not included in the current edition of the *Thesaurus of ERIC Descriptors* (I-48). Many of the articles in CIJE are available from University Microfilms International (UMI).

Electronic access: Current Index to Journals in Education (CIJE) is available online and on CD-ROM. The CD-ROM version includes the *ERIC Thesaurus*.

I-67 **Resources in Education**. Phoenix, AZ: Oryx Press, 1975- . Monthly with annual and multiyear cumulations (print version).

Resources in Education (RIE) is the other major component of the *ERIC* database (I-68). Like *CIJE* (I-66), *RIE* provides indexing and abstracting coverage of information gathered by the ERIC Clearinghouses. It consists of resumes, each of which is assigned a unique ED (ERIC Document) number. The resumes provide descriptions of each document and abstracts of their content. Whereas *CIJE* concentrates on journal articles, *RIE* covers books, theses and dissertations, guides, bibliographies, and other types of educational materials, such as unpublished and published research reports, papers presented at meetings, in-house documents, tests, questionnaires, and selected government publications. *RIE* thus controls a lot of otherwise elusive and inaccessible educational material.

Arrangement of *RIE* is by specific aspects of education and sequentially assigned ED accession numbers. An index section provides access by subject, author, institution or sponsoring agency, publication type, and Clearinghouse number. As with *CIJE*, descriptors are controlled by the *Thesaurus of ERIC Descriptors* (I-48). In addition, *RIE* has appended pages that include *Thesaurus* additions and changes. Publications announced in *Resources in Education* are available in paper or on microfiche from the ERIC Document Reproduction Service.

Results of studies funded prior to 1965 are found in *Office of Education Research Reports, 1956–65: Indexes, Resumes* (Government Printing Office, 1967), and results of projects funded between 1966 and 1974 are found in *Research in Education* (Government Printing Office, 1966–1974).

Electronic access: Available online and on CD-ROM.

I-68   **ERIC**. Washington, DC: Educational Resources Information Center (ERIC), Office of Educational Research and Improvement (OERI), U.S. Department of Education, 1966- . Updated monthly. Electronic format.

The *Educational Resources Information Center (ERIC)*, established by the federal government in 1966, is a comprehensive national bibliographic database providing access to abstracts of more than 700,000 documents and journal articles in education and education-related literature. It is the largest source of education information in the world and can be retrieved manually or by computer (batch, online, or CD-ROM). *ERIC* collects all types of print materials, mostly unpublished, that deal with education, such as descriptions and evaluations of programs, research reports and surveys, curriculum and teaching guides, instructional materials, position papers, and resource materials.

There are sixteen clearinghouses and four adjunct clearinghouses in the nationwide ERIC network, each specializing in different, multidisciplinary educational areas. These centers of educational expertise, located mostly at universities or professional associations, "identify, acquire, and process educational information in specific subject areas such as reading and communication skills, science and mathematics, social studies, and in such other areas as elementary, secondary, higher, rural, and urban education."

With the help of the controlled vocabulary provided in the *Thesaurus of ERIC Descriptors* (I-48), users can manually search the printed indexes in *Resources in Education* (*RIE*) (I-67) and *Current Index to Journals in Education* (*CIJE*) (I-66). Computer searches of the online or CD-ROM *ERIC* database allow review of part or all of the files with a single query. *ERIC* does not provide full-text searching of the whole document but rather searching of individual words in the document resumes. *ERIC* document texts are usually available from the ERIC Document Reproduction Service. However, the texts of the *ERIC* journal articles are available from the journals themselves or through reprint services.

Beginning in 1989, "ERIC Digests" began appearing in Dialog's online ERIC file in their full-text form. These are short reports prepared by the ERIC clearinghouses on topics of primary interest in education, such as "Qualities of Effective Writing Programs," "Grade Retention and Promotion," and "Full-Day or Half-Day Kindergarten?" AskERIC Virtual Library (I-160) is an Internet question-answering service sponsored by the ERIC Clearinghouse of Information and Technology.

I-69   **State Education Journal Index and Educator's Guide to Periodicals Research Strategies**. Westminster, CO: State Education Journal Index Publications, 1963- . Semiannual.

This privately printed index focuses on periodicals not indexed in other sources such as *Education Index* (I-65) or *Current Index to Journals in Education* (I-66). Coverage is primarily of publications from state departments of education, state education associations, state teachers' associations, and state school board associations. Entries are brief, consisting of article title, author name, journal title (with state name in parentheses), and page citation. Access is by subject, a few cross-references are provided, and there is no author index. Brief annotations are provided only for articles with vague or misleading titles, such as "Accidents will happen" (district officials need to know liability issues affecting schools).

An interesting addition to the preface is a five-page guide to conducting a periodical literature search, which is an adapted and excerpted version of Phi Delta Kappa Fastback #192—*Library Research Strategies for Educators* by Alexia M. Kartis and Annette Jones Watters (Phi Delta Kappa, 1984). In addition, there are both a guide to abbreviations and a list of the journals with frequency, publisher, address, phone number, and price.

Despite its limitations in format and indexing, this index provides subject access to information in state education publications by focusing on material largely ignored by other abstracting and indexing services.

I-70 **Educational Administration Abstracts**. Newbury Park, CA: Sage, 1966- . Quarterly.

Published in cooperation with the University Council of Educational Administration (UCEA), this abstracting journal covers approximately 200 professional journals (including some British), plus monograph series and selected OECD (Organisation for Economic Co-operation and Development) publications. Until 1977, *Educational Administration Abstracts* also listed dissertations completed in educational administration at UCEA schools.

Numbered citations are arranged alphabetically by author under sixteen broad subject headings such as student personnel, curriculum, testing, professional and staff development, performance and program evaluation, government and law, and special programs. Issues contain approximately 350 abstracts, with access provided by author and subject indexes that are cumulated annually. The fourth issue of each volume also provides a list of the journals covered.

I-71 **Higher Education Abstracts**. Claremont, CA: Claremont Graduate School, 1984- . Quarterly.

Higher Education Abstracts documents materials containing current research and theory in the field of higher education. "Materials are selected that 1) are of more than narrow interest and apply to more than one institution, state, or field of study, 2) include original research or newly formulated theory, 3) are issued within the previous two years, and 4) appear in a scholarly journal, are delivered at an association conference, or are issued as a published or unpublished monograph or report." The journal does not include dissertations, annual reports, book reviews, editorials, interviews, commentaries, rebuttals, symposia, news items, historical studies, program descriptions, case studies, "how to" articles, test descriptions, or reliability and validity studies. Selection is based on relevance only. Descriptions, without abstracts, are provided for books, compilations, research reviews, and bibliographies.

Abstracts are from 100 to 300 words long and are arranged in four broad subject categories: students, faculty, administration, and higher education. Indexing is by author and subject, with a yearly cumulative index provided in the summer issue. The first volumes, covering 1965 to 1984, were published under the title *College Student Personnel Abstracts* (Claremont Institute for Administrative Studies).

I-72 **Exceptional Child Education Resources (ECER)**. Reston, VA: Council for Exceptional Children, 1977- . Quarterly.

ECER serves as a bibliographic database that cites current professional literature and dissertations relating to every aspect of disabled and gifted child education. The Council for Exceptional Children scans considerably more than 200 journals, research reports, curricular materials, dissertations, texts, and nonprint media for material concerning exceptional children. About half of the articles are indexed and submitted for announcement in *Current Index to Journals in Education* (I-66). Beginning with volume 24 in 1992, coverage of book and journal literature was increased by about one-third; the time lag between source publication and date of announcement was cut in half; and coverage of nonprint media, especially software and video products, was increased. Access is by author, title, and subject, with a six-year subject, author, and title index presently in production in both microfiche and diskette formats.

Electronic access: ECER became available on CD-ROM in 1996. It is recommended that users scan newly added material listed in the *ECER* announcement journal to refine search strategies.

I-73 **Child Development Abstracts and Bibliography**. Washington, DC: National Research Council, 1927- . Triannual.

This reference tool, a publication of the Society for Research in Child Development, contains abstracts from professional periodicals and reviews books related to the growth and development of children. Arrangement is alphabetical by author under such broad subject headings as biology, health, and medicine; cognition, learning, and perception; social psychology and personality; education; psychiatry and clinical psychology; and theory, methodology, and review. Coverage is international in scope. Each issue also includes book notices, author addresses, and indexing by subject and author. The last issue in each volume includes a list of journals regularly searched and cumulative author and subject indexes for the volume.

I-74 Fabiano, Emily. **Index to Tests Used in Educational Dissertations**. Phoenix, AZ: Oryx Press, 1989.

Fabiano's work indexes more than 50,000 test title occurrences in the educational dissertations from 1938 to 1980 appearing in *Dissertation Abstracts International (DAI)* (A-39). For volumes 27 on, only those dissertations found in section A, "Humanities and Social Sciences," have been indexed. Dissertations from related disciplines, such as psychology, are not included. The volume is divided into two sections. "Section I: Test Title Index" provides test title, test population, *DAI* volume and page number, and dissertation author. "Section II: Keyword/Name Index" provides cross-references for test authors, keywords in test titles, or acronyms by which tests are known, referring the user to the test title used in section I. This index provides assistance to anyone looking for information on the use of tests in research.

I-75 **Australian Education Index**. Melbourne, Victoria: Australian Council for Educational Research, 1958- . (Vol. 40, 1997). Quarterly.

This is a comprehensive index of materials on Australian education and Australian authors published as journal articles, monographs, conference papers, government reports, research reports, and curriculum documents. Abstracts for many documents are provided. There is an author and institution list. Subject terms, which are very comprehensive and inclusive, are drawn from the *Australian Thesaurus of Education Descriptors*.

Electronic access: Available online.

I-76 **British Education Index**. Edited by Phil Sheffield. Leeds, England: University of Leeds, 1954- . Quarterly.

This index lists and analyzes the subject content of all articles on subjects of permanent interest to educators that are published in the British Isles and some internationally published periodicals. Standard index information such as title, author, number of pages, issue number, and date is provided. There are an author list, a subject list of articles, and a list of periodicals and publishers. These lists enhance access to materials covered by the index. Subject terms are drawn from the *British Education Thesaurus*. Scholars and educators will find *British Education Index* a useful source of information on British educational practices and research.

Electronic access: Available online.

I-77 **Canadian Education Index/Repertoire Canadien Sur l'Education**. Toronto: Micromedia, 1965- . Quarterly.

This index provides bibliographical references and abstracts to Canadian education literature of both research and practical value, including journal articles; monographs; theses; dissertations; research reports; government reports from federal, provincial, and territorial departments; curriculum documents; and forthcoming titles. It serves as an awareness tool to current information for teachers, administrators, researchers, and academics. The index includes a list of journal titles indexed, the corporate and personal names indexes, a comprehensive subject index in both French and English, and document delivery services information for contributors. Subject terms are drawn from the *Canadian Education Thesaurus*.

I-78 **Sociology of Education Abstracts**. Abingdon, Oxfordshire, England: Carfax, 1965- . Quarterly.

This is an international indexing service that draws from a wide range of international sources, but with an emphasis on materials originating from the United Kingdom. It aspires to meet the information needs of all practitioners, researchers, and everyone interested in the sociological study of education. It serves as an awareness tool for identifying, locating, and verifying important new and old publications on the theoretical, methodological, and policy developments in the field of sociology of education. The coverage is extensive and covers over 600 periodicals articles and books annually. There are an author index and a subject index.

I-79 **Research into Higher Education Abstracts**. Abingdon, Oxfordshire, England: Carfax, 1966- . 3/yr.

This abstracting service provides an index to books, journal articles, monographs, chapters in a book, and theses and dissertations relevant to the theory, research, and practice of higher education. Abstracts are also provided for the materials indexed. Although it is international in scope, the focus is on higher educational literature published in or dealing with the British Commonwealth and Europe. Over 600 abstracts are produced annually. They are divided into eight main headings: national systems and comparative studies, institutional management, curriculum, research, students, staff, finance and physical resources, and contributory studies and research approaches. There are subject and author indexes, which enhances access. There is also a list of journals with addresses on which abstracts are based.

Dissertations and Theses

I-80 **American Dissertations on Foreign Education: A Bibliography with Abstracts**. Edited by Franklin Parker and Betty June Parker. Troy, NY: Whitston, 1971–1990.

Each volume in this series is dedicated to an individual country and attempts to examine and abstract all locatable doctoral dissertations completed in the United States, Canada, and some European countries. Included are dissertations that deal with the work and influence of educational, scientific, and cultural agencies; individuals; and movements in the field of education. Arrangement is alphabetical by author, and each volume includes abbreviations used in the series and a subject index. The twenty volumes deal with Canada; India; Japan; Africa; Scandinavia; China; Korea; Mexico; South America; Central America, West Indies, Caribbean, and Latin America; Pakistan and Bangladesh; Iran and Iraq; Israel; Middle East; Thailand; Asia; Pacific; Philippines; Australia and New Zealand; and Great Britain.

Although dissertation information needs in education are well served by *Dissertation Abstracts International* (*DAI*) (A-39), this source is noteworthy for three reasons: It concentrates solely on education dissertations; it is more international in scope than *DAI*; and it is a convenient, one-stop source for people working in comparative and international education. One drawback is that many of the countries covered in the 1970s and 1980s are in need of updating.

I-81 **Master's Theses Directories: Education**. Cedar Falls, IA: Herbert M. Silvey, 1991–1992.

This directory, published from 1952 to 1990 as *Master's Theses in Education*, includes both master's and educational specialist degree theses available via interlibrary loan. Arrangement is by seventy-one broad subject categories, with indexes by author, subject, and institution (by state). Each citation gives entry number, author, title, and institutional code. General information about locating master's theses is included in the introduction to each volume.

DIRECTORIES

Education as a field is overwhelmed by directories, particularly those of institutions. Coverage overlap is tremendous. Because only a select few can be discussed here, it is recommended that for a more extensive discussion readers refer to Sarah Barbara Watstein and Barbara Wurtzel, "Higher Education Directories: An Overview," *Booklist* 89, no. 6 (November 15, 1992): 518–624.

Evaluation

I-82   Gourman, Jack. **Gourman Report: A Rating of Undergraduate Programs in American and International Universities**. 8th rev. ed. Los Angeles: National Education Standards, 1993.

I-83   Gourman, Jack. **Gourman Report: A Rating of Graduate and Professional Programs in American and International Universities**. 6th rev. ed. Los Angeles: National Education Standards, 1993.

Each of these reports covers more than 150 undergraduate and more than 100 graduate academic disciplines at a large number of institutions and provides both rankings and a single overall numerical score for each program. Schools in the United States are arranged by discipline, foreign schools by country. The volume contains ratings for professional programs and covers the fields of law, dentistry, medicine, veterinary medicine, nursing, optometry, and pharmacy. Arrangement is by country and academic programs by subject field. Each entry provides the institution's name, address, a description, and evaluation by the author.

These directories and their previous editions are at the center of a storm of controversy revolving around the author's refusal to give more than a vague indication of his sources of information or his methods of analysis and evaluation. Even though their credibility is questioned, the reports are well known primarily because few of the other commonly used general guides to graduate study offer such ratings.

I-84   **Cass & Birnbaum's Guide to American Colleges**. New York: Harper Perennial, 1964- . Biennial.

The purpose of this directory is to provide prospective students and their parents with analytical and comparative data on more than 1,500 accredited four-year colleges and undergraduate programs. Emphasis is on the scholastic achievements of the student body, the academic opportunities offered by the institutions, and the quality of the faculty.

Arrangement is alphabetical by college. Description of each college is preceded by an introductory statement; admission information, including indication of level of selectivity, brief admission requirements for some, and average SAT/ACT scores; academic environment, including degrees conferred, percentage who graduate, and special programs like those designed for the returning adult student; graduates' career data; varsity sports; campus life, including composition of the student body in terms of geography; race, and religion; annual costs; and general institutional data. Indexing is provided by state, religious orientation, and selectivity. Also included is a comparative listing of majors.

The selectivity index, which is one of the most useful features of this reference tool, is based on percentage of applicants accepted by the college, the average test scores of recent freshman classes, the ranking of recent freshmen in their high school classes, and other related data that measure the scholastic potential of the student body.

I-85   **Educational Rankings Annual: 3000 Rankings and Lists on Education**. Edited by Lynn C. Hattendorf. Detroit: Gale, 1994.

ERA is a source on ranking information that includes not just source citations but also the actual rankings. It covers 3,000 national, regional, local, and international lists and rankings for all levels of education. The studies are primarily U.S., but some relevant studies from Canada and other countries are included. A useful outline of the contents is provided in the front of the volume, followed by the educational rankings, which are arranged alphabetically by subject. Each entry includes ranking title, ranking basis/background, remarks, number listed, ranking, and source. The index has been expanded to include the schools, programs, and states and ties the descriptive entry titles to what is being ranked.

I-86 **Rugg's Recommendations on the Colleges**. By Frederick E. Rugg. Compiled and edited by the College Staff of Rugg's Recommendations. Sarasota, FL: Rugg's Recommendations, 1980- . Annual.

Written by a secondary school college counselor, the current edition of this reference work covers sixty-eight majors at 541 four-year colleges. Covered are the 240 colleges that have a Phi Beta Kappa chapter and more than 300 other colleges that were determined to be as good as the Phi Beta Kappa colleges or that had excellent specialized programs based on student opinion and counselor input. Arrangement is alphabetical by academic field, subdivided by selectivity, and identified as to size of enrollment. Selectivity is based on SAT/ACT scores and high school averages. Following the eighty or so recommended programs are an alphabetical listing of schools with the SAT/total recommended major and a number of appendixes.

Although there may be more suitable sources, this guide is often requested by students, parents, and high school counselors.

I-87 **An Assessment of Research Doctorate Programs in the United States**. By the National Academy of Science. Edited by Brendan Maher, Marvin Goldberger, and Pamela Ebert Flattau. Washington, DC: National Academy Press, 1995.

This new one-volume edition covers all of the same broad subject areas as the previous five-volume edition. It continues to be sponsored by the Conference Board of Associated Research Councils, which is composed of the American Council of Learned Societies, the American Council on Education, the National Research Council (NRC), and the Social Science Research Council. Unlike the Gourman reports, the techniques and measures used by this tool are fully explained and placed in the context of the existing literature of higher-education evaluation.

A comparison is provided of the quality of programs in thirty-two disciplines and more than 200 doctorate-granting universities. Programs are judged on the basis of size, characteristics of graduates, reputation, library size, research support, and faculty publication record. Each of the five volumes provides a brief introduction detailing the number of programs studied, average total statistics for the field, and an explanation of the tabular data. Each type of statistical test is explicitly identified. Following the tables are discussions of needed future studies, additional debate on the validity of some of the measures, and copies of the survey instruments.

Elementary and Secondary Education

I-88 **The Handbook of Private Schools**. Boston: P. E. Sargent, 1915- . Annual.

"Porter Sargent," as this handbook is popularly called, is the most respected private school directory available. The 1994 edition lists 1,684 schools plus 250 more in a "Private Schools Illustrated" section. Arrangement is by geographical region, state, and city. Each city or town is described with relevant or interesting information. Each entry lists the name of the admissions officer; grades offered; academic orientation, including whether the curriculum is college preparatory, pre-preparatory, general academic, or specialized; number of yearly admissions in each grade; total student enrollment; number of faculty; number of students in the previous year's graduating class; number of those who went to college; and tuition information.

The "Private School Illustrated" section serves as a supplement in which 300 schools pay for space to stress features they consider most significant. Entries are divided into categories: coeducational, girls, boys, underachiever, and schools abroad. This is followed by a "Concise Listing of Schools," for those schools that do not have enough information or that do not qualify for the

"Leading Schools" section. There is also a section for classified directories of firms and agencies, and an index of schools completes the book.

I-89 **Patterson's American Education**. Mount Prospect, IL: Educational Directories, 1904- . Annual.

I-90 **Patterson's Elementary Education**. Mount Prospect, IL: Educational Directories, 1989- . Annual.

These two guides provide a comprehensive list of schools in the United States. The only schools that are not represented are special-needs schools and private and parochial schools with fewer than 100 students. Entries contain the school name, mailing address, contact person, student enrollment, grade range, type of school, and perhaps additional descriptive material supplied by the school. It is important to read the two sections in the front of the book, "How to Use This Directory" and a "Guide to Editorial Style," in order to understand the codes provided in the entries. Indexing is provided in *Patterson's American Education* for universities and colleges, community and junior colleges, career schools, hospitals, and preparatory schools. *Patterson's Elementary Education* covers kindergarten schools, primary schools, elementary schools, middle schools, and K–12 schools; the 1995 edition covers more than 13,500 school districts; 58,000 public, private, and Catholic elementary schools; and 13,000 junior and middle schools.

Part I of the 1995 *American Education* contains information from 11,400 school districts on approximately 19,000 public, private, and Catholic high schools and 15,000 junior and middle schools arranged alphabetically by state. This is followed by territorial secondary schools, religious school superintendents, and educational associations and societies. Part II includes "Patterson's Schools Classified," listing more than 7,000 postsecondary schools. An updated version of this section is published separately in paperback.

Postsecondary Education

I-91 **Accredited Institutions of Postsecondary Education, Programs, Candidates**. Washington, DC: American Council on Education, 1964- . Annual.

This publication is the most comprehensive and authoritative tool available for determining the accreditation status of public, private, two-year, four-year, and vocational education institutions in the United States, as well as U.S. chartered schools in fourteen countries. The list, which also includes candidates for accreditation, is provided by U.S. accrediting agencies recognized by the newly formed Commission on Recognition of Postsecondary Accreditation (CORPA), the successor to the Council on Postsecondary Accreditation (COPA). The current edition includes more than 5,000 entries divided into two sections: degree-granting and nondegree-granting institutions. Each entry includes the name and address of the institution, a brief description, date of first accreditation or date and status of admission, type of accreditation and name of accrediting body, type of academic calendar, levels of degrees offered, specialized accreditations, name and title of chief executive officer, latest enrollment figure, and professional accreditation. Appendixes provide an explanation of accreditation, a reprint of the Joint Statement on Transfer and Award of Academic Credits, and a list of the accrediting groups recognized by CORPA.

I-92 **American Universities and Colleges**. Washington, DC: Walter de Gruyter, 1928- . Quadrennial.

Profiles of more than 1,900 institutions of higher education that are accredited and offer a baccalaureate or higher degree are represented in the latest edition of this standard directory for U.S. colleges and universities. Entries are arranged alphabetically by state and institution. Descriptions include the school's regional, professional, and institutional accreditation; characteristics; brief history; institutional structure in terms of governance and composition; calendar; characteristics of freshmen; admission and degree requirements; distinctive educational programs; ROTC; degrees and other formal awards conferred; fees and other expenses; financial aid; departments and teaching staff; enrollment; foreign students; student life; publications; library collections; finances; buildings; and the name of the chief executive officer. Preceding the listing are a series of introductory essays on higher education in the United States and a section describing the accreditation activities in each professional field represented by a specialized accrediting agency recognized by the Committee on Recognition of Postsecondary Accreditation (CORPA). Appendixes include essays on academic codes and ceremonies, tables of earned doctorates, ROTC programs, summary data on institutions appearing in the main section, and a brief description of the American Council of Education. General and institutional indexes are provided at the end of the volume. This work remains a standard in the field, with no other college guide providing as much detail about institutions.

I-93 **Peterson's Annual Guides to Graduate Study**. 6 vols. Princeton, NJ: Peterson's Guides, 1976- . Annual.

One of the few directories solely dedicated to graduate study, this comprehensive work provides current information on graduate and professional programs in more than 31,000 administrative and academic units at more than 1,500 accredited institutions in the United States, U.S. territories, Canada, Mexico, Europe, and Africa. It consists of six volumes: an overview; humanities, arts, and social sciences; biological and agricultural sciences; physical sciences and mathematics; engineering and applied sciences; and business, education, health, and law.

Each volume has a section called "The Graduate Adviser," which provides information on application, financial aid, and tests; a directory of programs; profiles of institutions; essays; institutional changes; abbreviations; and indexes of profiles and directories. Arrangement in volumes 2–6 is alphabetical by field and then by institution. Volumes can be purchased individually or as a set.

Electronic access: Peterson's full graduate database is also available as a CD-ROM from Peterson's, *Peterson's GRADLINE*, CD-ROM from SilverPlatter, *GradSearch CD*, and online through two Dialog and CompuServe's Knowledge Index.

I-94 **Peterson's Guide to Two-Year Colleges**. Princeton, NJ: Peterson's Guides, 1983- . Annual.

I-95 **Peterson's Guide to Four-Year Colleges**. Princeton, NJ: Peterson's Guides, 1983- . Annual.

These two widely consulted college guides provide detailed information for more than 1,400 accredited public and private two- and four-year institutions in the United States and Canada. Both include introductory essays, followed by maps and descriptions of the institutions, which are now arranged alphabetically by state. One of the most useful features is the in-depth description of some of the colleges. Also included are institutional changes since the previous edition and an index to the institutions. The two-year guide has a new section with hints on taking standardized tests and survival tactics for adult learners.

The four-year guide now includes a 3.5-inch IBM diskette containing Peterson's College Application Planner, with college snapshots, inquiry letters, and other resources.

Electronic access: Comparable information to that found in these two guides is available online as Peterson's *College Database* through such services as BRS, Dialog, CompuServe's Knowledge Index, and Dow Jones News/Retrieval. It is also available on CD-ROM and diskette.

I-96 **The College Blue Book**. New York: Macmillan, 1923- . Biennial.

Published since 1923, this directory is one of the major standard guides to two- and four-year institutions in the United States and Canada. More than 3,000 schools are covered in the first two volumes. *Narrative Descriptions* provides entrance requirements, term system, faculty-student ratios, student body data, and special programs; *Tabular Data* gives examination scores, percentage accepted, admission plans available, application deadlines and fees, required high school units, housing data, library statistics, ROTC opportunities, and athletics; and *Degrees Offered by College and Subject* lists majors and the institutions granting them. *Occupational Education* lists almost 8,000 business, trade, and technical schools, and *Scholarships, Fellowships, Grants and Loans* lists more than 2,600 primarily private sources of financial aid, grouped by field of study.

> *Electronic access:* CD-ROM access is available for four of the databases: *The College Blue Book, Occupational Education, Occupational Education State Regulations,* and *Scholarships, Fellowships, Grants and Loans.*

Specialized Guides

I-97 Mitchell, Robert. **The Multicultural Student's Guide to Colleges: What Every African-American, Asian-American, Hispanic, and Native American Applicant Needs to Know**. New York: Farrar, Straus & Giroux, 1993.

This guide offers in-depth profiles of most of the "country's top schools" and addresses the academic support services, financial aid opportunities, and availability of organizations for students of color, plus indications of diversity reflected in the curriculum.

More than 200 colleges and universities are profiled, with information provided by admissions offices and students. Categories for each school consist of a statistics section describing the usual features, plus such topics as percentage of tenured and nontenured faculty who are African-American, Asian-American, Hispanic, or Native American; percentage of nonwhite students over the past five years; most popular majors among students of color; retention rate of nonwhite students; scholarships exclusively for nonwhite students; remediation programs; ethnic studies programs and courses; organizations for nonwhite students; notable nonwhite alumni; and percentage of faculty and administration that is nonwhite. The narrative section covers such subjects as a college's academics, cultural organizations, faculty and staff support, extracurricular activities, and location. Arrangement is alphabetical by state.

Even though many high-quality schools are excluded, and only five of the best-known black colleges are listed, this is a useful tool when used with some of the more comprehensive college directories.

I-98 **The Black Student's Guide to College Success**. Revised and updated by William J. Kekler. Edited by Ruby D. Higgins et al. Westport, CT: Greenwood Press, 1994.

This new, updated, and expanded edition of *The Black Student's Guide* now covers more than 950 colleges and universities. Almost one-third of this guide is devoted to essays on how to succeed in college. It covers such topics as choosing a black or an integrated college, financing, special issues for the black athlete, housing, and getting along with non-blacks on campus. This is followed by a separate part on how certain notable African Americans succeeded in college.

Part 3 contains a directory of colleges and universities in the United States. Also included is a list of prestigious undergraduate institutions; the top ten historically and predominantly black colleges and universities; universities in Africa, Central America, and the Caribbean; and black Greek letter organizations.

I-99 **Directory for Exceptional Children**. Boston: Porter Sargent, 1954- . Irregular.

Comprehensive data on 3,000 facilities and organizations in the United States serving children with special needs are provided in the 1994–1995 edition of this directory. Coverage includes schools and clinics for the learning disabled; private, state, and public facilities for the emotionally disturbed and the mentally retarded; and speech and hearing clinics.

Each section is arranged alphabetically by state, cities, and facilities. Entries include name, address, category, sex and age range, name of facility director, type of handicaps accepted, grades offered, academic orientation, curriculum, therapy offerings, enrollment, staff, rates and financial aid, summer programs, organizational structure and establishment, and a description of the programs and services. Following the entries for facilities is a listing of associations, agencies (including a list of federal and state agencies), and societies and foundations. Indexing is provided for schools and facilities.

I-100 **Peterson's Colleges with Programs for Students with Learning Disabilities**. 4th ed. Edited by Charles T. Mangrum II and Stephen S. Strichart. Princeton, NJ: Peterson's, 1994.

This directory, which now comes with an IBM-compatible disk, is an excellent starting place for those in the college selection process who are looking for colleges and universities that accept and serve students with learning disabilities (LD). It contains descriptions of nearly 1,600 such programs. Information was gathered by mailing questionnaires to all (more than 3,250) accredited two- and four-year colleges and universities in the United States and U.S. territories. The volume begins with some brief essays on college opportunities for LD students, how to select a college, and what it takes to succeed. A quick-reference table of colleges, organized by state, precedes the college profile listings, which are divided into two sections: colleges with comprehensive programs and colleges with special services. The newest edition now includes sections on graduate-level options, financial aid, and special services at Canadian schools. Indexing is provided at the back of the volume.

I-101 **Complete Learning Disabilities Directory: Products, Resources, Books, Services**. Edited by Leslie Mackenzie. Lakeville, CT: Grey House Publishing, 1993/1994- . Annual.

This handy directory provides a list of resources for people with physical or mental disabilities; it is particularly useful due to the comprehensive coverage and the descriptions included with most listings. Included are schools, learning centers, vocational training programs, associations, organizations, and relevant government agencies. The first edition of this directory was titled *Complete Directory for People with Learning Disabilities*. The 1995/1996 edition includes chapters on teaching materials and texts; computers; professional periodicals and texts; schools; testing resources; toys and games; and programs for the learning disabled, including camps and summer programs, conferences and workshops, exchange programs, adult literacy, transition skills, and employment programs.

Indexing by entry and subject is provided at the back of the volume. The subjects in the subject index are too broad and have too many listings to be of more than limited usefulness. However, this directory is a useful tool for people looking for a guide to such resources.

Electronic access: A computerized version that can be merged with most database software programs is now available.

I-102 Burgess, William E. **Oryx Guide to Distance Learning**. Phoenix, AZ: Oryx Press, 1994.

The focus of this directory is on courses offered via media-assisted teaching. Information was gathered from 298 accredited U.S. institutions offering 1,507 courses that grant academic credit or are used for transfer to other institutions. Unlike many directories, the guide provides complete descriptions of courses available through distance learning. Formats include courses available on audiocassettes, audiographic conferencing, e-mail, videocassettes, broadcast television via local cable stations, computer tutorials, and online interaction via modems. Descriptions include the geographic access area, courses offered, delivery methods, accreditation, admission requirements, tuition, application of distance credits to degrees, grade/exam system, and library services. Indexing is provided for subject, delivery system, and institution. An appendix lists institutions that provide nationwide or worldwide course access.

Financial Aid

I-103 **The College Blue Book: Scholarships, Fellowships, Grants, and Loans**. New York: Macmillan, 1975- . Triennial.

This volume, which is part 5 of *The College Blue Book* set (I-96), is divided into nine broad subject areas: area studies, environmental studies, humanities, life sciences, medical sciences, minorities, physical sciences, social sciences, and technology. These sections are preceded by a general section that lists sponsors who do not restrict their awards to the study of a specific subject. More than 1,800 awards are included, and entries in the latest edition provide name and address of the organization offering the aid; brief background of the organization; title of the award; area, field, or subject; level of education for which award is granted; number, amount, and type of award; eligibility requirements and application procedures; and deadlines. Indexing is provided for subject, level of education, sponsoring organization, and title of awards.

Although this directory concentrates primarily on private sources of financial aid, the introduction points out that there is a lot of assistance available from other schools and all levels of government, and it recommends other sources of information regarding federal, state, and college institutional funds.

I-104 **College Costs and Financial Aid Handbook**. New York: College Entrance Examination Board, 1980/1981- . Annual.

Formerly titled *The College Cost Book*, this guide to financial aid planning is one of the most respected resources available. The majority of this directory is in the form of tables, arranged by state and institution, including data on tuition and fees, books and supplies, costs of campus residency, home costs, number of students receiving aid, need-based aid, grants and scholarships, financial aid application deadlines, and documentation requirements. Indexing is by institution and includes schools offering tuition and fee waivers and special tuition payment plans. Also included are sources of information about state grant programs.

I-105 **The Grants Register**. New York: St. Martin's Press, 1969/1970- . Biennial.

This highly regarded reference tool is intended for graduates or postgraduates who are nationals of the United States, Canada, United Kingdom, Ireland, Australia, New Zealand, South Africa, and the developing countries. Focus is on scholarships, fellowships, and research grants; exchange opportunities, vacation study awards, and travel grants; grants and grants-in-aid; competitions, prizes, and honoraria; and professional, vocational, and special awards. Awards that are restricted to students of a particular university or college are excluded.

The 2,000-plus entries, arranged alphabetically by award or award-granting institution, include the name of the award, purpose, subject, number of awards offered, frequency, value, length, eligibility, and contacts for further information. The subject index has been improved by listing awards according to eligibility and under broader subject headings. Three appendixes provide information about institutions that have terminated their funding schemes, institutions whose information arrived too late to be included in the main text, and institutions that did not reply but may still offer awards.

I-106 Cassidy, Daniel. **The Scholarship Book**. 4th ed. Englewood Cliffs, NJ: Prentice Hall, 1993.

Information for this book was gathered from the National Scholarship Research Service (NSRS), one of the largest private-sector college financial aid research services. The scholarship and award listings include a condensed description of the award, its eligibility requirements, deadline dates, and where to get more information or an application. Awards that do not specify a particular field of study in their eligibility requirements are listed in a large "general" section. Also included are two sections listing helpful publications and organizations that can provide other types of guidance information. Three indexes are provided: "quick find," based on the most common eligibility requirements; field of study; and alphabetical.

For information on financial aid for study outside the United States, readers can consult Cassidy's *International Scholarship Book: The Complete Guide to Financial Aid for Study Anywhere in the World*, 3d ed. (Career Press, 1993).

I-107 Schlachter, Gail Ann, with R. David Weber. **Directory of Financial Aids for Minorities**. San Carlos, CA: Reference Service Press, 1984- . Biennial.

This unique directory concentrates on programs designed primarily or exclusively for Asian Americans (including Chinese, Japanese, Vietnamese, and Koreans), African Americans, Hispanic Americans (including Chicanos and Puerto Ricans), Native Americans (including Eskimos, American

Indians, Hawaiians, and Samoans), and minorities in general. "Excluded are awards available equally to Caucasians and minorities and financial aid programs administered by individual academic institutions solely for the benefit of their currently enrolled students."

The 1995–1997 directory is divided into four sections: a descriptive list of financial aids designed primarily or exclusively for minorities (scholarships, fellowships, loans, grants, awards, and internships), a list of state sources of educational benefits, an annotated bibliography of directories listing general financial aid programs, and a set of six indexes (program title, sponsoring organization, residency, tenure, subject, and calendar). Reference Service Press also publishes two other directories: *Directory of Financial Aids for Women* (1970- ; biennial) and *Financial Aid for the Disabled and Their Families* (1988- ; biennial).

International Study

I-108 **Academic Year Abroad**. New York: Institute of International Education, 1987- . Annual.

I-109 **Vacation Study Abroad**. New York: Institute of International Education, 1983- . Annual.

The Institute of International Education is the largest U.S. agency devoted to educational exchanges at the postsecondary level and has been in existence for more than sixty-five years. These annual series have been around since the 1960s and have been published under a variety of titles and formats. The two volumes can be used together or separately and provide one of the most comprehensive sources for international study.

Academic Year Abroad includes information on more than 2,100 postsecondary study programs in other countries, most sponsored or cosponsored by colleges and universities accredited in the United States. *Vacation Study Abroad* focuses on more than 1,600 summer study programs and short courses that are geared to undergraduates, graduates, adults, and professionals. Arrangement is by the geographical region in which the programs take place, subdivided alphabetically by county, then by city, town, or region. Entries are numbered and indexed by sponsoring institutions, consortia, fields of study, special options, and cost ranges. Both titles indicate whether eligibility is limited, if academic credit is available, in which language the course is taught, costs, housing, deadlines, and availability of financial aid.

I-110 **The World of Learning**. London: Europa; distr., Detroit: Gale, 1947- . Annual.

This unique reference work, long considered the standard international organizational directory, is the source of choice for questions about foreign scholarly institutions. It covers more than 150,000 higher-education personnel from more than 26,000 institutions and organizations. The first of the two parts of the directory covers international organizations (e.g., UNESCO) and is arranged alphabetically by field of endeavor, giving names, statements of objectives, addresses, and publications. National organizations—including universities, museums, galleries, research institutes, academies, technical institutes, and libraries—are listed in the second part alphabetically by country and then by institutional name. Entries include institutional names and addresses, names of prominent administrators and faculty, library holdings, and other data. A comprehensive 100-page index provides access to all of the institutions covered.

The foreword of the most current edition includes comments on recent political upheavals, the dissolution of the Soviet bloc and Yugoslavia, and national reorganizations of education systems.

I-111 **Guide to American Educational Directories**. 8th ed. Edited by Barry Klein. West Nyack, NY: Todd Publications, 1999.

This is a directory of directories that provides a guide to the major educational directories of the United States and major foreign directories. Its goal is to assist educational organizations and associations, teachers, professors, and researchers in finding current and accurate sources of information in the field of education. There are over 1,000 new directories included in this edition, and approximately 500 directories in the previous edition have been canceled. Entries are grouped into more than 100 educational headings that are arranged topically from accounting to zoological and animal sciences. Each entry includes brief description of the title and full publisher and distributor information including the addresses, telephone numbers, and price. The subject and alphabetical title indexes enhance access to the titles contained in the directory.

I-112   Directory of Curriculum Materials Centers. 4th ed. Edited by Beth Anderson. Chicago: Association of College and Research Libraries, 1996.

This directory lists and describes curriculum materials centers (CMCs) or collections at 278 institutions in the United States and Canada. Each CMC supports the teacher education program in the institution by its collection, which is a representation of the instructional materials in the pre-K–12 schools. The institutions in the United States are listed before the ones in Canada. They are arranged by state or province. The entries are arranged alphabetically within the states or provinces. Each entry includes the name of the curriculum material center or collection, the type and size of the collection, the address and telephone number, and other vital information such as the format of the bibliographic records. The name, title, and e-mail address of the supervisor are also provided. The directory includes an appendix, which is the questionnaire used to gather the data for the directory. The institution index provides quick access to the institutions included.

I-113   Directory of ERIC Resource Collections. Washington, DC: Office of Educational Research and Improvement, National Library of Education, U.S. Department of Education, 1996- . Irregular.

This directory continues *Directory of ERIC Information Service Providers*. It lists 984 organizations that provide access to the *ERIC* database and other related resources. The purpose of the directory is to serve as a quick locating tool to nearby organizations that provide access to ERIC and other related resources and services. The organizations included have to meet one of the following criteria: provide electronic access to *ERIC* database on a regular basis; maintain sizable collections of ERIC microfiche; and/or subscribe to and collect ERIC publications, including *Current Index to Journals in Education* (I-66), *Resources in Education* (I-67), the *Thesaurus of ERIC Descriptors* (I-48), and/or ERIC Clearinghouse publications. Entries are arranged geographically and divided into three groups: the United States; outlying territories, and other countries. Within the U.S. group, entries are arranged alphabetically by state and city. Within the outlying territories entries are arranged alphabetically by territories. The entries within other countries group are arranged alphabetically by country and city. These arrangements provide quick referral and location of ERIC resource collection providers.

I-114   Directory of Graduate Programs. 17th ed. Princeton, NJ: Educational Testing Service, 1999/2000. Biennial.

Directory of Graduate Programs is published under the sponsorship of the Graduate Record Examinations Board (GRE) and the Council of Graduate Schools. It continues the official GRE/CGS directory of graduate programs. It is designed as a source of information for individuals who are thinking of entering a graduate program. The directory helps the user find out about numerous institutions and programs. The seventeenth edition features detailed information on over 800 accredited institutions in the United States and Canada that supplied data about their graduate programs of study.

The directory is published in four volumes: *Volume A: Natural Sciences; Volume B: Engineering & Business*; *Volume C: Social Sciences & Education*; and *Volume D: Arts & Humanities and Other Fields.* There are six sections in each volume: "Comparison by Program," "Comparison by Institution," "Institution Descriptions," "Addresses," "Resources," and "Index of Programs." Information is provided in tabular format and in narrative format. Information provided under each entry includes graduate programs offered, graduate degree requirements, tuition/academic fees, financial assistance, campus housing, and institutional contacts. This is a valuable resource for prospective graduate students and their parents.

I-115 Schlachter, Gail A. **Publication Directory of Financial Aids for Women, 1999–2001**. El Dorado Hills, CA: Reference Service Press, 1999. Biennial.

This directory focuses specifically on financial aid programs that are primarily designed for women. It is intended to be used to locate financial aid programs for women. It lists over 1,700 scholarships, fellowships, loans, grants, personal grants-in-aid, awards, and internships reserved exclusively for women. The information provided is current and accurate. Information from the previous edition of the work has been updated. Over 225 new entries are included in this edition. Women at all educational levels, from high school to postdoctoral and professional levels, are eligible to apply for the financial aids listed in the directory. It is divided into three parts: financial aid programs primarily or exclusively for women; annotated bibliography of general financial aid directories; and indexes. There are six indexes: program title, sponsoring organization, residency, tenability, subject, and calendar. They are arranged word-by-word alphabetically. The indexes enhance the ease of use and the accessibility of the directory.

I-116 **Cabell's Directory of Publishing Opportunities in Education**. 5th ed. Edited by David W. E. Cabell. Beaumont, TX: Cabell Publishing, 1998.

This directory serves as a source of information on more than 440 potential journals in which novice and veteran authors can publish. The goal of the directory is to help authors publish their ideas. The information provided in the directory enables authors to compare the needs of each journal included and the characteristics of their articles. Such comparison helps authors to identify the journal or journals that could be interested in publishing their articles. Entries are grouped under twenty-seven subject disciplines. Each entry provides vital information on the publisher, editor, address for submission, telephone and fax numbers, e-mail address, circulation data, manuscript topics, publication guidelines, manuscript guidelines/comments, and review information. This directory can also serve as an awareness tool to education journal literature.

I-117 Schlachter, Gail Ann, and R. David Weber. **Financial Aid for African Americans, 2001–2003**. El Dorado Hills, CA: Reference Service Press, 2001.

I-118 Schlachter, Gail Ann, and R. David Weber. **Financial Aid for Asian Americans, 2001–2003**. El Dorado Hills, CA: Reference Service Press, 2001.

I-119 Schlachter, Gail Ann, and R. David Weber. **Financial Aid for Hispanic Americans, 2001–2003**. El Dorado Hills, CA: Reference Service Press, 2001.

I-120 Schlachter, Gail Ann, and R. David Weber. **Financial Aid for Native Americans, 2001–2003**. El Dorado Hills, CA: Reference Service Press, 2001.

These four titles continue the *Directory of Financial Aids for Minorities*, which was the only comprehensive and current listing of funding sources open to African Americans, Asian Americans, Hispanic Americans, and Native Americans. The goal of the directory was to serve as an awareness tool for financial aid programs that are exclusively for minorities. It became a reliable and invaluable source of funding information for students, scholars, librarians, researchers, and academic advisers. As a result of the rapid increase in the number of financial aid programs set aside for minorities, the directory became continuously fatter.

In 1997, *Directory of Financial Aids for Minorities* split into four volumes: *Financial Aid for African Americans*; *Financial Aid for Asian Americans*; *Financial Aid for Hispanic Americans*; and *Financial Aid for Native Americans*. *Financial Aid for African Americans* lists and describes scholarships, fellowships, loans, grants, awards, and internships that are available primarily or exclusively for African Americans. *Financial Aid for Asian Americans* lists and describes scholarships, fellowships, loans, grants, awards, and internships that are available primarily or exclusively for Americans of Chinese, Japanese, Korean, Vietnamese, Filipino, or other Asian origins. *Financial Aid for Hispanic Americans* lists and describes scholarships, fellowships, loans, grants, awards, and internships that are available primarily or exclusively for Americans of Mexican, Puerto Rican, Cuban, or other Latin American descent. *Financial Aid for Native Americans* lists and describes scholarships, fellowships, loans, grants, awards, and internships that are available primarily or exclusively for American Indians, Native Alaskans, and Native Pacific Islanders as well as Native Hawaiians and Samoans.

I-121 Atwell, Robert H., and David Pierce. **American Community Colleges: A Guide**. 10th ed. Phoenix, AZ: Oryx Press, 1995.
This directory continues *American Community, Technical, and Junior Colleges: A Guide*. The American Council on Education and the American Association of Community Colleges jointly produce it. Two-year colleges that are members, or could be members, of the American Association of Community Colleges are included. There are 1,181 entries of public, private, and private proprietary institutions in the United States and its territories. The main entry section is organized alphabetically by state and city in which the institution is located. Under each entry the information provided includes contact information, history of the institution, type of control, administrators, grounds, and type of accreditation. The information under academic information includes calendar, admission requirements, student inquiries, teaching staff, areas of study, program awards, enrollment, student life, and library/learning resource center. Information is also provided on tuition and fees and student financial aid. The subject index is extensive and it is arranged alphabetically by subject headings based on major field of study. The institution name index is arranged alphabetically. *American Community Colleges: A Guide* is a useful source of information on two-year institutions.

HANDBOOKS

I-122 **Handbook of Research on Social Studies Teaching and Learning**. Edited by James P. Shaver. New York: Macmillan, 1991.
This well-organized and authoritative handbook does an excellent job of achieving its stated purposes of providing a comprehensive view and analysis of research in the field and presenting a synthesis of past research and identification of needed future efforts. A project of the National Council for the Social Studies, the essays are written by specialists and are intended for use by researchers, including professors, graduate students, and policy makers at all levels. It consists of eight sections and begins with chapters focusing on the quality and productivity of research in the field. Articles in section 1 cover such issues as historiography; philosophical inquiry; theory; and critical, qualitative, and quantitative research. The next two sections relate to students and teachers, with articles on cognitive, emotional, and social development from several different perspectives; social studies for culturally diverse, at-risk, disabled, and gifted students; research and history of teaching in the field; and teacher characteristics, education, and competence in social studies education. Section 4 includes seven essays on the contexts of social studies education. Section 5 centers on the issue of instructional outcomes and how to achieve them. Sections 6 and 7 discuss components of instruction and interrelations between social studies and other curriculum areas. The final section provides international perspectives on research on social studies, with an essay on cross-national social studies research and other essays on research in England, Eastern Europe, and Africa.

I-123 **The International Encyclopedia of Educational Evaluation**. Edited by Herbert J. Walberg and Geneva D. Hartel. Tarrytown, NY: Pergamon Press, 1990.
The International Encyclopedia of Educational Evaluation is in the form of a handbook and provides an easily accessible, current, and comprehensive discussion of significant topics in educational evaluation. Consisting of more than 150 signed articles by well-known specialists in the field, it provides practical and scholarly information for student and researcher alike. The arrangement is one of the strengths of the volume. The preface provides the historical background on the subject, and the work is then divided into eight major parts. Parts 1 through 3 provide an overview of evaluation, the role of the evaluator and dimensions of evaluation practice, and how curriculum and school setting affect the design and execution of education evaluation studies. The next four parts

contain articles on the practice of evaluation research, from measurement theory and measurement applications to types of tests and examinations and research methodology. Part 8 deals with educational policy and planning, considering the purposes and impacts of evaluation research. Indexing is provided for names, subjects, and contributors.

I-124 **Handbook of Educational Ideas and Practices.** Edited by Noel Entwistle, Ruth Jonathan, and others. New York: Routledge, Chapman & Hall, 1990.

The 101 essays contained in this handbook focus on compulsory schooling, with a separate section provided for issues related to early childhood, postsecondary, and adult and continuing education. The essays, intended for both practitioners and students, cover a wide range of topics and provide summaries of current thinking, research findings, and innovative practices. The beginning chapters discuss the current social, political, and economic forces affecting education. The next series of essays covers the organization and management of institutions. Section 3 centers on the learning environment, and the last section discusses the individual learner and how education can address the requirements of children with special needs.

I-125 **Handbook of College and University Administration.** 2 vols. Edited by Asa S. Knowles. New York: McGraw-Hill, 1970.

The purpose of a handbook is to provide nuts-and-bolts information for practitioners while simultaneously enlightening them about the conceptual basis for daily tasks. Quite simply, a good handbook shows practitioners both the shape and substance of their activity. Knowles's handbook, with its signed articles written by authorities in the field, is excellent and serves as a starting place for a quick view of higher-education administration in the United States. Volume 1 is devoted to general administration, including sections on planning, public relations, physical plant, business and finance, the law, and alumni relations. Volume 2 covers academic topics such as programs, standards, faculty, and student personnel. There is an abundance of real and hypothetical examples, sample forms and documents, tables, charts, and outlines.

This landmark work is aging and is, therefore, lacking information on some of the more current trends and issues. In addition, the indexing is topical (no names) and somewhat shallow. In spite of these caveats, Knowles's achievement remains impressive even after three decades.

The Handbook of School Psychology. 2d ed. Edited by Terry B. Gutkin and Cecil R. Reynolds. New York: John Wiley, 1990. (See J-66)

This edition of *The Handbook* is a complete revision and reorganization of the first edition published in 1982. More than half of the volume covers new authors or new topics of interest, and all of the chapters that were retained have been updated and revised to reflect contemporary views of the field. Of particular interest is the inclusion of a section devoted to the science of psychology and how it influences school psychology theory and practice.

The work is intended to serve school psychologists, and is divided into five major sections: current perspectives; scientific study of behavior: contributions of theory and practice; psychological and educational assessment; school psychological interventions: focus on children; and school psychological interventions: focus on staff, programs, and organizations. Each section contains signed articles on a spectrum of subtopics. The approach is descriptive rather than speculative, but the authors represent a wide variety of philosophical perspectives.

That this work is solidly grounded in the literature of school psychology is evidenced by references in the articles and an extensive bibliography. A name index is provided. The only disappointment in this otherwise superlative handbook is the very short index, surely somewhat superficial for a volume of more than 1,200 pages.

I-126 **Handbook of Research on the Education of Young Children.** Edited by Bernard Spodek. New York: Macmillan, 1993.

Handbook of Research on the Education of Young Children, which is thorough and well organized, is intended for scholars, practitioners, and policy makers. It is a compendium of critical reviews of relevant research and identifies implications of this research for practice and policy development for the field of early childhood education. The volume is divided into four parts, with a total of thirty-three articles written by recognized researchers and scholars in the field. Part I focuses on child development and includes articles on cognitive development, motor development, and peer relationships. Part II centers on curriculum issues and includes articles on the role of play, language, literacy, mathematics, social studies, arts, music, science, multicultural education, and electronic media and how these topics relate to early childhood education. Part III relates to educational policy, with articles on such topics as testing, tracking, and retaining; readiness screening; play environments; child care; parental influence; diversity; and teacher preparation. The final section discusses research strategies and methodologies, including standardized and nonstandardized measurement instruments, qualitative research, trends, and a case study of Chinese and Japanese kindergartens. Name and subject indexes are provided at the back of the volume.

I-127 **International Handbook of Early Childhood Education**. Edited by Gary A. Woodill, Judith Bernhard, and Lawrence Prochner. New York: Garland, 1992.

International Handbook of Early Childhood Education consists of fifty-six articles on early childhood education in forty-seven countries on five continents. Following two introductory essays on historical perspectives and current themes, the volume provides authoritative, signed essays by recognized experts in the field from each of the countries represented. Organization of the articles is alphabetical by country; topics covered include curriculum, teacher training, parental involvement, special education, staffing, and funding. Concentration is on current early childhood education practices from the countries represented, so this is a useful tool in a time of an increasing emphasis on global education. The volume concludes with a helpful bibliography on comparative early childhood education, biographies of the contributors, and an index.

I-128 **Special Education Handbook: An Introductory Reference**. Philadelphia: Open University Press, 1991.

Intended for students of special education, experienced teachers, advisors, and people who work with children with special needs, this handbook contains more than 1,000 terms covering twelve different fields of special education. Entries on individuals and the majority of societies and associations are excluded. There are a number of entries, primarily North American, relating to legislation, projects, tests, and reports. Entries appear in alphabetical order.

I-129 **Handbook of Research on Curriculum: A Project of the American Educational Research Association**. Edited by Philip W. Jackson. New York: Macmillan, 1992.

A project of the American Educational Research Association, this authoritative handbook is similar in format and organization to the research handbook *Education of Young Children*. It too relies on essays written by respected researchers and scholars in the field. The thirty-four signed essays are divided into four parts: conceptual and methodological perspectives, how the curriculum is shaped, the curriculum as a shaping force, and topics and issues within curricular categories. This valuable tool is enhanced by the inclusion of historical information, current bibliographies, and implications for future research in each of the chapters.

I-130 **Handbook of Gifted Education**. Edited by Nicholas Colangelo and Gary R. Davis. Needham, MA: Allyn & Bacon, 1991.

The purpose of this comprehensive and highly respected handbook is to serve as a text for upper-level undergraduate and graduate courses and as a resource for researchers in the field. Consisting of thirty-one signed essays, the book is divided into seven main sections: an introduction, including a historical overview and a discussion of issues; definitions and identification; instructional models and teaching practices; creativity and thinking skills; psychological and counseling services; special topics that deal with special populations; and future trends. Author and subject indexes are provided at the back of the volume.

I-131   Ambert, Alba N. **Bilingual Education and English As a Second Language: A Research Handbook, 1988–1990**. New York: Garland, 1991.

Covering a two-year period of research on the education of language minority students, this volume discusses culturally diverse populations beyond the realm of language and includes societal and acculturative factors affecting these children. Topics covered include issues of early childhood education, gifted and talented, teacher training, and psychoeducational assessment of language minority children. Appendixes provide a list of multifunctional resource centers, organizations, and journals and newsletters in the field. Indexing is by author and subject.

I-132   Willis, Barry. **Distance Education: A Practical Guide**. Englewood Cliffs, NJ: Educational Technology Publications, 1993.

This handbook is a good place to start for faculty and administrators considering using distance education as a means of delivery of instruction. It begins with an introduction and historical overview, followed by a discussion of summaries of research in the field and roles and responsibilities of the "key players." The next chapters provide a step-by-step description of how to develop and adapt distance-delivered instruction, including selection of the appropriate teaching tools and technology, and strategies for effective teaching. The last chapter is a discussion of the future of distance education.

I-133   **International Handbook of Teachers and Teaching**. 2 vols. Edited by Bruce J. Biddle, Thomas L. Good, and Ivor F. Goodson. Dordrecht, The Netherlands: Kluwer Academic, 1997.

This resource is a representative collection of a cross-section of recent thinking, and studies on teachers and teaching. The authors of the chapters are renowned individuals in the field of education and teacher education. Their biographical sketches are presented in the preliminary pages of the first volume. The rapidly changing world and position of teachers is examined from different perspectives. Contributors focused on issues such as the professional behavior, lives, and careers of teachers; feminism; reform initiatives; multiculturalism; students; and political, social, and economic situations. The articles are well-researched, and several references are provided at the end of each article. There are also name and subject indexes, which serve as access points to the information contained in the international handbook. This handbook is a useful source for educators, scholars, teacher educators, teachers, and graduate students to gain a better understanding of teaching and teachers.

I-134   **International Handbook of Education and Development: Preparing Schools, Students and Nations for the Twenty-First Century**. Edited by William K. Cummings and Noel F. McGinn. New York: Elsevier Science, 1997.

The Development Dictionary influenced the writing of this international handbook. According to the editors it is a unique collection of thinking about education and development and the contradictions in the constructs of education and development. Contributors, who are outstanding international educators, attempt to document the interrelated impact of education and society. The forty-nine chapters are divided into two sections. Section 1, "Modern Education Reformed," is divided into four subsections: "The Construction and Diffusion of the Modern School"; "Reforming Modern Education: General Issues"; "Reforming Modern Education: Issues in Specific Countries"; and "The Changing Relationship Between Education and Development." Section 2, "Modern Education Replaced," is subdivided into "Changes in the Environment for Education" and "Possibilities for the Future Organization and Operation of Education." There are author and subject indexes.

I-135   Farrell, Michael, Trevor Kerry, and Carolle Kerry. **Blackwell Handbook of Education**. Oxford: Blackwell, 1995.

This handbook is a source of information and clarification of areas and topics of education in the United Kingdom. The goal of this resource is to present factual information, recent data, and important studies in an easy-to-read style. The handbook covers eight major areas: 1) education: concepts, issues, disciplines, types, and phases; 2) schools and other institutions and their organization; 3) roles and people; 4) rules, regulations, and conditions; 5) individual differences (among learners); 6) curriculum and assessment; 7) pedagogy; and 8) resources. There are four sections in the book. The first contains A to Z entries on educational terminology relevant to education in the United Kingdom. The terms are explained in either a dictionary or an encyclopedic format. The second section is a listing of acronyms and abbreviations. The third section is a directory of British and Welsh organizations. The fourth section, which is in chronological order, is a description of education legislation in Britain and Wales. *Blackwell Handbook of Education* is a useful resource for professional teachers, researchers, students, administrators, academics, inspectors, advisors, politicians, and educational psychologists seeking information on education in the United Kingdom.

I-136   **Handbook of World Education: A Comparative Guide to Higher Education and Educational Systems of the World**. Edited by Walter Wickremasinghe. Houston, TX: American Collegiate Service, 1992.

This handbook is a one-volume, compact reference source of current information on the major aspects of educational systems around the world. One of the goals of this work is to enhance international understanding by fostering global fluidity in education. The main audience for the handbook consists of scholars, students, and teachers who need information on foreign educational systems. A chapter is devoted to each country, and an educator native to that country wrote it. Information provided under each entry is grouped into sections: background, primary and secondary education, higher education, issues and trends, and a brief bibliography. The main focus is on higher education level, although lower education levels are described. The information provided on higher education includes general characteristics, governance, undergraduate studies, student facilities, costs, funding, faculty, advanced studies, and research. The information provided on the primary and secondary education includes information on educational administration, primary and secondary education, curriculum, examinations, funding, and policies pertaining to teachers. Each chapter has a section on issues and trends, which talks about contemporary issues and concerns in that country. There is a bibliography at the end of each chapter.

I-137   **Handbook of Research on School Supervision**. Edited by Gerald R. Firth and Edward F. Pajak. New York: Simon & Schuster/Macmillan, 1998.

According to its preface, this handbook simultaneously serves to explore the antecedents, establish the parameters, and speculate on the destiny of supervision in educational settings. One of the goals of the handbook is to pull together in one volume the major research in the field of school supervision. It provides a synopsis of school supervision, its history, philosophy, practice, trends, and future. There are fifty-two chapters, grouped under nine sections: "Supervision As a Field of Inquiry," "Foundations of Supervision," "Supervision As Professional Practice," "Specialized Areas of Supervision," "Levels of Supervision," "Relationships to Affiliated Fields," "Supervision As an Organized Profession," "Theories of Supervision," and "Forces and Factors." There are name and subject indexes, which enhance accessibility to the information contained in the handbook.

BIOGRAPHICAL SOURCES

To begin a search for background information on a person in the field of education, it is first necessary to define *education* in the context of the research question. Are you searching for information on someone who is, for example, a professor of education, an educational administrator, or a teacher in an educational institution?

Not many biographical tools available provide comprehensive coverage for either past or present people in the field of education. Retrospective information can be found in a number of sources in addition to the ones listed below. Researchers should be referred to standard general biographical reference sources, including the biographical tools from other disciplines, for cases in which the individual under investigation may have cross-disciplinary affiliation.

None of the current sources gives the breadth of information provided retrospectively by *Leaders in Education* (I-138). Only one of the two current sources listed below, *Who's Who in American Education* (I-142), gives such biographical information as basic data, activities, accomplishments, and lists of publications. The other one, *The National Faculty Directory* (I-141), is primarily a directory, providing only names, positions, and addresses. For individuals associated specifically with education as a discipline, however, the researcher may find some useful biographical information in certain educational encyclopedias or dictionaries, such as *The Encyclopedia of Education* (I-52), *The International Encyclopedia of Education* (I-53), *American Educators' Encyclopedia* (I-55), *The Facts on File Dictionary of Education* (I-37), *An International Dictionary of Adult and Continuing Education* (I-40), and *Concise Encyclopedia of Special Education* (I-57).

Retrospective

I-138 **Leaders in Education**. 5th ed. Edited by Jaques Cattell. New York: R. R. Bowker, 1974.

This major retrospective biographical directory for the field of education was first published in 1932. Successive editions appeared in 1941, 1948, and 1971 before this, the final edition. Nearly 17,000 biographical sketches of U.S. and Canadian educators appear in this volume. Included are officers and deans of accredited institutions of higher education, education professors, directors and staff of educational research institutes, public and private school officials, officers of education-related foundations, officials of the Office of Education and major educational associations, and selected authors. Criteria for inclusion were based on the individual's stature in the field as demonstrated by positions held, memberships in professional associations, and research activity. Arrangement is alphabetical, and indexing is provided by geographical areas and subject specialty.

Because of its emphasis on administrators, this is an especially useful source for research in the area of leadership, such as determining what jobs university chief executive officers tend to hold immediately prior to assuming a presidency.

I-139 **Directory of American Scholars**. 8th ed. 4 vols. New York: R. R. Bowker, 1982.

First published in 1942 under the auspices of the American Council of Learned Societies, *Directory of American Scholars* is one of the most important retrospective biographical reference tools for U.S. humanities scholars. Unlike *Leaders in Education* (I-138), whose emphasis is primarily administrative achievement, *American Scholars* focuses on scholarship. This set profiles more than 37,500 U.S. and Canadian scholars who were active in teaching, research, and publishing.

The directory is divided into four subject volumes: history; English, speech, and drama; foreign languages, linguistics, and philosophy; and philosophy, religion, and law. Entries are arranged alphabetically and provide primary discipline; vital statistics; education; honorary degrees; past and present professional experience; concurrent positions; membership in international, national, and regional societies; honors and awards; research interest; publications; and mailing address. Each volume includes a geographical index by state and city, and volume 4 has an alphabetical index to scholars in all four volumes.

Entrants were selected on the basis of recommendations from entrants in former editions, academic deans, or citations in professional journals.

I-140   Ohles, John F. **Biographical Dictionary of American Education**. 3 vols. Westport, CT: Greenwood Press, 1978.

The *Biographical Dictionary of American Education* provides bibliographical data on 1,665 U.S. educators from colonial times to 1976. Entrants come from all levels of education but are limited to people "who had been engaged in education, were eminent, and had reached the age of sixty, had retired, or had died by January 1, 1975." Each entry includes birth and death dates; educational background; professional career, including contributions to education; and selected reference works. Appendixes are provided in volume 3 for place of birth, state of major service, and field of specialty; chronology of birth years; important dates in U.S. education; and a general index. This biographical dictionary is particularly useful because of its efforts to include women and minority educators.

Current

I-141   **The National Faculty Directory**. Detroit: Gale, 1970- . Annual.

The twenty-fifth edition of this directory provides an alphabetical list of more than 615,000 members of teaching faculty at approximately 3,600 U.S. colleges and universities, and about 240 Canadian institutions using English-language instructional materials. *NFD* is compiled from current class schedules and academic catalogs; is verified and updated continuously throughout the year; and has as its stated purpose to serve as mailing lists for textbook, academic, technical book, and computer software publishers. Coverage is limited to faculty with classroom teaching responsibilities; entries list name, departmental affiliation, and institutional address. Preceding the faculty entries is a "Roster of Colleges and Universities," arranged alphabetically by state.

Since the demise of *Faculty White Pages* (Gale Research, 1989–1991) and its predecessor, the twelve-volume *Faculty Directory of Higher Education* (Gale Research, 1988), *NFD* serves as the primary directory of higher-education faculty in the United States and Canada.

I-142   **Who's Who in American Education**. New Providence, NJ: Marquis Who's Who, 1988- . Annual.

Outstanding educators at all levels of education, administrators, selected officials from the U.S. Department of Education, state superintendents of education, presidents and superintendents of state boards of education, librarians, and program directors are represented in the 1994–1995 edition of this directory. Selection criteria for the 28,000 sketches are based on position of responsibility held and level of achievement attained.

Entries include name; occupation; vital statistics; parents; marriage; children; education; professional certifications; career; career-related items; writings and creative works; civic and political activities; military; awards and fellowships; professional and association memberships, clubs, and lodges; political affiliation; religion; home address; and office address. Following the biographical profiles is a professional index arranged alphabetically by specialty and then subdivided by state and city. At the end of the volume is a list of more than 170 awards from ninety-five granting agencies of national and regional importance.

I-143   Gordon, Peter, and Richard Aldrich. **Biographical Dictionary of North American and European Educationists**. London: Woburn Press, 1997.

This biographical dictionary assembles in one single volume prominent educationists in North America and Europe. Entries are limited to deceased prominent educators from 1800 onward. Each biography is approximately a page in length. Most of them have a bibliography at the end of the article. Although educationists are drawn from twenty countries, the coverage is not balanced. Over half of the entries are American. Educationists from Germany, Canada, France, Switzerland, Russia, and Belgium are fairly covered. This resource is not useful for seeking information on educationists from countries such as Bulgaria, Czechoslovakia, Finland, and Greece.

I-144   Ohles, Frederik, Shirley M. Ohles, and John G. Ramsay. **Biographical Dictionary of Modern American Educators**. Westport, CT: Greenwood Press, 1997.

This resource continues the *Biographical Dictionary of American Education* (I-140). The subject of this dictionary is educators who made a distinctive contribution to the field of education in the United States. The goal of the dictionary is to have representation from the breadth and variety of society as represented in American educational ideas, practices, and institutions. Therefore much care was taken to include individuals from diverse groups of educators, from different areas of education, from all the fifty states, and from different backgrounds. There are 410 individuals included in the dictionary who were born before January 1, 1935, or who are deceased. The sketches highlight the unique and significant impact they made on education in the United States. The basic information provided under each entry includes personal history, distinctive contribution to education, brief outline of education and career, scholarly activities and publications, awards and honors received, and some references. Professional relationships among the biographees are identified by the use of "q.v.," which means to see another biographical entry in the dictionary. Accessibility is enhanced by the five appendixes: place of birth, states of major service, field of work, chronology of birth years, and important dates in American education. There is also an index that has some cross-references.

I-145   Peltzman, Barbara Ruth. **Pioneers of Early Childhood Education: A Bio-Bibliographical Guide**. Westport, CT: Greenwood Press, 1998.

This resource provides short biographies and bibliographies of selected pre-modern and modern individuals and organizations that had a significant impact on early childhood education. Pioneers included are now deceased. The narratives on the pioneers promote the understanding of the theories and practices presented in the context of the time in which they are written. One of the goals of this resource is to provide information on the recent and distant past of early childhood education. Entries are organized alphabetically. Each entry consists of a brief biographical sketch of the biographee's distinct contribution to early childhood education, primary sources, and secondary sources, which are in chronological order. Each of the sources included has a full bibliographic citation and is annotated. There is an appendix, which is a chronological list of pre-modern and modern pioneers. There are also a bibliography and an index at the end of the work.

STATISTICAL SOURCES

I-146   **Digest of Education Statistics**. Washington, DC: U.S. Department of Education, Office of Educational Research and Improvement, Center for Statistics, 1962- . Annual.

Anyone beginning a search for statistical information on any aspect of U.S. education should start with this source. It reports and summarizes data gathered from within and outside the federal government, especially the results of surveys collected by the National Center for Education Statistics (NCES). The NCES covers all levels of education and has as its purpose, which is set by statute, "to collect, analyze, and disseminate statistics and other data related to education in the United States and in other nations." Topics include numbers of educational institutions, teachers, enrollments, graduates, educational attainment, finances, federal funds for education, employment and income of graduates, libraries, and international education. The supplemental information on population trends, attitudes on education, education characteristics of the labor force, government finances, and economic trends provides background for evaluating education data. To qualify for inclusion, material must be nationwide in scope and of current interest and value. Appendixes provide definitions and guides to the tables and sources.

If this title does not provide sufficient information, the searcher can move on to other NCES series, such as *The Condition of Education* (I-147), *Projections, Education Statistics* (Department of Health and Human Services, U.S. Government Printing Office, 1983/1984- ; annual), and *Degrees and Other Awards Conferred by Institutions of Higher Education* (U.S. Department of Education, Office of Educational Research and Improvement, 1994- ; annual).

I-147   **The Condition of Education**. Washington, DC: U.S. Department of Education, Office of Educational Research and Improvement, Center for Education Statistics, 1975- . Annual.

Data for this report, which provides a broad overview of the educational enterprise, draw on the same sources as *Digest of Education Statistics* (I-146). There are indicators measuring the health of education, monitoring important developments, and showing trends in major aspects of education. These indicators are divided into six areas: access, participation, and progress; achievement, attainment, and curriculum; economic and other outcomes of education; size, growth, and output of educational institutions; climate, classrooms, and diversity in educational institutions; and human and financial resources of educational institutions. Key data on issues in elementary, secondary, and postsecondary education are integrated into each of the six sections.

Whereas *Digest of Education Statistics* includes more than 400 statistical tables, plus figures and appendixes, *The Condition of Education* is limited to no more than sixty indicators in each year's report. Some of the new indicators are participation in adult education, international comparisons of reading literacy, educational attainment of Hispanics, education and labor market outcomes of high school diploma and GED graduates, participation in school decision making, and time in the classroom. Each indicator has text, tables, charts, technical supporting data, supplemental information, and data sources. The appendixes include supplemental tables and notes, an annotated listing of data sources, a glossary, and a general index.

I-148   **Almanac of Higher Education**. Chicago: University of Chicago Press, 1989- . Annual.

Produced by the editors of *Chronicle of Higher Education* (Chronicle of Higher Education, 1966-), the *Almanac* provides current statistics relating to higher education in an easy-to-use format. The volume is divided into three major sections: the nation, including data on students, faculty, and staff, resources, and institutions; the states, including sources and notes; and enrollment by race at more than 3,100 colleges and universities. Brief introductions with descriptions of background, current trends, and issues are included in both the national and individual state sections.

I-149   **Annotated Bibliography of National Sources of Adult Education Statistics. Bibliographie Annotée des Sources Nationales de Statistiques sur l'Education des Adultes**. Paris: UNESCO; distr., Lanham, MD: UNIPUB, 1989.

Prepared by UNESCO in the Division of Primary Education, Literacy and Adult Education and Education in Rural Areas, this English-language work excludes the United States but is a valuable source of adult education statistics from sixty-three countries around the world, including Africa, the Middle East, Asia, Europe, and Latin America and the Caribbean. The intended audience is administrators, planners, policy advisers, decisionmakers, and research workers in the field of adult education. Data were gathered by means of a specially designed questionnaire to the member states of UNESCO. There is information on students, teachers, graduates, student-hours, operating income, expenditures, institutions, age, sex, marital status, and so forth.

I-150   **Condition of Teaching: A State-by-State Analysis, 1990**. Princeton, NJ: Carnegie Foundation for the Advancement of Teaching, 1990.

The goal of this report is to present the views of teachers on the current state and concerns of the teaching profession. The report is drawn from a survey of teacher opinions of education. It contains the highlights of the survey and state-by-state comparisons. The survey highlights are "Teachers Today: Attitudes and Values"; "The Students"; "Academics: Learning and Instruction"; "Working Conditions: School Climate"; "Working Conditions: Buildings and Materials"; "Teacher Involvement in Decision Making"; "The Status of the Profession"; and "Achieving Excellence." A narrative summary preceding the tables enhances the information contained in them.

I-151 **Educational Rankings Annual 1999**. Edited by Westney Hattendorf and C. Lynn. Detroit: Gale, 1998.

The rankings information in this title is drawn from reputable books, publishing, periodicals, dictionaries, encyclopedias, hospitals, libraries, museums, employment, and other educational and published sources. There are 3,700 rankings and lists, arranged alphabetically by subject. The topics about the quality of education, which the rankings address, include reputation, faculty publications, tuition rates, library facilities, test scores, alumni achievement, faculty salaries, and admissions selectivity. The scope is international and all levels of education are included. Each entry includes the ranking title, ranking basis/background, number listed, ranking, and sources. There is a comprehensive index, which includes topics and institutions being ranked.

I-152 Andersen, Charles J. **Fact Book on Higher Education 1997**. Phoenix, AZ: American Council on education and the Oryx Press, 1998.

Compiled from federal and state government agencies and nongovernment and private research organizations and professional associations, this resource provides statistical information on baseline trends in higher education. One of the special features of the *Fact Book* is the comparisons over time that it provides. It is divided into four categories: "Demographic and Economic Data"; "Enrollment Data"; "Institution and Finance, Faculty, Staff, and Students"; and "Earned Degrees." At the beginning of each section there is a highlights section that identifies noteworthy changes in that category. Each table is followed by a graphic display of the data presented in the table. There is a "Guide to Sources" at the end of the *Fact Book*, which identifies the major information sources. The descriptive table of contents and the index enhance the accessibility and ease of use of this *Fact Book*.

I-153 Nettles, Michael T., and Laura W. Perna. **African American Education Data Book**. Fairfax, VA: Fredrick D. Patterson Research Institute, The College Fund/UNCF, 1997.

This data book assembles in one source information on the education of African Americans. The research carried out by the Frederick D. Patterson Research Institute focuses on the educational status and attainment of African Americans from preschool to adulthood. The goal of the data book is to disseminate research information that will guide educators, the general public, and policy makers in developing programs, activities, and initiatives that have the potential to improve educational opportunities and outcomes for African Americans. It is the first of its kind. The data book consists of three volumes, each with a unique focus. The first volume focuses on higher education and adult education; the second on the educational status of African-American preschool, elementary, and secondary school children; and the third on the transitions from school to college and from school to work. Each of the volumes has a separate executive summary.

I-154 **UNESCO Statistical Yearbook 1998**. Paris: United Nations Educational, Scientific and Cultural Organization, 1998.

This international statistical yearbook provides information on the educational, scientific, and cultural life and activities of approximately 200 countries and territories. The data contained in the yearbook are drawn from UNESCO questionnaires and special surveys. The statistical sources are divided into ten parts: "Reference Tables," "Education," "Education by Country," "Public Expenditure on Education," "Research and Experimental Development," "Summary Tables for Culture and Communication Subjects by Groups of Countries," "Printed Matter," "Films and Cinema," "Broadcasting," and "Cultural Paper." There are also seven appendixes: "Member States and Associate Members of UNESCO," "School and Financial Years," "Exchange Rates," "List of Selected UNESCO Statistical Publications," "Tables That Have Appeared in Past Editions of the Yearbook," "Introductory Texts in Russian," and "Introductory Texts in Arabic." The introductory texts to each chapter and some table texts are translated into Russian and Arabic.

YEARBOOKS

I-155 **World Yearbook of Education**. New York: Taylor & Francis, 1965- .
Annual.

This general source was called *Yearbook of Education* between 1932 and 1964. It suspended publication between 1941 and 1947 and between 1975 and 1978. However, it remains a well-respected source of authoritative summaries of current developments in international education. Each year's volume has a different editor, is devoted to a current educational theme of international interest, and contains articles by experts from several countries. Recent volumes include *Urban Education* (1992); *Special Needs and Special Education* (1993); *Gender Gap in Higher Education* (1994); *Youth, Education, and Work* (1995); and *Evaluation of Higher Education Systems* (1996). Essays are addressed to the intelligent general reader.

World scholars contribute the signed articles, which include abstracts and chapter references. In addition, each volume has a bibliography, author biographies, and an author/title index. The editor provides an overview of the volume as a whole in an introductory essay. Although it has a British perspective, this is a good source for international and comparative education and can be profitably used in conjunction with *The International Encyclopedia of Education* (I-53).

I-156 **Educational Media and Technology Yearbook**. Englewood, CO: Libraries Unlimited, 1985- . Annual.

Published in cooperation with the ERIC Clearinghouse on Information & Technology and the Association for Educational Communications and Technology, this yearbook continues to do an excellent job of carrying out its function of chronicling the previous year's trends and issues in the field of educational media and technology. For example, the 1994 volumes contain essays on such topics as "Analysis of Computers in Education as a Cultural Field," "Alternative Assessment and Technology," and "Telecommunications and Distance Education." It also serves as a reference tool for reports on the seven major professional associations in North America in the field. The reference section lists more than 200 professional organizations and associations in North America; graduate programs, including graduate programs in educational computing; and coverage of scholarships, fellowships, and awards. Each volume also contains a "mediagraphy" of the previous year's important print and nonprint publications. A single alphabetical index provides access to associations and organizations, authors, titles, and subjects, identified by boldface type.

For an international perspective on current trends and issues in the field of educational media and technology, readers should consult *International Yearbook of Educational and Training Technology* (Kogan Page, 1976- ; annual).

I-157 **The Yearbook of Education Law**. Topeka, KS: National Organization on Legal Problems of Education, 1933- . Annual.

Continuing *Yearbook of School Law* (1950–1987) and absorbing *Yearbook of Higher Education* (1977–1981), *The Yearbook of Education Law* "provides bias-free summaries of state appellate court cases and federal trial and appellate court cases affecting the operation, management, and governance of elementary and secondary schools as well as postsecondary institutions." Each section is written by an education specialist in the areas under discussion. The 1995 edition covers such topics as employees, bargaining, pupils, individuals with disabilities, torts, sports, education, and federal and state legislation. Summaries seem to be mostly descriptive, although some analysis is provided. A subject index and a table of cases are found at the end of the volume.

I-158 **Making Standards Matter: An Annual Fifty-State Report on Efforts to Raise Academic Standards**. Washington, DC: American Federation of Teachers, 1995.

This resource analyzes and reports the status of academic standards in the United States. It highlights the progress each of the fifty states is making toward the improvement of academic standards.

The information contained in the report is grouped under five sections. The first section describes the American Federation of Teachers' criteria for assessing state reform initiatives. The second section presents a synopsis of the situation. The third section presents suggestions for improving educational reform efforts. The fourth section gives an overview of the current condition of each state on the subject of standards. The fifth section reproduces the feedback from each of the fifty education departments.

INTERNET RESOURCES

The number of people who have access to the Internet is expanding daily, and Internet-based sources of information for the field of education are growing at an increasingly rapid rate. Listed in this section are a few of the largest and most useful education-related Internet information sources currently available to online users.

I-159 Arizona State University. Tempe: Arizona State University. URL: http://info.asu.edu.

ASU is a major site for educational information. Its *Resource for Educators* (http://olam.ed.asu.edu/~casey/links.html) includes "Electronic Journals & Other Full Text Resources," "Employment Opportunities & Grants," "K–12 School/District Web Sites," "Resources for K–12 Educators," and "Educational Technology and Other Education Sites."

I-160 AskERIC Virtual Library. Syracuse, NY: Syracuse University Educational Resources Information Center. URL: http://ericir.syr.edu.

This Internet-based question-answering service for anyone involved in education is sponsored by ERIC (I-39) and provides information resources within forty-eight working hours. Content includes "AskERIC Lesson Plans," *ERIC Digests*, ERIC publications, archives of education-related listservs, "AskERIC InfoGuides," and the *ERIC Bibliographic Database* (*RIE* and *CIJE*).

I-161 California State University. Carson: California State University. URL: http://nis.calstate.edu.

The *K–12 Kaleidoscope* (http://www.coreplus.calstate.edu/KALEIDO/Nav.html) is a collection of World Wide Web sites divided into academic subjects with search and reference tools on "Arts & Artisans," "Current Events," "Education Info," "Kids Resources," "Language Arts," "Physical Education," "Science," "Social Studies," "Teachers," and "Technology." The link to *Education Info* (http://www.coreplus.calstate.edu/ KALEIDO/Education.html) provides access to many other useful resources. Some of these are *At Risk Institute, Education Center, EdWeb K–12, The Kids on Campus, School Net, Talented and Gifted*, and *Web of Addictions*.

Another CSU Internet site with additional education information is the World Wide Web Search tool EINet Galaxy Link to Social Sciences (http://galaxy.einet.net/galaxy/Social-Sciences.html). This will lead to resources on such topics as adult education, higher education, measurement and evaluation, and special education.

I-162 Educom. Washington, DC: Educom. URL: http://www.educom.edu.

Founded in 1964, Educom is an organization devoted to information technology in higher education and represents a wide range of institutions. Its focus for the 1990s is twofold: to increase "individual and institutional intellectual productivity through access to and use of information resources and technology," and to ensure "the creation of an information infrastructure that will meet society's needs into the twenty-first century." Available through this server are Educom publications such as the *Educom Update, Edupage* electronic newsletter, conference and seminar schedules, archives of *Educom Review*, and news about their corporate affiliates.

I-163 **FIE (Federal Information Exchange)**. Gaithersburg, MD: Federal Information Exchange. URL: http://gopher.fie.com.
Federal agency information on research programs, contact information, educational programs and services, equipment grants, procurement notices, and minority opportunities are available through FIE. A database accessible through FIE is *MOLIS*, which contains information on colleges and universities for minorities.

I-164 **Canada's SchoolNet**. Carleton: SchoolNet Support Group. URL: http://schoolnet2.carleton.ca.
SchoolNet was developed as a cooperative venture between the Canadian government and industry. Its primary purpose is to introduce elementary and secondary school students and teachers to the Internet. It is a user-driven resource free to teachers, students, and educational organizations.

I-165 **ED. U.S. Department of Education, World Wide Web Server**. Washington, DC: U.S. Department of Education, Office of Educational Research and Improvement, National Library of Education. URL: http://gopher.ed.gov.
This directory contains education software contributed to the OERI Electronic Bulletin Board by educators. Descriptions of the software are supplied by the contributors, and files are free to be downloaded and used by anyone. In addition, there is information related to research findings, statistical data, and teaching materials. The intended audience is primarily users interested in K–12 education. One directory, "A Teacher's Guide to the U.S. Dept. of Education," includes information about *GOALS 2000—National Education Goals*. Another directory, "Researcher's Guide to the U.S. Department of Education," offers information on ED programs, ED fellowship programs, and services and resources.

I-166 **The University of Michigan Library**. Ann Arbor: University of Michigan. URL: http://gopher.lib.umich.edu.
The University of Michigan Library's MLink project (http://mlink.hh.lib.umich.edu/main-index.html) provides a wealth of information on education and the social sciences. The education link leads to such subjects as adult education, distance learning, higher education, K–12 education, research in education, resources for educators, and educational statistics.
The University Library's ULibrary gopher provides links to *Social Sciences Resources* (gopher://una.hh.lib.umich.edu:70/11/socsci), which contains many education-related links. Included are a number of full-text journals, such as the *Journal of Statistics Education* and the *Journal of Technology Education*.

I-167 **American School Directory (ASD)**. URL: http://www.asd.com/asd/asdhome.htm.
ASD is a comprehensive listing of and Internet guide to over all 108,000 K–12 schools in the United States. Coverage includes public and private schools, schools with or without Internet access. This site provides vital information on all the schools. One can access school calendars, maps, pictures, menus, contact information, wish lists, and student artwork. It is a useful source of information for families planning to relocate. Search options include School Search, School of the Day, Product Guide, Education Connection (learning activities), Alumni Directory, Free email, and Homework Help.

I-168 **Chinese Educational Resources Information Centre Project: Chinese ERIC**. URL: http://www1.fed.cuhk.edu.hk/en/index.htm.
This *C-ERIC* (Chinese ERIC) is a site that mirrors the Educational Resources Information Center database. The goal of the C-ERIC project is to provide a free electronic database of educational studies in Chinese communities. The target audience for this product consists of educational researchers, policy makers, teachers, practitioners, administrators, media staff, support staff, and students. *C-ERIC* currently contains 8,000 educational articles from seventeen leading journals from Hong Kong, Chinese Mainland, and Taiwan, dating back to 1990, and a small number of theses and dissertations

dating back to 1980. Documents such as proceedings and conference papers are not yet included. C-ERIC Thesaurus of Key Words is still under construction, with search terms classified as keywords rather than descriptors.

I-169 **Education Virtual Library**. URL: http://www.csu.eduau/education/library .html. Australia: Charles Stuart University.

This Web site provides links to numerous education sites globally. It allows access to educational resources such as books, databases, funding, tutorials, methodology, software, and educational technology. Access can be made alphabetically by site, educational level, resources provided, type of site, and country. Gopher sites provide links to related virtual libraries and newsgroups. There are also links to the top fifty educational sites.

I-170 **Educational Information Resources Information Center: ERIC**. Washington DC: National Library of Education. URL: http://accesseric.org:81/.

ERIC is a national information system designed to provide ready access to an extensive body of education-related literature for educators, librarians, administrators, counselors, instructional media staff, support personnel, educational researchers and policy makers, parents, and students. The ERIC system, the world's largest source of education information, through its sixteen subject-specific clearinghouses, associated adjunct clearinghouses, and support components, provides research summaries, bibliographies, reference and referral services, computer searches, and document reproduction. The *ERIC* database contains nearly 1 million abstracts of documents and journal articles on education research and practice and is updated monthly. This Web site has added links to Special Projects, Resources, Parent Brochures, the Department of Education, and the National Library of Education.

I-171 **EROD: Educational Resource Organizations Directory**. Washington, DC: US Department of Education. URL: http://www.ed.gov/Programs/EROD/.

The major goal of EROD is to serve as a site for identifying and contacting organizations that provide information and assistance on an extensive range of topics relevant to the field of education. The intended audience for this site includes teachers, librarians, researchers, and students. There are links to information on the types of organizations the directory covers and the fields of information provided for each of the organizations. Input is solicited from users. As of June 21, 2000, there were 2,792 entries. Information on this site is updated at lease once a year.

I-172 **National Assessment of Educational Progress (NAEP)**. Washington, DC: National Center for Education Statistics, U.S. Department of Education. URL: http://nces.ed.gov/nationsreportcard/site/home.asp.

NAEP, or The Nation's Report Card, is the only national body that reports on the academic performance of fourth, eighth, and twelfth graders to an audience of administrators, principals, policy makers, and teachers. It also provides information on the instructional dependent variables that influenced academic performance. This Web site includes summary data tables in the areas of geography, the arts, civics, mathematics, reading, science, U.S. history, and writing. NAEP's goal for the year 2000 is to have all the fifty states take part in the mathematics and science state assessments at grades 4 and 8. The information on the site can be accessed by audience and subject under the "Starting points for . . . " feature.

I-173 **College and University Home Pages**. URL: http://www.mit.edu:8001 /people/cdemello/univ.html.

This site provides access to the home pages for over 3,000 universities and colleges throughout the world that maintains an Internet presence. The site has access to "Full List of Universities," "Geographical Listings of Universities," "Frequently Asked Questions and Their Answers," "Survey Results," "Compressed Tar File of All Files," and "Gzipped Tar File of All Files." Accessibility by the alphabetical listing of colleges and universities is further enhanced by the possibility to view the institutions under a particular letter.

I-174 **College and University Rankings**. University of Illinois at Urbana-Champaign: Education and Social Science Library. URL: http://www.library.uiuc.edu/edx/rankings.htm.

The goal for this site is to assemble and provide context to various ranking services, educate users about rankings in general, and promote the use of the ranking services. The College and University Rankings page provides ranking information that can be searched by categories such as general and undergraduate, graduate/research programs, business, law, and international (non-US). There are links to print sources and bibliography as well as a cautionary page containing viewpoints on the accuracy of rankings.

I-175 **NCBE; National Clearinghouse for Bilingual Education**. URL: http://www.ncbe.gwu.edu/.

This is one of the initiatives of the NCBE designed to address vital issues and concerns relating to the education of students from linguistically and culturally diverse backgrounds. This site also provides a broad range of information that is a great resource to those who are involved with or who work for programs such as foreign-language programs, ESL (language as a second language) programs, Head Start, Title I, migrant education, and adult education programs. There is information on how to access the NCBE resources, NCBE partners, and contact information. NCBE also provides links to an online library, *AskNCBE*, "Language and Education Links," "Databases," "Success Stories," "In the Classroom," "State Resources," *NCBE Newsline*, and "NCBE Roundtable Forums."

I-176 **World Lecture Hall**. Austin: University of Texas. URL: http://www.utexas.edu/world/lecture/index.html.

The World Lecture Hall is a comprehensive site that publishes links to course materials Web pages that are developed by teachers from all over the world. Some of the courses are delivered virtually, on site, and some fall somewhere in between. The intended audience for the World Lecture Hall includes faculty developers, adventurous students, and any member of the general public. "Useful Links" is a special feature on this site.

I-177 **GEM: The Gateway to Educational Materials**. URL: http://www.thegateway.org.

This is a significant one-stop, any-stop access to first-rate educational resources such as lesson plans, curriculum units, instructional activities, and projects. Subject, keywords, title, and grade level serve as access points to the information accessible through this site. The intended audience for the site includes teachers, parents, and administrators.

I-178 **ED/Office of Elementary and Secondary Education (OESE)**. URL: http://www.ed.gov/offices/OESE/.

The Office of Elementary and Secondary Education (OESE) promotes quality education at the elementary and secondary school levels and disseminates timely information on relevant programs and issues.

I-179 **National Center for Education Statistics (NCES)**. URL: http://nces.ed.gov/.

This is a division of the U.S. Department of Education. It is the primary federal unit dedicated to collecting and analyzing data related to education in the United States and other countries.

I-180 **Gateway to Educational Materials**. URL: http://www.thegateway.org.

This site provides a comprehensive access to high-quality lesson plans, curriculum units, and other education resources on the Web site. There are over 14,000 lesson ideas and learning resources from over 200 organizations on this site. The materials on this site can be accessed by performing basic, browse subject and browse keywords searches. One can also search topic and grade levels.

I-181 **NCATE (National Council for the Accreditation of Teacher Education).** URL: http://www.ncate.org/.

This is the home page for NCATE, the only national body charged with the responsibility for maintaining standards and ensuring accountability and continuous improvement in teacher preparation programs. It provides standards to improve the quality of teachers and the education students get in K–12. Information on almost everything educators and students need to know on standards, indicators, as well as current articles on teacher education-related issues are posted on this site.

I-182 **Annotated Links for Elementary Education.** URL: http://www.students .dsu.edu/hoferan/annotate.htm.

This site provides access to links to information, activities, and resources relevant to elementary education.

I-183 **Elementary education teacher materials at ClassroomDirect.com.** URL: http://www.classroomdirect.com/elementary.htm.

This is the Web site to visit to access information and resources for the elementary school classroom, teacher resources, and elementary education. The focus of the materials on this site is elementary education. ClassroomDirect.com sells, at great discount rates, all types of teacher materials and supplies such as arts and crafts supplies, audiovisual equipment, and computer learning games.

I-184 **IPL Science Fair Project Resource Guide.** URL: http://www.ipl.org /youth/projectguide/.

This is the Internet Public Library Science Fair Project Resource Guide Web site. It serves as a guide to a variety of Web site resources that facilitate student participation in science fairs.

I-185 **School Science Fairs Projects Homepage.** URL: http://www.stemnet .nf.ca/sciencefairs/.

This is a project of the Eastern Newfoundland Science Fairs Council. Educators and students can visit this site to find ideas for school science fair projects. The projects are grouped into primary, intermediate, and senior projects. This Web site also provides access to "cool links."

I-186 **CyberFair: A Resource for and by Elementary Science Students.** URL: http://www.isd77.k12.mn.us/resources/cf/steps.html.

This is a virtual science fair site. Students can go to this site to learn how to complete a project, see samples of projects, and access other useful information.

I-187 **DiscoverySchool.com: Parents, Teachers, Students.** URL: http://school .discovery.com/schoolhome.html.

This is a site for teachers, students, and parents to visit for "fresh ideas to enhance learning." There are links from this site to Student Channel, Teacher Channel, and Family Learning Store. Students can get information to help them complete assignments, teachers can access a rich collection of teacher-approved creative curriculum resources, and parents can purchase items to enhance their children's academic achievement.

I-188 **Division of Science Resources Studies (SRS).** URL: http://www.nsf .gov/sbe/srs/stats.htm.

This site fulfills the legislative mandate of the National Science Foundation Act to provide a central clearinghouse for the collection, interpretation, and analysis of data on scientific and engineering resources. The division compiles, analyzes, and disseminates quantitative information about domestic and international resources devoted to science, engineering, and technology.

I-189 **Earth Science Information Centers (ESIC). Ask USGS.** URL: http://ask
.usgs.gov/.

ESIC is the gateway to the United States Geological Survey (USGS). It provides information
on USGS map products and earth science publications. ESIC provides information about geologic,
hydrologic, topographic, and land use maps, books, and reports. It also supplies information about aerial,
satellite, and radar images and related products

I-190 **SciEd: Science and Mathematics Education Resources.** URL: http://
www-hpcc.astro.washington.edu/scied/science.html.

This site provides access to numerous resources to teach each of the science discipline areas.

I-191 **The Teacher Education Yearbook.** URL: http://www.siu.edu/departments
/coe/ate/yearbk.html.

This site includes access to research report on topics of high interest to teachers at all levels.
Acquisition information is also provided online.

I-192 **Center for Education Reform.** URL: http://edreform.com.

This site provides access to resources, support, and guidance to communities involved in
school improvement across the United States.

I-193 **The MASTER Teacher World Wide Web Site.** URL: http://www
.masterteacher.com/index.html.

This is the site where educators can gain access to the most comprehensive behavior and
discipline resource online.

I-194 **Discipline with Dignity.** URL: http://www.disciplineassociates.com/
index.htm.

This is the site for the activities and resources of Dr. Richard Curwin and Dr. Allen Mendler,
who are well-known internationally for providing thousands of educators and parents with practical,
proven ideas to effectively manage children's behavior in a manner that respects the dignity of each
individual.

I-195 **Teachnet Classroom Management Page.** URL: http://www.teachnet
.com/how-to/manage/index.html.

Here is access to some interesting ideas about class management, links, and ways of managing
classes by computers.

I-196 **Reaching Today's Students: Building the Community Circle of Caring.**
URL: http://www.teachereducation.com/courses.html.

Building the Community Circle of Caring is an exciting synthesis of the most current theories,
strategies, and practices to comprehensively address the needs of children and youth at risk in educational settings. It is put together by the Teacher Education Institute.

I-197 **Selected ERIC Abstracts on Discipline and Classroom Management.**
URL: http://www.ascd.org/services/eric/manage.html.

This is a site maintained by Association of Supervision and Curriculum Development. It
provides access to articles, reports, surveys, and other useful educational documents.

I-198 **Educational Leadership Resource Library**. URL: http://www.coe
.missouri.edu/~cpe/ed_leadership.html.

Educational Leadership Resource Library provides the link to online information and journal articles relating to all aspects of educational leadership, including instructional leadership.

I-199 **Effective Instructional Leadership Manual (EIL)**. URL: http://www
.kde.state.ky.us/olsi/leaders/eil/weilmanualdl.asp.

Effective Instructional Leadership Manual (EIL) is the technical assistance manual for education administrators, professional development coordinators, and providers for the 1998–2000 cycle.

I-200 **Yahoo! Internet Life Magazine**. URL: http://www.zdnet.com/zdsubs
/yahoo/tree/yc9.html.

Yahoo! Internet Life Magazine maintains a Web site that offers a free CD-ROM containing the directory of the best fifty sites on promoting teaching and learning through the use of technology.

I-201 **MathWorld**. URL: http://mathworld.wolfram.com/.

A convenient, comprehensive, and interactive mathematics encyclopedia of mathematics equations, terms, and derivations intended for students, educators, math enthusiasts, and researchers.

I-202 **Math Archives**. URL: http://archives.math.utk.edu/k12.html.

This site provides access to rich collections of materials that can be used in the teaching of mathematics to the K–12 grades. These materials include lesson plans, software, and relevant topics in mathematics.

I-203 **MathSciNet**. URL: http://www.ams.org/mathscinet/basicsearch.

This Web site provides access to reviews, abstracts, and bibliographic references to journal articles, conference proceedings, and books in pure and applied mathematics, computer science, and statistics.

NOTES

1. L. Cremin, *A Public Education* (New York: Basic Books, 1976), 3.

2. G. T. Page and J. B. Thomas, *International Dictionary of Education* (New York: Nichols, 1977), 112.

3. C. V. Good, *Dictionary of Education* (New York: McGraw-Hill, 1973), 202.

4. K. Ryan and J. M. Cooper, *Those Who Can, Teach*, 8th ed. (Boston: Houghton Mifflin, 1998), 549.

5. D. E. Kapel, C. S. Gifford, and M. B. Kapel, *American Educators' Encyclopedia* (Westport, CT: Greenwood Press, 1991), 439.

6. Educational scholars also use humanistic and natural science methodologies and resources, but these are outside the scope of this book.

7. *Encyclopedia of Higher Education* (Tarrytown, NY: Pergamon, 1992); *Encyclopedia of Educational Research* (New York: Macmillan, 1992); *The International Encyclopedia of Education* (New York: Elsevier Science, 1994).

8. Kapel, Gifford, and Kapel, *American Educators' Encyclopedia*, 430.

9. F. Watson, *The Encyclopedia and Dictionary of Education* (London and New York: Sir Isaac Petman, 1921), 1: 520.

10. C. A. Baatz, *The Philosophy of Education: A Guide to Information Sources* (Detroit: Gale, 1980), 2.

11. *Encyclopedia of Education* (New York: Macmillan, 1971), 519.

12. *International Encyclopedia of Higher Education* (San Francisco, CA: Jossey-Bass, 1977), 4: 1378.

13. *Howard Gardner Topics Menu: Howard Gardner's Multiple Intelligence Theory.* Accessed December 19, 2000. URL: http://www.ed.psu.edu/insys/ESD/Gardner/MItheory.html.

14. Austin Independent School District, *The Eight Strands of the Guidance and Counseling Curriculum (Instructional Support: Austin Independent School District 1998).* Accessed December 19, 2000. URL: http://www.austin.isd.tenet.edu/curriculum/guidance/strands.html.

15. Kapel, Gifford, and Kapel, *American Educators' Encyclopedia*, 599.

16. *International Encyclopedia of Higher Education*, 5: 1361.

17. Ibid., 7: 3963.

18. Kapel, Gifford, and Kapel, *American Educators' Encyclopedia*, 362.

19. Ibid., 45–46.

20. D. Ravitch, *A New Era in Urban Education? Policy Brief #35*—August 1998. Accessed December 20, 2000. URL: http://www.brook.edu/comm/PolicyBriefs/pb035/pb35.htm.

21. C. R. Morris, "The Coming Global Boom," *Atlantic* 264, no. 4 (October 1989): 53–54.

22. R. F. Arnove and C. A. Torre, eds. *Comparative Education. The Dialectic of the Global and the Local* (Lanham, MD: Rowman & Littlefield, 1999), 16.

23. *International Encyclopedia of Education*, 2: 1007.

24. Consult the sources listed in this chapter, such as N. P. O'Brien, *Core List of Books and Journals in Education* (I-3) and M. E. Collins, *Education Journals and Serials: An Analytical Guide* (I-7) for specific journal titles or the names of organizations involved in the production of professional and scholarly literature in education.

25. *The Condition of Education* (I-148).

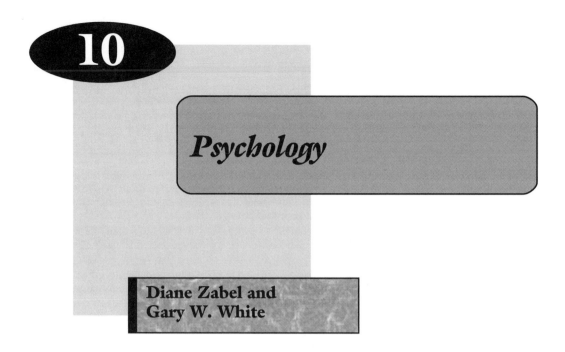

10

Psychology

Diane Zabel and Gary W. White

ESSAY

Psychology is the scientific study of human and animal behavior and is concerned with the mental, social, and biological processes influencing behavior. Hermann Ebbinghaus, a nineteenth-century German psychologist, characterized psychology as having "a long past but only a short history."[1] Philosophers and physicians in ancient Greece theorized about the relationship between mind and body. However, psychology did not emerge as a distinct discipline until the late nineteenth century. Thomas Hardy Leahey's account of psychology's history is a good choice for those who wish to know more about the development of psychology as a discipline.[2]

The association between psychology and philosophy is evident in the treatment of psychology as a branch of philosophy in the Dewey Classification System. The literature of psychology is expansive because psychology has linkages to numerous disciplines beyond philosophy. There are connections to other social sciences, particularly sociology, anthropology, education, and business. Sociologists, anthropologists, and psychologists study behavior in societies, although from different perspectives. Educators and psychologists are concerned with learning. Business has applied psychology to determine what motivates employees or why consumers behave as they do.

Psychology, more than any other social science, has strong ties to the biological and natural sciences. Both physiology and psychology examine the relationship between the brain and behavior. Zoologists and psychologists study animal behavior, although psychologists are generally more interested in using animals as substitutes for human populations when the conditions of an experiment make the use of human subjects inappropriate. The integration of mathematics and psychology has been recognized as a separate division of psychology. Because psychology measures and compares various mental processes in individuals and groups, statistics are an important tool. These strong links to the sciences have affected the dissemination of information in psychology. Many types of materials prevalent in the sciences, such as handbooks and annual reviews of research, are also used heavily in psychology.

The interdisciplinary nature of psychology is reflected in the diversity of its major divisions. Research in experimental psychology concentrates on basic processes such as learning, motivation, and perception. Physiological psychology focuses on the relationship between the body and the mind, particularly the roles of the brain and the nervous system in controlling behavior. Developmental psychologists study human development across the life span, from infancy to old age. Social psychologists observe how people interact with others and how society influences behavior, particularly attitude formation. The diagnosis and treatment of mental and emotional disorders is the subject of clinical psychology. Educational psychologists study learning and develop instructional materials and teaching methods. Industrial/organizational psychology is concerned with people in the workplace. Psychometrics involves the design of tests and measures for the measurement of psychological variables such as intelligence, personality, and aptitude.

Psychology is not only a discipline but also a profession. In 1988, this dual quality led to a schism within the American Psychological Association (APA), the premier professional organization for psychologists in this country. Academic psychologists charged that the APA was dominated by practitioners and formed a separate group, the American Psychological Society, for psychologists whose focus is teaching and research rather than private practice.[3] Academic psychologists formerly made up the majority of the APA's membership. This shift parallels a dramatic shift in psychology. Since World War II, applied psychology has grown dramatically. The subfields of clinical, counseling, educational, and school psychology have experienced the greatest growth.[4] Alan Bellack and Michael Hersen, editors-in-chief of a monumental clinical psychology encyclopedia published in 1998, note in their preface to the first of eleven volumes that there has been not only a phenomenal increase in the number of students and professionals in clinical psychology but a corresponding explosion in publishing in this area.[5] They report that hundreds of books are published annually in clinical psychology, and there is a proliferation of specialty journals relating to specific areas of clinical psychology. In fact, this increasing specialization is an important trend.

Although there may be tensions among factions of the profession, all subfields of the discipline have a common methodology. Psychology uses empirical methods to obtain data. Direct observation and experimentation are standard techniques used in psychological research. Information may also be obtained from case studies, questionnaires, interviews, and standardized tests.

Some psychologists make use of machine-readable data files. Although there is no central source of information on datasets relevant to psychology, psychologists use well-known data archives such as the Inter-University Consortium for Political and Social Science Research (ICPSR), which is located at the University of Michigan, and the Henry A. Murray Research Center of Radcliffe College.[6]

Almost two decades ago, Anne K. Beaubien outlined the nature of psychology literature in an essay on the research process employed by social scientists.[7] Much of what she wrote is still valid. Researchers often contact colleagues directly to exchange findings, but most of the controlled literature exists in the form of journal articles. Psychologists often collaborate on research; multiple authorship of an article or book is common. Psychologists are anxious to disseminate research results quickly, and books take too long to publish. Because the results of empirical research are published in research journals, articles are regarded as primary rather than secondary sources of information. An emphasis on current research contributes to the heavy reliance on journal literature. An early study of citation analyses in the social sciences documented that up to 69 percent of all citations from scholarly research in psychology were to journal articles.[8] In comparison, the citations to journal literature for the social sciences in general ranged from 29 to 43 percent.[9] There is a large body of literature in psychology (published in both psychology and library science journals) using citation analysis as a tool to predict journal usage, determine core psychology journals, and guide collection development decisions. One of the best ways to identify these studies is through the excellent bibliography accompanying Margaret Sylvia's 1998 case study on citation analysis as a methodology for assessing a journal collection in the behavioral sciences.[10] Sylvia analyzed the bibliographic citations to journal articles found in research papers written by undergraduate and graduate students in psychology. She found an overwhelming reliance on recent articles. In her study, 60 percent of the citations were to publications from the 1990s; 31 percent were to articles from the 1980s.[11] Prior to this, Sylvia (in conjunction with Marcella Lesher) had conducted a citation analysis of master's theses and dissertations authored by psychology and counseling students to determine journal usage patterns of graduate students in psychology.[12]

This article is important because it serves as a model that can be used in other disciplines. Two Israeli researchers also employed a citation analysis of master's theses in psychology to determine how graduate students in psychology use library collections.[13] They found that graduate students made significant use of material from fields outside of psychology, reinforcing the notion that psychology is interdisciplinary. What is most interesting is their finding that these students make rather extensive use of publications that are at least twenty years old. This Israeli study showed much greater use of retrospective material (that is, publications that were published two or more decades ago) than Sylvia's study. At the same time, however, their data indicated that there is limited use of publications published more than fifty years ago. Like other studies, their research demonstrated that the majority of citations were to journal articles. This pattern was also confirmed in a more recent citation analysis of dissertations in the field of clinical psychology. This Wright State University study found that 35 percent of the references were to books and book chapters while 62 percent were to journal articles.[14]

Monographs and retrospective bibliographies are viewed as less important for research in psychology. Books often take the form of a collection of readings that are directed to the undergraduate user. However, in the late 1980s the American Psychological Association noticed a trend toward more publishing in the form of chapters within books. The Association estimated that as much as 30 percent of the literature in psychology was in the form of books and book chapters.[15] This finding led to APA's development of *PsycBOOKS* in 1989, an index of books and book chapters in psychology. Although *PsycBOOKS* was only published for four years, book and chapter indexing was added to *PsycINFO*, the major database in psychology, beginning in 1992. Another trend noted by experts is the notable increase in the number of edited books in psychology, perhaps a reflection of psychology's collaborative tradition.[16]

There are several important German-language and many non-English-language monographs published in psychology, but research has indicated that U.S. psychologists rely almost exclusively on English-language material.[17] Professional associations play an important role in the transfer of knowledge. The American Psychological Association alone publishes more than twenty-five research journals and is an important monographic publisher.

Psychology is one of the disciplines that made early use of the Internet to disseminate information. There are vast resources on the Web relating to psychology, many about common psychological problems. Several articles on Internet resources in psychology have addressed this proliferation of sites and the need for review of these sites. Lorrie Knight's 1997 article on the Internet as a reference tool in psychology is still useful for background on this topic.[18] Another excellent evaluative article on psychology Web sites appeared in a 1998 "Webwatch" column of *Library Journal.*[19] In addition to browsing this column, psychology librarians will want to look for articles on Internet resources (as well as other articles pertaining to collection development, reference service, and bibliographic instruction) in *Behavioral & Social Sciences Librarian*, a scholarly journal focusing on the dissemination and use of information in the social and behavioral sciences.

GUIDES

Guides explain the research process in a discipline and advise users on the preparation of research papers. Some are bibliographies, listing the core literature in the discipline.

J-1 Reed, Jeffrey G., and Pam M. Baxter. **Library Use: A Handbook for Psychology**. 2d ed. Washington, DC: American Psychological Association, 1992.
Library Use: A Handbook for Psychology is a guide for finding psychology-related materials in a college library. Most of the 600 sources included will be found in college libraries with collections of 100,000 to 300,000 volumes. There are sections on how to select and define a research topic, locating a book, using *Psychological Abstracts*, using other psychology-related indexing and abstracting services, using citation indexes, searching government information, and using psychological tests and measures. Information about libraries, and library services such as interlibrary loan, is also included. Major sources are well-illustrated with search examples. This reference book bridges a gap not typically addressed in most research methods texts. Although written prior to the rise of the Internet as a research

tool and medium, its message is still relevant for today's psychology students. See the "Indexes, Abstracts, and Databases" section in this chapter for an overview of *Psychological Abstracts* (see J-75n).

J-2   Sternberg, Robert J. **The Psychologist's Companion: A Guide to Scientific Writing for Students and Researchers**. 3d ed. Cambridge, MA: Cambridge University Press, 1993.

Barron's Educational Series first published *The Psychologist's Companion* in 1977 with the title *Writing the Psychology Paper*. This edition, like its predecessors, addresses the mechanics of writing the research paper. Chapters include information on library research papers, experimental research papers, commonly misused words, the style format of the American Psychological Association, guidelines for data presentation, and common misconceptions about psychology papers. Four new chapters added for this edition cover tips for writing better journal articles, writing grant or contract proposals, finding a book publisher, and advice on writing better lectures. There is also an appendix listing guidelines for writing for British and European journals. This guide will benefit not only students writing papers for courses but also graduate students and faculty members submitting articles for publication.

J-3   **Publication Manual of the American Psychological Association**. 4th ed. Washington, DC: American Psychological Association, 1994.

The *Publication Manual of the American Psychological Association* (*APA*) is intended to aid authors in the preparation of manuscripts. *APA* format is often required for papers in psychology and the social sciences. With its roots in the 1920s, this publication is now in its fourth edition and has been updated by a Web site. There are more general chapters containing guidelines for the content and organization of manuscripts, the expression of ideas, and *APA* editorial style. Chapters also contain examples of papers, manuscript preparation instructions, copyright information, APA journal review policies, and a discussion of ethics. There is also a bibliography and appendixes for citing format types and checklists for authors. This standard source belongs in every library's reference collection.

> ***Electronic access:*** A supplement to the *Manual, APA Style.Org*, is available at http://www .apastyle.org/elecref.html. It is updated regularly to provide changes, additions, or clarifications to APA style guidelines for electronic resources. Examples are given to illustrate the guidelines. This site also features tips of the week, an "ask an expert" service, and a free e-mail notification service about APA changes. Also available is *APA Style Resources* at PsychWeb, at http://www.psychwww.com/resource/apacrib.htm, which lists a series of links to various Web sites providing APA style guidelines and help sheets. This useful list of links, written primarily by academics, is intended to further clarify APA's guidelines through the use of specific examples.

J-4   McInerney, Dennis M. **Publishing Your Psychology Research: A Guide to Writing Journals in Psychology and Related Fields**. London: Sage, 2001.

McInerney outlines the publishing process step by step. Among the topics he covers are what editors look for in a scholarly article, how to write a publishable article, the review process, and how to approach journals. This handbook on scholarly publishing will be heavily used, especially by graduate students and beginning faculty, who are often new to academic writing.

J-5   Scott, Jill M., et al. **The Psychology Student Writer's Manual**. 2d ed. Upper Saddle River, NJ: Prentice Hall, 2002.

This handbook has been designed for students enrolled in undergraduate psychology courses. It provides detailed instructions on preparing short writing assignments, term papers, and experimental research papers. The second edition is a substantial revision. There is a new section on resources for distance learning students, as well as one that explains literature reviews. There are also several new writing exercises. Given the heavy use it will receive, many academic libraries will want to purchase multiple copies of this title.

J-6 Sternberg, Robert J., ed. **Guide to Publishing in Psychology Journals**. New York: Cambridge University Press, 2000.

This guide is written to assist authors in preparing higher quality manuscripts to improve the chances for acceptance into refereed psychology journals. The book consists of fourteen chapters, each written by an expert in the field. Part one, consisting of two chapters, provides an introduction to writing empirical articles and writing a literature review. Part two, comprising chapters three through ten, analyzes the various parts of an article. Included are chapters on preparing titles and abstracts, writing the introduction, outlining theories and hypotheses, preparing a section on research design, conducting data analyses, writing results, preparing an effective discussion section, and providing appropriate citations and references. Part three discusses dealing with the referees of a journal. Included are chapters on how to write for your referees, dealing with rejection, and rewriting papers. The final chapter is a series of fifty tips covering all areas of preparing manuscripts. This is an extremely helpful guide for faculty and students preparing articles for submission to refereed journals in psychology. Not only does it address the nuts and bolts issues of preparing manuscripts, it also provides a good overview of what to look for before beginning research, such as deciding if the research idea is interesting and applicable to the field. This book should be in the library of any academic institution supporting psychology programs.

J-7 Cone, John D., and Sharon L. Foster. **Dissertations and Theses from Start to Finish: Psychology and Related Fields**. Washington, DC: American Psychological Association, 1993.

This manual is authored by two professors with a combined thirty-five years of experience in supervising theses and dissertations. The fifteen chapters provide valuable advice on finding and refining a topic, time management, selection of a chairperson and committee members, developing a proposal, reviewing the literature, methodology, data collection and analysis, presentation of the results, oral defense, the presentation of findings at professional meetings, and the submission of manuscripts based on a thesis or dissertation for publication consideration. Appendixes include the APA's ethical standards relating to research in psychology; lists of bibliographic databases and statistical software; and a bibliography listing resources on research design, measurement, statistics, and writing style. This is an essential title for libraries serving graduate programs in psychology and related fields.

DICTIONARIES AND ENCYCLOPEDIAS

Psychology has many single and multivolume general encyclopedias. The following section is not intended to be an exhaustive inventory of general encyclopedias but rather a descriptive listing of some outstanding titles. In addition, psychology has many dictionaries that help define terms and concepts.

General

J-8 Cardwell, Mike. **The Dictionary of Psychology**. Chicago: Fitzroy Dearborn, 1999.

The Dictionary of Psychology begins each entry with a sentence that starts with the term, creating a short, concise definition. Length of entry depends on relative importance of the term. Some, such as "zygote," are one-sentence long. Others, such as "behaviorism," are over a page in length. Most entries, however, are two to three sentences long. There are ample cross-references and illustrative examples. This work was originally published in 1996 in the United Kingdom.

J-9   Colman, Andrew M., ed. **Companion Encyclopedia of Psychology**. 2 vols. London: Routledge, 1994.

This work aims to provide a comprehensive overview of all the major branches of psychology. It is divided into thirteen subject sections, among them biological aspects of behavior, sensation and perception, cognition, learning and skills, individual differences and personality, social psychology, developmental psychology, and abnormal psychology. Each section begins with an overview of the topic and a chapter outline, followed by five or six units. Included are suggestions for further reading and an extensive bibliography. Also included are special topics such as parapsychology and hypnosis. This work serves as a wonderful overview of the field of psychology and would be useful as a study guide for the GRE.

J-10   Corsini, Raymond J. **The Dictionary of Psychology**. Philadelphia: Brunner/ Mazel, Taylor & Francis, 1999.

Raymond Corsini, who also published the four-volume *Corsini Encyclopedia of Psychology* (J-11), spent seven years compiling this one-volume dictionary. At over 1,100 pages long, it is fairly comprehensive. Definitions are short, averaging thirty-one words. Corsini also includes appendixes containing prefixes, suffixes, and affixes; DSM-IV Terms; the Greek alphabet; medical prescription terms; a list of systems of treatment; a list of measuring instruments; a symbols directory; and a directory of short biographies. This is a handy, ready reference guide that is more affordable than the four-volume set.

J-11   Craighead, W. Edward, and Charles B. Nemeroff, eds. **The Corsini Encyclopedia of Psychology and Behavioral Science**. 3d ed. 4 vols. New York: John Wiley, 2000.

The *Corsini Encyclopedia of Psychology and Behavioral Science* is one of the standard reference sources for the multifaceted field of psychology. The third edition is arranged in four volumes and contains over 1,200 entries written by more than 700 experts. Entries consist of both subjects and significant contributors to the field. There are over 600 new or revised entries, making up over 60 percent of the material. There is extensive cross-referencing throughout the set, and each entry contains a bibliography. This work has received high recommendations from all of the standard reviewing sources and will be of great use to both researchers and students of psychology.

J-12   Kazdin, Alan E., ed.-in-chief. **Encyclopedia of Psychology**. 8 vols. Washington, DC: New York: American Psychological Association; Oxford University Press, 2000.

This massive undertaking by hundreds of expert psychologists in the United States and abroad took seven years to compile. The result is an alphabetical list of 1,500 articles ranging from 500 to 7,000 words in length and almost 400 biographies. Each article provides in-depth coverage of the topic as well as an extensive bibliography. Major areas covered are psychology as a discipline, research design and statistics, psychological testing and assessment, developmental psychology, social psychology, cross-cultural psychology, clinical psychology, and psychology and other disciplines. The preface of the book states that "a useful reference work on psychology should merge into one source the topics, methods, findings, advances, and applications that characterize the broad field of study." This work, a collaboration between the American Psychological Association and Oxford University Press, succeeds in this mission. It is the new standard psychology encyclopedia; a copy belongs in any library supporting psychology-related programs.

J-13   Magill, Frank N., ed. **Psychology Basics**. 2 vols. Pasadena, CA: Salem Press, 1998.

This set consists of 110 articles arranged alphabetically by subject and written by subject experts. Topics are drawn from seventeen areas of psychology, among them cognition, consciousness, developmental psychology, emotion, intelligence, language, learning, memory, motivation, personality, sensation and perception, social psychology, and psychotherapy. The articles average six pages in length, beginning with information on type of psychology and the particular field of study for the topic. There are also a brief, italicized summary and a list of key terms and definitions. The text of each article is divided into three sections. The "Overview" section introduces and explains the topic, the "Applications" section explains how the topic is used in practice, and the "Context" section places the topic in the field as a whole. There is also a bibliography at the end of each entry. A glossary of more than 500 terms and an index are located at the end of volume two. The arrangement allows users to quickly gain insight into a given topic, find a key concept or term, or read the entire entry for a more comprehensive overview. Institutions with psychology programs will find this to be a useful reference work.

J-14   Roeckelein, Jon E. **Dictionary of Theories, Laws, and Concepts in Psychology**. Westport, CT: Greenwood Press, 1998.

This reference work is primarily designed to provide a very brief introduction to concepts in psychology and to provide access to the literature on the concepts that "explicitly employ the generalized descriptors of law, theory, hypothesis, effect, doctrine, and principle in the field." Entries range from broad theories ("Schizophrenia, Theories Of") to theories of individuals ("Horney's Theory of Personality"). Each entry is typically about a page in length, allowing users to read a fairly quick overview. The original references given are the heart of this work, providing citations to the theories so that users can retrieve the original publications. This unique work is a handy ready reference tool for locating information on psychological concepts. Each concise entry contains an overview that is in greater depth than a general dictionary or textbook.

J-15   Statt, David A. **The Concise Dictionary of Psychology**. 3d ed. New York: Routledge, 1998.

This is the perfect pocket dictionary for psychology. There are more than 1,300 entries in this 140-page book. Definitions are clear, to the point, and typically not more than two sentences long. The author also includes appropriate "See" and "See also" references throughout the work. There are also some figures used to illustrate concepts. The abundance of entries in this relatively short dictionary makes this an attractive and relatively inexpensive acquisition for libraries.

J-16   Stratton, Peter, and Nicky Hayes. **A Student's Dictionary of Psychology**. 3d ed. New York: Arnold, 1999.

The authors intend that this guide be used as a tool to help students, particularly those without previous experience with psychology, to better understand psychological terms and lingo. Each entry in this dictionary contains definitions written in a clear, simplified format that contains an illustration of how the term is used in psychology. The authors provide an abundance of "See" and "See also" references. This is an excellent work for the beginning psychology student or anyone interested in basic-level psychology information.

J-17   Strickland, Bonnie R., ed. **The Gale Encyclopedia of Psychology**. 2d ed. Detroit: Gale Group, 2001.

This encyclopedia is geared to the nonspecialist. Its readability and ease of use make it an ideal choice for high school and public libraries. Academic libraries serving primarily undergraduate courses in psychology will also want to consider it for purchase. There are more than 650 articles, approximately two-thirds of which are new or revised from the first edition. They cover theories, terms, important case studies and experiments, notable people, applications of psychology, and career information. Entries range in length from 250 to 1,500 words. Charts, graphs, and photographs enhance the text. An expanded index, a revised glossary, and an updated directory of organizations round out this edition.

Specialized

Psychology has many specialized encyclopedias and dictionaries, reflecting the discipline's growing trend toward greater specialization.

J-18   Bellack, Alan S., and Michael Hersen, eds.-in-chief. **Comprehensive Clinical Psychology**. New York: Pergamon, 1998.

This title truly deserves its reputation as a publishing landmark. It comprises eleven volumes, representing years of labor by the editors-in-chief, who oversaw the progress of each volume and the work of individual volume editors. Prominent psychologists from around the world contributed to it, both as authors and volume editors. Several factors contributed to the decision to undertake this mammoth project. First, clinical psychology has undergone substantial change in the past three decades. In addition, there has been an explosion in the number of programs granting master's degrees in clinical psychology. As a result, the number of practicing clinical psychologists has dramatically increased. These factors have contributed to the publishing explosion in clinical psychology, making it difficult for students and practitioners to keep current. Consequently, the editors-in-chief felt that the time was right for a comprehensive work in clinical psychology. There are ten volumes of text and an entire volume (volume 11) that serves as an exhaustive index. This volume also contains information about the contributors. Each of the ten subject volumes represents one of the following broad fields: foundations of clinical psychology; professional, legal, and ethical issues; research and methodology; assessment; behavioral disorders in children and adolescents; behavioral problems and interventions with adults; clinical geropsychology; health psychology; clinical work with diverse populations; and cross-cultural psychopathology and interventions. Since this set costs approximately $3,500, it is a title that will only be found in large academic and research libraries supporting clinical psychology.

J-19   Cole, Robert, ed. **The Encyclopedia of Propaganda**. 3 vols. New York: Sharpe Reference, 1998.

Propaganda is a subject covered not only in psychology courses but also in mass media, advertising, political science, speech communication, sociology, and history courses. This set contains 510 articles on the psychological, social, cultural, artistic, and historical aspects of propaganda. The alphabetically arranged entries range in length from 300 to 2,500 words. Entries cover a variety of topics: the abortion debate, antiwar campaigns, bias, Bertold Brecht, brainwashing, Fidel Castro, courtroom trials, demagoguery, fascism, graffiti, historical falsification and revisionism, language policies, mass psychology, objectivity, political campaigning, ritual, scapegoating, statistics, television news, tobacco industry, truth, war crimes, and xenophobia. The third volume includes a categorical list of entries, a detailed index, a bibliography, and a filmography. The filmography is particularly interesting because it lists films (from 1984 through 1994) with propaganda themes. This set will be popular with many undergraduate students.

J-20   Everitt, B. S., and T. Wykes. **Dictionary of Statistics for Psychologists**. London; New York: Arnold; Oxford University Press, 1999.

Although there are many textbooks relating to statistical methodology in the behavioral sciences, this is the only recently published English-language dictionary that focuses on statistical terms used in psychological research and practice. This dictionary defines more than 1,500 terms, often providing a numerical or graphical example to clarify the meaning of a term. Cross-references are used to refer users to synonyms or related terms. One special feature is the inclusion of references to a term's use in a book or journal, a feature allowing users to obtain further information on the application of a particular statistical methodology. This dictionary will be useful to psychology students, practicing psychologists, and other students and professionals in related disciplines.

J-21 Friedman, Howard S., ed. **Encyclopedia of Mental Health**. 3 vols. San Diego, CA: Academic Press, 1998.

Library Journal named this comprehensive, multivolume encyclopedia a "Best Reference Source" for 1998, concluding that it was an essential acquisition for academic, health science, and large public libraries. The Reference and User Services Association's (a division of the American Library Association) Reference Sources Committee also named this an "Outstanding Reference Source" for 1999. This encyclopedia is distinguished by its ability to make complicated material understandable to specialists and nonspecialists alike. In addition, it takes a broad approach, examining the psychological, biological, social, and cultural factors relating to mental health. Among the topics covered are aggression, agoraphobia, behavioral genetics, brain development and plasticity, the psychosocial aspects of caffeine, cognitive therapy, day care, exercise and mental health, hypertension, infertility, legal dimensions of mental health, middle age and well-being, obesity, psychopharmacology, smoking, television viewing, and wellness in children. Each entry follows a standard format, containing an outline, glossary, cross-references, and a bibliography. Articles are substantive, ranging from ten to twenty pages in length. A detailed index can be found in the third volume. Students, researchers, practitioners, and lay readers will use this timely set.

J-22 Honig, Alice Sterling, Hiram E. Fitzgerald, and Holly Brophy-Herb. **Infancy in America: An Encyclopedia**. (The American Family). 2 vols. Santa Barbara, CA: ABC-Clio, 2001.

This encyclopedia is scheduled for publication in 2002. It is one of a half-dozen titles that constitute ABC-Clio's The American Family series. These titles are being marketed as comprehensive reference works for general readers, students, scholars, and professionals. The purpose of the series is to provide multiple perspectives on the history and state of the American family. Several titles in the series focus on specific developmental stages, such as this set on infancy. Each title in the series has its own advisory board comprising distinguished researchers. The editors of *Infancy in America* are leading educators and researchers in the area of child development, specifically infant-toddler development. According to information supplied by ABC-Clio, each title in the series will be richly illustrated with abundant indexing and references for further reading. The publisher also promises that articles will be cogent, free of bias, and not laden with jargon. The goal is to offer a fresh approach to issues relating to the family. ABC-Clio's intent is to eventually make the series available on the Web. This series is being designed for high school, public, and academic libraries. Obviously, an encyclopedia set on infancy has wide appeal to parents, educators, child caregivers, students enrolled in child development courses, and a wide range of professionals who need an understanding of how babies develop.

J-23 Houdé, Olivier, ed. **Dictionary of Cognitive Sciences**. London: Fitzroy Dearborn, 2001.

This is a translation of the distinguished French reference work titled *Vocabulaire de Sciences Cognitives*. The expected date of publication is November 2002. According to information supplied by the publisher, this source will provide detailed definitions of more than 120 topics. More than sixty scholars have contributed to the work. Entries range from abduction to writing and cover multiple disciplines given the interdisciplinarity of the field of cognitive sciences. There are terms relating to psychology, philosophy, linguistics, artificial intelligence, and neuroscience. This dictionary promises to be an important source for the cognitive sciences.

J-24 Kagan, Jerome, ed. **The Gale Encyclopedia of Childhood and Adolescence**. Detroit: Gale Research, 1998.

Kagan is one of America's most preeminent researchers in child development. Along with being a prolific writer, he has been a strong advocate for children. This comprehensive encyclopedia assembles 800 signed articles by renowned experts on a range of topics relating to the development of children from birth through adolescence. Among the topics covered are acting out, Action for

Children's Television, Bayley Scales of Infant Development, boredom, breastfeeding, child abuse, diaper rash, hallucinogens, intelligence quotient, mental retardation, nutrition, rites of passage, sexually transmitted diseases, sun protection, undesirable language, and video games. Articles range in length from a single paragraph to 5,000 words. The organization of material is excellent. Entries are alphabetically arranged, abundantly cross-referenced, and enhanced by illustrations and sidebars. Most of the entries list sources for further study, including books, popular magazine articles, and professional journal articles. Some entries also include audiovisual materials, Web sites, and organizations. Overall, the work is marked by clarity and balance. In the case of controversial topics, authors present both views. This encyclopedia will be found in many high school, public, and academic libraries. It is a valuable source for students enrolled in child development courses, teachers, child care workers, health care providers, practicing child psychologists, educational counselors, and even parents.

J-25 Kahn, Ada P. **Stress A-Z: A Sourcebook for Facing Everyday Challenges**. New York: Facts on File, 1998.

Stress is so pervasive that is has become a public health issue. This clear and concise volume on the most common sources of stress (ranging from life-changing events such as divorce and death to everyday nuisances such as traffic snarls and telemarketers) will have a wide audience. The more than 500 entries cover stress producers, methods for reducing or treating stress, and individuals in the area of stress management. There are entries as varied as aromatherapy, back pain, boredom, Deepak Chopra, downsizing, eating disorders, elderly parents, hair pulling, M. Scott Peck, pets, prayer, shift work, shopaholism, sick building syndrome, stuttering, success, and vacations. Entries range in length from a paragraph to several pages. Articles are abundantly cross-referenced, and many entries also include sources for further reading as well as information on relevant organizations. In addition, there are an extensive bibliography (organized by subject) and an index. Since stress affects virtually everyone and is also a topic of interest to a wide range of students, researchers, and practitioners, this volume is appropriate for public and academic collections. Many librarians may recognize the author's name, as she has co-authored three other Facts on File publications: *The A-Z of Women's Sexuality* (1990); *The Encyclopedia of Phobias, Fears and Anxieties* (2000); and *Midlife Health: Every Woman's Guide to Feeling Good* (1987).

J-26 Kastenbaum, Robert, ed. **Encyclopedia of Adult Development**. Phoenix, AZ: Oryx Press, 1993.

Library Journal named this one-volume encyclopedia "A Best Reference Source for '93." Kastenbaum co-edited another award-winning encyclopedia, the *Encyclopedia of Death*, a title published by Oryx in 1989. Adult development is another of his research interests. He has served as the editor of the *International Journal of Aging and Human Development*. Although this encyclopedia covers human development from infancy through old age, the focus is on adult development. More than seventy contributors in 106 articles share ideas and research findings about a wide range of topics relating to development across the life span. This variety in topics no doubt reflects the diversity of the contributing authors. The contributors include specialists in the disciplines of communications, education, psychology, history, sociology, gerontology, family studies, anthropology, communication disorders, physiology, psychiatry, nursing, medicine, and the health sciences. This interdisciplinarity is reflected in the inclusion of articles on alcohol use and abuse, cardiac health, divorce, exercise, gender differences in the workplace, humor, language development, menopause, political beliefs and activities, religion and coping with crisis, sleep and dreams, taste and smell, vision, and widowhood. Each article includes a bibliography, and abundant *see also* references refer readers to related articles. This single-volume encyclopedia will be found in many academic and large public libraries.

J-27 Kurtz, Lester, ed.-in-chief. **Encyclopedia of Violence, Peace, and Conflict**. 3 vols. San Diego, CA: Academic Press, 1999.

This multidisciplinary, multivolume encyclopedia on violence, war, and peace examines these phenomena from various perspectives including psychological, anthropological, biomedical, economic, historical, cultural, political, sociological, and legal. Among the topics covered are violence toward animals, political assassinations, chemical and biological warfare, the impact of television on children, changing attitudes toward crime and punishment, drugs and violence, the economic costs and consequences of war, gangs, hate crimes, violence towards homosexuals, juvenile crimes, legal theories and remedies, peace education, peaceful societies, peace movements, religion and peace, sports, trade wars, war crimes, and women and war. The structure of this work is exemplary. Each chapter begins with an outline followed by a glossary. The text begins with a statement that defines the topic and summarizes the content of the article. The quality of writing is excellent. All of the articles have abundant cross-references and include a basic bibliography. The third volume contains a comprehensive subject index. This is an essential source for college and university libraries.

J-28 Lawry, John D. **Guide to the History of Psychology**. Totowa, NJ: Littlefield, Adams, 1981.

Although this title was published two decades ago, this concise (approximately 100 pages in length) reference still serves as a good introduction to the history of psychology for students and general readers with an interest in psychology. In an outline format, the *Guide* delineates the history of psychology from antiquity through the early twentieth century. The book is organized into five parts. The first part provides sketches of more than 100 major contributors to the development of the discipline. These profiles are followed by a chronological listing of the "fathers of psychology" and a series of fun questions in question-and-answer format. The next section is a glossary of philosophical terms that will be helpful background for psychology students given the discipline's linkages to philosophy. Also, these terms are not often found in the glossaries of introductory level psychology textbooks. Section IV is an annotated and chronological listing of classics in the history of psychology. This list begins with Hippocrates's *On the Sacred Disease* (c. 400 B.C.E.) and concludes with Koffka's *The Principles of Gestalt Psychology* (1935). The final section is an annotated bibliography of sources in the history of psychology. There are two indexes, of names and of subjects. All libraries that own it should retain this brief guide.

J-29 Lerner, Richard M., Anne C. Peterson, and Jeanne Brooks-Gunn, eds. **Encyclopedia of Adolescence in America**. New York: Garland, 1991.

Although Richard Lerner and Jacqueline Lerner recently edited *Adolescence in America: An Encyclopedia* (2 v., Santa Barbara, CA: ABC-Clio, 2001), this 1991 encyclopedia remains the core reference work on adolescence. It is interdisciplinary in scope, examining adolescence from many perspectives. More than 200 articles cover the psychical, psychological, and social development of adolescents.

The study of adolescence has emerged as a separate field of scholarship, and this encyclopedia includes biographical articles on prominent individuals (e.g., Erik Erikson, Anna Freud, Sigmund Freud, Jean Piaget) who have contributed to the development of theory and scholarship. Most colleges and universities now offer undergraduate or graduate level courses on adolescence. There are several scholarly journals focusing on the study of adolescence as well as numerous treatises and textbooks. The Society for Research on Adolescence has also been established.

The publisher of this encyclopedia assembled experts from numerous universities and research centers, including psychologists, sociologists, biologists, physicians, and researchers in other disciplines. The diversity of this work is reflected in the inclusion of articles on academic achievement, adrenarche, AIDS and HIV infection, cognitive development, delinquency, diabetes, exercise and fitness, adolescence in nineteenth-century America, pregnancy and childbearing, religion, risk-taking behaviors, television, and unemployment. Articles range in length from two to fifteen pages and conclude with substantial bibliographies. Abundant cross-references, effective illustrations, an extensive subject index, and excellent layout and design enhance the book's usefulness. This specialized encyclopedia is essential for any academic library serving programs in psychology, education, and family studies. It is also useful to a wide range of practitioners, including clinical psychologists, school counselors, and teachers.

J-30 Levinson, David, James J. Ponzetti Jr., and Peter F. Jorgensen, eds. **Encyclopedia of Human Emotions**. New York: Macmillan Reference USA, 1999.

This exceptional encyclopedia received a starred review in *Library Journal*. It is a comprehensive work on human emotions, bringing together almost 150 articles on specific emotions, emotions across the life span, and emotions in society and the human experience. There are also biographical entries on individuals who have contributed to the study of emotions. There are articles on a variety of topics: aggression; ambivalence, annoyance, attachment, the biochemistry of emotions, cognitive perspective, cross-cultural patterns, dance, emotional intelligence, flirtation, genetics, health and illness, intimacy, jealousy, loneliness, music, pain, propaganda, sports, trust, and the visual arts. Among the individuals profiled are Aristotle, Augustine, John Bowlby, Charles Darwin, Erik Erikson, Hans Eysenck, Anna Freud, David Hume, Friedrich Nietzche, Plato, and Spinoza. Articles are highly readable and enhanced by the inclusion of photographs and drawings. Because these well-written articles are so accessible, this work will be useful to general readers, high school students, college students, and specialists.

J-31 McGuigan, F. J. **Encyclopedia of Stress**. Boston: Allyn & Bacon, 1999.

The late Frank McGuigan was a renowned expert on progressive relaxation, a stress management technique. He served as the director of the Institute for Stress Management at the United States International University in San Diego. McGuigan published widely on the topics of stress and tension control. He was twice nominated for the Nobel Prize in physiology. In the introduction, he notes that stress has been called "the twentieth-century disease." Millions of people in this country alone suffer from stress-related illnesses, and stress management is a topic of wide interest. This encyclopedia has a broad scope, attacking the topic of stress from multiple perspectives. It provides information on a range of stress topics, from the nature of stress to strategies for reversing the toll that stress can take on the body. Among the 200 topics covered are absenteeism, alcoholism, Alzheimer's disease, asthma and stress, backache, the stress of downsizing, exercise, executive stress, hypertension, infertility, insomnia, menopause, stress management techniques, stuttering, ulcers, workplace stress, and yoga. For each stress disorder, there is a description and discussion of causes and treatments. Articles are very readable and amply cross-referenced. Readers are directed to sources of additional information. This clear and concise source on a topic of interest to many nonspecialists and an array of students and professionals should be considered for all academic and medium- to large-sized public libraries.

J-32 Runco, Mark A., and Steven R. Pritzker, eds.-in-chief. **Encyclopedia of Creativity**. 2 vols. San Diego, CA: Academic Press, 1999.

Runco, a professor of child and adolescent studies, is the founder and continuing editor of the *Creativity Research Journal*. He is a prolific writer and has published widely in the area of creativity. Pritzker is a creativity consultant and writer who has worked with major companies, helping them develop strategies that foster creativity in the workplace. He holds a doctoral degree in educational psychology and has authored numerous popular and academic publications related to creativity. *The Encyclopedia of Creativity* is the only encyclopedia of its kind. This set has filled an important gap given the proliferation of literature relating to creativity and the need for a reference source that will survey the field. Since 1960, more than 10,000 journal articles and 600 books have been published on the topic of creativity. The editors assembled a small but prestigious advisory board that included Harvard University's Howard Gardner and Yale University's Robert J. Sternberg. This multifaceted encyclopedia has been written for a broad audience. It will be an important source for many disciplines: psychology, education, business, the arts, and the health sciences. Articles cover a range of topics: theories relating to creativity; thought processes associated with creative thinking; creativity in specific domains such as dance, acting, architecture, art, and music; tests of creativity; and the relationship between creativity and individual circumstances such as genetics and birth order. In addition, there are biographical sketches of individuals who personify creativity. Articles are alphabetically arranged and are heavily cross-referenced. Each article contains a brief bibliography. The visual presentation of the set is striking. The layout and design is very attractive. The second volume contains multiple appendixes and indexes. There is an appendix that is a chronological listing of important events, ideas, and works in creativity. It begins in 1859 with the publication of Sir Francis Galton's *Hereditary Genius* and concludes in 1999 with the publication of this encyclopedia. Another appendix selectively reviews tests, inventories, and rating scales used to assess creativity. There is also a listing of contributors in the back of Volume II. Most are psychologists, but there are also creativity experts from the fields of business, the arts, and education. Name and subject indexes are provided. Although there is some unevenness in the quality of the writing, this is an admirable effort and an important contribution to this area of psychology. This is a title that all academic libraries will want to consider for purchase.

J-33 Squire, Larry R., ed.-in-chief. **Encyclopedia of Learning and Memory**. New York: Macmillan, 1992.

This well-designed single-volume encyclopedia is more specialized than standard encyclopedias in psychology. The concise and well-written articles provide a good overview of topics relating to learning and memory and provide biographical sketches of twenty-six individuals who have contributed to our understanding of this subject. Among the individuals profiled are Aristotle, Frederic Bartlett, Hermann Ebbinghaus, Sigmund Freud, Edwin R. Guthrie, William James, Karl Lashey, Jean Piaget, B. F. Skinner, Edward Thorndike, and John B. Watson. The 189 signed articles vary in length from 500 to 2,000 words. Although the emphasis is on human memory, there is coverage of research on vertebrates and invertebrates. The breadth of coverage is impressive. There are articles on learning algorithms, Alzheimer's disease, aphasia, birdsong learning, development of memory in children, drugs and memory, head injury, imprinting, language learning, mental retardation, mnemonic devices, neural computation, phobias, school learning, spatial learning, and tip-of-the-tongue phenomenon. *See* and *see also* references are abundant, and the extensive subject index helps users locate specific subjects. The entries conclude with up-to-date references. Figures and photographs are also included. This highly readable and attractively designed encyclopedia can be found on the shelves of many college and university libraries.

J-34 Sternberg, Robert, ed.-in-chief. **Encyclopedia of Human Intelligence**. New York: Macmillan, 1994.

Although intelligence is a topic covered in virtually every encyclopedia in psychology, this is the only specialized encyclopedia in this major area of psychology. It assembles 250 signed articles on various aspects of intelligence, among them abilities and aptitudes, achievement testing, animal intelligence, bilingualism, crime and delinquency, dyslexia, fetal alcohol syndrome, giftedness, information processing, legal issues in intelligence, musical ability, race and intelligence, schooling, test-taking strategies, underachievement, and verbal ability. There are also biographical articles on major theorists and researchers, including Anne Anastasi, Alfred Binet, Arthur B. Jensen, and Edward L. Thorndike. Articles include bibliographies. Although entries are arranged alphabetically, a detailed index has been provided. This outstanding specialized reference source will be found in most academic libraries serving students in psychology and education.

J-35 Taublieb, Amy Beth. **A to Z Handbook of Child and Adolescent Issues**. Boston: Allyn & Bacon, 2000.

Taublieb, a practicing clinical psychologist, is frequently interviewed by the popular press for her opinion on parenting topics ranging from thumb-sucking to arguments over clothing. She is also the author of "Ask Dr. Amy," a weekly newspaper column. She has worked extensively with children, adolescents, and parents. In addition, she has taught undergraduate psychology courses and has written a textbook on child and adolescent psychopathology. The *A to Z Handbook of Child and Adolescent Issues* has been designed as a nontechnical guide on the psychology of children and adolescents. It covers hundreds of topics relating to common behaviors (thumb-sucking, temper tantrums, and arguing between siblings) and behaviors that are pathological in nature (e.g., adolescent suicide, childhood depression, childhood schizophrenia, school phobia). The scope is comprehensive, including articles as diverse as adolescent mood swings, allowance, anatomically correct dolls, burping, day care, family therapy, fear of the dark, homework problems, learning disorders, puberty, spanking, terrible twos, and Zoloft. Articles are alphabetically arranged and include many cross-references. Taublieb provides suggestions for dealing with common behavioral problems and guidelines as to when to consult professionals. This practical guide will be useful to parents, child care workers, teachers, guidance counselors, pediatricians, social workers, and students studying child and adolescent development. It belongs in all public and academic libraries.

J-36   Ulijaszek, Stanley J., Francis E. Johnston, and Michael A. Preece. **The Cambridge Encyclopedia of Human Growth and Development**. Cambridge, UK: Cambridge University Press, 1998.

Many disciplines study human growth and development: psychology, biology, anthropology, education, and health. The editors of this comprehensive encyclopedia on human growth and development include a nutritional anthropologist, a biological anthropologist, and a growth physiologist. Librarians working in the behavioral sciences need to have some familiarity with this work because it covers the behavioral and cultural factors relating to human growth. In fact, an entire section focuses on behavioral and cognitive development. This section includes articles on cognitive development, motor development and performance, language development, nutrition and cognitive development, the development of sexuality, and psychosocial factors influencing growth and development. Other sections also include articles of interest to behavioral scientists. For example, there are articles on menopause, aging as part of the developmental process, and growth and psychosocial stress. This reference work, which will be found in large academic libraries, is a good example of the linkage between psychology and the biological sciences.

J-37   Wilson, Robert A., and Frank C. Keil, eds. **The MIT Encyclopedia of the Cognitive Sciences**. Cambridge, MA: MIT Press, 1999.

Cognitive science is an interdisciplinary field that emerged in the 1970s. This landmark encyclopedia is the first comprehensive reference work to pull together cognitive research from six disciplines: psychology; philosophy; neurosciences; linguistics and language; culture, cognition, and evolution; and computational intelligence. There are long introductory essays for each of these disciplines. The body of the work contains more than 450 essays written by experts in the cognitive sciences. Among the various topics covered are aging and cognition, animal communication, aphasia, blind sight, cognitive architecture, cognitive linguistics, evolution, fuzzy logic, imagery, language acquisition, mental retardation, pain, sleep, stereotyping, thalamus, vagueness, and working memory. Each article was rigorously reviewed. Entries have numerous "see" and "see also" references along with a list of further readings. Name and subject indexes are provided. This interdisciplinary encyclopedia is an essential resource for academic collections.

Electronic access: The publisher provides free access to the online version of the encyclopedia with the purchase of the print or CD-ROM version of this important encyclopedia.

J-38   Zusne, Leonard. **Eponyms in Psychology: A Dictionary and Biographical Sourcebook**. New York: Greenwood Press, 1987.

An eponym is a concept, technique, or syndrome named after an individual or a place. Some examples from this fascinating dictionary are Antigone complex, Apgar Score, Cornell technique, Hawthorne effect, jabberwocky, Jackson's Law, Jastrow cylinders, rolfing, and Romeo and Juliet effect. There are almost 900 terms in total. Entries are uniform, presenting a definition of the eponym and a short paragraph about the individual or place for which a term has been named. Some sources are real; others originate in literature or mythology. In addition to being useful as both a topical and biographical dictionary, this unique source is fun to browse.

HANDBOOKS

Handbooks can serve as a quick source of facts for ready reference questions or may supplement general texts and encyclopedia articles by providing a detailed summary of a broad topic. Handbooks are prevalent in psychology. Some of the handbooks described in the chapter 8 may also be useful to psychologists, such as *Designing and Conducting Survey Research* (H-41), the *Handbook of Survey Research* (H-43), and *Handbook of Marriage and the Family* (H-46).

J-39 Pashler, Hal, ed. **Stevens' Handbook of Experimental Psychology**. 3d ed. 4 vols. New York: John Wiley, 2002.

This is a revision of the now-classic handbook edited by Stanley Smith Stevens in 1951. Although there are separate handbooks within specializations of experimental psychology (e.g., perception), this remains the most comprehensive summary of developments in experimental psychology. The original was composed of thirty-six chapters in six sections; this edition consists of sixty-seven chapters. The third edition has expanded to four volumes, reflecting the tremendous growth in experimental psychology, neuroscience, and related disciplines since publication of the two-volume second edition in 1988. Volume 1 covers sensation and perception, with chapters on vision, hearing, taste, and smell. Volume 2 focuses on memory and cognitive processing. Among the topics covered are kinds of memory, spatial cognition, language processing, psycholinguistics, problem solving, reasoning, and cognitive development. Volume 3 covers learning, learning instincts, spatial learning, temporal learning, language acquisition, the anatomy of motivation, social behavior, and addiction. Volume 4 focuses on research methods in experimental psychology, discussing a range of methodologies used to measure psychological, social, behavioral, and cognitive processes in humans. This handbook is a fundamental source for any library serving graduate students and researchers in experimental psychology.

J-40 Balter, Lawrence, and Catherine Tamis-LeMonda. **Child Psychology: A Handbook of Contemporary Issues**. Philadelphia: Psychology Press, 1999.

This handbook provides a good summary of core topics in developmental psychology, such as infant-parent attachment, early language development, cognition, and social and emotional development. It also reviews research on controversial and new topical areas such as cross-cultural perspectives on child rearing, racial socialization, solo mother families, lesbian mother families, and families created by assisted reproduction. The twenty-four chapters are grouped into five sections: infancy; early childhood; middle childhood; cross-cutting themes (which addresses topics such as parenting, children's knowledge of gender stereotypes, and the impact of poverty and community violence on children); and new frontiers (which includes cutting edge research on topics ranging from new family forms to insights about behavior from studies with Rhesus monkeys). *Child Psychology* will be a critical source for upper-level undergraduate and graduate students in developmental psychology, educators, and development scholars.

J-41 Birren, James E., and K. Warner Schaie, eds. **Handbook of the Psychology of Aging**. 5th ed. (The Handbooks of Aging). San Diego, CA: Academic Press, 2001.

This handbook synthesizes the literature on the psychology of adult development and aging. It is one of the three volumes in the publisher's Handbook of Aging series. The companion volumes are *Handbook of the Biology of Aging* and *Handbook of Aging and the Social Sciences*. Some topics covered in the first, second, and third editions of *Handbook of the Psychology of Aging* have been dropped in this latest edition. This edition has fewer chapters as a whole because the editors tried to keep the size manageable. There is less emphasis on topics relating to the clinical psychology of aging; the authors note that this topic is more comprehensively covered in the 1992 *Handbook of Mental Health and Aging*. Birren and Schaie's handbook is divided into three parts. Part 1 covers the history of the geropsychology (the psychology of aging) as a discipline and discusses theory and methodology. Part 2 examines the effects of heredity, health, biology, and environment on the aging process. Part 3 examines behavioral processes in aging, including vision, hearing, motivation, cognitive and motor performance, attention, learning, memory, language processing, and intellectual development. There are also chapters on social influences such as religion and spirituality. In addition, there are two new chapters in this section on creativity and wisdom and on technological change and the older worker. This remains the standard handbook in this rapidly growing subfield of developmental psychology.

J-42 Brown, Steven D., and Robert W. Len, eds. **Handbook of Counseling Psychology**. 3d ed. New York: John Wiley, 2000.

This is the leading handbook on counseling psychology in clinical and educational settings. The editors, both major scholars in the field, have published extensively on topics in career and counseling psychology, including school-to-work transitions and career choices. Both are fellows of the American Psychological Association and serve on editorial boards of prestigious journals in their field. Brown and Lent surveyed a large group of researchers and practitioners to determine how the handbook could be improved. They used data from this survey to make decisions about which topics and chapters should be retained and what topics and chapters needed to be added to this edition. As a result of their consultation with users of the handbook, this edition underwent major revisions in content and organization. One of the most significant changes was the elimination of the separate section on career and educational counseling. The editors decided to take a cross-disciplinary and integrative approach, so chapters on career and education topics are now dispersed throughout the handbook. The third edition had been updated to include greater coverage of diversity themes such as the role of gender, sexual orientation, ethnicity, race, social class, and culture within the context of counseling. In addition, several chapters have been added to reflect new or substantially revised areas in counseling psychology and related fields. These new topics include qualitative research methods, preventive intervention with school-aged youth, the school-to-work transition, the process and outcomes of group counseling, and processes and outcomes in couples and family therapy. This is a requisite source for students, researchers, and practitioners in career and counseling psychology.

J-43 Burack, Jacob A., Robert M. Hodapp, and Edward Zigler. **Handbook of Mental Retardation and Development**. Cambridge, UK: Cambridge University Press, 1998.

This is the most current handbook in the field of mental retardation. It focuses on developmental issues associated with mental retardation. In fact, it is the first handbook to exclusively cover retardation from a developmental perspective. The twenty-six chapters are organized around four themes: general developmental issues surrounding mental retardation, cognitive and linguistic development, social and emotional development, and family and environmental contexts (including a chapter on the impact of mental retardation on the family). Readers can find essays on neurological development, genetic perspectives on mental retardation, sensorimotor development, early and later language development, symbolic play, friendship, self-image, life-span development, maladaptive behavior, mother-child interaction, siblings of children with mental retardation, and raising a child with retardation. Detailed author and subject indexes are provided. This is a primary handbook for any library supporting students and professionals researching mental retardation. In particular, it will be in heavy demand by upper-level undergraduate and graduate students in psychology, special education, human development and family studies, and social work.

J-44 Carr, Alan. **The Handbook of Child and Adolescent Clinical Psychology: A Contextual Approach**. New York: Routledge, 1999.

This handbook on contemporary child and adolescent clinical psychology is 1,000 pages long. Carr, the director of the doctoral program in clinical psychology at Dublin's University College, has designed this as a core text for postgraduate psychology students in clinical training and practitioners in child and adolescent clinical psychology. The topics covered in this handbook are core to clinical child psychologists not only in Ireland but the United Kingdom, Europe, and North America. This comprehensive text consists of six sections: frameworks for practice; problems of infancy and early childhood, problems of middle childhood, problems in adolescence, child abuse, and adjustments to major life transitions. Among the topics covered are sleep problems, attention and over-activity problems, fear and anxiety problems, drug abuse, anorexia and bulimia nervosa, physical abuse, sexual abuse, foster care, separation and divorce, and grief and bereavement. Because the focus is on practice there are separate chapters on classification, epidemiology, and treatment effectiveness; the consultation process and intake interviews; and report writing. Numerous cases, tables, and figures are included to assist practitioners in diagnosing problems and identifying treatment options. An impressive fifty-page bibliography can be found at the end of the book. This advanced comprehensive handbook is a source that will be found in libraries supporting graduate-level programs in clinical psychology and practitioners in this area.

J-45 Christianson, Sven-Ake. **The Handbook of Emotion and Memory**. Hillsdale, NJ: L. Lawrence Erlbaum Associates, 1992.

This handbook fills a gap in the literature on the influence of emotion on memory. Although there are books and articles on this topic, this is the only exclusive reference work on this increasingly important area of psychology. The handbook consists of nineteen chapters written by prominent authorities in the field of emotion and memory, including Daniel Schacter, George Mandler, James Pennebaker, and Michael Eysenck. The book is divided into four parts: general perspectives, methodological issues, biological aspects, and clinical observations. Chapters cover a variety of issues, including the interaction between emotion and learning, eyewitness memory, traumatic events, the biological aspects of emotion and memory, and emotional disorders and memory. This valuable work is appropriate for all college and university libraries serving undergraduate and graduate students in the behavioral sciences.

J-46 Damon, William, ed.-in-chief. **Handbook of Child Psychology**. 5th ed. 4 vols. New York: John Wiley, 1998.

This handbook has been a standard reference work for more than half a century. It is regarded as the most important handbook in developmental psychology. The first edition, edited by Leonard Carmichael, was published in 1946 under the title *Carmichael's Manual of Child Psychology*. The fifth edition represents a significant expansion from the previous edition. In the preface, Damon outlines the *Handbook's* long and illustrative history. The fifth edition is the work of 112 authors from around the globe. Like previous editions, the scope is comprehensive. The biggest change with this edition is that an entire volume is devoted to issues relating to the practice of child psychology. Each volume covers specific aspects of child development. Volume 1 details theories of human development and the history of developmental psychology. Volume 2 focuses on cognition, perception, and language. Volume 3 provides coverage of topics relating to social, emotional, and personality development. Volume 4 is devoted to child psychology in clinical and educational practice. This volume in particular will be useful to a range of research-oriented practitioners (e.g., psychologists, sociologists, educators, neurobiologists, anthropologists, and psychiatrists). Each volume has a detailed table of contents, and individual chapters have detailed topical breakdowns. Chapters conclude with substantive bibliographies. Because each volume can be used independently, each volume has its own author and subject indexes. This classic belongs in all college and university libraries.

J-47 Denmark, Florence L., and Michele A. Paludi, eds. **Psychology of Women: A Handbook of Issues and Theories**. Westport, CT: Greenwood Press, 1993.

Many universities offer courses in the psychology of women. There are several behavioral science journals relating to women and gender. Both the American Psychological Association (APA) and the American Psychological Society have women's divisions. Denmark is a past president of the APA and one of the founding members of the American Psychological Association's Division of the Psychology of Women. Paludi has written widely on the topics of sexual harassment on campus and in the workplace. The editors refer to the list of contributors as a "Who's Who of Women in Psychology." These prominent psychologists have produced the definitive handbook on the psychology of women. The eighteen chapters in this volume are organized into six parts. Part 1 includes chapters outlining theory, research methodology, and the history of the psychology of women. Part 2, "Society's View of Women," includes chapters relating to the themes of sexism and gender stereotypes. The chapters in part 3 relate to women's social, personality, and cognitive development across the life span. Part 4 reviews the research on women's mental and physical health. The theme of part 5 is the victimization of women, with chapters on sexual harassment, battering, and rape. The chapters in the last section, "Achievement Motivation, Career Development, and Work," discuss issues such as gender bias in education, bias in career counseling and testing, and women's labor force participation. This important handbook is essential to any academic collection supporting psychology or women's studies.

J-48 Drenth, Pieter J. D., Henk Thierry, and Charles J. de Wolff, eds. **Handbook of Work and Organizational Psychology**. 2d ed. 4 vols. Hove, East Sussex, England: Psychology Press, 1998.

This is an extensive revision of the first edition, which was published in Dutch in the early 1980s and subsequently translated into English. This handbook is still the most comprehensive European handbook in the area of work and organizational psychology. However, the market for this title extends beyond Europe. It is useful to upper-level students and practitioners in industrial and organizational psychology worldwide. This set contains fifty-one chapters. Volume 1 is a comprehensive introduction to work and organizational psychology. Volume 2 is devoted to work psychology. Among the topics covered are the psychological aspects of workload, ergonomics, industrial safety, absenteeism, occupational stress, the older worker, and discrimination in the workplace. Volume 3 focuses on personnel psychology, with detailed articles on the selection process, personnel appraisal, job analysis, the development of managers, career guidance, women and work, work and health psychology, participatory management, negotiation, and conflict management. Volume 4 concentrates on organizational psychology. There are chapters on theories of organizations and the behavior of individuals and groups in the workplace. This set will be found in large academic collections supporting graduate-level programs in industrial and organizational psychology.

J-49 Dunnette, Marvin D., and Leaetta M. Hough, eds. **Handbook of Industrial and Organizational Psychology**. 2d ed. 4 vols. Palo Alto, CA: Consulting Psychologists Press, 1990–1994.

This remains a comprehensive handbook in industrial and organizational psychology. The first edition of this standard work was published in 1976. This set has been carefully edited, and undergraduates can easily understand the well-written chapters. Volume 1 covers theory, measurement, and research methodology. It contains chapters on motivation theory, learning theory, individual differences theory, quasi-experimentation, item response theory, and multivariate correctional analysis. Volume 2 looks at individual behavior, with chapters on job analysis, personnel assessment, recruitment, training, employee performance, and personality and personality measurement. Volume 3 includes chapters on leadership in organizations, consumer psychology, conflict and stress in organizations, and strategic decision making. Volume 4 focuses on cross-cultural issues. This multivolume handbook belongs in all college and university libraries serving programs in industrial and organizational psychology, management, and marketing.

J-50 Durso, Francis T., ed. **Handbook of Applied Cognition**. New York: John Wiley, 1999.

This is an important work because it is the only handbook in applied cognitive psychology. Cognitive psychology is applied to many domains: computers and technology, education and information, business and industry, and health and law. It is a growing field. Not only does this handbook synthesize the research in cognitive psychology, it also reviews the research in cognitive engineering. Among the general topics covered are knowledge and expertise, memory, judgment and decision making, human error, and social cognition. Subsequent chapters provide in-depth coverage of cognition applied in four key areas: business and industry, computers and technology, information and instruction, and health and law. Sample essays cover applied cognition in consumer research, instructional technology, reminding devices, medical cognition, eyewitness testimony, and the cognitive aspects of aviation. This summary of research in applied cognition will be in high demand in academic libraries. It is relevant to students in psychology, education, industrial engineering, computer science, business, and other applied disciplines.

J-51 First, Michael B., ed. **Diagnostic and Statistical Manual of Mental Disorders**. 4th ed., text rev. Washington, DC: American Psychiatric Association, 2000.

Commonly referred to as *DSM*, this is the standard manual used by psychiatrists, clinical psychologists, physicians, social workers, and other mental health professionals to define and diagnose mental disorders. This source belongs in the core collections of both public and academic libraries because the guidelines are accepted not only by mental health professionals but also by insurance companies, disability boards, and the courts. The first edition was published in 1952 and described approximately 100 disorders. The fourth edition of the DSM (1994) describes more than 300 disorders. The text revision integrates new research findings about disorders and conditions.

J-52   **Getting In: A Step-by-Step Plan for Gaining Admission to Graduate School in Psychology**. Washington, DC: American Psychological Association, 1993.

This practical guide to graduate school admission can serve as a companion volume to *Graduate Study in Psychology* (J-94), an annual directory published by the American Psychological Association. The book is organized around five major steps. The first step is determining whether graduate school is the right choice. Step 2 is identifying an area of concentration and a degree to pursue. The third step is targeting programs to apply to. Step 4 is the completion of applications to these programs. The final step is attending preselection interviews and deciding which program to attend. This chapter also addresses what to do if you are not accepted by any of the programs to which you have applied. Although this guide is directed to those considering graduate work in psychology, much of the advice is useful to anyone applying for graduate study regardless of discipline. Most college and university libraries will own at least one copy of this helpful handbook.

J-53   Gilbert, Daniel T., Susan T. Fiske, and Gardner Lindzey. **The Handbook of Social Psychology**. 4th ed. 2 vols. Boston; New York: McGraw-Hill; Oxford University Press, 1998.

This is the classic handbook in the area of social psychology. The first edition, edited by Carl Murchison, was published in 1935. Whereas the second edition consisted of five volumes, this title was pared down to two volumes beginning with the third edition. However, the fourth edition differs significantly from the third. First, the editorship has been expanded from two to three editors. Gardner Lindzey edited the previous edition along with Elliot Aronson. Aronson retired and was replaced by Daniel Gilbert and Susan Fiske. In addition to this change in editors, there have been significant changes in contributors. Many new contributors were recruited for this edition. In fact, the majority of the chapter authors are new and represent diversity in experience, orientation, and background. The result is a handbook that is essentially new in content. The editors note that approximately twenty of the thirty-seven chapters have no direct counterpart in the previous edition. Among the new topics covered are the self, emotions, automaticity, social stigma, memory, and evolutionary social psychology. This handbook belongs on the shelves of all academic libraries because it is useful to students and researchers in a wide range of social science disciplines, including psychology, sociology, communications, political science, and anthropology.

J-54   Groth-Marnat, Gary. **Handbook of Psychological Assessment**. 3d ed. New York: John Wiley, 1997.

This handbook has been designed as a reference guide to the most frequently used psychological tests. Among the assessments covered are the Wechsler Intelligence Scales, the Millon Clinical Multiaxial Inventory, the California Psychological Inventory, the Minnesota Multiphasic Personality Inventory, the Rorschach, the Thematic Apperception Test, and projective techniques such as the Draw-A-Family and Kinetic Family Drawing Tests. In addition to the chapters on specific assessment techniques, there are chapters covering topics such as the ethical practice of assessment, test bias and use with minority groups, computer-assisted assessment, the assessment interview, behavioral assessment, and the writing of psychological reports. The inclusion of an overview, guidelines, and comparison on assessment techniques makes this tool useful to clinical psychologists; other mental health practitioners; and psychology, education, or counseling students enrolled in courses covering psychological measurement.

J-55 **Handbook of Cross-Cultural Psychology**. 2d ed. 3 vols. Boston: Allyn & Bacon, 1997.

The second edition of this work has been extensively revised. The first edition was published in 1980. This edition covers topics not found in the first edition, for example, new chapters on methodology. In addition, some subjects covered in the previous edition (e.g., sex and gender issues; aggression, crime, and warfare; and intergroup relations) are now treated in separate chapters. Volume 1, *Theory and Method*, covers theoretical developments and methodological issues. There are chapters on the history of cross-cultural psychology, the theoretical frameworks of cross-cultural psychology, various approaches, empirical methods, and data analysis. Volume 2, *Basic Processes and Human Development*, summarizes research on developmental processes. Among the topics covered are perception; cognition; emotions; language acquisition; socialization; and the development of identity, education, and literacy. Volume 3, *Social Behavior and Applications*, examines the role of biology and socialization in behavior and relationships. Among the topics explored are individualism and collectivism; acculturation; gender roles; cross-cultural training and education; the built and natural environment; aggression, crime, and warfare; management and organizational behavior; intergroup behavior across cultures; social cognition; and the cultural, social, and psychological factors relating to health, illness, and disease. Each volume has its own name and subject indexes. This set will be found in large academic libraries supporting curricula in ethnopsychology, comparative anthropology, and sociobiology.

J-56 Hochberg, Julian E., ed. **Perception and Cognition at Century's End**. (Handbook of Perception and Cognition). San Diego, CA: Academic Press, 1998.

This handbook serves as a core reference for advanced undergraduates, graduate students, and faculty in perception and cognitive science. It is part of Academic Press's Handbook of Perception and Cognition series. There are more than twenty volumes in this series. Recent titles in the series include the second edition of *Cognitive Science* (1999), *Seeing* (2000), and *Human Performance and Ergonomics* (1999). The initial chapters of *Perception and Cognition at Century's End* chronicle the historical development of these major fields of psychology. Other chapters examine new concepts and recent empirical research relating to perceptual and cognitive development. There is also a discussion of future directions. This handbook and other titles in this series should be considered for all academic libraries supporting curriculum relating to cognition and perception.

J-57 Hogan, Robert, John Johnson, and Stephen R. Briggs, eds. **Handbook of Personality Psychology**. San Diego, CA: Academic Press, 1997.

There has been renewed interest in personality psychology since the late 1980s. Personality psychology emerged as a separate field in the 1930s. The first chapter of this handbook (written by Don P. McAdams) provides an excellent conceptual history of the field. Subsequent chapters cover topics relating to conceptual and measurement issues in personality, developmental issues, biological determinants of personality, social determinants of personality, dynamic personality processes, personality and the self, and applied psychology. For example, there are chapters on emotion, genetics, cross-cultural perceptions, the psychology of getting along, and the relationship between personality and health. There are thirty-six chapters, all authored by leaders in the field of personality psychology. Given the clarity of writing overall, articles are accessible to undergraduates and students in fields other than psychology. This handbook is a standard source in any academic behavioral science collection.

J-58 Kendall, Philip C., James N. Butcher, and Grayson N. Holmbeck. **Handbook of Research Methods in Clinical Psychology**. 2d ed. New York: John Wiley, 1999.

The first edition of this handbook (published in 1982) was well-received, and this work quickly became a core reference source for graduate students and researchers in clinical psychology. This edition has been updated to include expanded coverage of specific methods and topics as well as new areas of research. For example, there are new chapters on item response theory, publishing and communicating research findings, community-based treatment and prevention, and meta-analysis. Chapters in part One focus on general issues in clinical research. Part Two concentrates on assessment.

Treatment is the focus of part Three. Part Four explores issues relating to psychopathology and health. The last part discusses research issues pertaining to special populations, specifically children, adolescents, older adults, couples, and families. This handbook remains a standard source for libraries serving graduate students and researchers in clinical psychology, social work, and other mental health disciplines.

J-59 Keren, Gideon, and Charles Lewis, eds. **A Handbook for Data Analysis in the Behavioral Sciences: Methodological Issues**. Hillsdale, NJ: Lawrence Erlbaum Associates, 1993.

This handbook has become a standard source for graduate students and researchers in the behavioral and social sciences. It focuses on methodological issues in data analysis. Chapters are organized into four parts. Part 1 deals with mathematical models and the measurements of psychological attributes. Part 2 examines issues, some controversial, underlying social science methodology. Part 3 includes chapters relating to the topic of intuitive statistics. Part 4 focuses on problems associated with hypothesis testing.

J-60 Koocher, Gerald P., John C. Norcross, and Sam S. Hill, eds. **Psychologists' Desk Reference**. New York: Oxford University Press, 1998.

This handbook has been designed for practitioners. It is useful not only to psychologists but also to other mental health professionals and physicians. The chapters were contributed by experienced clinicians. The volume is organized in eight sections. Part 1 contains chapters relating to assessment and diagnosis. Part 2 covers psychological testing. Psychotherapy and treatment are covered in Part 3. Part 4 focuses on pharmacotherapy. Ethical evaluation and testimony are discussed in Part 6. Experts offer advice on managing a practice in Part 7. Part 8 leads users to professional resources. This handbook is a core resource for collections serving practicing psychologists and for academic libraries supporting graduate level programs in clinical psychology.

J-61 McGovern, Thomas V., ed. **Handbook for Enhancing Undergraduate Education in Psychology**. Washington, DC: American Psychological Association, 1993.

This is the first comprehensive study of the undergraduate psychology curriculum since the publication of the Kulik Report in 1973. It is the result of a 1991 national conference on undergraduate education in psychology. One of the goals of the American Psychological Association (APA) National Conference on Enhancing the Quality of Undergraduate Education in Psychology was the publication of a practical handbook for psychology faculty involved with undergraduate instruction. This handbook includes chapters on curriculum assessment, student advising, the recruitment and retention of minorities, faculty development, collegiality between faculty, active learning techniques, and the transformation of the undergraduate curriculum. Many college and university libraries have acquired this thought-provoking book. Many of the chapters are relevant to all undergraduate faculty, not just faculty who work with psychology undergraduates.

J-62 O'Donohue, William T., and Richard Kitchener, eds. **Handbook of Behaviorism**. San Diego, CA: Academic Press, 1999.

Although the behaviorism movement gained its momentum in the early to mid-twentieth century (roughly from 1920 to 1960), there is currently renewed interest in studying the views of individual behaviorists and the history of this movement. This handbook pulls together essays on the various schools of thought as well as the views of specific theorists. There are fifteen chapters in total. One can find substantive essays on the views of Watson, Tolman, Hull, Skinner, Wittgenstein, Ryle, and Quine as well as articles on interbehaviorism, interbehavioral psychology, empirical behaviorism, teleological behaviorism, theoretical behaviorism, biological behaviorism, contextualistic behaviorism, and logical behaviorism. All academic libraries supporting graduate programs in psychology will want a copy of this specialized handbook.

J-63   Puente, Antonio E., Janet R. Matthews, and Charles L. Brewer, eds. **Teaching Psychology in America: A History**. Washington, DC: American Psychological Association, 1992.

This unique handbook does not chronicle the history of psychology but rather the history of the teaching of psychology. Many of the thirty-one contributors have used archival records to enhance the historical analyses. The chapters are grouped into five divisions: general issues, key individuals, conferences on the teaching of psychology, scholarly and professional organizations in psychology, and key publications in the teaching of psychology. There are chapters on the evolution of the psychology curriculum, student advising, teaching methods, the development of psychology in other countries, the impact of women on the teaching of psychology, multiculturalism, the role of the American Psychological Association (APA), and the development of important publications (such as APA's journal *Teaching of Psychology*, introductory textbooks, and psychological handbooks). Psychology faculty and scholars will find this history interesting, especially because many of the recommendations made in the past by national conferences and surveys are still relevant today. Librarians responsible for developing collections supporting psychology programs will also find this handbook useful, particularly those chapters outlining trends in the curriculum and the evolution of textbooks and handbooks.

J-64   Rappaport, Julian, and Edward Seidman, eds. **Handbook of Community Psychology**. New York: Kluwer Academic/Plenum, 2000.

Community psychology has emerged as a field distinct from community mental health. The APA created a separate division for community psychology in 1966, and two major journals in the field, the *American Journal of Community Psychology* and the *Journal of Community Psychology*, were launched in 1973. This is the only handbook in the area of community psychology. Much of the literature is in the form of textbooks or books of readings about social problems and social interventions rather than reference works. This handbook assembles the ideas of a wide range of authors around these broad themes: conceptual frameworks; empirically grounded constructs; intervention strategies and tactics; social systems; design, assessment, and analysis; cross-cutting professional issues; and contemporary intersections with community psychology. The thirty-eight chapters are the work of 106 authors including academics and practitioners form a range of settings (e.g., small colleges, large research universities, government agencies, grassroots organizations). There are articles on topics as diverse as community and neighborhood organizations, the school reform movement, and the farm crisis and rural America. This unique handbook will be useful to advanced undergraduates, graduate students, and practitioners in programs ranging from community psychology to public policy.

J-65   Reis, Harry T., and Charles M. Judd, eds. **Handbook of Research Methods in Social and Personality Psychology**. New York: Cambridge University Press, 2000.

This handbook covers traditional and new research methodologies employed in social and personality psychology. There are the standard chapters on design, measurement, and analysis, as well as chapters on less traditional techniques such as daily experience methodology, cognitive mediation, and psychophysiological measures. There are nineteen chapters grouped into three parts. Chapters in part one focus on research design, inference, and issues of validity. Part two covers specific procedures, ranging from small group research to content analysis and narrative analysis. Essays in part three focus on data analysis strategies. Separate author and subject indexes are provided. This handbook is so complete that it could easily serve as a textbook on methodology in social psychological research.

J-66   Reynolds, Cecil R., and Terry B. Gutkin, eds. **The Handbook of School Psychology**. 3d ed. New York: John Wiley, 1999.

The first edition of this handbook was published in 1982, and the second edition (which was essentially a complete revision of the first edition) was published in 1990. For almost two decades, this has been a basic source for practicing school psychologists as well as students training to become school psychologists. Some chapters have been updated; others have been reworked and given new focuses. Also, new chapters have been added, including chapters on secondary prevention (specifically, intervention assistance programs and inclusive education), psychopharmacology with school-aged children, and the impact of recent research in biological psychology. The forty-three chapters are grouped into four general sections: current perspectives; scientific study of behavior: contributions to theory and practice; psychological and educational assessment; school psychological interventions: focus on children; and school psychological interventions: focus on staff, programs, and organizations. The contributors represent a diversity of experience and background. Chapter authors include faculty in a range of disciplines (e.g., curriculum and instruction, psychiatry; human development; pediatrics, social work) as well as practicing school psychologists. Author and subject indexes are provided. This handbook will remain a core reference work.

J-67 Schabracq, Marc, J. A. M. Winnubst, and Cary Cooper, eds. **Handbook of Work and Health Psychology**. New York: John Wiley, 1996.
   Work and health psychology have generally been treated as two separate subfields of psychology. This handbook serves to integrate the two fields. This integration is logical given that work-related health problems are a major concern to businesses across the globe. Part I introduces the reader to the concepts, defining work and health psychology and establishing a theoretical framework. Chapters in part II examine theories and constructs such as the relationship between job control and health, individual differences in coping, and the role of social support and organizational culture. Part III focuses on the diagnosis of stress. The next part of the handbook looks at interventions and current issues such as new technologies and stress, stress among managerial and professional women, and gender differences in coping. The final part focuses on preventive programming, including strategies ranging from biofeedback to the design of healthy work environments. This handbook will be useful to graduate students, researchers, and professionals in organizational psychology and human resource management as well as practitioners in corporate wellness, worksite health promotion, and employee assistance programs. The latter constitute a growing rank of professionals in all types of worksites: business, industry, government, and health care.

J-68 Sternberg, Robert J., ed. **Handbook of Creativity**. New York: Cambridge University Press, 1999.
   Creativity is a growing area of research in psychology, biology, education, and the arts and humanities. This handbook, edited by one of America's most esteemed educational psychologists (Sternberg is IBM Professor of Psychology and Education at Yale University), provides a comprehensive overview of the history of the study of creativity, approaches to the study of creativity, issues in the field, and the future of creativity research. The twenty-two chapters (all written by prominent behavioral scientists) are grouped into six parts. The first part of the book introduces readers to the field of creativity. The second part contains chapters on methods for studying creativity, including psychometric approaches, experimental studies, case studies, and historiometric perspectives. Part III examines the origins of creativity. The next part of the volume looks at the relationship between creativity, the individual, and the environment. Part V covers a range of special topics in creativity, including cross-cultural studies, prodigies, and computer models of creativity. The final part summarizes the past half-century of creativity research. This handbook is an important source for students and researchers in any discipline concerned with the development of creative thinking.

J-69 Sternberg, Robert J., ed. **Handbook of Intelligence**. Cambridge: Cambridge University Press, 2000.
   This handbook complements and updates in part the *Encyclopedia of Human Intelligence* (J-34), the 1994 encyclopedia edited by Sternberg. It also supersedes Sternberg's 1982 work, *The Handbook of Human Intelligence*. This new handbook provides broad topical essays on the nature of intelligence, the measurement of intelligence, and how intelligence affects society and culture. Over the past two decades, several areas of study have developed within the field of intelligence studies. Consequently, this 2000 handbook covers new areas of intelligence such as social intelligence, practical intelligence, emotional intelligence, and the teaching of intelligence. In addition, it incorporates articles

on topics that were excluded from the 1982 work. For example, there are articles on giftedness, animal intelligence, the neuropsychology and psychophysiology of intelligence, tests of intelligence, and the relation of intelligence to wisdom and creativity. This broad handbook has been designed for multiple audiences and purposes. It has been written for psychologists, educators, cognitive scientists, other social scientists, and the nonspecialist. It can be used as a reference or read cover to cover by anyone taking a course on human intelligence.

J-70   Tulving, Endel, and Fergus I. M. Craik, eds. **The Oxford Handbook of Memory**. New York: Oxford University Press, 2000.

These two Canadian scholars are world authorities on memory. Tulving and Craik have collaborated before, co-authoring articles on episodic memory. The publication of this handbook is very important because it is the first comprehensive handbook of memory ever published. It is 700 pages in length and all-encompassing. It covers all aspects of memory, summarizing research findings from early behavioral studies to recent research using brain-scanning techniques. The handbook covers the development of memory, its contents, the study of memory in the laboratory environment, memory in daily life, the decline of memory, and the organization of memory. This title does an excellent job of explaining why research relating to memory is so important to professionals in medicine, engineering, and law. There are articles on methods of memory research, short-term memory, the encoding and retrieval of information, recollection, memory in infancy and early childhood, spatial memory, memory in the dementias, the neuroanatomy of memory, and episodic memory. Although memory studies have emerged as a relatively new specialty, human memory has been studied for more than a century. This well-written, authoritative handbook is an essential purchase for any academic library serving students and others in psychology, the neurosciences, and the field of memory research.

J-71   Walker, C. Eugene, and Michael C. Roberts, eds. **Handbook of Clinical Child Psychology**. 3d ed. New York: John Wiley, 2001.

This handbook covers normal and abnormal development in infancy, childhood, and adolescence as well as the assessment, diagnosis, and treatment of children's psychological problems. It includes a review of research on these topics as well as guidelines for practice. Given the explosion of research in this area of clinical psychology, a new edition of this classic has been needed for some time. This new edition will no doubt continue this title's legacy as a core reference in clinical child psychology. It serves as a comprehensive reference on the intervention in and management of children's psychological problems and has sometimes been adopted as a textbook in this field. The third edition will be useful not only to graduate students but also to practicing clinical psychologists, pediatric psychiatrists, and other mental health professionals who work with children and adolescents. It will also be useful to students and others studying for board certification.

REVIEWS OF RESEARCH

Reviews of research critically discuss research that has been conducted in specific areas. They are indispensable to psychologists because they document the past and present state of knowledge on a topic. Given the proliferation of journal literature, many psychologists may have to depend on this secondary source to keep abreast of the status of research in a given area. Review publications are abundant in psychology and can be recognized by titles that include words such as *advances*, *progress*, and *review*. Three important review publications are described below. Fortunately, the *PsycINFO* (J-75) database allows searchers to retrieve literature review articles published in many review periodicals.

J-72   **Annual Review of Psychology**. Palo Alto, CA: Annual Reviews, 1950- . Annual.

Although the *Annual Review of Psychology* is published annually, it is not intended to be a summary of the year's research. Rather, the editors select articles as they relate to the group's master plan, which is composed of twenty major topic areas. Members of the editorial committee nominate chapter authors. The resulting chapters therefore cover some topics more frequently than others. Articles are international in scope, and substantial bibliographies are typically included. There are indexes for the current volume as well as cumulative indexes for the series. This standard source should be available in any library supporting psychology programs. It is also a good source for identifying current topics in the field.

J-73   **The Psychological Bulletin**. Washington, DC: American Psychological Association, 1904- . Bimonthly.

Published by the APA, the *Psychological Bulletin* publishes review articles that summarize the research that has been conducted on given topics in psychology. The literature reviews are scholarly and directed at professionals, researchers, and students. Most academic libraries subscribe to this journal. Original, theoretical works are published in the companion publication, *The Psychological Review*.

J-74   Columbus, Frank, ed. **Advances in Psychology Research**. Huntington, NY: Nova Science Publishers, 2000- . Annual.

The preface to the first volume in this series states that it is "intended to provide a forum for substantial research contributions dealing with current research in psychology." Each of the thirteen chapters in Volume 1 is a previously unpublished working paper or conference paper. Subjects range from social psychology ("A Social Norms Extension of the Investment Model") to abnormal psychology ("Body Image and Anxiety in Paranoid Schizophrenia") to cognitive psychology ("Cognitive Processing Anomalies in Depressive Mood Disorders"). Authors are primarily academics and include professors from Canada, Australia, Germany, Belgium and Switzerland. Volume 2, published in 2001, contains eleven chapters on topics from the validity of type A behavior to a psychohistorical account of Hitler's lifestyle. Like the *Annual Review of Psychology*, this work provides another snapshot of the year's research activities in psychology.

INDEXES, ABSTRACTS, AND DATABASES

The need for currency, and the importance of research journals, may have contributed to the development of *Psychological Abstracts* (and *PsycINFO*, its online counterpart), a model indexing and abstracting service. Bibliographic control of journal literature is excellent in psychology. *PsycINFO* provides thorough access to scholarly articles in psychology. Core journals in psychology are also indexed in general social science databases and databases in other social science disciplines.

J-75   **PsycINFO**. Washington, DC: American Psychological Association.

PsycINFO is a series of related information services produced by the American Psychological Association. *PsycINFO* consists of *Psychological Abstracts*, *PsycLIT*, *PsycINFO* database, *The Thesaurus of Psychological Index Terms*, and several additional publications.

Psychological Abstracts/PsycLIT. Washington, DC: American Psychological Association, 1927- . Monthly. Print, online, and CD-ROM formats available.

Thesaurus of Psychological Index Terms. 9th ed. Washington, DC: American Psychological Association, 2001.

PsycINFO Database. n.d. Monthly. Online format.

Psychological Abstracts is regarded as the premier periodicals index in the field of psychology. It indexes and abstracts journal literature in all areas of psychology and covers the related disciplines of sociology, anthropology, education, management, and communication. Approximately 1,300 journals are scanned annually for coverage. Abstracts are arranged under twenty-two broad classification categories. The interdisciplinary nature of this index is reflected in the inclusion of various diverse categories: psychology and the humanities, communication systems, educational psychology, sport psychology and leisure, military psychology, consumer psychology, engineering and environmental psychology, and intelligent systems. Psychological Abstracts also indexes and abstracts the book literature in the behavioral sciences. Author, subject, and title indexes are provided.

Beginning in January 1988, foreign-language material appears only in *PsycINFO*, the corresponding online database. *PsycINFO* also includes dissertations. Dissertations were included in the print index until 1980. Book coverage also ceased in 1980 but was resumed in 1992. The current paper version of *Psychological Abstracts* indexes and abstracts English-language journal articles, books, and book chapters. *PsycLIT*, a subset of the full *PsycINFO* database, is distributed in CD-ROM format. *PsycLIT* includes references to journal articles, books, and book chapters. *PsycINFO* is available in electronic format including the Web and is updated monthly. The database contains over 1.5 million citations and abstracts. Although it is not full text, it remains the most comprehensive database in psychology and related disciplines. It indexes and abstracts journals, books, book chapters, technical reports, and dissertations. It also covers disciplines related to psychilogy (e.g., management, business, education, social work, medicine, law). *PsycINFO* is available through several commercial vendors. For more information on how to obtain access, consult the APA Web site at www.apa.org.

The vocabulary of psychology is diverse because of the interdisciplinary nature of the field. There is also a need for precise terminology because psychology deals with both human and animal populations. The American Psychological Association developed *Thesaurus of Psychological Index Terms* in an attempt to control this vast vocabulary. It lists descriptors (i.e., established subject headings) that are used in the indexing of all documents appearing in *Psychological Abstracts*, *PsycLIT*, and *PsycINFO*. More than 7,700 index terms are listed in the ninth edition of the thesaurus. The thesaurus also includes notes defining the terms, hierarchies that explain the relationships between terms, an indication of when a term was established, and an indication of how many times the term has been used.

PsycFIRST is another product from the APA consisting of the latest three years of the *PsycINFO* database. *ClinPSYC* is a clinical psychology subset of *PsycINFO*.

J-76 **Ageline**. Washington, DC: American Association of Retired Persons (AARP), 1978- . Bimonthly. Electronic format.

Ageline, also known as *AARP Ageline*, contains over 50,000 citations and abstracts in the field of social gerontology, specifically the social and psychological aspects of aging. The economics of aging, including welfare, Social Security, and public policy issues, are also included. The database is in English, although it is international in scope. Coverage is from 1978 to the present and approximately 500 records are added bimonthly. It is available on CD-ROM and through the Web as well as other information providers including Dialog.

J-77 **Child Abuse and Neglect**. Washington, DC: U.S. National Clearinghouse on Child Abuse and Neglect Information, 1965- . Semiannual. Electronic format.

This database contains citations and abstracts to materials related to all facets of child abuse and neglect. Included are journal articles, books, government publications, conference papers, and other materials. Audiovisual materials, including audio and videotapes and anatomically correct dolls, are included. There is also a thesaurus of standardized terms. The database contains approximately 25,000 records from 1965 to the present and is updated semiannually. It is available free on the Internet or on CD-ROM.

J-78 **Child Development Abstracts and Bibliography**. Ann Arbor, MI: Society for Research in Child Development, 1927- . 3 times/yr.

Child Development Abstracts and Bibliography covers research and book reviews from 275 English-language and non-English-language journals in all areas of child development.

Electronic access: Available online to members of the organization.

J-79 **Exceptional Child Education Resources (ECER)**. Reston, VA: Council for Exceptional Children, 1969- . Quarterly. Electronic format.

ECER contains over 100,000 citations and abstracts related to exceptional children, including gifted children; those with artistic or other talents; and children with physical or mental disabilities, mental disorders, or behavior problems. In addition, there is coverage of health issues including AIDS and cancer. Records are in English. It is available on CD-ROM and via several information providers.

J-80 **Linguistics and Language Behavior Abstracts (LLBA)**. Bethesda, MD: CSA, 1973- . Monthly. Electronic format.

LLBA contains over 250,000 citations and abstracts on language, linguistics, speech, communication, and related topics. Coverage is from 1973 to the present. *LLBA* is available on the Web, CD-ROM, or through various information providers including Dialog and SilverPlatter.

J-81 **Mental Health Abstracts**. Wilmington, NC: IFI/Plenum Data, 1969- . Monthly. Electronic format.

Mental Health Abstracts contains over 500,000 bibliographic citations and abstracts to the international literature on mental health. Information is derived from over 1,200 journals, books, conference proceedings, and other works. Coverage is from 1969 to date. Mental Health Abstracts is available on CD-ROM or through Dialog.

J-82 **The Psychological Index: An Annual Bibliography of the Literature of Psychology and Cognate Subjects**. New York: Psychological Review, 1894–1934.

Although there is some overlap with *Psychological Abstracts* (see J-75n) (from 1927 to 1934), this source provides an index to the literature of psychology beginning with the late nineteenth century. The index was published annually. The book is divided into broad categories, each of which is subdivided into more specific subjects. Within these subdivisions, entries are arranged alphabetically by author's last name. Each citation includes author's name(s), title of the work, name of publication, volume number, and page numbers. Each edition contains an author index. This series is invaluable to those researching the history of psychology or those seeking to find original citations to early works. Although no longer in print, it should be available in larger academic and research libraries.

BIBLIOGRAPHIES

Bibliographies list resources on a topic and can be especially useful in locating specialized material. In addition to reference work, they may be used for collection development decisions. Bibliographies are produced less frequently in psychology than in other social science disciplines because of psychology's emphasis on current information.

J-83 Baxter, Pam M. **Psychology: A Guide to Reference and Information Sources**. (Reference Sources in the Social Sciences). Englewood, CO: Libraries Unlimited, 1993.

This guide is part of Libraries Unlimited Reference Sources in the Social Sciences series. More than 600 sources (both print and electronic) are listed with descriptive and evaluative annotations. The guide is divided into four parts: general social science reference sources, relevant reference works in other social science disciplines, general psychology reference sources, and special topics in psychology. This last part constitutes the bulk of the work, with descriptions of almost 400 sources (e.g., guides, bibliographies, indexes/abstracts, databases, handbooks, dictionaries, encyclopedias, directories, biographical sources) in more than twenty subfields of psychology. There are author/title and subject indexes. This guide to the literature is useful for undergraduate and graduate students, researchers, practicing psychologists, and librarians.

J-84 **Bibliographic Guide to Psychology**. New York: Macmillan, 1975- . Annual.

Publications cataloged by the Library of Congress and the Research Libraries of the New York Public Library are reviewed annually for inclusion in this subject bibliography. G. K. Hall previously published this title as part of its Bibliographic Guides series. Coverage is restricted to items in the LC classification BF. English-language and non-English-language books and serials in all forms are included. All entries are alphabetically arranged with access by main entry, added entries, title, series title, and LC subject headings. Full catalog records are provided for the main entry; secondary entries have abridged records. Librarians may want to use this guide for verification purposes as well as to aid collection development work.

J-85 **Bibliographies in Psychology**. Washington, DC: American Psychological Association, 1988- .

Each bibliography in this series provides references and abstracts on a specific topic. The books include references from journal articles, dissertations, and books and book chapters. There are also indexes for authors and subjects. The search strategies used to produce the results are also included so that users can perform updates searches on *PsycINFO* (see J-75). As of November 2000, there were twenty-one titles in the series. Recent subjects include cancer, gay and lesbian issues, and emergency medical services for children.

J-86 Caton, Hiram. **The Bibliography of Human Behavior**. Westport, CT: Greenwood Press, 1993.

This annotated bibliography focuses on biologically oriented studies of human behavior. Among the subjects covered are human evolution, cultural evolution, sociobiology, behavior genetics, parenting, sexuality, neurology, psychiatry, social psychology, and politics. Most of the references selected for inclusion were published after 1979. However, some classic works are also listed. The documents included are books, book chapters, and journal articles. Because of the interdisciplinary perspective, this source would be of interest to a wide range of researchers, including psychologists, sociologists, anthropologists, and biologists.

J-87 McInnis, Raymond G. **Research Guide for Psychology**. Westport, CT: Greenwood Press, 1982.

This comprehensive guide to sources in all areas of psychology includes coverage of approximately 1,200 titles published through 1979. Bibliographic essays focus on subdivisions of the field and list sources according to the type of information they contain. Although dated, this work is still useful because of its comprehensiveness. This extensive guide is appropriate for upper-level undergraduates, graduate students, faculty, researchers, and librarians. However, students needing a general library guide for the discipline would be better served by *Library Use: A Handbook for Psychology* (J-1).

J-88 **Psychology: An Introductory Bibliography**. Lanham, MD; Pasadena, CA: Scarecrow Press; Salem Press, 1996.

This annotated bibliography has a subject arrangement, including sections on the history of psychology, biological bases of behavior, sensation and perception, emotion, motivation, learning, cognition, memory, language, developmental psychology, social psychology, psychological assessment, personality, psychopathology, and psychotherapy. Each section is also subdivided so that users can more easily locate materials of interest. Most of the citations are from the 1970s to the 1990s, but major historical works are also included. There are author and subject indexes. This work is especially valuable for more recent works and should be used in conjunction with one of the historical bibliographies listed below.

J-89   Viney, Wayne, Michael Wertheimer, and Marilyn Lou Wertheimer. **History of Psychology: A Guide to Information Sources**. Detroit: Gale, 1979.

The authors of this work chose to focus on the inclusion of general reference materials and psychology-specific reference materials, general histories of psychology, major schools of thought, histories of specific content areas, and histories of related fields. The result is a bibliography of about 3,000 entries, 1,200 of which are annotated and divided into the five content sections above. Included are name, title, and subject indexes. The exclusion of materials written in languages other than English is a drawback, but this is still a valuable reference tool that will be of use to those studying the history of psychology and related disciplines.

J-90   Watson, Robert Irving. **Eminent Contributors to Psychology**. 2 vols. New York: Springer, 1974–1976.

Volume one of this set, *A Bibliography of Primary References*, was published in 1974, and volume two, *A Bibliography of Secondary Reference*, was published in 1976. Volume one contains 12,000 references produced by 538 individuals living between 1600 and 1967. It is arranged alphabetically by last name and the citations are not annotated. Volume two builds on volume one, containing about 55,000 selected secondary references to the work of the same 538 individuals. Volume two is also arranged alphabetically by last name. This reference set is a core reference title in the history of psychology.

BOOK REVIEWS

The following book review journal offers critical reviews of scholarly books in psychology. Several databases can also be used to retrieve citations (and sometimes the full text) to reviews, notably, *Social Sciences Abstracts* (H-50) and *ProQuest Direct*.

J-91   **Contemporary Psychology: APA Review of Books**. Washington, DC: American Psychological Association, 1956- . Bimonthly.

Contemporary Psychology contains critical reviews of books, films, videotapes, and other materials relevant to psychology. Reviews are written by invitation from the editorial review board. Each review is typically two to three pages in length, and most contain references. The journal was formerly divided by subject areas. Recent issues, however, are not. The preface to the journal states that its mission is to represent a broad cross-section of psychological literature. A recent issue reviews books on such topics as developmental psychology, educational psychology, measurement, research methods, social psychology, cognition, learning; personality, and cross-cultural psychology. Each review contains a complete bibliographic citation and price as well as institutional affiliation of the work's principle authors. This journal is indexed in *Book Review Index*, and the December issue contains cumulative author/reviewer and subject indexes.

DIRECTORIES

In psychology, an increasing amount of directory information is being made available on the Internet.

J-92   **Directory of the American Psychological Association**. Washington, DC: American Psychological Association, 1916- . Quadrennial.

The official directory of the APA is published every four years. The 1997 edition lists over 82,000 members. Biographical information includes address, birth date, highest degree attained, major field, areas of specialization, states where licensed or certified, current employment, past employment, and membership status. Data items are collected from survey questionnaires sent to members.

A geographical index and divisional rosters are also included, as are the APA bylaws, code of ethics, and standards for psychological practice.

J-93 **APA Membership Register**. Washington, DC: American Psychological Association, 1967- . Annual.

The *APA Membership Register* is a current roster of APA members. It is published with the purpose of updating the *Directory of the American Psychological Association* (J-92), and is published every year except those in which the Directory is published. Each entry lists addresses, telephone numbers, membership status, and divisional affiliations. Biographical information is not included except for new members.

J-94 **Graduate Study in Psychology**. Washington, DC: American Psychological Association, 1968- . Annual.

This definitive guide to graduate psychology programs is currently in its thirty-third annual edition. The bulk of the work is a state-by-state listing of psychology programs arranged alphabetically by college or university name. Each listing provides a description of the programs and degrees offered; application information; student information, including total enrollment, number of applications, and students admitted; degree requirements; admission requirements, including courses, test scores, GPA, and other criteria; tuition; housing and day care; and financial assistance. The preface also contains APA's policy on graduate education, information about accreditation and professional licensing, and a discussion of selecting an appropriate program and tips for successfully applying to a graduate program. This works belongs in the library of any college or university offering an undergraduate psychology program.

J-95 Buskist, William, and Amy Mixon. **Allyn & Bacon Guide to Master's Programs in Psychology and Counseling Psychology**. Boston: Allyn & Bacon, 1998.

This guide is intended for students who wish to pursue a terminal master's degree in psychology or those who want to apply to such programs as a backup in case they are not accepted into doctoral programs. The first part of the book is a listing of academic programs by state and a listing by program type. There is also a glossary of common graduate school terms. The main body of the work is divided by geographic region: North Atlantic, South Atlantic, North Central, South Central, Mountain Pacific, U.S. Territories, and Canada. States or provinces are listed alphabetically within each region. Entries contain information on how to obtain application materials; a contact person; number of openings each year; a description of the campus and faculty; degrees offered and program orientation; GPA and GRE information; required undergraduate courses; information on the interview process, letters of recommendation, and relevant experiences; degree requirements; financial information; number of applicants and those accepted into the program; and the program director's comments. This is a useful complement to *Graduate Study in Psychology* (J-94).

J-96 **CyberPsychLink—Organizations**. URL: http://cctr.umkc.edu/user/dmartin /organ.html.

CyberPsychLink is run by Dawn Martin, who started collecting psychology-related links while a graduate student at the University of Missouri, Kansas City. This site resides on the university's Academic Computing Department Web server. The "Organizations" link currently contains sixteen links to professional organizations and associations including the APA and American Psychological Society; governmental sites, including the National Institutes of Health and the National Science Foundation; and educational sites including Psi Chi, the psychology national honor society. Most sites contain a brief description, most of which are one or two sentences in length. This is a useful Web directory and users should also explore the main CyberPsychLink pages (http://cctr.umkc.edu/user /dmartin/psych2.html) (see J-159).

J-97 **PsychRef—Professional Associations & Societies**. URL: http://maple
.lemoyne.edu/~hevern/psychref1-3.html.

PsychRef was created and is maintained by Vincent W. Hevern, who is in the Psychology
Department at LeMoyne College in Syracuse, New York. The Professional Associations & Societies
page is alphabetical by name of the organization, besides the APA and APS, which are listed at the
top of the page. This site is useful because in addition to pointing to the main pages, there are also
links to other areas of an organization's Web site. The APA section, for instance, provides about
twenty-five links to various APA pages, including its divisions and student information section. The
arrangement is hierarchical, with underlying pages indented under the main link. This site is also international in scope, including links to various organizations and professional associations in several
foreign countries. This is a useful listing of professional psychology organizations, and the hierarchical
arrangement is especially helpful for going directly to a desired site without having to wade through
from the main page. Users need to be aware that Hevern recently posted a message on his site indicating
that he will not be updating it until he makes some decisions about the site's future.

J-98 **Social Psychology Network—Organizations and Conferences**. URL:
http://www.socialpsychology.org/psych.htm.

The Social Psychology Network is maintained by Scott Plous of Wesleyan University. The
organizations and conferences page contains links to and descriptions of over twenty professional
organizations, including links to the main page and to some other pages within the organization. Each
description lists the number of members and the date and place of the national conference. There are
also links to the conference sites when available and a separate link to membership information for
each organization. A separate link directs users to social psychology organizations located outside of
the United States. This site is especially good for social psychology faculty and students, as is the parent
site, Social Psychology Network (http://www.socialpsychology.org).

J-99 **Psychology Departments on the Web**. URL: http://www.psychwww
.com/resource/deptlist.htm.

This page, part of *Psych Web* (J-162), contains links to the psychology departments of over
1,100 universities and colleges in the United States and abroad. The list is alphabetical by the institutional name. There are no listings under "University of . . ." because they are listed by place name. A
disclaimer at the top states that the site was last updated in 1999, but this doesn't appear to be a problem
since the Web site addresses probably do not change often. Departments related to psychology but
having different names (i.e., counseling) are not included. Sites suspected of having broken links are
identified with an asterisk. This is a useful site, especially for students or prospective students looking for appropriate programs or faculty seeking academic positions.

J-100 **PSYCLine: Your Guide to Psychology and Social Science Journals
on the Web**. URL: http://www.psycline.org/journals/psycline.html.

This site is an index to over 1,600 psychology and social sciences journals. Based in Germany,
there are also mirror sites in Great Britain, the United States, Japan, and Spain. Search options appear
in a frame on the left of the screen. Users can search by keyword or subject or can browse by journal
title. It is important to realize that searches do not result in individual articles but to titles of journals.
There is also a link to search journal home pages to find information such as subscription prices, publication schedule, editorial information, and manuscript submission requirements. This site is very
useful for those wishing to submit a manuscript for publication or to find information on accessing or
subscribing to a journal. There is also an article locator. Users can search free tables of contents and
abstracts databases provided by journal publishers.

J-101 **Journals in Psychology: A Resource Listing for Authors**. 5th ed. Washington, DC: American Psychological Association, 1997.

This directory is designed to assist authors in finding an appropriate journal to which to submit manuscripts. The fifth edition contains information on 355 journals arranged alphabetically by title. Each listing contains the publisher and contact information; editor and contact information; editorial policy; selective notes on submissions; journal frequency, number of articles, and total pages published per year; total number of subscribers; an indication whether book reviews are accepted; and the rejection rate. This is an essential title for libraries supporting psychology programs and related disciplines.

J-102 **CyberPsychLink—Software**. URL: http://cctr.umkc.edu/user/dmartin /software.html.

CyberPsychLink's software site currently consists of twenty links to various software programs or to other lists of sites describing software available for psychology research. The listings range from psychology specific (e.g., *APA StyleSheets for WinWord*) to more general (e.g., *Health Sciences Software*). There are also several links to companies producing specific software packages as well as to statistical software packages. This is a great resource for faculty and other researchers seeking information on software packages for use in psychological research.

J-103 **PsycLink Software Information Service for Psychology**. URL: http:// plaid.hawk.plattsburgh.edu/psyclink/.

Peter Hornby of the State University of New York at Plattsburgh maintains PsycLink, originally established in 1987. The site is intended to serve as a comprehensive resource for psychology-related software, as a site organizing Web-based resources, and as a directory for software users. The main search area is divided into six sections, one each for PsycLink Resources (i.e., software), Web sites, submissions, questions and announcements, a guest book, and a search engine to search the PsycLink files. The main PsycLink Resources link is divided into sections for finding descriptions of software (i.e., software catalog) and to download software. Descriptions, divided into twenty-two browseable subject sections, contain title, author, publisher, description, price information, hardware requirements, contact information, and Web sites when available. A cautionary note is that although the site has an update date of 2000, most resources are from 1997 or earlier. Nonetheless, this site should serve researchers, instructors, and practitioners who seek psychology-related software.

J-104 VandenBos, Gary R., ed. **Videos in Psychology: A Resource Directory**. Washington, DC: American Psychological Association, 2000.

This directory was published by the APA in response to the growing demand for psychology-related multimedia resources, particularly videos. The directory is arranged alphabetically by name of the video. Included are year of production, series (if applicable), abstract, narrator and participants, accompanying materials, licensing and purchasing information, intended audience, format (e.g., VHS), time, any awards given, ISBN (if available), and producer. At least one distributor is listed with contact information. There is a topic index to find videos by subject. This useful directory fills a void in psychology reference materials. The inclusion of prices would have enhanced the work.

BIOGRAPHICAL SOURCES

Works listed in this section provide biographical information on living and deceased psychologists as well as on individuals who have influenced the field.

J-105 Sheehy, Noel, Antony J. Chapman, and Wendy A. Conroy, eds. **Biographical Dictionary of Psychology**. New York: Routledge, 1997.

The editors have created a dictionary describing the impact that some 500 individuals have had on psychology. Not all of the individuals included may regard themselves as psychologists, but all have dramatically affected the discipline. The editors have succeeded in taking a global perspective, including psychologists who may not be well-known in North America or Europe. The individuals profiled include both living and deceased figures. However, given publication deadlines, individuals included had to achieve recognition by the early 1990s. The editors conducted a rigorous process to determine whom to include. They surveyed colleagues, reviewed histories of psychology and textbooks published between 1950 and 1990, used citation analysis, searched major library catalogs, and reviewed the lists of recipients of awards recognizing major contributions to the discipline. Each biographical entry shares a standard format: name; date and place of birth; main area of interest in psychology; death date, if appropriate; nationality; education; appointments and awards; principal publications; sources that could be consulted for a further understanding of the person's work; and an analysis of the individual's intellectual development, main ideas, and influence. Each biographical entry is signed. The editors have written those that have no attribution. Four indexes are provided: of names; of interests (allowing users to search by broad areas within psychology); of key terms (linking individuals to concepts); and of institutions (linking individuals with academic and professional institutions). This biographical dictionary should be part of any core reference collection in an academic library supporting the behavioral sciences.

J-106 Zusne, Leonard. **Biographical Dictionary of Psychology**. Westport, CT: Greenwood Press, 1984.

This is a revision of Zusne's 1975 *Names in the History of Psychology: A Biographical Sourcebook* (Hemisphere), a dictionary listing 526 deceased contributors to the field of psychology. A panel of prominent psychologists selected biographies. The revised edition retains most of the entries from the first edition and adds 101 new names. Entries are arranged alphabetically, an improvement over the original edition, which had a chronological arrangement. Along with standard biographical data there is a description of the individual's contribution, influence, research, and publications. Sources providing additional information are listed. Zusne's dictionary is a source of lasting value in the history of psychology. All libraries that own this title should retain it.

J-107 Nordby, Vernon J., and Calvin S. Hall. **A Guide to Psychologists and Their Concepts**. San Francisco: W. H. Freeman, 1974.

Nordby and Hall provide brief biographical sketches of forty-two psychologists who have influenced the development of contemporary psychology. The majority are American, and the major fields of psychology are represented. Biographical data are followed by an identification of the concepts associated with each individual. Each concept is then fully explained, and a list of references (generally books written by the biographee) is given. The subject index provides access to the more than 400 concepts defined in this guide. The writing is clear and understandable and assumes no background in psychology. High school, public, and academic libraries should have this book on their shelves.

J-108 Watson, Robert I., and Rand B. Evans. **The Great Psychologists: A History of Psychological Thought**. 5th ed. New York: HarperCollins, 1991.

This is the long-awaited revision of Robert I. Watsons's *The Great Psychologists*. Although Watson planned to update the fourth edition (which was published by Lippincott in 1978), he died in 1980. Evans, a former colleague of Watson's, has carried on the work. Although all the chapters have been revised and updated, Evans has tried to retain the flavor of the fourth edition, and when possible, has retained Watson's words. *The Great Psychologists* remains a readable and authoritative account of the development of psychology from ancient Greek times to the modern period. The history of psychology is outlined through biographical chapters focusing on major contributors to the discipline. Articles are more substantial than those appearing in Zusne's *Biographical Dictionary of Psychology* (J-106) or *A Guide to Psychologists and Their Concepts* (J-107). Evans's revision of Watson's classic is appropriate for all academic collections.

J-109   Murchison, Carl, ed. **History of Psychology in Autobiography**. Volumes 1-3. New York: Russell & Russell, 1930–1936.

J-110   Boring, E. G., et al., eds. **History of Psychology in Autobiography. Volume 4**. New York: Russell & Russell, 1952.

J-111   Boring, E. G., and Gardner Lindzey, eds. **History of Psychology in Autobiography. Volume 5**. New York: Appleton-Century-Crofts, 1967.

J-112   Lindzey, Gardner, ed. **History of Psychology in Autobiography. Volume 6**. Englewood Cliffs, NJ: Prentice-Hall, 1974.

J-113   Lindzey, Gardner, ed. **History of Psychology in Autobiography. Volume 7**. San Francisco: W. H. Freeman, 1980.

J-114   Lindzey, Gardner, ed. **History of Psychology in Autobiography. Volume 8**. Stanford, CA: Stanford University Press, 1989.

Each volume in this series contains approximately thirteen autobiographies of prominent psychologists. Some of the most eminent individuals in psychology discuss the evolution of their work. Among the people profiled are Marty Whiton Calkins, Jean Piaget, B. F. Skinner, John B. Watson, Carl Rogers, and Eleanor Maccoby. Articles average about twenty pages in length. Essays conclude with a list of selected publications.

J-115   Cohen, David. **Psychologists on Psychology**. London: Routledge & Kegan Paul, 1977.

Cohen's introduction provides an engrossing history of the development of psychology as a discipline and profession. The psychologists that he interviewed for this collection of sketches reflect a wide range of perspectives. Among the influential psychologists profiled are David McClelland, H. J. Eysenck, Leon Festinger, Liam Hudson, Michel Jouvet, R. D. Laing, Harald Leupold-Lowenthal, Neal Miller, B. F. Skinner, Henri Tajfel, and Niko Tinbergen. Cohen includes his own tentative conclusions from his study of some of the world's premier psychologists. One intriguing theme that Cohen identified was that many of these renowned figures became psychologists by accident. A bibliography is also provided. This compendium of provocative interviews should be found in any academic library supporting the behavioral sciences.

J-116   Cohen, David. **Psychologists on Psychology**. 2d ed. New York: Routledge, 1995.

In this second edition, Cohen has interviewed ten leading psychologists. These eminent figures include Sandra Bem, Donald Broadbent, Hans Eysenck, Howard Gardner, Liam Hudson, R. D. Laing, Robert Ornstein, Patricia Smith Churchland, Herbert Simon, and Burrhus Skinner. Broadbent, Eysenck, Hudson, Laing, and Skinner were also interviewed for the first edition. These new interviews allow readers to find out whether these major thinkers have altered their views. The inclusion of new profiles (including two women) provides a broader view of contemporary figures in the field. Cohen retains the structure of the original edition with the inclusion of an essay summarizing his conclusions and a bibliography. Since some of the individuals profiled died in the 1990s (e.g., Donald Broadbent, B. F. Skinner, and R. D. Laing), this collection of interviews is even more valuable as a resource.

J-117   Birren, James E., ed. **A History of Geropsychology in Autobiography**. Washington, DC: American Psychological Association, 2000.

The psychology of aging became recognized as a subfield of psychology after World War II. Fortunately, many of the scholars who laid the groundwork for this field of study are still alive.

This collection of autobiographies by leaders in the field of geropsychology serves as a history of this discipline. The selection criteria required that any individual included had to be over the age of fifty. Although the majority of autobiographies are American, there was an effort to include geropsychologists from other countries. In addition, all subfields of geropsychology are included and a deliberate effort was made to ensure that pioneering women in the field were included. Courses focusing on the psychology of aging are being taught by an increasing number of psychology departments. Since interest in geropsychology will continue to grow, any academic library supporting faculty, scholars, and upper division and graduate students in the psychology of aging should acquire this volume.

J-118 Thompson, Dennis, and John D. Hogan. **A History of Developmental Psychology in Autobiography**. Boulder, CO: Westview Press, 1996.

The editors undertook the development of this biographical/historical source because they believed that developmental psychology was underrepresented in textbooks chronicling the history of psychology. Two reference series served as models: the long established The History of Psychology in Autobiography and the more recent The History of Clinical Psychology in Autobiography. Thompson and Hogan also thought that the time was right for a book on contemporary developmental psychology because the field has undergone significant changes. The international psychologists included in this work represent various specialties within developmental psychology. There are autobiographies from ten influential contemporary developmental psychologists: Louise Bates Ames, James Emmett Birren, Marie Skodak Crissey, David Elkind, Dale B. Harris, Lois Wladis Hoffman, Cigdem Kagitcibasi, Lewis P. Lipsitt, Paul Mussen, and Seymour Wapner. These personal accounts provide great insight into the work of these prominent figures. This collection of mini-memoirs is an essential source for all academic libraries supporting curriculum in developmental psychology.

J-119 Krawiec, T. S. **The Psychologists. Volumes 1–2**. New York: Oxford University Press, 1972–1974. **Volume 3**. Brandon, VT: Clinical Psychology Publishing, 1978.

Each volume contains approximately twelve autobiographies of prominent psychologists. These autobiographical essays are even more substantial than those found in *History of Developmental Psychology in Autobiography* (J-118). Most are thirty to forty pages in length and include an extensive bibliography of publications. A photograph of the individual is often supplied. The index is particularly helpful because it allows users to locate information about other individuals that is embedded within the essays.

J-120 Kimble, Gregory A., Michael Wertheimer, and Charlotte White, eds. **Portraits of Pioneers in Psychology. Volume 1**. Washington, DC; Hillsdale, NJ: American Psychological Association; Lawrence Erlbaum Associates, 1991.

This work brings together biographical sketches of twenty-two men and women who were pioneers in psychology. Among those profiled are William James, Ivan Petrovich Pavlov, Mary Whiton Calkins, Joseph Jastrow, Edward L. Thorndike, C. G. Jung, John B. Watson, Max Wertheimer, Edna Heidbreder, and Robert Choate Tyron. The chapters are actually revisions of addresses presented at a convention of the American Psychological Association. These addresses were enormously popular (drawing standing-room-only crowds), and APA members urged the Association to publish them. This publication was planned so it release (in 1992) would coincide with the APA's centennial celebration. Although writing styles vary from chapter to chapter, the overall quality is excellent. Undergraduates, graduate students, and scholars will find this collection engaging and interesting. Although these prominent men and women are included in standard reference sources and collective biographies, and most have been the subject of individual biographies, this volume continues to serve as a nice introduction to psychology's pioneers.

J-121 Kimble, Gregory A., C. Alan Bonaeau, and Michael Wertheimer, eds. **Portraits of Pioneers in Psychology. Volume 2**. Washington, DC; Hillsdale, NJ: American Psychological Association; Lawrence Erlbaum Associates, 1996.

This volume follows the format established in the inaugural volume (J-120). However, the content of this volume is more varied, both in terms of the time periods when these pioneering psychologists lived and their interests within psychology. One-third of the psychologists in volume 2 were born in the twentieth century, and the diversity of interests is reflected by the inclusion of a social reformer (Dorthea Dix) and a parapsychologist (J. B. Rhine). Only one of the individuals covered in volume 2 (John Dewey) was a founder of a traditional school of psychology. Among the twenty-one men and women profiled in volume 2 are Lightner Witmer, William Stern, Lillian Gilbreth, Edwin Ray Guthrie, Carl Murchison, Barbara Stoddard Burks, Donald Olding Hebb, and Silvan Tomkins. Like the first volume, the overall quality of writing is excellent. Most of the chapters are revisions of papers presented at conventions of the American Psychological Association. Upper-division under-graduates and graduate students, faculty, and scholars will find this follow-up volume useful. Since the pioneers profiled provide interesting source materials for a range of courses in psychology, faculty may want to use chapters as supplementary readings.

J-122 Kimble, Gregory A., and Michael Wertheimer, eds. **Portraits of Pioneers in Psychology. Volume 3**. Washington, DC; Hillsdale, NJ: American Psychological Association; Lawrence Erlbaum Associates, 1998.

Like previous volumes (J-120 and J-121), this collection of biographical sketches of pioneers in the field can be used as a reference source of supplementary reading for undergraduate- and graduate-level courses in the history of psychology. Some of the individuals included have affected other disciplines (e.g., biology, sociology, anthropology), so other students and faculty will find this resource helpful. Unlike previous volumes in this series, most of the chapters have been written specifically for this volume; they are not revisions of conference presentations (with the exception of two chapters). This volume brings together essays (ranging from sixteen to twenty-four pages in length) on the professional and personal lives of twenty preeminent psychologists. Among the men and women profiled are: Charles Darwin, Herman Ebbinghaus, Alfred Binet, Jean Piaget, Mytle McGraw, Henry Nissen, Kenneth Spence, David Krech, and Benton Underwood. This collection of interesting and well-written profiles is an essential acquisition for any library holding previous volumes in this series. However, if libraries lack the first two volumes, this volume can stand alone.

J-123 Kimble, Gregory A., and Michael Wertheimer, eds. **Portraits of Pioneers in Psychology. Volume 4**. Washington, DC; Hillsdale, NJ: American Psychological Association; Lawrence Erlbaum Associates, 2000.

This volume is modeled after previous volumes. It profiles twenty-one nineteenth- and twentieth-century men and women who contributed to the development of psychology. The individuals represent a range of subfields. Among those included are Evelyn Hooker (a leader in the gay rights movement), Francis Cecil Sumner (the first African American to earn a doctoral degree from an American university), and Roger Sperry (a neuroscientist and Nobel Laureate).

J-124 Fuller, Ray. **Seven Pioneers of Psychology: Behaviour and Mind**. New York: Routledge, 1995.

This volume assembles substantive critical essays on seven influential psychologists. Fuller decided to omit any psychologist still living. The psychologists selected for inclusion are Francis Galton, William James, Sigmund Freud, Konrad Lorenz, Nikolas Tinbergen, B. F. Skinner, and Jean Piaget. Those profiled contributed major concepts to psychology, and their influence on the field has been profound. For example, Galton (regarded as the founder of eugenics) contributed to psychology's understanding of heredity and intelligence. This collection of essays on the founding fathers of psychology will be found in many academic libraries.

J-125   Wade, Nicholas. **Psychologists in Word and Image**. Cambridge, MA: MIT Press, 1995.

The idea for this book grew out of a 1992 exhibition in Brussels on the history of psychology. The International Congress of Psychology hosted the exhibit. This exhibit graphically represented the history of the discipline through "perceptual portraits" combined with motifs reflecting each individual's contribution to psychology. This book includes some of the portraits from this unique international exhibit. However, this volume is broader, assembling more than 100 perceptual portraits. This interesting graphic technique, combined with narrative, creates an unconventional but effective way of linking a phenomenon (be it the publication of a book, development of a concept, or invention of an apparatus) with an individual. For example, a schematic face is used to introduce Egon Brunswick, a functionalist theorist who conducted research on the perception of schematic faces. The earliest psychologist covered is Francis Bacon (1561–1626) and the latest born psychologist covered is David Courtenay Marr (1943–1980). This title is appropriate for academic collections serving upper-level undergraduate and graduate students in psychology.

J-126   Popplestone, John A., and Marion White McPherson. **An Illustrated History of American Psychology**. 2d ed. Akron, OH: The University of Akron Press, 1999.

For more than three decades, the authors have staffed and administered the Archives of the History of American Psychology at the University of Akron. They have also taught psychology at the University of Akron, and both have served as presidents of the American Psychology Association's Division of the History of Psychology. In addition to drawing upon the resources of the Archives, this source brings together images from archives at other universities as well as commercial companies. This unique photographic collection of people, events, and artifacts graphically depicts the history and development of American psychology roughly from 1875 to 1975. This fascinating collage of images (ranging from photographs of old laboratory equipment to copies of correspondence from some of psychology's giants) is an essential and absorbing source for any academic behavioral science collection.

J-127   O'Connell, Agnes N., and Nancy Felipe Russo, eds. **Models of Achievement: Reflections of Eminent Women in Psychology**. **Volume 1**. New York: Columbia University Press, 1983. **Volume 2**. Hillsdale, NJ: Lawrence Erlbaum Associates, 1988. **Volume 3**. Mahwah, NJ: Lawrence Erlbaum Associates, 2001.

These three volumes contain autobiographical essays about distinguished women in psychology. *Models of Achievement* highlights the accomplishments of women in various specialties of psychology, including child development, clinical psychology, cognition, perception, personality, experimental psychology, tests and measurements, industrial/organizational psychology, and psychotherapy. Supplemental chapters written by the editors discuss the role of women in the development of psychology, similarities and differences in the lives of the women included in the volume, barriers to their achievements, and how each woman overcame these obstacles. This is one of the few monographs to focus on the contributions of women in psychology (the idea for this title evolved from a special issue of *Psychology of Women Quarterly*, authored by the editors). The essays here will supplement biographical sketches found in standard biographical sources as well as profiles in collective biographies.

J-128   Stevens, Gwendolyn, and Sheldon Gardner. **The Women of Psychology**. 2 vols. Cambridge, MA: Schenkman, 1982.

This set provides biographical sketches of women (many of whom are not included in standard biographical sources) who contributed to the development of psychology. More than 130 women are included. Not all of these women were psychologists by training. For example, Margaret Mead is included because her work contributed to psychology. The first volume, *Pioneers and Innovators*, begins with an overview essay on women in psychology. However, the bulk of the volume consists of thirty-seven biographical essays on women pioneers, most of whom were influential in the late nineteenth and early twentieth centuries. Among the women profiled are Dorthea Lynde Dix, Mary Whiton Calkins, and Maria Montessori. Essays vary in length from less than a page to more than ten pages. Volume 2, *Expansion and Refinement*, includes shorter entries for 100 women born between 1881 and 1940. This is an important set because it includes biographical information not easily located elsewhere.

J-129 O'Connell, Agnes N., and Nancy Felipe Russo, eds. **Women in Psychology: A Bio-Bibliographic Sourcebook**. New York: Greenwood Press, 1990.

This work is an extension of *Models of Achievement: Reflections of Eminent Women in Psychology* (J-126). This latest work provides biographies of thirty-six prominent women in psychology. A typical entry includes date and place of birth; family background; education; major professional positions; significant influences, events, mentors, etc.; awards and professional recognition; important works and contributions; critical evaluations of these contributions and achievements; marital status; names and birth dates of children; and interests outside psychology. In addition, there is a bibliographical chapter listing important sources of information on women in psychology. Several appendixes group biographees by date of birth, place of birth, and major fields of psychology.

WORKS ON TESTS AND MEASUREMENTS

These works describe psychological tests; some cite reviews of them. Tests that are widely used in psychology, education, and industry tend to be published and are commercially available. However, thousands of tests are unpublished and are created primarily for research purposes.

J-130 **FAQ on Locating Psychological Tests**. URL: http://www.apa.org/science /faq-findtests.html.

The American Psychological Association (APA) has constructed this Web site to assist users in finding and using psychological tests. It is divided into two main sections: published tests and unpublished tests. Under published tests, the APA offers advice under the following categories: "Finding Information on a Particular Test," "Finding a Particular Type of Test," "Locating a Specific Test," "Locating Test Publishers," "Purchasing Tests," "Test References," "Available Software and Scoring Services," and "Additional Information on the Proper Use of Tests." The second section provides information on how to find unpublished tests, which are primarily those cited in journal articles by individual researchers. A final note covers the responsibilities of those administering tests. This is a very useful explanatory guide for researchers, students, or others seeking information on locating and using psychological tests.

J-131 Buros, Oscar Krisen, ed. **Mental Measurements Yearbook**. 1st–8th eds. Highland Park, NJ: Gryphon, 1938–1974. Irregular.

J-132 Mitchell, James V., Jr., ed. **The Ninth Mental Measurements Yearbook**. Lincoln: Buros Institute of Mental Measurements, University of Nebraska, 1985.

J-133 Conoley, Jane Close, and Jack J. Kramer, eds. **The Tenth Mental Measurements Yearbook**. Lincoln: Buros Institute of Mental Measurements, University of Nebraska, 1989.

J-134 Conoley, Jane Close, and Jack J. Kramer, eds. **The Eleventh Mental Measurements Yearbook**. Lincoln: Buros Institute of Mental Measurements, University of Nebraska, 1992.

J-135 Colony, Jane Close, and James C. Impara, eds. **The Twelfth Mental Measurements Yearbook**. Lincoln: Buros Institute of Mental Measurements, University of Nebraska, 1995.

J-136 Impara, James C., and Barbara S. Plake, eds. **The Thirteenth Mental Measurements Yearbook**. Lincoln: Buros Institute of Mental Measurements, University of Nebraska, 1998.

J-137 Impara, James C., Linda L. Murphy, and Barbara S. Plake, eds. **The Supplement to the Thirteenth Mental Measurements Yearbook**. Lincoln: Buros Institute of Mental Measurements, University of Nebraska, 1999.

J-138 Plake, Barbara S., and James C. Impara, eds. **The Fourteenth Mental Measurements Yearbook**. Lincoln, NE: Buros Institute of Mental Measurements, University of Nebraska, 2001.

The development of this landmark series by Oscar Buros was a response to the need for evaluative reviews of psychological and educational tests. Coverage is limited to commercially published English-language tests. Each edition of the *Mental Measurements Yearbook* (*MMY*) contains critical test reviews, many with bibliographies, written by professionals. There are also excerpts of reviews that have appeared in scholarly journals. Descriptive data are presented for each test, including information on audience, use, administration, scoring, and cost. In addition, many of the specific tests have a list of references. Tests are organized under broad classifications such as achievement, intelligence, and personality. Each *MMY* supplements rather than supersedes previous volumes. The fourteenth edition contains a bibliography of 430 available tests. Although the first nine editions were published irregularly, the Buros Institute has established a publishing schedule with the goal of publishing a yearbook every two years and a supplement in alternating years.

MMY is the most important tool available for persons needing assessments of tests. It is recognized as the standard source for factual and evaluative information on commercially available English-language tests used in psychological and educational assessments. Although Buros is deceased and others have carried on his work, library patrons continue to ask for "Buros" when they want information on tests.

J-139 Buros, Oscar Krisen, ed. **Tests in Print: A Comprehensive Bibliography of Tests for Use in Education, Psychology, and Industry**. Highland Park, NJ: Gryphon, 1961.

This classified bibliography lists commercially published English-language tests that were in print and out-of-print as of 1961. Entries include cross-references to information published in the *Mental Measurements Yearbooks* (J-131 through J-138). Consequently, it serves as an index to the first five volumes of *MMY*.

J-140 Buros, Oscar Krisen, ed. **Tests in Print II: An Index to Tests, Test Reviews, and the Literature on Specific Tests**. Highland Park, NJ: Gryphon, 1974.

This volume lists tests in print as of 1974 and tests that have gone out-of-print since the publication of *Tests in Print* (J-139) in 1961. It is an index to the first seven volumes of the *Mental Measurements Yearbooks* (J-131 through J-138).

J-141 Mitchell, James V., Jr. **Tests in Print III: An Index to Tests, Test Reviews, and the Literature on Specific Tests**. Lincoln: Buros Institute of Mental Measurements, University of Nebraska, 1983.

The third volume in this series indexes the first eight volumes of the *Mental Measurements Yearbooks* (J-131 through J-136). It lists tests that are commercially available as of 1983. Tests hat have gone out-of-print since the publication of *Tests in Print II* (J-140) are also included.

J-142   Murphy, Linda L., Jane Close Conoley, and James C. Impara. **Tests in Print IV: An Index to Tests, Test Reviews, and the Literature on Specific Tests**. Lincoln: Buros Institute of Mental Measurements, University of Nebraska, 1994.

The fourth edition indexes the first eleven *Mental Measurements Yearbooks* (J-131 through J-138) and contains a listing of commercially available tests as of 1994.

J-143   Murphy, Linda L., James C. Impara, and Barbara S. Plake. **Tests in Print V: An Index to Tests, Test Reviews, and the Literature on Specific Tests**. 2 vols. Lincoln: Buros Institute of Mental Measurements, University of Nebraska, 1999.

The most recent entry in this series (now two volumes) serves as a comprehensive index to the *Mental Measurements Yearbook* (J-131 through J-138), including the recent thirteenth edition. It lists tests commercially available as of 1999 as well as those that have gone out of print since *Tests in Print IV* (J-142) was published. The authors indicate a plan to publish *Tests in Print* every five years.

J-144   Maddox, Taddy. **Tests: A Comprehensive Reference for Assessments in Psychology, Education, and Business**. 4th ed. Austin, TX: Pro-Ed, 1997.

Tests is a good starting point for those needing basic information on commercially available testing instruments. Divided into the three broad subject areas described in the title, *Tests* provides information on approximately 4,000 English-language tests. Each entry includes title, author, copyright date, population (i.e., audience for the test), purpose, description, format (how the test is administered), scoring, cost, and publisher information. Unlike *MMY* (J-131 through J-138) or *Test Critiques* (J-145), reviews of tests are not included. The fourth edition does include expanded indexes, including an index of test titles; an index of tests not in the fourth edition; an index of publishers not in the fourth edition; an index of tests available in foreign languages; an index of computer-scored tests; and indexes of authors, publishers, and cross-references.

J-145   Keyser, Daniel J., and Richard C. Sweetland. **Test Critiques**. 10 vols. Austin, TX: Pro-Ed, 1991- .

This series, produced by the publisher of *Tests* (J-144), is designed to be used in conjunction with that work. *Test Critiques*, now in ten volumes, provides details not included with the *Tests* directory, including a discussion of the application, administration, scoring, and implementation of the test as well as a discussion of reliability and validity studies. Each entry concludes with an overall critique and bibliography. The indexes in the final volume, including subject, title, and author, are cumulative. There is also a listing of test publishers along with contact information. *Test Critiques* can be used along with *MMY* (J-131 through J-138) to obtain critical and evaluative information about commercially available tests.

J-146   **Buros Institute of Mental Measurements**. URL: http://www.unl.edu /buros.

The Buros Institute, publisher of *Mental Measurements Yearbook* (J-131 though J-138) and *Tests in Print* (J-139 through J-143) serves to provide professional assistance, expertise, and information to users of commercially available psychological tests. The main Web page has information and search engines for locating information on tests, test reviews, and test publishers. There is a subject index to tests along with citations to the *Mental Measurements Yearbook*. A section on articles contains several full-text publications related to psychological assessment. Buros also provides a fee-based fax service for test review, which is accessible at this site. This handy, Web-based guide to the tests in the *MMY* relieves users of the necessity of using the print guide and is an alternative to electronic versions of the *MMY*. This site will probably be of most use to individual practitioners and psychological measurement researchers.

J-147 **ERIC Clearinghouse on Assessment and Evaluation**. URL: http://ericae.net/.

The ERIC Clearinghouse on Assessment and Evaluation is located at the University of Maryland, Department of Measurement, Statistics and Evaluation and is one of sixteen subject-oriented clearinghouses operated by the United States Department of Education, Office of Educational Research and Improvement. ERIC/AE is charged with gathering the papers presented by educational researchers and preparing information resources discussing research and methodology related to assessment. There is an online library of over 400 full-text articles and book citations arranged by subject. This site is primarily educational in focus and does not deal exclusively with psychological tests. There is a search engine to find information about tests as well as recent news items related to educational testing. There is also a link to search the *ERIC* database, which originated in 1966. Overall, this site will be of most use to educators and researchers in educational psychology. The availability of full-text resources is a definite bonus, as are the test locators.

J-148 Corcoran, Keith, and Joel Fischer. **Measures for Clinical Practice: A Sourcebook**. 3d ed. 2 vols. New York: Free Press, 2000.

The first volume of this two-volume work provides an introduction and overview and reproduces testing instruments designed for use with couples, families, and children. The second volume presents instruments to be used with adults when the primary issue is not couple or family relationships. Because actual copies of tests are so rarely reproduced (for both validity and copyright reasons), this compilation is a great asset to graduate students, researchers, and practitioners. Together these two volumes provide access to more than 400 instruments that are brief and easy to administer.

J-149 **Health and Psychosocial Instruments (HAPI)**. Pittsburgh, PA: Behavioral Measurements Database Services, 1985- . Quarterly updates. Electronic format.

This database provides information on rating scales, questionnaires, interview forms, projective techniques, and other measurement instruments used in psychology, social work, sociology, business and industry, communication, nursing, medicine, and public health. It can be used to retrieve information on measurements that is hidden in journal articles. It is particularly useful because it is interdisciplinary in scope, drawing from journals in both the psychosocial sciences and health sciences.

Electronic access: Online and CD-ROM formats available.

J-150 Goldman, Bert A., John L. Saunders, and John C. Busch. **Directory of Unpublished Experimental Mental Measures. Volumes 1–3**. Washington, DC: American Psychological Association, 1996.

J-151 Goldman, Bert A., William L. Osborne, and David F. Mitchell. **Directory of Unpublished Experimental Mental Measures. Volumes 4–5**. Washington, DC: American Psychological Association, 1996.

J-152 Goldman, Bert A., and David F. Mitchell. **Directory of Unpublished Experimental Mental Measures. Volume 6**. Washington, DC: American Psychological Association, 1996.

J-153 Goldman, Bert A., David F. Mitchell, and Paula E. Egelson. **Directory of Unpublished Experimental Mental Measures. Volume 7**. Washington, DC: American Psychological Association, 1997.

This reference work is a collection of noncommercial testing instruments in use by researchers in the behavioral and social sciences. For the latest volume the authors pulled information from thirty-seven scholarly publications. Volume 7 is divided into twenty-four subject chapters. Each entry includes test name, purpose, number of items on the test, format, reliability, authors, article citation, and related research. Entries are also numbered throughout the series. Volume 7 has entries 5364 through 7441. There are also cumulative author and subject indexes. This work should be used in conjunction with *MMY* (J-131 through J-138).

INTERNET RESOURCES

The number of Internet sites relating to psychology can be overwhelming. The following section is intended as a guide to some of the best sites, including several excellent megasites.

J-154   Whitford, Fred W., and Doug Gotthoffer. **Allyn & Bacon Quick Guide to the Internet for Psychology**. 2d ed. Boston: Allyn & Bacon, 2000.

This book is one-half psychology sources and one-half guide to the Internet in general. The first part instructs users on what the Internet is, how to search Web directories, how to use e-mail, how to use ftp, how to do research, and how to locate and use newsgroups and listservs. The second part of the book covers specific Web sites for psychology for numerous disciplines such as sensation and perception, memory and learning, child and adolescent development, and social psychology. Each section also has an activity for users to test their skills. There are a glossary and an index of all URLs mentioned in the book. This concise guide (just over 100 pages) packs a lot of useful information and is especially good for those beginning research using the Internet.

J-155   Birnbaum, Michael H., ed. **Psychological Experiments on the Internet**. San Diego, CA: Academic Press, 2000.

Psychological Experiments on the Internet is not a listing of resources, or even experiments, but rather a guide to using the Internet as a medium for conducting behavioral research. The foundations of the book grew out of experiments that utilized the Internet to conduct research and collect high-quality data. By mid-1999, the American Psychological Society's Web site listed sixty-five such experiments. This book is intended for psychologists who are interested in the experiences of those who have used the Internet for research. The first section of the book covers general issues covering such issues as the validity of Web research, a history of experimentation on the Web, and advantages and disadvantages of using the Web. The second section addresses individual differences; covers cross-cultural studies; and includes chapters on using the Web to conduct personality research, human sexual behavior, and facial features. This section provides a good overview of conducting Web-based research, providing many concrete examples. The final section covers computer techniques for Internet experimentation, including techniques for creating and using questionnaires and a chapter on server issues. There are also chapters discussing two online laboratories. Each chapter contains numerous examples, Web sites, and a reference section. This work fills a unique niche in the current psychology literature and is an invaluable guide to those interested in using the Internet to conduct psychological research.

J-156   **PsychCrawler: Indexing the Web for the Best in Psychology**. URL: http://www.psychcrawler.com.

PsychCrawler, produced by the American Psychology Association, is a combination search engine and subject listing of authoritative psychology Web sites. Site indexes include the APA; National Institute of Mental Health; and the U.S. Department of Health and Human Services, Center for Mental Health Services. There is an extensive online user's guide that covers search techniques, including basic keyword searching and advanced query building. Results are ranked by relevance. The site is still under development at the time of this writing but should emerge to be a primary Internet resource for psychology.

J-157 **American Psychological Association**. URL: http://www.apa.org.
The APA is the world's largest professional psychology association. Based in Washington, D.C., there are over 159,000 members. The APA's Web site is among the most useful for psychology-related information. The main page is divided into three main sections. "Psychologists" contains information for educators, scientists, practitioners, and other mental health professionals such as information about joining the APA, the annual convention, and classified ads. There is also a members-only area to search *PsycINFO* (J-75), find information on APA members, and find APA articles online. The "Public" area contains information such as the APA style guidelines, information on issues such as depression and AIDS, and ordering information for APA products. The "Students" section contains information about psychology programs, summer internships, research assistance, and financial aid information. There is also a search box to search for press releases and summaries of research.

J-158 **American Psychological Society**. URL: http://www.psychologicalscience .org.
APS was started in 1988 as a professional organization for those interested in "scientific psychology." It now has over 15,000 members, primarily academics, graduate students, and Ph.D. candidates. A doctorate or evidence of significant contribution to the advancement of scientific psychology is required for membership. The Web site contains information about its publications and the latest edition of the APS *Observer*. There are also employment ads, information on annual meetings, and information on the student caucus. A member's-only area provides access to journals and the membership directory.

J-159 **CyberPsychLink**. URL: http://cctr.umkc.edu/user/dmartin/psych2.html.
This site links to educational programs, grant information, electronic journals and news, statistics, listservs, and software. It has been maintained by Dawn Martin since 1995 and resides on a server at the University of Missouri, Kansas City. (See also J-96)

J-160 **PsychREF**. URL: http://www.psychref.com.
PsychRef is a guide and index to psychology-related resources on the Web. Maintained by Vincent Hevern at Le Moyne College in Syracuse, New York, *PsychRef* is a useful guide for any researcher in psychology but is geared toward academics. Hevern started *PsychRef* in July 1995, and it has grown considerably since that time. Statements on the site indicate that there are between 300 and 1,000 visitors per week and that the 100,000th visit occurred in July 1999. The sites are arranged under four broad categories: general resources, faculty—teaching and scholarly activities, students and academic advisors—online resources, and topics and subfields in psychology. Hevern has also created symbols to signify "outstanding" and "very fine" resources. This should be a first stop for students or faculty seeking Web-based psychology resources. Users should be aware, however, that in spring 2001 Hevern posted a notice on this site indicating that he would not be updating it until he was certain about the site's future direction. See also *Teachpsych.org* (J-164), another site maintained by Hevern.

J-161 **PsycSite**. URL: http://stange.simplenet.com/psycsite/.
PsycSite, maintained at Nipissing University in Ontario, Canada, is a nonprofit site aimed at researchers and students interested in the science of psychology. A disclaimer states that sites dealing with self-help or parapsychology are not included. *PsycSite* is arranged in "rooms," which users are directed to enter by selecting a link on a table. There is an information link, providing links to lists of psychology resources on the Web, as well as a communications link providing access to bulletin boards and chat rooms. A "student centre" has links to academic departments, tips on applying to graduate school, and a list of resource persons containing contact information and subject specialties. A "professional centre" has links to software, information on setting up a Web-based research study, and a professional resources link that directs users to another extensive table of resources. This site is geared toward academics and will be of assistance to both faculty and students.

J-162 **Psych Web**. URL: http://www.psychwww.com/.

Psych Web is another collection of psychology-related Web resources, created and maintained by Dr. Russell A. Dewey of Georgia Southern University. The main subject areas are arranged alphabetically in a frame on the left side of the page. Topics include APA style resources, departments (at colleges and universities), books, journals, megalists, sports psychology, and tip sheets. The main page consists of a "What's New" section, which contains the date that materials were posted. Although it appears that most items were added between 1997 and 1999, there is also a Fall 2000 date, indicating that the site is currently maintained. The inclusion of dates, including dates of complete overhauls of the site, makes this a valuable tool for faculty and students of psychology.

J-163 **PsycCentral: Dr. Grohol's Mental Health Page**. URL: http://psychcentral .com/grohol.htm.

Dr. John Grohol's Mental Health Page was first formed in 1994 when the Web began to rise in popularity. A note on the page describes itself as "best annotated guides to the most useful Websites, newsgroups, and mailing lists online today in mental health, psychology, social work, and psychiatry." There are between 3,000 and 4,000 visitors a day and almost 2 million total visitors. The main "resources" page is divided into more than twenty-five subject areas containing nearly 1,500 links. The site also lists online articles, book reviews, chats, and online forums. Although originally an academic, Grohol is now CEO of HelpingHorizons.com, an online counseling firm that sponsors this site. Visitors are able to assign ratings to the sites included, providing a convenient and fast assessment tool. This site has won a number of Internet awards. Although the resources are great, the layout of the page contains a large number of graphics to other sites, making the resources on this site more difficult to find. Once users learn to navigate the site, the resources are quite impressive.

J-164 **Teachpsych.org: The Society for the Teaching of Psychology**. URL: http://www.teachpsych.org.

Dr. Vincent Heverne at Le Moyne College maintains this site. *Teachpsych.org* is the official Web site for The Society for the Teaching of Psychology (STP). STP "represents the interests of psychologists in academic institutions from the secondary through the graduate level." According to this site, STP also " promotes teaching excellence, research on teaching, and professional identity and development; and sponsors and co-sponsors teaching-related programs at national and regional psychology conventions." The Society also publishes several journals and books. This site is geared to members of the Society and primarily provides information about the organization, its activities, and its publications. There is not a lot of information available for nonmembers.

J-165 **The Psychology Jumping Stand**. URL: http://www.indiana.edu /~iuepsyc/topics/topic.htm.

The Psychology Jumping Stand is a collection of psychology links arranged under approximately fifteen broad categories, such as biopsychology, psychologists and their work, social psychology, sensation and perception, and learning and memory. Some listings are quite extensive, such as that for biopsychology, which is divided into a number of subcategories with a number of links. However, other listings are not extensive. Social psychology, for instance, has only five links. Dates on the site indicate that it has not been updated since 1999. Although there is a lot of good information here, users will likely encounter a number of nonworking links.

J-166 **Galaxy Psychology Links**. URL: http://www.galaxy.com/galaxy/Social -Sciences/Psychology.html.

Galaxy provides this Yahoo-like directory of psychology-related Web sites. In addition to an alphabetical listing, there are also nine categories that users can browse. The alphabetical listing is useful in that there are descriptors explaining what something is, such as discussion group, organization, collection, or event. Although the listing of resources is similar to that found on other sites, the descriptors add a valuable service to this site.

NOTES

1. David Hothersall, *History of Psychology* (New York: Random House, 1984), xiv.

2. Thomas Hardy Leahey, *A History of Psychology: Main Currents in Psychological Thought*, 3d ed. (Englewood Cliffs, NJ: Prentice-Hall, 1992).

3. Katherine S. Mangan, "Rift Among Psychologists Prompts Academics to Form New Society: 2,000 Are Said to Join," *The Chronicle of Higher Education* (September 1, 1988): A10.

4. Albert R. Gilgen and Carol K. Gilgen, eds., *International Handbook of Psychology* (New York: Greenwood Press, 1987), 537–538.

5. Alan S. Bellack and Michael Hersen, eds.-in-chief, *Comprehensive Clinical Psychology*, Vol. 1 (New York: Pergamon, 1998), viii.

6. Constance C. Gould and Mark Handler, *Information Needs in the Social Sciences: An Assessment* (Mountain View, CA: Research Libraries Group, 1989), 37.

7. Anne K. Beaubien, "The Research Process in the Social Sciences," in *Learning the Library* (New York: R. R. Bowker, 1982), 135–151.

8. Shirley A. Fitzgibbons, "Citation Analysis in the Social Sciences," in Robert D. Stueart and George B. Miller, eds., *Collection Development in Libraries: A Treatise* (Greenwich, CT: JAI, 1980), 302.

9. Ibid.

10. Margaret J. Sylvia, "Citation Analysis As an Unobtrusive Method for Journal Collection Evaluation Using Psychology Student Research Bibliographies," *Collection Building* 17, no. 1 (1998): 20–28.

11. Ibid., 25.

12. Margaret Sylvia and Marcella Lesher, "What Journals Do Psychology Graduate Students Need?: A Citation Analysis of Thesis References," *College & Research Libraries* 56 (July 1995): 313–318.

13. Bluma C. Peritz and Dina Sor, "The Use of Libraries by Graduate Students in Psychology As Indicated by Citations," *Collection Management* 12, nos. 3–4 (1990): 11–23.

14. Jeffrey M. Wehmeyer and Susan Wehmeyer, "The Comparative Importance of Books: Clinical Psychology in the Health Sciences Library," *Bulletin of the Medical Library Association* 87, no. 2 (April 1999): 187–191.

15. *PsycBooks 1987: Books & Chapters in Psychology. Vol. I: Experimental Psychology: Basic and Applied* (Arlington, VA: American Psychological Association), ix.

16. Ellen D. Sutton, Richard P. Feinberg, and Cynthia R. Levine, "Bibliographic Instruction in Psychology: A Review of the Literature," *Reference Services Review* 23, no. 3 (Fall 1995): 13–22.

17. Raymond G. McInnis, "Psychology," in Patricia A. McClung, ed., *Selection of Library Materials in the Humanities, Social Sciences, and Sciences* (Chicago: American Library Association, 1985), 215.

18. Lorrie A. Knight, "Reference Sources on the Internet: Psychology," *The Reference Librarian* 57 (1997): 63–67.

19. Deborah Kelley-Milburn, "Webwatch," *Library Journal* (February 1, 1998): 31–32.

Part 4

Those Disciplines with Recognized Social Implications

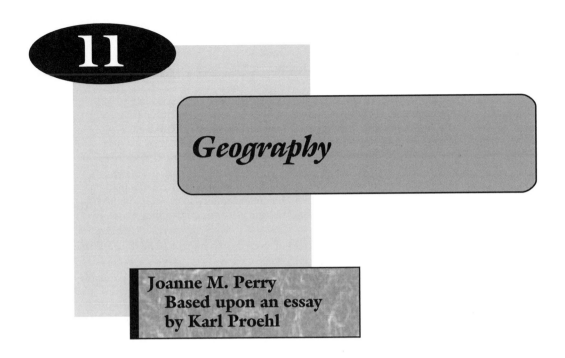

11

Geography

Joanne M. Perry
Based upon an essay
by Karl Proehl

ESSAY

Although the common perception of geography is that it is merely a collection of place names and lists of products or the recounting of explorers' adventures, it is important to understand what geography is really about. Geography is the study of the Earth and all that is upon it, but it focuses on the significance of location, distribution, and subsequent patterns of identifiable phenomena. The researcher compares and contrasts differences from place to place and associates patterns of one particular phenomenon to other patterns within the area. The essence of geography, then, lies in the importance of places and regions, and the interconnections among places and regions.[1]

Gilbert Grosvenor, chairman of the board and former president of the National Geographic Society, wrote:

> Geography deals with the physical and cultural realities of the world.
> It helps us to understand the varied and complex environments of the
> Earth. It gives meaning to location and establishes a context for under-
> standing the connections of places.[2]

Grosvenor added that an understanding of the significance of location and place is important; otherwise the consequences of human activities within the physical environment is lessened. Geography provides a frame of reference. It explores, describes, analyzes, and interprets the imprint and the processes of human activities on the land.

Novelist and former social studies teacher, the late James Michener, noted:

> The more I work in the social studies field the more convinced I become that geography is the foundation of all. . . . When I begin work on a new area . . . I invariably start with the best geography I can find. This takes precedence over everything else, even history, because I need to ground myself in the fundamentals which have governed and in a sense limited human development. . . . The virtue of the geographical approach is that it forces the reader to relate man to his environment. . . . It gives a solid footing to speculation and it reminds the reader that he is dealing with real human beings who are just as circumscribed as he.[3]

Geography as an interdisciplinary field of study has an interest in both the physical and the cultural worlds. Although geography's physical side is not specifically covered in this chapter, many of the items cited will cover the entire discipline, not just the study of human activity on the Earth that is the focus of geography as a social science.

During the twentieth century a number of fundamental themes evolved within geography. A traditional definition of the discipline is given in the essay "Geography" by Norton Ginsberg, found in *A Reader's Guide to the Social Sciences* (A-1). In the new two-volume edition, published in December 2000, the geography chapter has been radically rewritten with essays that focus on feminist geography, geographical information systems, residential segregation and urban social geography, and human geography. Geographers also point to a presentation by William Pattison entitled "The Four Traditions of Geography" as a help in defining the discipline.[4] It is also traditional for the current president of the Association of American Geographers to present a presidential address that defines the nature and state of the discipline, which is then published in the *Annals* of the AAG.

Regional and Systematic Geography

Within the social sciences the study of geography is divided into regional geography and systematic geography. The regional approach has traditionally formed the core of geography and reflects its essential character.[5] The main purpose of regional studies is to concentrate on the geographical character of areas and to focus on critical distinctive features. Regional studies usually include a number of topics: location, natural environment, population, political status, type of economy, internal arrangement and organization, external connections and relationships, characteristic landscapes and their origin, world importance, potentialities, and problems.[6]

Alternatively, systematic geography is focused on the phenomenon and how it is spatially distributed. Systematic geography experienced significant growth during the twentieth century, with research interests splitting off from each other as geographers became increasingly specialized. For instance, the main subfield, human geography, was subdivided into cultural, economic, historical, political, population, and urban geography.

CARTOGRAPHY AND GEOGRAPHIC INFORMATION SYSTEMS (GIS)

If cartography is concerned with the making and use of maps, then it is not just concerned with visual products; it is equally concerned with the process of mapping from data collection, transformation, and simplification through to symbolism as with map reading, analysis, and interpretation. These intellectual processes are expressed in terms of prevailing technologies, and computer-based information technology is fast becoming the dominant technology of the day.[7]

Cartography is the art and science of map making, both the tool and the product of the geographer. The history of the map extends back into prehistory. The history of the printed map begins somewhat later, during the fourteenth and fifteenth centuries. Between the earliest map and the present, the need for spatial expression has been a constant; it is the technology used to express this need that has undergone immense changes. From sticks and binding ties to parchment and inks, to computers and plotters, the means of production has been transformed.

Geographic research relies on the analysis of its data to provide answers to the questions researchers ask. In the past researchers used paper and pencil to array their data and produce maps; in today's world the computer is able to provide assistance in this analysis. Geographic Information Systems (GIS) are software packages that enable the researcher to more quickly analyze data by connecting them to a location (georeferencing) and then mapping their distribution. The data can be used to model theoretical outcomes or to inventory an existing situation.

K-1   Curry, M. R. **Digital Places: Living with Geographic Information Technologies**. London: Routledge, 1998.
This work is a philosophical examination of the ability and potential of GIS in society.

K-2   Dorling, Daniel, and David Fairbairn. **Mapping: Ways of Representing the World**. (Insights into Human Geography). London: Longman, 1997.
This is an introductory work on how maps are used to understand, describe, and control the world. Individual chapters include annotated suggested readings; the volume is indexed and has a bibliography.

Although utilizing a GIS can be a valuable tool for any discipline that is concerned with the distribution of a phenomenon, its use is generally taught in the geography department in conjunction with cartography classes. Many academic and public libraries provide GIS support to their users because an increasingly large amount of demographic information is available digitally, either online or on CD-ROM.

There are a number of GIS packages available on the market. Although *ArcInfo* and *ArcView*, developed by Environmental Systems Research Institute (ESRI), are very popular and used by many universities, federal and state agencies, and commercial companies, there are a number of other packages available, including *Idrisi32*, *MapInfo*, *Intergraph*, and *GRASS*.

K-3   Davis, David E. **GIS for Everyone: Exploring Your Neighborhood and Your World with a Geographic Information System**. Redlands, CA: Environmental Systems Research Institute, 1999.
This book is an introduction to GIS using *ArcExplorer* (included on disk), written for the beginner. Enthusiastic text is accompanied by many colorful graphics.

THE MAP: THE BASIC TOOL OF GEOGRAPHY

It tells the truth by lying, like a poem
With bold hyperbole of shape and line—
A masterpiece of false simplicity.
Its secret meanings must be mulled upon,
Yet all the world is open to a glance.
With colors to fire the mind, a song of names,
A painting that is not at home on walls
But crumpled on a station wagon floor;
Worn through at folds, tape patched and chocolate smudged
(What other work of art can lead you home?)
—A map was made to use.[8]

The map, the principal tool of geography, puts information in its place. Maps and related cartographic materials such as aerial photographs are important in understanding any geographical area because they help locate and identify places by recording and communicating locational information in a systematic and stylized manner. Maps are particularly useful because they reduce the dimensions of an area to a human scale, so people can observe what would otherwise be outside the normal range of human vision, and they translate into visual form statistical information derived from systematic studies. The result is a research tool that provides a frame of reference and a means of summarizing large quantities of data into one comprehensible form. This tool may be printed on paper or exist digitally on a CD-ROM or online.

Three vital characteristics of maps must be understood to be able to appreciate the information that is arrayed on them: map generalization, map scale, and map projection.

Cartographers have developed many mapping conventions through the years to assist map users in understanding the messages that maps portray. As a result, maps are not merely pretty pictures, they are complex documents that include data that are carefully chosen before being added to the final product. Because it is obvious that not everything that exists in even a small area can be noted on a piece of paper, cartographers must be selective in what they choose to record; they must simplify, *generalize*, and hint at reality. Reading a map should be approached as though reading a page in a foreign language, thoughtfully and with an eye to detail.

Map scale is a ratio that explains the relationship of the printed map to the physical world. Maps are reductions of reality, and the scale can be represented as a representative fraction (1:250,000 or 1/250,000), a verbal scale (1 inch equals 16 miles), or on a linear bar scale. Because scale is a fraction, the larger the denominator, the less detailed the information that can be portrayed (1/250,000 of a pie is a much smaller slice than 1/24,000). Thus a small scale map (1:250,000) shows a larger area but with less detail possible than a large scale map (1:24,000). The smaller the scale, the wider and more synoptic the view, but at the expense of detail.

Projections are mathematical transformations that permit the three dimensional Earth (a sphere) to be represented in two dimensions (as a plane). However, during this transformation either distance, shape, or area must be stretched or distorted. As a result, no single projection can show the entire Earth flat with area, distance, and shape exactly as it should be; at least one of the three must be sacrificed. In many instances this is of small importance to the map user but if, for example, distribution data are plotted on a map projection that is not equal area, the impression of the map is faulty, and incorrect assumptions and decisions may be made by the map user.

Maps are categorized by their scale, their function, or what they represent. The following conceptual scheme is a functional one that is useful but should not be considered as exhaustive or superior to any other scheme; it is merely a tool for learning about maps:[9]

- *Inventory maps* (also known as general reference maps). Maps in this category serve primarily to describe an area by displaying a selection of diverse geographical elements. Many categories of information may be included, but the basic use is that of locational information, answering the "where" questions. This category includes base maps, topographic maps, and road maps.

- *Analytical maps* (often known as thematic maps). Maps in this category facilitate geographic knowledge by providing a view of distribution, trends, patterns, and anomalies, with analytical operations performed on the data before they are mapped. These maps answer many questions about a single phenomenon and generally lack or have only a little additional locational information. Maps in this category would be many of the traditional distribution maps such as agricultural production maps, land use maps, and rainfall maps.

- *Synthesis maps* (often known as thematic or statistical maps). Maps in this category would portray two or more sets of data that attempt to answer the question "why" by showing correlation or causal relationships. This category would include settlement maps that include relief or transportation routes or maps of disease that also indicate pollution or insect distributions.

Discussions about the strengths and weaknesses of maps and projections may be found in many books.

K-4   Monmonier, Mark S. **Cartographies of Danger: Mapping Hazards in America**. Chicago: University of Chicago Press, 1997.

K-5   Monmonier, Mark S. **Drawing the Line: Tales of Maps and Cartocontroversy**. New York: Henry Holt, 1995.

K-6   Monmonier, Mark S. **How to Lie with Maps**. Chicago: University of Chicago Press, 1991.
Mark Monmonier's books on cartography disclose the subtleties of maps and suggest how people may be deceived by them. These titles provide interesting insights into the uses and abuses of maps.

K-7   Monmonier, Mark S. **Mapping It Out: Expository Cartography for the Humanities and Social Sciences**. Chicago: University of Chicago Press, 1993.
This book makes the social scientist aware of the importance of cartographic information in scholarly communication. It is a collection of essays on principles and practices relevant to the social sciences.

K-8   Monmonier, Mark S. **Maps, Distortion, and Meaning**. Washington, DC: Association of American Geographers, 1977.

K-9   Tufte, Edward R. **Envisioning Information**. 3d printing with revisions. Cheshire, CT: Graphics Press, 1992.

K-10   Tufte, Edward R. **The Visual Display of Quantitative Information**. Cheshire, CT: Graphics Press, 1983.

K-11   Tufte, Edward R. **Visual Explanations: Images and Quantities, Evidence and Narrative**. Cheshire, CT: Graphics Press, 1997.
Not all geographic data are arrayed cartographically, and the researcher must decide how to best graphically display his or her material. These titles have become classics in illustrating methods of visual communication and should provide imaginative as well as reliable assistance in making decisions about graphic representation.

THE WEB: THE NEW SOURCE OF INFORMATION

During the 1990s a new source of information emerged, the World Wide Web. The power of the Web lies in its vastness and speed; queries made to any one of a number of search engines (e.g., AltaVista, Ask Jeeves, Excite, Google, GoTo, LookSmart, Lycos, or Yahoo) seem to instantaneously pull thousands of pages of information out of thin air. Very quickly imaginative displays are suddenly available, with links to other sites that make following a trail of interrelated topics very easy. The downside is that no single search engine can search the entire Web, so any search is only a partial search, making it possible to miss valuable or useful information. In addition, there is no overall authority that checks the information on the Web for error, so researchers need to critically evaluate the information that is found. Older information is not readily available on the Web and must be found through other, more traditional, methods.

Although much of the information found on the Web is free, many information providers do charge for access to their proprietary databases. In these cases users must either subscribe individually or have access through their public or university library or place of employment.

K-12 **United States Geological Survey**. URL: http://ask.usgs.gov.

K-13 **United States Census Bureau**. URL: http://www.census.gov.

K-14 **Library of Congress**. URL: http://www.loc.gov.
Most federal, state, and local agencies have Web sites available through the Internet. Although URLs may change, searching by jurisdiction and/or agency name should yield a home page with access to much valuable information.
Several important ones follow.

K-15 **American Congress on Surveying and Mapping**. URL: http://www .acsm.net.

K-16 **The Association of American Geographers**. URL: http://www.aag.org.

K-17 **British Cartographic Society**. URL: http://www.cartography.org.uk.

K-18 **Canadian Association of Geographers**. URL: http://zeus.uwindsor.ca /cag/cagindex.html.

K-19 **Institute of Australian Geographers**. URL: http://www.ssn.flinders.edu .au/geog/IAG.

K-20 **International Geographical Union**. URL: http://www.igu-net.org.

K-21 **Royal Geographical Society/Institute of British Geographers**. URL: http://www.rgs.org.

K-22 **Society of Cartographers**. URL: http://www.soc.org.uk.

K-23 **Colorado School of Mines, Arthur Lakes Library**. URL: http://talus .mines.edu/academic/library.

K-24 **Pennsylvania State University, University Libraries**. URL: http:// www.libraries.psu.edu.

K-25 **University of Washington, University Libraries**. URL: http://www .lib.washington.edu.

K-26 **University of Waterloo, The Library**. URL: http://www.lib.uwaterloo.ca.

K-27 **Carleton University. Department of Geography**. URL: http://www .carleton.ca/geography.

K-28 **Pennsylvania State University. Department of Geography**. URL: http://www.geog.psu.edu.

K-29   **University of California at Berkeley. Department of Geography**. URL: http://www-geography.berkeley.edu.

K-30   **University of Texas at Austin. Department of Geography**. URL: http://www.utexas.edu/depts/grg/html/index_f.html.
The home pages of professional associations and university libraries and geography departments are also good beginning search sites.

BASIC GUIDES TO THE DISCIPLINE

The first three titles in this section are classic works in geographic research. Although dated, they have not been replaced by more current publications and should be consulted by those attempting to be comprehensive in their research. It is prudent to remember that due to their age they will not reflect the new developments in geography and cartography, specifically the personal computer in Web searching and Geographic Information Systems (GIS).

K-31   Durrenberger, Robert. **Geographical Research and Writing**. New York: Thomas Y. Crowell, 1985.
Durrenberger covers the main types of geographic material in simple listings, valuable for bibliographies and periodicals before 1985.

K-32   Harris, Chauncy Dennison. **Bibliography of Geography**. Chicago: University of Chicago, Department of Geography, 1976.
This title is especially helpful because it is organized by type of publication, with an introduction for each category explaining its importance to the field. The bibliography includes 585 main entries and cites numerous subentries under the major ones.

K-33   Wright, John Kirkland. **Aids to Geographical Research: Bibliographies, Periodicals, Atlases, Gazetteers, and Other Reference Books**. Westport, CT: Greenwood Press, 1971.
Originally published in 1947 and reprinted in 1971, this was the first bibliographic guide to geographical literature and emphasizes regional bibliographies and reference materials published prior to 1946.

K-34   Brewer, James Gordon. **The Literature of Geography: A Guide to Its Organization and Use**. 2d ed. Hamden, CT: Linnet Books, 1978.
This is a well-balanced introductory guide. Initial chapters stress the understanding of the structure of both the discipline and the literature. It has a British orientation.

K-35   Lock, C. B. Muriel. **Geography and Cartography: A Reference Handbook**. 3d ed. Hamden, CT: Linnet Books, 1976.
Lock focuses on geographical scholarship and the contributions that helped shape the discipline. Entries pertain to significant publications; biographical notes are concerned with academic and bibliographical achievements rather than with personal details. International in scope, with a British orientation.

K-36   Goddard, Stephen, ed. **A Guide to Information Sources in the Geographical Sciences**. Totowa, NJ: Barnes & Noble, 1983.
Goddard's guide contains a selective collection of bibliographic essays by specialists in the various subfields of geography; a good supplement to other guides.

STUDY AND TEACHING

K-37 Hay, I. **Communicating in Geography and the Environmental Sciences**. Melbourne, Australia: Oxford University Press, 1996.

This is a basic introduction to presentation skills for students in geography, providing explanations and insights into faculty expectations. The chapters clearly explain how to write and present essays, research, reviews, bibliographies, posters, examinations, and oral presentations. Although it is oriented toward the Australian system of higher education, American students can only benefit by applying the author's suggestions.

K-38 Williams, M., ed. **Understanding Geographical and Environmental Education: The Role of Research**. London: Cassell, 1996.

Editor Williams produces a comprehensive text by an international group of scholars on geographical research traditions, paradigms, and methods. Each essay has its own list of references, and there is a general index to the entire volume.

K-39 Gerber, R., and G. K. Chuan, eds. **Fieldwork in Geography: Reflections, Perspectives and Actions**. (The GeoJournal Library). Dordrecht: Kluwer Academic, 2000.

This work is a collection of essays by a group of international scholars on the importance of fieldwork in geographical research.

K-40 Mikesell, Marvin W., ed. **Geographers Abroad: Essays on the Problems and Prospects of Research in Foreign Areas**. (Research Paper, no. 152). Chicago: University of Chicago, Department of Geography, 1973.

These essays are based on a conference held in 1972.

K-41 Howell, N. **Surviving Fieldwork: A Report of the Advisory Panel on Health and Safety in Fieldwork, American Anthropological Association**. Washington, DC: American Anthropological Association, 1990.

Surviving Fieldwork is a valuable work that examines the dangers as well as the practicalities of living in the field. Most applicable to those researching in remote or foreign destinations but of interest to any potential field worker who will have to temporarily change home location.

BIBLIOGRAPHIES

Bibliographies provide subject access to journal articles, books, government documents, dissertations, and other publications.

K-42 Conzen, Michael P. **A Scholar's Guide to Geographical Writing on the American and Canadian Past**. Chicago: University of Chicago Press, 1993.

This text is a comprehensive bibliography with more than 10,000 entries of geographical writing on Canada and the United States. Includes books, dissertations and articles from 1850 to 1990. Organized regionally and then by subject with extensive index.

K-43 **Geographical Bibliography for American Libraries**. Washington, DC: Association of American Geographers, 1985.

Geographical Bibliography remains the most comprehensive one-volume bibliography in the field, covering general geography and its subfields. With more than 2,900 annotations, its focus is on works published for the period 1970 to 1984; its predecessor, *A Geographical Bibliography for American College Libraries* (1970), from the same publisher, provides access to earlier publications. Includes an extensive index.

K-44   **Research Catalogue of the American Geographical Society**. 15 vols. Boston: G. K. Hall, 1962.

This library catalog is the most comprehensive regional geographical bibliography for the years 1923 to 1960. It includes books, journal articles, pamphlets, and government documents on topics and regions of geographical interest. The first two volumes focus on the subfields of geography; regional geography is covered in volumes 3 through 15. Map indexes are included to allow the user quick access to a particular country or region. A two-volume supplement updates the bibliography to 1971. It is continued by *Current Geographical Publications* in paper and online at http://geobib.lib.uwm.edu.

K-45   Sitwell, O. F. G. **Four Centuries of Special Geography: An Annotated Guide to Books That Purport to Describe All the Countries in the World Published in English Before 1888, with a Critical Introduction**. Vancouver, BC: UBC Press, 1993.

This is an attempt to list every English-language book whose author described every country— special geography before it became modern geography. Text entries are in alphabetical order by author, indexed chronologically and by short title.

DICTIONARIES

"One expression of the maturation of geography as an independent scholarly discipline," writes Chauncy Harris, "is the recent publications of many high-quality dictionaries."[10]

Each discipline, and geography is no exception, has its own jargon that is continuously evolving. Discipline-specific dictionaries help students and researchers remain current as new terminology enters the discipline's vocabulary. Chauncy Harris's statement is as valid now as it was in 1986, as proved by the substantial number of recent dictionary publications.

K-46   Clark, Audrey N. **New Penguin Dictionary of Geography**. 2d ed. London: Penguin, 1998.

Clark covers the entire field of geography in this text and provides a large number of concise definitions for the field.

K-47   Driever, Steven L. **Spanish/English Dictionary of Human and Physical Geography**. Westport, CT: Greenwood Press, 1994.

This dictionary includes words not found in standard Spanish-English dictionaries, giving more precise geographical definitions. Current and historical meanings are given.

K-48   **The Houghton Mifflin Dictionary of Geography: Places and Peoples of the World**. Boston: Houghton Mifflin, 1997.

This dictionary contains more than 10,000 entries organized alphabetically. Geographic names and terms as well as ethnic, linguistic, and national names are defined in a concise yet clear manner in this work. A small black-and-white outline map of each country is provided. An appendix with an abbreviations list, a geographic features list, a currency table, and a measurement table is included.

K-49 Johnston, Ronald J., ed. **Dictionary of Human Geography**. 4th ed. Oxford: Blackwell, 2000.

Covering the entire social science aspect of geography, this dictionary is a redesigned and rewritten edition with over 200 new entries charting the emergence of new themes, including GIS and GPS. Lengthy definitions; many have references or suggested readings.

K-50 McDowell, Linda, and Joanne P. Sharp. **A Feminist Glossary of Human Geography**. London: Arnold, 1999.

A guide to the theories, concepts, and terms used in geographical writing about gender relations, this volume includes over 400 definitions. Entries vary in length and often contain references to related terms and to source materials listed in this extensive bibliography.

K-51 Meynen, E., ed. **International Geographical Glossary = glossaire geographique international = Internationales geographisches Glossaruim**. Stuttgart: F. Steiner, 1985.

Meynen's multilingual dictionary of geographic terms provides definitions in German, with comparable terms given in English, French, German, Italian, Japanese, Spanish, and Russian. It includes bibliographies and an important index.

K-52 Skinner, Malcolm, David Redfern, and Geoff Farmer. **Dictionary of Geography**. London: Fitzroy Dearborn, 1999.

Skinner, Redfern, and Farmer cover the entire field of geography with this text; they also provide in it a significant number of diagrams explaining physical phenomena.

K-53 Small, Ronald John. **A Modern Dictionary of Geography**. 3d ed. London: Arnold, 1995.

K-54 Stamp, L. Dudley, and Audrey Clark. **A Glossary of Geographical Terms**. 3d ed. Harlow, England: Longman, 1979.

When published in 1979, *A Modern Dictionary of Geography* was considered to be the most scholarly geographical dictionary available. The glossary contains alternative meanings and references to origin, then current usage, and cites the sources of information.

K-55 Starr, N. S. **The Traveler's World: A Dictionary of Industry and Destination Literacy**. Englewood Cliffs, NJ: Prentice-Hall, 1996.

An interesting selection of terminology is defined in this book for the business traveler. Included in alphabetical order are geographical place names, travel industry abbreviations, and jargon, as well as international foods.

K-56 Wheeler, James. **Dictionary of Quotations in Geography**. Westport, CT: Greenwood Press, 1986.

Quotations from prominent geographers are chosen here to characterize a variety of themes in geography during the twentieth century. Wheeler uses Pattison's four traditions of geography as an outline for this work.

DIRECTORIES

Most professional organizations publish memberships lists, which are provided to members and are available for purchase by nonmembers. Organizations with Web sites may make their membership directories available electronically, although they might not be accessible to nonmembers.

K-57   Association of American Geographers. **Guide to Departments of Geography in the United States and Canada. AAG Handbook and Directory of Geographers**. Washington, DC: Association of American Geographers, 1984- . Annual.

This publication by the Association of American Geographers provides detailed information on most of the academic departments in the United States and Canada that grant degrees in geography (entries include size of department, contact person, program and facilities, and faculty). The book includes a chart of program specialties, a list of titles of thesis and dissertations completed during the previous year organized by institution, and results of a survey of geography programs. The handbook portion contains the organizational manual of the AAG, including lists of officers; committees; the mission statement; and the membership list, which includes biographical data.

K-58   Ehlers, P. D. E., ed. **Orbis Geographicus = World Directory of Geography**. Wiesbaden, Germany: Franz Steiner Verlag, 1992/1993- . Irregular.

This international directory of geographers is organized by country and includes, in addition to traditional professional information, specific fields of research.

ENCYCLOPEDIAS AND HANDBOOKS

Encyclopedias and handbooks attempt to be comprehensive in coverage while providing relatively brief entries. They may cover the entire globe or focus on a single subdivision of geography or a single topic. They provide a good starting place for research.

K-59   **Geographica: The Complete Illustrated Atlas of the World**. New York: Welcome Rain Publishers, 2000.

Although called an atlas, this volume is much more than a collection of maps covering the globe. The text begins with a series of essays on the Earth as a physical and cultural place to live. There is a multipage description for each continent, with photographs, as well as a small physical map with location globe, flag, text, and fact file (official name, form of government, capital, demographic data, etc.).

K-60   **The Houghton Mifflin Dictionary of Geography: Places and Peoples of the World**. Boston: Houghton Mifflin, 1997. (See K-48)

Although actually a dictionary, its breadth of coverage of ethnic, linguistic, and national names, accompanied by small black-and-white outline maps make this work a first choice for basic information on each country. Features like an appendix with an abbreviations list, a geographic features list, a currency table, and a measurement table are all included.

K-61   National Geographic Society. **The National Geographic Desk Reference**. Washington, DC: National Geographic, 1999.

This informative collection of essays about physical and human geography includes a helpful "Places" section as well as specific country data. This desk reference makes good use of maps, graphs, and photographs. It also includes some bibliographies and is indexed.

K-62   Weaver, David Bruce. **Encyclopedia of Ecotourism**. Oxon, UK: CABI, 2001.

This work is composed of topical chapters and includes bibliographic references and an index.

HISTORIES AND BIOGRAPHIES

The history of the discipline and the people who guided its development are topics of continuing interest to researchers. Publication focused on the history of geographic thought is particularly strong.

Biography

K-63   Freedman, Thomas W. **Geographers: Biobibliographical Studies**. Bronx, NY: H. W. Wilson, 1977- .

The biographies of eminent geographers provided in this source present the reader with a better understanding of the development of geography as a discipline. Each biography is about six pages long, and a helpful bibliography accompanies each. For similar information on contemporary geographers, see *AAG Handbook and Directory of Members* (K-57). For obituaries see *Annals* (AAG) (K-88) and *The Geographical Journal* (RGS) (K-96).

History of Geographic Thought

K-64   Brown, Eric H. **Geography Yesterday and Tomorrow**. New York: Oxford University Press, 1980.

This title is a useful and popular text used by both graduate and undergraduate students.

K-65   Dreiver, Felix. **Geography Militant: Cultures of Exploration and Empire**. Oxford: Blackwell, 2001.

Geography Militant looks at historic exploration, the institutions and explorers, and what they have become in today's world.

K-66   Dunbar, Gary S. **The History of Modern Geography: An Annotated Bibliography of Selected Works**. New York: Garland, 1985.

This title covers general and systematic geography, geography in various countries, and biographies. The biographical section greatly supplements the Freedman bio-bibliographical annual biographical series (K-63).

K-67   Hanson, S., ed. **Ten Geographic Ideas That Changed the World**. New Brunswick, NJ: Rutgers University Press, 1997.

This collection of ten essays discusses a basic geographic idea that has had a major impact on the world constitutes this work. It is not meant to be inclusive of the field but rather to provide insight into the breadth of the discipline, it is written for the non-geographer.

K-68   James, Preston Everett, and Geoffrey Martin. **All Possible Worlds: A History of Geographical Ideas**. 3d ed. New York: John Wiley, 1993.

James and Martin provide an excellent survey of the history of geography from ancient times to the present. Included are a good topical bibliography and a section of concise biographies of eminent geographers.

K-69   Unwin, T. **The Place of Geography**. Harlow, Essex, England: Longman Scientific & Technical, 1992.

This text is an introduction to the history of geographic thought, written for the undergraduate student. It includes bibliographical references and an index.

Historical Geography

K-70   Meinig, Donald William. **The Shaping of America: A Geographical Perspective on 500 Years of History**. 4 vols. New Haven, CT: Yale University Press, 1986- .
In this ongoing work Meinig discusses the transformation of America. Includes bibliographies and indexes in all volumes.

    V. 1 *Atlantic America, 1492–1800*. n.d.

    V. 2 *Continental America, 1800–1867*. n.d.

    V. 3 *Transcontinental America, 1850–1915*. 2000.

    V. 4 *Global America 1915–1992*. Forthcoming.

GEOGRAPHICAL SOCIETIES

Information about professional societies linked to geography and specific details about their members can be found in the following four works.

K-71   Bryan, Courtlandt Dixon Barnes. **The National Geographic Society: 100 Years of Adventure and Discovery**. Updated and enlarged ed. New York: Abrams, 1997.

K-72   James, Preston. **The Association of American Geographers: The First Seventy-Five Years**. Washington, DC: Association of American Geographers, 1978.

K-73   Wright, John Kirkland. **Geography in the Making: The American Geographical Society, 1851–1951**. New York: American Geographical Society, 1952.

K-74   Steel, Robert. **The Institute of British Geographers: The First Fifty Years**. London: The Institute, 1984.

TRAVEL LITERATURE

There are many books currently available to assist travelers in any and all parts of the world. Two interesting titles that focus on personal histories of travelers across the ages are included here.

K-75   Campbell, M. B. **The Witness and the Other World: Exotic European Travel Writing, 400–1600**. Ithaca, NY: Cornell University Press, 1988.
This survey of European travel writing from 400 to 1600 includes the works of pilgrims, crusaders, merchants, and explorers. The author's thesis is that writers not only documented conquest but made it possible; he also hypothesizes that travel literature contributed greatly to the development of the modern novel and the modern life sciences.

K-76   Elsner, J., and J. P. Rubies, eds. **Voyages and Visions: Towards a Cultural History of Travel**. London: Reaktion Books, 1999.
In this collection of essays on the history of travel, Elsner and Rubies cover a time period from the sixteenth century to the present day.

GAZETTEERS

Gazetteers are locational guides, designed to help users quickly identify and find the location of a specific geographic feature. Such works vary greatly in scope and content. Older editions of gazetteers remain valuable to geographic researchers because they provide access to historical information and help document name changes. A number of gazetteers are now available online, but the choice of which format to use is a personal one.

K-77   Abate, Frank R., ed. **American Places: A Guide to 45,000 Populated Places, Natural Features and Other Places in the United States**. 4 vols. Detroit: Omnigraphics, 1994.

Editor Abate organized this guide by region, then alphabetically by state, county, and city or town in that order. Indexing is by state as well as by volume, with a general index to all volumes included in volume 4. Individual entries include ZIP code, latitude/longitude, population in 1980 and 1990, land and water area, general description, and name origin if available.

K-78   Cohen, Saul B., ed. **The Columbia Gazetteer of North America**. New York: Columbia University Press, 2000.

Based on the three-volume *Columbia Gazetteer of the World* (K-79), this volume has 50,000 entries on places in North America arranged in alphabetical order. Geographic information is on Canada, United States, Mexico, and Caribbean. Includes maps.

K-79   Cohen, Saul B., ed. **The Columbia Gazetteer of the World**. 3 vols. New York: Columbia University Press, 1998.

This is the long-awaited new edition of the classic *Columbia-Lippincott Gazetteer of the World* (Leon E. Sulzer, ed. Columbia University Press, 1962). It represents the standard in world coverage gazetteers with over 165,000 entries. Known for its descriptive and factual information, its entries include places names, political subdivisions, and geographic features; variant spellings; pronunciations; population (with date); geographic location; trade; industry; history; and other significant data.

Electronic access: It is also available as a CD-ROM and online by subscription. Electronic editions provide multiple search options, and the online version will be continuously updated.

K-80   **Getty Thesaurus of Geographic Names Browser**. Online format. URL: http://www.getty.edu/research/tools/vocabulary/tgn/index.html.

This site includes international place names, originally focused on names particularly important in art and architecture. Entries include a geographic hierarchy.

K-81   Hobson, Archie, ed. **Cambridge Gazetteer of the United States and Canada: A Dictionary of Places**. New York: Cambridge University Press, 1995.

This dictionary of geographical place names in the United States and Canada also includes some literary place names.

K-82   U.S. Board on Geographic Names. **Gazetteer**. Washington, DC: Government Printing Office, 1955- . Irregular.

This is the most comprehensive set of gazetteers ever published, covering more than 150 foreign countries. The purpose of the project is to provide uniform usage of geographic names throughout the U.S. government. The U.S. Board on Geographic Names operates through several committees to standardize names of geographic features in foreign areas, Antarctica, and extraterrestrial bodies. Locational information includes geographic coordinates and first-order administrative units. It is available in paper and microfiche.

K-83 **National Imagery and Mapping Agency (NIMA)**. URL: http://www
.nima.mil/gns/html; http://gnpswww.nima.mil/geonames/GNS.
Known as *GEOnet Names Server*, this is a database of international place names established
by the U.S. Board on Geographic Names for use in government publications.

K-84 U.S. Geological Survey. **The National Gazetteer of the United States**.
(Professional Paper 1200). Reston, VA: The Survey, 1982–1990. Online format.
The National Gazetteer began as a series of individual state gazetteers, in interim form, no
longer available in paper. Final versions were published for only nine of fifty states. All states are
available for free downloading from http://geonames.usgs.gov. The *Geographic Names Information
System* (*GNIS* [K-85]), first as a CD-ROM and now as a Web-accessible database, has taken the place
of the individual state volumes.

K-85 **Geographic Names Information System (GNIS)**. Online format. URL:
http://mapping.usgs.gov/www/gnis.
The *GNIS* database, developed by the U.S. Geological Survey (USGS), contains records of
approximately 2.1 million names in the United States, presumably all place names found on the
USGS 7.5-minutes scale maps. Information on each place name includes name, feature type (e.g.,
populated place, stream), county, and geographic coordinates. The CD-ROM version, *Geographic
Names Information System Digital Gazetteer*, initially available from the USGS, was last published
in July 1999, with no further versions planned.

Bibliographies of Gazetteers

K-86 Meynen, Emil. **Gazetteers and Glossaries of Geographical Names: Bibliography, 1946–1977**. Wiesbaden, Germany: Franz Steiner Verlag, 1984.
This bibliography includes member countries of the United Nations and is useful for locating
sources on foreign countries and worldwide gazetteers. The four-part bibliography not only includes
titles to gazetteers but also cites indexes to maps and atlases that may be overlooked in searching for a
place name. The four sections include lists of country and territory names, world gazetteers and indexes
(gazetteers by continents, regions, and oceans, indexes or world atlases and maps), gazetteers and indexes
by country, and glossaries of geographical names.

K-87 Sealock, Richard B., and Margaret S. Powell. **Bibliography of Place-
Name Literature: United States and Canada**. 3d ed. Chicago: American Library
Association, 1982.
This text is a very comprehensive bibliography of published material in place name lists;
both books and periodical articles are included, as are some manuscript compilations, along with library
location. This compilation has been prepared to assist librarians, historians, and genealogists in locat-
ing information about place names—local, state/province, or regional—in the United States and
Canada. Two helpful indexes, of place names and subjects, are provided.

SERIALS

Serial publications are the main medium for the publication of current geographical research
because they provide timely access to what is new and exciting in the discipline. It is in the serial literature that new concepts, methods, and data are presented to other geographers for their criticism
and review. The growth of the Web as a research tool has not yet reduced the reliance of researchers
on the serial literature.

As with any healthy discipline, geography has many journal titles from which to choose when doing research. Some journals publish research from every area of the discipline; others focus on a single subfield. Some titles are published by professional associations and others are commercial in nature; some are scholarly and others are more popular. A selection of current geographic titles is provided in this section.

K-88 **Annals**. Association of American Geographers, 1911- . Quarterly.
Premier publication of the AAG.

K-89 **Antipode: A Radical Journal of Geography**. Blackwell, 1969- . Quarterly.

K-90 **Applied Geography**. Elsevier Science, 1981- . Quarterly.

K-91 **Australian Geographical Studies**. Blackwell, 1963- . 3/yr.

K-92 **The Canadian Geographer**. Canadian Association of Geographers, 1951- . Quarterly.
Premier publication of the CAG.

K-93 **Ecumene**. Arnold, 1994- . Quarterly.

K-94 **The Explorers Journal**. The Explorers Club, 1921- . Quarterly.

K-95 **Geographical**. Royal Geographical Society, 1935- . Monthly.

K-96 **The Geographical Journal**. Royal Geographical Society, 1893- . Quarterly.
Premier publication of the RGS.

K-97 **Geographical Review**. American Geographical Society, 1916- . Quarterly.
Premier publication of the AGS.

K-98 **Geography Review**. Philip Allen, 1987- . 5/yr.

K-99 **Geopolitics**. Frank Cass, 1998- . 3/yr.

K-100 **Journal of Cultural Geography**. Bowling Green State University, 1980- . Biannnual.

K-101 **Journal of Geography**. National Council for Geographic Education, 1902- . Bimonthly.
Premier publication of the NCGE.

K-102 **Journal of Geography in Higher Education**. Taylor & Francis, 1977- . 3/yr.

K-103 **Journal of Historical Geography**. Academic Press, 1975- . Quarterly.

K-104 **National Geographic**. National Geographical Society, 1888- . Monthly.
Premier publication of the NGS.

K-105 **Research in Geographic Education**. Gilbert M. Grosvenor Center for Geographic Education, 2000- . Biannual.

K-106 Tourism Geographies: An International Journal of Tourism Space, Place and Environment. Routledge Journals, 1999- . Quarterly.

K-107 Urban Morphology: Journal of the International Seminar on Urban Form. The Seminar, 1997- . Biannual.

BIBLIOGRAPHIES

K-108 International List of Geographical Serials. 3d ed. Compiled by Chauncy D. Harris and Jerome D. Fellman. Chicago: University of Chicago, Department of Geography, 1980.

Although quite dated, this title lists approximately 3,500 serial titles representing more than 100 countries and 55 languages. Organized by country, each entry provides the serial's name(s), both current and closed, dates and frequency, inclusion of abstracts, cumulative indexes, and addresses for active periodicals.

K-109 Harris, Chauncy D. **Annotated World List of Selected Current Geographical Serials**. 4th ed. (Research Paper no. 194). Chicago: University of Chicago, Department of Geography, 1980.

This helpful publication cites more than 450 geographical journals having the "greatest scholarly interest" to the discipline. Annotations indicate the subject content, scope, and status of each title. These journals publish research articles that adhere to high standards of scholarship and make an important contribution to geographic knowledge.

K-110 American Geographical Society. **Geographical Review**. 1916- . Quarterly.

This journal publishes an annual review of new journals in geography.

Electronic access: The archives are now searchable online at http://www.geography.unr .edu/GR/grhome.html.

INDEXES AND ABSTRACTS

Bibliographic indexes and abstracts provide subject access to journal articles as well as books, government documents, proceedings, and other hard-to-locate materials. Many of the traditional bibliographic indexes are now available on the Web as well as in printed format. Libraries with online catalogs are beginning to expand their cataloged materials so that subject access that once was only available through printed indexes may now be found in their online catalog.

K-111 Current Geographical Publications: Additions to the Research Catalogue of the American Geographical Society. Milwaukee: American Geographical Society Collection at the University of Wisconsin—Milwaukee, 1938- . 10 issues/ yr., noncumulating.

Current Geographical Publications provides subject and regional access to books, articles, government documents, maps, and atlases in the American Geographical Society Collection at the University of Wisconsin—Milwaukee.

Electronic access: Originally a noncumulating paper publication, it became available online in 1985. The years 1985 to date are available at http://geobib.lib.uwm.edu. The current issue of *CGP* may be searched at http://leardo.lib.uwm.edu/cgp.

K-112 GeoBase. New York: Elsevier Science, 1980- . Monthly. Online format.
This electronic database covers journals, books, monographs, conference proceedings, and reports. It includes 812,000 records, with over 600,000 records having abstracts. Subject coverage includes cartography, environment and ecology. See *Geographical Abstracts* (K-113).

K-113 Geographical Abstracts. Norwich, England: Elsevier/Geo Abstracts, 1989- . Monthly.
This bibliographical journal provides approximately 11,000 abstracts annually from 1,100 core journals plus books, theses, and proceedings. It has gone through a number of changes in name and scope of geographical coverage since 1960; it has been known variously as *Geomorphological Abstracts* (1960–1965), *Geographical Abstracts* (1966–1973), *Geo Abstracts* (1974–1988), and then *Geographical Abstracts* again in 1989. Under the first title the publication dealt only with physical geography. Geography as a social science began to appear only in the later series, where coverage included economic geography as well as social and historical geography in 1966, and regional and urban planning in 1972. Currently the abstracts are published monthly in two separate publications subtitled *Human Geography* and *Physical Geography*, which are also available in CD-ROM format.
Electronic access: Current entries are also available on *GeoBase* (K-112).

K-114 Bibliographie Géographique Internationale. Paris: Laboratoire d'Information et de Documentation en Géographie, Centre National de la Recherche Scientifique, 1891- . Annual.
Bibliographie Géographique Internationale is the oldest of these bibliographies and best chronicles the development of modern geography. This abstracting publication provides the fullest coverage of geographical serials. Although most of the entries and brief annotations are in French, the table of contents and headings are in English.

Dissertations

Most geographical dissertations are developed around very specialized topics, and they usually contain substantial data not previously compiled under one title. An important element found in dissertations is the methodology section, which provides researchers with new ideas for exploration within the discipline.

In general dissertations have been difficult to locate due to inadequate cataloging by libraries as well as the fact that they were not commercially published, thus limiting the number of copies available. Access to dissertations has improved because University Microfilms reproduces dissertations and provides indexing and/or abstracts them, and many libraries provide improved access to their thesis and dissertation publications through their online catalogs.

Current

Dissertation Abstracts International (DAI). Ann Arbor, MI: University Microfilms, 1938- . (See A-39)

K-115 Dissertation Abstracts Ondisc. Ann Arbor, MI: University Microfilms, 1989. Electronic format.
DAO began with three archival disks covering January 1861 to December 1988.

K-116 ProQuest Digital Dissertations. Ann Arbor, MI: UMI, 1997.
This primary source for 1.4 million doctoral dissertations (abstracts 1980-) and selected master's theses (abstracts 1988-) from over 1,000 North American and European universities is available through subscription to authorized users.

Older Dissertation Sources

K-117 Browning, Clyde E. **A Bibliography of Dissertations in Geography, 1901–1969: American and Canadian Universities**. (Studies in Geography, no. 1). Chapel Hill: University of North Carolina, Department of Geography, 1970.

K-118 **Studies in Geography**. Chapel Hill: University of North Carolina, Department of Geography, 1983.

K-119 Stuart, Merrill. **A Bibliography of Master's Theses in Geography**. Tualatin, OR: Geographic and Area Study Publications, 1973.

CARTOGRAPHY AND GEOGRAPHIC INFORMATION SYSTEMS

Guides to the Literature

K-120 Perkins, C. R., and R. B. Parry, eds. **Information Sources in Cartography**. London: Bowker-Saur, 1990.
Extensive bibliographic essays on cartography that encompass all aspects of the discipline are included in this guide. The book is divided into six parts: general, history of cartography, map production, types of mapping, map use, and promotion. Appendixes include cartographic periodicals, cartographic societies, and an international list of map publishers.

K-121 Hodgkiss, A. G., and A. F. Tatham. **Keyguide to Information Sources in Cartography**. London: Mansell, 1986.
Not just a bibliography of cartography, this book contains essays as well as annotations of major works of interest to anyone researching any aspect of maps.

Bibliographies and Indexes

Many of these bibliographies are in the form of book catalogs and are reproductions of the original catalog cards in the holding library's card catalog. At one time these volumes were the only way to locate maps held by other institutions, but the advent of the online library catalog and OCLC reduced the need for these volumes to be published. These are therefore most useful for retrospective searching. For current holdings the easiest search is using OCLC's WorldCat, a subscription-based service accessible at most libraries.

K-122 **Bibliographia Cartographica**. New York: K. G. Saur, 1974- . Annual.
This annual provides "international documentation to cartographical literature." The bibliography is divided into thirteen chapters: bibliography, map collections, documentation, general publishers list, history of cartography, institutions and organizations of cartography, theoretical cartography, cartographic technology, topographic and landscape cartography, thematic maps and cartograms, atlas cartography, use and appreciation of maps, and reliefs and other globes. It replaces *Biblioteca Cartographia*, which was issued from 1957 to 1972.

K-123 **Bibliography of Cartography**. 5 vols. Boston: G. K. Hall, 1973. **Supplement**. 2 vols. Washington, DC: Library of Congress. Geography and Map Division, 1980.

A comprehensive bibliography to cartographical literature, this work covers materials published from the early nineteenth century through 1971. It provides author and subject access to books and journal articles about maps and all phases of map making, interpretation, use, preservation, and history. Covered best is early American cartography, including biographical information on explorers, surveyors, cartographers, printers, and publishers. The supplement adds information from 1971 to 1980.

K-124 **Guide to Cartographic Records in the National Archives**. Washington, DC: National Archives and Records Service, 1971.

This publication describes materials that were in the cartographic branch of the National Archives as of 1966. The arrangement is by government agency and is followed in alphabetical order by subordinate organizations with agency: legislative branch, judicial branch, executive branch, independent (e.g., existing, World War I, those established in 1920–1939 and later terminated, World War II), and other sources. The publication has an extensive table of contents and a keyword index.

K-125 **Index to Maps in Books and Periodicals**. 10 vols. Boston: G. K. Hall, 1968. **Supplement 1**. 1968–1971. **Supplement 2**. 1972–1975. **Supplement 3**. 1976–1986.

This index is based on the *American Geographical Society Map Catalog* and is an indispensable reference tool in the field of cartobibliographies. It is the only comprehensive source that cites maps in books and periodicals. The index complements cartographic bibliographies that list only separately issued maps and atlases. Entries are arranged into sixty-seven areas and subjects in one alphabet.

K-126 Library of Congress. **National Union Catalog: Cartographic Materials**. Washington, DC: Library of Congress, 1983- . Quarterly.

This microfiche catalog contains the retrospective *LC MARC MAP* database from 1969 to date. It is a continuing record of the cataloging of cartographic materials held by LC and other participating libraries. Records are included on single maps; map series; manuscript maps; maps issued in microformat; and maps issued by international, national, and local government bodies. All imprints, regardless of date, are included with the source of their cataloged serial.

The catalog consists of a register and five indexes. The register displays the full cataloging information of each record. The five indexes consist of name, title, series, LC subject, and geographic classification code.

K-127 **A List of Geographical Atlases in the Library of Congress**. 9 vols. Washington, DC: Library of Congress, 1909–1994.

This is the most extensive bibliography on atlases ever published. The basic work was in four volumes (1909–1920), arranged first by general atlases of special subjects, followed by general atlases of the world in chronological order; then covering continents arranged in the same manner. Volume 5 (1958) supplements the world atlas section with items received from 1920 to 1955. Volume 6 (1963) includes materials on Europe, Asia, Africa, Australia, Oceania, the polar regions, and the oceans acquired from 1920 to 1960. Volume 7 lists atlases of the Western Hemisphere from 1920 to 1967. Volumes 8 and 9 are indexes. This is an outstanding resource for locating cartographic materials housed in the Library of Congress collection. The set was reprinted in 1970 by Theatrum Orbis Terrarum.

K-128   Seavey, Charles Alden. **Mapping the Transmississippi West, 1540–1861: An Index to the Cartobibliography**. Winnetka, IL: Speculum Orbis Press, 1992.
   The answer to a researcher's prayer, this is an index created to assist in the use of the massive work by Carl Irving Wheat, *Mapping the Transmississippi West, 1504–1861* (K-131).

K-129   Stams, W. **National and Regional Atlases: A Bibliographic Survey**. Enschede, Netherlands: International Cartographic Association, 1985.
   This survey lists more than 2,000 atlases of major regions of the world. State and national atlases as well as district and city atlases are included.

K-130   Otness, Harold M. **Index to Early Twentieth Century City Plans Appearing in Guidebooks, Baedeker, Muirhead-Blue Guides, Murray, I.J.G.R. Etc. Plus Selected Other Works to Provide Worldwide Coverage of Over 2,000 Plans to Over 1,200 Communities, Found in 74 Guidebooks**. Santa Cruz, CA: Western Association of Map Libraries, 1978.

K-131   Wheat, Carl Irving. **Mapping the Transmississippi West, 1540–1861**. 5 vols. San Francisco: Institute of Historical Cartography, 1957.
   This extraordinary cartobibliography on the mapping of the expanding United States includes reproductions of many maps. Reprinted in 1995 by Maurizio Martino Publishers. Not well indexed; see K-128.

K-132   Wheat, James Clements. **Maps and Charts Published in America Before 1800: A Bibliography**. New Haven, CT: Yale University Press, 1969.
   This bibliography includes maps and charts published separately as well as illustrations in books, pamphlets, atlases, gazetteers, almanacs, and magazines.

Dictionaries

K-133   **Glossary of the Mapping Sciences**. Prepared by a Joint Committee of the American Society of Civil Engineers, American Congress on Surveying and Mapping, and American Society for Photogrammetry and Remote Sensing. Bethesda, MD: American Society for Photogrammetry and Remote Sensing, 1994.
   This glossary provides definitions for nearly 10,000 terms used in surveying, mapping, and remote sensing.

K-134   Neumann, J. **Enzyklopadisches Worterbuch Kartographie in 25 Sprachen = Encyclopedic Dictionary of Cartography in 25 Languages**. Munchen, Germany: K. G. Saur, 1997.
   This multilingual dictionary of cartographic terminology provides full definitions in German, English, French, Spanish, and Russian. Equivalent terms are given in Algerian, Moroccan Arabic, Bulgarian, Danish, Chinese, Finnish, Hindi, Italian, Classical and transliterated Japanese, Croatian, Dutch, Norwegian, Polish, Portuguese, Swedish, Slovakian, Thai, Czech, and Hungarian. It is arranged by subject groups and indexed by main language.

K-135 **A Practitioner's Guide to GIS Terminology : A Glossary of Geographic Information System Terms**. Federal Way, WA: Data West Research Agency, 1994.

This reference book contains over 6,100 definitions used by those in the GIS community.

K-136 Wallis, H. M., and A. H. Robinson, eds. **Cartographical Innovations: An International Handbook of Mapping Terms to 1900**. [s.l.]: Map Collector Publications, 1987.

A marvelous work of scholarship, this volume is a dictionary of cartographic innovations. The innovations are grouped into eight sections (three for maps, reference systems, symbolism, techniques, method of duplication, and atlases), with each entry consisting of three parts (definition, history of its development, and bibliographic citations).

Directories

K-137 Loiseaux, Olivier, ed. **World Directory of Map Collections**. 4th ed. (IFLA Publications no. 92/93). Munchen, Germany: K. G. Saur, 2000.

Contains references to 714 map collections in 121 countries. The entries are arranged alphabetically by country and city except for Australia, Canada, and the United States, which are subdivided by state or province and city. Each entry includes the address and contact information as well as staffing, history of the collection, subject strengths and specializations, bibliographic control, reference services, copying and interlibrary loan information, storage equipment, conservation procedures, and publications.

K-138 **GIS World GeoDirectory**. 3 vols. Fort Collins, CO: GIS World, 1997.

This set (*Products and Services*, *Academic Institutions*, and *Data Sources*) replaces the *International GIS Sourcebook* by the same publisher. Information is acquired from the annual GIS Industry Survey.

Histories and Biographies

K-139 Barber, P., and C. Board. **Tales from the Map Room: Fact and Fiction About Maps and Their Makers**. London: BBC Books, 1993.

This is a companion book to the TV series *Tales from the Map Room* (first broadcast in spring 1993). Contains six chapters, or themes, with examples from the British Library, to explain the role of maps in society.

K-140 Campbell, Tony. **Map History and History of Cartography**. URL: http://www.ihrinfo.ac.uk/maps. (Accessed March 23, 2001).

Maintained by Tony Campbell, retired map librarian at the British Library, this site provides access to scholarly and commercial articles and Web sites on "early, old, antique, and antiquarian maps." It is a major source for information.

K-141 Tooley, R. V. **Tooley's Dictionary of Mapmakers**. Tring, England: Map Collection Publications, 1979.

K-142   Tooley, R. V. **Tooley's Dictionary of Mapmakers. Supplement**. New York: Alan R. Liss, 1985.
With 21,450 entries, this is the major source for information on cartographers, engravers, and publishers from earliest times to 1900. The supplement adds approximately 4,000 names to the original publication.

K-143   Wilford, John Noble. **Mapmakers**. Rev. ed. New York: Alfred A. Knopf, 2000.
This is an updated edition of a classic work on cartographers and the history of cartography.

K-144   Harley, J. B., and D. Woodward, eds. **The History of Cartography**. 4 vols. Chicago: University of Chicago Press, 1987- .

Volume 1. *Cartography in Prehistoric, Ancient, and Medieval Europe and the Mediterranean*. 1987.

Volume 2, Book 1. *Cartography in the Traditional Islamic and South Asian Societies*. 1992.

Volume 2, Book 2. *Cartography in the Traditional East and Southeast Asian Societes*. 1994.

Volume 2, Book 3. *Cartography in the Traditional African, American, Arctic, Australian, and Pacific Societies*. 1998.

Exhaustive research on the development of cartographic expression by a group of international scholars is presented in this series. All volumes are highly illustrated and each includes extensive bibliographies. There are six volumes planned. Volume 3, *Cartography in the European Renaissance*, is forthcoming.

K-145   Suarez, S. **Early Mapping of Southeast Asia**. Singapore: Periplus Editions (HK), 1999.
A detailed examination of the history of mapping of Southeast Asia from earliest times through the nineteenth century is presented in this work. Included are numerous color reproductions of many maps with detailed cartobibliographical information on each title. A bibliography and an index are provided.

K-146   Wolter, J. A., and R. E. Grim, eds. **Images of the World: The Atlas Through History**. New York: McGraw-Hill, 1997.
This work is a scholarly collection of fifteen essays on the evolution of atlases as a cartographic and cultural artifact. Illustrations and bibliography are included.

Serials

Serials provide access to the most recent research and the newest techniques in a discipline. The following are some of the journals publishing in the areas of cartography and GIS.

K-147   **The Cartographic Journal.** The British Cartographic Society, 1964- .
Biannual.
Premier journal of the BCS.

K-148   **Cartographic Perspectives**. North American Cartographic Information Society, 1989- . 3/yr.

K-149   **Cartographicia**. The University of Toronto Press, 1980- . Quarterly.
Continues the numbering of the *Canadian Cartographer*.

K-150   **Cartography**. Mapping Sciences Institute, Australia,1954- . Biannual.
Premier journal of the MSI.

K-151   **Cartography and Geographic Information Science**. American Congress on Surveying and Mapping, 1999- . Quarterly.
Previously *American Cartographer* (1974–1989) and *Cartography and Geographic Information Systems* (1990–1998). Premier journal of the ACSM.

K-152   **Geoinformatica**. Kluwer, 1997- . Quarterly.

K-153   **Geospatial Solutions**. Advanstar Communications, 2000- . Monthly.
Previously *Geo Info Systems*, 1990–2000).

K-154   *GEOWorld*. Adams Business Media, 1998- . Monthly.
Previously *GIS World* (1988–1998).

K-155   **Imago Mundi: The International Journal for the History of Cartography**. Imago Mundi, 1935- . Annual.

K-156   **International Journal of Geographic Information Science**. Taylor & Francis, 1997- . 8/yr.
Formerly *International Journal of Geographical Information Systems* (*IJGIS*).

K-157   **Mercator's World: The Magazine of Maps, Exploration, and Discovery**. Aster Publishing, 1996- . Bimonthly.

K-158   **SoC Bulletin**. The Society of Cartographers, 1990- . Biannual.
Previously *Bulletin of the Society of University Cartographers* (1967–1989). Premier journal of the SC.

Map Design and Interpretation

K-159   Campbell, John. **Map Use & Analysis**. 3d ed. Boston: WCB/McGraw-Hill, 1998.
In this book Campbell presents a classic teaching text with twenty-three chapters, eight appendixes, a glossary, and an index. Discusses the basics components of maps and their production, design, and use. Includes chapter on cartograms and special purpose maps as well as the misuse of maps. Remote sensing, computer-assisted cartography, digital map applications, and GIS are also covered. The final two chapters are on map producers and foreign maps, with the land survey in Canada covered in chapter 4.

K-160   Muehrcke, Phillip C., and Juliana O. Muehrcke. **Map Use: Reading, Analysis, Interpretation**. 4th ed. Madison, WI: JP Publications, 1998.
Like Campbell's *Map Use & Analysis* (K-159), this text is a classic teaching text, with the chapters on map analysis and map interpretation particularly useful. It includes instruction on grids, GPS, and navigation. Appendixes include map scale, remote sensing of the environment, and map projections.

K-161   Robinson, Arthur H., et al. **Elements of Cartography**. 6th ed. New York: John Wiley, 1995.

The classic teaching text *Elements of Cartography* is composed of thirty-one chapters, six appendixes, and a comprehensive index. Also included are overviews on the nature of cartography, history of cartography, and map projections. Sources of data, data processing, map design, cartographic abstraction and production, as well as ground survey methods, remote sensing, and map digitizing are provided. Digital databases and their management and GIS are covered in the latest edition.

Map Projections

K-162   Snyder, J. P., and P. M. Voxland. **An Album of Map Projections**. (U.S. Geological Survey. Professional Paper 1453). Washington, DC: Government Printing Office, 1989.

This is a catalog of some ninety basic projections in over 130 different aspects. Entries include graphic representation and text that discusses the projection (including classification, the graticule, scale, distortion, usage, and origin and alternative names).

K-163   Yang, Q. H., J. P. Snyder, et al. **Map Projection Transformation: Principles and Applications**. London: Taylor & Francis, 2000.

Based on the Chinese book *Ditu touying bianhuan yuanli yu fangfa*, this text has been rewritten and revised. Explanations of the principles of mathematically transforming map projections are particularly useful to researchers using computer-aided cartography and GIS/LIS. This scholarly work is not written for the novice.

Atlases, Maps, and Aerial Photographs

Identifying and locating maps and aerial photographs is a frustrating process. Although most atlases can be found in *Books in Print*, there isn't any reference volume or database that is truly comprehensive, listing all the commercial and government publications, for maps or aerial photographs. However, one particular title, *World Mapping Today* (K-164), by Parry and Perkins, certainly attempts to provide as much information for maps as one physical volume can. For easier access to tourist maps, acquiring the catalog of a map dealer or searching their Web sites is very useful. *Geo Katalog 2*, from GeoCenter in Stuttgart (http://www.geokatalog.de/intgeo2.htm), is a subscription-based catalog with international coverage, but there are many other map dealers who also have substantial catalogs that are not as expensive to acquire. Search the International Map Trade Association Web site (http://www.maptrade.org) or use their printed membership directory to identify appropriate dealers. To view and download free U.S. Geological Survey topographic maps, use http://www.topozone.com. If customized USGS topographic maps are desired they can be found at TopoFactory, a subscription-based service for CAD and GIS users, that is linked from TopoZone. Aerial photographs for the United States are available online at http://terraserver.com. Other sources of information about aerial photographs may be requested from any Earth Science Information Center (ESIC); call 1-800-USA-MAPS or check out the Web site at http://mapping.usgs.gov/esic/esic_html. The U.S. Geological Survey's Web site is http://ask.usgs.gov.

K-164   Parry, R. B., and C. R. Perkins. **World Mapping Today**. 2d ed. London: R. R. Bowker, 2000.

Newly revised and nearly double in size, this long-awaited second edition presents an overview of the availability of maps around the world. The volume begins with essays on the state of world mapping and its accessibility before the individual continent and country entries. Entries are generally two to four pages long; include a brief essay on the history of mapping in a particular country; provide addresses of mapping institutions; and list a sample of atlas, gazetteer, and map or map series titles.

Many countries have index maps for standard map series. This edition includes URLs for agencies and commercial companies. State level coverage for many countries (Canada, Great Britain, Germany, Mexico, United States, etc.) significantly increases the overall length of the country entry.

K-165 Makower, J. **The Map Catalog: Every Kind of Map and Chart of Earth and Even Some Above It**. New York: Vantage Books, 1992.

This illustrated sampler of maps shows the wide array of maps that are published by government agencies as well as commercial companies. This work includes many full citations, ordering addresses, and prices at the time of publication.

K-166 **Manual of Federal Geographic Data Projects**. Falls Church, VA: ViGYAN, 1993. Looseleaf.

Although not updated since its initial publication, this manual provides a comprehensive and standardized description of cartographic and spatial data available from U.S. government agencies. It includes contact addresses with phone and FAX numbers but not URLs.

K-167 Bohme, R., ed. **Inventory of World Topographic Mapping**. 3 vols. London: Elsevier Science, 1989–1993.

This work, organized geographically, provides a history of the topographic mapping of each nation. Illustrated with index maps.

K-168 Larsgaard, M. L. **Topographic Mapping of Africa, Antarctica, and Eurasia**. Sacramento, CA: Western Association of Map Libraries, 1993.

Topographic Mapping is an overview of the history of topographic mapping for Africa and Eurasia at scales 1:250,000 or larger. An extensive bibliography is provided.

K-169 Larsgaard, M. L. **Topographic Mapping of the Americas, Australia, and New Zealand**. Littleton, CO: Libraries Unlimited, 1984.

Like the previous text by the same author (K-168), this work is an overview of the history of topographic mapping in the Americas, Australia, and New Zealand at scales 1:250,000 or larger. It also provides an extensive bibliography.

Atlases

An atlas is a collection of maps, generally bound in book form or stored loose in a box, having a distinct purpose. There are essentially three types of atlases: *world* (general reference), *regiona* (including national atlases and state atlases) and *subject-oriented* (thematic).

World atlases provide quick access to basic environmental and locational information. In this type of atlas, the major portion of the work consists of inventory maps, often indicating elevation by the use of shading, in a selection of uniform scales that permits the reader to gain an understanding of the physical situation of a place. A standard practice is to include a series of world or continental maps indicating the distribution of natural and cultural resources, and an index, or gazetteer, to place names. Additional information in the form of essays or tables may be included. Scholarship aside, there is no best atlas on the market, there are only atlases that are better or worse due to the personal needs and preferences of the reader. Nearly all of today's publishers use the computer to design maps, which has led to the improvement of visual clarity, enhanced relief shading, the use of more subtle colors, and easier placement of place names. Oversized atlases that have satellite photography and additional essays, tables, or overview maps cost more than atlases that are smaller and limit their use of graphics.

K-170   **Book of the World**. Rev. 2d ed. New York: Macmillan, 1999.
The most expensive and impressive world atlas published in many years, the *Book of the World* has spectacular satellite photographs and uses a limited number of scales on its maps: world at 1:35,000,000, continents and oceans 1:12,000,000, the entire world at 1:4,000,000, the United States at 1:2,000,000, selected international cities on full-page spreads with a page of text and photographs for each. It includes a CD-ROM version.

K-171   **Macmillan Centennial Atlas of the World**. Rev. ed. New York: Macmillan, 1999.
Notable for its spectacular satellite photographs and choice of scales (provides the world at 1:4,000,000, adds the United States at 1:2,000,000, selected international cities at 1:20,000) this is a compact version of *The Book of the World* (K-170), first published in 1996.

K-172   **The Times Atlas of the World. New International Atlas**. 10th comprehensive ed. New York: Times Books, 1999.
This classic work is an entirely new edition, computer-generated from world and regional databases, with the allocation of map plates reflecting recent changes in the political world and satellite photography. There is an extensive place name index. It is much improved over older editions.

K-173   **National Geographic Atlas of the World**. 7th ed. Washington, DC: National Geographic Society, 1999.
Redesigned, digitally produced, and having satellite photography, this is the latest edition of the well-known and well-loved NGS *Atlas of the World*. It has an index with 140,000 entries, with revised notes for every country. The interactive atlas on National Geographic Society's Web site (http://www.nationalgeographic.com) will provide map updates.

K-174   **Hammond World Atlas**. Maplewood, NJ: Hammond Incorporated, 2000.
Notable for its new design and addition of shaded relief maps at the continental scale, this atlas has a softer look than many of the others listed here. Enhanced by satellite photography and a small amount of text for each two-page spread, the atlas includes world thematic maps and a place name index. Accompanied by a CD-ROM.

K-175   Goode, J. Paul. **Goode's World Atlas**. 19th ed. Chicago: Rand McNally, 1995.
This classic student atlas is noted for its thematic world and continental maps and its extensive place name index.

National Atlases

National atlases are government-sponsored publications and focus on a single country. These atlases represent the national character of their country and provide extremely detailed physical and demographic information as well as many unique maps that cannot be found elsewhere. They are important sources of information and may provide information at the county as well as state/provincial level. Because they are a major research endeavor, not every nation has been able to publish a national atlas. For the researcher they are an important source of information.

K-176   **National Atlas of Canada**. Ottawa, ONT: Natural Resources Canada, 2000.
The latest edition of this atlas is located on the Web at http://atlas.gc.ca/english.

K-177   **National Atlas of Wales**. Cardiff, South Glamorgan: University of Wales Press, 1980.
This atlas is available in paper.

K-178   **National Atlas of Japan**. Rev. ed. Tokyo: Japan Map Center, 1992.
This atlas is available in paper.

K-179   United States Geological Survey. **National Atlas of the United States**. Washington, DC: The Survey, 1970.
Out-of-print and with much of its information out-of-date, this is the only edition in paper. The new format will be online only, although selected map sheets are available for individual purchase from USGS. The digital *National Atlas* is a joint project by the government and a commercial firm. The official government site is http://nationalatlas.gov, but there is also a commercial site at http://www.usatlas2000.com that requests a lifetime subscription fee of $9.00.

K-180   **Vietnam: Atlas Quoc Gia = National Atlas**. Ha Noi: Tong cuc dia chinh, 1996.
This atlas is available in paper.

State Atlases

State atlases are similar to national atlases in that they focus on a single jurisdiction and examine it in great detail. They are often published by a university or a state agency rather than by a commercial company, although they may be funded by grants that may derive from the commercial sphere. The format of this type of atlas parallels that of the national atlases. There is an overview map of the study area accompanied by a proliferation of topical maps depicting the physical and cultural environment. Information is generally given at the county level, and there is often an historical section. Tables, graphs, text , bibliographies or reference lists, and a subject index generally complete the publication.

K-181   **Atlas of Hawaii**. 3d ed. Honolulu: University of Hawaii Press, 1998.
Exceptionally well-designed, this atlas focuses on a single state and its natural and human resources. As befits a state-level atlas, many of the topics are unique to Hawaii. Many photographs and graphics are included, as are statistical tables, references organized by subject, and a gazetteer.

K-182   **Atlas of Kentucky**. Lexington: The University of Kentucky Press, 1998.
Also exceptionally well-designed, this *Atlas of Kentucky* focuses on a single state and its natural and human resources. As befits a state-level atlas, many topics are unique to Kentucky. It includes photographs, graphics, glossary, and list of references, and cites sources of maps, tables, graphs, and photographs. It is indexed.

K-183   **The North Carolina Atlas: Portrait for a New Century**. Chapel Hill, NC: The University of North Carolina Press, 1999.
Although it has more text than maps, this is still an excellent representative of the state/regional atlas.

Road Atlases

Road atlases, covering a nation or a single state, are published by a number of companies, with DeLorme and Rand McNally two of the best-known providers. These atlases are frequently updated and relatively inexpensive. They are often available in both paper and electronic format (CD-ROM and on the Web). Personal preference will determine which product is more acceptable, as all perform the same basic functions.

K-184   DeLorme. **Indiana Atlas & Gazetteer**. Yarmouth, ME: Delorme, 1998.
This is just one of several state topographic/road atlases published for the recreational user who requires more than just highways. Included are tables of recreational sites with descriptions and index (gazetteer) to place names; newer editions include GPS grids.

K-185   DeLorme. **Street Atlas USA 9.0**. Yarmouth, ME: Delorme, 2000. Online format.
The latest version (2000) of DeLorme's very popular electronic database of U.S. streets permits routing for trip planning as well as the custom printing of maps and travel plans. the latest versions of the software are generally available for review at http://www.delorme.com.

K-186   Rand McNally. **Rand McNally Road Atlas: United States, Canada, Mexico**. Chicago: Rand McNally, 2001.
This atlas is an annual publication by the largest commercial map publisher in the United States. It has individual maps of each state/province in the United States and Canada, a single map for Mexico, and includes detailed city maps and extensive county and city indexes.

Thematic Atlases

Thematic atlases are subject-oriented; almost any subject can be depicted in cartographic format. The following list is a sample of recent thematic atlases.

K-187   Benewick, R., and S. Donald. **The State of China Atlas**. London: Penguin, 1999.
This is one of the *"The State of . . ."* atlases that have been popular for the past decade or so. Known for flashy graphics, these are flamboyant reference works that provide a wide range of statistical information. This particular volume has a spreadsheet of world statistics in eighteen categories (from land area and population to energy use and carbon dioxide emissions) as well as a commentary section that explains, in essay form, the significance of the maps and how they were derived.

K-188   Bradbury, M., ed. **The Atlas of Literature**. London: De Agostini Editions, 1996.
This atlas, with its extensive essays, focuses on the places that are important to literature. Outlined are the places where literature was born or developed, and the homes and landscapes of the authors as well as the landscape of their works. It is organized chronologically ("Middle Ages and Renaissance," "Age of Reason," "The Romantics," "Age of Industrialism and Empire," "Age of Realism," "Modern World," "After the Second World War," and the "World Today"). Also included are a section of brief biographies of authors discussed but not featured in the essays, a list of places to visit, a list of further readings (organized geographically), and an index.

K-189   **The Cassell Atlas of World History**. Oxford: Andromeda Books, 1997.
Essays and maps in this work provide a global view and then focus in on regional historical events from 4,000,000 B.C.E. to 1997.

K-190 Dartmouth Medical School. Center of the Evaluative Clinical Sciences. **The Dartmouth Atlas of Health Care 1998**. Chicago: American Hospital Publishing, 1998.

This atlas is a thought-provoking examination of the distribution of health services and costs in America. It includes a CD-ROM.

Electronic access: The Web site, http://www.dartmouthatlas.org, includes electronic copies of hard-to-find references as well as summaries of research.

K-191 **Hammond Atlas of the 20th Century**. 2d ed. London: Time Books, 1999.

Essays, maps, graphs, and photographs in this atlas review significant political events around the world.

K-192 Moseley, Christopher, ed. **Atlas of the World's Languages**. New York: Routledge, 1994.

This atlas is the first comprehensive mapping of the world's languages in book format. It aims to present an up-to-date picture of the linguistic composition of the world.

K-193 Myers, N., ed. **The Gaia Atlas of Planet Management**. London: Gaia Books, 1994.

An atlas with a difference, this book is divided into seven topics (land, ocean, elements, evolution, humankind, civilization, and management) that are examined from three perspectives: potential as a sustainable resource, crises, and management alternatives. An environmentalists' guide to geographic dishonor and disaster (achieved or pending) is provided.

K-194 Kidron, Michael, and Ronald Segal. **The State of the World Atlas**. New rev. 5th ed. London: Penguin, 2000.

The latest edition of the highly graphic social atlas of the world. This atlas has been one of the most thought-provoking examples of cartographic publication for many years, with graphics that are by turns moody, garish, and in-your-face.

Topics covered include people, global economy, work, politics, society, and sustaining the Earth. Author, title, and publisher vary for previous editions.

K-195 **National Geographic Atlas of World History**. Washington, DC: National Geographic Society, 1997.

Surprisingly few maps enhance this timeline of world historical events explained through essays, art, and photographs.

K-196 Pillsbury, Richard. **Atlas of American Agriculture: The American Cornucopia**. New York: Simon & Schuster, 1996.

This atlas is an examination of America's agricultural regions, with essays and maps. Two-thirds of the volume is organized by product; it includes a bibliography and index.

K-197 Sanders, R., and M. T. Mattson. **Growing Up in America: An Atlas of Youth in the USA**. New York: Simon & Schuster Macmillan, 1998.

Growing Up in America is an atlas with extensive text and charts that profile the lives of America's children. It includes such topics as mortality, adoption, poverty, homelessness, runaways, teen suicide, birth defects, juvenile court system, American school system, and student performance. Appendixes include sources, references, and an index.

K-198 Stephenson, Richard W., and Marianne M. McKee, eds. **Virginia in Maps: Four Centuries of Settlement, Growth, and Development**. Richmond, VA: The Library of Virginia, 2000.

Stephenson and McKee have edited a work that contains essays and superb reproductions of maps illustrating the evolution of the state of Virginia. This atlas is an excellent example of historical research.

K-199 Talbert, Richard A., ed. **Barrington Atlas of the Greek and Roman World**. Princeton, NJ: Princeton University Press, 2000.

A landmark atlas that re-creates the classical world known to the Greeks and Romans, this atlas provides ninety-nine topographic maps that cover a broad range from the British Isles to the Indian subcontinent and into North Africa. Its scales are 1:500,000 and 1:1,000,000, and it is accompanied by a *Map-by-Map Directory* on CD-ROM that provides supplemental information about each map as well as all place names. It is also available as a separate two-volume paperback publication.

K-200 **National Geographic Maps: Every Foldout Map from National Geographic Magazine on CD-ROM**. Washington, DC: National Geographic Society, 1998.

In this work eight computer laser optical discs reproduce over 500 maps, including all the supplemental maps published from 1888 until 1997. Interactive map tours and timelines provide additional information.

Electronic Data

Finding electronic data is time consuming and frustrating because data are being developed so fast and by so many players that it is difficult for a single person to keep abreast of all the potential providers. In addition, although much information is available, some free and some quite expensive, it often doesn't cover the geographic area required or isn't for the correct time period.

In general there are two ways to begin searching for electronic data: by going to a library or by trying to directly locate a federal or state agency that is producing the data. Because the federal government provides an immense amount of free electronic information on CD-ROM to depository library collections throughout the United States, it is useful to consider a local library as a primary source for information on digital spatial data. To begin a traditional library search, begin with the library's online catalog (which may very well be searchable via the Web) to identify materials the library may have in-house as well as by asking for assistance from the reference staff (this may be accomplished in person, by e-mail, or by telephone).

To locate specific federal and state agencies, it is only necessary to identify the name of the agency and search for its Web site, because most agencies have Web sites and provide varying levels of metadata (descriptive information about the data) to enable the user to determine if the information is appropriate to use. Not every agency provides information, but it is becoming more commonly available. If nothing is apparent, most sites have contact links and specific requests can be sent to the agency requesting further assistance. In addition, consortia are beginning to evolve that provide access to digital data. Try the *Geography Network* (http://www.geographynetwork.com) as a starting place.

An example of a state data site is *The Pennsylvania GeoSpatial Data Clearinghouse*, often referred to as PASDA (for Pennsylvania Spatial Data Access), at http://www.pasda.psu.edu. This site is a joint effort by many the statewide GIS professionals to make their data easily available to each other as well as to the general public. Data are continually being added from federal and state agency projects.

Geography departments and map libraries at many universities, as well as professional organizations, have Web sites that assist researchers trying to locate spatial data. Due to the fluid nature of such "publishing," it is foolish to try to produce a definitive bibliography of sites, so only a brief sample is given in this section.

In June 2000, the Map and Geography Round Table of the American Library Association posted a list of electronic sites for free geospatial data at http://www.sunysb.edu/libmap/freedata2.html. Some of the sites suggested for initial investigation were *Center for Advanced Spatial Technologies*, University of Arkansas (http://www.cast.uark.edu/local/hunt); *Map Library*, Clark University (http://maplib.clarku.edu/links.html); and *Infomine, Scholarly Internet Resource Collections*, University of California, Riverside (http://Infomine.ucr.edu).

For reaching downloadable data, try the following sites:

Ciesin (Center for International Earth Science Information Network, Columbia University), http://www.ciesin.org

GIS Data Depot, http://www.gisdatadepot.com

Directions Magazine, http://www.directionsmag.com/datacenter

UNEP/GRID (United Nations Environmental Program, Global Resource Information Database), http://grid2.cr.usgs.gov (user restrictions apply)

U.S. Census, http://www.census.gov/datasets/datalist/php3

TOOLS FOR THE MAP LIBRARIAN

Being a good map librarian includes organizing a map collection so that materials can be found as well as providing reference assistance using both traditional and electronic resources. The following materials will assist the beginner in getting started, since proper tools are necessary to do a job well.

Basic Guides

K-201   Farrell, Barbara, and Aileen Desbarats. **Guide for a Small Map Collection**. 2d ed. Ottawa, ONT: Association of Canadian Map Libraries, 1984.

Although dated and definitely pre-computer revolution, this is an excellent basic manual designed as a series of checklists. Particularly helpful to the novice who needs to focus on a particular problem quickly.

K-202   Hodgkiss, A. G., and A. F. Tatham. **Keyguide to Information Sources in Cartography**. London: Mansell, 1986.

Chapter 6, "Map Care," is of particular interest to map librarians because it discusses acquisitions, classification, and cataloging as well as reference services.

K-203   Larsgaard, Mary Lynette. **Map Librarianship: An Introduction**. 3d ed. Littleton, CO: Libraries Unlimited, 1998.

Now a classic, this provides an overall introduction to map librarianship, especially strong for acquisitions, reference, preservation, and marketing. Includes extensive bibliography.

K-204   Parry, R. B., and C. R. Perkins, eds. **The Map Library in the New Millennium**. London: Library Association Publishing, 2001.

The next classic book on map librarianship, this is a volume of essays by fourteen international authors, examining the impact of digital data and GIS on the traditional map library environment.

Cataloging

K-205   Andrew, Paige G., and M. L. Larsgaard, eds. **Maps and Related Cartographic Materials: Cataloging, Classification and Bibliographic Control**. Binghamton, NY: Haworth Press, 1999.

This collection of articles on map cataloging and classification provides practical instruction on the bibliographic control of maps, atlases, globes, aerial photographs, remote sensing images, and digital cartographic materials. Articles include abstracts, references, and examples where appropriate. This volume is indexed. It was simultaneously published as *Cataloging & Classification Quarterly*, volume 27, nos. 1/2 and 3/4 (1999).

K-206   **Cartographic Materials: A Manual of Interpretation for AACR2**. Chicago: American Library Association, 1982.

This ALA publication remains the most detailed explanation of how to interpret the AACR2 cataloging rules for maps and atlases. A greatly revised and expanded second edition is expected in 2001–2002.

K-207   Hughes, Glenda Jo Fox, and C. Demetracopoulos. **Map Cataloging Bibliography: Selectively Annotated**. (Special Publication No. 4). Washington, DC: Special Libraries Association, Geography & Map Division, 1997.

This massive collection of citations on map cataloging, some annotated, was compiled from book and journal sources and consists of nine chapters, each introduced by an essay. Four chapters are organized by chronological time period, five chapters by topic. An index to all citations is included.

K-208   **Library of Congress. Schedule G**. Washington, DC: Library of Congress, 1976.

Schedule G is the official classification schedule (the call number scheme) for maps and geographical information, developed by the Library of Congress and used by most academic libraries. A revised paper edition of *Schedule G* is expected soon.

Electronic access: An online version, available by subscription only, is included on *The Cataloger's Desktop*.

K-209   **Map Cataloging Manual**. Washington, DC: Library of Congress, 1991.

This manual still remains "the Rules" for map cataloging in the library.

Electronic Reference

No matter how large the collection or how experienced the librarian, sometimes finding the right answer requires help from other sources. The following are a few sites that will provide links to many other cartographic or geographic sites of interest.

K-210   **Geography**. URL: http://geography.about.com.

Has links to sites on all aspects of geography, including chat rooms, forums, and quizzes.

K-211   **Geography Home Page**. URL: http://geography.miningco.com/science /geography.

Has links to over 700 sites on all aspects of geography.

K-212   **Oddens List**. URL: http://oddens.geog.uu.nl/index.html.

Had over 15,000 links to cartographic sites in January 2002.

K-213 **TOWD**. URL: http://www.towd.com.
Tourism Offices Worldwide Directory site. Lists only official tourism offices, visitor bureaus, and chambers of commerce that provide free and unbiased travel information.

K-214 **Road Map Collectors Society of America**. URL: http://www.roadmaps .org/links/state-links.html.
Searchers can link to tourist bureaus from this site.

Map librarians generally work in single-librarian departments and, when they need reference help, cannot easily ask a nearby colleague for assistance. As a result, most map collections have taken advantage of the Web to post home pages that have many useful reference links. The following home pages are good examples from among the many available.

K-215 Arthur Lakes Library. Map Room. **Colorado School of Mines**. URL: http://www.mines.edu/academic/library/maproom.

K-216 **Library of Congress. Geography and Map Division**. URL: http:// lcweb.loc,gov/geogmap.

K-217 **Map Librarian's Toolbox**. URL: http://www.waml.org/maptools.html.

K-218 **Pennsylvania State University. Maps Library**. URL: http://www .libraries.psu.edu/crsweb/maps.

K-219 **University of Washington. Map Collection & Cartographic Information Services**. URL: http://www.lib.washington.edu/maps.

K-220 **University of Waterloo, University Map & Design Library**. URL: http://www.lib.uwaterloo.ca/locations/umd.html.

Professional Organizations

The following are the primary professional organizations for map librarians. Although there are a number of smaller "map-oriented" organizations and GIS or cartographic organizations that might also be of interest to map librarians, that depends on individual work assignments and/ or specific research interests.

K-221 **ACMLA (Association of Canadian Map Libraries and Archives)**. URL: http://www.sscl.uwo.ca/assoc/acml/acmla.html.
Established in 1967, ACMLA is the major professional organization for map librarians in Canada. It meets annually with CCA (Canadian Cartographic Association) and publishes a journal, the ACMLA *Bulletin*.

K-222 **ALA, MAGERT (American Library Association, Map and Geography Round Table)**. URL: http://www.sunysb.edu/libmap/magert1.htm.
Established in 1980 as a Round Table of ALA, this is a major professional group for map librarians in the United States. This group meets annually and publishes a newsletter, *Base Line,* and a semiannual refereed journal, *Meridian*.

K-223 **SLA, G&M (Special Libraries Association, Geography & Map Division)**. URL: http://www.sla.org/division/dgm/index.htm.

Established in 1941 as a Division of SLA, this was once the only map-related group for map librarians. SLA published *SLA, G&M Bulletin* for many years, but ceased publication in 1997. The group meets annually in conjunction with SLA.

K-224 **WAML (Western Association of Map Libraries)**. URL: http://www.waml.org.

Established in 1967 by U.S. and Canadian west coast map librarians, this association holds two meetings each year (spring and fall). WAML publishes *Information Bulletin*, in paper, and *Electronic News and Notes*. Occasionally it has joint meetings with ACMLA. WAML also supports the Web site *Map Librarian's Toolbox.*

K-225 **NACIS (North American Cartographic Information Society)**. URL: http://www.nacis.org.

This is a professional organization of map librarians, cartography faculty, and professional cartographers (commercial, governmental, and freelance), founded in 1980. This group meets annually and publishes the refereed journal *Cartographic Perspectives.*

K-226 **IMTA (International Map Trade Association)**. URL: http://www.maptrade.org.

This is the trade association for book and map retailers, government and commercial map producers, and anyone interested in the map trade. International and U.S. meetings are held. The *IMTA Membership Directory* is an excellent guide to map dealers, particularly useful for answering reference and acquisitions questions.

E-mail Listservs

Map librarians have a number of electronic listservs that provide timely information. Some of the better known and most frequently used ones are the following:

Maps-L

GIS4Libraries

Lis-maps

Map-Hist

Directories

K-227 **A Directory of UK Map Collections**. 4th ed. (A Map Curators' Group publication No. 5). British Cartographic Society, 2000. Online format. URL: http://www.cartography.org.uk.

This directory provides no traditional publication information; it does provide an e-mail link for updating information under the heading "Publications."

K-228 **Directory of Canadian Map Collections = Repertoire des collections Canadiennes de cartes**. 7th ed. Ottawa, ONT: Association of Canadian Map Libraries and Archives, 1999.

Bilingual (English and French) alphabetical listing by province of Canadian map collections. Includes information on staffing, days and hours of service, clientele, scope of collections, publications, and Web sites.

K-229 American Library Association, MAGERT. **Guide to U.S. Map Resources**. 2d ed. Chicago: American library Association, 1990.

K-230 Carrington, David K. **Map Collections in the United States and Canada**. 4th ed. New York: Special Libraries Association, 1985.

For many years these two directories provided the primary source of access to map collections in the United States. They are not currently up-to-date and there seems to be no interest in revising them in the near future. Apparently, access to collections through Web sites has made some directories seem less necessary than others.

Maps and Map Collecting

K-231 Lobeck, Armin K. **Things Maps Don't Tell Us: An Adventure into Map Interpretation**. Chicago: University of Chicago Press, 1993.

This reprint, originally published in 1956 by one of the nation's premier cartographers, explains what geomorphology is actually behind the cartographic techniques and symbols found on maps.

K-232 Thompson, Morris M. **Maps for America**. 3d ed. Reston, VA: U.S. Geological Survey, 1988.

This work remains the best publication the U.S. government has ever written for the general public concerning government-published cartographic materials. The first part of the publication discusses the USGS topographic maps, followed by maps and related materials by other agencies, with text and color reproduction of each cartographic type.

K-233 Manasek, Francis J. **Collecting Old Maps**. Norwich, VT: Terra Nova Press, 1998.

In this text Manasek provides serious and practical advice from a seasoned map dealer on collecting antique maps. Included is basic information on important maps and the vocabulary of the antique map trade. It is well-illustrated, with extensive appendixes (mapmakers, recommended references, glossaries, map and paper chemistry, and addresses of map societies and organizations).

K-234 Rosenthal, Jon K., and Bernice M. Rosenthal, comps. and eds. **Antique Map Price Record & Handbook for 1999–2000: Including Sea Charts, City Views, Celestrial Charts, Battle Plans and Globes**. Amherst, MA: Kimmel Publications, 2000.

This annual publication began in 1984 and lists maps available and sold by map dealers as reported by the dealers. It provides a directory of dealers, both U.S. and international (by country).

Electronic access: Internet sales from the eBay site (http://www.ebay.com) are included beginning with this volume.

NOTES

1. Alan Jenkins and David Pepper, "No Special Place for Geographers—No Place at All," *Annals of the Association of American Geographers* 78 (December 1988): 516.

2. Gilbert M. Grosvenor, *Maps, the Landscape, and Fundamental Themes in Geography* (map poster) (Washington, DC: National Geographic Society, 1986).

3. James A. Michener, "The Mature Social Studies Teacher," *Social Education* 34 (November 1970): 760–767.

4. William Pattison, "The Four Traditions of Geography," *Journal of Geography* 36 (1964): 211–216.

5. James Gordon Brewer, *The Literature of Geography: A Guide to Its Organization and Use* (London: Bingley, 1973), 39.

6. Jesse Wheeler, *Regional Geography of the World*, 3d ed. (New York: Holt, Rinehart & Winston, 1975), 39.

7. M. Visvalingam, "Cartography, GIS and maps in perspective," *Cartographic Journal* 26, no. 1 (1989): 26–32.

8. Juliana O. Muehrcke, *Map Use: Reading, Analysis, Interpretation*, 4th ed. (Madison, WI: JP Publications, 1998), x. Reprinted with permission from *Map Use*, JP Publications, PO Box 44173, Madison, WI 53719.

9. John E. Isom, "A Framework for the Geographical Meaning of Maps," paper presented at the annual meeting of the National Cartographic Information Society, NACIS XX, Knoxville, TN, October 11-14, 2000.

10. Chauncy Dennison Harris, "A Review of Six Geography Dictionaries," *Annals of the Association of American Geographers* 76 (June 1986): 258.

Communication

Christine A. Whittington

ESSAY

Definition and History of Communication As a Discipline

In the previous editions of this book, "communication" was discussed as an emerging but evolving and maturing discipline within the social sciences. Although communication as an academic discipline is still emerging, defining itself, and evolving, communication itself—defined at its most basic level as interaction through messages—is "a process fundamental to the development of humans and human society."[1]

Connections with Other Disciplines

Communication is the broadest discipline within the social sciences, providing the basis for all other areas. Without communication of some sort, psychology, economics, sociology, and many other social processes would simply not exist. In 1968, Ray L. Birdwhistell wrote in the *International Encyclopedia of the Social Sciences* that "social scientists have generally accepted the communicative process as a given and have concerned themselves primarily with its success or failure."[2] In other words, communication was something that was so pervasive that it was not understood as a discipline in itself.

In their guide to communication research, Rebecca B. Rubin, Alan M. Rubin, and Linda J. Piele define "communication" as "how people arrive at shared meanings through the interchange of messages" and that communication researchers "examine the processes by which meanings are managed . . . how people structure and interpret messages and use language and other symbol systems. . . ." They further note that "when we define it as the process through which meaning and social reality are created, many things become communication events. Political scientists, educators, business executives, linguists, poets, philosophers, scientists, historians, psychologists, sociologists, and anthropologists . . . are concerned with communication within their specific areas of inquiry. It is little wonder that no other discipline of knowledge is quite as broad as communication."[3]

Although it was not labeled as the "discipline of communication," areas of study that we now place within the field of education were matters of great concern to ancient philosophers like Aristotle, the Greek philosopher, biologist, and inventor of logic. He also analyzed, classified, and defined the two areas of study relating to communication: rhetoric and drama. More than 2,000 years before market studies and audience research emerged as subdisciplines of the field of communication, Aristotle's work on oratory, *Rhetoric*, discussed the effect of rhetoric on the emotions and techniques the speaker can use to persuade an audience.

Communication in the University Curriculum

Lectures on journalism were taught at Leipzig University in 1672, and a doctoral dissertation on "the press" was presented there in 1690, but the emergence of communication as a discipline followed the growth of mass media.[4] The first academic programs in communication were practical courses of study preparing students for careers in journalism and broadcasting. Gerbner and Schramm identify the field of communication as "an area of scholarship and research whose purpose is to contribute to the critical understanding of interpersonal and social communication and its politics as well as to the practical skills of media production."[5] In the United States, when practical communication curricula entered the academic environment, students were required to take courses in the liberal arts curriculum, including philosophy, history, and politics. As communication curricula became more traditionally academic, it began to be accepted as an academic discipline on its own rather than as a component of other disciplines. The University of Iowa approved the first doctoral dissertation in communication in 1945, and within ten years doctoral programs existed at four other large universities. By 2001 there were 163 institutions offering doctoral degrees in journalism or mass communication.[6]

Areas of Study Within Communication

Although communication is a fairly new academic discipline, there is a relative degree of agreement about the subfields, both among scholars and in reference sources. Nomenclature can vary, with journalism sometimes considered a subfield within communication and sometimes a separate department. Distinctions are a bit clearer between the fields of *communications* with an "s," which usually focuses on the technological means of communication without the human element, and communication disorders, which is a more medically oriented discipline involved with, for example, speech and hearing disorders. One interesting exception is the placement of the Communication Department at Cornell University within the College of Agriculture. As a Land Grant institution, Cornell had an obligation to educate New York residents, including those involved with farming. Because the university believed that farmers should be able to speak well in public and represent their concerns in the legislature, the discipline of communications was placed under the jurisdiction of agriculture.[7]

Current reference books and academic departments generally place the following subdisciplines within the field of communication: interpersonal communication (relationships and interactions between and among people), small group communication (communication within groups of three or more persons), language and symbolic codes (meaning and transmission of symbols), organizational communication (communication within formal structures), public communication (nonmediated public speaking such as rhetoric and public address), and mass communication (communicated through mediated channels such as television or print media).[8]

Research Methods and Scholarly Communication

As communication took its place within the academic liberal arts curriculum, its students and faculty began to develop research interests as well as focusing on its more practical aspects. Communication students now use many of the research methods used in other areas of the social sciences, such as surveys and sampling. In fact the survey has become a well-known technique for judging the commercial success of mass communication media such as television and radio. Communication researchers perhaps use techniques such as interviewing, oral history, and narrative more than some other disciplines within the social sciences (with the exception of anthropology and folklore). As in other areas of the social sciences, communication researchers exchange information through electronic discussion groups, e-mail, and at conferences of national and international organizations. Also as for other disciplines, the availability of electronic databases, full-text resources, and other information on the World Wide Web has made communication research richer and more complex.

Selection of Sources

Many of the resources listed in previous editions are also included in this one. Those dropped include outdated references that have been superseded by other sources, periodical indexes or annuals that have ceased publication, and print indexes that have evolved into electronic formats. Included here are a few older, out-of-print sources that are useful for historical information or that are so well known as classics in the field that students and researchers in the field of communication should know of their existence and importance.

Because communication is indeed the broadest discipline, difficult decisions had to be made about including excellent reference sources in its subdisciplines. In general, reference sources are included that met criteria for excellence if they covered the subdiscipline broadly or covered major components of the subdiscipline. For example, sources on advertising and market studies that did not have a communication component (e.g., a connection to the mass media) were excluded. Reference books on advertising expenditures included in previous editions were also excluded because of their specialized nature and because of the appearance of more current, newer publications. English-language publications predominate, and arrangement is by content of the reference source and how researchers are likely to use it, regardless of its format.

RESEARCH GUIDES AND BIBLIOGRAPHIES

General

L-1 American Communication Association. **Communication Studies Center**. American Communication Association, 2000- . Continuous. Online format. URL: http://www.uark.edu/~aca/acastudiescenter.html.

The *Communication Studies Center* Web site is a centralized index of Internet resources on communication research and practice. A guide to cybersources, the *Communication Studies Center* is organized into subfields that reflect current society and technology: business communication, communication education technologies, computer mediated communication, gender and communication, film studies, language and linguistics, research methods, rhetorics of science and technology, statistical and data archives, social scientific communication research, independent media centers, and mass media and culture. Some categories are further subdivided; for example, "mass media and culture" includes links to pages on mass media, culture, film/television, and radio. Pages are signed by their creators, and links are annotated to a greater or lesser degree, depending on the creator and the subject.

L-2   Block, Eleanor S., and James K. Bracken. **Communication and the Mass Media: A Guide to the Reference Literature**. (Reference Sources in the Humanities series). Englewood, CO: Libraries Unlimited, 1991.

Now ten years old, Block and Bracken is still the most comprehensive and thoroughly annotated guide to the literature of communication. Sources selected include those published after 1970 that are relevant to communication curricula at colleges and universities in the United States, including courses in communication theory, interpersonal and small group communication, organizational communication, mass communication, speech and rhetoric, applied linguistics, and international and intercultural communication, as well as affiliated disciplines such as public relations, journalism, and advertising. The guide includes both general and specialized sources such as reference materials on topics such as religious broadcasting, stereotyping in television, historical rhetoric, and satellite communication.

The guide is organized according to publication type, including bibliographies (e.g., research guides, bibliographies and bibliographic series, annual reviews); dictionaries, encyclopedias, and handbooks; indexes and abstracts; biographical sources; library catalogs; directories and yearbooks; online and CD-ROM databases; core periodicals; research centers and archives; and societies and associations. Author/title and subject indexes, as well as an appendix listing database service suppliers and vendors, are provided.

L-3   Gitter, A. George, and Robert Grunin. **Communication: A Guide to Information Sources**. (Psychology Information Guide series, vol. 3). Detroit: Gale, 1980.

For many years, Gitter and Grunin's work was the primary bibliography for the general field of communication. It is divided into chapters on communication research, international communication, interpersonal communication, political communication, attitude change, mass communication, and reference works. Now more than twenty years old, Gitter and Grunin is useful for its coverage of journal articles in the field through the 1970s. Brief annotations to some books are also included. Author, title, and subject indexes are provided.

L-4   Rubin, Rebecca B., Alan M. Rubin, and Linda J. Piele. **Communication Research: Strategies and Sources**. 5th ed. Belmont, CA: Wadsworth Thomson Learning, 1999.

Although this work is intended to be a textbook for undergraduate and graduate communication research courses, it is also an excellent guide to reference sources in all subject areas within the discipline and sources in other fields (e.g., psychology, law) that are useful to communication students. The authors define communication to include interpersonal communication, small-group communication, language and symbolic codes (e.g., semiotics, nonverbal communication), organizational communication, public communication (e.g., rhetoric, public address, performance), and mass communication (journalism, broadcasting, film, popular culture).

Communication Research is divided into three major sections covering communication research strategies, sources, and processes. Included in these sections is information on such topics as searching the communication literature, using the Internet for communication research, communication periodicals, and designing the communication research project. The section "Communication Research Sources" serves as a guide to the literature, updated with references to Web sites and electronic databases. Other sections of *Communication Research* also include references to information sources. For example, "Structure of Professional Communication Organizations" includes descriptions of associations such as the National Communication Association, with references to their Web sites, activities, and publications. Wadsworth's Communication Café Web site (http://www.communication.wadsworth.com), intended to update this guide,[9] includes links to online resources.

Specialized

L-5 Cates, Jo A. **Journalism: A Guide to the Reference Literature**. Englewood, CO: Libraries Unlimited, 1997.

Jo Cates was the founding director and Chief Librarian for The Poynter Institute for Media Studies in St. Petersburg, Florida, and is now Director of Research for Entertainment Enterprises. Indispensable since publication of its first edition in 1990, Cates's guide is a "selected, annotated bibliography and reference guide to the English-language reference literature of print and broadcast journalism" from the late 1960s to 1995. The second edition's 789 entries are arranged in sections on bibliographies, encyclopedias, dictionaries, indexes and abstracts, commercial databases and Internet sources, biographical sources, directories and yearbooks, handbooks and manuals, stylebooks, catalogs, and core periodicals. It also includes information about research centers, archives, media institutes, societies, and associations. Cates's annotations are thorough, insightful, and pithy, enriched by an insider's knowledge of sources like the *Associated Press Stylebook and Libel Manual* and Brigham's *History and Bibliography of American Newspapers, 1690–1820.*

L-6 Sterling, Christopher H., James K. Bracken, and Susan M. Hill, eds. **Mass Communications Research Resources: An Annotated Guide**. Mahwah, NJ: Lawrence Erlbaum Associates, 1998.

This research guide is intended to be a "road map for researchers who need to find specific information about American mass communication as expeditiously as possible," including information on 1,400 of the "most important and useful" resources on American mass communication. Newer electronic media as well as newspaper, magazine, radio, television, and cable are within the guide's scope. It also includes resources on mass communication history, technology, economics, audience research, and policy. It complements Cates (L-5) in that it includes references to primary sources, organizations, documents, reports, secondary books, and electronic sources as well as reference literature. The book is arranged in topical chapters, including history, technology, industry and economics, research and audiences, and policy and regulation.

L-7 National Press Club. Eric Friedheim Library. **Reporter's Internet Resources**. 2000- . Continuous. Online format. URL: http://npc.press.org/what/library/reporter.htm.

L-8 Guss, Dave. **Webgator: Investigative Resources on the Web**. 1996- . Continuous. Online format. URL: http://www.webgator.org/.

L-9 Foundation for American Communications (FACSNET). **FACSNET**. 1996- . Continuous. URL: http://www.facsnet.org/.

L-10 Tudor, Dean. **MEGASOURCES: Surfing for Information and Journalism Resources**. 1994- . Continuous. Online format. URL: http://www.ryerson.ca/journal/megasources.html.

L-11 Poynter Institute. **NELSON: The Search Tool for Journalists**. URL: http://www.nelsonsearch.org/index.htm.

L-12 Investigate Reporters and Editors. **Reporter.org**. 2001- . Continuous. Online format. URL: http://www.reporter.org/.

Although varied in arrangement and focus, these six Web sites are all gateways to a wide variety of Internet resources for communication and journalism students and professional journalists. *Reporters' Internet Resources* is arranged according to the standard reporting format of "who, why, where, what, and when." *Webgator* focuses on resources for investigative reporting. *FACSNET* is especially useful for journalists working with issues regarding education: business and economics, science and technology, and environment and land use. Compiled by Dean Tudor, journalism professor at Ryerson Polytechnic University in Toronto, *MEGASOURCES* is a gateway to a massive amount of information for journalists, notable for its Canadian emphasis. NELSON is a specialized search engine for journalists that searches several hundred news, journalism-related, and beat-oriented sites on the Web. *Reporter.org* includes links to organizations and resources plus *News on the Net, The Beat Source Guide*, arranged by "beats" such as crime and healthcare, and *Global Beat* for international journalists.

Resources linked to these gateways include official government agencies and disseminators of statistics (Federal Emergency Management Association, Centers for Disease Control and Prevention, the White House), advocacy groups (Electronic Freedom Frontier, Christian Coalition), and other organizations and services (American College of Forensic Examiners, Experts.com: the Online Expert Registry).

L-13 Duffy, Bernard K., and Halford Ross Ryan. **American Orators Before 1900: Critical Studies and Sources**. New York: Greenwood Press, 1987.

L-14 Duffy, Bernard K., and Halford R. Ryan. **American Orators of the Twentieth Century: Critical Studies and Sources**. New York: Greenwood Press, 1987.

Speech communication students frequently need to find information about the rhetoric of a particular person, the texts of the person's speeches, information about the context of the speech, and critical analyses. It can be time consuming and frustrating for students to find this information in general biographical sources, especially if the person is a public figure known for many other things (e.g., Abraham Lincoln, Henry Kissinger). These two volumes include articles on American orators: their historical context; their training; their causes; the social, political, and legal effects of their rhetoric; their contributions to the theory or practice of rhetoric; and a critical examination of the person's rhetoric, including style, delivery, preparation, and the use (or not) of speechwriters. Each entry includes references to information sources, such as research collections and collected speeches (e.g., *Great Debates in American History, Congressional Record*), critical studies, and bibliographies. A chronology of major speeches includes references to the collections or publications in which they can be found. Each volume also includes "Basic Research Sources in American Public Address" and a glossary of rhetorical terms such as *jeremiad* and *call and response*.

DICTIONARIES AND ENCYCLOPEDIAS

General

L-15 Barnouw, Erik, ed.-in-chief. **International Encyclopedia of Communication**. 4 vols. New York: Oxford University Press, 1989.

Possibly the single most important reference work to have appeared in the field of communication, this set includes approximately 550 articles covering all areas of communication. Although relatively comprehensive, the depth of treatment of individual topics is not consistent. Volume 4 includes a topical guide that lists articles under thirty-one broad categories, including international communication, advertising and public relations, media, political communication, and nonverbal communication. It also includes a detailed subject index of more than 15,000 entries. This joint publication of Oxford University Press and the Annenberg School of Communications at the University of Pennsylvania has become a standard source for the field.

L-16 DeVito, Joseph A. **The Communication Handbook: A Dictionary**. New York: Harper & Row, 1986.

The Communication Handbook provides essays of several pages and extended entries on major concepts and brief definitions of more specialized terms. Arrangement is alphabetical, but the dictionary includes a "Guide to Selected Essays" by topic. Topics include interpersonal communication, language and verbal messages, mass media, nonverbal communication, organizational communication, persuasion, public speaking, and small group communication. Individual articles are listed under each topic. For example, under the topic "Nonverbal Communication" are listed articles on *Body Type*, *Color Communication*, and *FAST (facial affect scoring technique)*. Topics with shorter definitions include scholarly, practical, and slang terms such as *Prisoner's Dilemma*, *Idiot Card*, *Code Switching*, *Cryptography*, *Sin License*, *Cuneiform*, *Culture Shock*, and *Nonce Word*. Some definitions—both short and long—include bibliographic references. Although this dictionary is older than the others listed here, it is useful for its thematic articles on communication concepts and coverage of more specialized terms that may not be included elsewhere.

L-17 Hollis, Daniel Webster. **The ABC-CLIO Companion to the Media in America**. Santa Barbara, CA: ABC-Clio, 1995.

Hollis's encyclopedia of multimedia history focuses on topics in the history of media in America, including media organs (e.g., newspapers, periodicals, networks, organizations) and biography. It also includes articles especially relevant to American students and researchers, such as *presidential debates*, *TV Guide*, *tabloids*, *space program*, *muckrakers*, and *talk media*. Chronological coverage begins with the colonial period and extends to the present. A chronology begins with the British Licensing Act of 1662, which allowed censorship of printing, and ends with the media frenzy surrounding the O. J. Simpson murder trial in 1995. The thorough articles include "see also" references and suggestions for further reading. Information on the history of magazines, newspapers, and other media organs is notoriously hard to find, and articles such as *Chicago Defender*, *Time*, and *Louisville Journal-Courier* are most welcome. The guide includes a chronology and an index to terms discussed within articles. Hollis complements Blanchard (L-19), which has an international perspective.

L-18 Watson, James, and Anne Hill. **A Dictionary of Communication and Media Studies**. 5th ed. New York: Oxford University Press, 1997.

Watson and Hill's latest edition includes up-to-date definitions. This dictionary offers more diverse terms and thorough definitions than do some of the other dictionaries listed in this section. Its British emphasis accounts for terms like British government reports (*Longford Committee Report on Pornography*, *Lindup Committee Report on Data Protection*) and the brevity or omission of some U.S.-related terms such as *Federal Communication Commission* and *Arbitron*. The dictionary offers excellent definitions of communication theories and terms relating to them (*postmodernism*, *text*, *discourse*) as well as technical terms (*footprint* in reference to communication satellites, *bandwidth*). Some definitions include bibliographic references, and some are accompanied by illustrations. This edition includes a chronology of media events, key moments in mass media, and many new entries.

Specialized

L-19 Blanchard, Margaret A. **History of the Mass Media in the United States: An Encyclopedia**. Chicago: Fitzroy Dearborn, 1998.

Blanchard's historical encyclopedia is an important contribution to mass media history. It includes signed articles by distinguished contributors encompassing both the informational and the recreational functions of mass media, defined as advertising, books, broadcasting in general, cable, magazines, motion pictures, newspapers, photojournalism, public relations, radio, and television. Coverage begins in 1690, when the first newspaper was founded in Boston, and ends in 1990, with a few exceptions (e.g., *Internet*, *Persian Gulf War*). Entertainment articles tend to be shorter than those "on the traditional media for the communication of ideas that influence the body politic" such as the historical overviews *Mass Media and the Antiwar Movement* and *Mass Media and Tobacco Products*. Some entertainment topics are discussed within more general articles. For example, soap operas are discussed in the articles on *Radio Entertainment* and *Television Entertainment*, and all comic strips, from the "Yellow Kid" to "Pogo" and "Doonesbury," are treated in a one-page article on *Comic Strips*. The encyclopedia also includes articles on the technological, legal, legislative, economic, and political developments that have affected or have been affected by the media; articles on major organizations and institutions; concepts; and theories. It excludes biographies of many—though not all—historical figures, leaving this function to major biographical dictionaries.

Each article includes "see also" references and suggestions for further reading. Many excellent photographs and illustrations enhance the encyclopedia. An index helps readers find information on topics within other articles, such as a discussion of George Carlin's "Seven Filthy Words" monologue and the resulting Supreme Court case (*FCC V. Pacifica*) in the articles on *Broadcast Regulation*, *Censorship of Broadcasting*, and *Decency Issues in Electronic Media*.

L-20   Ellmore, Terry R. **NTC's Mass Media Dictionary**. Lincolnwood, IL: National Textbook, 1995.

L-21   Weiner, Richard. **Webster's New World Dictionary of Media and Communications**. Rev. and updated ed. New York: Webster's New World, 1996.

Both Ellmore and Weiner offer concise, up-to-date, definitions for terms in all areas of mass media. They are spirited and practical, rather than theoretical, in orientation. The dictionaries are similar in purpose. Ellmore was "written to aid writers, broadcasters, publishers, film and video makers, printers, advertisers, . . . as well as teachers, students, and others interested in the vocabulary of the mass media." Weiner defines terms "essential to several million communications professionals" from all fields of media and communications (public relations, advertising, broadcasting, film, and newspapers and other publications). Although both provide excellent coverage of general and specialized terms that communications professionals might encounter in their daily work, they don't entirely overlap in the areas of slang, jargon, and verbal shorthand. Both define *hack* ("a writer hired to do commercial or routine work" or "a hired writer; usually willing to accept any assignment for money"), but only Ellmore notes that hacks are also called *word jobbers* or *word slingers*. Only Weiner defines *dis* ("to gossip or defame"), and *four hankie movie* (a film that "excels in its tearfulness"). Definitions in both are concise and to the point, for example, "*lhp*" (left-hand page) and "*eow*" (every other week).

L-22   Museum of Broadcast Communications. **Encyclopedia of Television**. 3 vols. Chicago: Fitzroy Dearborn, 1997.

The Museum of Broadcast Communication was founded in Chicago in 1987. The constant use and expansion of the Radio and Television Archive in the Museum's A. C. Nielsen, Jr., Research Center led to the publication of the landmark *Encyclopedia of Television*. The editor, Horace Newcomb of University of Texas at Austin, and an advisory committee selected 1,000 topics to address, focusing on English-speaking, television-producing countries. The encyclopedia includes articles on countries (Australia, Canada, Egypt, Russia) actors and television personalities (Groucho Marx, Jack Paar), television programs (*Gunsmoke, Candid Camera, Twilight Zone*), and other topics (*Reality Programming, Quiz Show Scandals, Sexual Orientation and Television, Religion on Television*). Articles are signed and include suggestions for further reading and, as appropriate, cast lists and programming history. The articles make fascinating reading, addressing the significance of each topic as well as just the facts, for example the enduring product development that came out of *The Flintstones* (vitamins, cereal), Ed Sullivan's "ability to capitalize on teenage obsession" by introducing rock and roll to his variety show, and the inclusion of important issues of legitimate use of violence, treatment of minorities, and the power of religious commitment addressed by America's longest-running western, *Gunsmoke*.

Electronic access: The encyclopedia is also available online at http://www.mbcnet.org /ETV/nav/Encyclopediatv.htm. The A. C. Nielsen, Jr., Research Center also has an online catalog, accessible at http://www.mbcnet.org/archives/archivepages/researchp1.htm.

L-23 Brown, Les. **Encyclopedia of Television**. 3d ed. Detroit: Gale, 1992.

Brown's work is intended to be a "one-stop source for information on the television industry . . . both on screen and behind the scenes." It provides relatively brief entries on the people, events, and programs that shaped television history. This latest edition features approximately 900 new entries as well as revisions of previous entries, a general subject index, and an expanded bibliography. It also includes an appendix of statistical tables covering topics such as worldwide TV advertising expenditures, Super Bowl rating history, and network subscriber counts. The third edition of this standard work is now nearly ten years old, and some of the articles seem a bit dated, or at least not as fresh as they did ten years ago (Max Headroom, MTV/VH-1), and the reader finds *The Real McCoys* when looking for *Reality TV*, and *Cop Rock* instead of *Cops*.

L-24 Reed, Robert M., and Maxine K. Reed. **The Encyclopedia of Television, Cable, and Video**. New York: Van Nostrand Reinhold, 1994.

The Reeds note that "although television, cable, and video use different technology to reach an audience, they have the same objective—communication," and also share production techniques, engineering equipment, and distribution processes. Their encyclopedia includes more than 3,100 entries within ten areas relating to electronic media: advertising; agencies, associations, companies, and unions; broadcasting and cablecasting; educational and corporate communications; engineering; general terms and processes; government and legal; home video; production; and programming. Terms defined include *pay per view (PPV)*, *PEG* (i.e., public access) *channels*, *VHF television stations*, *infomercials*, *docudrama*, *video superstore*, and *shrinkage* (loss of inventory over a period of time in the home video retail industry). The encyclopedia includes a handy list of abbreviations and acronyms, including BTA ("best time available") and EBS ("emergency broadcasting system").

L-25 Slide, Anthony. **The Television Industry: A Historical Dictionary**. Westport, CT: Greenwood Press, 1991.

Slide indicates that this book is about " 'things' rather than people," a "what's what" of television industry history offering 1,000 entries on production companies, distributors, organizations, genres, and technical terms. This is a good source to go to for hard-to-find historical information on networks (A&E Cable Network, Nickelodeon), stations (KUHT, the first educational television station in the United States), programming (the comedy troupe Second City's SCTV), corporations (Westinghouse broadcasting operations), and resources (the UCLA Film and Television Archive, the NBC Radio Archive at the Museum of Broadcasting). There is some coverage of foreign television. Many entries include brief bibliographies, and there is a bibliography of reference books about television.

L-26 Hudson, Robert V. **Mass Media: A Chronological Encyclopedia of Television, Radio, Motion Pictures, Magazines, Newspapers, and Books in the United States**. New York: Garland, 1987.

Hudson presents a chronological compilation of historical facts about mass media in the United States from "The Founding Period" (1638–1764) to "Economic and Legal Challenges" (1974–1985). Synopses of significant events, achievements, people, and dates are provided in the context of the development of books, broadsides, pamphlets, newspapers, magazines, motion pictures, radio, and television. It is arranged within time periods reflecting U.S. history (e.g., New Nation, 1783–1799; Cold War Period, 1946–1953). Within those periods, a year-by-year listing of entries is provided, divided by medium (magazines, radio and television, etc.). Entries vary in length and are dense with facts, dates, statistics, and citations to court cases. Some entries, such as the famous libel case *New York Times v. Sullivan* (1964), have substantive entries., Others are brief, including references to the first broadcasts of the *Batman* and *Mission Impossible* television shows (both in 1966) and "man's first landing on the moon a live telecast" (July 20, 1969). In addition to the chronology, Hudson includes "Trends in Mass Media History" and "Selected Firsts in Mass Media." A detailed index leads readers from subjects like "drive-in theaters" or "Sesame Street" to the appropriate entry in the chronology.

L-27 Givens, David. **Nonverbal Dictionary of Gestures, Signs, and Body Language Cues**. Spokane, WA: Center for Nonverbal Studies. 1998- . Continuous. Online format. URL: http://members.aol.com/nonverbal2/diction1.htm#The NONVERBAL DICTIONARY.

From *Adam's-Apple-Jump* to *Zygomatic Smile*, the *Nonverbal Dictionary* discusses a variety of ways in which people (and some nonhumans) communicate nonverbally and also supplies bibliographic references to the work of "anthropologists, archaeologists, biologists, linguists, psychiatrists, psychologists, semioticians, and others who have studied human communication from a scientific point of view." Many of the entries in this online dictionary are fascinating ones that users are not likely to find elsewhere easily, at least not so thoroughly and with references. They include gestures; body movement; food; clothing; body language; and aroma, touch, and taste cues (*high heel, apocrine odor, bite, body adornment, arm cross, lawn display* and five different levels of *love signals*). Among the most interesting entries are those for consumer products like *Coca Cola* ("a hand-held consumer product with incredible presence in the media") and *Arpege* perfume ("a classic consumer product for the nose"). It not only mentions all the reasons the *Barbie Doll* is a contemporary icon, but some we had not thought of (pointed feet like the Willendorf Venus), and provides references as well. The *Nonverbal Dictionary* is a fascinating source that will become even more useful as entries are added.

L-28 Burton, Gideon. **Silva Rhetoricae: The Forest of Rhetoric**. [Provo, UT]: Brigham Young University. 1996- . Continuous. Online format. URL: http://humanities.byu.edu/rhetoric/silva.htm.

Silva Rhetoricae is a guide to the terms and concepts of classical and renaissance rhetoric. Its title comes from the fact that "it is difficult to see the forest (the big picture) of rhetoric because of the trees (the hundreds of Greek and Latin terms naming figures of speech, etc.) within rhetoric." It includes two sections: subject "trees" for major categories and concepts (*audience, persuasive appeals of logos, pathos, and ethos*) and "flowers" for specific terms (*hyperbole, onomatopoeia*). A scholarly work, *Silva Rhetoricae* provides the name of each term in English and Greek (modern and ancient). Each "tree" entry provides a definition, a sample rhetorical analysis in terms of the concept being defined, related figures, and connections to other aspects of rhetoric.

L-29 Enos, Theresa. **Encyclopedia of Rhetoric and Composition: Communication from Ancient Times to the Age**. New York: Garland, 1996.

This dictionary includes 467 scholarly articles signed by 288 contributors on all aspects of rhetoric ("the strategic presentation of ideas and choice of language") from the classical period to the present, including its connections with tangential disciplines such as anthropology, psychology, and philosophy. Articles cover key rhetorical concepts (*persuasion, public speaking, the philosophy of rhetoric*), the theories and contributions of rhetoricians and scholars of rhetoric from all periods (*Sappho, Umberto Eco*), types of rhetoric (*homily, liturgy*), and the influence rhetoric has had on individual fields of scholarship (*Postmodernism, Environmental Rhetoric*). Each article includes references for further reading, and there is a comprehensive index.

DIRECTORIES

L-30 **Communication Serials: An International Guide to Periodicals in Communication, Popular Culture, and the Performing Arts**. Virginia Beach: SovaComm, 1992–1993.

This source covers more than 2,700 English-language popular and scholarly communication-related serials dating from the early 1800s to the early 1990s in such categories as advertising, cable television, communication law, communication research, instructional communication, magazines, marketing, public relations, and telecommunications. Although the book is now almost ten years old, it is still useful for its annotations, which provide information on the serial's history, audience, objectives, subtitles and title changes, dates, historical publishing patterns, departmental features ("Under Hedda's Hat" as a feature of *Photoplay*), publication schedule, supplements, ISSN, and abstracting and indexing sources. For example, the magazine *Hollywood* ("Official organ of the Hollywood Foreign Press Correspondents Association") is described as "one of the most unusual serials of Hollywood, containing stories on film, the foreign press corps, local Arabic news, world developments of Lebanon, religion, and other subjects that one might not expect in a Hollywood magazine." Each entry also includes five typical article titles. A typical issue of *Hollywood*, for example, included articles on Arabic news from Jacksonville, Florida, and a reprint of a 1947 interview with Father Divine. The list appears in alphabetical order, but numerous indexes, including by abstracting/indexing service, by association, by columnists, by subject (using broad headings), by publishers, and by country of origin, are provided. This is an impressive scholarly effort that should prove of value to communication researchers generally and particularly to those conducting historical communication research.

L-31   **Burrelle's Media Directory. Vol. 1: Daily Newspapers, Vol. 2: Non-Daily Newspapers, Vol. 3: Broadcast Media: Radio, Vol. 4: Broadcast Media: Television and Cable, Vol. 5: Magazines and Newsletters**. Livingston, NJ: Burrelle's Information Services, 1995- . Annual.

L-32   **Working Press of the Nation. Vol. 1: Newspaper Directory, Vol. 2: Magazines and Internal Publications, Vol. 3: TV and Radio Directory**. New Providence, NJ: R. R. Bowker, 1945- . Annual.

L-33   **Gale Directory of Publications and Broadcast Media**. 4 vols. Detroit: Gale Research, 1869- . Annual.

L-34   **Willings Press Guide**. 2 vols. London: Willing Service, 1874- . Annual. Available on CD-ROM.

L-35   **Benn's Media Directory**. 3 vols. Tonbridge, England: United Business Media, 1846- . Annual.

These five multivolume annual publications are directories of print, broadcast, and electronic mass media. *Burrelle's Media Directory* is the most comprehensive directory for the United States, including print and broadcast media. *Working Press of the Nation* also provides U.S. coverage, focusing on news media. *Willings Press Guide* and *Benn's Media Directory* both have volumes for the United Kingdom and for other countries.

Burrelle's directory is intended to be used by journalists and business and public relations professionals. It lists more than 2,100 daily and 10,300 non-daily newspapers arranged by state, with indexes of staff names by beat. The radio and television/cable volumes include information on 1,200 radio stations, 1,700 television stations, cable systems, local radio and television station programming, national radio and television network and syndicated programming, radio and television program providers, and network affiliations. The volume on magazines lists more than 13,500 magazines and newsletters, including consumer magazines, trade publications, professional publications, and college magazines. Subscriptions to *Burrelle's* include free updates available on the Web.

Currently, *Working Press of the Nation* consists of three volumes: *Newspaper Directory*, *Magazines and Internal Publications Directory*, and *TV and Radio Directory*. The newspaper directory covers 8,268 daily, weekly, special interest, religious, ethnic, and foreign-language newspapers; feature syndicates; newspaper-distributed magazines, and 130 news services, feature syndicates, and photo services. It provides contact information, circulation, frequency, wire services, material requirements, deadlines, personnel, and area population. It also includes indexes of newspapers by ADI and editorial personnel by subject. The magazines and internal publications directory provides information on more than 5,700 magazines, grouped by subject areas. It also covers more than 2,500 corporate, government, association, and organization publications. The TV and radio directory covers more than 14,000 television and radio stations, 230 networks, and more than 11,000 local programs. Among other information, it includes station area population, ownership, network affiliation, wire services used, and management and programming personnel.

Journalism librarian Jo Cates calls the *Gale Directory* the "granddaddy of periodical directories." It was first published by N. W. Ayer and Son and is known to veteran librarians as the *Ayer Directory* of publications. It has had many variations of that title since its initiation, becoming the *Gale Directory* in 1987. The *Gale Directory* is especially useful for its listings of newspapers, periodicals, and radio and television stations by city. Arrangement is by state, then city, with both print and broadcast media listed under the cities in which they originate.

Each entry for print media includes publication title, company, contact information, a description, date founded, frequency, print method and other physical characteristics, key personnel, ISSN, subscription rates, advertisement rates, circulation, and e-mail and Web addresses. Entries for broadcast media also include format (commercial or public), network affiliates, operating hours, cities served, and Areas of Dominant Influence (ADI). *The Gale Directory* also includes a master name and keyword index, a publishers index, subject indexes, and a regional market index arranged by publication or broadcast type.

The United Kingdom volume of *Willings* indexes periodicals by title and classification (e.g., music trade, transportation) and newspapers by frequency and area. The major section of the book contains entries for all media arranged alphabetically. Each entry includes the publisher, address, e-mail address, ISSN, format (e.g., print, electronic), frequency, price, circulation, a summary of the content, language, target audience, and advertising rates. A section on broadcast media includes television, cable and satellite, radio, news sources, online services, and hospital and student radio. Other features include a list of UK publishers, advertising representatives, and broadcasters. The international volume offers the same arrangement, except that in the major section of the book print media are listed by country first, then alphabetically.

Benn's has volumes for the *United Kingdom* (volume 1), *Europe* (volume 3), and *World* (Americas, Africa, Asia, Australasia) (volume 3). Formerly titled *Benn's Press Directory*, it became *Benn's Media Directory* in 1986 (volume 134) when it began to cover media and electronic publications. It includes sections on international and in-flight media, media Web sites, and subject classifications of periodicals. The major parts of the *International* and *World* volumes are arranged by country, and include useful contacts, newspapers, consumer periodicals, business and professional periodicals, and broadcasting. The *United Kingdom* volume provides detailed coverage, including national, regional, and local newspapers, periodicals, and media services. The broadcasting section covers the BBC, commercial television, radio, and electronic publishing.

L-36 United Nations. Department of Public Information. **World Media Handbook**. New York: United Nations, 1995.

World Media Handbook includes basic statistical data for countries that host or are served by United Nations Information Centres and Services (UNICS) and United Nations Development Programme (UNDP). Statistics include population data; student population data; illiteracy rates; and telephone, newspaper, and broadcasting data. A maximum of sixteen major newspapers and twenty magazines, with standard directory information for each, are listed for every country. Also included is a list of major journalism/mass communication education and training programs from around the world, most at universities. It also lists participation in UN organizations from 1946 to the present.

L-37 **Broadcasting & Cable Yearbook**. New Providence, NJ: R. R. Bowker, 1935- . Annual.

This successor to *Broadcasting Cablecasting Yearbook* and other title variations is an important directory of statistical and legal information for the broadcasting industry. Currently a one-volume source, it contains ten sections: industry overview, television, cable, radio, satellites and other services, programming services, technological services, brokers and professional services, associations and events, and law and regulation. It also includes a brief overview of the broadcasting industry and the "year in review" for broadcasting and cable. Sections on television and cable include full station listings arranged by state and city, with indexes by call letter index, maps, and marketplace statistics. These sections also include listings for special topics such as "College, University, and School-Owned

Television Stations" and radio stations by format, so that users can find, for example, a country radio station in Bar Harbor, Maine. Listings for services (e.g., satellites, programming) provide standard directory information, including e-mail addresses and URLs where available. The section "Law and Regulation and Government Agencies" includes a directory of FCC staff, FCC regulations, industry professional codes, and lists of government agencies of interest to the broadcasting and cable industries.

L-38 **Standard Rate and Data Services**. Skokie, IL: SRDS, [various dates]. Most publications are monthly.

Standard Rate and Data Services (SRDS) produces more than thirty directories and databases, including the following:

> *Business Publication Advertising Source*
>
> *Canadian Advertising Rates and Data*
>
> *Circulation*
>
> *Community Publication Advertising Source*
>
> *Consumer Magazine Advertising Source*
>
> *Direct Marketing List Source*
>
> *Hispanic Media and Market Source*
>
> *Interactive Advertising Source*
>
> *Mexican Audiovisual/Print Media Rates and Data*
>
> *Newspaper Advertising Source*
>
> *Out-of-Home Advertising Source*
>
> *Print Media Production Source*
>
> *Radio Advertising Source*
>
> *Technology Media Source*
>
> *TV and Cable Source*

These sources are designed for ease in placing advertising. Although there is some variation among the different SRDS sources, they generally provide market data summaries, advertising rates for specific types and sizes of ads (e.g., inserts, color), special feature issues policies, and deadlines. *Circulation* provides some unique information about circulation and penetration of major daily newspapers in metropolitan areas, counties, and individual newspapers.

Electronic access: Available online to subscribers at www.srds.com.

L-39 **O'Dwyer's Directory of Corporate Communications**. New York: J. R. O'Dwyer, 1976- . Annual.

L-40 **O'Dwyer's Directory of Public Relations Firms**. New York: J. R. O'Dwyer, 1960- . Annual.

O'Dwyer's Directory of Corporate Communications provides information on larger corporations' and trade associations' corporate communication or public relations departments. For some companies, it lists outside public relations counsel in addition to the standard directory information. *O'Dwyer's Directory of Public Relations Firms* is a comprehensive directory of more than 2,300 U.S. public relations firms and public relations departments of advertising agencies. Also included is information on approximately 750 public relations firms in seventy-seven foreign countries. In addition to standard directory information such as address, phone and fax numbers, e-mail addresses and URLs, and number of employees, the main entry for each firm lists firm branches and major clients. Also included are rankings of public relations firms by net fees, with breakdowns by geographic area and specialization.

Public Relations Firms includes indexes by type of service (e.g., media monitoring, video production), specialization (e.g., beauty and fashion, political candidates), geographical indexes, and a cross-reference index from the name of the client to PR firm so that the user can discover, for example, that Eddie Bauer works with Edelman Public Relations Worldwide.

L-41   Plunkett, Jack W. **Plunkett's Entertainment & Media Industry Almanac, 2000–2001**. Houston, TX: Plunkett Research, 2000.

The first part of this business-oriented media directory includes an overview of the entertainment and media industry, trends affecting the industry (e.g., digitization, deregulation), new technology, new media, budgeting, careers, and industry contacts. Industries include film and video; music; radio and television; cable and satellite; books and magazines;, online publishing; and sports, gaming, and gambling. The second part consists of summaries of the "Entertainment and Media 400," public U.S. companies chosen for their dominance of the entertainment and media field. Examples of such companies are America Online, Bureau of National Affairs, and entertainment companies like Churchill Downs and Cineplex. Information in each company capsule includes business activities, types of business, brands, divisions or affiliates, growth plans or special features, competitive advantage, salaries and benefits, sales and profits, and "other thoughts" such as whether there are women or minority officers or directors. The company profile section includes indexes by industry rank, geographic location, subsidiary or brand name, and a list of companies noted as "hot spots for advancement for women and minorities." This almanac will remain useful as long as it is kept current. The first edition was published in 1998; this edition is the second. The second edition includes a CD-ROM.

L-42   American Journalism Review. **American Journalism Review (AJR) Newslink**. Mount Morris, IL: American Journalism Review, n.d. Continuous. URL: http://ajr.newslink.org/.

AJR Newslink provides links to Web sites of newspapers, radio, and television stations and networks, online newspapers worldwide, campus newspapers, magazines, news services, articles from current issues of *AJR*, and starting points for journalists. Links are arranged geographically, by format (e.g., public, news/talk), and "most-linked-do" Web sites.

INDEXES, ABSTRACTS, AND BIBLIOGRAPHIC DATABASES

Communication researchers who have access to *ComIndex* (L-43) and *ComAbstracts* (L-44) will probably want to start their journal literature reviews with those sources. Depending on the specific nature of their research, most communication researchers will need to consult additional indexes., reinforcing the notion of the interdisciplinary nature of the field of communication and the necessity for careful topic analysis when doing research in this area.

L-43   Communication Institute for Online Scholarship. **ComIndex**. Rotterdam Junction, NY: Communication Institute for Online Scholarship, 1993- . Continuous. Online format. URL: http://www.cios.org/www/comindex.htm.

L-44   Communication Institute for Online Scholarship. **ComAbstracts**. Rotterdam Junction, NY: Communication Institute for Online Scholarship, 1997- . Continuous. Online format. URL: http://www.cios.org/www/abstract.htm.

ComIndex uses menu-driven software to provide bibliographic citations to articles in seventy-four journals from the core literature of the communication field (journalism, speech, communication studies, rhetoric, and mass communication). Time period covered is from the initial publication date of the journal or 1970, whichever date is later. *ComIndex* provides bibliographic citations, but not abstracts or full-text articles. This is an inexpensive ($100 for individuals and $1,000 annually for campus-wide access) and critical source for libraries that support communication programs.

ComAbstracts provides indexing and abstracts for fifty-three communication journals. Chronological coverage varies from journal to journal; coverage of *Public Opinion Quarterly* begins with volume 30 (1966), for example, but coverage of *Research on Language and Social Interactions* begins with volume 33 (2000).

Author, wild card, and Boolean searching are available in both *ComIndex* and *ComAbstracts*. Words in abstracts are searchable, and the abstracts are enriched with additional key words to increase the likelihood of success.

L-45 National Communication Association. **CommSearch**. 3d ed. [CD-ROM]. Annandale, VA: National Communication Association, 1999.

CommSearch is a database on CD-ROM that comprises six different datasets, all searchable with the same software. The datasets include the full text (usually from 1991 to 1997) and abstracts (generally from volume 1 to 1997) of articles published in the journals *Communication Education, Communication Monographs, Critical Studies in Mass Communication, Journal of Applied Communication Research, Quarterly Journal of Speech, Text*, and *Performance Quarterly*. It also includes searches by a table of contents, author/contributor, and keywords for twenty-six journals, derived from the print Matlon index (*Index to Journals in Communication Studies Through 1995* [L-47]). *CommSearch* is "the beginning of a long-range effort by the National Communication Association to offer a compilation of communication research in a format the permits searching and full-text retrieval."

L-46 **Communication Abstracts**. Beverly Hills, CA: Sage, 1978- . Bimonthly.

Superbly annotated, *Communication Abstracts* may nevertheless be losing some users to easy-to-use electronic indexes. Although it does not index a set group of periodicals, *Communication Abstracts* indexes and abstracts a wide variety of communication-related articles, books, book chapters, and reports, selected by an academic editorial advisory board and published with the cooperation of the Department of Communication Science and the School of Communications and Theatre at Temple University. The sources indexed are listed in the fifth issue of each volume, and include some that may not ordinarily appear in communication indexes (e.g., *Space Policy* and *Suicide and Life-Threatening Behavior*). All areas of communication are within the scope of *Communication Abstracts*, from communication theory to advertising and marketing, to organizational communication. Arrangement is by subdiscipline (e.g., political communication or health communication), so that researchers can peruse the section of *Communication Abstracts* pertaining to their work. Subject indexing, which cumulates in the last issue of each volume, is a bit cumbersome, with fifty or so abstract numbers listed after broad topics like "research trends" or "television programs," so using this abstracting service usually takes a little longer than other sources. On the other hand, students who find a topic in the index that intrigues them—"tornadoes" or "celebrity endorsements," for example—will know that the article abstracted will have something to do with communication aspects of that topic.

Electronic access: Communication Index is now available electronically, although not entirely satisfactorily, through online periodical indexes such as *Academic Search Elite* and *FirstSearch*. They tend to treat *Communication Abstracts* as a journal itself and each section as a full-text "article," which makes it difficult to pinpoint a reference to one specific article.

L-47 Matlon, Ronald J., and Sylvia P. Ortiz, eds. **Index to Journals in Communication Studies Through 1995**. Annandale, VA: Speech Communication Association, 1997.

This is the fifth edition (previous editions having been published in 1975, 1980, 1985, and 1990) of a unique and valuable index for communications research, commonly known as the "Matlon Index" after its primary editor.

The most recent edition is composed of three parts. Part I consists of the tables of contents of twenty-four communication studies journals, arranged alphabetically by journal title, from *Argumentation and Advocacy* to *Women's Studies in Communication*. Each journal title has a two-letter code (e.g., CQ for *Communication Quarterly* and AA for *Argumentation and Advocacy*). Tables of contents for each journal begin with the first issue published, for example 1964 for *Argumentation and Advocacy*. Each article in the table of contents is numbered; hence, the first article in the first issue of *Argumentation and Advocacy* (volume 1, January 1964) is designated AA1; the last article in the last issue covered (volume 32, Fall 1995) is AA562. Part II is an author index, and Part III is a keyword index, both alphabetical. Each of these parts indicates the journal title by its two-letter code and the entry number of the article. The author index generally does not include book reviewers. The classified index of previous editions has been dropped in favor of the simpler keyword index. Like the *Communication Abstracts* index, the keyword index is encumbered by lists of a hundred or so articles under some keywords ("Freedom of Speech" for example), but the indication of journal allows researchers to select articles in the journals that interest them the most.

L-48   Vanderbilt University. **Television News Archive**. Nashville, TN: Television News Archive, Vanderbilt University, 1968- . Continuous. Online format. URL: http://tvnews.vanderbilt.edu/index.html.

The Television Archive at Vanderbilt University is "the world's most extensive and complete archive of television news," with a collection of more than 30,000 videotapes of individual network evening news broadcasts and more than 9,000 hours of news-related special programming. It provides brief abstracts of news reports and is accessible through three indexes: *Network Television Evening News Abstracts*, *Special Reports*, and *Periodic News Broadcasts*. Each index provides the option for searching by individual day, or by a year combined with a keyword search.

L-49   Sutton, Roberta Briggs. **Speech Index: An Index to 259 Collections of World Famous Orations and Speeches for Various Occasions**. 4th ed., rev. and enlarged. New York: Scarecrow Press, 1966.

L-50   Mitchell, Charity. **Speech Index: An Index to Collections of World Famous Orations and Speeches for Various Occasions. 4th edition supplement, 1966-1980**. Metuchen, NJ: Scarecrow Press, 1982.

The *Speech Index* and its supplement index cover standard collections of speeches, single volumes of speeches by specific authors, and books about public speaking containing speeches. The fourth edition incorporates all the materials in the three previous editions (1935, 1935–1955, and 1961), and updates it with new publications. The 1966–1980 supplement indexes 115 additional titles. The main body of each *Speech Index* consists of speaker and subject listings in a single alphabet, with the main entry under the name of the speaker. All chronological periods are covered.

Communication students and researchers will find it especially useful for its inclusion in the index of types of speeches (Persuasive Speeches, Sermons, Commemorative Addresses) in addition to topics (*Battle of New Orleans*, *Freemasons*, *Lynching*). The main entry includes references to the collections indexed, which are listed in the beginning of the book. A "selected list of titles" at the end of the volume lists speeches that the compiler thought would be difficult to locate if the author is not known, if the title bears no resemblance to the topic of the speech, and if they could not be readily located by a subject search ("Big Stick" speech by Theodore Roosevelt; "Blood, Sweat, and Tears," by Winston Churchill).

L-51   Manning, Beverly. **Index to American Women Speakers, 1828–1978**. Metuchen, NJ: Scarecrow Press, 1980.

L-52   Manning, Beverly. **We Shall Be Heard: An Index to Speeches by American Women, 1978–1985**. Metuchen, NJ: Scarecrow Press, 1988.

These two volumes index women's speeches in conferences and symposia, anthologies, documentary histories, and government documents. Each book includes four parts: a list of books indexed and author, subject, and title indexes. Most of the author entries refer the reader to the complete bibliographic citation for the speech in the list of books indexed. There is an author index. If the speaker was someone other than the author (for example, Susan B. Anthony often read Elizabeth Cady Stanton's speeches), the reader is noted after the author's name. The first volume (1828–1978) indexes about 200 sources and the second (1978–1985) more than 350 sources. Both include a generous number of congressional hearings and conference proceedings as well as anthologies.

ABI/INFORM. Ann Arbor, MI: University Microfilms, 1971- . (See D-43)

Business Periodicals Index. Bronx, NY: H. W. Wilson, 1958- . (See D-42)

ERIC. Washington, DC: Educational Resources Information, 1966. (See I-68)

Humanities Index. Bronx, NY: H. W. Wilson, 1974- . Quarterly. (See A-25)

Psychological Abstracts. Arlington, VA: American Psychological Association, 1927- . (See J-75n)

Social Sciences Index. Bronx, NY: H. W. Wilson, 1974- . (See A-24)

Sociological Abstracts. San Diego: Sociological Abstracts, 1953- . (See H-49)
These indexes cover communication-related topics within other disciplines. They are discussed in depth in the chapters relating to their subject areas. *Business Periodicals Index* and *ABI/Inform* are especially useful for their coverage of organizational and workplace communication. *ERIC* indexes a number of communication journals and can also be useful to those investigating communication in K–12 and academic environments, communication research, interpersonal communication, communication skills, and communication instruction. *Humanities Index* is probably most useful for journalism-related topics, such as photojournalism, which may fall inside or outside the scope of the social sciences, depending on the emphasis of the research in question. *Psychological Abstracts* is an outstanding source for many communication-related topics, including communication theory and nonverbal, interpersonal, and group communication. *Social Sciences Index* and *Sociological Abstracts* are useful for finding information on group and social communication. Still other indexing and abstracting services will be useful to communication researchers—depending again on the focus of their research. For example, various print and electronic newspaper indexes, including *World News Connection* for foreign broadcasts and articles, may be useful to the communications researcher studying political communication.

HANDBOOKS

L-53 Kalbfeld, Brad. **Associated Press Broadcast News Handbook**. New York: McGraw-Hill, 2001.

L-54 **The Associated Press Stylebook and Libel Manual: Including Guidelines on Photo Captions, Ailing the Wire, Proofreaders' Marks, Copyright**. Fully updated and rev. ed. Reading, MA: Addison-Wesley, 1998.

L-55 United Press International. **UPI Stylebook: The Authoritative Handbook for Writers, Editors & News Director**s. 3d ed. Lincolnwood, IL: National Textbook Company, 1992.
News service style guides define clear news writing for journalists, broadcasters, and others in communication professions. The UPI book covers both print and broadcast journalism; AP offers a separate guide for each format. The books consist primarily of sections on usage, including capitalization (capitalize U.S. Congress but not congressional hearing), using generic names instead of trade names (artificial grass rather than AstroTurf; trash bin rather than Dumpster), gender (mail carrier rather than mailman) and age issues (use "girl" and "boy" only until the eighteenth birthday; use "elderly" and

"senior citizen" with caution). The AP and UPI stylebooks have sections on libel, and the *UPI Stylebook* also has sections on news, sports, writing for broadcast (including pronunciation), pictures, and audio. The AP *Broadcast News Handbook* is arranged in two parts. The first part covers news writing, pictures, and sound; field reporting; the newsroom, structure, style, and production. The second part is a usage guide similar to that in the AP *Stylebook* and *UPI Stylebook*. Style guidelines in the *UPI Stylebook* tend to be more detailed than those in the other two.

L-56   Berger, Charles R., and Steven H. Chaffee, eds. **Handbook of Communication Science**. Beverly Hills, CA: Sage, 1987.

The work is divided into five sections that provide overviews, levels of analysis, functions, contexts, and a conclusion for major concepts in the field of communication. The authors of each chapter provide four levels of analysis for their topics: individual, interpersonal, network/organizational, and macrosocietal. Chapters focus on such specific subject areas as "The Macrosocial Level of Communication Science," "Persuasion," and "Organizational Assimilation." Particularly valuable for the conceptual overviews it provides and the extensive bibliographies that conclude each chapter, this is an impressive and important work for communication studies. Author and subject indexes are provided.

YEARBOOKS AND ALMANACS

L-57   Communication Yearbook. New Brunswick, NJ: Transaction Books, 1977- . Annual.

Prior to 1988, *Communication Yearbook* consisted of essays, reviews, and commentaries as well as refereed papers from the International Communication Association's (ICA) constituent divisions and interest groups. Since 1988 each volume has contained state-of-the-art reviews of the latest communication research on a topic of concern to communication scholars. Recent volumes have included review articles on cross-cultural communication and on the relationship between communication and emotional processes. *Communication Research* is most valuable as a current awareness tool for students and scholars, including librarians, who want to be familiar with current communication issues and research.

L-58   Progress in Communication Sciences. Norwood, NJ: Ablex, 1979- . Biannual.

Progress in Communication Sciences is a self-described "twice a year series dedicated to presenting high-quality state-of-the-art reviews of the literature in the fields of communication and information science." Each volume includes approximately ten essays. The essays are very specialized, but they reflect the broad-based, interdisciplinary nature of the communication discipline and have ranged from such topics as advances in telecommunications to gender and power in organizational communication.

COMMUNICATION LAW AND ETHICS

L-59   Bureau of National Affairs. **Media Law Reporter**. Washington, DC: The Bureau, 1977- . Weekly, with annual cumulations.

Media Law Reporter indexes and provides full text for most federal and state court and administrative agency decisions relating to media law. A topical index to commonly used terms (e.g., "gag orders," "reporter's privilege") provides classification numbers that correspond to a more detailed "Classification Guide." The "Classification Guide" is divided into the major areas of regulation of media content, regulation of media distribution, news gathering, and media ownership. Each area is broken down into subdivisions with individual classification numbers. An "Index Digest," arranged in the same classification scheme as the "Classification Guide," consists of headnotes of decisions assigned to each classification number. Each headnote includes the page number of the full decision. A table of cases and a table of cases by jurisdiction (e.g., Supreme Court, circuit courts, state courts) are included. *Media Law Reporter* first appears in looseleaf form and is then cumulated in bound volumes.

L-60 Federal Communications Commission. **FCC Record: A Comprehensive Compilation of Decisions, Reports, Public Notices and Other Documents of the Federal Communications Commission of the United States**. Washington, DC: Government Printing Office, 1986- . Biweekly.

The *FCC Record* was known as *Federal Communications Commission Reports* from 1934 to 1985. It provides details on all Federal Communications Commission (FCC) actions and decisions. The FCC also maintains a Web site (www.fcc.gov) on which it posts a "Daily Digest" consisting of brief synopses of Commission orders, news releases, speeches, public notices, and all other FCC documents that are released each business day. Other documents, such as orders, are available on the Web page of the relevant FCC bureau (e.g., Mass Media Bureau). FCC Court Opinions are available through the Office of General Counsel Web page (http://www.fcc.gov/ogc/recopin.html).

L-61 **Pike & Fischer Radio Regulation**. Bethesda, MD: Pike & Fischer, 1947- . Looseleaf.

Usually referred to simply as *Pike & Fischer*, *Pike & Fischer Radio Regulation* provides the text of laws, regulations, FCC and court decisions, and other documents affecting the broadcasting industry. Despite its name, it does in fact cover the television and cable casting industries. To some extent this source acts as a composite of the two previous sources because it includes both information on FCC regulations (those taken and under consideration) and court decisions. It also uses a looseleaf format.

COLLECTIONS

L-62 Safire, William. **Lend Me Your Ears: Great Speeches in History**. New York: Norton, 1992.

This collection provides the texts of speeches from the ancient world to the present arranged in thirteen categories, including "Memorials and Patriotic Speeches" (e.g., "Mark Twain Celebrates the Fourth of July"), War and Revolution Speeches (e.g., "George Washington Talks his Troops Out of Insurrection"), Trials ("Job Pleads the Record of a Good Life Against God's Inexplicable Punishment"), Gallows and Farewell Speeches ("John Brown Has a Few Words to Say About His Death Sentence"), and Political Speeches ("Barry Goldwater Ignites the Conservative Movement"). Safire introduces each speech. An index to speakers and subjects is included.

L-63 Straub, Deborah Gillan. **Voices of Multicultural America: Notable Speeches Delivered by African, Asian, Hispanic, and Native Americans, 1790–1995**. New York: Gale, 1996.

High school and college speech communication instructors sometimes assign their students to find speeches given by members of ethnic minorities. Unless the student has a particular individual in mind, it is difficult to find something that will fit the student's needs. This volume pulls together and prints in their entirety, where possible, 230 "noteworthy and compelling" speeches delivered by 130 individuals from the late 1700s through 1995. Included are a speech by African-American journalist and anti-lynching advocate Ida B. Wells-Barnett, Native American actor and Salish tribal chief Dan George's speech at the celebration of Canada's centennial, and Japanese American attorney and U.S. Representative from Hawaii Patsy Takemoto Mink on the right of Americans to engage in dissent. Each speech is introduced by experts in oratory and in the cultural traditions of the speaker. The volume also includes indexes by ethnicity (including individual Native American tribes), by speech category (topic or type of speech, such as commencement speeches), a keyword index (e.g., "guns" or "Buffalo

Soldiers"), and a timeline of events so that speeches can be placed in context, incorporating the name of the speaker in boldface. Four introductory essays on African American, Native American, Hispanic American, and Asian Pacific oratory and public discourse are excellent introductions for beginning students.

L-64   Price, Gary. **Speech and Transcript Center**. Washington, DC: George Washington University, 1998- . Continuous. Online format. URL: http://gwis2.circ .gwu.edu/~gprice/speech.htm.

Gary Price of George Washington University created and maintains this gateway to an enormous collection of links to full text—and sometimes audio and video—speech and transcript resources. Categories include Television/Radio Transcripts (National Press Club Luncheon Speeches, Washington Week in Review), international government (arranged by country and organization), business (speeches by company executives arranged by company name), professional and trade associations (AFL-CIO, American Medical Association), and Historical Material (Fireside Chats, speeches of individual presidents).

L-65   Public Agenda. **Public Agenda Online**. New York: Public Agenda, 1997- . Continuous. Online format. URL: http://www.publicagenda.org/.

Like librarians, journalists often need to be come experts in an unfamiliar field about which they are expected to find information. Public opinion and policy analysis are covered for journalists in nineteen major policy areas including abortion, crime, gambling, illegal drugs, abortion, and the federal budget. Pages for each issue include an overview, a digest of recent news stories, a fact file, different perspectives on the issue, sources and resources ("who the players are and how to reach them"), people's chief concerns, major proposals, red flags (e.g., cautions about surveys), areas of consensus and division, and selection criteria for the items included in the guide. *Public Agenda* is "a nonpartisan, nonprofit public opinion research and citizen education organization based in New York City. It was founded in 1975 by social scientist and author Daniel Yankelovich and former Secretary of State Cyrus Vance."

L-66   Public Broadcasting Service. **Great American Speeches: 80 Years of Political Oratory**. Alexandria, VA: Public Broadcasting Service, 2000- . Continuous. Online format. URL: http://www.pbs.org/greatspeeches/timeline/index.html.

L-67   Linton, Liz, and Tom Solomon. **Gifts of Speech: Women's Speeches from Around the World**. Sweet Briar, VA: Sweet Briar College, n.d. Continuous. Online format. URL: http://gos.sbc.edu/.

L-68   Douglass Project. **Douglass: Archives of American Public Address**. Evanston, IL: Northwestern University, n.d. Online format. URL: http:// douglass.speech.nwu.edu/index.html#go.

These Web sites are collections of full-text speeches, each with a slightly different focus. *Great American Speeches*, from the Public Broadcasting Service, provides transcripts, background information, and some audio and video of more than 100 speeches from the 1890s to the present, from Booker T. Washington's speech at the 1895 Cotton State Exposition to Elie Wiesel's 1999 speech on the "perils of indifference." Some speeches have links to background, audio, and video (e.g., John F. Kennedy's 1963 speech promising to defend the citizens of West Berlin). Speeches are listed within a chronological timeline that provides context for the speech.

Sweet Briar's *Gifts of Speech* provides full text of speeches by influential, contemporary women. Its creators request speeches from women chosen through a selection process. The speeches are then digitized and loaded on the *Gifts of Speech* Web site. Speeches can be searched by name (e.g., Jane Fonda, Madeleine Albright) or keyword (e.g., Vietnam, menopause), or browsed alphabetically by name of speaker or by year. There is also a list of Nobel lectures and the "Top 100 Speeches of the

20th Century" (compiled by Texas A&M). Within these lists, there are links to the full texts of speeches by women. There is as yet no audio or video on this Web site.

Northwestern's *Douglass* is an electronic archive of American oratory and related documents intended to serve general scholarship as well as courses in American rhetorical history at Northwestern University. Full-text speeches can be retrieved chronologically, by speaker, by title, or by issue. They range in date from John Winthrop's "On Liberty" (1645) to President Clinton's "Map Room Speech" (1998). Issues include care for the poor, women's suffrage, temperance, and slavery. "Speech Guides and Research Notes" includes notes to sections of *Outline of American History*, published by the U.S. Information Office. A section of references provides links to other Web resources (e.g., the *Harry S. Truman Page*, the White House's *Presidents of the United States* Web site for presidential speeches).

STATISTICS

L-69 Beville, Hugh M. **Audience Ratings: Radio, Television, and Cable**. rev. ed. Hillsdale, NJ: Lawrence Erlbaum, 1988.

L-70 Webster, James G., Patricia Phalen, and Lawrence W. Lichty. **Ratings Analysis: The Theory and Practice of Audience Research**. 2d ed. Hillsdale, NJ: Lawrence Erlbaum, 2000.

Library users frequently ask for television and radio ratings information and how to interpret that information. These two publications do excellent jobs in providing readers with background information on ratings services and how ratings information is used. *Ratings Analysis*, sometimes used as a broadcasting text, provides an overview on types of audience research; examples of common audience research reports; how ratings are used in advertising, programming, and the social sciences; the methodology of collecting ratings; and analytical techniques. It also addresses use of ratings in advertising, programming, and other areas of the social sciences. It includes an appendix listing national ratings research companies and their products as well as a glossary and author and subject indexes.

Beville's value currently lies in the historical perspective it provides on established services like Nielsen and Simmons (L-71). The new edition of Webster, Phalen, and Lichty makes it a better choice for up-to-date information. Library users seeking information on ratings services will probably also want to seek periodical articles on the topic as well as referring to one of these two works, because ratings and ratings methodologies have come under increasing scrutiny in recent years, especially ratings provided on the World Wide Web.

L-71 **Study of Media and Markets**. New York: Simmons Market Research Bureau, 1979- . Annual.

This multivolume set, commonly known as "Simmons," reports the results of yearly surveys of the product and media use of more than 19,000 consumers. It cross-lists media use with demographic information product information so that, for example, users can figure out what magazines or television shows consumers of flea powder or greeting cards are most likely to be exposed to. Conversely, it also tells users the demographic characteristics of individuals who use various types of products or media. Thus, its usefulness lies in its ability to target market groups and the media to use for reaching those groups. The set consists of "M" (media) and "P" (product) volumes. Media volumes provide audience data for magazine, newspaper, and supplement reading; television viewing; and radio listening. The set provides household and consumption rates and usage for various goods, television viewing, and radio listening. Product volumes provide market data for categories of products, cross-listed with data about media use so that researchers can found out, for example, whether readers of the *New York Times Magazine* or *Field and Stream* are more likely to purchase flea and tick powder. Simmons is the most detailed source of such information commonly available to library users, because it makes older editions available to libraries and journalism schools at reduced cost. Market research compilations such as Simmons are extremely expensive to compile and to purchase. Library users need to be aware, therefore, that this information will always be outdated. Simmons has recently been making the *Study of Media and Markets* available to libraries only on a CD-R disk, which has been a challenge to use.

   Electronic access: Also available on CD-ROM.

L-72   Niles, Robert. **Finding Data on the Internet: A Journalist's Guide**. 1996- . Continuous. Online format. URL: http://www.robertniles.com/data/.

   Robert Niles's Web site provides basic statistical information for journalists and other writers who need a Stat 101, including "statistics every writer should know" (mean, median, percent), "how not to get duped" (per capita, margin of error), and frequently asked questions (statistical tests and sample sizes). The section on finding data on the Internet is arranged by topic, including "basic stuff" (FedStats), agriculture (USDA state fact sheets), Crime (FBI, Bureau of Justice Statistics), health (National Center for Health Statistics), and tracking campaign contributions

L-73   Statistical Assessment Service. **STATS: Statistical Assessment Service**. 1997- . Continuous. Online format. URL: http://www.stats.org/.

   The Statistical Assessment Service is a nonpartisan, nonprofit research organization in Washington, DC, devoted to the accurate use of scientific and social research in public policy debate. It "seeks to weed out bad data and research before it enters the media stream" and, to that end, offers analyses for journalists of current statistical and scientific disputes, including data distributed by the media. It also fields queries from journalists. One section of the Web site, "STATS Spotlight," consists of pieces of extensive, unpublished STATS research, mostly debunking statistical studies that have appeared in the news. "Newsclips" provides full text of news articles published by or reflecting the work of Statistical Assessment Service researchers. "Asides" includes "assorted commentary and esoteric interests" (an article statistically supporting the statement that "most strangers are not evil"). There is also a list of "Dubious Data Awards" from 1995 to 2000, including a special "Millennial Misconceptions" article. STATS has a topic index (e.g., crime, environment, social issues) and a search engine. A page of links lead to other statistical sites, including skeptical sites (e.g., *Skeptic.com* and Cecil Adams's *The Straight Dope: Fighting Ignorance Since 1973*).

NOTES

1. Geroge Gerbner and Wilbur Schramm, "Communications, Study of" in Erik Barnouw, ed., *International Encyclopedia of Communication* (New York: Oxford University Press, 1989), 358.

2. Ray L. Birdwhistell, "Communication," in *International Encyclopedia of the Socail Sciemnces* (New York: Macmillan, 1968), 3: 24.

3. A. B. Rubin, A. M. Rubin, and L. J. Piele, *Communication Research: Strategies and Sources*, 5th ed. (Belmont, CA: Wadsworth, 1999), 3.

4. Gerbner and Schramm, "Communications," 359.

5. Ibid.

6. From a search on *College Source* [online database].

7. Information from a tour of Cornell University, April 24, 2001.

8. Rubin, Rubin, and Piele, *Communication Research*, 6. This guide to the literature of communication includes a further breakdown of each category.

9. Ibid., xii.

Author Index

Reference is to entry number. The letter "n" indicates that the name is found in the annotation. If a page number (p.) is referenced, the author is mentioned in the essay section or an unnumbered entry.

Abate, Frank R., K-77
Abdel-Khalik, Rashad, D-9n
Aby, Stephen H., H-1
Accardo, Pasquale J., I-46
Administrative Office of the U.S. Courts, F-82
Aker, James R., F-1
Aldrich, Richard, I-43
Ali, Sheikh R., B-67, B-176
Alkin, Marvin C., I-54
Ambert, Alba N., I-131
American Bar Association and the Association of American Law Schools, F-81
American Communication Association, L-1
American Economic Association, C-9
American Geographical Society, K-110
American Journalism Review, L-42
American Library Association. Government Documents Roundtable, B-144
American Library Association, MAGERT, K-229
Anderegg, M. L., I-47
Andersen, Charles J., I-152
Anderson, Andy B., H-43
Anderson, Beth, I-112
Anderson, Lorin W., I-60
Andrew, Paige G., K-205
Andrews, William G., p. 48
Andriot, John, A-45n
Appleton, Andrew M., B-129
Archeology and Ethnography Program, National Park Service, G-31
Argyris, Chris, D-9
Asher, R. E., G-79
Association of American Geographers, K-57
Association of College and Research Libraries, Anthropology and Sociology Section, G-95
Aston, Mick, G-88
Atkins, Helen, p. 261
Atkinson, G. B., H-31
Atwell, Robert H., I-121
Auerbach, Susan, I-59

Bahn, Paul, G-62
Baker, Colin, I-62
Balachandran, M., D-2
Balay, Robert, E-8
Balter, Lawrence, J-40
Banks, Arthur, B-93
Bankston, Carl III, H-5
Bankston, Carl L., H-14

Barber, P., K-139
Barbuto, Domenica M., D-177n
Barfield, Thomas, G-59
Barkan, Elliott Robert, H-15
Barker, Graeme, G-63
Barnard, Alan, G-73
Barnouw, Erik, L-15
Barone, Michael, B-131
Barrow, Robin, I-38
Barzun, Jacques, E-1
Bateson, Ann, F-5
Baxter, Pam M., J-1, J-83
Bealey, Frank, B-8
Beers, Henry Putney, E-9
Bell and Howell, F-67
Bellack, Alan S., J-18
Benamati, Dennis C., F-105
Benewick, R., K-187
Benewick, Robert, B-6
Bengtson, Hermann, E-2
Bennett, Peter D., D-26
Bensen, Clark H., B-39
Berger, Bennett M., H-66
Berger, Charles R., L-56
Berger, James L., I-9
Bernhard, Judith, I-127
Bernice M. Rosenthal, K-234
Bernstein, Mark F., B-132
Berry, Dorothea, p. 295, I-4, I-6n
Besterman, Theodore, A-8n
Beville, Hugh M., L-69
Biddle, Bruce J., I-133
Birnbaum, Michael H., J-155
Birren, James E., J-41, J-117
Biskupic, Joan, F-91, F-92
Black, Henry Campbell, F-20
Blake, David, I-41
Blanchard, Margaret A., L-19
Blau, Judith, H-6
Blaug, Mark, C-11, C-12, C-14
Blausten, Albert P., B-98
Blazek, Ron, E-3
Block, Eleanor S., L-2
Board, C., K-139
Bohme, R., K-167
Bonaeau, C. Alan, J-121
Borgatta, Edgar F., H-7
Boring, E.G., J-110, J-111
Bosch, Reva, F-8

Title Index

Reference is to entry number. The letter "n" indicates that the title is found in the annotation. If a page number (p.) is referenced, the title is mentioned in the essay section or an unnumbered entry.

Subject Index

Reference is to page numbers.